Following the Flag
An Air Force Officer Provides an Eyewitness View of Major Events and Policies during the Cold War

LLOYD R. "DICK" LEAVITT
Lieutenant General, USAF, Retired

Air University Press
Air Force Research Institute
Maxwell Air Force Base, Alabama

March 2010

Muir S. Fairchild Research Information Center Cataloging Data

Leavitt, Lloyd R.
    Following the flag : an Air Force officer provides an eyewitness view of major events and policies during the Cold War / Lloyd R. "Dick" Leavitt.
        p. ; cm.
    Includes bibliographical references and index.
    ISBN 978-1-58566-205-0
        1. United States—Air Force—Officers—Biography. 2. Air pilots, Military—Biography. 3. Generals—United States—Biography. 4. Cold War. I. Title.

    358.4/0092—dc22

Disclaimer

Air University Press
Air Force Research Institute
155 N. Twining Street
Maxwell AFB, AL 36112-6026
http://aupress.au.af.mil

*Dedicated to our Country
Where hopes and dreams
can become reality*

Contents

Illustrations

Tables

Thirty-Five Years in Uniform

Wing commander, Vietnam War

Vice-Commander in Chief, SAC

U-2 pilot, chief of standardization

F-4 assistant division commander for operations, USAFE, 36th Tactical Fighter Wing

West Point cadet

Flight commander, Korean War

Preface

After nearly two years of listening to service rivalries, Pres. Harry Truman pushed Congress into passing the National Security Act of 1947, thus establishing the Department of Defense and three military services—Army, Navy, and Air Force. Stuart Symington became the first secretary of the Air Force on 18 September 1947, and the United States Air Force was born.

The years from 1947 through the beginning of the twenty-first century witnessed the USAF steadily progress until it became the preeminent air force in the world. With less than 400,000 active duty personnel, the USAF has capabilities and tasks today that were not imaginable six decades ago. The World War II legacy from the Army Air Forces, epitomized in the familiar Air Force song lyrics "off we go into the wild blue yonder, climbing high into the sky!" is not forgotten. However, a strong professional image and unparalleled responsibilities in air and space are far more descriptive of today's USAF.

From time to time, people ask about my Air Force career. These conversations led me to believe most Americans know too little about the many challenges and responsibilities in an Air Force career. Sure, the public has TV and sees "smart bombs" dropped and missiles launched, or goes to movies that mimic aerial combat, or suffers through a TV drama with a Dr. Strangelove-type officer committing treason or another heinous crime. Given these snapshots of Air Force activities, true and fictional, do they really portray the Air Force? Would going back 50 years and tracing the path of progress by citing personal experiences and observations along the way paint a more authentic picture? Perhaps an individual can describe with some degree of accuracy what is personally experienced. Beyond that, conjecture, opinion, and hearsay take over.

Friends suggested my personal experiences might interest veterans who may have shared similar experiences, as well as persons with or without a military background who have a historical interest in these same events or young people who might be interested in a military career. In response to their suggestions, I have written this book but claim no special insight, talent, or skill that was denied my contemporaries. My best credential is simply the coincidence of having been in a variety of different jobs, in combat and peacetime, when important and interesting changes were happening during the Cold War. The book focuses on my own experiences and is biased in that regard.

What I have attempted to do is open up the period of history called the Cold War by tracing my personal experiences. In my opinion, the biggest mistake a career-oriented person can make is staying in one job and ignoring other opportunities for fear of failure. For that reason, I volunteered whenever an opportunity was offered. It would be misleading to portray my career as unblemished—no failures, no mistakes, no disappointments. I have included some of my more memorable mistakes. (Those who know me can probably recall more than I have included.)

Every life is unique, and the only distinction that separates one life from another is what happened along the way. Because of this reality, I have tried to clarify—or at least share a different view of—the crises, wars, and political events that characterized the Cold War. Many accredited historians have written extensively on these same subjects. They typically authenticate their opinions and conclusions with footnotes or endnotes by referring to interviews, books by other authors, public records, and newspaper reports the author has researched. Since so much has been written, authors can pick and choose whatever source fits their own predispositions. If an author presented this information in a courtroom, much would be treated as hearsay evidence. Therefore, I have limited the use of endnotes to clarify, to describe key personnel, and to disclose the source for statistical data. Instead, the opinions, conclusions, and events described are usually drawn from my own experience. My hope is the reader will find the chronicling of one Air Force career during the years of change not only informative but also interesting.

To understand a military career, you must understand that the American military is subject to national policies that override and are inherently more important than what might be a preferred "military policy." Because we live in a republic that responds to the electorate, national policies change periodically. If decision making were perfectly synchronized, American foreign policy and American military policy (which is guided by foreign policy) would always walk hand in hand without stumbling. Rarely does that happen. Our State and Defense Departments contain talented people with different opinions, motivations, backgrounds, and axes to grind. Once convinced of the necessity for change, the president must turn to Congress for the money. Congress may or may not agree with the president's proposed policy, but military people have no choice. We may personally disagree with a commander in chief's new policy, but our oath demands we accept it.

During the years I spent on active duty, three different foreign policies strongly influenced both foreign relations and military operations: containment, deterrence, and flexible response. Each of these policies changed the Air Force. Each had its day in the sun. Superseded policies did not die; they just became less important. A time lag exists between the primacy of an old policy and the evolution to an effective new policy. Albert Einstein once said, "The only reason for time is so that everything doesn't happen at once." Einstein's comment is certainly applicable when applied to creating a military force structure necessary to support a new foreign policy.

The book is organized chronologically and follows my experiences at West Point and subsequent assignments during my Air Force career. The title, *Following the Flag*, alludes to an officer's responsibility whenever a major policy shift occurs. I have attempted to explain the reason for each shift, define the policy, and describe the impact on the Air Force. The reader may wonder if it was simply a coincidence that my assignments followed the changes in national policy. My answer is no. I wanted to be in the front ranks of the parade, not in the last. I intended to accept whatever challenges the Air Force offered as the most satisfying way to spend my career and to do my best in each new assignment. At times, this was hard on my wife and shifted to Anne's shoulders much of the responsibility for raising three children. Thankfully, Anne is a strong, patriotic woman and always accepted the responsibility that went with being my Air Force partner. Wives of Cold War warriors, regardless of their husbands' service or rank, were the unsung heroes of those dangerous years that threatened our nation's future.

Acknowledgments

Although the primary sources for *Following the Flag* are my personal experiences, opinions, and observations, many times I have turned to others for their aid, their own recollections, and welcome advice. The book spans 35 years from 1946 through 1981. This means that many contemporaries and most of my supervisors are no longer around for interviews. Despite this fact of life, since the Air Force system renders officer effectiveness reports (OER) at frequent intervals—a year or less apart—my personal OER file is an official "memory stick" for dates, places, activities, and names of supervisors. Filling the gaps between the official records and orders are scrapbooks, letters, pictures, and my wife, Anne. She has been a strong supporter throughout this project, not only for keeping track of our life in the military but offering her talents in proofreading and making suggestions about content and context.

Oral History Interview

In December 1984, three years after I retired from the Air Force, Lt Col David Greenberg, a student at the Air War College, conducted an oral history interview. Greenberg was well prepared with questions based upon my 35 years in the military—four years at West Point and 31 years in the Air Force. A year later, the USAF Historical Research Center returned a manuscript and recording from Greenberg's interview. It had gone through a security review in the meantime and was now ready for my final editing and approval. I declined signing an Office of Air Force History release that would "voluntarily give, transfer, convey, and assign all rights, title and interest in the memoirs and remembrances contained in the aforementioned magnetic tapes and manuscript." In the back of my mind was the notion that someday I would find the 245 pages of his questions and my answers written by Colonel Greenberg a useful tool in writing a biography based upon my Cold War experiences. Nearly two decades later when I began writing this book, this proved to be the case, thanks to Colonel Greenberg's efforts, patience, and questions.

Support from US Strategic Command Historian

This book includes major portions of my Air Force career that were involved with the Strategic Air Command (SAC). From 1954 to 1962, it was crew duty with SAC fighters, U-2s, and B-52s. From 1963 to 1967, roughly one-half of my first Pentagon tour was spent on strategic aircraft and missile studies. From 1972 to 1974, the Joint Chiefs of Staff (JCS) assignment was highlighted by SAC's role in Linebacker II. From 1974 to 1976, while commanding Chanute Technical Training Center, our principal job was to train aircraft and missile technicians for SAC. From 1978 to 1981, my last assignment was Vice-Commander in Chief, SAC.

SAC was disbanded in June 1992 and its assets distributed between the newly formed Air Combat Command and other operational commands. It was replaced at Offutt by the US Strategic Command, a unified command with broad responsibilities. In 2001 Dr. Jerome Martin became the command historian for US Strategic Command. Historical records for the old SAC remain at Offutt.

From 1976 to 1978 at Headquarters United States Air Forces in Europe (USAFE), I wore "two hats" as the deputy chief of staff for both operations and intelligence. It was a dangerous time because of the Warsaw Pact buildup of both conventional and nuclear forces. Every morning the senior staff in USAFE would get an update on intelligence as a first order of business. One young captain, Jerome Martin, stood out for his concise presentations and thorough subject knowledge. Martin later served three tours at the Air Force Academy teaching military studies and commanding a training group, interrupted by three years at Ohio State University where he earned a PhD in military history and by attendance at the Air War College. When young, talented Captain Martin was now Dr. Martin, command historian, I immediately established contact.

I have visited Jerry Martin three times at Offutt and telephoned him many times for information. He has graciously responded to my many requests by providing important information, now declassified, as well as studies, pictures, and other historical data. The data he furnished provides accuracy and authenticity to what I have written and fills memory gaps that otherwise would have existed. As an experienced military historian, Jerry realizes this important part of Cold War history needs to be recorded while my generation of SAC leaders is still alive.

Classmates and Contemporaries

During my four years at West Point, lasting friendships were established with many classmates—future Army and Air Force officers—who would spend much of their adult lives serving their country. For those who chose the Air Force upon graduation, our friendships were enhanced in pilot training and in subsequent assignments. Contacts and memories have since been refreshed at frequent class reunions. If Army details about the Korean or Vietnam wars needed confirmation or explanation, retired Generals Wally Nutting, Volney Warner, and John Wickham were helpful. My prime source for information about Air Force classmates has been Brig Gen Michael DeArmond, who has collected detailed biographies of Air Force classmates. Lt Gen Winfield "Skip" Scott, the longest-serving Air Force officer in the class before retirement, has also been a dependable source for information.

Maj Gen Patrick Halloran, USAF, retired, and Lt Col Anthony Bevacqua, USAF, retired, have been very helpful about dates, places, and names for the U-2 program. Lt Col Jack Mudie, USAF, retired, has been an excellent source for B-52H crew duties and Cuban missile crisis data. Col Charlie Spicka, USAF, retired, has provided pictures and data on the AC-130 gunships, as well as technological developments. Col "Iwo" Kimes, USAF, retired, has been an invaluable source for information about the early involvement of the Air Force in Vietnam.

Vice Adm Jerry King, the J-3 during my two years in the JCS, patiently answered many questions about our activities during those years that ended the Vietnam War. Working for Jerry King was always challenging, but he offered me opportunities well beyond my rank at the time. I thoroughly enjoyed knowing and becoming a friend of this talented, great American who died in July 2008.

After my final draft was completed, I asked four highly respected retired Air Force generals, who served with distinction during various phases of the Cold War, to evaluate *Following the Flag*. They are Gen Ronald R. Fogleman, former USAF chief of staff; Gen John T. Chain, former Commander in Chief, Strategic Air Command; Gen Michael P. C. Carns, former USAF vice chief of staff; and Gen John A. Shaud, former chief of staff, Supreme Headquarters Allied Powers Europe. Their positive responses and encouragement made publishing this book possible.

Air University Press

The Air University Press provided the technical expertise and editorial support for *Following the Flag* that I needed as a novice author. The *Air University Style and Author Guide* led the way on punctuation, abbreviations, and other stylistic issues. Daniel Armstrong and Susan Fair of the Design Branch put a great deal of skill and effort into improving the figures and many photos, some being half-century-old snapshots. Carolyn Burns checked the technical aspects in her review of the manuscript. Last, but not least, is Ann Bailey, typesetter for the project, who expertly turned hundreds of pages of text and illustrations into a professional publication.

For the past six months, Jeanne Shamburger has been my editor. Her pleasantly delivered suggestions, encouragement, useful questions, and good humored corrections have made this a better book. Although she works at Maxwell AFB, Alabama, and I reside a thousand miles away in Texas, her adept use of e-mail has made it possible to progress through the editing process in a timely manner, disturbed only by my absences. Thank you, Jeanne, for your outstanding efforts.

Chapter 1

West Point
Cadet—1946–50

From Cadet Grey to Air Force Blue

While I was mowing the lawn at our home in Michigan on a hot day in August 1945, my mother opened the screen door and said, "Dick, the Japanese have surrendered. The war is over!" My emotions were mixed and conflicting. The sensible emotion was thankfulness—no more wartime casualties. World War II had seriously impacted our family. My father, an automobile dealer in civilian life, was commissioned shortly after the Pearl Harbor attack. As an Army captain, he had suffered a disabling heart attack in May 1944 while running a gas obstacle course on his way to the war in Europe. My sister Jeanne's husband had been killed in action in June 1945 while piloting a B-29 in a firebomb raid over Japan. My sister Helen's husband, an Army first lieutenant, was headed for Okinawa as part of the Japan invasion force. My Navy uncle had survived the numerous kamikaze attacks in the great sea battle off of Okinawa that summer. Too many of our friends and neighbors had suffered similar, or worse, tragedies in their families.

I suppressed the other emotion—envy. I was envious of those who had served in the war. They would always be veterans of the greatest war in history. And I would always be a 16-year-old kid who wasn't old enough to fight in a truly *world* war—a war where America had extended its powerful reach across both the Atlantic and Pacific oceans and crushed Germany and Japan. Even though I missed the main feature, was there a way to experience the show in some vicarious way? Even if there were no more wars, would a military career offer challenges and opportunities not available in civilian life? Was there a "right way" to start?

A lifelong interest in military aviation began in 1940. The First Pursuit Group of the Army Air Corps (AAC) did its gunnery training at Phelps-Collins Airport near my hometown of

Alpena, Michigan.[1] My father would frequently visit the airport where we could watch the new P-38s fly and meet the fighter pilots and other officers he knew. The First Fighter Group was transferred to Clark Field in the Philippines in the fall of 1941. The surprise Japanese attack on 8 December 1941 destroyed many aircraft and support facilities there. An early wartime hero, 1st Lt Boyd "Buzz" Wagner, a pilot in the First Fighter Group, became the first US Army Air Forces (USAAF) ace of World War II on 16 December 1941 by shooting down five Japanese aircraft before Clark Field went out of business.

My freshman and sophomore years in high school, 1942–44, were spent in Orlando, Florida, where my father was stationed at Orlando Air Base after being commissioned in the USAAF. Orlando was the home of the AAF School of Applied Tactics, and there were many opportunities to see airplanes and talk about flying. One day, Dan Barnes's father, a brigadier general, let us sit in the cockpit of the newest fighters while he explained the switches, guns, instrumentation, and controls. I was sold! When the war ended, my heroes included Dwight Eisenhower, Douglas MacArthur, Hap Arnold, and Omar Bradley—the only five-star generals of World War II—and they were West Point graduates. Why not try to follow in their footsteps?

The goal became reality. With help from family, high school teachers, and coaches, I was appointed to West Point in the fall of 1945, passed the entrance exams, and entered on 1 July 1946 with 952 other new members of the Class of 1950. Fifty-six "turnbacks and comebacks"—former members of the Class of 1949—joined us. Turnbacks were cadets who had failed one academic course the previous year, been reexamined, and been allowed to enter with the following year's class. Comebacks were cadets who had been placed on leave of absence, usually for sickness, and allowed to enter with the following year's class. Total class size at the beginning of freshman ("plebe") year was 1,008.

The Class of 1950 was the first class to enter West Point after the end of World War II.[2] Approximately one-third were WWII veterans. The veterans included 45 former officers of various ranks ranging from second lieutenant to major. Former officers were expected to resign their commissions before becoming cadets, although a few discretely managed to keep a reserve (inactive) commission during their cadet years. Most of the 45 had been officers in the Army ground forces during World War II and returned to the Army upon graduation in 1950. When the United States Air Force became a separate service in 1947, several former officers in the AAF were offered regular commissions in the new service. Cadet Roy Clark, a former major and now a plebe, was in this group. Roy resigned after completing plebe year and accepted a regular USAF commission. Colonel Clark served with distinction prior to retiring in 1974. Jim Carter, a former captain, also accepted a regular USAF commission after resigning from West Point in July 1947. On 15 April 1958, Maj James B. Carter was killed in an aircraft accident. Most former AAF officers, including Al Packer, a WWII fighter pilot and ex-POW, continued as cadets and were commissioned in the USAF upon graduation. Al Packer served as a Navy exchange pilot on the USS *Bon Homme Richard* during the Korean War and was the first graduate from the Class of 1950 to be promoted to major. Col Allan R. Packer retired in 1975 after completing a distinguished career in the Air Force and Air National Guard (ANG).

July and August are months remembered as "Beast Barracks" by plebes. It is an intentionally severe indoctrination period designed to transform young civilians into cadets. The summer is spent on physical training, care and cleaning of equipment and uniforms, close-order drill, basic weapon knowledge, plebe knowledge as found in the *Blue Book*, squad-level field training, and complete understanding of the Honor Code, *Academy Regulations*, and customs. During Beast Barracks, the enforcement of discipline and training is left to the First Class (seniors) under the overall supervision of officers from the Tactical Department.

My roommate in Beast Barracks, Boyd Bashore, had been a first lieutenant in the 82d Airborne Division before resigning his commission to become a cadet. The last weeks of Beast Barracks were devoted to field training—all old stuff to Boyd. Summer training ended with the plebe hike, a road march covering the several miles from our summer training area back to West Point. The goal was to look "soldierly" as we marched along carrying backpacks and rifles—no more raw recruit stuff. We were 1,000 strong and glad to have passed at least one difficult phase of our cadet life. As we marched through a small Hudson Valley village, it started to rain. It soon became a real downpour. Boyd and I were marching side by side and grousing about the rain when no upperclassmen were around. Now and then, our company commander, a First Classman named Bill Cronin, would walk back along the troop column and check our progress. He stopped abruptly when he came abreast of where Boyd was marching.

"Mister Bashore!" Cronin growled. "They may do that in the 82d Airborne Division, but we don't allow it at West Point!" A quick glance to my left showed that the ever-practical Boyd had taken a condom and drawn it over the end of his M-1 rifle, thus stopping rain from rusting the rifle bore. (In those simpler days, carrying condoms probably violated the public image of a West Point cadet.) After a ripple of laughter ran through the entire company, order was restored, and Bashore's solution to combat readiness went back into his pocket. To our regret in later years, Lt Col William B. Cronin was killed in action in Vietnam, 27 April 1967. Col Boyd T. Bashore's distinguished career as an infantry officer included two tours in Vietnam before he retired in 1971. Boyd remained a close friend until his death in May 2001 after a long illness. If Boyd were alive today, he would smile at his former roommate's suggestion that a 21-year-old ex-paratroop lieutenant was treated with significantly more deference by upperclassmen than a 17-year-old kid from a small town in Michigan! And rightly so, I must add.

At the end of Beast Barracks, we were assigned to permanent companies for the academic year. A notice on our K-1 Company bulletin board stated that any plebe wanting to become an assistant football manager should report the next day to the practice football field. In stark contrast to the Army teams of recent years, West Point in 1946 was ranked number one in the preseason polls after winning the national championship in 1945. These were the "golden years of Army football" under famous coach Col "Red" Blaik. The team was loaded with star players. Halfback Glenn Davis and fullback "Doc" Blanchard, both Heisman Trophy winners, were starting their last year along with quarterback Arnold Tucker, an All-American candidate. Recruiting efforts had brought forth some great plebe talent that promised continued success for Army football. For example, my roommate, Bobby Gene Vinson, had been chosen as the 1945 outstanding Texas high school football player and was expected to replace Glenn Davis at running back after Davis graduated. Unfortunately, Bobby wiped out a knee during one of the early games in 1946. Colonel Blaik shifted him to defensive safety to save his knee from further damage, and he excelled at that position for the next three seasons. A truly gifted all-around athlete, Bobby ranked first (one of 771) at the end of plebe year and first (one of 672) in the final order of merit in military physical efficiency when we graduated in 1950.

Although I had played football in high school as the second-string quarterback on a conference championship team, playing for Army was way beyond my skill level. Maybe I could become an assistant manager and in some small way help the team? After I had been on the sidelines for a while watching practice, one of the assistant coaches asked why I was standing there. My answer about wanting to be an assistant manager caused him to ask if I knew how to pass. "Yes, sir!" was my enthusiastic reply. "OK," he said, "Go over there and pass a ball back and forth with your classmate Arnold Galiffa. Warm him up until he gets called into the scrimmage." Wow! What an opportunity.

I picked up a football and passed it over to Galiffa, who was standing about 10 yards away. It was my best pass and although somewhat like a sick duck, it did reach Arnie. He caught it and tossed it back. After picking myself off the ground, I knew two things: One, I had no idea a human being could throw a football that hard. Two, I was not good enough to even play catch with these guys. Thus ended my football-managing audition. Galiffa became Army's starting quarterback the following year, led the team to an undefeated season in 1949, fought in the Korean War as an infantry officer, resigned in 1953, and joined the New York Giants at quarterback. Sadly, Arnold Galiffa died from a brain tumor in September 1978. He was elected to the Football Hall of Fame in 1983.

West Point is the oldest engineering school in the United States. During the years that I was a cadet, the curriculum was the same for all cadets except for two years of training in a foreign language. A cadet had to pick one of five foreign languages to study: Spanish, French, German, Portuguese, or Russian. In addition, every plebe took mathematics, English, military topography, graphics, physical training, and tactics. The heaviest emphasis was on mathematics—90 minutes daily with the last 30 minutes being a graded test. One of the entrance requirements was a credit for trigonometry. My high school did not teach trigonometry, so I arranged with the principal to get credit for the course by buying a trigonometry book, teaching myself, taking the quiz at the end of each chapter, and paying the algebra teacher to grade each quiz. I passed the course with a high grade and received the credit required for entrance.

At the beginning of the academic year, math professors reviewed trigonometry for a few days. It quickly became obvious that I didn't know a damn thing about trigonometry. Things got worse before they got better. We were issued a complex slide rule to solve trigonometry and other math problems. I had never used a slide rule before and realized I had probably bitten off more than I could chew! Somehow, I squeaked by first semester math and was out of danger by the end of the year, ranking 536 of 771 in math. Fifty-one former classmates were eliminated for being deficient in mathematics that year.

Plebe year had its lighter moments. The entire corps was bussed to Yankee Stadium one Saturday morning for the Army–Notre Dame football game. Both teams were undefeated, and the national championship hung in the balance. To everyone's regret, the game ended in a tie, but we had a few hours of freedom before the bus ride back to West Point. Rufus "Rufe" Smith and I walked to Times Square dressed in our cadet uniforms. Without much trouble, we found two female companions along the way and headed for the famous Colony Club. Rufe and I had decided earlier that we would split the bill. The legal age for drinking was 18 in New York, but reality was "big enough to put your money on the bar, old enough to drink!" We had a few drinks, danced with the girls, and ate dinner. When it was time to go, the waiter presented the bill—$60 for the four of us!

I passed the bill over to Rufe along with my $30. Rufe put five dollars on top of my $30 and gave the money and the bill to the waiter. The waiter looked horrified and quickly disappeared. The headwaiter came to our table and said we had not paid our entire bill. We agreed. He then asked Rufe four questions. First: "Did you like the music and dancing?" Second: "Were your drinks good?" And third: "Did you enjoy dinner?" Rufe answered, "Yes, sir," to each question. "Then why don't you pay your whole bill?" the headwaiter asked. "Because I don't have any more money," was Rufe's answer. "Did you think that five dollars would cover an expensive evening in the Colony Club with a pretty girl like her?" he asked, while eyeing Rufe's new friend who looked ready to disappear under the table. "Sir," Rufe said, "In Fort Huachuca, Arizona, you can dine and dance all night for five bucks!" The headwaiter laughed, tore up the check, and told us to bring more money next time! Who said New Yorkers have no heart? Slightly more sophisticated and certainly more sober, we caught the bus in time and headed back to West Point.

Alan Ladd, a famous leading man in the '40s and '50s, starred in a movie about West Point that was filmed during the spring of plebe year. The handsome Mr. Ladd was not tall enough to be a cadet, even with his elevated shoes. Cadets were assigned to companies by height; "flankers" were in tall companies and "runts" in short. The reason for this arrangement was purely cosmetic. When the corps marched in parades, everyone would appear to be the same height, an illusion no longer politically correct or feasible now that female cadets comprise about 20 percent of the corps. Acting as a cadet company commander in the movie, Mr. Ladd marched several paces ahead of his company, which minimized the height difference and also required minimal marching skills. The Big Day in the movie had Mr. Ladd leading his company in the graduation parade. Company K-1 (the runt company I called home) had won the annual drill competition and was given the dubious honor of marching in full dress uniform behind Ladd one hot, sunny afternoon.

As each company approaches the reviewing stand, the company commander is supposed to command, "Eyes . . . right!" and draw his saber from its scabbard with his right hand, raise the saber until the hilt is opposite his jaw and the blade is pointing vertically upward, turn his head to the right, and salute the reviewing officer. Ladd led K-1 past the reviewing stand several times but always flunked the saber salute. To his credit, he did not stab himself, hurt any bystanders, or leave lasting saber holes in the ground after dropping the saber every time we passed in review.

7

Soon, a new invisible problem made itself known. The smell from 120 sweaty wool uniforms became obvious to all as time after time we marched by the reviewing stand on this hot spring day. Clearly irritated by Ladd, the weather, and the smell, the director changed the cast. Our cadet company commander took over from Mr. Ladd and successfully completed the scene. While we were making the final pass by the reviewing stand, Mr. Ladd retreated to his quarters, probably seeking a stiff drink.

Maj Gen Maxwell Taylor was the new superintendent at West Point during my first two years. General Taylor was destined to be Army chief of staff and later chairman, Joint Chiefs of Staff (JCS). On D-Day, Taylor had jumped into Normandy with the 101st Airborne Division. When he became superintendent, he brought a cadre of young paratrooper colonels and lieutenant colonels with him. Those he picked were clearly superior officers, and they served as excellent role models. It did not take long for cadets to nickname West Point the "101 Ranch."

General Taylor instituted several badly needed reforms during his tour as superintendent. One reform was a modified Fourth Class system (plebe year). The stated objectives of plebe year were not controversial: instill perseverance, discipline, devotion to duty, personal integrity, and the ability to overcome adversity. The academy motto of Duty, Honor, Country summarized these individual responsibilities. A major goal of plebe year was to instill the motto so deeply in the individual cadet that it would become his lifelong criteria for acceptable behavior.

The motto and the objectives did not require reform. However, the leadership techniques used by upper-class cadets and condoned by the tactical department were often counterproductive and needed reform. In a technical sense, hazing was forbidden—meaning no upperclassman could *physically* abuse a plebe. There was no beating with paddles or other rites of passage used by some college fraternities. While obeying the letter of the law, some upperclassmen skirted the law with practices that were immature, abusive, and demeaning.

When all is said and done, the overriding objective of the academy, beginning with plebe year, was to train military leaders. Despite the "in-your-face" screaming by Hollywood drill sergeants as frequently portrayed in TV advertisements and "boot camp" movies, our armed forces do not consider personal abuse an effective form of leadership. I have often wondered how many West Point graduates from that era failed as career officers because they could not reconcile their negative leadership experiences at West Point with the positive leadership required in the armed forces. To the credit of subsequent superintendents, tactical departments, and faculty members, leadership training at West Point today is a far cry from that earlier era.

The ending of plebe year on 30 June 1947 was the time to count plebe "casualties" (Army jargon for losses). There had been 130 resignations, 83 discharges for deficiency in studies, 14 discharges for physical disability, six discharges for deficiency in conduct, and four discharges for other reasons. Remaining were 771 cadets ready to begin their sophomore year ("yearlings" in cadet jargon). Another 101 would be discharged or would resign in the next three years. Not me. A military career was still my goal despite the post–World War II atrophy of our armed forces.

Camp Buckner, located on the large West Point Military Reservation, was the site for field training exercises and weapons training in the summer months for the Fourth and Third Classes. Each summer, upper-class groups would visit selected Air Force bases and Army forts. These "show and tell" visits were useful in familiarizing cadets with the roles and missions of each service. Since prior to graduation cadets must select either the Air Force or a branch of the Army in which to serve, the visits helped steer cadets into a career best suited to their personal aspirations and abilities.

Summer training occasionally offered unexpected thrills. In 1948 we joined Annapolis midshipmen on a joint operation at the Navy/Marine base at Little Creek, Virginia, where Sailors and Marines trained for amphibious operations. Among other things, we learned how Marines from a larger ship transferred to a smaller ship by climbing down a rope net hanging over the side of the larger ship. After training on the upcoming operation, we boarded a landing ship, tank (LST).

The sea was moderately rough on Exercise D-Day for the amphibious assault. Cadets wore or carried combat gear—steel helmets, combat boots, M-1 rifles with bayonets, canteens, and backpacks. This much weight made falling into the ocean something to avoid. The first task was to climb down the net hanging from the LST and get into the landing craft, infantry (LCI) that was bobbing up and down next to the LST.

The LCI would rise in the water and bang against the LST hull as big waves rocked the two boats. After each big wave passed, about eight more cadets would climb down the net and climb into the LCI. I was assigned the farthest left position on the net. After climbing halfway down the net, a large wave caused the left side of the net to flip over and pin me between the net and the LST. If the next wave slammed the LCI against the LST before the net returned to the normal position, I could be crushed. Luckily, the net flipped back to the normal position when the large wave receded. Before another large wave came, I finished climbing down the net and jumped into the LCI. Close call!

Another summer we went to Fort Benning, Georgia, for paratrooper training and airborne operations. Our training did not include actually jumping from an aircraft. Cadets were not allowed to qualify for jump wings during my years as a cadet, a restriction that no longer applies. To give some taste of reality, we took a familiarization ride in a troop-carrying glider. These gliders were the same type used with poor results and high casualty rates during the Normandy invasion.

An Air Force C-47, the proverbial "Gooney Bird," towed our glider using a long cable stretched between the two aircraft. The glider pilot provided a little extra thrill by performing "evasive action" maneuvers as in combat, such as rapidly climbing and descending several times a minute while being towed about 600–1,000 feet above the Georgian pine woods.

The glider had open windows along each side of the troop compartment. It was a hot summer day. Before long, one classmate—with his complexion now matching his green fatigue uniform—reacted strongly to the heat and mild acrobatics. Lacking an "urp cup," he resolved his problem by attempting to toss whatever remained of his lunch out the open window to his left. As might be expected at 150 miles per hour, his intended contribution to glider sanitation and Georgia farming did not go out the open window. Instead, the wind stream bounced it back onto the man sitting directly behind him, a master sergeant, now wearing a very pained look on his face. Recognizing his error, the cadet sheepishly turned and said,

"Gee, I'm really sorry, sergeant. I thought it would go out the window." The master sergeant's response was terse, specific, and nonquotable!

At that same moment, the cable connecting the glider to the C-47 snapped. The broken cable whipped into the windscreen sending broken glass from the cockpit into the troop compartment. The broken glass seriously injured nobody, but a question arose. All we could see below were pine forests. Would we crash into the trees?

My friend Rufe Smith and I started to stand up. We were going to display our newfound parachute skills by bailing out the rear door. The same master sergeant anticipated our action. "Damn it! Sit down and strap in!" We did. Within seconds the pilot steeply banked the glider over a farmer's small field and attempted to land. The glider hit the ditch at the edge of the field and flipped over amidst a great cloud of Georgian red dust. We all climbed out, dirty but unhurt, and thanked the pilot for a great job! Important lesson learned: pay attention when master sergeants speak.

The summer of 1949 began my last year at West Point. About two dozen First Classmen were assigned to Fort Knox, Kentucky, as platoon leaders in the Third Armored Division. Our job: teach basic training to recruits. It was a great personal experience and afforded many leadership opportunities. The downside was a genuine eye opener. Not obvious to cadets was the steady deterioration of Army capabilities during the three years we had been at West Point. The magnificent Army of World War II was now scraping bottom. Plain and simple, the Army was broke. One manifestation of Army problems was a shortage of qualified recruits.

After a few days on the job, we compared notes. It was obvious to us that many recruits were underage and should not be Soldiers. When this fact was brought to the attention of the battalion commander, he told us the unwritten Army policy. "If they're big enough to carry a rifle and can pass basic training, they can stay unless their parents come to Fort Knox and take them home." Somewhat nonplused by the lieutenant colonel's answer, we went back to work.

Too many recruits were poorly educated, borderline illiterate, and lacked normal cultural development, especially recruits from the mountainous regions of Kentucky, Pennsylvania, West Virginia, and North Carolina. Basic training at Fort Knox was my first exposure to this segment of American society. Their poor reading and writing skills, coupled with limited exposure to normal American living standards, severely handicapped their progress in basic training. Several examples stick in my memory.

On his third night in the Army, one young Soldier in my platoon relieved himself and hid the feces under his bunk in the open bay barracks. He had ignored using the latrine available at the end of the barracks. During morning inspection the next day, the company commander identified what had happened, and the floor was quickly cleaned. After the recruit returned from the field in late afternoon, I told him what we had found and asked for an explanation. He professed to have never seen or used indoor plumbing before joining the Army, did not know how to flush a toilet, and was too embarrassed to ask for help. So, when three days constipation became unbearable, he relieved himself and hid it under the bed. After his squad leader thoroughly trained him in the use of latrine facilities, he successfully avoided further incidents.

One Sunday, I was officer of the day for the battalion. The phone rang, and an excited voice asked me to come to his barracks right away—"a big fight was under way" between recruits who temporarily were acting as noncommissioned officers (NCO) and the other recruits. (Recruits doing well in basic training were given this recognition as an incentive and wore an armband indicating their status.) Sure enough, lots of pushing and shoving was under way when I walked behind the barracks.

There were several trees behind the barracks where the scuffling was occurring. After calming things down, I discovered the problem. A recruit had arranged for his wife to "service" all the recruits in his platoon. As they waited their turn standing in line at the edge of the woods, he watched all the activity. The fighting started when she had grown tired and would only deal with the temporary NCOs—"the guys wearing armbands." I broke up the "party," sent everyone back to their barracks, and had the military police haul away the loving couple. Neither my prior life nor cadet years had quite prepared me for this experience!

Prior to the end of basic training, we could nominate highly qualified recruits for a special training course leading to early promotion to corporal if they passed a rather simple, multiple-choice quiz. One recruit in my platoon was truly outstanding. He did everything well, and I enthusiastically nominated him. The day after he took the written test, the company commander called me to his office. "Mr. Leavitt, how in hell could you recommend Jones? He missed every question and scored zero on the test!"

I couldn't understand why Jones did so poorly and asked him to explain. "Sir, I'm really sorry," he said with tears in his eyes. "I can't read. The Navy found out just as I finished boot camp and discharged me. I was hoping the Army wouldn't find me out."

I never knew whether Jones was discharged following this incident, but the memory of his personal tragedy lingered in my mind. Twenty-five years later, as a major general commanding the large Air Force technical training center at Chanute AFB, Illinois, I arranged individual training with modern teaching techniques and equipment for young men and women with learning difficulties. Individual training was needed despite the fact that all had earned high school diplomas before enlisting in the Air Force.

After returning to West Point, our company tactical officer, a very nice lieutenant colonel whom I respected, called me to his office. He said the reports on my performance at Fort Knox were exceptional and maybe I should stay in the Army rather than transferring to the Air Force. Naturally, I was pleased to hear about the reports. I told him the assignment to Fort Knox was a great experience, but I would probably stick with the Air Force. When the Korean War started, I thought about the recruits at Fort Knox and understood why many Soldiers sent to Korea were ill prepared and not combat ready.

Separated? Yes! Equal Treatment? No!

Many ways to organize black Soldiers into Army units were tried during World War II. The professed objective of all these experiments was to separate the black Soldiers from the white but treat them as equals. When General Eisenhower was Army

13

chief of staff, he detailed the difficulties and inefficiencies of a segregated Army. By denying the black minority the opportunity to serve in an equal status with white service members, the manpower pool of combat-capable Soldiers was reduced by approximately 15 percent. Furthermore, racial tensions increased as blacks recognized that "separate but equal" was discriminatory and actually denied them equality while serving their country.

On 27 July 1948, Pres. Harry S. Truman announced to a special session of Congress that he had issued an executive order ending discrimination in the armed forces. There were only a few black cadets during my years at West Point—only two in the Class of 1950. Most cadets realized that ending discrimination in the armed forces was worthwhile. Not all, as I would soon find out.

First Classmen (seniors) were assigned the responsibility of maintaining discipline and order in the cadet areas. One night I was senior officer of the day (SOD). Among other tasks, the SOD closed the First Class Club after taps, turned the lights off, and locked the club. The First Class Club overlooked the concrete courtyard below and the surrounding barracks. As I turned off the lights, two cadets ran from their barracks across the courtyard and placed a burning cross in front of the barracks where my two black classmates, David Carlisle and Robert Green, lived. I ran down the stairs and quickly entered the courtyard. When they saw me, the two cadets dragged the burning cross across the courtyard and tossed it under their barracks. Both cadets disappeared before I could reach their barracks.

The next morning, I reported the incident to Col Paul D. Harkins, commandant of cadets, and suggested to him that the racial implications of this cross-burning incident at West Point would play poorly in the press.[3] He agreed. I suggested that my classmates living in that area might tell me who burned the cross. After further discussion, Harkins authorized immunity to the cadets if they would come forward and apologize to Carlisle and Green. I passed all this information to several classmates who lived in the barracks where the two cadets disappeared.

At noon, I was standing guard at Washington Hall—the cadet dining hall—at the entrance opening to North Area. Two nervous Third Classmen (sophomores) wandered over to me. A rather sheepish looking one said, "We heard someone was burning a cross near our barracks last night. Is that true?"

"It happened. What do you know about it? " was my response.

"Well, maybe we know who did it. Is it true that whoever did it will not be punished if they apologize to the black cadets?" the other asked.

"Yes. If you are the guys who did it, you will have to apologize. Don't you know the Ku Klux Klan threatens blacks by burning crosses?"

"OK," he said. "We did it but didn't mean any harm. We saw a picture in a magazine of a burning cross and did it for a prank. We're not in the Klan. We'll apologize to the black cadets right away." With this promise, I let them go.

I reported all this to Colonel Harkins. We both assumed the two cadets would do as they promised, so Harkins closed the incident. A year or two before Dave Carlisle died in 2002, I reminded him of the cross-burning incident and the agreement to apologize. To my total surprise, Dave never knew about the cross-burning in front of his barracks, and no one ever apologized to him or to his roommate![4]

Dave Carlisle suffered other indignities during his cadet years that did not surface until years later. On 1 July 1946, when Dave entered West Point and began "Beast Barracks," he was the only black cadet in our class. Cadets were assigned to companies by height and within the company to roommates by class. Dave was assigned two white roommates. On 10 July, a second black cadet, Bob Green, joined our class. Dave describes this event in his brief biography published for the 50th class reunion.

> Immediately, to my roommates' and my consternation, it was decided by some authority unknown to us to effect a change in our living arrangement. Bob, despite being a few inches taller than others in our unit, had been assigned to Eighth New Cadet Company. Now, he was to become my sole roommate. My three ex-roommates, despite their objections, went to other rooms. . . . Suddenly I was forced to join a long line of segregated blacks back to the late 19th century.

I appealed this decision to, successively, my company tactical officer, my regimental tactical officer, and even to the Commandant of Cadets. This august personage . . . listened patiently . . . then said, "Well, yes, you can discuss this matter with General Taylor if you wish. But it won't do you any good."

In one sense, the continual and pervasive mistreatment with occasionally a pleasant interlude that I experienced at West Point was a curiously appropriate form of preparation for an initial tour of Army duty that turned out to be an extension of the segregated experience.

After graduating, Lieutenants Carlisle and Green were assigned to Korea in the Army's last segregated regiment in the 25th Infantry Division (ID). Both were decorated for their combat service in Korea. Captain Carlisle resigned in 1958. Captain Green returned to civilian life in 1955, remained active in the Army Reserve, and retired as a colonel in 1978.

During my Air Force career, problems associated with racial discrimination, real or alleged, continued to surface. Successfully resolving these problems has been a challenge to commanders. Despite occasional setbacks, there has been great progress. It is unlikely that senior officers today would make the decisions that adversely affected Carlisle and Green. In the final analysis, Truman's 1948 executive order mandating desegregation forced the military to lead the rest of American society in ending racial discrimination.

Military History and Career Choice

Perhaps the highest quality and most unique course taught at West Point was military history. Not surprisingly, military history taught in the late 1940s was weighted toward the way the Army fought World War II in Europe and the Pacific. Augmenting various textbooks and lectures by World War II leaders were a series of pamphlets, complete with campaign maps and analyses, published by the Department of Military Art and Engineering (MA&E).[5] These texts, covering major campaigns and war strategies dating from Napoleon's era through World War II, were generally based upon material furnished by the Historical Division, Department of the Army. From other sources, the contributions of naval and airpower were objectively reported and given appropriate credit. For example, the *War in*

Western Europe textbook quotes the United States Strategic Bombing Survey as an overall assessment of airpower's role in defeating Germany.

> Allied air power was decisive in the war in western Europe. In the air its victory was complete; at sea, its contribution, combined with naval power, brought an end to the enemy's greatest naval threat, the U-boat; on the land it helped turn the tide overwhelmingly in favor of Allied ground forces. Its power and superiority made possible the success of the invasion. It brought the economy that sustained the enemy's armed forces to virtual collapse, although the full effects of this collapse had not reached the enemy's front lines when they were overrun by Allied forces. It brought home to the German people the full impact of modern war with all its horror and suffering. Its imprint on the German nation will be lasting.[6]

The Army officers assigned to the MA&E department were not out-of-bounds by including in the same textbook their views on the effectiveness of airpower in fighting Germany. In an outstanding example of "fair and balanced reporting," the editors had this to say:

> But although air power provided a decisive factor in the victory, the conclusive element in the German surrender was the Allied ground strength. Until the infantry of the Western Allies and Russia joined at the Elbe, Germany's will was unbroken. However, it is useless to attempt an assessment of the credit due each of the various arms services or nationalities. Later victory was dependent upon the early refusal of Soviet Russia and England to accept defeat and upon their retention of vital areas. The naval roles of securing the sea lanes and participating in the amphibious attack were also essential. The importance of air operations has already been stated. Nothing could have been accomplished without the logistical support of the service forces. Civilian industry provided the sinews for all.[7]

The *War with Japan* textbook focused on General MacArthur's campaign in the Southwest Pacific and Adm Chester W. Nimitz's "island hopping" campaign across the Central Pacific. Summations stressed the importance of air and naval power in ending the war.

> Final Collapse, 15 August 1945. Constantly increasing air bombardment destroyed the industrial areas of practically all the cities of Japan, and air-sown mine fields sealed the principal seaports. An atomic bomb was dropped on Hiroshima on 6 August and another on Nagasaki on 9 August. On the latter date the Russians attacked in Manchuria. Japan surrendered on 15 August 1945 (14 August in the United States).[8]

17

Army leadership in 1950 was still refighting the successful World War II battles, particularly the Normandy invasion in 1944 and subsequent battles in Northern Europe. Perhaps more attention should have been paid to the 1943 battles in North Africa—Operation Torch—where a poorly trained and equipped Army without adequate air support was badly mauled by a smaller German/Italian army supported by Stuka dive-bombers, Messerschmitt 109 fighters, and hundreds of Luftwaffe transports. The Army learned bitter lessons from these early defeats. Leadership was strengthened, and more troops and millions of tons of supplies and new equipment were sent from the states. When the German and Italian armies in North Africa finally surrendered in May 1943, Army ground forces took proper credit for overcoming the many obstacles leading to victory. Less recognition was given to the AAF for gaining air superiority over North Africa, stopping aerial resupply from Germany, and destroying German and Italian ships as they crossed the Mediterranean. Unable to supply ammunition, tanks, fuel, and troop reinforcements, Hitler sacrificed his stranded African forces. The lesson learned from Torch seemed to be that Army ground forces could be decisive in the forthcoming invasion of Europe if Allied air forces gained and maintained air superiority.

The shrunken fiscal year (FY) 1950 defense budget sharply limited Army modernization after the war. In stark contrast, the Air Force was modernizing with jet-engine bombers and fighters, experimental aircraft propelled by rocket engines, long-range transports, and guided missiles. Capt Chuck Yeager had busted Mach 1, the sonic barrier, in 1947, and the Strategic Air Command (SAC) had inherited the primary responsibility for delivering nuclear weapons. Technology being developed in the research and development (R&D) community promised dramatic improvements in the effectiveness of aircraft and air-delivered weapons.

I went to West Point because of a strong interest in the strategy involved in fighting our country's wars. The reputation West Point had gained for building bridges and other Corps of Engineers projects were not my primary interest—probably a good decision considering my mediocre grades in mathematics. The infantry had appeal as a career choice, and I agreed that "boots on the ground" was a necessary factor in winning wars. Working with troops had a special attraction after my Fort Knox experience.

Why did I choose to leave the Army and join the Air Force? The increasingly important role that aircraft played in World War II indicated to me the decisive factor in winning future wars would be airpower. The Air Force was my choice but made without resentment toward the Army. I viewed the Army with great respect and would have proudly served in a "green suit." Topping all these cerebral reasons was the emotional challenge to fly jet fighters in some future war.

April 1950 came up fast. It was time to make a career decision. The five largest quotas available for assignment were infantry—199, Air Force—167, engineers—84, field artillery—74, and cavalry—41. The selection process was in order of class academic standing. The number one graduate in 1950, Bill De-Graf, chose the infantry. Bill was the youngest officer in World War II to earn a battlefield commission, edging Lt "Audie" Murphy by 19 days. A platoon leader in the European theater in World War II, Bill saw combat in both the Korean and Vietnam wars before retiring as a colonel. He is one of the few individuals to have earned three Combat Infantryman Badges.

Traditionally, the highest ranking cadets upon graduation chose the Corps of Engineers, although there have been numerous exceptions. In 1950, 84 graduates who chose Corps of Engineers included numbers two, three, and four by class ranking. The future president of the Philippines, Fidel Ramos, also chose the Corps of Engineers.

Three infantry officers became four-star generals—Paul F. Gorman, Volney F. Warner, and John A. Wickham, the Army chief of staff from 1983 to 1987. One cavalry officer, Wallace Nutting, gained four stars. John Murphy, first captain of the cadet corps and our class president, also chose infantry. In the Korean War, Murphy won the Distinguished Service Cross, two Bronze Star Medals for Valor, the Purple Heart, the Combat Infantryman's Badge, and a Commendation Medal. After resigning from the Army in 1956, Murphy was elected to Congress in 1963 and served eight terms in the House of Representatives.

Two USAF officers became four-star generals—Charles A. Gabriel, the Air Force chief of staff from 1982 to 1986, and Bennie L. Davis, Commander in Chief, SAC, 1981–85. The most famous member of the class was probably Col Frank Borman, a National Aeronautics and Space Administration (NASA) astronaut from 1962 to 1970. He commanded the first spacecraft to rendezvous in space in December 1965 and the first spacecraft to make a circumlunar orbit. On Christmas Eve 1968, Borman and his fellow astronauts during the first lunar orbit each read a verse from Genesis 1 and stirred the hearts of millions throughout the world: "In the beginning, God created the heavens and the earth. . . ." In addition to many NASA decorations and other recognitions, Borman received the Congressional Space Medal of Honor in 1978.

The Howitzer 1950, *US Military Academy yearbook*

My 1950 classmates in K-1 Company. One of 24 companies in the corps of cadets. *Standing on left*, Peltz, Barrett, Dunn; *standing on right*, Hirsch, Talbott, Leavitt; *first row sitting*, Garrett, Laccetti, Harrell, Hutcheson, Paulger, Vinson; *second row*, Blank, McFarland, Lockwood, Warner, Webster; *third row*, Hufnagel, McDowell, Newcomb, Price, Shemwell; *fourth row standing*, McDaniel, Weight, Dowe, Sweidel, Smith. Wartime losses: Lt Courtney L. Barrett, Jr., 2d Infantry Division (ID), KIA Korea, 27 Sept 1950; Lt Warren Webster III, 7th ID, KIA Korea, 21 Feb 1953; and Lt Col Bobby G. Vinson, USAF, MIA North Vietnam, 24 Apr 1968, DED 1977, Colonel. Of the 28 members of the Class of 1950 who graduated and were commissioned, 21 retired (75 percent) with 20 or more years' military service, 15 fought in the Korean War (includes two KIA and one POW), 16 fought in the Vietnam War (includes one KIA), 10 fought in both the Korean and Vietnam wars, and four resigned in 1953–54 after the Korean War.

Bill DeGraf
First in class

Jack Murphy
First captain of cadets

Fidel Ramos, DG 2000
Philippines president

Frank Borman, DG 1996

Charlie Gabriel, DG 2001

Dave Hughes, DG 2004

John Wickham, DG 2005

Dick Trefry, DG 2007

Wally Nutting, DG 2008

Class of 1950 ranking West Point cadets and distinguished graduates (DG). "DG" awards are for accomplishments after graduation. (*The Howitzer 1950*, US Military Academy yearbook)

Graduation day finally arrived on 6 June 1950. Of the 1,008 who entered four years earlier, 670 (66.4 percent) graduated. Four days earlier, 172 Annapolis graduates had been commissioned in the Air Force and would join us for pilot training. Nevertheless, in an amazing display of inter-service cooperation, 167 West Point graduates transferring to the Air Force were sworn in as second lieutenants at a very low-key ceremony on 2 June, thus gaining the same date of rank (DOR) as Annapolis contemporaries joining the Air Force. In exchange for this act of kindness, we were cautioned not to "pull rank" on Army classmates who would not be commissioned until 6 June. When the "secret" commissioning ceremony leaked out—five minutes after we were sworn in the Air Force—no Army classmates were seen leaping with joy over our good fortune!

The principal academy objective is to produce motivated leaders who will devote a major part of their lives to military service. Newly commissioned graduates must complete an active-duty commitment, the length of which has varied from time to time. For example, active-duty time has been reduced if the officer would join the Reserve or National Guard. Ideally, academy graduates would satisfy their minimum commitment, receive periodic promotions, and stay until eligible for retirement. In reality, many graduates leave before reaching retirement. Careers must have met or exceeded expectations for West Point classmates who chose the Air Force; only 38 (22.7 percent) resigned before reaching retirement.

Looking back on cadet days offers an opportunity to assess the impact of West Point on my later life. The Duty, Honor, Country motto has served as a constant reminder of my obligations to society. The emphasis on self-discipline and physical training made it easier to tolerate stressful situations in both combat and peacetime. The jam-packed daily schedules at West Point taught how to prioritize the competing demands a successful leader will encounter. When the four long years ended, I felt prepared for an Air Force career—my original purpose in attending.

Peacetime Snooze Gets Cold War Wake-Up

Startling events between World War II and the Korean War pushed the United States into roles not visualized by previous generations of Americans. As World War II drew to a close in 1945, the "Big Three" Allies—United States, Great Britain, and Soviet Union—held two important conferences. The first was held in January 1945 at Yalta on the Black Sea prior to the German surrender in May 1945. The second was in July in the Berlin suburb of Potsdam before Japan surrendered in August. The conferences resulted in the Yalta and Potsdam Declarations, two agreements whose unforeseen consequences included the boundaries of the 45-year Cold War.

Joseph Stalin, general secretary of the Communist Party of the Soviet Union, immediately violated the Yalta Declaration concerning the boundaries of postwar Poland. After Pres. Franklin D. Roosevelt died, his successor, Harry S. Truman, believed that the United States must comply with the Yalta Declaration despite Soviet noncompliance. He informed Prime Minister Winston Churchill on 9 May 1945 that American troops would pull back from their positions on the Elbe to new locations approximately 150 miles to the west.[9] Churchill saw this as a terrible mistake. Wisely or not, the Yalta Declaration split Europe—democracy to the West and Communism to the East.

How had the United States been trapped into signing the Yalta Declaration with its onerous consequences for the postwar era? Hindsight being better than foresight, we now realize that President Roosevelt's deteriorating health prevented him from being at the top of his game at Yalta. Moreover, Vice President Truman did not participate with Roosevelt, Stalin, and Churchill at that January 1945 conference. President Roosevelt did not return from the conference until the end of February 1945. Truman met with Roosevelt only twice between Roosevelt's return from Yalta and his departure for Warm Springs, Georgia, where he died. At neither time was the Yalta Conference discussed.[10]

On 12 April 1945, immediately following President Roosevelt's death, Vice President Truman had taken the presidential oath of office. He had little opportunity during the 82 days remaining before the Potsdam Conference to understand the possible ramifications of the Yalta Declaration. Truman had never met Stalin. On the other hand, Churchill, an early skeptic about Soviet intentions, realized the threat to Western civilization was real. He wrote of the "Iron Curtain" in a 12 May 1945 message to Truman and warned of the impending Cold War. Churchill in his famous speech at Westminster College, Fulton, Missouri, on 5 March 1946, reiterated and amplified his opinions to the press and the audience present, which included Truman.

President Truman knew the first nuclear explosion at Alamogordo, New Mexico, on 16 July 1945 had been successful the day after he arrived at Potsdam and before negotiations began. Truman believed the only accomplishment at Potsdam was to bring the USSR into the war against Japan. Eisenhower advised Truman not to beg the Russians into the war. Whether Truman fully understood the impact the bomb would have on ending the war is not clear. Some years later, he told Margaret Truman that he would not have wanted the USSR in the war against Japan if he had known what the bomb would do.

Potsdam had another secret agreement with long-term, bad implications. The Potsdam Declaration ruled out either the unification or independence of Vietnam. It was decided that Vietnam would be divided, with China in charge north of the 16th parallel and British forces in charge in the south. By so doing, the French were given the opportunity to return. The quid pro quo for France joining the North Atlantic Treaty Organization (NATO) was Truman's pledge that America would support the French against Ho Chi Minh. During 1952–53, I served on the operations staff in Headquarters (HQ) Far East Air Forces (FEAF) and witnessed this support operation. FEAF implemented Truman's agreement by flying supplies to French Foreign Legionnaires fighting Ho Chi Minh forces in Vietnam. USAF aircrews wearing civilian clothes flew USAF transport aircraft in this sensitive operation.

President Truman left Potsdam believing he could work with Stalin and was convinced Stalin would honor both the Yalta and Potsdam Declarations. "I like Stalin. He is straightforward," he wrote in a letter to Bess Truman.[11] "Stalin was a fine man who wanted to do the right thing," Truman told Henry Wallace.[12]

From 1946 to 1950, the United States moved from crisis to crisis with our aggressive former ally—the Soviet Union. During this time, "containment" became our foreign policy. Containment's objective was to limit further Communist expansion, particularly Stalin's attempts to communize Europe. We would build alliances with other free nations and deter Soviet aggression with our nuclear monopoly, confident the USSR was the only clear threat to world peace. With this geopolitical fence around the Communist world, we could avoid war and wait for Communism to collapse.

In late 1945 and 1946, with a collective sigh of relief, the United States had demobilized. The rapid, almost chaotic demobilization drastically reduced the size of the Army and the Air Force. When "Johnny came marching home again," the greatest military force in the world reverted to prewar impotence—with one exception. We had the *Bomb*. Without great debate or much foresight, America quickly reverted to traditional, prewar foreign and defense policies. Core beliefs were to avoid entangling alliances and to keep the US Navy (USN) as America's first line of defense.

Stalin also reduced Soviet armies but maintained a force structure several times larger than our own and a wartime economy. In 1948 the United States swallowed a large dose of reality when the Soviets blockaded Berlin. The Berlin Airlift kept Berlin alive. After 321 days, on 12 May 1949, Stalin abandoned the blockade and seemed to accept a stabilized Germany.

Being the only nation possessing the "atom bomb" minimized the risk of war in the minds of many policy makers. General Bradley, Army chief of staff in 1948, seemed to ignore the fact that the USSR had neither nuclear weapons nor a long-range bomber force. He offered the following strange testimony to Congress during hearings on the FY 1949 Military Appropriations Bill.

> [We] must consider the possibility that the United States will be subject to air and air-borne attack at the outset. The likelihood and the practicability of this kind of attack increases daily. . . . We would have to immediately secure bases from which an enemy might attack us by air. Next, we will have to launch an immediate counterattack . . . predominantly through the air. . . . To make our counterblows we will need bases which we do not have now. The seizing and holding of these bases . . . will require Army combat elements.[13]

The ending of World War II had shuffled the principals in world politics. Left standing in dominant positions were the United States and Soviet Union. Great Britain was unable to assume anything more than a secondary role because of severe economic problems. Strong Communist parties in France and Italy threatened democracy in both nations. Civil war raged in Greece between Communist guerrillas sponsored by the USSR and a royalist government backed by British forces.

Following the British withdrawal of troops in 1946, American aid became an imperative if democracy was to survive in Greece. Turkey was similarly threatened and needed American support. Civil war between Nationalist and Communist armies kept China in chaos. With colonialism dead or dying, former European colonies in Asia, the Middle East, Indian Ocean, Southeast Asia, and Africa struggled to develop their own political systems and economies. Truman addressed a joint session of Congress on 12 March 1947 and asked for $400 million to aid Greece and Turkey. The Truman Doctrine was the first postwar recognition of our superpower responsibilities.

America reacted strongly to other attempts by Stalin to communize Europe. Our containment policy included economic, political, and defense initiatives. The Marshall Plan began bolstering Western European economies with billions in aid. Slowly but surely, Western Europe came alive. After extensive negotiation, the NATO Treaty was signed on 4 April 1949 and ratified by the US Senate on 21 July 1949. Signing nations had agreed on an "all for one and one for all" promise to defend against aggression.

The Korean War Begins

Pres. Theodore Roosevelt served as the mediator of the peace conference in 1905 that formally ended the Russo-Japanese War. The resulting Treaty of Portsmouth recognized Japanese control of Korea. In the closing days of WWII, the USSR reversed its 1905 losses to Japan and occupied Korea before the United States could land troops there. Army colonel Dean Rusk, later the secretary of state in the Vietnam War, negotiated an agreement with the Soviets in 1945. Japanese troops north of the 38th parallel would surrender to the Soviets, and Japanese troops south of the 38th parallel would surrender to the United States. The Soviets then created a Communist government in the north called the Democratic People's Republic of Korea (DPRK).

During 1946 and 1947, after sending the surrendered Japanese troops below the 38th parallel back to Japan, the United States developed a provisional government in South Korea under Syngman Rhee. In December 1948, President Truman authorized the withdrawal of the last American troops from South Korea. On New Year's Day 1949, he recognized the Republic of (South) Korea (ROK) under US military protection. Intentionally or by oversight, General MacArthur, Far East commander, omitted the Korean Peninsula in his March 1949 definition of our defense responsibilities: "Our line of defense runs through the chain of islands fringing the coast of Asia. It starts from the Philippines and continues through the Ryukyu Archipelago, which includes its main bastion Okinawa. Then it bends back through Japan and the Aleutian Island chain to Alaska."[14]

After withdrawing all forces from Korea, Secretary of State Dean Acheson outlined a "defensive perimeter" in January 1950 that defined the nations vital to our national security. Korea was not included.[15] In his speech before the National Press Club, Acheson not only consigned Korea to being outside the American defense perimeter but specifically abjured any intentions of guaranteeing areas located on the mainland of Asia, stating that "so far as the military security of other areas of the Pacific is concerned, it must be clear that no person can guarantee these areas against military attack. But it must also be clear that such a guarantee is hardly sensible or necessary within the realm of practical relationship.[16]

When Acheson and MacArthur announced that Korea was not in our defense perimeter, it left the ROK with no guarantee against attack. Kim Il Sung, Communist premier of the DPRK, wanted to unify Korea by conquering South Korea. He knew Soviet Union assistance with planning, materiel, and technical support would guarantee success against the poorly led and equipped South Korean army. Stalin, aware of America's denials of protection for South Korea, went along with Kim.

If Stalin needed further proof the United States would not go to war over Korea, he could refer to American policy toward the civil war in China. We had accepted Chairman Mao Tse-tung forcing Chiang Kai-shek to retreat to Taiwan and did not intervene despite Nationalist China being a World War II ally of the United States. When American policies toward Asia from 1948 to 1950 are fully considered, it is understandable why Communist leaders in Moscow and Pyongyang might have expected nothing more than a diplomatic protest from the United States when North Korean troops crossed the 38th parallel and invaded South Korea.

Not well known at the time was the active Soviet participation in the Korean War. In 1976, the Defense Nuclear Agency released *A Study of Breakthrough Operations* that detailed the USSR's role in the initial phase of the Korean War.[17] A high-ranking group of Soviet staff officers prepared and directed the surprise attack. Overall control was the responsibility of Gen Aleksei Antonov, chief of staff of the Soviet General Staff. Most of the high-ranking North Korean officers had served as line or staff officers in the WWII Soviet armed forces and were ex-Soviet citizens. All the armament and equipment were made in the Soviet Union and provided to the North Korean People's Army (NKPA). Soviet advisors continued to play an active role as the war progressed.

The US defense budget for 1949 was totally inadequate to support a conventional war in Korea. The total defense budget proposed in 1949 by Truman's controversial defense secretary, Louis Johnson, and approved for FY 1950 was only $13 billion.[18] In April 1950, a report by the National Security Council (NSC), NSC-68, sharply criticized the military strength of the United States and called for a large military buildup costing $40 to $50 billion ($274 to $342 billion in 2003 dollars) per year. Truman chose not to act on the NSC report. By accepting Johnson's proposal, Truman forced the Defense Department to shoot craps with the Soviets and North Koreans with only $13 billion in our defense pockets.

The North Korean army crossed the 38th parallel and invaded South Korea at 4:00 a.m., 25 June 1950, a Sunday morning (Saturday in Washington). On Monday the administration decided to provide air and naval support to South Korea and seek a supporting United Nations (UN) resolution. By Tuesday North Korean tanks were in Seoul, the South Korean capital. That night the UN Security Council voted 9-0 in favor of using armed force to stop the invasion. Truman stated on 27 June 1950 that "the attack upon Korea makes it plain beyond all doubt that Communism has passed beyond the use of subversion to conquer independent nations and will now use armed invasion and war. It has defied the orders of the Security Council of the United Nations issued to preserve peace and security.[19]

At a Thursday, 29 June, press conference, Truman agreed to be quoted after stating with emphasis, "We are not at war." A reporter asked if it would be correct to call this a "police action" under UN auspices. Truman answered, "Yes. That is exactly what it amounts to."[20] This intentional downplaying of what turned out to be the fifth largest war in US history created a long-term controversy. On Friday, 30 June, President Truman approved General MacArthur's request and committed ground troops to combat in Korea.

In addition to committing ground and air forces in the Korean War, Truman sent our Seventh Fleet to protect Taiwan from invasion and increased military aid to French Indochina where the French Foreign Legion was fighting Ho Chi Minh. Truman's objective was to stop Communist aggression. Mao may have seen these moves by Truman as evidence we intended to over-throw his Communist government and reinstate Chiang Kai-shek and the Nationalist government that had fled to Taiwan.[21]

In August 1950, the United Nations Command (UNC) was fighting desperately to save South Korea. Seoul had fallen quickly to North Korean forces, and refugees flooded the roads leading south. American and ROK ground forces had been driven back to the southeastern perimeter of South Korea de-fined by the Naktong River. A major battle along the perimeter was in progress to keep Pusan, the destination port for Ameri-can reinforcements and war materials, from being captured. Without reinforcements and supplies, the outmanned and out-gunned American and ROK troops would be doomed.

From July through September 1950, UNC tactical air forces were significantly increased. During the battle for the Naktong Perimeter, the principal airfield left in South Korea was at Taegu. Called "K-2," it later developed into a jet fighter base, but in the fall of 1950 was only suitable for conventional aircraft. F-51 fighter-bombers staging through K-2 played a major role in stabilizing the battle and preventing the North Korean army from breaking into the UNC defensive positions along the Naktong.

On 13 July, B-29s from the 22d and 92d Bomb Groups began their strategic bombing campaign against North Korean industrial centers. The 98th and 307th SAC Bomb Groups deployed to FEAF in early August. By 26 September 1950, there were no targets left on the strategic target list. Only one B-29 was lost to enemy action during these three months.

The North Korean air force (NKAF) was destroyed in the first month of the war. It had started the war with approximately 140 World War II Russian fighters and attack aircraft. NKAF air bases became unusable because of repeated B-29 bombing attacks. Their obsolete aircraft and ill-trained pilots were no match for the better equipped and trained USAF and Navy fighter pilots. We totally dominated the skies over North Korea at that point—a situation that would change when the MiG-15 entered the air war.

General MacArthur pulled a rabbit out of the hat on 15 September 1950. Bypassing most of the North Korean army, he launched an amphibious assault at Inchon, near Seoul. Combining luck and audacity, the landing achieved all objectives. Within a few days, the successful invasion force cut in two the North Korean army forces invading South Korea. UNC forces recaptured Seoul by the end of September and began moving rapidly north toward the Yalu River.

MacArthur's success forced the United States and its UN allies to reevaluate their reason for entering the war. The UN resolution on 25 June was to stop North Korean aggression and restore the 38th parallel as the boundary between North and South Korea. Routing the North Korean army after the Inchon invasion put a different face on the war. A JCS message dated 27 September 1950 gave permission to MacArthur to cross the 38th parallel. "The destruction of the North Korean Armed Forces" became the new objective. On 7 October, the UN passed a resolution that called for reunifying Korea by force. This most important political decision probably brought China into the war.

The first months of the Korean War severely impacted the West Point Class of 1950. The Army had canceled many graduation leaves and sent these young lieutenants directly to Korea. Thirteen were killed before the year ended.

Notes

(All notes appear in shortened form. For full citation, see the appropriate entry in the bibliography.)

1. The AAC became a subordinate element to the Army Air Forces (AAF) on 20 June 1941 and was not disestablished until 18 September 1947. AAF personnel remained assigned to the AAC until assigned to the USAF on 18 September 1947. "USAF Almanac 2000," 45.

2. During the four years that I was a West Point cadet, a total of only 1,855 cadets graduated. During WWII, the curriculum had been reduced to three years. After the war, the four-year program was restored and the Class of 1947 was split in half, primarily by age. The revised Classes of 1947 and 1948 had 310 and 301 graduates, respectively. The Classes of 1949 and 1950 had 582 and 670 graduates, respectively. Classmates shared similar academic, social, athletic, and military experiences. While cadets, they fostered friendships that extended into their military careers.

Perhaps the major distinction between the Class of 1950 and its predecessors was the high percentage of WWII veterans. This provided an experience factor that was lacking in earlier classes. I was a 16-year-old senior in high school when the war ended. I learned a great deal from these older, veteran classmates. The West Point Association of Graduates publishes annually the *Register of Graduates*, which includes a brief resume of each graduate's career. It has been an invaluable source of information as I searched for names, assignments, dates, and career accomplishments.

3. Gen Paul Harkins was commandant of cadets from 1948 to 1951. Harkins also served in WWII and the Korean War and was the commanding general of the US Military Assistance Command, Vietnam (MACV) and MAC, Thailand, from 1962 to 1964. He was awarded two Distinguished Service Medals and three Bronze Star Medals during his 35 years of active duty. He died on 21 August 1984.

4. The cross-burning incident led to long conversations with Dave Carlisle in later years. Since he was unaware of the incident when it happened, it did not add to his already well-developed sensitivity to racial discrimination. He was more resentful of his Korean War experience serving in the last segregated Army regiment.

5. MA&E faculty was composed of Army and Air Force officers who had served in the various wartime theaters during World War II. The faculty published campaign summaries of World War II, such as *The War with Japan* and *The War in Western Europe*. These summaries captured significant details while they were fresh in the memories of the authors who typically had participated in the campaigns. They also published *Great Captains before Napoleon*; *Jomini, Clausewitz and Schlieffen*; *Supplemental Material on the First*

31

World War; and other texts that provided a basis for understanding the principles of war. Because there was no Air Force Academy at that time, the role of airpower in WWII was afforded equal treatment. In addition to the MA&E faculty, nearly every officer at West Point was either an Army or Army Air Force combat veteran of WWII.

6. US Military Academy, *War in Western Europe*, 123.

7. Ibid.

8. US Military Academy, *War with Japan*, 87–90.

9. McCullough, *Truman*, 469. Several historians have written about the Yalta and Potsdam Declarations creating the circumstances that led to the Cold War. These books include excellent biographies of Churchill, Roosevelt, Truman, Marshall, Eisenhower, and Stalin. They generally concur on the unforeseen consequences of Yalta and Potsdam, particularly in underestimating Stalin's treachery. For the purposes of this book, I have summarized the principal events for the reader using McCullough's *Truman* for specific details concerning this postwar period.

10. Ibid., 422.

11. Ibid., 546.

12. Ibid.

13. Gen Omar Bradley, Army chief of staff, testimony to Congress, hearings on the FY 1949 Military Appropriations Bill, 1948.

14. Kissinger, *Diplomacy*, 475–79.

15. McCullough, *Truman*, 726, 777, 785–86, 799.

16. Kissinger, *Diplomacy*, 476. From *U.S. Department of State Bulletin*, vol. XXII, 116.

17. Historical Evaluation and Research Organization, *Study of Breakthrough Operations*, 83–87.

18. In 1950, $13 billion would be equivalent to approximately $90 billion in 2003. Defense budgets after the Cold War were typically in the mid-$300 billions.

19. Truman, *Memoirs*, vol. 2, *Years of Trial and Hope*, 339.

20. President's news conference, 29 June 1950.

21. Borowski, *Harmon Memorial Lectures in Military History*, 217–27.

Chapter 2

Flight Training
2d Lieutenant—1950–51

Basic: Gold Bars and Horse Manure

The Texas sky was blue, and the warm wind drifting off the flight line carried the sound of T-6 engines beginning their day's work. It was 2 August 1950. I closed the car door and walked toward the operations ("ops") building at Goodfellow AFB. My emotions fluctuated between exhilaration and trepidation! More than a car door had closed. Left behind were the "growing up" years in Michigan and Florida and the rigorous but structured life of a cadet at West Point. My exciting new life included not only switching from Army fatigues to Air Force flight suits and sporting the gold bars of a second lieutenant but marrying Anne Sullivan during graduation leave. Anne and I had arrived only yesterday at San Angelo, home of Goodfellow, where I would begin basic flight training with Class 51-E.

The World War II wooden, one-story ops building where I was to report served several purposes. It faced and was conveniently close to the flight line. Also, it contained the administrative offices for our flying training Class 51-E and had individual briefing rooms for instructors and their students, a locker room for flight gear and personal equipment (PE), and bulletin boards for posting flying and academic schedules. When I opened the door to ops, at that moment I joined my "real world"—the world of flying and fighting for the United States Air Force.

About 80 new second lieutenants, called student officers in Air Training Command (ATC) lingo, reported that morning. After everyone had signed in and met their instructors, we were told to assemble outside, facing the ops building. The captain in charge of training 51-E addressed us briefly and introduced a master sergeant who would give further instructions. The master sergeant called us to attention and told us to line up in alphabetical order. He dismissed the officers with names beginning with A through K after telling them to go to the flight line, meet their instructors, and spend the morning learning about the T-6 aircraft.

He then turned to those whose names began with L through Z—the alphabetically disadvantaged. His immortal words still ring in my ears. "At ease, all you Ls through Zs. See that pile of horse manure over there? Take those rakes and shovels and spread it all over the grass in front of ops. And finish by noon. Dismissed!" Leavitt being my name, I met the alphabetical qualification required and made the team as a horse-manure spreader—my first duty assignment in the Air Force!

We all reassembled in front of ops after lunch. The same captain appeared but this time obviously very angry. He pointed out in rather dramatic terms that one of us had squealed about the horse manure–spreading and that we would really regret getting him into trouble with the base commander. Shortly afterwards, we found out what had happened. L through Z manure spreaders that morning included Lt Robert Luckese. Bobby had called his father in New York during the morning break and told about having to shovel manure. His father called his congressman, Vito Marcantonio, who called Secretary of the Air Force (SECAF) Stuart Symington. Then Symington called Gen Hoyt Vandenberg, USAF chief of staff. Vandenberg, in turn, called Goodfellow AFB and raised hell with the base commander for making those new lieutenants shovel horse manure! The base commander then passed Vandenberg's tight-jawed message to our new boss, the captain. After hearing the captain's threatening remarks, some of my early morning exhilaration disappeared and was replaced by a heavier dose of trepidation!

This incident had several interesting aspects. Lieutenant Luckese decided that he had a fear of flying and self-eliminated from flight training. (USAF policy, then and now, allows personnel who declare a fear of flying to be excused from aircrew duties.) Senator Estes Kefauver had hearings about organized crime in America. Among other things, the hearings alleged that Luckese's father, Thomas, was the notorious "Three-Finger Brown," leader of the Lucchese Mafia family in New York City.[1] Bobby Luckese was immediately transferred from Goodfellow to Lackland Air Force Base where he trained basic recruits. Later, as a budget officer, he served honorably in various Air

Force assignments before resigning in 1955 to enter the family garment business.[2]

The manure-spreading episode did not improve relations between permanent party and student officers. Clearly, attitudes diverged as to how student officers should be treated. This clash of attitudes between permanent party and student officers continued to be a problem throughout flight training. West Point and Annapolis graduates had spent four years earning their commissions, and they resented occasions when the permanent party degraded their officer status. In the new lieutenants' minds, *student officer* seemed to have two meanings—one acceptable, the other not. The acceptable meaning was an *officer* training to become an Air Force *pilot*. The unacceptable connotation was a *student* training to become an *Air Force officer and a pilot.*

A better understanding of the problem can be gained by analyzing the growth and composition of the officer corps from the prewar Army Air Corps to the wartime US Army Air Forces and then to the new USAF. In January 1939, there were only 1,600 officers, mostly pilots, in what was then called the Army Air Corps. The large demand for pilots during World War II had to be satisfied quickly. Fortunately, thousands of young men volunteered and met the physical and mental requirements for flying training.

The year-long wartime Flying Cadet training program was intentionally rigorous. The transition from civilian life to the military was crammed into preflight training, not totally unlike the boot camp used in the other services. As the cadets progressed through primary, basic, and advanced training, at each new phase they flew higher performance aircraft. The jam-packed training schedule necessarily limited their exposure to other issues, such as administration, customs of the service, and leadership training. Assuming all the hurdles were jumped successfully, these new pilots usually faced a combat assignment in a wartime theater or instructor duty in the states.

Pilot supply exceeded demand in 1944. As a result of the rapid buildup and sudden decline in pilot training, the newly formed USAF officer corps in 1947 had a very narrow band of experience. Most field grade officers (major or higher) were pilots commissioned in 1940–43. Most junior officers (lieutenants and captains) were pilots commissioned in 1943–45. This large "hump" of officers that were separated by only five years' or less experience, but separated in rank from lieutenant to general, caused major personnel problems in the new USAF. The hump lasted until significant numbers began to retire with 20 or more years of commissioned service in the 1960s.

Because of the hump, promotions were rare during the austere years between VJ Day and the Korean War—especially promotions beyond first lieutenant. In the summer of 1950, our flight instructors were generally lieutenants, and their supervisors were captains. The majority had been commissioned in World War II after completing flight training. Some had attended college, but a degree was not required.

The senior leaders of the newly formed USAF recognized the need for an Air Force academy to provide educated career officers and began soliciting support. Both the Army and Navy agreed to allow a percentage of their academy graduates to transfer to the Air Force until the Air Force Academy could graduate its first class. Under this agreement, the principal sources for Regular Air Force second lieutenants after the Air Force became a separate service in 1947 were West Point and Annapolis. Strong chief of staff support for this policy continued until the Air Force Academy's first class graduated in 1959.[3]

Another factor after World War II influenced the relationship between the small minority of West Point officers and the large majority commissioned from other sources. In the early days of military aviation, the Army air services were generally commanded by West Point graduates. As World War II approached, the demand for pilots and line officers from other sources, especially the Reserve Officer Training Corps (ROTC), greatly increased. During World War II, many officers from other sources succeeded in command and staff positions and then stayed in the newly formed USAF. Some West Point graduates were seen by these officers as autocrats who expected to get ahead because of their graduation from West Point and not from their competitive abilities. Called "ring knockers," they could often be identified by wearing their West Point class rings. Although there may have been good reasons for resentments and prejudices of this nature, they were seldom openly stated. To avoid the allegation and offending other officers, many West Point graduates in the Air Force, including myself, chose not to wear their West Point rings.

After receiving the gold bars of an Air Force second lieutenant in June 1950, we were granted graduation leave until August, when flight school began. Married student officers lived in the city of San Angelo, and I asked a friend living there for help. He found a small second-floor apartment that was available, and we immediately rented it. Bachelor student officers lived at Goodfellow AFB in two-story wooden barracks built in World War II. Called BOQs for bachelor officers' quarters, the barracks were partitioned into small, individual rooms—one per officer, separated from his neighbor's room by a plywood partition. Everyone shared an "18 hole" latrine with showers located at the end of a hall that ran through the center of the building. The lieutenants living in BOQs knew their housing was rather primitive but took it in good spirits—except for one issue. Every Saturday morning, the captain in charge of 51-E inspected the BOQ and each officer's room. This was too reminiscent of cadet and midshipmen days. One Saturday morning, the captain opened the door to the barracks and found straw spread over all the floors in rooms and the hall.

"What the hell is going on!" he demanded. One of the lieutenants, a West Point football player who 30 years later became a four-star Air Force general, answered, "If you stop treating us like animals, we'll stop behaving like animals." His point was made, and Saturday morning inspections stopped.

As time went on, the relationships between instructors and student officers at Goodfellow improved. The angry captain cooled down and turned out to be a good guy. The students came to learn how to fly, and the instructors responded by teaching us to the best of their abilities. Ground school filled the hours when not flying or briefing to fly. Many hours were spent in classrooms learning about theory of flight, flight controls, weather, navigation, flying regulations, piston engines and engine instruments, instrument flying and flight instruments, parachutes, radio procedures, and Morse code. I still remember the acronym CIGFTR (pronounced *sig-feeter*) for the T-6 pretakeoff cockpit check: controls, instruments, gas, flaps, trim, and radio. Morse code training was another memory-stretching exercise. *Dah* meant *dash*, *dit* meant *dot*, and *ditty* meant two *dots*. Thankfully, by the 1960s improved radios and navigation aids generally negated the need for Morse code.

Flight training was a wonderful new world after spending four years at West Point. Student officers shared a common interest—learning to fly. Although our focus was on flying, the newfound freedom was more than welcome. Gone was the "Army versus Navy" rivalry, and strong, new friendships were quickly formed. Married couples lived in apartments or small houses in San Angelo and socialized with other newlyweds and bachelor buddies. Among other lifestyle adjustments, young wives learned to cope with husbands who seemed to have only two interests, one of which was flying.

Monthly pay in 1950 for second lieutenants on flying status was $240 base pay and $100 flight pay. It seemed like a lot compared to four years of cadet pay at $75 each month. Our food budget was $15 per week, and the rent was $90 a month. Friday night signaled an opportunity to party, and we enjoyed the West Texas hospitality, country fried steak dinners for 95 cents, and 15-cent Lone Star and Pearl beers. Allegations to the contrary, they were brewed with water from "genuine artesian wells," and horses had nothing to do with the brewing process or the flavor. We bought our first dog, a cocker spaniel named Woof because of his distinctive bark. Woof was not the best name for a dog. Whenever he was outside and Anne called "Woof! Woof! Woof!" our next-door neighbors had reason to question the heredity of this lieutenant's young wife.

The T-6 "Texan" was an advanced trainer in World War II, and we were using it for basic flight training. By present standards, it is quite an anachronism. The T-6 was a "tail dragger"; it landed on two front wheels located under the wings and a tail wheel in the rear—no tricycle landing gear like modern aircraft. A piston engine provided the power, not a jet engine. The engine powered a propeller that created "torque." When the propeller was spinning, it caused the aircraft to pull to the right. The faster the propeller turned, the harder the T-6 pulled to the right. This pulling movement was "trimmed out" in flight but had to be taken into serious consideration while taking off. The student pilot had to apply opposite rudder smoothly during takeoff, or the T-6 might "ground loop"—a loss of directional control followed by one of three levels of remorse. Lowest:

if the instructor had to intervene to keep the T-6 pointed in the right direction, a severe butt chewing usually followed. Medium: if the T-6 left the runway and stopped but suffered no damage, a severe butt chewing plus a failing grade for the day and contemptuous glances from the other student pilots. Big Time: if the student lost control and the T-6 ground looped and was damaged, the student probably faced career changes.

My instructor, Lt John Amadon, was both brave and patient. John had been a Flying Cadet who had earned his wings and commission about the same time I graduated from West Point. Immediately after earning his wings, he went to instructor school, and Class 51-E was his first time instructing. Since I had never piloted an aircraft before, everything was a new thrill for me. The basics came easily. Turns, climbs, descents, stalls, spins, barrel rolls, snap roles, and in-flight procedures were all performed to some acceptable level. The big test was learning how to land without bouncing the airplane, stalling it too high, landing too fast, or otherwise terrorizing the onlookers. ATC expected students to solo somewhere between 16 and 20 hours of dual flight instruction. At the end of my 16th hour of instruction, a not particularly memorable flight where we made several landings, John waited for me in the debriefing room. "Lieutenant Leavitt, have you ever thought about being a shoe salesman?" At that point, he walked out. Was my romance with flying over after16 hours? What had gone wrong? Was I going to be washed out?

The following morning, feeling apprehensive because of Amadon's remarks, I reported at the usual time to the briefing room and approached him. "Get your gear, we're going out to the flight line," he said without further explanation or briefing. We walked around the T-6 doing the regular preflight inspection. He said, "Get in!" I climbed into the front cockpit. He was still standing on the wing, looking in my cockpit. "I'm tired of you scaring me. Go scare yourself—and make six good landings while you're at it!" I was soloing! The landings went well, and after the last landing, he congratulated me on a good flight. No selling shoes for this second lieutenant!

One of the sad things about Air Force life—maybe it's a good thing at times—is the constant shuffling of friends and acquaintances as they are transferred to other air bases in the states or overseas. Friendships develop, people move, and the cycle starts over again. The frequency of moves increases in wartime as requirements change to meet new demands. I thought John Amadon was a fine man and an excellent instructor, and I had hoped our paths would cross again after I earned my wings. It never happened. Someone told me later that John was married in San Angelo and resigned from the Air Force after the Korean War.

After soloing, student pilots would frequently practice landings—called "touch and goes." During training, there might be as many as eight or 10 T-6s in the traffic pattern. Once the airplane landed and was firmly on the ground ("touch"), the student would cram the throttle forward and take off again ("go"), headed in the same direction he landed. After reaching altitude, the student would turn and reenter the traffic pattern following the aircraft ahead. One day when I was about halfway down the final approach to landing, the T-6 that was landing directly ahead of me ground looped. To my amazement, after the ground-looping T-6 had spun around 180 degrees, the pilot added power and successfully took off. Nice recovery except for one problem: he was climbing in the opposite direction of landing, directly toward my descending aircraft! The two T-6s, one climbing and the other descending, passed very close to each other. So close, I could see the face of my good friend and fellow student, Jack Dille, as his T-6 passed by. That evening, Jack, our wives, and I shared a toddy or two. As usual with self-proclaimed hotshot pilots, the talk soon turned to the daily flying adventures and exploits. (Appropriately called "hangar flying," this practice frequently drove our young wives to distraction.) After complimenting Jack on his skill in overcoming the ground loop, I asked, "Jack, please give me a warning when you feel the urge to demonstrate 'how to recover from ground loops.' Next time I want to watch from the ground!"

The remaining weeks at Goodfellow passed quickly. Night flying, acrobatics, instrument flying, and navigation training were introduced and practiced. Cross-country flying at night was very primitive by modern standards. Well-traveled routes—San Angelo to San Antonio for example—had powerful lights along the route, spaced at about 10-mile intervals. Following these lights kept these future Magellans from getting lost. I suppose the lights were installed when airmail began. Instrument training was practiced in a "Blue Box" with fake wings and mounted on a swivel, also called a Link Trainer. Once seated in the simulated cockpit, the roof to the box was closed, and the student would "fly" the Link Trainer by referring to the artificial horizon, airspeed indicator, and heading indicator. Comparing the Link Trainers to today's sophisticated flight simulators makes one wonder whether they had the same genes!

Most of us completed the basic flying training successfully, but not all. Thirty-seven of 167 West Pointers were washed out and sent to navigator training or other schooling. One classmate, Lt James Smyly, had fallen behind because of an appendectomy. Jim asked to stay at Goodfellow for a few days and make up the missed flights rather than be turned back to the next flying school class. When we reported for advanced pilot training, we learned the sad news that Jim and his instructor had been killed in a T-6 accident on 6 February 1951. His death in an aircraft accident was the first in Class 51-E and served as a grim reminder that piloting military aircraft was a dangerous business.

Those who successfully completed basic flight training were assigned to one of three different schools for advanced training: Advanced Single-Engine Pilot School (F-80 jet fighter) at Williams AFB, Arizona; Advanced Single-Engine Pilot School (F-51 piston-engine fighter) at Craig AFB, Alabama; and Advanced Multi-Engine Pilot School, Vance AFB, Oklahoma (B-25 twin-engine bomber).[4] I asked for F-80s at Williams and got it.

Thank you, Lt John Amadon!

The War Changes—Korean Stalemate
Fall 1950–Spring 1951

In October and early November, American and ROK troops were rapidly moving toward the Yalu River. When North Korean units began their helter-skelter retreat to the north, the air effort shifted from close air support (CAS) to interdiction. The new objective was to destroy the bridges and cut the supply lines the North Korean army required during its retreat.

Although the JCS generally gave MacArthur a free hand in his advance into North Korea, an exception was guidance to use only South Korean units as his UN Command approached the Yalu. The JCS was concerned about the Chinese reaction to American troops being positioned on the Yalu River boundary between Korea and China. Ignoring the JCS guidance, MacArthur used American troops as the spearhead of his advance. His rationale for not following JCS guidance was a 29 September message from Gen George C. Marshall, at that time the secretary of defense (SecDef), stating, "We want you to feel unhampered tactically and strategically to proceed north of the 38th parallel."

President Truman met with General MacArthur at Wake Island on 15 October 1950. When Truman asked MacArthur what were the chances for Chinese or Soviet intervention, he answered,

> Very little; had they interfered in the first or second months it would have been decisive. We are no longer fearful of their intervention. . . . The Chinese have 300,000 men in Manchuria. Of these probably not more than 100,000 to 125,000 are distributed along the Yalu River. They have no Air Force. Now that we have bases for our Air Force in Korea, if the Chinese tried to get down to Pyongyang there would be the greatest slaughter.[5]

It seems strange that the president of the United States was not better prepared to discuss this issue with his Far East Commander in Chief. General MacArthur's remarks about the People's Republic of China (PRC) lacking an air force were overstated and ignored the possibility the Soviets would augment the Chinese air force with jet fighters and combat experienced pilots. Far East Air Forces had previously submitted an intelligence estimate showing the PRC with 300 combat aircraft. On 18 October, an RB-29 aircrew counted 75 fighters at Antung airfield on the Manchurian side of the Yalu.

Chinese army "volunteers" began to appear in the Korean War in October 1950. Their initial probing was against South Korean divisions, but on 2 November they attacked the American 1st Cavalry Division near the Yalu River. On 3 November, they attacked the 24th Infantry Division located south of Sinuiju. On 4 November, my former West Point roommate Lt Mike Dowe, a platoon leader in the 24th ID, was captured after running out of ammunition in a day-long battle with the Chinese. Mike spent nearly three years as a POW under extremely difficult conditions before repatriation in September 1953.

Forward elements of the Eighth Army were quickly overrun by thousands of Chinese soldiers who crossed the Yalu bridges into North Korea on 26 November. Army and Marine forces began to withdraw back to the 38th parallel. At this time, FEAF controlled the skies over the battle area. Fighter-bombers provided close support for the retreating ground forces and attacked the supply routes for the Chinese army after it crossed the Yalu River bridges into North Korea. Our heavy air attacks forced the Chinese to shift their attacks from day to night.

Too little attention had been paid to the logistic problems facing the advancing Eighth Army. An amphibious landing at Wonsan a few weeks after the successful Inchon landing was poorly planned, leaving the X Corps critically short of supplies. Gen Walton Walker's Eighth Army was on the west coast of North Korea near Sinuiju and Maj Gen Edward Almond's X Corps with the First Marine Division was heading up the east coast beyond the Chosin Reservoir when the Chinese struck. Splitting his ground forces prevented MacArthur from concentrating defensive efforts when the Chinese exploited the gap between the Eighth Army and X Corps. The First Marine Division ran the gauntlet of Chinese fire as it retreated from the Chosin Reservoir. Despite extremely cold weather, constant fire from Chinese forces, and heavy casualties, the Marines fought their way back to friendly lines. During their retreat, USAF transports air-dropped critical supplies to them.

The PRC attacks should not have surprised MacArthur, Truman, or the JCS. Chou En-lai's warning was given substance when Chinese "volunteers" were reported to be in North Korea in early October 1950. MacArthur's intelligence staff is usually blamed because it failed to anticipate the Chinese intervention. In its defense, his staff's job was to provide intelligence about the enemy belligerent—North Korea. The Central Intelligence Agency (CIA), State Department, and other intelligence agencies were responsible for providing intelligence about nonbelligerent nations.

The new JCS chairman, General of the Army Omar Bradley; Army chief of staff, Gen Lawton Collins; and Air Force chief of staff, Hoyt Vandenberg, were generals in the European theater during World War II and had not served with or under General MacArthur. MacArthur's success at Inchon, his World War II reputation, and his lengthy experience in the Far East made it difficult to challenge his judgment.

The first indication that the air war was intensifying had occurred on 1 November 1950 when six MiG-15s from Antung attacked a flight of F-51s. These early air battles demonstrated that the fast, highly maneuverable MiG-15 threatened our air superiority. One serious consequence was that daylight reconnaissance by RB-29s was stopped. The USAF answered the threat by quickly deploying from the United States the 4th Fighter Interceptor Wing (FIW) equipped with our newest fighter, the F-86A, and manned with experienced pilots, including several World War II aces. The 4th entered action on 15 December and temporarily restored air superiority.

The UNC rules of engagement (ROE) did not allow our aircraft to attack the MiG-15 bases in Manchuria or to pursue MiG-15s across the Yalu. This ROE provided MiGs a safe haven in Manchuria throughout the Korean War. The F-86 forward air bases were overrun after the PRC entered the war and the 4th FIW went to Japan, where it remained until 6 March 1951. During its absence, the Chinese air force controlled the air between the Yalu and the middle of the peninsula. "MiG Alley" became the ominous nickname for this chunk of North Korea.

On 23 December, General Walker was killed in a jeep accident and replaced by Gen Matthew Ridgway. By mid-January 1951, Ridgway had stabilized the Eighth Army situation and turned what might have been a rout into an orderly withdrawal to the 38th parallel. The Army chief of staff, General Collins, flew to Korea to talk with Ridgway in early January 1951. Collins returned with an optimistic report. "Eighth Army is in good shape and improving daily under Ridgway's leadership. Morale very satisfactory. On the whole Eighth Army now in position and prepared to punish severely any massed attack."[6]

In March 1951, President Truman sought to end the war with a cease-fire proposal that was sent in draft form to the other 17 UN member nations involved in Korea. The draft specifically ruled out a war with the PRC. After MacArthur received the draft message, he issued his own proclamation to the PRC stating among other things that "the enemy, therefore, must by now be painfully aware that a decision of the United States to depart from its tolerant effort to contain the war to areas of Korea, through an expansion of our military operations to his coastal areas and interior bases, would doom Red China to the risk of imminent military collapse."[7] This proclamation sealed MacArthur's fate. MacArthur was fired on 11 April 1951. He had gone too far in pressing his own view to widen the war. He had preempted the serious proposal of his president to negotiate the end to war following a cease-fire.

MacArthur went home to a hero's welcome. The American public was split between those who were concerned that any expansion of the war would lead to World War III and those who were dissatisfied with accepting anything less than victory. Congress called hearings in the spring of 1951, the so-called MacArthur Hearings. Among other things, MacArthur pointed to our reluctance to place priority on winning the war in Korea because we were strengthening our position in NATO. "You have got a war on your hands, and you just can't say, 'Let that war go on indefinitely while I prepare for some other war.'"[8] General Bradley, chairman of the Joint Chiefs of Staff (CJCS), testified at the MacArthur Hearings. He cited three options: "Either to get out and forsake Korea, try to fight it out in general where we are now without committing too great forces, or going to all-out war and committing sufficient forces to drive these people out of Korea. At the present time, we are following the second course." Referring to the possibility that a general war could result over Korea, Bradley said it "would involve us in the wrong war, at the wrong place, at the wrong time, and with the wrong enemy."[9]

Truman in his memoirs said that "every decision I made in connection with the Korean conflict had this one aim in mind: to prevent a third world war and the terrible destruction it would bring to the civilized world. This meant that we should not do anything that would provide the excuse to the Soviets and plunge the free nations into a full-scale all-out war."[10]

The die was cast at the MacArthur Hearings. There would be no major escalation in the Korean War as long as Truman was president. Bradley's "try to fight it out where we are now" philosophy confirmed Truman's position. It would not change for the 19 months remaining in Truman's presidency.

Lacking a cease-fire, major fighting continued near the 38th parallel. Lt Wally Nutting, a tank platoon leader in the 2d Armored Division, was seriously wounded in May during a Chinese attack.[11] Later he told me, "The hills were swarming with Chinese soldiers. So many, it reminded me of thousands of ants coming out of an anthill!"

From Texan to Shooting Star

February–August 1951

After leaving San Angelo, Anne and I drove to Williams AFB, Arizona, located a few miles from Chandler, a town of about 10,000, not far from the larger cities of Tempe and Phoenix. The day we arrived was graduation day for the previous class, 51-D. The sky was filled with a long line of F-80 Shooting Stars chasing each other in one final rat race through the skies over the air base. As these F-80s flown by graduating students and their instructors landed, four other F-80s at treetop level roared over our heads and, in diamond formation, pulled up into a loop.

The Acrojets, wings overlapping, were at work demonstrating their skill in formation acrobatics. In the early '50s, several Air Force major commands had their own aerial demonstration teams. The world-famous Thunderbirds were later formed to manage the public relations aspect and to reduce the total costs associated with aerial demonstrations. When the major air command teams were disbanded, some Acrojet pilots were transferred to the Thunderbirds. Being a Thunderbird was a true accolade and often the high point of a fighter pilot or maintenance man's career.

Seventy-two West Point and Annapolis graduates in Class 51-E reported to Williams AFB in February 1951. "Willie" was a well-equipped air base with more modern facilities than Goodfellow, including a modern hospital with a large maternity ward. After signing in, Col Leon Gray, the pilot training group commander, addressed us in the base auditorium. He noted, among other things, that we must have all been on the same picnic together since there were so many pregnant wives in

51-E. "Wives should be like laundry bags. Draw one from base supply when you report to a base; turn one in when you leave." Furthermore, he didn't want anyone asking to be excused from flying just because his wife was having a baby that day. Young, sometimes pregnant, wives received Gray's off-the-cuff comments with something less than enthusiasm. When my daughter's arrival time occurred several months later, I followed half of Gray's advice. Chris was born at 4:15 a.m., and I made an on-time takeoff at 7:00 a.m. However, when we left Willie, Anne was not "turned in" at base supply. She spent the next 30 years as an exemplary Air Force wife—and still is.

One Saturday night shortly after arriving at Willie, we were at the O'Club with our wives and bachelor friends. Suddenly the dining room and dance floor became quiet. Colonel Gray, microphone in hand, was going to make an important announcement. Maybe he was going to say something nice like, "Have a drink on me!" No, that would have been way out of character. How about, "Glad to see you're having a good time!" Not even close. Instead, we were greeted with, "It's nine o'clock. All second lieutenants and their wives leave the club!" Guess what— we all left, muttering to our wives about how "we pay dues," and "damn it, we're club members, too," and "Gray can't do this"—and maybe a few disrespectful things about Gray and his antecedents.

Most of us had never met anyone quite like Colonel Gray—a flamboyant personality with exceptionally strong political support in Arizona.[12] In college days, Gray had been a Golden Glove champion boxer from the Phoenix area. During World War II, he commanded a reconnaissance unit in North Africa. His executive officer in North Africa was FDR's son Elliot, and they maintained contact after the war. Another contact was Senator Barry Goldwater, a pilot in World War II who maintained an active role in the Reserve. With big-time Democrat and Republican friends and a powerful reputation locally, Col Leon Gray was apparently bulletproof, or at least immune to normal administrative controls. Although his style of leadership gradually disappeared as the Air Force matured, stories about "Leon the Peon" (nickname given by students) inevitably surface whenever old fighter pilots swap tales.

Switching to jets was not a difficult transition for pilots experienced in flying WWII fighters such as the P-51 and P-47. However, moving from the two-cockpit, 150-knot piston-engine T-6 to the single-cockpit, 400-knot F-80 jet fighter was quite a jump for student pilots without an instructor on board to supervise the transition. Lockheed answered the requirement for a two-place trainer by building the T-33, basically an F-80C modified with a rear cockpit. The rear cockpit allowed an instructor to supervise the student pilot during his first few flights in a jet and during instrument flight training. Unfortunately, there were not enough T-33s in 1951 to satisfy all USAF fighter wings as well as ATC. A gap filler was needed until more modern aircraft became available for basic training.

Preceding the arrival of Class 51-E by only a few days were new, North American T-28A trainer aircraft—the gap filler. The T-28As had been delivered earlier but were grounded until an engine modification was completed. We were the first class to train in this new aircraft, and our instructors were still checking out the T-28A when we arrived. The T-28A was much faster than the T-6, with a cruising speed approximating the earlier fighters of World War II, and was equipped with modern instrumentation and communications, tricycle landing gear, and a large radial engine.

One of the first chores a flyer had to complete when reporting to a new assignment was drawing PE from base supply—parachute, helmet, face mask, flying boots, gloves, flying suits, anti-G suit, survival kit, and whatever else the local situation requires. Two lines were in the PE building at Willie. One line issued PE to the student pilot about to begin advanced training. The other line was for returning PE to base supply. While standing in the first line to draw my PE, I noticed my friend and classmate Bob Williams standing in the second line. Bob had arrived at Willie a few days earlier than I although we were both in 51-E. "Hey, Bob! What are you doing in that line?" His answer shocked me, "A couple of rides in a T-28 and they washed me out."

The T-28A was excellent for instrument training and a good aircraft for teaching formation flying. Although the T-28A was a big step up from the T-6, the aircraft was somewhat of a disappointment to the Air Force because of limited engine power.

Captain Roberts, a member of the Acrojets, was my assigned instructor. Every now and then, you meet an individual with overwhelming talent and a personality to match. Roberts had that impact on me. After our first meeting, he asked if I would like to play golf with him the following Saturday. Was this a golden opportunity for me to bridge the huge gulf between instructor and student? Maybe, even find a new friend? "Yes, sir—I'd really like to play!"

My too-quick response masked my limited golfing ability—best described as dismal—but triggered an invitation from Roberts for a Saturday golf match at San Marcos Golf Club—an outstanding golf resort in Chandler. It turned out that Captain Roberts was a "scratch" golfer, a level of expertise resulting in a par 72 for him that Saturday morning. Meanwhile, after 18 humiliating holes, I escaped with 98 strokes. There's an old saying, "No good deed shall go unpunished." Round one for Roberts!

Professional pilots, even student pilots, can hardly wait for their first flight in a new aircraft. If they don't have that curiosity and sense of adventure, they probably are in the wrong business. The experience is somewhat like a blind date—she's never quite like what you expected. By the time we flew our first T-28 flight, hours had been spent in the cockpit simulator learning T-28 "switchology," emergency procedures had been memorized, and a closed-book exam had verified our aircraft knowledge. When the Big Day came, I was ready. And so was Captain Roberts.

The T-28 accelerated quickly down the runway and was soon airborne. With gear retracted and flaps moving up, I turned out of traffic. Hey, this was great! Any initial concerns about being able to fly this complex beast were rapidly disappearing. Within a few minutes, Roberts interrupted my self-congratulatory reverie by calling, "I got it!" and took control of the aircraft.

The next half-hour was an eye-opener. Roberts could make the aircraft perform as if it were somehow connected to his brain. He did his entire bag of tricks with never a miscue. Stalls, spins, chandelles, high-speed dives, loops, Immelmans, rolls, high-G turns, and so on. We finished the flight by flying instrument approaches and touch-and-go landings. As we taxied to the ramp area, the golf game flashed through my mind. The fighter pilot shot par, and the student scored 98. Captain Roberts had shown me what a great pilot could do in the T-28A. The other side of the coin—I had a lot to learn. Round two for Roberts!

After a few T-28A flights devoted to aircraft familiarization and instrument training, I was hospitalized with jaundice. A week in the hospital cured some symptoms. However, a second week in the hospital would mean being washed back to Class 51F, and I didn't want that to happen. The flight surgeon reluctantly approved my request to return to flying status. I ignored his caution that flying duties would be challenging because of the aftereffects of the sickness, primarily weakness and nausea.

"Doc" was right. The first flight after returning to duty was an absolute nightmare. As we rode back to the operations building after landing, Captain Roberts critiqued the flight. His criticisms were undoubtedly accurate, but they went in one ear and out the other. All I felt was great relief; the physical ordeal was over, and I could go home to bed! The next two flights with Roberts went somewhat better, and I was scheduled for an instrument check with Maj Al Brown. After passing the instrument check, I moved on to the next phase—formation flying with a new instructor, Capt P. J. Mercier. He was an excellent instructor, and this phase was completed without incident.

Captain Roberts had been assigned a new training responsibility. Because of the Korean War, fighter pilots in the Air Force Reserve with World War II experience were being called back to active duty. Most needed jet qualification before being assigned to an active-duty fighter wing. On one of these training flights, Roberts was landing a T-33 with an Air Force Reserve pilot aboard when the landing gear would not extend. He decided to "belly land" the aircraft with the gear retracted rather than eject. The T-33 had drop tanks (detachable fuel tanks) fastened on the tip of each wing. As the aircraft slid to a stop, one drop tank caught fire. The fire rapidly spread through the wing toward the fuselage. To escape the fire, the two pilots needed to jettison the aircraft canopy, rapidly climb from their cockpits, and run away from the burning aircraft. The unexpected happened. The canopy release mechanism had jammed during the belly landing and would not open. Both pilots were trapped in the burning cockpits. They were seen trying to break open the canopy without success and died in the rapidly spreading fire. I sincerely regretted the death of Captain Roberts—an outstanding pilot with a bright future cut short by this fatal accident.

Roberts's accident had an unusual aftermath. The Air Force needed a way for a trapped pilot to break open the canopy during an emergency if the canopy would not open by normal means. Rube Goldberg would have been proud of The Fix. A wooden bat, smaller than a baseball bat and larger than a rolling pin, was fastened on the canopy rail inside the F-80 cockpit. In time of need, pilots were to disconnect the bat and bash the canopy until it broke open. Students viewed The Fix with a mixture of skepticism and gallows humor. Later, The Fix was replaced with a modification that corrected the problem.

With T-28 training over, it was finally time for jets. Captain Mercier was in the backseat of the T-33 for my first ride in a jet. The most vivid memory is how fast the ground was moving by as we practiced landings. After a second transition ride in a T-33, I soloed an F-80B and loved the speed, power, and responsiveness of the aircraft. In later years, I was fortunate in being able to fly some truly remarkable aircraft, including the world's fastest, the Mach-3 SR-71. None left a fonder memory than that first solo flight in that F-80B. The remaining flying time at Williams was spent in F-80s practicing formation flying, short navigation flights, acrobatics, and night flying.

Academics at Willie focused on the knowledge required to fly the new jet fighters and to understand their limitations. During WWII, the German Me-262 jet fighter had proven its effectiveness as an interceptor but was never fielded in sufficient numbers to stop the Allied bomber offensive. Nevertheless, the startling performance of the Me-262 wiped out any indecision within the Air Force about shifting to jets as quickly as production would allow. By 1945 the Lockheed P-80 was flying, and 16 were deployed to an American base in Italy in the last few days of the war. By 1950 the F-80 and F-84 had become the standard fighters in the Air Force, and F-86 production was under way.

Safely flying the F-80 and F-84 required a thorough understanding of their limitations. Both aircraft drank too much fuel, were inefficient at low altitude, accelerated slowly, lacked power (thrust), and could not carry much payload. The differences between the two aircraft were slight, although the newer

F-84 could carry more payload and fly farther than the F-80. Aircraft limitations had to be fully understood and carefully considered on each flight. For example, on a hot day in Denver, where the airport is a mile above sea level, a fully loaded F-80 or F-84 might not be able to reach takeoff speed before running out of runway.

Academic instructors taught the budding jet fighter pilots how to plan routine training flights and combat missions that included many variables—for example, taxi and takeoff data; fuel used in climb; climb distances; cruise and descent; time in the target area; the effect of temperature and winds on true airspeed, ground speed, and aircraft headings; fuel allowances to alternate destinations; the effect of various weapon loads on performance; navigation aids en route; selection of appropriate maps and charts; flight publications, including approach and letdown procedures; landing minimums at destination; parking, taxi, and runway details at home or destination bases; tower and en route radio frequencies; and current "Notices to Airmen." Students were carefully taught all these important details and required to satisfactorily pass examinations before graduating. This training was the most important I ever received in a classroom. There was a special incentive for working hard. The top 10 percent could choose the longest leave granted between advanced and gunnery training.

One of the World War II pilots who reported to Williams for jet upgrading was an outgoing young colonel carrying credentials that validated his great war record and total flying experience. He soon became a favorite with the instructors because of his friendly demeanor and modest explanations at the O'Club bar of his past heroics. Because of the colonel's extensive flying background, he skipped flying the T-28 and started flying the jet-powered T-33 under the supervision of one of the best instructors. After a few flights, this instructor commented to his supervisor, "Jeez, the colonel seems to have forgotten a lot about flying since World War II, and his jet transition is progressing at the speed of smell!" Another instructor who overheard the comment said, "Give him to me. I can solo anybody like that guy in two rides."

After two more rides, the new instructor advised, "Well, the colonel still has a few problems, but he's probably OK to solo the

T-Bird." The next day came, and the colonel took off alone. After several landing attempts failed, despite lots of concerned advice from his instructor who was manning the radio in mobile control, someone joked, "We're going to have to shoot him down!" Nearly out of fuel, he made one final attempt. After bouncing down the runway in a "controlled crash," the T-Bird finally stopped. When nail-biting stopped, the finger-pointing began.

"How did this happen?" A quick call to the Pentagon disclosed the "colonel" was an impostor carrying forged records. He had never flown an aircraft before arriving at Willie! This same man had posed as a surgeon in an earlier adventure and had pretended to be qualified in other scams despite lacking necessary qualifications. After the Williams incident, screening the records of recalled officers was tightened, and similar incidents were apparently avoided. As students, we got a big kick out of hearing how the "colonel" had hoodwinked the system. We could not help admiring his guts, if not his common sense. A student proposed making him student of the month, but cooler heads prevailed.

Passing an instrument check flight in a T-33 was the final hurdle before graduation. After a few minutes of checking my basic instrument flying, the instrument check pilot asked, "Have you ever flown acrobatics under the hood?" My negative response brought forth his second question, "Would you like to try?" "Yes, sir!" led to 15 minutes of loops, rolls, chandelles, lazy 8s, and Immelmans—all under the hood. But the real meaning of this departure from the ordinary was that the last hurdle had been jumped—those "silver wings" were nearly on my shirt. We landed, had a friendly debriefing, shook hands, and I raced home to brag to Anne about how good her fighter pilot husband was!

Physical recreation at Willie was somewhat limited in the early fifties, so we welcomed off-duty exercise opportunities. Frank Borman, a native of Arizona, offered to take "Bolo" Brunson, Carroll Griffin (a Navy grad), and me waterskiing. Willie was located in an agricultural area with no lakes, but Frank had found an ingenious way to water-ski. We drove to one of the large irrigation canals around Chandler. A road ran parallel to the canal. By fastening a rope to the rear bumper of the car, we were able to tow a skier down the canal. There was one problem. Every quarter-mile the main canal had sluice gates controlled by a large capstan on the top of each gate that allowed water to flow into the adjacent cotton fields. This obstruction required snaking the rope over the capstan, or otherwise the rope would snag and spill the skier. Borman, Brunson, and Leavitt mastered the "snaking," but our Navy friend flunked "Snaking 101"—a source of constant amusement and heckling by his "Army" buddies. Moderate tow speeds were a little too tame, so we kicked up the car speed. Spilling at 55 miles per hour was borderline cruel and inhuman punishment, so we made a gentlemen's agreement not to drive over 50 mph. Exploring one's physical limits seemed important at that age.

A day or two before graduation, a clerk noticed that several students in 51-E needed one more night flight to satisfy ATC hourly minimums. Takeoffs and landings had to be after dark. I was the next to last to take off and was flying alone in an F-80. After flying locally for over an hour, I returned to Willie and let down to enter traffic. The landing procedure involved entering on initial approach about five miles from the air base. Once on initial approach, the procedure was to slow down by extending the speed brake, bank sharply to the left after crossing above the end of the runway at 1,000 feet, and call the control tower—for example, "Knothead 3, on the break, landing three zero left." I entered on initial and approached the end of the runway at 1,000 feet before realizing the speed brake had not been extended and airspeed was too high. Pride whispered in my ear, "Don't let the tower know you screwed up your last traffic pattern at Willie and had to go around." With this brainstorm, I ignored calling the tower and left the traffic pattern. Five minutes later, I reentered traffic, followed the proper procedures, and made a nice landing. After parking the F-80, I strolled into ops congratulating myself on successfully completing advanced training.

No sooner had I entered ops than several angry instructors and their supervisors started yelling at me. "Where in the hell have you been? Where were you at 11:40 when you were supposed to call the tower? You live in Chandler don't you? We know you were buzzing Chandler at that exact time! You buzzed right down the main street. You were the only solo student flying—we know it was you. Do you realize we have hundreds of phone calls complaining about your buzz job?" From time to time, I tried to explain but to no avail. My confession about entering traffic earlier and failing to call the tower sounded pretty feeble, even to me. The "third degree" continued until I began to wonder whether it would ever end.

Eventually, they let me go home with the warning to report in a blue uniform, not a flying suit, because Colonel Gray, who was not noted for his benevolent disposition, would decide what to do with me in the morning. What would Colonel Gray do? Wash me out? Prefer charges against me? Upon arriving at home, my angry wife accused me of buzzing our home and scaring the entire neighborhood. After a sleepless night, I put on my blue uniform in the morning and headed for ops. The whole incident reminded me of the French Revolution, with an innocent man facing the guillotine.

As soon as I entered ops, it was clear the atmosphere had totally changed. A very friendly group of instructors and supervisors (last night's interrogators) greeted me. My instructor, Captain Mercier, offered a cup of coffee and said, "You are going to be a great fighter pilot, Dick!" Flattery or not, I appreciated his kind words. Others shook hands and wished me well in gunnery training. No one mentioned a word about the buzzing. What had caused the big change overnight?

There was one other airplane flying about the time I was to land, a T-33 flown by a young lieutenant instructor with student Lt Bud Knapp in the rear cockpit. Bud, a Naval Academy graduate also in 51-E, had heard about my troubles and convinced the instructor to confess that he had buzzed Chandler, not me. I suppose the young instructor was chastised after we left Willie, thus ending the incident. With a big sigh of relief, I thanked Bud for "saving my butt."

The first year of my Air Force career had ended on a happy note. I was a jet fighter pilot. A year earlier upon entering basic flying training, my emotions had fluctuated between exhilaration and trepidation. The afternoon I graduated and received my silver wings changed my emotions. Exhilaration was still there, but trepidation was gone. It had been replaced with confidence. Sure, there would be problems that wouldn't disappear overnight, but I felt confident about the future. A better Air Force lay ahead, and I would be part of it. I realized the Air Force was truly my home.

Thank you, Captain Roberts, Captain Mercier, and especially Bud Knapp!

How Did Class 51-E Do?

On 4 August 1951, the graduates of Class 51-E from advanced flying schools located at Williams AFB, Arizona (F-80), Craig AFB, Alabama (F-51), and Vance AFB, Oklahoma (B-25) were awarded Air Force pilot wings. Flying Cadets in the class were commissioned as second lieutenants in addition to receiving pilot wings.[13]

The alumni associations at West Point and Annapolis track their graduates and are a fairly reliable source for information concerning their subsequent military careers. No similar association exists for tracking the Air Force careers of the Flying Cadets who represented about 20 percent of 51-E. Therefore, 51-E statistics relate only to graduates from the two academies. Despite lack of specifics, we know many Flying Cadets in 51-E served with distinction in the Korean War and afterwards.

Only a few Annapolis graduates had transferred to the Air Force until 1950, when the 25 percent quota was filled with 172 officers. One hundred nineteen were assigned to 51-E for pilot training; the remainder went to navigator training or chose nonrated duties. After completing advanced flight training one year later, 67 were awarded pilot wings.

Reporting to 51-E were 160 second lieutenants from West Point. Six other 1950 graduates had been Army Air Force pilots in World War II and went directly to refresher training. Another graduate, 2d Lt Lynn Camp, had been killed in an automobile accident on 25 July 1950. After completing advanced flight training one year later, 119 were awarded pilot wings.

Most of 51-E assumed if they passed basic flying training, they were relatively safe from elimination while in advanced flying training. This assumption was partially correct. There were no student officer washouts in either the Advanced Single-Engine Pilot School (F-51 piston-engine fighter) at Craig AFB or the Advanced Multi-Engine Pilot School (B-25 twin-engine bomber) at Vance AFB. It was a different story for those assigned to advanced single-engine (jet) training at Williams AFB, where 18 of the 81 second lieutenants who entered were eliminated.

Several possibilities could account for the statistical differences between training bases. Was the transition from T-6 to T-28 to F-80 too difficult for student pilots with only 120 hours' total flying time? Or were the eliminated student officers not suitable for flying jet fighters but would have been suitable for conventional fighters or twin-engine bombers? Or were student officers encountering a cultural bias at Williams AFB similar to that encountered in basic flying training?

One of the West Point graduates eliminated, 2d Lt George Vlisides, decided to challenge his elimination. George headed for Washington, DC, seeking an audience to plead his case. Bypassing the Pentagon, George went directly to the Air Force chief of staff's home at Fort Myers, Virginia. One can only surmise what General Vandenberg was thinking when he found a second lieutenant knocking on his door on a Sunday night. After hearing this determined young officer, General Vandenberg directed ATC to review the elimination process at Williams AFB. The review resulted in seven of the 14 West Pointers being reinstated in the jet training program at Willie. All seven graduated with a later class and were assigned to fighter units.

One West Point graduate was killed in basic flying training. One hundred nineteen graduated from pilot training with Class 51-E. Seven pilots were killed in action (KIA) in Korea, two were KIA in Vietnam, and 13 in aircraft accidents. Cadet pictures of those killed are shown in the following pages.

Sixty-seven pilots from Annapolis graduated with Class 51-E. Three were KIA in Korea; one was KIA in Vietnam, and seven in aircraft accidents:

2d Lt James R. Bowers, training accident, B-25, 19 December 1951
2d Lt Hamilton E. McDowell, training accident, F-80, 21 December 1951
1st Lt Donald S. Kobey, KIA, Korea, F-84, 6 March 1952
1st Lt Wilbur R. Spradling, KIA, F-80, Korea, 22 July 1952
1st Lt James W. Wills, KIA, Korea, F-84, 4 December 1952
Capt Edward C. Hotz, training accident, F-86, 5 May 1953
1st Lt Cedric A. Peterson, aircraft accident, Japan, 7 December 1953
1st Lt William S. Taylor, aircraft accident, F-80, 1 December 1954
1st Lt Lorenzo J. Daleo, aircraft accident, F-86, 7 December 1954
Capt George W. Duncan, aircraft accident, B-45, 30 January 1956
Lt Col Christopher Braybroke, KIA Vietnam, C-130, 8 August 1967

2d Lt James W. Smyly III
Training accident, T-6
6 February 1951

2d Lt Henry E. Tisdale, Jr.
Training accident, F-80
14 September 1951

2d Lt John M. Garrett, Jr.
Aircraft accident, F-84
6 November 1951

2d Lt Elliot R. Knott
Aircraft accident, Japan, F-80
12 December 1951

1st Lt Russell E. Leggett
Aircraft accident, B-45
12 December 1951

1st Lt Thurston R. Baxter
MIA-KIA Korea, F-51
21 December 1951

1st Lt Medon A. Bitzer
KIA Korea, F-51
8 January 1952

1st Lt George B. Eichelberger, Jr.
KIA Korea, F-51
15 January 1952

2d Lt Harry E. Rushing
KIA Korea, F-51
3 March 1952

1st Lt John M. McAlpine
KIA Korea, F-51
24 June 1952

1st Lt John A. Dille, Jr.
Aircraft accident, Korea, F-80
13 April 1952

1st Lt William B. Slade
KIA Korea, F-80
12 May 1952

1st Lt Gene A. Dennis
KIA Korea, F-84
28 September 1952

1st Lt Thomas F. Casserly
Aircraft accident, Korea, F-86
1 October 1952

1st Lt Robert A. Williams
Aircraft accident, Korea, F-84
1 October 1952

1st Lt Anderson O. Hubbard
Aircraft accident, France, B-26
23 October 1952

Maj Lewis A. Page, Jr.
Aircraft accident, T-33
20 June 1953

Capt William S. Todd, Jr.
Aircraft accident, B-57
8 February 1955

Capt Eugene C. Etz
Aircraft accident, T-33
7 September 1955

Capt Robert D. Willerford
Aircraft accident, T-33
24 September 1956

Lt Col Carl B. Mitchell
KIA Vietnam, B-26
14 January 1964

Maj George F. Vlisides
Aircraft accident, Vietnam, A-1E
27 January 1965

Lt Col Bobby G. Vinson
KIA Vietnam, F-4D
12 September 1977

West Point classmates killed in aircraft. (*The Howitzer 1950*, US Military Academy yearbook)

Class 51-E had a total of 34 fatalities from both academies, of which 25 were fighter pilots (73.5 percent). The total number of fighter pilots killed by type of aircraft they were flying are F-80, seven; F-84, five; F-51, five; F-86, three; T-33, three; A-1E, one; and F-4, one.

Members of Class 51-E served between 1950 and 1987. Their Air Force careers varied. They gradually assumed leadership roles in command, operations, training, personnel, maintenance, research and development, logistics, and intelligence. As the years passed, the accidents and combat losses so common to the early days of jet aviation were dramatically reduced. Graduates from both academies worked toward this goal and shared another common experience—helping the Air Force rise to its preeminent position in the world today.

Putting the "Fight" in Fighter Pilot
August–October 1951

The 30-day leaves promised for the top 10 percent in academics was cut to three days just before graduation. My bachelor classmate Joe Green voluntarily swapped his 10-day leave for my three-day leave so I could drive Anne and Chris to Little Rock, Arkansas, where they would stay while I was in Korea. After arriving at Nellis AFB, near Las Vegas, I was immediately immersed in fighter gunnery training.

Sometimes fighter pilots are described as "scarf in the wind" egoists who fly hugely expensive airplanes for the sole purpose of destroying enemy aircraft and becoming aces. Such criticism ignores reality. Modern fighters are expensive, but they do more than shoot down enemy aircraft. Most fighter sorties have attacked enemy ground forces, interdicted supply routes, destroyed command and control centers, suppressed air defense systems, knocked down bridges, and bombed infrastructure. The Korean War was the last war where fighter pilots fought enemy aircraft in large numbers. Because American fighter pilots have been able to dominate the skies overhead, the payoff has been huge. *No American Soldier has been killed by enemy aircraft since World War II.*

Training at Nellis included a lot of attitude development. The nature of combat requires a fighter pilot to be aggressive and self-confident. It simply is not enough to be able to fly a fighter aircraft safely. Whether the combat mission is against enemy ground targets or enemy aircraft, the fighter pilot must be willing to fly into harm's way and destroy the assigned target. Later in combat, I saw a few skilled pilots either unwilling or unable to perform their assigned missions because they were intimidated by external factors having nothing to do with their flying abilities.

Two months' training at Nellis developed the specialized skills a fighter pilot must learn: high- and low-angle strafing, air-to-air gunnery at various altitudes, dive-bombing and low-angle

61

bombing, rocket firing, and fighter tactics. Eighty hours of intensive flying (103 F-80 sorties) focused on learning these skills. The training paid off. Scores were averaged for each event at the halfway point and again for the second half. For example, my direct hits from low-angle bombing increased from 12 percent the first half to 50 percent the second half; air-to-air gunnery hits increased from 7 percent to 20 percent. When Nellis training ended, I knew how to deliver fighter weapons.

Firing machine guns on strafing passes and dive-bombing small targets on a ground gunnery range with three other aircraft—all flying around 400 knots and spaced a few seconds apart in a gunnery pattern—require absolute concentration. The body, as well as the mind, gets a good workout. The constant turning, diving, and climbing at high speed subjects the aircraft and pilot to gravitational (G)-forces. Although advances in technology—such as better aircraft, improved means of target acquisition, on-board computers, all-weather delivery systems, and "smart" munitions—have greatly improved the effectiveness of fighter attacks since the 1950s, the demands upon today's fighter pilot have not lessened and in some instances have increased.

One G is the normal gravitational force on earth. The acceleration of gravity occurs when an object changes direction. Two Gs equal twice the force of gravity and cause a 180-pound body to weigh the equivalent of 360 pounds. As the jet fighter turns at high speed, very high G-forces are possible—five, six, seven, or more Gs. The faster it changes direction, the greater the G-force. To counter the G-factor, fighter pilots wear G-suits. The suit senses G-forces and then inflates automatically. The inflated G-suit squeezes the legs and abdomen, keeping blood flowing in the upper torso.

If too many Gs are encountered, the pilot may temporarily lose vision (gray out) or become unconscious (black out) as blood flow decreases to the brain. The possible bad effects of high G-turns were hammered home on an early training mission at Nellis. My instructor, 1st Lt Carl G. Schneider, had recently returned from a combat tour in Korea.[14] He was an ideal role model for "wannabe" fighter pilots. The training lesson one day was simulated air-to-air combat. Our four-ship flight led by Schneider split into two elements. He led one element, and a student led the other. After splitting, the elements flew in opposite directions for a few seconds, then reversed course and started a dogfight.

At one point in the dogfight at about 10,000 feet altitude, I was closing rapidly on Carl's F-80 from his "5 o'clock" (right rear). Seeing this, he broke hard to the right. *Breaks* in fighter pilot lingo are high-G turns to escape a threat. To avoid hitting his aircraft, I pulled hard on the F-80 control stick while rolling over into a "split-S." A split-S maneuver rolls the airplane on its back and starts a steep, high-speed dive.

I pulled too many Gs doing the split-S. The last thing I saw before "graying out" was the G-meter registering around 10 Gs and the altimeter rapidly unwinding as the F-80 headed nearly vertically toward the ground. Could I think? Yes. Could I see? No. Best chance was to level off somehow before plowing into the desert. I reduced power and gradually applied enough back pressure on the stick to stop the dive without tearing the wings off or getting into high-speed stalls. As the overdose of Gs began to wear off, my vision returned and the F-80 leveled off about 1,000 feet above the terrain. Without the G-suit minimizing the effect of 10 Gs, I probably would have been unconscious. Close call. Lesson learned: know your limitations.

West Point classmate Lt Henry E. Tisdale was killed at Nellis on 14 September 1951. The F-80 accident was judged pilot error with a contributing factor being lack of crew rest. The Korean War was now a year old, and new fighter pilots were badly needed for replacements. This created considerable pressure on Nellis to compress the training program and produce more fighter pilots. Hank had a very heavy flying schedule the previous day, as well as the day he was killed. Because of accidents like Tisdale's, the Air Force has developed firm policies to protect crew rest.

Las Vegas in those days was a small town but a great place for having fun. The casinos welcomed our business, meals and drinks were cheap, and floor shows were great. The Thunderbird casino had "adopted" our training squadron, and other casinos treated other squadrons with similar hospitality. Uncle Sam paid us all our per diem a day or two before leaving Nellis. Per diem is additional money paid the military for each day on temporary duty (TDY). Jack Dille and I received about $130 each—our pay was about $350 a month in 1951, so $130 extra was a real family bonanza.

Sensing an opportunity, Jack and I invested five dollars in a miniature roulette wheel. Practicing with pennies for dollars, we convinced our wives that we had a Surefire Method to win at roulette. We would stick with one color—red, for example. Bet one dollar. If the ball stopped on red, take the dollar won and set it aside. If the ball stopped on black, double the bet. Continue doubling the bet until the ball stopped on red again. Set the winning dollar aside. Don't be greedy. Be patient. Settle for modest winnings.

We pooled our per diem money, reassured our wives, and headed for the Strip with our Surefire Method and a $260 stake. The first open roulette table looked lucky. We bet $1 on black; the ball stopped on red. No sweat, we bet $2 on black; the ball stopped on red. Things were getting serious, but we stuck with The Surefire Method. A $4 bet on black turned sour when the ball stopped on red again. Bets of $8, $16, $32, and $64 in rapid succession all were the same sad story. Should we bet $128 on black? Surely, red couldn't come up eight straight times! We bet—red came up. We had five dollars left and two angry wives. Fortunately, they calmed down by the time we left for Korea two days later.

After winning his wings and completing fighter gunnery training at Nellis Air Force Base, Jack was assigned to the 8th Fighter-Bomber Wing (FBW) at K-13 Air Base, South Korea, as an F-80 pilot. 1st Lt John A. Dille was killed on 13 April 1952 while ferrying an F-80 back to Japan. He left behind his wife, Barbara, young son, John, and many close friends.

Before leaving for Korea, we had a boisterous picnic on the top of Mount Charleston near Las Vegas. Underlying all the horseplay and beer drinking was the realization that things would never be quite the same. We were closely knit and had shared similar experiences for more than five years. We had sympathized with those who were eliminated, mourned the loss of friends who died in training, and jumped high hurdles in the process of becoming jet fighter pilots. And now, it was time to go halfway around the world and fight a nasty war that our president called a "police action."

Notes

1. Sifakis, *Encyclopedia of American Crime*, 442.

2. US Military Academy, *Register of Graduates*; and Buccolo, *Memories of West Point and Its Impact on the Class of 1950*.

3. During the war and the transition years from the USAAF to USAF through 1961, all Air Force chiefs of staff were West Point graduates and pilots: General of the Air Force (five-star) Henry H. Arnold, chief of staff, 1941–46; Gen Carl Spaatz, chief of staff, 1947–48; Gen Hoyt S. Vandenberg, chief of staff, 1948-53; Gen Nathan F. Twining, chief of staff, 1953-57; and Gen Thomas D. White, chief of staff, 1957–61.

4. The term used to describe our skill was "jet fighter pilot." Somehow the media has since turned jet aircraft and pilot descriptions to "fighter jets" and "fighter jet pilot." To me, this is like describing a truck as "truck diesel," or an orange tree as "tree orange," or a brain surgeon as "surgeon brain"!

References to the treatment of "student officers" and "flying cadets" are based upon conversations with many West Point and Annapolis classmates, including Michael DeArmond, Brunson, and Pierce Hodnette. Before his death in 2004, Lt Gen A. J. Russell discussed the genesis of the ring-knocker problem that he too experienced in the early forties. The problem is nonexistent in today's Air Force since all pilot trainees are officers.

5. McCullough, *Truman*, 804–5.

6. Ibid., 835–36.

7. Senate, *Military Situation in the Far East*, MacArthur Hearings.

8. Ibid., pt. 2, 938.

9. Ibid., pt. 3, 1,720.

10. Truman, *Memoirs*, vol. 2, *Years of Trial and Hope*, 345.

11. Gen Wallace Nutting, recovered from his wounds, returned to duty and served 35 years in his distinguished military career. He retired in 1985 as Commander in Chief, US Readiness Command.

12. By 1951 Williams AFB had earned a reputation for being a little out of control, primarily because Col Leon Gray, the flying training group commander, frequently ignored Federal Aviation Administration (FAA) and USAF regulations and rode roughshod over second lieutenants. He ran the jet training program like the hazing phase prior to joining a "great fraternity"—a phrase Gray used in a congratulatory letter to us on graduation.

13. Brig Gen Michael E. DeArmond, USAF, retired, has compiled a detailed history, yet unpublished, of the USAF careers of many 1950 West Point graduates. His gracious help has been my prime source concerning flying assignments, eliminations from flight school, fatalities, and career progress. A highly talented track and swimming athlete at West Point, Mike was asked to compete for the 1952 Olympic Team. Instead, he volunteered to go to Korea and fly F-86s. He was shot down near the Yalu River in April 1952 by a Russian MiG-15 pilot, a fact confirmed a few years ago. Mike was a POW for the remainder of the war.

14. Lieutenant Schneider did an excellent job of indoctrinating his students. He had a series of fighter assignments during his career before moving into several important assignments in logistics. His last assignment was commander of the Oklahoma City Air Logistics Center, and he retired as a major general in December 1978.

Chapter 3

Korean War
1st Lieutenant—1951–54

Korea-Bound, Japanese Detour
November 1951–January 1952

Camp Stoneman, near San Francisco, was the out-processing center for Korea-bound pilots. We decided to commemorate our departure by drinking champagne toasts at the Top of the Mark at the Hampton Hotel. The romantic atmosphere of the Mark added to our little melodrama. Less romantic was the long flight that started from Travis AFB, California, to Haneda Airport, Tokyo, Japan. Sitting in bucket seats on a C-124 flying at 150 knots across the Pacific for two days could be where the term "pain in the butt" originated!

We landed at Haneda Airport on 5 November 1951 and then boarded a GI bus for the reception center at Fuchu where Air Force personnel were processed. Many thoughts raced through my mind. When will we leave for Korea? Is this how Japanese cities really look? The streets are terribly narrow, bumpy, not well lighted, and are filled with people riding bicycles, pulling carts, driving trucks, weaving in and out on motorbikes, and chugging along on three-wheel contraptions. There don't seem to be any sidewalks. Their flimsy little houses sit close to the street and to the house next door. No wonder B-29 firebombing was so effective.

My curiosity was interrupted by a man pulling a two-wheeled cart with long handles crossing directly in front of our moving bus. The bus hit the cart, spun it around, and flung the man, spread-eagled, against the closest house. The bus stopped. To everyone's surprise, the man shook himself loose from the house, came over to the bus, bowed two or three times, and apologized to the bus driver, another Japanese, for getting in his way. No police, no lawyers, no ambulance, and no crowd— how un-American!

Once again the fighter pilots were split into two groups by very scientific means—last names beginning with letters. "A-K" pilots went to Itazuke Air Base at Kyushu, Japan, to learn how to fly the F-84. The "L-Z" pilots were assigned to the 41st Fighter Interceptor Squadron (FIS), flying F-80s, at Johnson AB, Honshu, Japan. The 41st FIS provided air defense from Johnson AB near Tokyo and Niigata Air Force Station (AFS) on the northwest coast of Honshu. I was disappointed about not going to Korea. It was like sending out wedding invitations and having the bride-to-be run off with another guy.

Johnson was a nice base with excellent facilities. A wartime trophy, the infamous "Baka Bomb" flown by kamikaze pilots in World War II, was displayed on a pedestal in front of the Officers' Club. After the pilot entered the Baka cockpit, the canopy was closed and locked with external wing nuts. Parachutes were extraneous, as was landing gear. Baka flying was a one-way trip.

The manager of the Johnson Officers' Club in 1951 was a kamikaze in 1945, with his orders to crash his Baka into a US Navy ship supporting our invasion of Okinawa. His last-minute decision to belly-land the Baka on an Okinawa sandy beach spared his life and possibly the lives of many American Sailors. An Army patrol found the unexploded Baka, unlocked the canopy, and took him prisoner.

The Japanese are an industrious and ingenious people. By 1951 much of the World War II bomb damage had disappeared. Factories were reopened, the economy was growing, and prices were cheap. However, Japan's current reputation for high quality had not yet been earned. I needed transportation around Johnson and bought a Japanese bicycle for 8,280 yen ($23). The bike looked nice, all shiny black enamel. After a week or two of rainy weather, the enamel began to peel off the fenders, and the familiar name and logo of "Budweiser" appeared. The fenders came from scrapped American beer cans!

Niigata AFS was near one of the few industrial cities in Japan not destroyed by B-29 raids. The squadron nickname for the station was "Eel Island" after a rather notorious base in Milton Caniff's popular comic strip *Steve Canyon*. Niigata was the location of the Allied POW camp where Gen Jonathan Wainwright, US Army, was confined after surrendering the Philippines in

1942. Although harsh conditions were imposed on all American prisoners, the Japanese kept Wainwright alive. They apparently believed General Wainwright would be a blue chip for future negotiations with the Allies.

Niigata AFS was bare bones, with minimal support facilities. Fighter operations for the F-80s standing strip alert at Niigata were controlled from a large tent located next to the runway. An elderly Japanese *papa-san* who had been Wainwright's orderly during his POW confinement kept the tent and latrines clean. Because the F-80 lacked radar and was not an all-weather interceptor, air defense alert was required only during daylight hours. We ate breakfast and lunch at the airfield. At night we lived in and ate our meals at a hotel rented by the Air Force.

Daylight hours were spent on strip alert. "Hurry up!—and wait" was how the military operated, according to many WWII veterans. A more accurate description for air defense operations would be "Wait—and hurry up!" A 4 December 1951 letter to Anne described my first "scramble" from alert at Eel Island.

> As soon as the phone rings, we run out to our planes wearing "G" suit and "Mae West." Helmet and mask are already plugged into the aircraft, so all we have to do is grab our 'chute. The APU (Auxiliary Power Unit) is next to the F-80. Two crewmen run to each plane—one starts the APU, the other starts the plane while I'm putting on my 'chute. I jump in and start taxiing as quickly as possible, while lowering wing flaps, raising dive flaps, strapping in, and completing the pre-takeoff and radio checks. We make running takeoffs—in formation, if both F-80s are ready. As soon as airborne, we raise the gear and turn to the course given by the radar controller while flaps are coming up. Pretty hairy the first time, because there was a low ceiling and we went right into the soup. The flight was uneventful. We only took four minutes from the time the phone rang until airborne and contact made with the radar controller, which isn't bad at all.[1]

One day at Niigata, Lt Cyril White and I were on alert; Cyril was flight leader, and I was wingman. Usually we passed the time playing ping-pong, gin rummy, writing letters, or reading. The "scramble" phone rang notifying us to get airborne immediately and report to the Air Defense Control Center (ADCC) for a "hot" mission. A hot mission might mean a Soviet intruder had left his base in the Sakhalin Islands north of Hokkaido and was probing the Japanese air defense network. We scrambled. After takeoff, the controller passed very unusual mission instructions.

A new Air Force Reserve C-82 crew had reported running low on fuel—too low to reach the nearest air base on the Kanto Plain. The aircraft commander had turned on the autopilot, headed the C-82 toward the mountain range to the northwest, and ordered the crew to parachute to safety. After recovering the crew, it was soon learned that it was not familiar with the correct procedure for C-82 fuel management. The C-82 actually had enough fuel to cross Japan and fly 500 more miles to the USSR. Our mission: shoot down the C-82 over the Sea of Japan.

The ground controller vectored us to a point where visual contact was established with the C-82. Cyril gave the order to arm the machine guns as we slowed down behind the C-82. As flight leader, Cyril had the "honors." At 200–300 yards behind the C-82, Cyril announced, "Watch this Red Two—I'm going to shoot out the left engine!" As he was talking, the "rat-a-tat-tat" from six machine guns was being broadcast over his radio. I said, "Nice shooting, Red Lead" and with a touch of irony added, "His *right* engine is burning!" The on-fire C-82 spun into the Sea of Japan. A few days later, we flew back to Johnson. Cyril, a 1949 Annapolis graduate and outstanding officer, left shortly afterwards for Korea. This time, flying F-86s, he would have the opportunity to shoot down enemy MiG-15s after live practice on a friendly C-82!

The Air Force had two promotion policies for second lieutenants during the Korean War. A second lieutenant with 18 months' service was automatically promoted to first lieutenant when his squadron commander initiated the action. In rare occasions, because of poor conduct or bad performance, this automatic promotion was withheld. The other policy applied in Korea. After 10 combat missions, a unit commander could recommend the officer for promotion from second to first lieutenant. Combat promotions were granted regardless of how much time in grade as a second lieutenant.

On 2 December 1951, all the West Point and Annapolis graduates in the 41st FIS had completed 18 months of service as second lieutenants. We learned through the rumor mill that we had not been submitted for promotion. After talking over this strange and disappointing news, we decided the discrimination experienced in flying school against regular officers was happening again. Two of the four flight commanders and the captain squadron commander had been WWII Flying Cadets and made offhand remarks about regular officers. I volunteered to ask the squadron commander why we were not being promoted. His answer was, "I don't know any of you well enough yet." My personal reaction was to write Anne, "It will be a pleasure to get out of the 'Tokyo National Guard' and over to Korea."

On 15 December, our flight was scheduled for ground gunnery practice at Mito Gunnery Range on the coast northeast of Johnson. I was element leader, and the wingman was my 51-E and West Point classmate 2d Lt Elliot Knott. I started a diving turn to begin my second strafing pass just as Elliot was pulling off the target after completing his first strafing pass. Then I saw a tragic scene that remains etched in memory. The fuselage on Elliot's F-80 was turning to the right, but the tail section was pointed straight ahead and tearing away from the fuselage. His aircraft snap rolled and cartwheeled into the ocean as the tail came off. Too low to eject, Elliot was killed when the aircraft crashed into the ocean seconds later. The Accident Investigation Board subsequently determined the bolts fastening the F-80 tail section to the fuselage were badly rusted and failed in the climbing turn after strafing.

A glimmer of hope about finally going to Korea occurred when the squadron published orders on 20 December 1951 relieving several combat-ready pilots from additional duties in the squadron. The peace talks were not going well, so we suspected a new round of transfers was in the mill. Christmas came and passed with no further news about transferring to Korea. Three of us were scheduled for a predawn takeoff on New Year's Day to replace pilots at Niigata. The flight leader, a WWII first lieutenant, celebrated New Year's Eve to the point where he could not ride his bicycle back to the BOQ, a matter of concern to the other wingman and me.

The hungover lieutenant managed to show up for briefing, and we took off as dawn broke. Instead of heading for Niigata, he kept us in close formation, and we made a high-speed, low-altitude pass over Johnson. Happy New Year everybody! The flight to Niigata that morning turned out to be a real challenge. The weather was marginal with a low ceiling and rain. We were having a difficult time picking up the signal from the radio beacon at Niigata. About 10 minutes prior to starting the letdown to Niigata, my F-80 had hydraulic failure. The flight leader told me to land while he and his wingman burned off fuel waiting for the weather to improve. As they pulled up and away, he gave me a wrong heading to Niigata. When my erratic radio compass did not agree with his heading advice, I called Niigata Tower for a direction-finding (DF) steer to the base.

A control tower with DF equipment can help an aircraft steer to an air base by measuring the bearing of radio transmissions coming from the aircraft. For example, if a pilot *north* of the base were transmitting for a DF steer, the aircraft heading to the base would be *south*. An inexperienced operator could mistakenly pass north, the reciprocal heading from the tower to the aircraft, rather than south, the heading from the aircraft to the tower. In this incident, the novice operator answered by providing the reciprocal heading, one that would take the aircraft away from Niigata and across the Sea of Japan. I corrected this heading error by cross-checking with the erratic radio compass and subtracting 180 degrees.

To add to the problem, the engine fire-warning light illuminated as the F-80 let down. The F-80 engine fire-warning system was not very reliable, but red lights on the instrument panel are difficult to ignore. A more immediate problem, though, was landing with hydraulic failure. The gear took a long time to come down but finally locked in place. With partial flaps and no hydraulic boost for the ailerons, I landed in a crosswind and stopped the aircraft on the 6,000-foot, wet runway without mishap. Sometimes flight pay was really earned.

Back at Johnson on 5 January, I badgered the squadron adjutant once more about going to Korea. The squadron commander heard us talking and said three sets of orders were now at group headquarters but would be held until our replacements arrived. At dinner that night he hinted that someone might go to F-86s, but "all the colonels and lieutenant colonels in the Pentagon and Far East Air Forces are going wild to get in F-86 outfits, even as wingmen." On 6 January 1952, I received orders to report to the 136th Fighter-Bomber Group (FBG) at K-2 (Taegu) Air Base, Korea, for combat duty as an F-84 pilot. At 0700, 8 January 1952, I was on a C-47 headed for K-2 (see fig. 1).

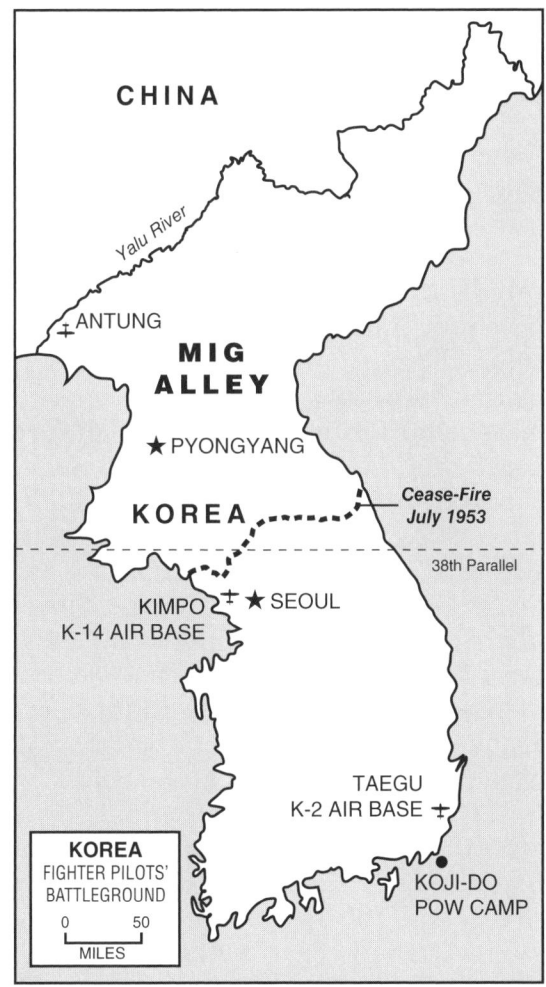

Figure 1. Korean Peninsula. The North Korean offensive was stopped in the summer of 1950 a few miles north of Taegu near the Naktong River. The runway on the small airfield (K-2) near Taegu was then lengthened and strengthened with pierced-steel planking (PSP). This allowed the heavier, longer-range F-84 fighter-bombers to be based in South Korea and reach targets as far north as the Yalu River border. The 136th FBG (ANG) and the 49th FBW, Tactical Air Command (TAC), were both equipped with the F-84E. ANG fighter squadrons came from Dallas-Fort Worth, San Antonio, and Little Rock. ANG pilots could rotate home after completing 100 combat missions, but their aircraft remained. USAF personnel gradually replaced guardsmen. The 136th became the 58th FBG in July 1951. The 38th parallel was the "official" border between North and South Korea, but battles raged on both sides of the 38th. Our shortest missions provided CAS about 175 miles north of K-2. Interdiction missions went farther north, ranging from Sariwon to the Yalu (350 miles). Antung was "safe haven" for MiG-15s. Koji-do was the island where enemy POWs were held and riots occurred in 1952.

Looking back on the two months spent in the 41st, I formed two conclusions. First, the flying experience gained in Japan was additional insurance for flying combat in Korea. Second, the way the squadron supervised day-to-day flying operations was troublesome. I doubted the 41st FIS had progressed very far since a disastrous accident on 13 June 1949 when it was equipped with F-51s.

An air defense exercise on that date required the 41st to escort B-26 bombers over a target near Misawa AB, Japan. When the B-26s aborted the mission because of bad weather, the 41st Squadron leader changed his mission from escort to fighter sweep and proceeded toward the target in tactical formation. The aircraft in tactical formations are spread further apart to improve pilot visibility, mutual support, and maneuverability.

The 12 F-51s in the 41st were attacked about 25 miles from Misawa by two "enemy" F-51s from the 8th Fighter Squadron defending Misawa. The 41st flights resisted the attack by turning toward the two F-51s. After the attackers passed, the 41st Squadron leader turned back on course and ended the fighter sweep after passing the designated target. He then moved his 12 F-51s into three flights in close formation for a flyby over Misawa—a change to the exercise plan made without an acknowledgment by radio from the "enemy" F-51s.

As the 12 F-51s in close formation approached the end of the Misawa runway, the 8th Flight leader and his wingman made another simulated attack. The wingman, flying slightly behind the leader, collided with the 41st Squadron leader and his wingman. The 41st's wingman crash-landed on the Misawa ramp, and the 8th's wingman crashed into a squadron of parked F-80s at Misawa, killing both pilots. Four Airmen working on the ramp were injured by falling debris and explosions. Five F-80s on the ramp were destroyed, and 13 more were damaged. Two F-51s were destroyed and three more damaged. The sad total: two pilots killed, four Airmen injured, and 23 aircraft destroyed or damaged. The Misawa accident remains an extreme example of poor air discipline, bad planning, faulty communications, and inadequate supervision.

After I had flown with the 41st FIS for two months in 1951, my opinion was that it suffered from many of the same weaknesses that had caused the 1949 disaster. The good news is that several of the other young officers whom the squadron commander "didn't know well enough" to promote to first lieutenant stayed until 1955. With a new squadron commander, they turned the 41st into an excellent fighter squadron.

K-2: New Guy Gets Going
January 1952

The Soviet deputy foreign minister had proposed an armistice in June 1951. Truman said in a speech at Tullahoma, Tennessee, on 25 June 1951, that our intentions were to end the war through negotiations and restore the prewar Korean borders. Less clear were the Chinese intentions. Would they use their manpower advantage and strong Soviet support to attack South Korea again?

A military axiom is that offensive operations require several times more logistical support than defensive operations. A new Chinese offensive would depend upon large quantities of supplies crossing the Yalu and moving 300 miles down the North Korean roads, railroads, and bridges before reaching the front lines. Stopping these supplies from reaching Chinese and North Korean troops might not win the war but would make it impossible for the Chinese or North Koreans to start a war-winning new offensive. Realizing they couldn't win the war, China would then quickly force North Korea to sign an armistice—an assumption that proved to be wishful thinking as the war dragged on for two more years.

Operation Strangle, the interdiction campaign, had started in the spring of 1951. The F-84s at K-2 at that time were the primary fighter-bombers used in support of Operation Strangle.

The C-47 left Johnson on 8 January 1952 with my one-way ticket to K-2, Korea. C-47s, affectionately called "Gooney Birds," shuttled mail, people, aircraft parts, and other supplies between USAF bases in Japan and Korea. We landed at K-2 in midday. The crowded ramp had nearly 140 F-84s parked wingtip-to-wingtip belonging to the 49th and 136th FBWs. After unloading quickly, I grabbed my bags and headed for base operations.

A typical fighter-bomber wing in the early fifties had four subordinate groups: a fighter-bomber group composed of a headquarters and three fighter-bomber squadrons (FBS) with 24 aircraft in each squadron, a maintenance and supply group, an air base group, and a medical group. The 49th FBW was the host organization with all its subordinate units at that base. In military jargon, the 49th had both "tooth and tail" at K-2.

The 136th FBG was the tenant organization at K-2. Wing headquarters and support organizations were at Itazuke Air Base, Japan. The group headquarters; three ANG fighter squadrons from Houston, Dallas-Fort Worth, and Little Rock; plus minimal maintenance and supply units were forward-based at K-2. Maybe the 136th fighter pilots were talking about this basing arrangement when they complained, "At K-2 we've got teeth, but no tail!"

My close friend Bolo Brunson soon arrived in a jeep. 2d Lt Carl L. Brunson from South Carolina, better known as Bolo, was the national gymnastics champion on the flying rings when a West Point cadet. He breezed through flying training and had the personality and flying skills that distinguish great fighter pilots. During the past two months at Itazuke, the "A through K" pilots had learned to fly the F-84E and became combat ready. By 8 January, they had all flown several combat missions.

"Hey, Ricardo, the 154th needs another FNG (slang for a new pilot)! Grab your stuff and let's go!" Bolo said in his deep Southern drawl. On the ride over to group headquarters, he explained that the 154th FBS had lost another pilot two days ago and maybe I could be the replacement. We talked about the differences between the F-80C and F-84E. Bolo said the F-84E was a "good bird" and he enjoyed flying it.

The 136th Fighter-Bomber Wing (ANG) belonged to the Texas and Arkansas Air National Guards. When the Korean War started, the 136th was called to active duty—federalized—for one year and sent to Korea. The Guard squadrons were beefed up with Air Force Reserve pilots, also called to active duty at the outbreak of war. The 136th authorization for active duty was due to expire in July 1952. By January 1952, many ANG and Reserve fighter pilots had already completed 100 combat missions and been replaced by recent pilot training graduates and pilots from the six SAC fighter-escort wings equipped with F-84s. The remaining ANG personnel at K-2 in July would be sent home. A famous World War II organization, the 58th FBW, would then be reactivated with the former 136th equipment and personnel.

At the 136th Group headquarters, the adjutant assigned me to the 154th FBS from Little Rock, Arkansas—Anne's hometown. Bolo, Joe Green, and Jim Caldwell, all 51-E classmates, were already assigned to the 154th. About that time, the squadron first sergeant, Allen Fury, appeared and said he had been looking for me. Allen worked for Anne's father in civilian life. Another sergeant observed that he had gone to high school with Anne's father. K-2 was beginning to feel like home with so many friends and acquaintances in the 154th.

Fury led the way to the 154th officer barracks. The open-bay concrete barracks had about 15 bunks lined up on each side of the middle aisle. Double doors at each end opened the barracks. Next door was a building with showers and latrines. About 100 yards away was the mess hall. The base was rather primitive when compared to the air bases in Japan but far better than living in a foxhole or tent like the Army.

A small pot-belly stove in the middle of the aisle heated the barracks during that cold Korean winter. A Korean guard, seated by the stove at night, kept the fire going by tossing in a lump of coal every now and then. The real-estate evaluation "location, location, location" had a special meaning in the barracks. Captains and senior first lieutenants had bunks nearest the stove. Second lieutenants shivered near the doors. The pragmatic "RHIP—Rank Has Its Privileges" was the trump card used to award an empty bunk when the prior resident headed for home, or was killed or missing.

I plunked my gear down by the only empty bunk. Drawn on the white plaster wall over the end of the bunk was an artistic rendition of an open champagne bottle, with bubbles and confetti floating above bars of music and "Lush" stylishly written below. I asked Sergeant Fury, "Who's Lush?" His terse answer restored reality, "Lieutenant Lush was killed a couple days ago." Falling asleep in Lush's bunk that night was difficult— and not because of the cold.

Joe Green occupied the bunk across the aisle. We talked about the missions he had flown. I thanked him again for swapping reporting dates for Nellis after graduating from advanced pilot training. As a result, Joe had arrived in Korea a few weeks earlier.

The next morning, I took the C-47 courier to Itazuke to in-process at 136th FBW headquarters and returned late in the afternoon of 11 January. While gone, I had been assigned to a flight commanded by Capt Clement Counts. Clem, a lawyer in civilian life, had been recalled to active duty from the Air Force Reserve when the Korean War began. During our meeting that evening, I asked him "Where's Joe Green?" Counts replied, "Sorry, Dick, I thought you knew. Joe was shot down this morning." Knowing she would soon hear about our friend Joe, I wrote Anne, "Joe Green was shot down yesterday on a rail cutting mission. He made a belly landing on the coast by Sinanju. He got out OK and started running south. They (other pilots in his flight) had him covered for quite a while, but it was too far north to get a helicopter to him. When the fighters left him for a while, he was gone, so the Reds probably have him as a POW, although we really don't know."

Helicopters were range limited, but the amphibious Grumman SA-16 Albatross was capable of landing close to the North Korean shoreline and rescuing downed aircrews. In Green's case, an SA-16 did not attempt the rescue because ocean spray on landing might have caused wing icing and prevented takeoff after rescuing Green. Col William T. Halton, our group commander, was furious over this Air Rescue Service decision and raised hell with Fifth Air Force. Despite his efforts, rescuing downed pilots on the west coast of North Korea remained a problem throughout my combat tour.

In September 1953, Joe was repatriated after 20 months as a POW. He had escaped the crash but was captured and forced to do slave labor for the North Korean army. He was turned over to the Chinese army in March 1952 and spent the remaining time with a small group of hard-core prisoners who refused to confess to germ warfare charges that were falsely alleged by the Chinese. Joe resigned from the Air Force in 1954 and retired from the University of Illinois in 1992 after a successful career as associate vice president for construction at all campuses.

There weren't any bright lights, floor shows, good restaurants, or other off-base activities worth mentioning at K-2. The nearest city was Taegu. Eighteen months of fierce fighting had taken its toll. Taegu was overrun with refugees. Desperate families were living in packing crates and cardboard boxes. Most people appeared ragged, hungry, and very poor. Taegu was truly an innocent victim of this terrible war.

At K-2 one could see the working side of fighter-bomber operations. Thousands of young Americans were busy flying and maintaining aircraft; loading bombs, rockets, and .50-caliber ammunition; pumping jet fuel; protecting the base from guerrillas; running a hospital; building an asphalt runway to replace the old pierced-steel planking runway; and performing clerical, planning, and administrative tasks on a wartime base.

Fighter pilots can do some outrageous things to let off steam. Three nights after arriving at K-2, I was sitting on my bunk writing a letter home. Crash! Someone was trying to drive a jeep through the closed barracks doors. Seconds later, another crash as he tried to drive the jeep through the double doors at the other end of the barracks. My flight commander jumped out of bed with his .45 pistol in hand shouting, "I'll shoot the SOB!" Our squadron commander, Maj Ray McNeil, a cool head, stood by his bunk and ordered, "Don't shoot; it's the deputy group commander!" A few minutes later the driver staggered into the barracks and apologized for the interruption.

The next few weeks provided a better understanding of the unwelcome stresses that some people suffer in combat—stresses that often influence their normal behavior in strange ways. One of our losses to antiaircraft fire during early March was this jeep-driving lieutenant colonel. A distinguished fighter pilot in World War II and an outstanding combat leader, he was truly a "tiger"—aggressive and fearless. His loss was keenly felt by all the officers and men who had worked and flown with him.

Hollywood's stereotype portrayal of WWII fighter pilots had lots of "wine, women, and song" interspersed with heroic aerial victories over ruthless foes. Fighter pilots at K-2 and their missions didn't quite fit the Hollywood stereotype. Lacking women, they did drink plenty of wine (really beer and Old Methuselah rye whiskey), and they did sing many raucous songs. But their ruthless foe was an unseen North Korean or Chinese antiaircraft gunner challenging the F-84 pilot as he dive-bombed the railroad track dropping 1,000-pound bombs. By the next day, North Korean laborers usually had repaired the cuts in the railroad tracks done by bombing. It was not a zero-sum game. Antiaircraft guns too often destroyed the aircraft and left the pilot forever dead. This was the situation at K-2 in the winter and spring of 1952. The 1978 Office of Air Force History report *Encyclopedia of US Air Force Aircraft and Missile Systems* describes the situation.

> In the spring of 1952, as the Fifth Air Force's fighter-bomber strength had been seriously depleted by logistical causes and excessive losses during the railroad interdiction campaign, . . . Headquarters USAF decided that Fifth Air Force would for 5 months receive a total of 102 F-84Ds as attrition replacements. Most of these aircraft were assigned *to the 136th Wing,* a former Air National Guard organization whose period of authorized service was running out."[2] (emphasis added)

For the 20 days spent in the squadron before flying a combat mission, I felt like the proverbial bastard at the family reunion. My ability to "talk the talk" was nonexistent without having "walked the walk." When the pilots returned to the barracks after a combat mission, their moods varied, and so did their talk. Some missions were "nothing exciting, one less to fly before going home." Other times their talk was exuberant—"Never seen so much flak! Flight got jumped by four MiGs. Shit hit the fan! F-86s got one—the other three headed for Antung!" And sometimes their talk was low key and sad—"He got hit in the middle of his bomb run, no chute, plane went straight in. No point in calling rescue. Good guy, known him a long time. I'll write his wife."

After a quick few days of F-84E ground school, my first F-84E flight occurred on 19 January. Soon after, I would first taste combat. Many thoughts were going through my head. The hazards were obvious. Nearly every day an F-84 from one of the two fighter-bomber wings at K-2 had been shot down. But listening to the pilots after they returned missions had raised unanswerable questions in my own mind: Would I see flak? Would I be afraid and not do a good job? Would I find the target and bomb accurately? In a strange way, the anticipation was reminiscent of my first high school football game or my first boxing match at West Point. On 1 February, after 10 training sorties totaling 15 hours in the F-84E, I flew my first combat mission. That night I wrote Anne, attempting a little gallows humor.

> Today was pretty interesting. After waking up in a slight sweat, they slapped a form fitting strait jacket on and carried me forth to battle. We had a relative milk run on a railway bridge and our flight got four hits out of eight bombs. After that we road recce'd and got a truck. Tomorrow, I have a mission with the Group as a whole and after that only 98 more.

> Charlie Gabriel and Jim German came through here today. They are flying F-51's up North. All of the boys who are grads of the '51 school are now up there. I feel sorry for them because the '51 is a pretty rough deal in combat.

The P-51 (nomenclature then) in World War II had excelled in air-to-air combat and was effective in air-to-ground operations despite a serious problem. Battle damage to the aircraft coolant system from small arms and antiaircraft fire quickly caused the liquid-cooled engine to fail. The other great AAF fighter in WWII, the P-47, was powered by a large, air-cooled engine that could better withstand battle damage. Because most P-47s had been retired from active-duty units before the Korean War started, the available F-51s went to war to fill the desperate need for fighter-bombers.

By 1951 China and the USSR had greatly improved the air defenses of North Korea. As Soviet radar, antiaircraft guns, and MiG-15s joined the war, the relatively slow and vulnerable F-51 became increasingly open to attack. Losses mounted. Of the small group of 51-E classmates who flew F-51s in Korea, five were killed: Lieutenants Thurston Baxter, Medon Bitzer, George Eichelberger, Harry Rushing, and John McAlpine. Lt John Streit became a POW.

In 1960 Capt Charlie Gabriel modestly described his Korean War experience in the Class of 1950's 10th anniversary yearbook: "I entered the police action in the saddle of an F-51 Mustang in January 1952. Being shot at so much and so often wasn't my idea of a gentleman's war and in May, 1952 my squadron converted to the F-86 to join the 'Glory Boys' above the flak. Fortunately, several MiGs obligingly flew in front of me to put my name on the scoreboard." Gabriel shot down two MiG-15s before completing 100 missions. Gen Charles A. Gabriel, chief of staff, USAF, 1982–86, died in 2003.

Farewell Nellis—hello K-2. Picnic at Mount Charleston after completing Nellis. *Left to right*: Carroll Griffin, Jimmy Wills, Mike DeArmond, Pierce Hodnette (*behind DeArmond*), Dick Leavitt, Bolo Brunson, and Pat McGill. Wills was KIA and DeArmond became a POW.

Bill Miller and I with "New Guy" looks. January was grim. Joe Green was shot down three days ago, and Bill inherited Joe's bunk.

A cold winter's day. *Left to right*: Bill Howard, Bolo Brunson, and Harry Garman. "Gar" was leading the flight in March when he was killed and I had to eject.

Experience Is the Best Teacher!

February 1952

The 1950 armed forces had shriveled to 10 percent of their World War II strength. Over 100,000 discharged pilots had returned to college, joined the airlines, or sought other peacetime pursuits. A minority of these pilots, for patriotic and other reasons, joined the Air National Guard and Air Force Reserve. Following the 25 June 1950 invasion, Far East Command did not have enough tactical airpower to offset the large North Korean advantage on the ground. The solution was to recall reservists and federalize ANG units. A disturbing aspect of the recall was that approximately 1,200 World War II pilots and navigators declared a fear of flying. In sharp contrast, the 136th FBW (ANG) was federalized, augmented with Air Force reservists, went to Korea, and joined the battle. Not all were happy warriors, but they fought with skill and courage. In World War II, the number of combat missions flown was usually the criteria for completing a combat tour. There were numerous exceptions to the overall policy, but this "light at the end of the tunnel" system worked well for most combat flyers.

A "carrot and stick" approach to combat missions was used in the Korean War. The carrot was a ticket home. Ignore the hazards, complete 100 combat missions, and you're on your way home. The stick was a full year in Korea if you dragged your feet or couldn't finish for reasons beyond your control. Griping when missions didn't come fast enough was a predictable by-product of this rotation policy.

My motivations were not necessarily the same as the ANG and Air Reserve pilots. I strongly believed that the United States had to stop the spread of Communist aggression not only in Europe but also in the Far East. As a career Air Force officer, flying combat to the best of my ability was an obligation and a rite of passage. It was an opportunity to learn about air warfare, particularly fighter operations, through first-hand experience. Since I wanted to learn, Maj "Giant" Cunningham, the assistant group operations officer, let me help him on nonflying days. Letter to Anne, 8 February:

> Today I briefed the Group for the mission and scheduled the flights for tomorrow. These are some of the duties of an operations officer that I'm learning. I also manned the tower when today's mission came back. Colonel Bill Halton saw me sitting on my duff in the office and stuck me with a job I've got to do tonight. He has a plan that he wants to take to Fifth Air Force Headquarters to improve operations, so he gave it to me to write up. Now I'm trying to scrounge a book on military correspondence to brush up on that lost art.

The first few missions removed most of my curiosity about flying combat, especially the third mission. After bombing the railroad track near the Yalu River and encountering moderate flak, we found and strafed some hidden trucks with good results. Flying number four in Elgin Red Flight, I was last to finish strafing. The flight was getting low on fuel, and we were a long way from K-2. The flight leader called, "Break it off, Elgin Red 4, and join up—we're heading for home plate."

I completed a long strafing pass on the trucks, turned south, and started climbing in order to catch Elgin Red Flight before it disappeared in the cloud deck above. Just then, four MiG-15s in close formation with their landing gear down popped out of the clouds. They were about a mile away, descending and heading in the opposite direction. Apparently the MiGs were on a radar approach to Antung, their base just across the Yalu.

What to do? "Dreams of glory—Alpena lieutenant gets four MiGs on his third mission!" passed through my mind. Could I turn 180 degrees, sneak up behind them, catch them with their gear down, and nail one, two, or more with the limited ammo I had left? Did I have enough fuel? Or should I call Elgin Red Leader, tell him about the MiGs, and see what he wants to do?

Discipline prevailed. "Elgin Red Leader, Red Four here. Four MiGs at your 9 o'clock are heading for Antung with their gear down." His answer ended the discussion and probably saved me from an extended visit to North Korea as a POW. "Roger, Red Four. I saw them. Join up; we're going home."

Lessons learned on that early mission helped me complete 100 combat missions in the Korean War and another 152 in the Vietnam War:

- Complete the assigned mission—first priority.

- Maintain air discipline—the flight leader is in charge.

- Know your limitations—fuel, ammo, aircraft, experience, and skills.

- Evaluate the enemy threat—how many? Ground or air or both?

- Make decisions correctly and quickly—combat at 500 knots demands fast actions.

Three days later, two missions were flown in MiG Alley, one in the morning and the other late in the day. Letter to Anne, 10 February:

> This afternoon we flew a real late mission to cut rails in MiG Alley. It was quite interesting. There were lots of MiGs, but the 86's kept them off of us. After bombing the railroad, we looked for stray vehicles, spotted two and worked them over. One blew up on my second pass which was satisfying to me. It is really amazing to see how fast the MiGs and 86's go when they are messing around. We watch their contrails and can keep fairly good track of them.

Lesson learned on that mission was that speed differentials between combat aircraft from past training exercises matter more than we could imagine. Both the F-86 and MiG-15 were swept-wing aircraft with approximately the same top speeds. The F-86F had a maximum speed of 600 knots, could fly slightly faster than the speed of sound in a dive, and could cruise over 500 knots. In contrast, the F-84E maximum speed was 521 knots, and its cruising speed while carrying bombs was around 375 knots.

Defending against MiG attacks was a three-dimensional problem. The F-84 flights generally cruised between 15,000 and 20,000 feet on their way to targets in MiG Alley. Flying above at 35,000 to 40,000 feet were F-86 flights providing top cover for the F-84s. Still higher, the lighter MiGs cruised above the F-86 top cover, waiting for the right moment to begin their attacks. Watching the contrails above, the F-84 pilots could often tell when a MiG attack was imminent. Aluminum external fuel tanks reflecting the sun would flutter down as F-86 pilots jettisoned them to increase speed and maneuverability before engaging the MiGs.

Suddenly, the MiG attack begins. Rolling over into near-vertical dives, MiGs flash through the F-86 cover at transonic speeds. F-86s in hot pursuit try their utmost to stop the MiGs before they can make a firing pass at the slower, bomb-carrying F-84s. The few seconds from the time you see the MiG until it completes firing cannons and passes through your flight leaves no time to counterattack. You can't stop a near-vertical attack when the MiG has an over 200-knot speed advantage. The bomb-loaded F-84 in level flight simply doesn't have enough energy to outmaneuver the diving MiG. You hope that the F-86 hot on its tail will screw up the MiG pilot's firing pass. The MiG misses you, with the F-86 chasing it, and you continue heading toward your target. Now you realize why close-flying escorts can't protect slower aircraft from attack in the Jet Age.

In World War II, P-51 and P-47 fighters protected bombers from enemy fighters by flying above or near the bombers. Because escort worked well in that war, SAC formed six fighter-escort wings (FEW) in the postwar era to protect SAC bombers. The Air Force learned a hard lesson in 1951 that should have been learned in exercises prior to the Korean War. Until the Chinese entered the war, SAC B-29 bombers in daylight raids were unopposed. Then MiG-15s made B-29 daylight bombing a high-risk operation. In December 1950, SAC's 27th FEW, equipped with F-84s, arrived to protect B-29s from MiG-15 attacks. Ten B-29s were shot up by nine MiGs on 1 March 1951. On 12 April, a daylight raid by 39 B-29s was conducted against railroad bridges at Sinuiju. B-29s were protected by a screen of F-84s and a high cover of F-86s. The high-flying MiGs dove through the F-86 cover and F-84 screen. Two B-29s were shot down and six more damaged. In October five B-29s were shot down in one week. After that, B-29 daylight bombing was terminated.

On one of the October missions, the B-29s were escorted by the 136th FBW. The group commander, Colonel Halton, a double ace from WWII, and Major Cunningham led two of the 136th flights. When the MiGs attacked, the slower F-84s repeatedly forced the MiGs to turn away from their B-29 targets. The desperate air battle continued as it moved from MiG Alley toward South Korea. The F-84s were running out of fuel when the MiGs began breaking off their attacks and headed for Antung.

Halton and Cunningham flew the last two F-84s countering the MiGs and covered the withdrawal of the other F-84s. After expending their ammunition, both pilots had barely enough fuel to reach the nearest air base. They throttled back, hoping to save enough fuel to reach K-14, now visible in the distance.

Just as things were looking better, Cunningham called Halton, "Red Lead, Blue Lead here. I've got four of them cornered—how about a little help?" The last flight of MiGs had found Cunningham flying alone. "Roger, Blue Lead, I'm on my way!" Halton answered, as he turned. Seeing Halton coming, the MiGs headed for Antung. Halton made a dead-stick landing at K-14 after his F-84 flamed out from fuel starvation. Cunningham was very low on fuel but landed safely at K-14.

Their heroism in this October battle was never officially recognized. Colonel Halton wanted to submit Major Cunningham for the Silver Star for his heroism. Major Cunningham would not accept the submission unless he could submit Halton for the Silver Star. Halton refused. Neither would concede, so nothing happened.

Road Gets Rougher
February–March 1952

My flight leader for several missions was Lt Charles A. Dunne, a black Air Force Reserve officer with World War II experience, assigned to the 154th when he was recalled. Charlie was an outstanding fighter pilot, a very cool head in combat and an exemplary flight leader. As Charlie and other ANG and AFR pilots reached the 100-mission mark, new flight leaders were appointed. In February and March, the new flight leaders usually were ANG or AFR pilots who needed only a few more missions to complete their 100 and were given the opportunity to lead flights their last few missions.

I was scheduled to fly mission number seven with one of the newly chosen flight leaders. His approach to leadership in combat could best be described as "every man for himself." On previous missions, he had earned a reputation for applying full power immediately after his dive-bomb run, climbing as fast and as far away as possible from the target, not checking the status of the other three pilots in the flight, and leaving them the challenging task of catching him as he ran for home at maximum speed.

By the time mission seven rolled around, I knew what to expect in terms of flak and MiGs while cutting railroad tracks in MiG Alley. A flight would normally dive-bomb in order—"One," the flight leader, followed by "Two," his wingman, then "Three," the element leader, followed by "Four," his wingman. New guys were wingmen; I was "Elgin Green Four." It didn't task my imagination to realize that antiaircraft gunners had polished their skills by the time "Four" dive-bombed the target. We bought longevity by "jinking"—abrupt turns left and right, up and down—until aligned for bomb release.

The weather was marginal in the target area near the Yalu River. We broke out of the clouds at about 4,000 feet. Clouds this low left only enough ceiling to make low-angle, glide-bombing attacks. Low ceilings also simplified ranging problems for antiaircraft gunners. One after the other, we began our glide-bomb runs, releasing bombs at about 1,500 feet. Just as my bombs were released, the F-84 was jolted by a direct hit from flak.

I called, "Elgin Green Lead—Green Four hit. I'm off the target, turning south!" No response came from Green Lead. The flak had caused a complete electrical failure. I looked for another F-84—someone to lead me home. No such luck. Green Lead had entered the clouds, and Green Two and Three were seconds away from disappearing in clouds. Without flight instruments, radio, or navigation aids, climbing into the clouds was not an option. I stayed below the clouds heading south on the magnetic compass, hoping to find K-14 near Seoul about 250 miles away before the fuel ran out or I ran into a stray MiG flight looking for stragglers. With a little luck, I made an emergency landing at K-14 about 40 minutes later and left the F-84 to be repaired.

My first order of business after returning to K-2 was to confront this poor excuse for a flight leader. I told him since he was either unwilling or unable to be responsible for the lives of the other pilots in his flight, he should never lead a flight again. When our squadron commander learned about the incident from one of the other pilots, he took appropriate action. Two days later, this ex-flight leader completed his 100th mission while flying Number Two in a low-threat area and left Korea. Lesson learned: combat leaders must ignore personal risk to protect their people.

Mission number nine was an example of how protecting each other can have a beneficial outcome. An F-84 was shot down in MiG Alley near the coast. Our flight flew rescue combat air patrol—circling over the downed pilot until he was rescued. We made it back to K-14, the closest American base, very low on fuel but feeling good about helping save another pilot. We flew back to K-2 that night and got a rousing response at the bar with the WWII ballad that says "throw a nickel on the grass, save a fighter pilot's ass! Oh, Hallelujah! Hallelujah! Throw a nickel on the grass and you'll be saved!"

Starting in 1951 and continuing through the spring of 1952, the Chinese and Russians greatly strengthened the air defenses within North Korea and around Antung. Two dozen early warning (EW) radar sites, many batteries of medium- and large-caliber antiaircraft artillery (AAA), 300 MiGs at the Antung complex of air bases, and a joint operations center (JOC) at Antung were in place. By the spring of 1952, approximately a dozen ground control intercept (GCI) radar sites became operational. The enemy air defense improvements increased fighter-bomber losses in our Operation Strangle.

A USAF radar site located on an island off the west coast of North Korea provided the only warnings available to USAF aircrews over North Korea. Radio calls would warn us whenever MiG flights took off. "One train leaving Antung" or "two (or more) trains leaving Antung" signified the number of MiG flights that had taken off. Whenever we heard, "Casey Jones with one train leaving Antung," we knew some flight was going to be in for a rough day. "Casey Jones" was the top Russian ace flying a MiG. Pilots approaching the 100-mission goal particularly felt the pressure. I wrote Anne, "Just went up to the mess hall for some coffee. The lad who is flying Number Three in my flight tomorrow (I'm Number Four) is getting his 100th mission—and he's a wee bit nervous tonight."

There was reason to be nervous. The next day's mission was bombing Namsi airfield. B-29 bombing destroyed Namsi and the other North Korean airfields early in the war. As long as the North Korean airfields remained inoperable because of our bombing attacks, MiG coverage from the Antung complex could only extend from the Yalu River as far south as the Chongchon River. This chunk of airspace was called "MiG Alley," a grudging tribute to the MiG 15. There was a "food chain" in MiG Alley— F-84s were eaten by antiaircraft guns and MiGs, and MiGs were eaten by F-86s.

Unless their supply situation improved, Communist troops could not resume an offensive against the well-equipped UN forces under General Ridgway. The Communists needed to gain air superiority over a much larger area of North Korea than MiG Alley. If the UN lost air superiority, our fighter-bombers and bombers would be unable to interdict the long supply lines extending from the Yalu River to Communist troop concentrations near the 38th parallel. Winning the air superiority battle raging in MiG Alley meant the UN could maintain the status quo between the two armies facing each other near the 38th parallel.

The weather approaching Namsi was nearly clear with a few scattered cumulus clouds. Our attack force was comprised of approximately nine flights of F-84s—36 aircraft. Both medium and heavy antiaircraft guns began firing as we approached the target at about 15,000 feet. In a few seconds, white gun smoke blanketed Namsi. It looked bad. Our flight leader rolled over and started his dive-bomb run. Two went next. What was Three waiting for? Just then, Three jettisoned his bombs and stayed at 15,000 feet. Seeing him do this disgusted me—every man a tiger? I rolled over into my dive-bomb run hoping the flak wasn't as bad as it looked.

The flight made it back to K-2 without a loss. Three, now happy but still shaky, had finished his 100! He left for home and civilian life the next day. The rest of the flight celebrated his departure with a bottle of Old Methuselah after he left.

By the end of February, the lack of replacement F-84E aircraft was beginning to be a problem. Several new pilots, mostly second lieutenants, had arrived as replacements for the departing ANG and AFR pilots who had completed 100 missions. Too many pilots and too few aircraft caused a lot of griping. I wrote Anne, "Didn't get to fly today, but got number 13 yesterday. Speaking of 13, my promotion to first lieutenant was effective on the 13th! We are really in tough shape as far as planes go. We lose a few here and there to battle damage and operational losses. We don't get any replacement airplanes to replace the losses, so now we have a full crew of pilots and only a few planes that can fly." On 28 February, I wrote Anne, mentioning the ever-present flak, "Today I flew number 16. Same sort of mission as usual, but slightly more exciting because of the overabundance of little red 'golf balls' in the air. I'm glad this is just a 'police action,' because I don't think I'd like a real war!"

The next mission required a predawn takeoff. An asphalt runway was under construction at K-2. In the meantime, we flew from a runway 75 feet wide and made of pierced-steel planking. For night operations, flare pots were spaced every few hundred yards outlining the edge of the PSP. Standard procedure was to make two-ship formation takeoffs because they reduced the time required for flights to rejoin and head for North Korea. I was the group commander's wingman on this mission. We started the takeoff roll, and after accelerating to 80 or 90 knots, I felt a thump. The nose of my F-84 started to drop, hit the runway, and scraped along on the PSP until stopping. I called the tower, "Elgin White 2, emergency abort on the runway, leaving the aircraft, switches off."

After disconnecting shoulder harness, parachute, helmet, and G-suit, I climbed from the cockpit to the wing and dropped to the ground. The 1,000-pound bombs had stayed on the bomb racks when the nose hit the runway. There was not much damage from the collapsed nose gear. I walked about 100 feet away and waited for the fire trucks.

Accident Board findings described the chain of events leading to the collapsed nose gear. On takeoff roll, the F-84 collided with a wheelbarrow left on the dark runway, causing the nose gear to collapse. Korean laborers had left the wheelbarrow on the runway after lighting flare pots. A lieutenant in another squadron had been designated mobile control officer for that day. His duties included checking the runway prior to predawn takeoffs. On the morning of the accident, the mobile control officer overslept, failed to check the runway, and did not discover the wheelbarrow.

Between missions, we passed the time in different ways. A postwar logistician must have heard we won World War II because aircrews received a ration of whiskey after each successful mission. The tradition continued in the Korean War. There was one problem—K-2 had no fruit juice but plenty of Old Methuselah rye whiskey. An enterprising pilot, known for his silver tongue, discovered the Army headquarters in Taegu had lots of canned fruit juice but lacked whiskey. Supply satisfied demand for both the Army and Air Force when our raconteur drove a jeep to Taegu and traded a case of Old Methuselah for several cases of grape juice. The grape juice was poured into a large metal pot and liberally diluted with Old Methuselah. Everyone but the chaplain called the colorful potion "Purple Jesus," but he enjoyed it anyway. Army–Air Force back-scratching continued for several weeks until the Army ran out of grape juice.

As promised, better bunks—closer to the pot belly stove—became available when pilots completed 100 missions or were killed or missing. The next empty bunk was given to me, the next pilot in the pecking order. Along with the new bunk came news about Joe Green. I wrote Anne on 27 February, "I moved my sack today farther down the BOQ aisle. It's a regular little Waldorf-Astoria here, complete with a GI bed with springs rather than the canvas cot. What a deal! I just heard that Joe Green is a prisoner which is good news, I guess. He would have had a heluva job walking out from that far north. Being a POW is probably better than freezing to death."

Fighter pilots tend to be somewhat superstitious, especially in combat—not quite neurotic but a little strange. Anne sent me two pairs of red pajamas for Christmas. Long johns in style, they made excellent underwear for winter flying. Not being immune to superstition and knowing Good Luck when I saw it, I wore the red pajamas for every mission until summer temperatures made them unbearable. Another oddity was the pilot in the BOQ who dressed before each combat mission by standing and holding his flight suit up with the front zipper open and facing him. He would carefully back into the flight suit by raising his left leg, making a half-turn to the right while putting his leg into the pant leg opposite his right hand, complete the turn, squeeze his shoulders together, stick his arms down the sleeves, and close the zipper. When queried about this strange ritual, his perfectly logical answer explained everything. "I've done that ever since I checked out in the F-84. It's worked so far, and sure as hell, I'm not going to change now!"

1st Lt Harry Garman slept across the aisle. Gar got his wings a class or two ahead of me and had been in the 154th since late fall. We became close friends with at least one thing in common—both from Michigan, we enjoyed arguing about the relative merits of the Army and Michigan football teams and similar trivia of national importance. When scheduled to fly the next day, we often spent the evenings playing gin rummy.

By early March, Gar was leading flights as the older flight leaders rotated back to the states. Known as a stand-up guy, his performance in combat had been exceptional. Other pilots trusted his judgment and were pleased to fly with him. From my viewpoint, Gar's only weak spot was his inability to win at penny-a-point gin rummy.

On 13 March 1952, the group was scheduled for a large mission in MiG Alley. Gar would lead one of the flights, and I was his wingman—Elgin Red Two. While we were putting on our flight gear, it occurred to me that it was Friday the 13th.

"Hey, Gar! I'm getting tired carrying all your gin rummy losses. You might get zapped on one of these missions, and I'd be screwed out of a hard-earned 20 bucks. And besides, today's

Friday the 13th." (We frequently lost track of the days of the week. I discovered later the day was really Thursday, not Friday.)

Taking my gallows humor in good spirit, Gar peeled two tens from his wallet. We walked over to group operations for the pre-flight briefing and listened to the usual operations, intelligence, and weather briefings. A cold front was creating marginal weather conditions across the entire Korean Peninsula. Low ceilings and snow were forecast for K-2 upon our return. Compared to the previous 22 combat missions, today's work seemed easy except for the weather.

Things went as advertised until we started our letdown into the target area. The target was obscured by lower clouds, and the group was diverted to the secondary target. The diversion was successful. Bad weather kept the MiGs on the ground at Antung, our bombs were dropped on target, and no planes reported being hit by flak. Upon reaching the radio beacon for K-2, the flights started their jet letdowns with one-minute separation between each four-ship flight.

Gar started the letdown for our flight on time. The K-2 Tower reported the ceiling and visibility were marginal but still OK for landing. We closed to a very tight formation while letting down because heavy snow was severely restricting lateral visibility. Just before we broke out of the low clouds, the squadron commander leading the flight behind us called the tower. "K-2 Tower, this is Elgin Blue Leader. My flight instruments have failed, and I'm declaring an emergency. Have the flight ahead of us make a missed approach so I can get on the ground." This lieutenant colonel had a reputation for being a poor instrument pilot and had used this excuse before when weather was marginal.

"Roger, Elgin Blue, this is K-2 Tower, you're cleared to land. Elgin Red, break off your approach. Report when back over K-2 beacon for letdown instructions." Gar added nearly full power; we accelerated and started a climbing turn to the left. By then, the heavy snowstorm was badly restricting visibility.

Number Four had problems staying in formation. He called, "Elgin Red Lead, Four here. I can't stay in formation and am breaking off." There was no response from Gar. Red Four left the formation, circled the area, found a hole in the clouds, let down through the hole, located K-2, and landed safely.

Meanwhile, Gar continued a climbing turn with nearly full power. A quick look at my altimeter and turn indicator showed we were passing through 16,000 feet and still turning. I was flying on the inside of the turn on Gar's left wing. Red Three was flying on the outside of the turn on Gar's right wing. The visibility in the heavy snowstorm continued to deteriorate, so I moved within a few feet of Gar with our wings overlapping. A few more seconds passed. Gar had not reduced power and had not made any radio transmissions since starting the missed approach. Something was wrong—we should be leveling off and slowing down! I took my eyes off Gar's F-84 for a second to check my instruments. Then, all hell broke loose.

"Red Lead, we're going through the Mach limit!" I called. Simultaneously, I saw Three's aircraft pitch sharply up to the right, while my out-of-control F-84 pitched down to the left. Gar disappeared quickly into the snowstorm.

The F-84E was design-limited to .82 Mach, about 520 knots (true air speed). The flight manual warned that the F-84E was uncontrollable over this Mach limit. The pilot could see when the F-84E was approaching the Mach limit by checking the flight instruments where a red line was prominently displayed at .82 Mach on the airspeed indicator. With his wingmen struggling to stay in formation in the heavy snowstorm, we had to depend upon our flight leader, Gar, to stay below the Mach limit.

My F-84 headed earthward as I fought to regain level flight. The altimeter rapidly unwound as the aircraft spiraled downward. For a second or two, it seemed recovery was possible when the nose seemed to rise in response to back pressure on the control stick. Suddenly, the aircraft pitched, rolled over, and headed downward for the second time. Moving the flight controls, rudders, and stick had no effect on changing the F-84 flight path. G-forces rapidly increased, and the airspeed remained around the red-line limit. It was time to go. I struggled to move my right hand to the ejection seat handle. My left arm and elbow were pinned under the canopy rail by the G-forces. Squeezing the handle, I ejected around 8,000 feet into the snowstorm.

With explosive force, the ejection seat cleared the aircraft. The 500-knot windblast felt like running full speed into a brick wall. The helmet and oxygen mask twisted 90 degrees on my head; I could not see—the helmet and earphones were covering my eyes. I ripped off the helmet and threw it away. Next step was unlocking the seat belt and shoulder harness that held me in the ejection seat. I unlocked, but the seat did not separate. The parachute and survival kit had become wedged in the seat. After kicking backward with my heels on the bottom part of the seat, the seat finally broke free, smacking me in the back of my bare head as a farewell gesture.

Although not sure how many seconds it took to eject and separate from the seat, I was damn glad to be out of the airplane and clear of the ejection seat. Falling in the snow cloud, I could only guess how high I was above the ground. I pulled the parachute ripcord when the windblast seemed less severe. The parachute snapped open. The opening shock ripped out two panels, but the open canopy was a joy to see.

Snowflakes within the cloud were falling in parallel lines. In contrast, my parachute and I were oscillating, or swinging, severely from left to right across these parallel lines of snow. Parachute training had taught how to control a parachute descent by pulling on the left and right risers. Stopping the oscillation by lining up with the parallel lines of falling snow seemed like a way to avoid a landing injury. After pulling on the risers a few times, the oscillation seemed to stop.

I broke out of the clouds—swinging wildly in big arcs from left to right, maybe 150 feet above the ground. My Snow Line Theory was a loser. I only had time to pull the right-hand riser and slow the oscillation before hitting the ground—hard. The terrain was difficult, a rocky mountainside overlooking a valley. Several Koreans appeared within minutes after landing. An anxious moment passed before determining they were friendly. They helped assemble my gear and carry it down the mountain. Soldiers from an Army convoy driving down a road in the valley met us coming down from the mountain. They saw the plane crash a few miles away, followed by a parachute dropping from the clouds.

An Army captain put me in the backseat of his jeep and headed the convoy into the next small village. He explained the convoy was hunting for guerrillas known to be in that village and declared I was lucky that they hadn't captured me. We entered the village. The Soldiers jumped from the jeeps, kicked open the doors of several houses, and fired into the houses. Under other circumstances, watching them operate would have been a fascinating experience, but my mind was still replaying the accident.

An Army sergeant drove me to a Marine air base shared with the South African Air Force. After I contacted the 136th Group about the accident, Koreans found a crash site about a quarter mile from my crashed F-84. Gar's body was in that aircraft. We never learned why Gar made no radio calls or whether something happened to his aircraft that led to his tragic loss of life.

A Marine flight surgeon examined me and decided my arm wasn't broken and that everything else was OK. Then he brought out a small bottle of brandy, telling me, "Drink this, it will prevent you going into shock." "No thanks," was my answer. "I don't like brandy." Our brief debate ended with, "Well, if you don't want it, I'll drink it." And he did. Semper Fi!

There was a great welcoming party that night. The South Africans insisted on teaching me the Zulu War Dance. Everyone stomped around in a circle, all the while loudly chanting, "Hold 'em down, you Zulu warriors. Hold 'em down, you Zulu chiefs, chiefs, chiefs!" The Marine courier flew me back to K-2 in the morning. Every bone in my body ached, but I was glad to be alive. I wanted to start flying immediately on the supposition that if a horse throws you, get right back on the horse. Colonel Halton said no and sent me on a five-day rest and recreation (R&R) to Johnson. Anne needed a low-key explanation for this unexpected R&R because returning ANG pilots from Little Rock often called her about happenings at K-2. Saturday evening, I wrote Anne, "By the way, the Group Commander ordered me to take an R&R because of a somewhat hairy experience. I made a 500 MPH bailout in weather from about 8,000 feet. No injuries and was picked up by South Koreans. Spent the night with Marines and South Afs. Am now a Caterpillar Club member!"

After returning from R&R, I started flying missions again. March continued to be a rough month. On one mission, a well-liked captain in our squadron was killed. Our flight had left the target area, was cruising about 15,000 feet, and was almost out of North Korea. Suddenly, a desperate cry broke radio silence. An antiaircraft shell had penetrated the cockpit and mortally wounded him in the stomach. We could do nothing.

His agonizing cries continued until his aircraft crashed a moment later.

Being unable to fly after being wounded is a hazard that goes with the job in a single-cockpit fighter. Rarely seen is a Purple Heart on a fighter pilot's chest. Unless the fighter pilot can eject and become a POW, chances of surviving a serious wound are slim.

Most of our missions in February and March were low-altitude bombing of the railroad tracks leading from Manchuria through MiG Alley to Pyongyang and Sariwon. These daylight raids arrived at their targets at approximately the same time each day during the winter months. The enemy loaded the area with AAA, making low-altitude bombing very dangerous, and the situation was getting worse. My aircraft was hit by flak five different times in the 20 rail-cutting missions I had flown through the end of March. Operation Strangle had lost 343 USAF aircraft in one year, the majority in the last few months. The laws of probability being what they are, there was slight chance to finish 100 missions unless the railway interdiction campaign changed.

The F-84 pilots understood why Operation Strangle was important. The Communists needed to build up supplies and to maintain a reliable resupply system in order to resume offensive operations. Our job was to attack their supply lines, prevent a supply buildup, and minimize the effectiveness of their resupply system. A simple plan, but the devil was in the details—the tactics and the planning.

It just did not make sense to trade a pilot and aircraft for a cut in railroad track that would be repaired overnight. Could targeting be varied? Were there other ways to hurt the enemy besides interdiction? Why not hit dams, power stations, and other infrastructure targets in North Korea? Why not fly more CAS missions against Communist troop positions?

The severe F-84 losses in the winter of 1952 finally caught the attention of Fifth Air Force. Targeting methods changed in the last part of March. It was like a breath of fresh air. Using a systems analysis approach to the problem, random numbers were drawn each day and determined which targets would be bombed. The purpose was to keep the enemy guessing when and where the next attack would strike. In addition, we started flying close air support, as well as interdiction missions. Fifth Air Force also added high-priority infrastructure targets as the months went by.

In combat it is very hard to relate your activities to the big picture. Instead, you plow ahead and hope your unit and the combined efforts of all units are making a positive difference. The present danger that a pilot could become a POW necessarily limits his access to plans and strategies. At squadron level, we called it "how to grow mushrooms"—keep 'em in the dark, water 'em frequently, and feed 'em B.S." Mushroom growing may explain the answer I sent Anne to one of her questions. "You asked me in your last letter if I thought this war was going to end soon. I doubt it, although it is hard to tell whether the Communists are building up their forces in order to further their power at the Peace Talks, or in order to give us hell in a spring offensive. The air war is going at an all-out tempo even though there is little movement at the 38th Parallel."

Combat losses and 100 mission completions created more vacancies in the squadron by the end of March. Bolo became squadron operations officer in recognition of his excellent job performance as assistant squadron operations officer. Meanwhile, I had been instructing in the training flight for the past several weeks. This involved a lot of extra flying time and provided flight-leading experience before leading flights in combat. After 28 combat missions, I became the flight commander for seven other pilots on 29 March.

New Faces—Big Changes
April–May 1952

By the end of March, most of the ANG pilots had finished their combat tours and returned to Little Rock. Maj Ray McNeil, the 154th Squadron commander, and 1st Lt Farris "Fearless" Fortner, a 154th Flight commander, were among the last to leave. Both officers were well regarded—not only nice guys but real tigers in combat. All the new replacement pilots were USAF officers, young and old, inexperienced and experienced. I wrote Anne about the personnel change and about close air support:

> It doesn't seem the same anymore without Major McNeil here. However, our new squadron commander, Major Don Booty is an experienced F-84 pilot and clearly knows what he is doing.
>
> Close air support missions are great stuff and really make you feel good if you have a successful one. The T-6 Forward Air Controller (FAC) gave us 85% effectiveness on today's strike which is damn good. It's amazing how the Commies are burrowed into these rugged mountains. You can see bunkers, trenches, guns, etc. that you are hitting and feel that you are doing the GI's about 500 yards away some good by beating the hell out of the Reds. Each F-84 carried two 500 pound bombs, four 5 inch rockets and 1800 rounds of machine gun ammunition. I slapped my two 500 pounders right into a bunker (glide bombing, a la Nellis) and the FAC almost went Able Sugar over the radio when he saw it blow! Another good thing about close support is that if you have any trouble, you are right by the front lines and can get out easily.

CAS missions were a welcome break. After cutting rails in MiG Alley, there was a tendency to minimize the dangers involved in CAS. On one CAS mission, I was orbiting over the front lines about 8,000 feet, waiting for the FAC to call in the flight. With oxygen mask unfastened, I lit a cigar, took a puff or two, looked down at the Red trenches, and speculated where the FAC would direct our attack.

"Ping!" A bullet came through the right side of the canopy, ricocheted around the cockpit, and fell into my lap. I doused the cigar, fastened the oxygen mask, and focused on the task at hand. If he had only known, some Commie soldier could have written home that he had cured forever this American fighter pilot from smoking in an aircraft. We finished the mission without any more trouble and flew home. The F-84 flew the next day after the canopy was repaired.

Col William T. Halton, 136th Group commander, was my hero. He epitomized everything that I had read or heard about leadership in combat. Despite the difficult times and heavy losses that winter of 1952, he was always upbeat and led by example. He filled his regular Sunday night meetings with all the fighter pilots with straight talk and rough humor. With Halton leading a mission, there was never a time when the results were in doubt. In the middle of March, we learned he was being transferred—a real blow to our group. Halton was assigned to the 18th FBW in April 1952 and was killed a short time later flying a close support mission in an F-51. Halton was a charismatic, brave leader, and I will always remember how he inspired us to do a difficult task in the hazardous months of early 1952.

With too few aircraft and too many pilots, most pilots had little to do. Our new squadron commander kept them busy building a pilots' lounge in an empty squadron building. There was much griping about having to saw, nail, and paint, but once the job ended, everyone had a positive reaction. Meanwhile, instructor duties were keeping me busy. All this, plus future R&R plans, was mentioned in a letter to Anne, written 8 April 1952. "I'm taking my instructor job quite seriously because the guys just out of Nellis and Luke [AFB, Arizona] don't know enough—most of the losses lately have been guys in their first few missions. I don't mean to say that I know everything by a long shot. However, I do know a few things picked up from the old heads that could save their lives. I'm going to write Jack Dille and ask him to go on R&R with Bolo, Mike and me the next time."

Two weeks later, I canceled any plans for an R&R with Jack Dille and Mike DeArmond. Jack died on 13 April, Easter Sunday, ferrying an F-80 to Itazuke AB. His son was born a few days later. A MiG-15 shot Mike down on 21 April near the Manchurian border. With his usual subtle humor, Mike later described this mishap, "Reported to 4th Fighter Group, 335th FIS (F-86s) at K-14 in December, 1951. Was shot down on April 21, 1952, on my 46th mission by an incredibly lucky MiG-15 pilot. I was repatriated in September, 1953, during Operation Big Switch."[3] Mike learned after the end of the Cold War that a Russian was flying the MiG.

The F-84E inventory continued to shrink because of combat and operational losses. By the middle of April, our squadron was down to 10 F-84Es against an authorization of 24. Our 10 F-84Es were sent to the 49th FBW to replace its losses. The Department of the Air Force decided to send 102 rebuilt F-84Ds to Korea over the next five months. We received the first few on 20 April. After two one-hour orientation flights, I flew the F-84D in combat on 30 April. The F-84D was lighter and shorter than the F-84E. The new Allison J-35-A-29 engine gave the F-84D slightly better acceleration and turning capabilities than the F-84E. However, an important advantage the F-84E retained over the F-84D was a much stronger wing—better able to withstand the repetitive, high-G loads necessary in combat.

Our pilots and maintenance crews called the F-84D "Harry Truman's war crime" because new F-84Es were sent to peaceful Europe and old, troubled F-84Ds were sent to our wing. This second-class treatment generated a lot of ill will and finger-pointing at the Truman administration. Discontent crept into my letters to Anne. She discussed my gripes with her father, a staunch supporter of Harry Truman, and mailed her father's reaction back to me. My response was emphatic but ended on a conciliatory note. Her parents were taking good care of Anne and Chris, for which I was very thankful.

Some new arrivals in the squadron were experienced pilots; others were not. A tall, rangy young lieutenant with an aeronautical engineering degree joined my flight. He had no trouble earning his wings at Williams AFB and satisfactorily completing F-84 gunnery training at Luke before joining the 154th. As often happened, the Old Boys gave him the NFG treatment at every opportunity. During the two-week stand-down from combat, they filled his ears with terrible tales of MiGs, flak, and all the conceivable rigors of combat. By the time he flew his first combat mission, the lieutenant was wild-eyed and shaking in his boots.

Our practice was to take newly assigned pilots on their first mission or two to the Haeju Peninsula in North Korea. There was seldom any flak encountered in Haeju and never a MiG. He passed this test without serious problems, calmed down, and seemed ready for the Big Time. His third mission was in MiG Alley against a lightly defended target. I assigned him to be my wingman, Elgin Red Two, where I could keep a close eye on him and help if he had any problems.

We started our dive-bombing attacks from out of the sun. After bomb release, each F-84 was to break either left or right, turn south, take evasive action while climbing, and rejoin in tactical formation for the ride home. I dropped my bombs, broke left, turned south, and started to climb. Where was Two? Then I spotted his aircraft. He had dropped his bombs, was climbing rapidly, and headed *north* toward the Yalu River! I called the element lead, "Elgin Red Three, you and Red Four rejoin and head for home. I'll catch Two and bring him home." Then I called, "Elgin Red Two this is Red Lead. You are heading in the wrong direction. Turn south and let me catch you. I'll lead you home." No answer came from Red Two. After chasing Red Two for three or four minutes, I pulled alongside his aircraft and signaled for him to join up. He complied and we turned south and landed later at K-2 without further incident. In the debriefing after landing, he said that after accidentally switching to the wrong radio channel, he became confused and headed in the wrong direction. I talked to the squadron commander about his performance. We agreed to give him another chance but for me to watch him carefully.

Two days later, we flew a similar mission. Once again, he was Red Two. After dropping his bombs, he headed north again. This time I deliberately circled the target after he bombed and was not far behind when he started climbing in the wrong direction. I caught him in a minute or two, he joined up, and we headed for home. After landing, we talked about the flight. He admitted being unable to control his actions under the stress of combat and didn't want to continue. The squadron commander agreed to send him back to Itazuke immediately before he killed himself or his flight leader.

In my opinion, a trained fighter pilot who fails the test of combat should not be retained as an Air Force pilot. I wrote words to that effect on his Officer Effectiveness Report (OER), which was endorsed by the squadron commander. Imagine my surprise five or six years later at Edwards AFB, California, when this same officer, now a captain, tapped me on the shoulder. After a brief hello, I asked him what he was doing at Edwards. His answer shocked me, "I'm a student in the test pilot school." I never saw him again and did not follow his subsequent career.

An ever-present danger in combat is thinking that the enemy will not change and will not improve. In fact, what worked well for you yesterday may not work at all today. The MiGs had no track record of using GCIs against our fighter-bomber attacks. Our intelligence sources indicated that MiG attacks against us were unlikely when we were flying between cloud layers because the Communists lacked GCI capability. This wishful thinking evaporated on 27 April when I was Baker Flight leader on a rail-cutting mission in MiG Alley.

Baker Flight was in tactical formation (F-84s were spread apart) and letting down to our target when six MiGs under GCI control popped out of a cloud layer from 6 o'clock low. Because of their position low and to the rear of our flight, no one saw them immediately. However, a burst of flak from the ground was close to our flight, causing Baker Four to look down. He saw the MiGs moving rapidly into tail chase positions on our flight. Four yelled over the tactical frequency, "Break, MiGs!" Probably every USAF airplane within 100 miles heard his call and broke. That is why radio discipline stresses that you must address a "break" call.

The flak burst had caused me to jink (take evasive action) at a very appropriate time. When Red Four was calling "Break!" cannon shells were passing so close to my canopy that I heard their shock waves snapping as they sailed by, soon followed by a MiG. After scissoring back and forth, I moved into firing position on the MiG. When I opened fire, the MiG seemed to shift into second gear, maintaining his bank angle while climbing steeply. My F-84 was no match. After the MiG attack ended, we found and bombed our target. The group commanding officer (CO) was pleased with Baker Flight for not jettisoning bombs when the six "red noses" hit us.

On 7 May, Communist POWs on Koje-do, an island south of Pusan, asked Brig Gen Francis Dodd, US Army, the camp commandant, to discuss various allegations of mistreatment. While Dodd was standing by the open gate to Compound 76, the POWs captured him. His capture and the subsequent negotiations for his release caused major problems at the Panmunjom armistice negotiations.

Nearly 170,000 North Korean and Chinese POWs were at Koje-do. They were divided into four enclosures, each enclosure containing eight compounds. Each compound was designed for 1,500 prisoners but contained as many as 6,000. The space between the compounds also held prisoners because of the shortage of available land. Given the huge prison population and the limited number of guards (6,000 US and ROK soldiers), the prisoners controlled the internal affairs of the prison and guards controlled the external.

The political implications of the POW riots were severe because they directly related to the ongoing armistice talks at

Panmunjom. The major unresolved issue was the exchange of POWs. North Korean negotiators at Panmunjom were insistent that all prisoners be returned, voluntarily or not. Only 70,000 of the 170,000 prisoners wanted to return to Communist control. The United Nations Command was unwilling to force the 100,000 anti-Communist POWs to return to North Korea and the PRC where they would face retribution for disloyalty. Armistice negotiations stalled over this issue.

Recognizing an opportunity to seize an advantage at Panmunjom, North Korea and the PRC had sent Communist agents to the front lines with orders to become POWs. These agents became the unseen leaders in the suppression of anti-Communist prisoners. The capture of General Dodd was a political victory for the hard-core Communist agents. On 9 May, they set up a trial accusing Dodd of 19 accounts of prisoner abuse.

Gen James Van Fleet quickly appointed Army brigadier general Charles Colson to replace Dodd. Over the next two days, Colson and Dodd negotiated agreements and made concessions. The POWs then released Dodd unharmed. The entire episode seriously undermined the UNC position at Panmunjom. The Department of the Army reduced both Colson and Dodd to the rank of colonel for mishandling the POW situation.

On 11 and 12 May, the UNC began screening prisoners. Resisting UNC orders, the POW waved flags, painted signs, and marched around singing their patriotic songs. On 13 May, the chain of command at Far East Command, Eighth Army, or Fifth Air Force suggested an air strike on the prison compound might stop the rioting.

On that morning, my flight had finished briefing for a rail-cutting mission. We were preflighting our four F-84Ds when a sergeant ran out with instructions to return to group operations immediately. The rail-cutting mission was canceled, and we were assigned the Koje-do strike mission. The operations staff speculated on what kind of ordnance to use in the air strike. Their first choice was to replace the 500-pound bombs on each F-84 with napalm. Memories of the Nuremberg trials ran through my head. Napalm attacks would have been a massacre of the first magnitude.

About this time, Fifth Air Force interceded with a more sensible order. All ordnance, including our .50-caliber machine gun ammunition, was downloaded. Three other instructors replaced the less experienced pilots in my flight. Our revised orders were to make low-altitude, high-speed passes over the compound, similar to strafing attacks. The objective was to impress the rioters, make them realize how vulnerable they were to air attacks as well as to ground attacks, and make it easier for the Army to restore control.

After the short flight to Koje-do, we circled Compound 76. Thousands of POWs were milling around in an area the size of a few city blocks. We began with a low pass or two over the compound. Our low passes seemed to stir them up. They began waving red flags and gathering in larger groups. Army officers from the 187th Airborne Regimental Combat Team (ARCT) told us later that POWs threw rocks and spears as each F-84 made a high-speed pass at very low altitude. Throwing rocks and spears at an F-84 had a very low probability of downing the aircraft, but the rock/spear throwers probably enjoyed the exercise.

One fearless POW stood on top of an exercise platform waving a red flag. A low pass over his head did not discourage him, even though I was close enough to see the expression on his face. I came around again, determined to dust him off the platform. He must have read my mind. As I leveled off about 50 feet above the ground, he jumped off the platform. With the air show over, the flight rejoined and headed for K-2.

While the Koje-do air show did not count as a combat mission, it was an interesting attempt to influence the outcome of a difficult situation. We used our gun cameras to film the rioting prisoners and their reactions. The films went to Fifth Air Force, but we never saw or heard the results from our mission.

Resistance ended two weeks later. In Compound 76, where Dodd was captured and where he made damaging concessions, the POWs were unofficially commanded by a North Korean, Col Lee Hak Koo. Compound 76 would serve as an example to POWs in the other compounds. On 10 June, the new US Army commandant of Koje-do ordered Colonel Koo to assemble the prisoners in groups of 150 and be prepared to move to a new location. Instead, Koo's men carried knives, spears, and tent poles into trenches, ready to resist the move. Paratroops from the 187th ARCT advanced on the trenches with concussion grenades, tear gas, bayonets, and fists. They overwhelmed the

POWs without firing a shot. Thirty-one POWs were killed, many by their Communist leaders, and 139 were injured. One US Soldier was killed, and 14 were injured. Captured weapons in Compound 76 included 3,000 spears, 4,500 knives, and 1,000 gasoline grenades, clubs, hatchets, wire flails, and hammers.[4]

On 17 May, an unwelcome incident reminded me, once again, that the administration was treating this "police action" as a low-priority event, not a war. I expressed my opinion in a letter to Anne.

> Yesterday was really a black day. The MiGs came out in great strength. They sent enough to keep the F-86s more than busy and the rest hit the fighter-bombers. It is the first time that we diverted from our target because we had lost air superiority. I'm really getting disgusted with the lackadaisical attitude the government has shown toward the Air Force in Korea. We get equipment *after* fighter units in the U.S., Europe and Japan are equipped—which needless to say, doesn't give us much. It seems to me that a greater effort could be made to help the firemen who are trying to put out this damn fire. Letting the war drag on is costing the lives of a lot of nice guys.

Author's personal photo

K-2 Air Base, South Korea, 1951–52. Mess hall and barracks. The squadron dog had a reputation—promiscuous.

Photo courtesy US Air Force

Briefing my flight for a CAS mission. *Left to right*: Eicher, Francis, Rice, and Leavitt.

Sayonara, Korea
June–August 1952

In June the frequency of flying combat missions increased with the arrival of the rebuilt F-84Ds. New targeting policies from Fifth Air Force had reduced our combat losses, meanwhile increasing the variety of targets. In addition to everyone flying more close air support and less interdiction, the more experienced pilots were assigned armed reconnaissance missions. "Armed recce" missions let the pilot hunt for targets and decide which targets to attack. Armed recce was usually flown at dawn or dusk with the expectancy of catching trucks or other vehicles on roads leading to Communist positions.

We also began flying night missions. There was never any doubt at night where the front lines were. While flying daylight missions, we could see flak bursts but not small-arms fire. At night, a steady stream of tracer bullets fired from machine guns and artillery explosions clearly marked positions on both sides of the 38th parallel. Bright flares illuminated wherever a serious firefight was in progress.

Except for the exciting opportunity to see ground warfare at night, these missions had little payoff. The F-84 had neither radar bombing nor electro-optical (EO) systems to help the pilot find targets at night. Occasionally, friendly troops on the front lines would fire flares into an area where they needed air support. We would then strafe or drop 500-pound bombs into the area designated. Being unable to see specific targets, we probably did little damage to the enemy at night.

The B-26, designated the A-26 in World War II, was more effective than fighter-bombers at night. B-26s flew 55,000 sorties during the war, mostly at night. A large number of vehicles, railroad cars, and locomotives were destroyed by these attacks. Verifying claims was difficult because the Chinese and North Koreans were adept at quick repair and replacement of losses. All in all, night fighting in the 1950s was very marginal and did not improve until the Vietnam War brought new technology.

F-84 attacks at dawn and dusk were a different story. The Communists moved men and material at night to avoid UNC fighter-bomber patrols during daylight hours. Summers in North Korea are short on darkness and long on twilight. Communist armies needed supplies regardless of the time of year, so traffic often moved in twilight. With the sun at our backs to maximize surprise, the flight would dive down on truck convoys with machine guns blazing. When we were sighted, Red soldiers would jump from the moving trucks into the nearest ditch. A second pass over the convoy was usually not worthwhile because soldiers were hidden and the trucks stopped. The trucks seldom burned—they kept little fuel in each truck to minimize the possibility of fire.

We continued cutting railroad tracks and railroad bridges. Instead of everyone being assigned to the same target, smaller flights of aircraft were used with better results and fewer losses. The hardest targets to destroy were railroad bridges. Suspension bridges were narrow and hung on exceptionally strong cables that were virtually immune to blast damage from our 500-pound bombs. The other bridges were supported by reinforced concrete and steel pilings with railroad tracks generally laid on top of steel girders.

One day, the target for my two-ship flight was a large suspension bridge in north-central North Korea. I descended in a long, shallow dive down to the height of the suspension tower at one end of the bridge. Flying directly down the railroad track, I released the first 500-pound bomb and tossed the second bomb into the tunnel leading into the mountain at the end of the track. The Good News: both bombs exploded—one blew pieces of railroad track into the air, and the other flew into the tunnel and exploded. The Bad News: the bridge and tunnel were out of business for only two days.

There seemed to be no progress in breaking the stalemate in armistice negotiations under way at Kaesong since mid-1951. American casualties had steadily risen after battle lines had stabilized along the 38th parallel. When MacArthur was fired in 1951, Americans killed in battle totaled about 10,000. By the time the armistice was signed at Panmunjom in July 1953 and fighting ended, 33,629 Americans had been killed in battle—more than half were killed after 1951 when armistice negotiations began. More than 20,000 Americans died from other causes, including the POWs in prison camps.

The possibility of a new Red offensive was on everyone's mind in the spring of 1952. UNC forces were in better shape than a year earlier, but so were the Communists. On 17 June, I wrote Anne, "Flew number 66 today—a close air support mission. We are concentrating on CAS these days so as to be well-trained and ready for the Red offensive, if it comes this month. As you can tell from press reports, there have been heavy probing attacks the last few days. They are usually the prelude to an offensive. Time will tell. I hope it happens soon, if it is going to happen."

Another indication of our preparation for the Red offensive was disclosed when Fifth Air Force ordered a stand-down because of a spare parts shortage. The next day, several F-84s arrived from Misawa AB and flew orientation missions. The stand-down stayed in effect until 23 June when targeting policy dramatically changed.

Prussian general Carl von Clausewitz's masterpiece *On War* included two doctrines that are often quoted but seldom recognized as possibly contradictory. His doctrine of "total war" meant that everything that comprised the enemy nation (people, property, and territory) was fair game to attack in every way possible. His second doctrine stated war was a political act and an extension of diplomacy. Therefore, political leaders should determine wartime objectives and control the prosecution of war.

World War II was a total war. The no-holds-barred approach to fighting in both Europe and Asia fitted the Clausewitz definition. This pattern was set by Japanese and German leaders early in the war and escalated by both sides until its violent ending in 1945. When Roosevelt announced at the end of the Casablanca Conference in 1943 that "unconditional surrender" was our wartime objective, any chance of ending the war through diplomacy was over.

The Korean War was not a total war, even though military forces on both sides were involved in fierce combat. Hanging over the heads of leaders on both sides was the possibility the war would spin out of control and turn the Cold War hot. Instead, de facto arrangements confined the fighting to the Korean Peninsula. National boundaries were usually respected after China intervened and the war stalemated on the 38th parallel.

After truce negotiations commenced on 10 July 1951, most of the infrastructure of North Korea was spared from bombing except for elements that directly supported the war effort, such as roads and railroads. North Korea's infrastructure was relatively untouched until 1952 compared to the damage inflicted on Seoul and other South Korean cities during the 1950 invasion. In contrast, North Korean cities were not badly damaged, there was enough food to feed the populace, and a well-developed hydroelectric system supplied electrical power to both North Korea and Manchuria.

F-84 pilots were cynical about UNC restraints on bombing. Whenever MiGs from Antung attacked, we knew they could fly safely home and the odds would still be stacked against us the next time we ventured into MiG Alley. Whenever lights dimmed in South Korea (a frequent occurrence), someone would say, "We probably didn't pay our monthly electrical bill to North Korea on time, again." Whenever we flew near the highly visible brick smokestack near Taejon, we suspected the gold mine at that location was in operation and selling gold on the international market. Whenever we passed near the undamaged power plants on the North Korean side of the Yalu, we knew it was business as usual in the hydroelectric business. Since the power plants were off-limits to our attacks, both North Korea and Manchuria would have electricity to run their command and control centers and GCI radars. Whenever we flew near the large dikes holding water for irrigating North Korean crops, we knew many more GIs would die before North Korean negotiators became hungry enough to get down to business.

The problems generated by our restrained approach to fighting the "police action" were finally coming home to Washington. The armistice negotiations were stalled, and our limited military actions were not putting enough pressure on the enemy to break the stalemate. The Communists were unwilling to settle the disagreement about POW exchange and other matters that would end the war. Nineteen fifty-two was an election year, and the electorate was tired of the never-ending casualty lists and lack of progress in negotiations. Something had to change. The rationale for a policy change was based upon several intertwined factors. Among other factors, the USSR had exploded the first nuclear fusion bomb—the H-bomb. Strengthening our strategic forces and NATO would take a big bite from the budget. More money would be available if the fighting in Korea would stop.

Increasing pressure was needed to resolve the stalemated negotiations. The JCS came through with approval to attack the North Korean hydroelectric plants along the Yalu River in June 1952. In preparation for the attack, the Navy connected large generators on ships in Pusan Harbor to the South Korean electrical grid. After the North Korean plants were damaged and electrical power was no longer being transmitted to South Korea, the plan was for Navy generators to keep essential electrical power flowing to South Korea. During the pretakeoff briefing, we were told about the Navy ships in Pusan Harbor. I wrote Anne on 24 June 1952,

> Yesterday and today were big days. Maybe you heard about them over the radio or read about them in the newspaper. Yesterday, we hit the biggest hydroelectric plant in the Far East. Today, we struck another big electrical facility by the Chosin Reservoir north of Wonsan. The plant yesterday was right on the Yalu, but we got in and out with no

sweat. Same today. Before yesterday, we were forbidden to bomb their hydroelectric plants. These attacks reflect a definite change in policy that originated with the Joint Chiefs in Washington.

We are sitting around with our fingers crossed these days. Tomorrow is the second anniversary of the war and it looks like the Commies might try a push. Early this morning, I also flew a close support mission by the infamous "Punchbowl," so now I have 69 missions.

When we returned from attacking hydroelectric complexes at Suiho, Chosin, Fusen, and Kyosen, K-2 had no electricity despite the briefing about Navy ships in Pusan Harbor. The grumbling about the Navy "SNAFU" ended an hour or two later when electricity was fully restored. The mission was highly successful. North Korea lost nearly all of its electrical power for two weeks and never regained full capacity until after the war ended in 1953. Manchuria lost nearly a third of its supply of electricity.[5]

The mail exchanged with Anne included the usual give-and-take between husband and wife. Anne had purchased a dachshund puppy a few months after arriving in Little Rock. The dog, Lieuty, was frequently mentioned in Anne's letters because of his many trips to the vet with minor health problems. My reaction to Lieuty's hypochondria was included in a 28 June letter that included a report on summer weather at K-2.

Naturally, I was greatly pleased to learn that Lieuty has now gone to the vet three more times than I have gone to North Korea! It is consoling to know that not only is the dog almost well, but also the vet was able to climb one income tax bracket. Do you think we should claim him as a dependent?

It's getting hot and humid over here and the mosquitoes have just surpassed flak as the Number One menace. However, I have discovered the sanctity of a mosquito net and am getting the last laugh on the little bastards.

We celebrated the Fourth of July with a memorable mission. Intelligence had learned that the North Korean military academy—their West Point—was having a class graduate that day. The academy was located in a narrow valley about 20 miles south of the Yalu. The attack was timed to strike while the cadets were having lunch.

Both wings at K-2—the 49th and 136th—totaling about 120 F-84s, comprised the attack force. Three 49th squadrons started the attack by dive-bombing the academy buildings. Within minutes the entire valley was clogged with smoke and dust from the explosions of more than 100 500-pound bombs. Three squadrons from the 136th followed the 49th bombing with low-altitude napalm attacks. Obscured visibility from the bombing made it difficult to find specific targets for our napalm attacks. All the F-84s made it safely back to K-2. The speculation at dinner that evening was about the possible long-term benefit of demonstrating USAF Airpower 101 to the North Korean cadets.

By the time my mission total was around 70, I occasionally was the squadron leader on missions comprised of three or more flights, with four F-84s in each flight. Being an eager young lieutenant and beginning to believe I was bulletproof and knew everything about combat in North Korea, the opportunity was welcome. With no radar controller providing headings, no photos of the target, no FAC to describe and direct you to the target, and, of course, no Global Positioning System (GPS)—the toughest job for the leader was often finding the target. I relayed this anxiety to Anne in a 14 July letter.

> I got the Spirit—76, that is! Just a few more and they'll report me for rotation back to the States. Today I was squadron leader and had the new Group C.O. flying in my flight. Needless to say, I was sweating out finding the damn target. It was a camouflaged supply dump hidden in the mountains with a cloud layer over it when we got there. Things went pretty well, but it took two passes before I finally managed to find it.

On 17 July, my friend Bolo rotated home after finishing 100 missions and doing outstanding work as a squadron operations officer. Lt "Jungle Jim" Caldwell, Navy grad in Class 51-E, and I had now been in the squadron longer than any other pilots.

On 20 July, our group flew an unusual mission. Intelligence reported that a Chinese infantry battalion was bivouacked in a North Korean village located on a hill at the end of a valley. We let down several miles past the village, reversed course, flew up the valley, and made a low-level napalm attack on the village. As the Chinese soldiers and villagers realized they were under attack, they ran from their houses into open areas, where they tried escaping the burning napalm. Intelligence reports later reported the attack was highly successful and made no comment about collateral damage.

Aerial warfare is said to be impersonal. Fighter-bomber pilots seldom see the people killed by their bombing or strafing.

When confronted with flak or missiles, they worry about their own skin, take evasive action, and hope nothing hits their aircraft. When the target happens to be an artillery or antiaircraft battery, their primary focus is probably on destroying the guns, not the soldiers manning them.

Aerial combat between fighter aircraft can become more personal—especially if the enemy fighter is firing at your airplane—but the adversary is still another machine, a MiG, or whatever, not an individual. The air war suddenly becomes much less abstract and far more personal when you are hit, or a friendly aircraft is shot down, or a friend is killed. The napalm attack on this village shocked many young fighter pilots. Seeing persons run for their lives and becoming engulfed in flames was a dose of reality not provided on the practice ranges at Nellis and Luke.

Shortly after the napalm mission, we flew a dive-bombing mission against the railroad-marshaling yard in downtown Pyongyang. The mission was difficult because Pyongyang, the North Korean capitol, was well-defended with many flak batteries. Six flights of four F-84s each, plus a spare flight with three F-84s, comprised the first attack force. Our squadron commander, now a new lieutenant colonel, Don Booty, was Elgin Leader. I was Elgin Spare Leader. Booty led two attacks against Pyongyang that day and earned a well-deserved Silver Star for his heroism.

Elgin Spare Flight was the source for airborne replacements in case F-84s aborted from earlier flights. Usually aborts occurred on the runway or shortly after takeoff. If no one aborted, Spare Flight would be the last flight to attack the target. If there were two aborts before reaching the target area, Spare Two and Three would join the other flights, and Spare Lead would return to K-2 and not attack the target.

On this mission, no one aborted until Spare Three, Lt Irving Tyndall, replaced Green Four in the flight ahead. A few minutes later, we were well into North Korea, and Pyongyang was clearly visible. Then, a second F-84 aborted, and Lt George Panas, my wingman, replaced Blue Four. After flying this far into North Korea and being close to the target, I decided to be "Tail-End Charlie" and follow Elgin Green, the last flight.

As expected, there was an overabundance of flak. As soon as Green Four was on his dive-bomb run, I rolled over and started down to the target. Looking ahead, I saw Green Four explode and crash into the rail yard below. Irv Tyndall did not eject and was undoubtedly killed in the crash. Seconds later, I heard George Panas call in a calm voice. "Mayday! Mayday! Blue Four here, I've been hit and am on fire. Going to have to eject!"

I recognized George's voice and saw a single F-84 pulling off the target. Breaking normal radio discipline so he would react to my voice, I called, "George, don't jump now. I have you in sight. Try to cross the railroad tracks and get away from Pyongyang, or they'll capture you right away. Over." George's F-84 kept climbing and crossed the tracks. "Roger, keep me in sight. I'm still on fire and need to get out of here." His F-84 was not far from the other F-84s, and still no flames were visible. "George, head for the coast. Air-Sea Rescue will be able to pick you up. I don't see any fire." "Roger, Lead. Keep an eye on me. I'll try to make it." Minutes later, I called. "George, you're near the coast. Turn south. I'm catching up to you and you're looking good."

A few more minutes and we passed near the Haeju Peninsula, not far from the closest air base, K-14. I called again. "George, you're going to make it. Start a letdown. I don't see any flames, and K-14 is only about 70 miles away. Over." George answered, "Where are you, Lead?" I responded, "Off your right wing, George." Long pause, then came his startling answer. "There's no one off my right wing!"

I had chased the wrong F-84 all the way from Pyongyang, not George Panas. The incident had a happy ending—George made a safe landing at K-14. The F-84 fire had apparently gone out after leaving the target area. George was mad as hell at me when the courier brought him back to K-2 the next day. "What if I had been killed by the fire?" It took a drink or two to persuade George that my mistake kept him out of a North Korean POW camp. Was it divine intervention, serendipity, or just blind luck?

Mission 79 was a challenge. Antiaircraft batteries had been set up around a large supply dump near Osan-ni, North Korea. Our assignment was to suppress these guns so a follow-on attack could successfully bomb the supply dump. As squadron leader, I circled the target area several times at low altitude in order to draw enemy fire. After pinpointing the gun positions as they opened fire, the squadron bombed and strafed them until we were out of ammunition. Several gun positions were destroyed by the bombing and secondary explosions. No aircraft were lost. My first Distinguished Flying Cross was awarded for leading this mission.

The 25th of July brought a big surprise. The new group commander, Lt Col Daniel Sharp, called me to his office. HQ Far East Air Forces wanted to know how soon I could report for duty in Tokyo as an operations officer. I pleaded for time to finish 100 missions. Sharp, an all-around great guy, gave FEAF a reporting date of 20 August and promised me priority to finish 100 missions. A courier took me to Tokyo the next day for interviews with Col (later Maj Gen) Oris B. "Obie" Johnson, the director of operational requirements, and his assistant, Col (later Lt Gen) James T. Stewart.

The flying weather was good upon returning from Tokyo on 31 July. Several times in August, I flew two missions a day. On 4 August, my flight bombed a factory in Pyongyang, scoring at least eight direct hits, and in the afternoon flew a successful CAS mission—number 86. Sorties were coming fast, and the proficiency of our flight was high. Mission 91 was a CAS mission, and the Army FAC awarded our flight a perfect score—100 percent effective. Mission 92, a solo armed reconnaissance mission, was a sobering reminder that war was still a two-sided game. I destroyed four trucks and a jeep but was hit for the seventh time. Damage was not severe, and the plane made it back to K-2.

I completed Mission 97 on 11 August. Finishing 100 in time to report to Tokyo on 20 August seemed to be a sure thing. The following day, disaster struck. Two of our best pilots died the same day over North Korea when the wings came off their F84Ds—the old aircraft we disdainfully called Harry Truman's war crime. HQ USAF permanently grounded all the remaining F-84Ds. New F-84Gs were scheduled to arrive in the near future, but probably not before my Tokyo deadline. With no aircraft and a typhoon approaching Japan, the cards were stacked against completing the last three missions. Dan Sharp came to my rescue and arranged for missions 98, 99, and 100 to be flown with the 49th FBW. On 17 August, I flew number 100 and wrote Anne that night,

Well, today was a big day. This morning I flew my 100th mission and now I'm an ex-combat pilot without a worry in the world. There was a nice welcoming committee when I taxied in. After a drink or two with the guys, I went to church. Felt that I should because I've had good luck on most missions and someone has helped me through the rougher ones.

This has been an interesting experience, but I've had enough combat and enough people shoot at me to last a long, long time. There were good breaks. I was never shot up too badly, never lost anybody in my flight when I led it, and flew some good missions. Sometimes things seemed to be going badly, like when we suffered heavy losses in the winter and spring months, again when things went too slowly because of no airplanes, and then, when we did get replacements, they were old and worn-out F-84Ds. With brand new aircraft, everything is looking better now. All in all, I've been fortunate and am very thankful—believe me.

I left two days later for the new assignment in Tokyo. Left behind at K-2 were the dedicated officers and Airmen who would continue to fight the air war until the truce was signed in 1953. Going with me were memories of fighter pilots killed, of courageous commanders providing leadership and inspiration, of NCOs and Airmen maintaining old F-84s under difficult conditions, of guardsmen and reservists accepting a year in

Photo courtesy US Air Force

One hundred missions! Thanking my young crew chief for his good work.

Congratulations from group CO Dan Sharp (*shaking hands*) **and squadron CO Don Booty**. Sharp arranged my 100th mission with the 49th Tactical Fighter Wing (TFW) when the 58th was grounded.

Korea as their patriotic duty, and of flight leaders and wingmen bravely carrying out each mission. It was an honor to know and to fly with these patriotic Americans.

Korean Air War—Did We Learn Anything?

The Air Force entered the Korean War without a clear idea of how to maximize the capabilities of the new jet fighters. One foot was still in World War II, while the other was in the Jet Age. The air war in Korea served as a transition laboratory, a field test, and a shakedown cruise for Jet Age equipment and doctrine. The results were mixed—some good, some indicating the need for new technology, and some unsatisfactory.[6]

The Chinese entered the war in late 1950 and drove UN forces back to the 38th parallel in early 1951. This situation created the most important USAF mission for the remainder of the war. Called Operation Strangle, our job was to reduce supplies flowing from the Yalu River to Communist armies near the 38th parallel. The goal was to keep supplies on hand below the level required to sustain a Communist offensive. At the same time, United Nations Command ground forces were also stronger and better prepared to counter a Red offensive than in 1951. The combination of these two factors may explain why the Communist leaders launched no major offensive after 1951. Instead, they turned to prolonged negotiations to achieve their political objectives.

Tactics and Planning Improved as the War Progressed

Tactics used on early missions in the war were reminiscent of *Twelve O'Clock High*—a WWII movie about Army Air Force B-17 and B-24 bombers escorted by P-51 and P-47 fighters and being attacked by FW-190s. Only this time, the bombers were B-29s, the escort fighters were F-84s, and the attackers were MiG-15s. Fighter escorts could not stop the much faster and more agile MiGs. Many escorted B-29s were lost, and SAC was forced to stop the B-29 daylight bombing raids.

F-86 units developed new air-to-air tactics. Double ace, Maj "Boots" Blesse (Maj Gen Frederick C. Blesse, USAF, retired) described these new tactics in his seminal manual *No Guts, No Glory!* Without F-86 dominance over the MiG-15, fighter-bomber operations in MiG Alley would have excessive losses, and Operation Strangle would have failed.

An important rule for offensive air operations is avoiding repetition. Most F-84 losses during the winter and spring of 1952 occurred while bombing railroad tracks protected by anti-aircraft fire. Targets were often located within 10 or 15 miles from the previous day's target. Attack times varied only a few minutes from day to day. Improved operational planning at Headquarters Fifth Air Force eventually reduced the losses.

Perhaps the most important change in fighter-bomber tactics was shifting away from the WWII practice of using large "gaggles" (squadrons and groups) to attack one target. This tactical change, begun in Korea, became standard practice in all subsequent wars. Small flights—two, three, or four fighter-bombers in each flight—are a more efficient way to employ fighters than a gaggle for several reasons.

Aggregate losses are less with smaller flights. When a large formation attacks one target, defenses may not be ready for the first attacking flight. But as successive flights attack, defenses improve their kill probabilities. Double your insurance policy if you are Tail-End Charlie in a gaggle!

Enemy air defenses will usually disperse if they need to protect more targets. Dispersal means fewer defenses at any one location, thus reducing offensive aircraft losses. If defenses do not disperse, many targets will be left undefended, and total losses will still decline.

Visual bombing is more effective if every pilot can see the target and make an individual bomb run. Too often, accuracy suffers when many bombs explode near a target, causing smoke and debris to obscure the target.

A large formation wastes fuel as it assembles. There never seems to be enough jet fuel in combat, and circling the field while waiting for more aircraft to join the group is a waste of time, fuel, and money.

Letting flight commanders, not squadron or group commanders, carry out the mission creates depth in an organization, develops leaders, and fosters new ideas.

A Large Requirement Was Defined
for New Technology

Successful air warfare depends on technology. The Korean air war uncovered many deficiencies in the application of air-power. Necessary solutions often required not-yet-invented technology and better tactical training. Correcting the deficiencies listed below occupied the aerospace industry and USAF for the rest of the twentieth century.

Teletype communication between higher headquarters and air bases was painfully slow. VHF radio frequencies were crowded with traffic, often garbled and hard to understand. Air-to-ground communication between USAF fighter-bombers and Army units was difficult or nonexistent. Communication security was cumbersome and unavailable in most instances.

Inaccurate bombing hindered the effectiveness of USAF combat missions. The inherent accuracy of an unguided general purpose bomb is poor. B-29 raids made up for bombing inaccuracy by saturating a target area with many bombs. Fighter-bombers compensated for bombing inaccuracy by dive-bombing targets from low altitude. Even with dive-bombing, the damage expectancy from a single bomb was low.

Armament and ordnance were unsuitable for maximum effect against many targets. Five-inch rockets from WWII were inaccurate. F-80s, F-84s, and F-86s had .50-caliber machine guns instead of rapid-firing cannons. Napalm was ineffective against many targets and dangerous to deliver. Radar-ranging gunsights in F-84E, F-86A, and F-86E fighters were only useful in low-angle off-tail chases. Too much time elapsed between discovering a target and attacking the target. The intelligence and mission approval cycle was complex and time-consuming.

Need for Realistic Training

Combat crew training emphasized individual skills but ignored enemy interaction. New USAF fighter pilots in the Korean War were reasonably proficient in acrobatics, navigation, and formation and instrument flying. They learned how to deliver weapons by practicing bombing, strafing, and aerial gunnery in combat crew training. There were no training facilities where pilots could interact with enemy equipment using combat tactics. This loss of realism resulted in high pilot losses during their first few combat missions.

Ops Requirements, Ike, and the 9th FBS

I arrived in Tokyo on 19 August 1952 and moved into the Tokyo Electric Building, living quarters for USAF junior officers. That evening, I dined at the University Club with squadron buddies on R&R from Korea. The University Club was an Air Force Officers' Club and quarters for senior officers. A rite of passage for fighter pilots on R&R was to eat a Kobe steak at the University Club, topped off with strawberry shortcake. The 10 or 12 pounds I lost in Korea were rapidly being replaced!

During the July interview with Colonel Johnson, he could not disclose for security reasons many details about my assignment to the Operations Requirements Directorate, FEAF headquarters. After reporting for duty in August, Johnson explained that the Air Force was moving the 9th FBS from K-2 in Korea to Komaki Air Base, near Nagoya. The 9th FBS would become the first FEAF unit with a tactical nuclear capability. Operations Requirements had the responsibility for making this happen. My primary job would be the liaison officer between Operations Requirements and the 9th FBS.[7] The move would not take place for about 90 days, so in the meantime I would have other duties.

Both Col "Obie" Johnson and his deputy Col "J. T." Stewart had rapidly been promoted in World War II and were now senior colonels, yet only in their early thirties. Johnson had commanded the first P-61 Black Widow night fighter squadron in the European theater, and Stewart had been a B-17 group commander in Eighth Air Force. Working in Operations Requirements for Johnson and Stuart opened my eyes to an Air Force that I had not seen as a lieutenant in Korea. Major projects under way included the 9th FBS acquiring a tactical nuclear capability, modifying the F-86F, raising aircraft in-commission rates in Korea, negotiating with the Japanese Foreign Office for gunnery and bombing ranges in Japan, adding new navigation aids at Korean air bases, developing and introducing arresting gear systems for fighter bases, planning the postwar force structure for FEAF, and developing munitions and fuel requirements.

123

Colonels Johnson and Stewart made life both interesting and pleasant. One day while I was briefly in his office with Colonel Stewart, Colonel Johnson asked me if I would like a cigar. He opened a new box of cigars. I took one, lit it, smoked a few puffs, and a few minutes later as we were leaving his office, snuffed out the cigar in the ashtray on his desk. As we walked from Johnson's office, Stewart had a shocked look on his face. "Dick, if you don't really like cigars, don't feel you have to take one . . . that is, if Colonel Johnson ever offers you one again. He imports them from Havana, it takes six weeks to get here, and they cost two bucks-and-a-half apiece." It never happened again!

From time to time, Colonel Johnson would take me on staff visits to our air bases in Japan and Korea. Although I never worked for Obie again, our paths crossed every few years. Obie was a great officer and a true gentleman. He retired as a major general and died in 1999, leaving behind many friends with fond memories.

Colonel Stewart was one of the most intelligent men I have ever known. In 1953 President Eisenhower sponsored a national competition for the best essays stating why the United States needed an interstate highway program. One afternoon Stewart closed his office door for an hour or two. When he emerged, he had in his hand the essay that won second prize nationally. Stewart also wrote an acclaimed book while in FEAF called *Airpower: The Decisive Force in Korea*. Colonel Stewart and his charming wife, Georgia, were very kind and helpful during our tour in Tokyo. In later years, Lt Gen James T. Stewart commanded the Aeronautical Systems Division at Wright-Patterson AFB, Ohio, until his retirement.

Lt Col Ken Chilstrom was in charge of the Fighter Requirements Division. Ken was one of the top test pilots in the Air Force prior to his assignment to FEAF. Ken and Chuck Yeager were contemporaries when the X-1 was being prepared to break the sound barrier in 1947. Ken had appealed to his boss, Col (later Maj Gen) Al Boyd, to fly the X-1. Boyd would not release him from the higher priority F-86 program scheduled to start testing about the same time as the X-1 in 1947.

Lt Col John Briggs, my immediate supervisor in Requirements, was an airline pilot recalled to active duty at the beginning of the Korean War. John needed a copilot to fly the C-47 with him on trips. Never having flown a twin-engine airplane, I jumped at the opportunity. Flying with John Briggs was a genuine learning experience; a superb instrument pilot, he was one of the best overall with whom I have ever flown.

Lt Col Paul Woodward was my supervisor for the last 200 days before my FEAF tour ended. Paul, once an English professor at West Point, now patiently supervised my transition into the bureaucratic world of military correspondence and staff work. After I returned to the United States, a letter arrived from West Point offering a master of arts in English literature from Columbia and a tour teaching English at West Point. Maybe Paul threw my hat in the ring. Anyway, I declined the offer. After more than a year out of the cockpit, flying fighters again was my goal.

Air Force policy encouraged personnel who had completed a Korean combat tour to stay in the Far East by offering a follow-on assignment accompanied by their family. Military dependents were furnished government travel and government housing in Japan as soon as housing became available. This extended tour lasted for one year after dependents arrived. I applied for dependent travel and government housing for Anne and Chris upon reaching Tokyo. Three months passed before they received travel orders.

My 24th birthday brought two great presents. Anne and Chris arrived at Yokohama on an Army troop ship. They had a memorable trip across the Pacific and were happy to be on land again. The difference between the three-month-old baby left in Little Rock and the one-and-one-half-year-old little girl who arrived in Yokohama was startling. Chris was more shocked than I was startled. Anne had explained to her for the past year that "Daddy" was this man in a picture frame. Seeing the real, live Daddy caused her to break into tears and shout, "You're not my Daddy!" People coming off the ship probably sensed a scandal in the making. Thank God, Chris looked like my offspring!

Bomber and fighter aircrews stationed in Japan depended upon air-to-air and air-to-ground ranges to practice weapons delivery. My job included negotiating with the Japanese Foreign Office and handling complaints. Although the Foreign Office was always cooperative and understood our training requirements, it was under constant political pressure to minimize our airspace requirements. Air-to-air gunnery ranges located over coastal waters were a constant source of friction between USAF fighter units and the Japanese fishing fleet. A typical complaint went something like this.

Able Flight from the 41st FIS was scheduled for air-to-air gunnery at 1000 hours, 21 November, in the aerial gunnery range off the east coast of Honshu. The range was a restricted zone, and fishing boats were not supposed to enter during hours of operation. When machine guns were fired, the spent bullets might fall on the fishing boats and kill a fisherman. Flight leaders were responsible for checking the area for fishing boats before live firing commenced. Able Flight aborted with no gunnery training accomplished because fishing boats were in the restricted zone. The 41st FIS filed a complaint.

The complaint reached my desk, and I called my contact in the Foreign Office for help. "Please, Ichisan, keep the fishing boats out of our restricted zone. Once again, we had to stop training before killing a fisherman. That's the third time this month."

"Very sorry, Lieutenant Leavitt. We tell the fishermen not to go into the restricted zone, but they keep going. Why don't you tell your pilots to fire anyway? If a fisherman gets killed, it's his own fault!" Of course, we could not comply with the Foreign Office solution. The conflict between fishermen and USAF gunnery practice never reached a satisfactory conclusion while I was in Japan.

With the 1952 presidential election only a few weeks away, the truce talks stalemated again. Our attention turned to planning the 9th FBS move from K-2 to Komaki. American media and Truman critics had frequently proposed ending the war by bombing North Korean and Chinese targets with tactical nuclear weapons. Truman was adamantly opposed to ending his "police action" by using, or threatening to use, nuclear weapons against North Korean or Chinese targets. He was concerned about Stalin's reaction and the possibility of starting a larger war in Europe where outgunned NATO forces faced larger Soviet forces.

The occupation of Japan had formally ended when the Peace Treaty went into effect on 28 April 1952, and normal diplomatic relations resumed between the United States and Japan. The 1952 decision to base a USAF fighter squadron in Japan capable of delivering tactical nuclear weapons seems inconsistent with Truman's reluctance to use, or even threaten to use, nuclear weapons to end the Korean War. The location of nuclear weapons was very sensitive to the Japanese because of the Hiroshima and Nagasaki bombings. It was agreed that *fully capable* nuclear weapons could not be stored in Japan.

Did Truman believe that training and maintaining a nuclear-capable squadron in Japan was not a violation of agreements with the Japanese government? Did Truman believe the Japanese would not discover and publicize our covert tactical nuclear capability? Did Truman decide to leave his successor the capability in case the political-military situation worsened? Or perhaps, training and equipping the 9th FBS was considered routine Air Force business, and Truman was not informed.

During his successful 1952 election campaign, president-elect Eisenhower became well aware of the national discontent over lack of progress in the truce talks. The American public clearly wanted an end to the war. Eisenhower had pledged to "go to Korea," and he made the trip in December 1952. Speculations arose about how the conduct of the war would change after Eisenhower met with Gen Mark Clark, US Army, and other commanders in Korea. It turned out that Eisenhower's approach to ending the war was less dramatic than some had expected. He decided an honorable armistice remained the best solution to ending the war. Instead of invading North Korea or choosing another aggressive military action, he would raise the pressure on the Communists through diplomatic means.

The legal authority to use nuclear weapons resides with the president of the United States. Shortly after assuming office, President Eisenhower warned the Soviet Union, Communist China, and North Korea that he expected immediate progress at Pyongyang to reach an armistice. His message made clear the United States would not accept further delays. According to Eisenhower's later writings, the warning messages stated that "we intended to move decisively without inhibition in our use of weapons, and would no longer be responsible for confining hostilities to the Korean Peninsula."[8] It was a clear threat to use nuclear weapons and end the war.

Eisenhower showed a determination to end the war that was lacking under Truman. Two threats in his messages—using

127

nuclear weapons and expanding hostilities beyond Korea—were especially threatening to the PRC. China had already suffered massive casualties and had no nuclear deterrent to counter Eisenhower's nuclear threat, and the PRC navy and air force were third-rate and incapable of protecting China's coast. Mao had to assume the Chinese Nationalists on Taiwan would invade if the PRC were defeated. North Korea would collapse without PRC participation.

On 3 December 1952, an Air Force transport flew to the F-84 bases in Korea, loaded on board the pilots selected for the 9th FBS with all their gear, and delivered them to Komaki. At a secure briefing after their arrival, their new commander disclosed the selection criteria and squadron mission. FEAF used four criteria to select F-84 pilots for this elite organization: completed at least 30 combat missions over North Korea, had at least one year remaining on their Far East tour, possessed the technical and flying ability to meet stringent training requirements, and recommended by the senior commander in their Korean-based group or wing.

A special weapons team from Sandia Base, ably led by Captains Senour Hunt and Robert Stewart, taught the pilots and maintenance personnel the necessary technical data about tactical nuclear weapons. This training was my first of many involvements with nuclear weapons. On 15 December 1952, 24 F-84G aircraft were delivered to the 9th FBS. These F-84Gs were modified for delivery of tactical nuclear bombs. Intensive flying training began on 18 December. Instructors loaned from the 20th Fighter-Bomber Wing stationed in England taught the special high-altitude dive-bombing and low-altitude toss-bombing required for the pilot to escape the nuclear explosion.

During the winter of 1952–53, the 9th FBS worked seven days a week. The crews flew long training missions into South Korea from Japan with KB-29 tankers providing air refueling. On simulated combat missions, the F-84Gs carried "shapes"—training devices with drag and weight characteristics of a tactical nuclear weapon. In March 1953, they were declared combat ready after passing an Operational Readiness Inspection (ORI). After passing the ORI, detachments were sent to Itazuke Air Base on the northwest coast of Kyushu and Misawa Air Base on the northeast coast of Honshu. Four F-84Gs stayed at each location, locked in classified hangars and isolated from other base activities. One of the four aircraft flew a test hop each day to check combat readiness. Pilots at Itazuke and Misawa had mission folders for assigned targets.

If the war-ending solution were to be an attack with nuclear weapons, what type would be used and who would do the bombing? Following the bombing of Hiroshima and Nagasaki, all the services were quick to realize the dominant role nuclear weapons would assume in world affairs. The Air Force claimed precedence and assigned SAC the responsibility for maintaining a nuclear weapon delivery capability, supported by appropriate operations and planning. The Navy and Army established their own requirements.

In 1949 the United States began developing the "H-bomb," a thermonuclear weapon using fusion to release immense amounts of energy—hundreds of times more powerful than the fission bombs used against Japan. The Eniwetok Island tests in 1952 of this powerful new weapon were successful. In 1953 the Soviet Union successfully tested its first thermonuclear weapons. The possession by both the United States and USSR of these powerful weapons created an unimaginable threat to both societies.

Political leaders, military strategists, and think tanks on both sides of the Iron Curtain seemed to agree that neither the Soviet Union nor the United States would willingly sacrifice millions of its citizens and their national infrastructure in a thermonuclear war. In a sense, *mutual deterrence* created the military requirement and justification for low-yield nuclear weapons—called tactical nuclear weapons. Advocates believed smaller weapons, if used, would not trigger a large-scale exchange of thermonuclear weapons. Succeeding administrations approved this rationale. The Army, Navy, and Air Force acquired thousands of "tac nukes" during the '50s and '60s.

If Eisenhower's threat became reality, tactical nuclear weapons would have been the preferred choice. Weapon yields could be limited in order to minimize collateral damage near target areas yet achieve desired damage levels. Yalu River bridges, MiG airfields, North Korean and Chinese troop concentrations, supply depots, and command and control centers were obvious targets. Confining attacks to these military targets and ignoring locations with Soviet personnel should avoid a nuclear response from the USSR.

Several options were available when assigning the mission. The most prominent and well-developed nuclear capability belonged to SAC. Choosing SAC required accepting two serious drawbacks. SAC involvement implied a much higher level of escalation to the Soviets than the United States desired. Using SAC might jeopardize deterrence at the thermonuclear level and risk Soviet intervention in Europe or Asia. An operational issue was whether the older SAC bombers could successfully attack targets defended by GCI radar, MiGs, and antiaircraft artillery.

Navy carrier attack pilots were also trained to deliver tactical nuclear weapons. Many likely targets were beyond the range of Navy aircraft flying from current carrier locations off the east coast of North Korea. Relocating a carrier to the Yellow Sea would detract from ongoing operations and expose the carrier to sea and air attacks from Communist China. The United States knew that Japan would strenuously object if our Yokosuka-based carriers were used for nuclear bombing missions.

After all the pluses and minuses were added, the 9th FBS was probably the logical choice for delivering tactical nuclear weapons to end the Korean War. 9th FBS pilots had Korean combat experience, frequently flew practice missions into Korean airspace, and were well trained in delivery tactics. Their air-refueled F-84Gs could reach all likely targets in North Korea, Manchuria, and coastal China. For security reasons, the 9th had trained at Komaki but kept mission-capable aircraft on alert at Misawa and Itazuke. If the president directed an attack with tactical nuclear weapons, the 9th FBS was ready except for a necessary component in each weapon. Until that component was installed, the bombs were not *fully capable* and complied with Japan's antinuke policy.

The American electorate expected Eisenhower to end the war. His threat after taking office to use nuclear weapons unless there was immediate progress toward an armistice and peace treaty confirmed that the three-year-old war was no longer a limited "police action." In May, Dulles repeated Eisenhower's warning, using India to convey the message to the Communist leadership.

This left one issue the Communist leaders needed to resolve. Was Eisenhower bluffing? The Communist leaders knew Eisenhower's reputation as a highly regarded military leader from World War II. They knew Eisenhower had played an important role in the Cold War as the Supreme Allied Commander in Europe. They knew Eisenhower had committed to ending the war during his election campaign. Given all they knew about Eisenhower, it certainly would have been a high-risk game to assume he was bluffing. Furthermore, the principal Communist leaders, especially in the Soviet Union, must have realized by 1953 that they would never be able to conquer all of Korea without escalating their commitment far beyond what was already involved. That being the case, Eisenhower's warning provided a face-saving way to end the fighting with an armistice.

If Eisenhower were bluffing, it was not for lack of capability. The 9th FBS was deployed and fully able to carry out nuclear attacks. Standing behind this small tactical force were the large deterrent forces of SAC and the Navy.

If he were bluffing, it was not because he thought nuclear attacks would be ineffective. The Chinese and North Koreans could not fight effectively if nuclear weapons destroyed their key military installations.

If he were bluffing, it was not because he thought world opinion would condemn our use of nuclear weapons as "surprise attacks." Eisenhower warned the enemy principals after his inauguration that he would not be inhibited in his use of weapons. His secretary of state, John Foster Dulles, repeated the warning.

In 1966, while I was a student at the National War College (NWC), former president Eisenhower addressed a joint session of the NWC and the Industrial College of the Armed Forces. Former secretary of state Dulles had already published his memoirs that confirmed the threatened use of nuclear weapons to end the war. Following Eisenhower's prepared address, he opened the floor to questions from the students.

Air Force colonel Ken Tallman asked, "Mr. President, would you have used nuclear weapons if the war hadn't ended when it did?"

Eisenhower's answer was blunt, to the point, and brought an enthusiastic response from the joint audience. "I didn't have to answer that question then, . . . and I sure as hell don't have to answer it now!"

Notes

1. The every-other-day-letter-to-Anne routine began during my brief tour in Japan before going to Korea and continued during the Korean combat tour. It served as a diary for specific events. Anne saved the letters, and they serve as a detailed record of my combat experience as a fighter-bomber pilot. Cross-checking the letters with my USAF individual flight records, copies of orders, Officer Effectiveness Reports, and combat citations has confirmed dates, places, and events.

2. Knaack, *Encyclopedia of US Air Force Aircraft*, vol. 1, *Post–World War II Fighters*.

3. From DeArmond's contribution to the 1965 West Point reunion book.

4. Hermes, *Truce Tent and Fighting Front*, chap. 11, "Koje-do."

5. Futrell, *United States Air Force in Korea, 1950–1953*.

6. Working in Operations Requirements for Brig Gen (later Gen) Jacob Smart (became TAC commander), Col (later Maj Gen) O. B. Johnson, and Col (later Lt Gen) J. T. Stewart (became commander, Aeronautical Systems Command) provided many opportunities to see the big picture. Stewart wrote a book while he was in Tokyo, *Airpower: The Decisive Force in Korea*, and occasionally asked me to contribute my thoughts. Johnson took me on trips to Korea and other bases in Japan and shared his views on the war. All in all, it was a great exposure to USAF successes and failures and strongly influenced my opinions.

7. As the liaison officer between HQ FEAF and the 9th FBS, I reported the 9th's progress in becoming a nuclear-capable fighter squadron, including during the ORI. Col Tyler Goodman, USAF, retired, was one of the pilots who deployed after they became combat ready. During recent interviews, he confirmed their training, deployment, and readiness.

8. Eisenhower, *White House Years*, vol. 1, *Mandate for Change*, 181.

Chapter 4

SAC Fighters
Captain—1954–56

Straight Wing to Bent—Hogs Again
1954–1957

The long-awaited orders to return to the states came in October. The Korean War was over, and as much as we enjoyed the tour in Tokyo, it was time for me to get back into the cockpit again. We left on a troop ship from Yokohama on 2 November 1953. Every day around 1700 (5:00 p.m.) the ship's captain would interrupt the monotony of the long sea voyage with his progress report: "This is your captain. In the past 24 hours the USNS *Buckner* has progressed 340 nautical miles across the broad Pacific. With continuing good weather, we estimate docking in Seattle at 1000 hours on 14 November."

One day we ran into a bad storm. The *Buckner* rocked and rolled, up and down, back and forth. Thoughts of capsizing ran through my head when our lower-deck cabin portholes went underwater. Anne and Chris took it in good stride and ate their meals with great relish. Not me. That day was long and miserable. I looked forward to the captain giving us some good news, as the storm seemed to subside around 1700. Instead: "This is your captain. In the past 24 hours, the USNS *Buckner* had to reverse course for 200 nautical miles because of the storm. We now estimate docking in Seattle at 0800 hours on 16 November."

An extra two days on this darn boat! Drowning my sorrows was not an option on the USNS *Buckner*. The voyage finally ended. Most fighter pilots returning from Korea to the States wanted an assignment to Tactical Air Command. TAC meant flying F-86s, shooting gunnery, taking cross-countries to Las Vegas, rat-racing, and telling war stories at the bar with kindred souls. My dreams about F-86s had vanished. Instead, my new assignment was to the 31st Strategic Fighter Wing (SFW) at Turner AFB, Albany, Georgia, flying F-84Gs (affectionately called "Hogs") in the Strategic Air Command (SAC).

In the fifties, SAC represented to the rest of the world America's nuclear deterrent. The Commander in Chief was the cigar-smoking, no-nonsense, hard-driving Gen Curtis E. LeMay who nourished SAC's well-deserved reputation with high standards, strict discipline, and rigorous training. SAC bombers and air refueling tankers rotated frequently from their home bases to air bases in Europe, Asia, and North Africa. With all these bombers, why did SAC have fighter wings?

The Army Air Forces' experience with daylight bombing raids over Germany had convinced bomber leaders of the value of escort fighters. After the war ended, the USAF procured 100 long-range F-82E escort fighters for the newly formed SAC.[1] In 1948 SAC selected the new F-84E as the escort fighter because of its longer range than F-80s and higher speed than F-82E Twin Mustangs. There were only two fighter wings in SAC.

When the Korean War started, the USAF increased the number of SAC fighter wings authorized from five to seven. Their primary mission was to "protect bombardment and reconnaissance aircraft engaged in combat operations from attack by enemy interceptor aircraft."[2] General LeMay selected an array of the top fighter aces from World War II to command these new wings. Colonels David Schilling (22.5 kills plus 10 on the ground), Gerald Johnson (16.5 kills), Hubert Zempke (17.75 kills), William Dunham (16 kills), and Gordon Graham (seven kills) were all stationed at Turner during the mid-fifties. Squadron commanders at Turner included Lt Cols Frank Klibbe (seven kills) and Charles Lenfest (5.5 kills) and Maj Billy Eden (seven kills). Fighter pilots with similar distinguished records commanded the other SAC fighter wings.

On 22 September 1950, Colonel Schilling—famous WWII ace and later the commander of the 31st FEW—became the first pilot to cross the Atlantic nonstop in a jet. He flew a modified F-84E using an experimental probe-and-drogue, in-flight refueling system and completed the flight in 10:02 hours. Schilling died in an automobile accident in the UK in 1956.

The first F-84E was delivered to SAC in August 1951 and incorporated the flying boom system with a receptacle on the left wing. Another modification allowed the F-84E to carry two large external fuel tanks on its inboard bomb shackles. The tanks held 230 gallons each and extended the aircraft range about 400 miles.

The first SAC fighter wing to deploy in the Korean War was the 27th FEW in December 1950 from Bergstrom AFB, Texas. Its 75 F-84Es were shipped across the Pacific to Yokosuka, Japan, on aircraft carriers.

From its rear echelon base at Itazuke, Japan, the 27th forward deployed to K-2 Air Base near Taegu, Korea. The 27th was replaced at K-2 in 1952 by the 49th TFW and the 136th TFW (ANG). Both fighter wings were equipped with F-84Es.

The 31st FEW from Turner AFB island-hopped to Japan with 58 F-84Gs supported by air refueling from KB-29 tankers. Called Fox Peter One, the 10,919-mile flight in 1954 established a fast, practical method to move fighter units overseas—a method commonly used since on fighter deployments.

SAC gradually replaced all F-84E aircraft with the F-84G beginning in 1952. In addition to other changes, the "G" model was the first fighter aircraft specifically designed to include an atomic weapon delivery capability.

The SAC requirement for escort fighters changed when F-84E escorts protecting B-29s over North Korea were unable to stop MiG-15 attacks. Escorting bombers in the Jet Age proved not to be a sound tactic. Just as the rationale for having fighters in SAC seemed to disappear, Republic in 1951 produced the first F-84Gs with air-to-air refueling and the capability to deliver the Mark 7 nuclear weapon. SAC assigned an important new role to these new F-84Gs fighter force—strategic bombardment.

In 1952 SAC had four fighter wings—the 12th, 27th, 31st, and 508th. Two more wings activated in 1953—the 506th and 407th. The USAF had canceled the seventh wing, the 413th, that same year. All fighter escort wings became strategic fighter wings on 20 January 1953. SAC placed a high priority on each wing becoming combat-ready with the Mark 7 nuclear weapon. The following instructions are extracted from a Headquarters SAC top-secret directive issued on 22 September 1953, since downgraded to unclassified.

Each strategic fighter wing is to achieve and maintain an atomic operational capability in accordance with the following factors:

1. Seventy-five assigned aircraft will be equipped to carry and deliver an atomic weapon in accordance with tactics described by this command.

2. Ninety-three combat crews will be trained in fighter atomic weapon delivery in the established Armed Forces Special Weapons Center course, or its equivalent, with continuous refresher training, and SAC Regulation 50-8 flying training.

3. Each strategic fighter wing will possess a capability to deliver 150 atomic weapons per month.

The top-secret directive became effective during a difficult time for SAC fighter wings. In 1952 HQ USAF had ordered SAC to rotate each fighter wing to Japan for three months for air defense operations. The 31st, 27th, 508th, and 12th each spent three months in Japan during 1953. This temporary duty was disruptive to "achieving and maintaining an atomic operational capability," as SAC directed. SAC asked to be relieved of the Japan rotation, but HQ USAF denied the request. This rotation policy to Japan cost each wing five months of nuclear weapons training.[3]

When I arrived at Turner, the 508th was preparing to leave for Japan the following week. Given the "opportunity" to return to Japan for three more months or to spend the next three months temporarily assigned to the 31st SFW at Turner, I chose staying at Turner and spent the next three months as an attached pilot in the 307th Squadron commanded by an outstanding officer, Maj Robert A. Krug.

Krug was killed in an F-84F accident approximately one year later. An electrical malfunction caused the ejection seat to fire at the same time he opened the canopy after landing. He died from severe injuries when his falling body impacted the concrete taxiway. His last words were, "What did I do wrong?" Nothing, Bob, the ejection system malfunctioned.

Perhaps the best pilot I had ever flown with was Lt Martin A. Knutson in the 307th. Marty was the first officer selected to be a U-2 crew member when it was a covert program under CIA direction. In later years, he became one of the top executives in NASA.

During the war, many experienced SAC F-84 pilots were transferred to F-84 wings in Korea as replacements. Their replacements in SAC were recent graduates from flying training or Korean War returnees. Rapidly expanding from two to six strategic fighter wings exacerbated the problem. With 900 hours' flying time and 100 combat missions, I was an "old head" compared to most of the young pilots in the 307th. Krug appointed me a flight commander, and time passed quickly while I was giving instrument checks in T-33s and leading F-84G training flights. The 307th was a great squadron and had some fine young officers. I tried to ignore the fact that my TDY would end when the 508th SFW returned from Japan.

After the 508th returned in late April, I asked Major Krug if I could transfer to the 31st and stay in his squadron. Krug said he would talk to Colonel Schilling, the 31st Wing commander. About 10 days later, there was the usual TGIF (Thank God It's Friday) assemblage at the Officers' Club. Schilling and Col Cy Wilson, 508th Wing commander, were sitting next to each other at the bar when I happened to walk by.

Wilson turned to Schilling, "Who's that lieutenant? I remember seeing him before we left for Japan." Schilling waved me closer to where they were sitting.

Schilling's introduction was encouraging. "His name is Dick Leavitt; he flew F-84s in Korea and has been TDY with the 307th while you guys were in Japan. Krug wants to keep him. How about letting him stay in the 307th?"

Wilson responded by passing a dice cup to Schilling. "OK, I'll roll you for him. One roll—aces wild." They rolled the dice and Schilling won. I went happily home with the good news and a new understanding of how the Air Force made personnel decisions!

The following morning, Colonel Wilson's adjutant called me at the 307th Squadron. "Lieutenant Leavitt. Colonel Wilson wants to see you in his office in ten minutes. You better be on time; he's really p----- off!"

It was not far from the 307th Squadron to 508th Wing headquarters. I walked into Colonel Wilson's office on time, cautiously saluted, and said, "Good morning, sir." Wilson's response was curt. "Leavitt, I'm going to give you a direct order. Are you going to obey it?" It did not take me long to answer, "Yes, sir!"

"Get your flying gear from the 307th and report to the squadron commander of the 466th not later than 1000 this morning. Dismissed." Leaving well enough alone, I left the office without reminding Colonel Wilson that Schilling won the dice roll. This ended my brief experience as an absent without leave (AWOL) pilot.

SAC was deep into aircrew training. For example, I attended arctic, jungle, water, and mountain survival and POW indoctrination. They varied in degrees of difficulty, but "swamp survival" was the most fun and least stressful. Turner AFB was not far from the Okefenokee Swamp. This large swamp was 40 miles long and averaged 20 miles wide. It was a sanctuary for all kinds of birds, small animals, big frogs, and fish, plus an overabundance of water moccasins. HQ SAC decided that we needed to learn how to survive in a swamp because we frequently flew over the Okefenokee and might have to eject.

Our grizzled old sergeant instructor knew all about swamps and did an excellent job of passing his knowledge to us. After demonstrating how to live and enjoy life in the swamp, he turned us loose. We carried the gear in our aircraft survival kits plus ponchos in case of rain, fishing poles, first aid kits, knives, and canteens. Two ponchos when fastened together became a pup tent. The inflatable two-man rubber life rafts were great for fishing. We used knives to sharpen spears for frog gigging. At twilight, we would light a fire, cook frog legs and fish, break out the hors d'oeuvres smuggled from home, pass around canteens filled with martinis, and shuffle the cards for a cutthroat game of hearts. Back home after two or three days, we would attempt to terrorize our wives with exaggerated stories of snake-infested waters and vicious alligators interrupting our well-deserved rest after a terribly hard day spent fishing.

The Air Force Survival School at Camp Stead, near Reno, Nevada, was a very tough program bearing little resemblance to swamp survival at Turner. Six fighter pilots from the 508th comprised our team. For the first few days, we focused on escape and evasion techniques. Then we learned how to survive in wooded, mountainous terrain with little food and clothing. The climax of the training was a long hike, lasting several days over difficult mountain terrain with minimal food and water. We navigated with a handheld compass and map.

Growing up in northeastern Michigan, I had liked hiking through the woods. However, foraging for food off the land instead of overeating in a hunting camp was a different experience. After eating most of our meager rations the first day, we had to scrounge for food. We killed, skinned, and roasted a porcupine one day. It tasted like pine oil—really bad. Fishing was poor, but we found leeches in the stream and cooked them—not too bad. Losing 10 or 12 pounds on the trek was typical.

An unwelcome surprise was a panic attack experienced by one of the lieutenants. After two days in the wilderness, he stopped eating and became very weak and depressed. We took turns carrying his gear and helping him along. When offered food, he would not eat. Failing to complete the trek had serious career consequences. We did not want him to quit. He was an excellent fighter pilot and a very competent officer. Because of his weakening condition, an instructor took him in a jeep to the base hospital at Camp Stead. After intravenous feeding and resting for another day, the doctors gave him the choice of self-eliminating or rejoining the team. He rejoined the team and finished the course. The head instructor told me that 5 to 10 percent of the trainees suffered similar reactions when confronted with a survival situation in unfamiliar surroundings.

The 508th SFW was well behind the SAC goals when it returned from Japan. Nevertheless, by the end of 1953, the 12th, 27th, 31st, and 508th Strategic Fighter Wings had acquired limited capabilities in delivering the Mark 7 nuclear weapon and were assigned Emergency War Plan missions.[4]

Training concentrated on the most important pilot capabilities for a successful mission—in-flight refueling, navigation, and bombing. A KB-29 refueling squadron was assigned to Turner, and pilots quickly qualified in this vital range-extender. Without in-flight refueling, the F-84G could not reach most Cold War targets from SAC bases in Europe, Alaska, North Africa, and Asia.

Unlike SAC bombers, the F-84G had no radar for navigation and bombing. An improved method of navigation was needed. SAC selected celestial navigation as the best solution to this problem and provided Col Charles Blair as our teacher.[5] Blair had flown solo across the Atlantic in a P-51 by flying the great circle route over the Arctic. He used a handheld sextant to take fixes on the stars en route. After he came to Turner, we spent several nights learning the constellations and finding the position and magnitude of prominent stars. Taking accurate celestial fixes with a sextant required stable flight for a minute or two. Celestial navigation training was discontinued because the F-84G autopilot could not keep the aircraft sufficiently stable for accurate fixes. A few years later, the early U-2 models successfully used celestial navigation on long-range reconnaissance missions.[6]

Since the profiles for weapon delivery required a high-speed run below 1,000 feet into the target area before releasing the bomb, the training program emphasized low-level navigation. Pilots used dead reckoning and pilotage—comparing a map and aerial photos with terrain features, road intersections, railroads, villages, and other identifiable items—en route to the target. As long as visibility was good, a proficient pilot could find these short-range targets without radar or external aids to navigation. This left unresolved the more difficult problem of navigating longer distances.

An F-84G could attack targets as far away as 565 nautical miles without aerial refueling by flying most of the mission above 32,000 feet. With only dead reckoning and pilotage as means to navigate, the pilot was dependent upon reasonably good weather to find the letdown point and attack the target at low altitude. The probability of having a successful mission was very dependent on weather and pilot skills.

The lowest probability of success involved targets around 1,000 nautical miles from home base that required two in-flight refuelings. If the pilot could not find the tanker on the way to the target, the mission would have to abort. Once refueled, the same problem of flying a long distance at high altitude and finding the letdown point existed. If the pilot could not find the tanker on the way home, he might not have enough fuel to return. How to navigate an F-84G to the point where the high-speed run should begin with a high probability of success was never resolved for high-altitude profiles.

When the marriage of the fighter-bomber and the tactical nuclear weapon first occurred, high-altitude dive-bombing was the preferred method of delivery. SAC rejected this method for two important reasons. High-altitude dive-bombing was subject to great inaccuracies, and success depended upon favorable weather conditions in the target area. SAC wanted to bomb from low altitude where weather was less likely to be a factor and accuracy was better. A very important issue for pilot safety was getting enough escape distance from the nuclear explosion. The development of a computing system called the Low Altitude Bombing System (LABS) gave the pilot two ways to bomb.

The first LABS method for releasing bombs from low altitude was "toss bombing." The pilot would approach the target flying at 1,000 feet above the ground and 480 knots airspeed. He would start a steep climb when 18,600 feet short of the target. As the climb angle reached 45 degrees, the LABS computer would automatically release the bomb—"tossing" it toward the target.

There was a serious problem with toss bombing. Ranging accuracy depended upon the pilot correctly estimating the distance from pull-up point to target. Pilot estimates of distance proved to be unreliable unless there was a point on the ground that the pilot could identify as the pull-up point. Since the F-84G is moving 810 feet per second at 480 knots, a five-second error in starting pull-up reduced bombing accuracy by an unacceptable error of approximately 4,000 feet.

Vertical angle release (VAR) offered a better application for bombing with the LABS computer. SAC directives described the maneuver as follows:

> VAR Delivery. The aircraft will approach the target at low level, high speed executing a 3 to 4 "G" pull-up so as to place the vertical path of the aircraft directly over the target. Release gyro in the LABS equipment will be set at the angle to release the bomb vertically over the target taking into consideration the speed, "G" force and weight of the aircraft at point of release. Following release, the aircraft will continue an Immelman maneuver heading straight away from the target until the effects of the weapon have dissipated.[7]

By the end of September 1954, the 508th Wing had enough people fully qualified to deliver the Mark 7 nuclear weapon. The wing deployed for the ORI to an airfield near Fort Campbell, Kentucky. At the deployment base, a simulated Mark 7 nuclear bomb would be loaded on each aircraft. After target briefings, the wing would fly 24 simulated nuclear strike missions against targets on one of the large bombing ranges at Eglin AFB, Florida. The 24 pilots scheduled for bombing were designated as "lead crews." Twenty-four combat-ready pilots flew as wingmen for the lead crews. All aircrews would air refuel between Campbell and Eglin. After bombing, we were to return to Turner AFB and land.

During the weeks prior to the ORI, we practiced VAR bombing. For every bombing mission the release gyro in the LABS computer had to set for the proper angle of release. Each degree equated to roughly 300 feet of correction at bomb impact, so it was very important to set the proper angle into the LABS computer. I did very well with VAR and had the lowest circular error probable (CEP) in the wing when we left for Fort Campbell.

The early morning briefing at Fort Campbell lasted longer than expected. I was scheduled for the first takeoff with Lt "Rip" Sewall as my wingman. It was close to Start Engine Time when the jeep arrived at my F-84. The pilot's job after the walk-around inspection was to climb a ladder and inspect the LABS computer setting located in the gun bay forward of the cockpit. Unfortunately, there was no ladder near my F-84G. By the time the crew chief found a ladder and brought it to the aircraft, it was Start Engine Time. Should I check the LABS computer and be late for takeoff, or should I climb into the cockpit and start the engine?

I remembered flying this same F-84 on a practice bombing mission two days earlier. Reaching in a pocket of my flying suit, I found the notes from the earlier mission. Today was supposed to have a gyro setting of 104.5 degrees. The gyro setting for the earlier mission was 103.5 degrees. What a break! I could simply adjust the pull-up point a few hundred feet. To save time, I skipped checking the LABS gyro, strapped in the cockpit, started engines, and took off on time. With Rip on my wing, we climbed on course and headed for the tankers. Air refueling went smoothly.

We let down in the Eglin complex right on time, headed for the target, and found the pull-up point. I made a slight adjustment in distance for the gyro setting and started the pull-up to 104 degrees vertical. Rip was flying right behind my aircraft when a rude shock disturbed my overconfident, complacent attitude. The training Mark 7 released from the F-84G bomb pylon when the climb angle reached *30 degrees, not 104 degrees*. The mock atomic bomb was on its way to some unknown impact point way downrange!

Rip, seeing what had happened, called with just a touch of sarcasm in his voice, "Hey, Red Lead. When is the bomb going to turn around?"

On the way back to Turner, many thoughts ran through my mind. I had not checked the LABS gyro setting as was required. Obviously, it was not set at 103.5 degrees. Somehow, it was set much lower between the previous bombing flight and today's flight. One thing was painfully clear; it was my fault for not taking the time to check the LABS gyro and dialing in the correct setting.

After landing back at Turner, a staff car drove to where I was parking the F-84. By the time the engine was winding down and the canopy was opening, Colonel Wilson, the wing commander, had climbed a ladder and placed his hands on the canopy rail. I took off my helmet, expecting the worst. He obliged.

"What the hell happened, Leavitt? You threw your bomb a couple miles long!" My answer was really a confession. "I'm sorry, Colonel. I didn't reset the LABS computer, and the bomb kicked off at 30 degrees during the pull-up." His answer was short and to the point. "I wish you'd crashed!" The next day, I learned the LABS technician had checked the computer and reset the gyro to 30 degrees, the nominal setting specified in the maintenance technical order. He had done his job properly. I had not done mine.

That same day, I was reduced from lead crew to non–combat ready. In addition, the list scheduled to fly F-84s to England on our forthcoming deployment no longer included my name. Instead, a C-124 would fly the advanced echelon (ADVON) to the Azores. I would be a spare F-84 pilot in the ADVON. The "long bomb" incident forced some soul-searching. Four years in the Air Force had passed quickly. The assignments had been interesting and rewarding. Along the way, supervisors had provided unusual opportunities for advancing my Air Force career. The new supersonic F-84F would arrive after we returned from England, and I was looking forward to flying it. Now, the future looked cloudy because of my gross error during the ORI. Maybe it was time to look for an airline job. After adding up the pluses and minuses, I decided to ride out the storm and recover if possible. The hidden motivation was probably to show Colonel Wilson that I could do better.

When the wing flew to England, the F-84s stopped at Lajes Air Base in the Azores before flying on to Royal Air Force (RAF) Station Sturgate. The ADVON had arrived several days earlier with the commander, two spare F-84 pilots, a maintenance officer, and maintenance crew. We completed our ADVON responsibilities in a few days and did some sightseeing.

It was the time of the year for the festival of San Fermin in the nearby city. As in Pamplona, Spain, the bulls run down cobblestone streets on their way to the bullring. There did not seem to be much danger to onlookers because, in contrast to Pamplona, the bulls were not turned loose. Instead, about a dozen men were hanging on a long rope connected to each rampaging bull. Their job was to slow down the bull before anybody was gored. Captain "Duffy" Ingalls and I stood on a street corner and watched the fun. A few minutes later, the first bulls headed our way. We decided to move a few feet down the side street, knowing the handlers would keep the bulls on the main street. One bull, disregarding the rules, turned the corner and headed our way. Not to worry—the handlers would pull on the rope before the bull could reach us.

Big Problem! The rope had broken, and the bull was free and headed toward us. The street was narrow, the cobblestones slippery, and houses were right next to the street. Duffy, running next to a house, vaulted over a gate. I looked back. A big, bad bull had me in his gunsight. I slipped on the cobblestones and fell—just as his head and horns passed over my head. The bull kept running down the street. As I brushed myself off, women were yelling out of their second-story windows, "Bravo! Bravo, Americano!" They did not realize this "bravo" Americano had just resigned from the bull-watching business. The mayor in the reviewing stand invited Duffy and me to join him. We accepted and enjoyed the rest of the show from a safe distance.

Our next stop was England. RAF Sturgate was an active air base in World War II. Located near Nottingham and Lincoln, the base and surroundings were reminiscent of the World War II movies involving the RAF. After a few days at Sturgate, to my surprise, I was included in the 24 aircraft scheduled to fly to Sola Air Station near Bergen, Norway. Not so pleasant was my position in the flights—number two in Colonel Wilson's flight! Since the bombing incident, I had kept a very low profile around the good colonel.

After takeoff and climb we leveled off at 25,000 feet, and the flights spread into tactical formation. On the way to Norway, we detoured over West Germany. The weather was reasonable, and between clouds cities and rivers were visible. I was concentrating on flying the best possible tactical formation when Cy Wilson's voice broke the radio silence. "Red Two, what's the name of that city at 10 o'clock?"

Since I had never been to Europe before and I had been spending more time watching Wilson's aircraft than navigating, his question caught me unawares. I glanced down and spotted a big city on a river. Cologne, where my father had served in the Army of Occupation in 1919, popped into my mind. He had described Cologne as being on the Rhine River. I quickly checked the map and answered, "Cologne, Germany, Red Lead." Wilson's response made my day, "Roger, Two."

We landed at an airfield near Bergen. Following the Nazi occupation of Norway, the Luftwaffe wanted an airfield near the seaport of Bergen. The Luftwaffe engineer in charge of building the airfield assumed the only runway would run west-east, the direction of the prevailing winds off the North Sea. He knew something about building airfields, but not quite enough. At the end of the W-E runway, there was a steep mountain slope. When the Luftwaffe landed its first aircraft at the new field, it discovered a huge error. The W-E runway was not safe for aircraft traffic because of the steep mountain. Norwegians say the German engineer committed suicide the next day.

We had a great time in Bergen. This was my Grandfather Hagen's hometown, and the people in Bergen liked to party. In 1954, World War II remembrances were still fresh in their minds. When they found out that our squadron commander and several other fighter pilots had flown against the Luftwaffe, the city lived up to its reputation.

Shortly after returning to Turner, the 508th began receiving F-84F swept-wing fighters. By the end of November, the F-84Gs were gone. During December we attended F-84F ground school and looked forward to being fully equipped in a month or two. Late one afternoon during the Christmas holidays, I met Colonel Wilson in the hall of the 508th Wing headquarters. He was on his way to the flight line. He stopped and asked pleasantly, "How are things going, Dick?"

This was only the second time he had spoken to me since the long-bomb incident in early October. My spirits lifted. Maybe I was on the road to recovery. "Just fine, sir. I'm looking forward to checking out in the F model." We exchanged New Year's greetings, and then he left for Barksdale AFB, Louisiana, in a newly arrived F-84F.

Deficiencies in the J-65 engine in late 1954 were delaying F-84F deliveries. Engine flameouts had occurred when flying in heavy precipitation or in severe weather. Colonel Wilson was flying back from Barksdale AFB at night when his engine flamed out near Maxwell AFB, Alabama. Despite his repeated attempts, the engine would not restart.

Cy Wilson could have ejected from the aircraft, but he decided to "dead stick" the F-84F into a farm area. Years before, under similar circumstances, he had been able to "belly in" a slower fighter aircraft and walked away without injury. Wilson informed the tower of his intentions and his belief that a relatively undamaged F-84F might lead to solving the flameout problem.[8]

Colonel Wilson made an excellent approach and touchdown into a farmer's field. When the aircraft slammed into the ground, the F-84F broke into large sections, throwing him forward in the cockpit. The crash tore off his helmet. His bare head struck the jagged edge of the broken canopy, causing fatal injuries. He died before the ambulance arrived. The crash destroyed most of the F-84F, but the cockpit was remarkably intact. He might have survived if he had locked his shoulder harness and his helmet had stayed fastened.

Wilson's heroic effort to save the aircraft for post-crash investigation was not in vain. The Accident Investigation Board was able to determine the cause of the J-65 engine flameouts. Engine compressor shrouds were shrinking when the aircraft flew through heavy moisture. As the shrouds shrank, they contacted the compressor blades, causing the engine to seize. Curtiss-Wright fixed the problem by "sanforizing" the engine— shortening the compressor blades slightly so they would not contact the shrouds. After modifying all J-65-W3 engines, the USAF released the F-84F for operations.[9]

Colonel Wilson's sudden death was a great loss to the 508th Wing. The 508th was a relatively new wing with many inexperienced young officers. His leadership style was "Follow me!" Wilson provided very strong, positive leadership, and the wing avoided most of the growing pains that new organizations suffer. The punishment that Wilson imposed on me for the long-bomb incident was well deserved and taught a lesson I did not forget. An exceptionally intelligent officer and an original thinker, he held a clear vision of the important role SAC fighters could assume in the Emergency War Plan. When he was on the air base, everyone sensed his presence and responded accordingly. When he was not on the air base, the wing tended to drift.

There was a definite contrast between the leadership styles of Schilling and Wilson. Col Dave Schilling was wing commander during the four months I was TDY with the 31st Wing. The 31st was an experienced organization with a long history of wartime successes. Its slogan, Another First for the 31st, reflected more truth than fiction. Schilling was better at delegating responsibility to subordinate commanders and staff. He was quick to accept good ideas from his subordinates. Although he usually took personal credit for successful ideas, Schilling would credit the wing's success to the officer who originated the idea when preparing OERs. The 31st seemed to run well whether or not Schilling was on the air base.

MBA gurus would probably label Wilson an "authoritarian" leader and Schilling a "participative" leader. Despite the differences in style, both were very effective wing commanders. In later years, after observing many other commanders, I concluded that labels do not mean much. More important is the chemistry and confidence that exists between leaders and their subordinates. Air Force organizations will adjust and respond to either personality as long as commanders are consistent, predictable, and competent.

Following Wilson's death, Col Gerald W. Johnson became the 508th Wing commander. His reputation as an outstanding officer—as well as one of the top aces in World War II—preceded his arrival. F-84F deliveries had accelerated, and the entire 508th was busy getting combat-ready with the new fighter. Johnson began flying the F-84F immediately and soon was very knowledgeable of the many technical problems associated with this new fighter.[10]

The development of the F model was plagued with problems from inception. Republic had proposed in 1949 to modify the F-84E by sweeping back the wing and tail surfaces. The changes proposed were reputed to be low-cost, rather modest changes that would permit the F to fly at supersonic speeds. Republic claimed that 55 percent of the F-model tooling would be the same tooling used to build the E model. The Air Force accepted Republic's proposal believing it had three big advantages: a fast R&D and production cycle, a supersonic fighter that could be built at low cost, and minimal wrangling with Congress because the F would simply be a production modification of the existing F-84E.

The Air Force allocated one F-84E from production in 1949 to Republic. This modified F-84E became the prototype YF-84F. Test flights in 1950 quickly proved the aircraft was badly underpowered with the J-35 engine and could not satisfy Air Force operational requirements. In mid-1950, the Armstrong-Siddeley "Sapphire" engine was selected as a replacement. This larger J-65 engine required redesigning the F-84F fuselage. As a consequence, instead of having 55 percent commonality with F-84E tooling, only 15 percent of the tooling proved to be common.

The F-84F was a single-cockpit aircraft. There was no two-seat trainer version of the F-84F. I flew the F-84F on 25 January 1955 for the first time and really liked the feel and performance of this new fighter. Flying the F-84F *safely* was a serious problem—not because the aircraft was particularly difficult to fly and not because of structural weaknesses. It had engineering design flaws that caused accidents and cost lives.[11]

In addition to the engine failure problem, the F-84F was plagued with hydraulic problems. Most aircraft separate the hydraulic pumps and lines between essential and nonessential systems; not so with the early F-84Fs. One interconnected system ran all aircraft hydraulics. A leak in any hydraulic line—essential or nonessential—required an immediate landing while sufficient hydraulic pressure remained.

To overcome this limitation, the F-84F had an emergency system that would allow the pilot to continue flying the aircraft without hydraulic power. An electric trim button on the control stick moved control surfaces. If hydraulic failure occurred, the flight handbook procedure was to land using the "electric-electric" trim system. Several pilots attempted emergency landings using this electric trim system. The attempts resulted in major accidents. The revised procedure instructed the pilot to eject from the aircraft rather than attempting to land using the electric trim system. One pilot assigned to my flight was killed after slowing the aircraft following hydraulic failure. He was unable to separate himself from the aircraft when the aircraft stalled and snap rolled. Later production models of the F-84F included a better hydraulic system. In the meantime, we flew the F-84F with one eye watching the hydraulic pressure gauge.

Photo courtesy US Air Force

SAC fighter air refueling

F-84F: Swept-Wing Widow-Maker

As flying safety officer, my job was to keep the squadron pilots prepared for in-flight emergencies. Since there was no flight simulator for the F-84F for practicing emergency procedures, we relied on written exams and oral quizzes. Every pilot had to pass an emergency procedures exam and cockpit check before his first flight in the F-84F. After that, the Wing Standardization Board reexamined each pilot and evaluated his flying once a year. In between these checks, there was a need for refresher

SAC receives the swept wing. The USAF procured 1,496 F-84Fs between FY 1954–57. Republic persuaded the USAF in 1949 that the F-84E could be modified at low cost and made supersonic. This was a very bad guess. The first of many problems traced to the J-35 engine with 5,300 pounds thrust, which was inadequate to reach supersonic speed. The more powerful J-65 engine was then selected and required a larger fuselage. Production problems continued through 1955. The end product was very fast but not supersonic.

Plans to set a speed record. Captain Leavitt expains to Vic Milam and the line chief the plan to set a speed record for a round-trip coast-to-coast flight across the United States. Leavitt took Milam's "F" when his engine failed to start. Tony Bevacqua was wingman. They air refueled twice and had an average speed of 579 mph for the 4,909 miles. The flight took eight hours and 29 minutes from takeoff to landing, cutting nearly three hours off the official record.

training. I developed a daily quiz game played at our morning pilots' meeting. Every day, I prepared an emergency procedure question, and the squadron commander rolled the dice. For example, if Red 2 and Green 1 came up, the flight commander of the second flight had to stand up and answer that day's question. Peer pressure being what it is, the pilots got very sharp on emergency procedures. *Flying Safety* magazine printed a favorable article on this safety program in January 1956.

In early January 1955, I attended the Armed Forces Special Weapons Course. While there, some friends in the 466th Squadron sent me a telegram. The annual promotion list to captain had been released. To their "shock and horror," I was now a captain! The 466th had more captains than flights to command, so I transferred to the 468th Squadron as a flight commander.

Although my previous record and excellent OERs warranted the promotion, the long-bomb incident was still hanging over my head. Transferring to a different squadron required a new OER. It came as no surprise when the previous squadron commander sent me on my way with a mediocre OER. Eighty-five days later, I received the required annual OER from the new squadron commander. He lifted the overall rating, and the wing commander, Colonel Johnson, added some nice words at the end of his comments. Maybe I was gradually getting out of the doghouse.

Nineteen fifty-five was a very good year. The highlight was the birth of my son, Lloyd R. III, on July 23d. We bought a new house near the air base. Living room, kitchen, three bedrooms, dining room, bathroom, and wooden floors—all for $12,500! Only problem was the front yard washed out every time it rained. Getting the red clay of Georgia to stay in one place remained an unsolved problem.

The 468th Squadron, commanded by Maj Floyd Herbert, was a well-disciplined fighter squadron with no military offenses charged against Airmen or officers for more than one year. An excellent example of personnel reliability was our periodic movement to Eglin AFB for gunnery training. Every quarter, a flight with five or six F-84s from our squadron would move to auxiliary airfield number six at Eglin for two weeks of gunnery training. A few days prior to the move, approximately 20 non-commissioned officers and Airmen would receive letter orders telling them to arrange their own travel for the 250-mile trip from Albany to Eglin.

Departure for Eglin began Friday afternoon after work. Maintenance and munitions personnel were to report to auxiliary number six not later than 0700 the following Monday. Pilots would fly the aircraft to the airfield on Monday morning and be met by maintenance and munitions crews. In my two years with the 468th, no Airman or NCO was ever late for this TDY assignment. When my Army classmates at Fort Benning would chide me about the Air Force lacking discipline, I would challenge them to turn an Army platoon loose some weekend from Fort Benning and see how many could make it to Fort Bragg (North Carolina) on Monday. Their disbelieving looks confirmed my point.

Our enviable squadron discipline record was shattered one day. A young black Airman appeared at the main gate and tried to enter without orders or military ID. After scuffling with the air police (later changed to security police [SP]), he convinced them his orders and wallet had been stolen. They checked and verified his story. He had been arrested in the District of Columbia for being in a riot and for fighting with a policeman. This apparently explained why he was AWOL and without orders or identification.

Assigned a bunk in the barracks, he later broke into the first sergeant's footlocker and attempted to steal a pistol. Major Herbert decided not to punish this latest offense after listening to the Airman's excuse. Instead, Herbert asked me to work with our "mini crime wave" and get him back on track.

After talking with the Airman, I was confident that he could overcome this bad start. He was very articulate while explaining "what really happened" and wanted a second chance. He described his underlying problem as a lack of money—all gone with the lost wallet. I was building a picket fence in my backyard and paid him $50 in advance to help build the fence. It turned out that his skills did not include fence building, but the 50 bucks improved his attitude. We met several times in the next few weeks for counseling, and each time he convinced me that his attitude and performance were improving. One day, the psychiatrist at the base hospital called.

"Captain Leavitt, have you been working with Airman B?" I assured him that I had. The psychiatrist said he had interviewed Airman B after his arrival and wanted to share his findings with me. His next question was disturbing. "Do you realize you are wasting your time? He's a psychopath and an incorrigible liar."

Not one to give up easily, I assured the doctor that Airman B had a bad start but was working hard to overcome his past. Every counseling session with B indicated steady improvement, and he was staying out of trouble. The doctor ended our conversation, "Good luck, but don't say I didn't warn you!"

Two nights later, my "steady improvement" comment took on new meaning. Airman B broke into the ladies dormitory at Albany State College and raped two black coeds. He received a stiff sentence and a dishonorable discharge. I learned two valuable lessons from this experience—do not practice psychiatry without a license, and learn to separate BS from music.

Eight years later, now a major, I was having lunch with two other officers at a Washington restaurant. As we left the restaurant, a mail carrier approached. "Captain Leavitt, you don't remember me, do you?" It was the psychopathic con man, the rapist! Totally surprised, my answer, "I'll never forget you!" ended this chance encounter. To this day, I wonder why he was released early and how he became a postal employee.

Flight commanders were responsible for the training and performance of five, six, or seven pilots. There were two or three new second lieutenants in each flight, recent graduates from advanced jet training and fighter gunnery school. They liked celebrating their newfound freedom—sometimes excessively. I arrived at work one morning and Brig Gen Thayer S. Olds, 40th Air Division (AD) commander, was sitting by my desk. I had taken General Olds in a T-33 to a conference at Nellis AFB a few weeks earlier and found him to be a very pleasant, considerate officer. I approached the desk assuming he had another trip in mind. His opening remarks focused my attention.

"Captain Leavitt, is Second Lieutenant Jones (not his real name) in your flight?" My answer, "Yes, sir," invited his second question. "How long have you known Lieutenant Jones?" My response, "Two days, General Olds; he just joined the squadron," led to the general's next question. "Did you know, Lieutenant Jones left the Officers' Club last night and at high speed, maybe 80 miles an hour, drove his brand new car into the perimeter fence while leaving the base? First, he knocked down 80 feet of cyclone fencing when he hit the fence and another 60 feet when he returned to the road."

"No, sir, I didn't know that," ended my contribution to the general's visit. General Olds left with an almost unnecessary suggestion, "Keep your eye on him!"

A few minutes later, young Lieutenant Jones and I had a man-to-man talk. Among other things, why did he knock down more fencing while driving out? His "rational" explanation seemed a little bizarre to me. Despite this rough start, Jones turned out to be one of the best officers in the squadron. He was an excellent pilot and left the Air Force with an unusually distinguished flying record when he retired years later.

No Guts, No Glory was an aerial combat manual by Korean War double ace Maj "Boots" Blesse. Effective air-to-air missiles were not available in the Korean War. F-86 pilots had to get behind a MiG in order to destroy it with machine gun fire. His manual described how high speed and maneuverable jet fighters could gain that advantage using the "fluid-four formation." Several lieutenants assigned to my flight were talented pilots, but my assistant flight commander, 1st Lt Buster E. Edens (called "Snede," Edens spelled backwards), was a superb fighter pilot.[12] We were both convinced that Blesse's tactics were far better than the air-to-air tactics passed down from World War II. I challenged the other flights in the squadron to mock dogfights for air-to-air combat training.

We would meet the other flight over an unrestricted airspace near Albany Radio at 40,000 feet at an agreed time. The two flights would fly in opposite directions for one minute, reverse course, and attempt to get on the other flight's tail. Once there, the name of the game was to stay in firing position behind the "enemy" fighters, regardless of their defensive maneuvering. Success depended upon good vision, well-trained wingmen, high-G maneuvering, aggressive tactics, and the ability to anticipate "enemy" reactions. The battle was over when you were on his tail and he lacked enough airspeed and altitude to escape. Most dogfights ended before the fighters had descended below 5,000 feet. Blesse's tactics worked every time.

Snede and I ran out of challengers after awhile, so we decided to fight each other. We met head-on just under supersonic speed at 40,000 feet. After trying our entire bag of tricks and scissoring back and forth, we were down to less than 1,000 feet. With no clear advantage to either Snede or me, I called it off. Snede earned the bragging rights.

Another exceptional pilot assigned to my flight was 1st Lt Francis Gary Powers. Gary made the 508th Wing gunnery team a year after receiving his wings and again the following year. Gary was a quiet, unassuming officer who married a local Southern belle while stationed at Turner. Shortly after their marriage, Gary reverted to Inactive Reserve status and entered the top-secret CIA U-2 program. At that time, all we knew was the CIA cover story that Lockheed had hired Powers and Edens. I never saw either Gary or Snede again.

Drinking beer and eating raw oysters at a hole-in-the-wall bar in Albany on Saturday morning after the mandatory pilot's meeting became a weekly ritual and a rite of passage for new guys. 2d Lt Anthony Bevacqua was the youngest pilot in the squadron and eager to join the gang. As the bartender cracked open the oyster shells, Tony acknowledged he had never eaten one of those slimy things. Amidst cheers of encouragement and chicken-like cackles, Tony bravely lifted to his mouth an oyster shell containing his first fresh, ice-cold blue-point oyster liberally doused in Tabasco sauce. The oyster traveled down— then up—then down again—then up again—before finally being swallowed! Tony was one of us!

Tony progressed rapidly in the training cycle and demonstrated his flying skills. He also showed a depth to his character seldom equaled—a character that provided new meaning to the term "friendship." On 19 July 1956, a T-33 crashed at Turner after flaming out on final approach. 1st Lt Richard Giordano, trapped in the rear cockpit, suffered near-fatal injuries after the aircraft burst into flames. The front-seat pilot helped Giordano from the burning aircraft and was also burned, but to a lesser degree than Giordano.

Evacuated to the Air Force general hospital at Maxwell AFB, Richard Giordano lingered between life and death for days. He finally recovered consciousness and began the long, painful struggle associated with recovering from serious burns. Tony made sure that pilots in the squadron wrote encouraging letters daily to "Gio." As weeks passed, as the letter writing tapered off, Tony picked up the slack. He wrote individual letters for the other pilots to sign. On weekends, Tony would drive to Maxwell and visit Gio. After six months at Maxwell AFB and two years at Lackland AFB, Giordano returned to active-duty and flying status. Years later, he commanded an American air base in the United Kingdom before retiring as a colonel.

The last year in the 468th Squadron was the best year from this fighter pilot's viewpoint. I persuaded the commander to ask SAC for permission to take the squadron to Puerto Rico for a short TDY. B-36s at Ramey AFB needed fighters to practice against, so our trip had a useful training purpose. SAC approved and made tankers available for air refueling en route. The squadron landed at San Juan Naval Air Station and enjoyed sightseeing and Caribbean nightlife. We flew intercepts against the high-flying, stripped-down B-36s before returning to Turner.

The two SAC fighter wings stationed at Turner regularly used the Eglin bombing ranges. The bombing ranges were a mile or so apart but ran in the same direction. One day, I was practicing LABS deliveries (a high-speed, low-level attack followed by an Immelman—steep climb into a half-loop followed by a half-roll at the top of the loop). As I started the steep climb, a B-47 on the parallel range was doing the same thing.

Muttering to myself, I flew back to Turner and told the disbelieving pilots about the B-47 doing LABS. SAC was rapidly acquiring B-47s. Was this new six-engine jet bomber capable of doing our job? The B-47 was nearly as fast as the F-84F, could fly further with or without air refueling, could carry more bombs, and was equipped with radar for bombing and navigation. The three-man crew permitted better safeguards against the unintentional or inadvertent release of nuclear weapons. To top it all, the B-47 could do LABS maneuvers! The die was cast: SAC fighters must be on their way out.

The F-84F and F-86H were the fastest operational fighters without afterburners in the Air Force in 1955. The F-84F had much longer range and with aerial refueling could fly several thousand nautical miles. When I added these facts together, it seemed appropriate to demonstrate F-84F performance to the public by breaking the round-trip speed record across the United States. The existing record for flying from coast to coast and back again was approximately 11 hours. I planned on breaking the record with a three-ship flight in about eight-and-a-half hours with two air-to-air refuelings.

Major Herbert liked the idea and so did Colonel Johnson, the wing commander, but Headquarters SAC was less than enthusiastic. It refused to approve or publicize our attempt to break the official round-trip coast-to-coast speed record with the F-84F. However, SAC did approve our plan as a "long-range training flight." We soon knew why it was low-keying our record attempt.

In 1956 SAC had 29 medium bombardment wings equipped with new B-47s and 11 heavy-bomb wings equipped with B-36s and B-52s. The USAF decided to transfer the SAC F-84F wings to TAC.[13] SAC was on the verge of becoming all bombers and no fighters. SAC publicizing an F-84F speed record would be like GM advertising Fords.

The morning of 27 January 1956, I briefed the flight. Two excellent pilots, Vic Milam and Tony Bevacqua, were wingmen. SAC arranged support for two aerial refuelings from KC-97s—one refueling heading west to the Pacific coast, the other heading east to the Atlantic. Weather was reasonably good, and the high-altitude jet stream was within acceptable limits. Federal Aviation Administration (FAA) facilities at Los Angeles, California, and Savannah, Georgia, had agreed to record our times as we passed overhead. We climbed into the cockpits, strapped in, and I signaled to start engines.

Damn! My engine would not start. After the time and energy spent planning and getting approval for this flight, aborting was not on my mind. Vic's aircraft had started all right. Regretfully, I told Vic I was taking his aircraft. Tony and I taxied out and hacked the time with Turner Tower on takeoff.

Everything went as planned. We kept the airspeed just under the maximum limit for level flight—around .94 Mach or 640 mph. To save time, we made high-speed letdowns and fast hookups with the KC-97 tankers. This meant flying over the top of the tankers at very high speeds; making a high-G, descending 360-degree turn with throttles back and speed brake out; and arriving in the receiver position ready to refuel with the refueling receptacle open and ready for business. These tanker crews were very skilled, and both air refuelings were over in minimum time. When we flew over Los Angeles, the FAA confirmed the time and location by radar. About eight hours and 10 minutes after takeoff, the FAA confirmed our time over Savannah.

Tony had discovered en route that his F-84F was slightly faster than mine. As we started a high-speed descent to Turner for landing, Tony showed his true fighter pilot spirit. He pulled abreast of my aircraft. "Hey Red Lead, I'll race you to Turner!" My answer reminded this brash, young friend the difference between flight leader and wingman. "Negative, Two. Get back on my wing, and enjoy the ride!" We landed at Turner eight hours and 29 minutes after takeoff. We had crossed the United States twice, air refueled twice, and completed the 4,909-mile flight at an average speed of 583 mph. Our "unofficial" record cut nearly three hours off the official record.

In February 1956, I volunteered for a top-secret program nicknamed Dragon Lady. Other than the requirements to be an experienced fighter pilot recommended by your wing commander and to be physically qualified for high-altitude flight, nothing was disclosed about the mission or the aircraft. Capt Warren "Goog" Boyd, a close friend, also volunteered. Several other Turner fighter pilots with Reserve commissions had suddenly "resigned" by this time without explanation. They included Jim Cherbonneaux, Buster Edens, E. K. Jones, Marty Knutson, Bill McMurray, Carl Overstreet, Gary Powers, and Carmine Vito. After volunteering, Goog and I scratched our heads and thought we had "solved" the mystery of the disappearing pilots and Dragon Lady.

Quemoy and Matsu are two small islands in the Formosa Strait between China and Taiwan. Although close to the PRC, Nationalist troops from Taiwan defended the heavily fortified islands. The skies over Formosa Strait were the scene for frequent dogfights between PRC MiG-15s and Nationalist F-86s. Ownership of Quemoy and Matsu was a hot political issue in the United States in the late 50s.

Further analysis involved a little detective work. There was a new prohibited area on the flight charts in northern Nevada. We knew Powers, Edens, Hall, Knutson, and others had left for California—not far from Nevada. We put two and two together and came up with five! The USAF must have a new, secret high-altitude fighter and was training pilots in that Nevada prohibited area. The project name, Dragon Lady, had an oriental slant. Probably a new Flying Tiger Group of experienced fighter pilots was forming to help Nationalist China. A short time later, Goog and I found out how wrong we were!

Project Dragon Lady changed my life. The first step after being conditionally accepted in Dragon Lady was being fitted for a partial-pressure suit. In February and March, the first 15–20 pilots went to the David Clark Company in Worcester, Massachusetts, that made our partial-pressure suits.

Modern day astronauts and U-2 pilots wear a "full" pressure suit. In 1956 the best available was the MC-3 "partial" pressure suit. The helmet and a bladder reaching to the lower torso were fully pressurized. The only protection for the arms and legs was the very tight-fitting, laced flight suit. If decompression occurred, external tubes running along the outside of the arms and legs inflated, causing the laces to tighten and squeeze the suit. The purpose of the tight fit and squeezing was to avoid blood pooling in the lower, unprotected extremities.

The company was best known for making Charmode ladies brassieres, girdles, and corsets. Since our partial-pressure suits had to be form-fitted, there was logic for using Clark, but it always brought smiles to the pilots' faces when the subject came up. After fitting, we were warned not to gain or lose more than five pounds, or the suit wouldn't fit. Each pilot's going-away present was a free Charmode bra for his wife. It turned out that fighter pilots, despite rumors to the contrary, were severely challenged when it came to estimating bra sizes. This impairment caused some uncomfortable moments and serious questioning when the wives unwrapped their presents!

Once we had our own pressure suits, we went to Maxwell AFB for high-altitude flight physicals. There are several levels of physiological concern linked to flight altitudes. The first is hypoxia. If the body suffers from an inadequate supply of oxygen in the blood, mental functions begin to deteriorate—a person can become unconscious and, in severe cases, die. Symptoms vary from individual to individual, but few can maintain a conscious state above 25,000 feet. Aircraft engines compensate for this danger by pressurizing the cabins and cockpits.

For example, a typical jet airliner may fly at 35,000 feet, but after climbing through 8,000 feet, the cabin altitude is maintained at a constant 8,000 feet. If the cabin begins to depressurize, oxygen masks pop out of the overhead compartments, and the pilot rapidly descends to a much lower altitude where normal breathing can occur.

Survival becomes increasing perilous above 48,000 feet after cockpit decompression. Lungs lack the strength to breathe normally, and oxygen must be furnished under pressure. As blood pressure drops in the lower extremities, the pilot's condition can quickly deteriorate to the point where he can lapse into unconsciousness.

Above 60,000 feet, body fluids will pool and ultimately boil unless the cabin pressure is maintained well below that altitude. High-altitude "bends" is another painful threat. Nitrogen bubbles blocking small veins and arteries and collecting in body tissues cause bends. In aircraft the bends are most apt to occur following a large increase in cabin altitude following a rapid decompression. Although pressure suits reduce the risk from bends, breathing 100 percent oxygen for at least one-half hour before the flight and eating a low-residue diet can significantly reduce the amount of nitrogen in the blood.

A final concern is the extreme drop in temperature following decompression. When this occurs, the canopy will instantly frost over if the air is humid, causing big-time visibility problems for the pilot. As long as the aircraft engine was running and kept the cabin pressure around 28–30,000 feet, the pilot did not need the pressure suit to inflate.

The aircraft we volunteered to fly—we still did not know what it was— cruised at a much higher altitude than any other aircraft. If the cockpit rapidly decompressed at 70,000 feet, the pilot would die unless he was wearing a partial-pressure suit. Our partial-pressure suits were designed to provide four hours' protection at high altitude *after* cockpit decompression. Long-term protection at altitude was needed if the cockpit decompressed over enemy territory.

Next stop was the high-altitude physical. In addition to the usual indignities that accompany a physical exam, each candidate had to sit for two hours in his partial-pressure suit in an altitude chamber that was depressurized to 70,000 feet. After this test began, a flight surgeon monitored the pilot's cardiovascular performance with an electrocardiograph. Because the partial-pressure suit bladder did not reach the lower extremities, blood could pool in the pilot's legs. His heart had to be strong enough to recirculate the blood. If the pilot passed out, the flight surgeon immediately brought the pressure chamber back to sea level, usually before the pilot realized he was unconscious. Several pilots failed the test and were eliminated from Dragon Lady.

After successfully completing both steps, I realized my days as a SAC fighter pilot were over. The three years spent at Turner filled in the gaps in my education as an Air Force officer and provided many opportunities to learn about the basic operational unit in the Air Force—the squadron.

One week was spent at Savannah. Air Force ROTC cadets from the University of Puerto Rico were receiving summer training at Hunter AFB. They were promised a ride in a jet while there, so Joe King and I volunteered to take two T-33s to Hunter and give them a "dollar ride." With one fuel load, we could take off, fly for 15–20 minutes, and land four times before shutting down the engine for refueling. After the cadet was strapped in the rear cockpit, we would ask each cadet, "What do you want to do—formation flight, acrobatics, or just straight and level?" Most would opt for formation or acrobatics.

One cadet had attracted a lot of attention. First, he was a real wise guy. Second, each day he slipped to the end of the line. Finally, after he could hide no more, he wound up with my last group of four cadets. The first two cadets were great and thanked me profusely for their rides. With the engine still running, the crew chief helped Mr. Wise Guy strap into the rear cockpit. As we taxied for takeoff, I asked him what he wanted to do.

No longer Mr. W. G., he politely said, "Please, Captain, just straight and level, no Gs, not too fast, no banking, and land as soon as you can." I resisted temptation and did as he asked. After the short flight and landing, I pulled into our parking spot, opened the canopy, and signaled the crew chief to help Mr. W. G. down. The engine was still running. The final cadet was standing by the ladder ready to get aboard when the crew chief walked to the front of the T-33. With a disgusted look on his face, he signaled to shut off the engine. I did, but wondered what the problem was.

Mr. W. G. had exceeded all expectations. In a 10-minute flight, he had wet his pants, thrown up all over the cockpit, and opened his parachute! Thank God, he didn't pull the ejection seat handle. My guess is that Mr. W. G. never applied for flight training.

The USAF expects junior officers with career intentions to complete the Squadron Officer School (SOS) conducted by the Air University at Maxwell AFB. Attending now would be an appropriate time before Dragon Lady interfered.

Squadron Officer School
April–July 1956

I flew the F-84F for the last time on 16 April, packed my bags, patted the dog, kissed my wife and kids goodbye, and drove to Maxwell AFB where SOS, part of the Air Command and Staff College (ACSC), was located. After in-processing and finding my room in the BOQ, the first order of business was a welcome-to-SOS party being given that evening by the staff.

The 600 lieutenants and captains in Class 56-B were divided into four groups. Upon entering the Officers' Club, we formed four long reception lines. The protocol was to shake hands with the group commander when your turn came and introduce yourself. I noticed a strange thing. There was no one assisting the lieutenant colonel commanding our group, yet he knew every student's name. When it was my turn to introduce myself, he beat me to the punch.

After the students in our group compared notes, we found the answer. Weeks before each student entered, we had to send a GI photograph of ourselves to SOS. Our group commander had memorized the name and face of each of the 150 officers in his group—an impressive performance.

The next day we took a long multiple-choice quiz to evaluate how much we knew about the Air Force. Capt John Andrus, our section leader, told me later that I had the highest score in Class 56B on the entrance exam. In my opinion, this simply reflected the varied and excellent assignments I had during the past six years.

SOS was a good balance between leadership training, communication skills, airpower doctrine, and the functions of a commander and staff. Each student was required to write an airpower report. Mine focused on the requirement for STOL and VTOL (short takeoff and vertical takeoff and landing) fighters. It was a bit visionary at the time but well received by the faculty.

In 1956, West Point was still furnishing 25 percent of each graduating class to the Air Force. Ninety-six seniors were spending two weeks at the Air University. The two weeks represented 70 percent of their total Air Force instruction. I was selected as a flight instructor for their stay. Frankly, two weeks with the cadets was fun, and I enjoyed playing hooky from the endless SOS lectures on Air Force doctrine and organization.

Air Force Manual (AFM) 1-2, *United States Air Force Basic Doctrine*, became a sore point between the SOS faculty and me. I wrote a paper criticizing the way AFM 1-2 was written. Speed, firepower, and maneuverability were described as unique attributes of aircraft. My paper argued, somewhat cynically, that to a certain degree these were also attributes of an Army tank or a Navy cruiser. The most important advantage of aircraft was the ability to operate in the third dimension of altitude, including space. Eventually, the USAF rewrote AFM 1-2 and recognized the importance of space.

About halfway through the course, I was called to the group commander's office. "Captain Leavitt, how would you like becoming an instructor in SOS?" was the opening remark by the lieutenant colonel with the great memory for names and faces. I answered, "No thanks, sir. I've already got a SAC assignment after SOS is over." His response carried a little threat. "Well, being an SOS instructor has a very high priority, so I'm submitting your name to Air Force personnel to get your SAC assignment changed."

Having passed the difficult Dragon Lady physical and now the proud possessor of two expensive GI pressure suits, I knew his was an empty threat. "With all due respect, sir, the SOS transfer is not going to happen. I volunteered and was accepted for a highly classified program and do not want to become an instructor at SOS." His request was refused by Air Force, and I stayed with Dragon Lady.

By 1956 I had received seven OERs—five written by squadron commanders and endorsed by wing commanders and two written by senior staff officers at HQ FEAF. Colonels endorsed all seven. SOS had a different twist. It not only rendered a training report prepared by your section leader, but in your section of 11 officers, each officer wrote two anonymous peer reports on every other student officer. The first report was written halfway through the course and the second prior to graduation. Although the peer reports did not become part of your permanent record, they provided valuable insight into what contemporaries thought about your strengths and weaknesses.

The peer rating report had the same five overall evaluation categories as the official OER—unsatisfactory, acceptable, dependable and typically effective, a very fine officer of great value to the service, and one of the very few outstanding officers I know. The overall evaluations on the final peer rating reports were quite similar to the seven OERs. More useful to me were the comments written on the back of several peer rating reports. One officer identified a personality problem, also mentioned by others, that plagued me throughout my career. "As indicated on the opposite page, this officer is one of the few outstanding officers I know. I believe his biggest asset is the ability to grasp the significant or important details in any situation. At times he is a little too outspoken with his ideas and could perhaps use a little more tact to keep from antagonizing certain individuals." He had a crystal ball; my career suffered from this weakness.

A big party preceded graduation day. The night before, Anne drove over from Albany for the party and graduation ceremony. I had reserved a room at the guest quarters for two nights but had not registered. When she arrived, the party was already in full swing. We waited until the party ended before driving over to the guest quarters and registering. With Anne in tow, I approached the desk to sign in.

A formidable-looking elderly woman was in charge. "Sign here," she commanded, pointing at the registration book. I signed, "Captain Lloyd R. Leavitt." The woman looked angry, "If you're going to take that young lady behind you into your room, Captain, she has to be signed in, too!" Embarrassed, I added, "and Mrs." after my name. Anne looked like she might kill me. The woman looked like she had thwarted a major sex crime. And I looked for the key and ran for the room.

SOS was a worthwhile experience. It provided an opportunity to examine the Air Force from a broader perspective, break away from the routine of squadron duties, and, at the same time, meet new friends and acquaintances. When I returned to Turner AFB, things had changed. The USAF had inactivated the 508th SFW on 14 May 1956 and transferred the aircraft to TAC. Most support personnel stayed at Turner in the newly formed 4080th Strategic Reconnaissance Wing, Light (SRW[L]).

On 15 May 1956, 34 F-84F pilots were transferred from the inactive 508th SFW to the 4029th SRW(L) of the 4080th Wing—a "paper squadron" with no aircraft and no mission. The 4029th was an intermediate assignment. First, four pilots, including Gary Powers, resigned from the Air Force and entered the top-secret CIA U-2 program. Next, three pilots transferred to the 4025th Strategic Reconnaissance Squadron (SRS) and began flying the RB-57D. Eight more pilots, including myself, stayed in the 4029th awaiting orders for Dragon Lady. The remaining pilots went to TAC, although a few left for other assignments or civilian life.

Winston Churchill once said, "Everyone has his day and some days last longer than others." This statement certainly fitted the history of SAC strategic fighter wings. The remaining five SAC fighter wings were either transferred to TAC or inactivated on 1 July 1957. The fighter business in SAC was over. Why did it end?

The B-47 fleet was building fast, and the B-47 was clearly a more capable bomber than the F-84F. Meanwhile, the SAC F-84F wings were plagued with engine problems and other issues that delayed combat readiness. It was June 1955 before five F-84F wings became combat-ready.

A major problem with the F-84F was the extremely high accident rate. Even by 1955 standards, it was a terrible record for peacetime operations. SAC owned 511 F-84F aircraft in June 1955. Their accident rate per 100,000 hours for 1955 was 57.1—more than *six times higher than the B-47 rate* of 8.9 per 100,000 hours. F-84Fs represented 40 percent of the total number of SAC accidents that year while having flown only 8 percent of the total SAC hours. *The entire Air Force accident experience for 1955 included 124 F-84s destroyed and 55 F-84 pilots killed.*[14] To place this in perspective, an average of only 23 USAF aircraft per year of all types were destroyed in accidents between 1993 and 2002, with fatalities averaging 28 per year. The hydraulic system and other problems were gradually corrected. The SAC F-84Fs were turned over to TAC and later to the ANG. Our allies bought and continued to fly the F-84F for over 10 years. A total of 852 F-84Fs were built before production was halted.[15]

What had SAC fighter wings contributed? Despite many problems, SAC fighter wings made significant contributions to Air Force history, including the first mass flights across the Atlantic and Pacific. These successful deployments of SAC jet fighter units to Europe, North Africa, and Japan aided by air refueling set the pace for subsequent USAF fighter movements. The 27th Strategic Escort Wing was the first F-84E wing to deploy and fight in the Korean War. Many SAC-trained F-84 pilots provided experience and leadership during their combat tours in Korea. During the Korean War, five SAC fighter wings rotated to Japan for 90 days at a time performing air defense alert for the Japan Air Defense Force. The experience gained with tactical nuclear training and development in SAC also benefited the other fighter commands—TAC, United States Air Forces in Europe (USAFE), and Pacific Air Forces (PACAF).

Photo courtesy US Air Force

End of an era—F-84F—last SAC fighter. SAC F-84F on display, National Museum of the US Air Force, Wright-Patterson AFB.

Notes

1. Knaack, *Encyclopedia of US Air Force Aircraft*, vol.1, *Post–World War II Fighters*, 13–14.

2. Headquarters SAC, *Developing an Atomic Capability*. Document is now declassified.

3. Ibid.

4. Ibid.

5. Colonel Blair was an Air Force Reserve officer with an extensive background in commercial airlines. Years later, he owned an amphibious airline flying passengers between Caribbean islands. He was killed in one of these aircraft. Blair was married to the famous Hollywood actress Maureen O'Hara.

6. A few years later, the early U-2 models successfully used celestial navigation on their long-range reconnaissance missions.

7. Headquarters SAC, *Developing an Atomic Capability*, 40. Document is now declassified.

8. *Dead stick* in the vernacular means landing without engine power. The pilot is forced to glide the airplane to the landing site. When attempting a dead-stick landing on unimproved terrain in a jet fighter, the pilot will usually retract the landing gear to avoid the aircraft flipping over on impact. For this reason, Colonel Wilson chose to "belly in" this flamed-out F-84F.

9. Knaack, *Encyclopedia of US Air Force Aircraft*, vol.1, *Post–World War II Fighters*, 39–40.

10. Lt Gen Gerald W. Johnson retired from the Air Force in 1974 after a very distinguished career and died in 2002. During WWII he destroyed 16.5 German aircraft in a shorter period than any other American ace. Johnson spent the rest of the war as a POW after ground fire shot down his fighter in 1944. "USAF Almanac 2008," 86.

11. Sixty-five F-84F pilots were killed in peacetime accidents the first two years the USAF was equipped with the aircraft—a rate of 20.22 per 100,000 hours. This is roughly twice the *total* number of all USAF flying fatalities experienced per year during the past decade. Information from SAC historian.

12. Lt Buster E. Edens reverted to Reserve status in 1956 and was one of the first pilots chosen by the CIA for the top-secret U-2 program. He was killed on 26 April 1965 at Edwards AFB practicing simulated aircraft carrier landings in a U-2. Pocock, 50 Years of the U-2, 206–7.

13. Hopkins and Goldberg, *Development of Strategic Air Command, 1946–1986*.

14. SAC Controller, *Summary of SAC Operational Data*, 1–3.

15. Mehuron, "Air Force in Facts and Figures," 88.

Chapter 5

U-2 Years
Major—1957–60

Toward the Unknown
1957–1960

The C-47 flight time from March AFB, California, to the "Ranch" was less than two hours. As the desert passed underneath, my mind shifted back to events of the last few months. Nearly a year had passed between volunteering for Dragon Lady and beginning U-2 flight training.[1]

After graduating from Squadron Officer School, I was assigned to the 4029th Squadron with the remaining F-84F pilots. Remaining at Turner, we then became the 4028th Strategic Reconnaissance Squadron, Light (SRS[L])—soon to be the only U-2 squadron in the Air Force. Our new squadron commander, Lt Col Jack Nole, was gone most of the time—where we didn't know—except his absence was tied to Dragon Lady.

Colonel Nole returned to Turner on 19 February 1957. In his absence I had performed many of the administrative duties of a squadron commander. Among other things, the new commander had been concerned about maintaining the morale and skills of our Airmen and junior NCOs while the squadron was waiting for new aircraft. We had discussed starting a school to prepare these men for their new responsibilities, and Nole mentioned the school in my annual OER: "The basic requirement for the school was foreseen by Captain Leavitt. The results have been noted through the last eight months by the improved performance, attitude, and sense of responsibility of these Airmen. I attribute the high reenlistment rate (75 percent for six months) of this squadron in large part to Captain Leavitt's school."

On Wednesday, 20 February 1957, Colonel Nole suggested we go to lunch. I was hoping he would have some information about Dragon Lady. Just before finishing lunch, he said, "By the way, Dick, I meant to tell you yesterday, but it slipped my mind. I want you to be at March Field by next Monday morning. Don't speculate or discuss any details with anybody. As you know, everything about Dragon Lady is top secret. I'll give you a phone number for Anne to use in an emergency."

"Colonel, that's really good news. I've been looking forward to this for a long time. Is it TDY?" His answer put me in high gear. "No, it's PCS [permanent change of station]. Orders are being cut tomorrow."

Wow! I drove home and told Anne we were leaving right away. The moving company was at the house by 4:00 p.m. Anne took care of the utilities and started packing her personal items. (She put them in the bathtub so the movers wouldn't pack them). I called a real estate agent and told him to sell or rent the house as soon as possible. Everything was packed or thrown in a box by the end of the day. Household goods were sent to government storage. The next day, Anne with our two kids and Trudy, our boxer dog, started driving to Little Rock for an indefinite-length visit with her parents.[2] I picked up Goog Boyd in my car, and we headed for LA, arriving at March AFB on Sunday. We were ready to begin our new adventure on Monday morning.

Anne and I often laughed in later years about the hurry-up move from Albany, Georgia. She accepted the indefinite separation lasting several months in good spirits without a lot of questions, trusting it would all be better in the future. After unexpectedly arriving in Little Rock, her friends (and maybe her family) assumed that we had split because Anne wouldn't explain where I was, what I was doing, or when she would see me again. It was one of many times Anne proved she was a perfect Air Force wife.

The 4028th SRS(L) had an interesting squadron patch. Written across the bottom were the words Toward the Unknown. Looking back at those early days of the U-2 program, I realize how appropriate the words were after leaving March AFB the following Monday morning on a C-47 for the Ranch.

The old Gooney Bird started to let down. Off the left wing, the Nevada Test Range could be seen. Above-ground atomic weapon tests had left circular imprints on the desert floor, a visible reminder of their awesome power. A few minutes later, as the aircraft circled for landing, we had our first look at the Ranch. A single black asphalt runway ran into a large dry lake—Groom Dry Lake. A parking ramp, a few small buildings, control tower, two hangars, and what looked like a trailer camp apparently comprised the entire site. No other signs of civilization were within eyesight. All in all, the Ranch (officially "Watertown Strip") was not impressive, but it certainly was isolated.

Climbing down from the C-47, we were met by the 4028th staff members, who would supervise the training program. Maj Floyd Herbert, former commander of the 468th Strategic Fighter Squadron, was the operations officer. He was assisted during our training by Majors Dick Nevett and Joe Jackson.[3] After chatting for a few minutes, processing began.

They pointed to a small building and told me to walk over there and knock on the door. After knocking, an ominous voice told me to enter. A man sitting behind a desk motioned me to come forward. The room was quite dark, and I could not see his face clearly. He did not ask me to sit down and did not identify himself. Clearly, this was not a social visit. So I stood in front of his desk wondering what was happening.

After a rather dramatic pause, he spoke. "Leavitt, you volunteered for this top-secret, extremely sensitive program. You better pay attention to what I say, or your ass will disappear from God's green earth. [This got my attention!] When you leave the Ranch, do not tell anyone where you have been, what you are doing, or anything about the U-2 or the Ranch—not your wife, not anybody. Do you understand? [I nodded my head affirmatively.] You will be going back to LA on weekends and staying at a motel. When you are there, you will be followed. We will watch you, and you'd better keep your mouth shut and do what I'm telling you. Do you understand?"

My "Yes, sir" ended the one-sided conversation. I left appropriately impressed by my first contact with someone I assumed was a CIA spook.

This Ranch Ain't Got No Horses
February–June 1957

A U-2 was parked in the nearby hangar. My first reaction was what a strange looking aircraft. The front end looked like an F-104 with its pointed nose and tiny cockpit. The fuselage was 50 feet long, about five feet shorter than an F-104. The tail as-

Photo courtesy Lockheed

The Ranch. The U-2 was manufactured at Lockheed's Burbank plant—"Skunk Works"—where tight security was kept for this top-secret program. Each aircraft was then disassembled into major components and airlifted in USAF C-124 transports to the Ranch, where Lockheed employees reassembled and tested each U-2.

Photo courtesy Lockheed

sembly looked normal, but the drooping, narrow wings spanned 80 feet in sharp contrast to the stubby, 22-foot wingspan of an F-104. And the landing gear looked like a pair of roller skates stuck under the fuselage.

The first day's ground training explained the whys and wherefores of the U-2. We later learned that the design peculiarities traced to three requirements which the CIA and Scientific Advisory Board had demanded and were subsequently used to gain Eisenhower's approval.

High Altitude. Performing aerial reconnaissance successfully over the Soviet Union in the late 1950s required flying well above Soviet air defense fighters. The long high-aspect-ratio wing would lift a U-2 powered by a J-57-P31 engine powered by 11,200 pounds thrust to a maximum altitude of 72,000 feet. The last few thousand feet were gained as aircraft weight decreased with fuel burn-off.

The -31 engines were still being modified in early 1957 and would not replace the -37s for several months. In the meantime, the J-57-P37 engines would power the U-2s we would fly. It was 400 pounds heavier than the -31, had 700 pounds less thrust, spread oil vapor on the inside of the cockpit windscreen, and had a nasty habit of flaming out at high altitude. Flameouts cause rapid decompression in the cockpit, fatal to the pilot if the partial-pressure suit and emergency oxygen system functioned improperly.

After initial level-off in the mid to high 60s, the U-2 would climb approximately 1,000 feet an hour as fuel burned off. During this climb, the pilot had to carefully monitor the exhaust gas temperature (EGT) gauge and gradually throttle back to keep EGT below the upper limit. The throttle quadrant had a vernier attached that permitted these very minor throttle adjustments. Large or rapid throttle movement could disturb engine airflow and cause a flameout.

These minor throttle adjustments continued in the slow climb to maximum altitude until the jet engine reached minimum fuel flow. At that point, the J-57 could flame out if fuel flow were further reduced. At maximum altitude the spread between Mach limit and stall speed was approximately 10 knots. In aviation lore this was called the "coffin corner." Ignoring either Mach or stall limits could result in catastrophic failure of the U-2.

Long Range. Reaching high-priority reconnaissance targets in the Soviet Union required flying very long distances. The U-2 wings held 1,250 gallons of jet fuel and the sump tank another 85 gallons. The U-2 burned about 140 gallons of jet fuel per hour on a typical high-altitude flight. For flight planning purposes, maximum range was about 4,000 nautical miles with the J-57-P31 engine. This was enough range to reach most Soviet areas from friendly air bases around the Soviet periphery. (Note: the comments and data apply to the early U-2 models flown by the author and not the U-2 models flown after 1960 or the larger and much more capable U-2 flown by today's USAF).

Superb Cameras and Electronic Sensors. Cameras and film were required that would provide exhaustive coverage in precise detail. The cameras, film, and signal intelligence sensors had to fit into the small equipment bay at the front of the aircraft. A 70 mm tracker camera invented by Perkin Elmer weighed only 55 pounds when loaded with film. It photographed the entire flight path and was useful in establishing exact coordinates and general intelligence. The prime camera system was the Hycon "B" camera with a 36" focal length. It cycled from left to right, taking as many as seven stereo photos in each cycle. Kodak invented Mylar film for the U-2 project. Two rolls of very thin Mylar film, each 4,000 feet long, fed the B camera. The installed cameras and film weighed only 540 pounds.

Everything about the U-2 was designed to save weight. The maximum flight altitude was dictated by aircraft design and construction, engine performance, and gross weight. Perhaps the 250-pound landing gear best illustrates the weight-saving efforts. The main gear, comprised of two small wheels and an axle, was installed well forward on the fuselage between the engine intakes. A much smaller two-wheel assembly was installed under the tail. Propping up the left and right drooping wings were freewheeling cantilever metal bars with small wheels attached at the bottom of each bar, called "pogos." Their purpose was to keep the wings reasonably level on takeoff roll. As the airspeed increased, the drooping wings would begin to lift. When this happened the pogos would fall out of their sockets and bounce down the runway, leaving only the main gear and tail wheel for landing.

Landing the U-2 was like landing a bicycle at 100 mph. Because the pogos had dropped off on takeoff, the pilot had to continue flying the U-2 on the runway after touchdown by keeping the wings level with aileron movements while steering with rudder. If fuel was not evenly balanced between the right and left wing tanks when landing, the heavier wing would drop as the aircraft slowed down. If the low wing touched the ground, the U-2 would swerve in that direction. This did not cause damage when the aircraft was moving slowly because the underside of each wingtip had a small skid. If the aircraft was moving fairly fast when the wing dropped, swerving could quickly turn into a ground loop and cause damage. Crosswind landings in high winds were particularly difficult and avoided whenever possible.

Each wing contained two fuel tanks. Fuel was gravity fed and boosted by a hydraulic pump into a fuselage sump tank. The sump tank quantity of 85 gallons could be read in the cockpit. The only other fuel measurement was a totalizer. The totalizer showed how much fuel was left at any moment by subtracting the gallons used from the total gallons on board at start engines. A full load was 1,335 gallons. A red light came on when fuel in the sump tank dropped to 40 gallons. There were no gauges for the wing tanks, so the pilot had to "feel" when they were out of balance and then use the transfer pump to crossfeed fuel from one wing to the other.

On my seventh U-2 flight at the Ranch, I experienced a serious deficiency in the fuel system. After a long night mission, the fuel totalizer at 70,000 feet indicated about 200 gallons—plenty of fuel to return to the Ranch, let down, and land. The low-level-fuel red light suddenly illuminated, indicating only 40 gallons of fuel remained. The engine flamed out a few minutes later. Fortunately, I was able to let down and make a successful "dead stick" landing on a dry lakebed near the Ranch with no damage. Maintenance located a fuel leak that caused 160 gallons to be lost before the fuel could flow through the totalizer. This incident was my "U-2 baptism of fire."

The Ranch was isolated and lacked the usual amenities found on an air base. The one mess hall at the Ranch was run by an exceptionally fine cook and his helpers. The food was

175

great, and meals were served from 0600 until 2100. We lived in air-conditioned house trailers, with three pilots per trailer. After we had flown the U-2 two or three times locally in the daytime, our training shifted to long-range, high-altitude night flights lasting eight hours. The schedule for an eight-hour night flight looked roughly like this:

0630–0800: Rise and shine. Eat breakfast.

0800–1200: Conduct flight planning.

1200–1300: Eat lunch.

1300–1900: Attempt to sleep; "tossing and turning" was easy.

1900–2000: Eat low-residue dinner (usually steak and eggs).

2000–2100: See flight surgeon for routine physical check; put on long underwear and partial-pressure suit, helped and checked by technicians.

2100–2230: Prebreathe 100 percent oxygen to avoid bends possibility.

2230–2250: Continue prebreathing on portable oxygen bottle, switch to aircraft oxygen system, check cockpit and instruments, pressure-check faceplate.

2250–2255: Start engine, check instruments, and taxi.

2300: Take off and begin climb to cruising altitude.

0630: Start letdown from max altitude.

0710: Land at Ranch.

0730–0830: Taxi to ramp after pogos are installed; cut off engine; disconnect from aircraft, return to personal equipment room; debrief maintenance and operations; remove pressure suit; complete paperwork; shower; and head for mess hall. The end of a long day!

By flying long training missions at night, we preserved the secrecy of the U-2 program. No other aircraft could see us at night because the U-2 was flying high above them. Our flight plans disclosed the route of flight in the United States, but the FAA didn't know how high we were or what kind of aircraft we were flying. Position reports to the FAA every half hour were limited to our call sign, location, and "above flight level 45 zero" (above 45,000 feet). Since no other aircraft were flying that high, flight level 45 zero effectively disguised our true altitude of 65,000–70,000 feet.

A practical issue was answering the "call of nature" in a partial-pressure suit. The pilot typically spent about 11 hours in his pressure suit from the time he dressed until he stripped after landing. One reason for the low-residue diet was to eliminate an unexpected "accident." A practical problem was urinating in flight since few pilots are equipped with an 11-hour bladder. Most single-place fighters have a pilot relief tube—not the U-2. Instead, a practical but time-consuming procedure was developed. It was important to pick a time when you would not be busy with higher priority chores. It required disconnecting the gloves from the pressure-suit sleeves and unfastening zippers on the flight suit and pressure suit. We carried a plastic bottle in the left pocket of the flight suit to contain the waste. After finishing and the zippers were zipped and the gloves reattached, we could get back to government business.

When a pilot began prebreathing, the seal around his faceplate was pressure-checked to rule out any possibility of leakage. A leaking seal would be fatal if cockpit pressurization were lost following a flameout. For that reason, the pilot was directed never to open the faceplate on his pressure suit helmet until well established at a lower altitude at the end of the long flight. This required a strong dose of self-discipline because oil and sweat from your face and forehead got in your eyes, an itchy or runny nose was really bad news, and the temptation to sneak a candy bar or some other form of nourishment after several hours with no food or water was always there. For the reader who says, "That ain't nothing," try driving for eight hours at high speed on an open freeway at night and never touch your face, rub your eyes, move out of your seat, stop and stretch, blow your nose, take your hands off the steering wheel, or eat anything.

On 4 April 1957, I was prebreathing prior to a night mission in the same room with Robert Seiker, a Lockheed test pilot. Seiker's U-2 flamed out that night at 65,000 feet, and the aircraft crashed. Four days later, the aircraft and Seiker's body were found after an extensive search. The subsequent investigation showed the faceplate clasp was open and Seiker had become hypoxic immediately after a flameout. Whether Seiker had opened his faceplate and the clasp had not been refastened properly or the clasp had failed when the suit inflated could not be absolutely determined. In either case, reengineering the clasp was the right course of action and was accomplished.

Designing the U-2 for this highly specialized mission required compromises that made it a difficult and sometimes hazardous aircraft to fly. The combination of long high-aspect-ratio wings plus a bicycle landing gear resulted in many accidents. Because U-2 missions did not require high-G maneuvering, weight was saved by building a lighter structure. U-2 operating limits were set at 2.5 Gs instead of six or more, as in fighter aircraft. Trading Gs for less weight resulted in a higher maximum altitude, but several U-2s broke apart in flight when subjected to unforeseen stress.

The original U-2 had few backup systems because they add weight and complexity and were unnecessary as long as everything was working normally. As the program matured, several changes were made in the interest of reducing fatalities and accidents. For example, an ejection seat was added after three pilots were killed in U-2s without them. And a much safer liquid oxygen system was installed after fatalities occurred following loss of cabin pressurization.

Life at the Ranch was all business from Monday morning through Friday noon. Weekends were spent in Riverside, San Bernardino, or Los Angeles. Only one in our group of seven pilots from the 4028th was eliminated from the project while training at the Ranch. During the low-level checkout phase, he became claustrophobic wearing the pressure suit helmet and had difficulty overcoming panic before landing the U-2.

The Ranch was downwind from the Nevada Nuclear Test Range because a series of small atomic weapons were undergoing tests that spring. We would leave the Ranch just prior to each test, fly to March AFB, and not return until it was determined the radiation level at the Ranch was safe. On 28 May, an unexpectedly large fireball of 900 feet caused more fallout than expected. With more tests scheduled, Headquarters USAF decided to transfer the U-2 training to Laughlin AFB at Del Rio, a small southwest Texas town on the Rio Grande.

The CIA and Lockheed were assigned operational and support responsibility for the U-2 program by President Eisenhower. The Air Force was not involved except as the source for CIA pilots. Assigning program management to the CIA was a bitter pill for Air Force leaders to swallow. The bureaucratic battle had a third participant—Lockheed's Kelly Johnson. An aeronautical engineering genius, he was equally gifted at cutting red tape. There was little doubt in Johnson's mind that he would have an easier and more profitable time working hand in hand with the CIA than with the Air Force. The Air Force finally got a foot in the door when a new Lockheed contract for 30 U-2s was assigned to the 4080th Wing at Laughlin.

The U-2 pilots trained at the Ranch for both the CIA and the USAF were generally experienced fighter pilots. No significant difference in their flying experience or background was apparent. Coordination between Lockheed, the CIA, and the USAF at the Ranch was both good and bad. When a problem involving a U-2 system needed fixing, Lockheed would provide a fix or a new or modified part with lightning speed. On the other hand, training at the Ranch fell far short of Air Force standards. Lacking was "professional grade" training from engineering, manufacturing, and operational staffs from Lockheed's Skunk Works. The high level of secrecy obscured

Photo courtesy Lockheed

U-2A cockpit. The cockpit was small and cramped. This limited the sitting height and movement of U-2 pilots wearing the partial-pressure suit and helmet. Steering the aircraft with a yoke instead of a "stick" was a novelty to most fighter pilots but not a problem.

both the training and aircraft deficiencies that plagued the early days of the U-2 program. After training, 15 pilots became the first USAF U-2 combat crews (see app. A).

Ace of Spades Trumps
Ace of Hearts
April–June 1957

Laughlin, a few miles from Del Rio, was a pilot training base until the 4080th SRW(L) took over the base in April 1957. The 4080th needed a remote location for security reasons, an airfield with two parallel runways and one crossing runway, and reasonably good flying weather. Laughlin met SAC operational requirements, but available housing was scarce.

The city fathers in Del Rio helped resolve the severe shortage of family housing by arranging for rental housing until base housing was constructed. Hunter Village, formerly occupied by itinerant workers, was vacated and leased to 4080th families. "Any port in a storm" was an appropriate maxim under the circumstances. We appreciated finding a place for our families and enjoyed the camaraderie in the much-less-than-luxurious Hunter Village.

Anne, daughter Chris, son Lloyd, and dog Trudy had already moved to Del Rio when Colonel Nole led a flight of four U-2s to Laughlin AFB. My pilot log shows the four-hour flight ended four months of family separation on 11 June 1957.

A surprise development was in store for us when we arrived at Laughlin. Col Hubert Zempke was our new wing commander. Zempke had been 40th Air Division commander at Turner AFB when we left for the Ranch in February. As such, he was responsible for both the 508th and 31st Wings. Everyone had expected Col

Photo courtesy US Air Force

Col Jack Nole. Nole was the first squadron commander of the 4028th SRS(L), the only U-2 squadron in the Air Force. He is wearing a partial-pressure suit and carrying his helmet. Not shown is the coverall worn over the pressure suit for suit protection.

Gerald Johnson, the 508th Wing commander until it was deactivated, to be the 4080th Wing commander since he was qualified in the RB-57D and was familiar with the mission and personnel in the 4080th.

In 1982 Jerry Johnson explained to me why the 4080th was given to Hub Zempke. After the 40th AD was deactivated, Zempke asked General LeMay, Commander in Chief, SAC (CINCSAC), to appoint him commander of the 4080th Wing in lieu of Johnson. Sensing a delicate situation developing between two highly decorated Air Force heroes, LeMay called both Zempke, a WWII ace with 17.75 kills, and Johnson, a WWII ace with 16.5 kills, to his office at SAC headquarters.

LeMay offered Zempke the command of a new B-47 air division, a position authorized for a brigadier general. Zempke turned it down, saying he still wanted to command the new 4080th Wing. Johnson told LeMay he wanted to retain command of the 4080th because he had taken the wing from inception and was best qualified to continue. LeMay then told Zempke the air division assignment would be good for his career since he was a very senior colonel and SAC B-47 air divisions were usually commanded by brigadier generals. Zempke thanked LeMay but stated again that he preferred commanding the 4080th. LeMay reluctantly agreed, saying he would defer to Zempke's request because he was senior in date of rank to Johnson. LeMay then transferred Johnson to a SAC air division as director of plans. Johnson later held a number of key staff assignments, commanded two SAC bomber wings, two SAC air divisions, and Eighth Air Force and was USAF Inspector General (IG) before retiring as a lieutenant general. Zempke retired as a colonel.

After General LeMay retired, he occasionally visited SAC headquarters when Gen Richard "Dick" Ellis was SAC commander and I was vice-commander. These encounters gave me an opportunity to know him better and understand why he used DOR to resolve the situation between Zempke and Johnson. LeMay was intensely loyal to people he respected, sometimes to a fault. Zempke and Johnson were both World War II heroes and fellow Airmen whom he truly respected. Date of rank provided LeMay a bureaucratic solution to the problem without being prejudicial to either officer. Whether it was the right decision became questionable in the light of later events.

Lt Gen Gerald W. Johnson. Johnson was the 4080th CO May 1956–April 1957 and the Eighth Air Force CO, Guam, during the Vietnam War.

Col Hubert Zempke. Zempke was the 4080th CO April–November 1957.

Lt Gen Austin J. Russell. Russell was the 4080th CO November 1957–December 1958. He later served as the USAF assistant vice CSAF.

Colonel Zempke took over a newly formed wing with a bushel basket full of problems. Because of the tight secrecy wrapped around Dragon Lady, U-2 accidents at the Ranch had not been investigated and reported through normal Air Force channels.

If SAC had known more about U-2 accidents at the Ranch, Zempke's problems might have been anticipated. Flight training began in June for newly assigned pilots being transferred from other SAC fighter wings.

A challenging task for any pilot was safely landing this "jet engine glider" on its bicycle landing gear. Tony LaVier, famed Lockheed test pilot, unintentionally demonstrated this difficulty the first time the U-2 was flown. Repeated attempts to land on the main gear caused the U-2 to bounce into the air every time the wheels touched the runway—not an enviable maneuver. LaVier finally landed safely. His wild first flight provided anecdotal evidence of the importance of proper landing technique to even the skeptical "world's greatest fighter pilot" that is found in every Air Force squadron.

Several U-2 limitations combined to cause landing difficulties: (1) poor visibility from the cockpit, particularly when wearing the pressure suit helmet, (2) little drag with gear down, speed brakes extended, and partial flaps, (3) too much engine thrust remaining despite the throttle being in idle, and (4) a landing gear only its mother could love.

An ideal landing in a jet fighter was stopping the descent several knots above stall speed, touching down on the main landing gear, and then allowing the nose gear to contact the runway as speed decreased. The ideal U-2 landing required the pilot to level off a few feet above the runway with throttle in idle, hold that attitude as the aircraft began to slow down, gradually increase back pressure on the yoke as it descended to a foot or two above the runway, and let the U-2 settle into the runway with a three-point landing—two main and tail wheels touching near simultaneously. While all this was happening, the pilot had to concentrate on keeping the wings level and offsetting crosswinds by "crabbing" the aircraft until touchdown. "Slipping" the U-2 was dangerous at low altitude because of its long wingspan and slow response to aileron movements.

A tradition in pilot training and in fighter operations was using pilots qualified in the unit aircraft to monitor takeoffs and landings. Known as mobile control officers (MCO), they insured that no air base hazards threatened flying operations. They monitored control tower and aircraft radio frequencies and were available for assistance during in-flight emergencies. The

4028th Squadron carried this duty a step farther. The MCO was located at the approach end of the runway, ready to roll in a souped-up Ford station wagon with the radio tuned to the landing frequency.

When a landing U-2 crossed the runway threshold, the MCO would advise the pilot how high the U-2 was above the runway and then call changes in the height as the speeding station wagon chased the U-2 down the runway. "You're about six feet, ease her down. Now about four feet, doing nicely. She's down to about two feet and looking good. You're about to touch. Nice landing—great job!" (Not all landings were that good!)

The 4080th suffered too many U-2, RB-57, and T-33 aircraft accidents the summer and fall of 1957. SAC senior leaders were shocked by the rash of accidents, especially in the U-2 squadron. Zempke was "kicking from deep in his own end zone" when Maj Gen John P. McConnell, the new commander of SAC's Second Air Force, paid a staff visit to Laughlin in early November 1957. While the 4080th Wing staff was waiting in front of base operations to greet McConnell, a B-57C trainer landed with gear up on one of the parallel runways. McConnell's C-54 circled the field while the runway was being cleared. A few minutes earlier, an RB-57D collapsed a wing on landing and closed the other parallel runway. While McConnell waited to land, Zempke never had an opportunity to learn the cause of either accident.

From our vantage point in 4028th Squadron Operations, several U-2 pilots were watching the excitement. Finally, the C-54 landed, and General McConnell disembarked. Zempke called his staff to attention and saluted. McConnell returned the salute and walked alone over to Colonel Zempke. They engaged in a brief conversation for a few minutes. As they turned and walked toward the waiting staff car, one of the U-2 pilots in our group said, "Zempke's smiling; he looks relieved." Truer words were never spoken.

Colonel Zempke never flew the U-2, although he commanded the wing from April to November 1957. He was obviously unsure about how to fix the U-2 accident problem. Brig Gen A. J. Russell was named our new wing commander the next day and arrived at Laughlin a few days later. One of Russell's first actions was checking out in the U-2 so he could fully understand the aircraft and its limitations. He instituted many needed changes in the 4080th Wing, and the reduction in the accident rate and subsequent improvement in aircrew performance during his tenure as wing commander testify to his effective leadership.

A stiff price in fatalities was paid for the high-altitude performing U-2. On 28 June 1957, 1st Lt Ford Lowcock was killed on his second U-2 flight. A few hours later, 1st Lt Leo Smith was killed. On 25 November 1957, Capt Benny LaCombe was killed. On 8 July 1958, RAF squadron leader Chris Walker was killed. The following day, Capt Al Chapin was killed. On 6 August 1958, 1st Lt Paul Haughland was killed. On 1 March 1962, Capt John Campbell was killed. On 27 October 1962, Maj Rudy Anderson was killed over Cuba. Of 38 pilots who began U-2 combat crew training in the 4028th Squadron during 1957 and 1958, eight were killed in U-2s during training or afterwards, and four more were eliminated for various reasons.

Troubles on the Rio Grande
June 1957–July 1958

On July 24th I tested the first U-2 we had received at Laughlin with the Pratt and Whitney J57-P-31 engine. We had looked forward to replacing the J-57-P-37, which was not specifically optimized for high-altitude flight. With only a light fuel load for my test flight and with the additional thrust from the P-31 engine, the U-2 climbed like a scalded eagle on this hot, humid day. The altimeter read 10,000 feet as the aircraft was climbing over the end of the takeoff runway. Heading north toward Abilene, the rapid climb continued. All the aircraft systems were working normally. I periodically recorded test data on the flight log. Gust controls were turned off above 45,000 feet, and the final climb to maximum altitude began.

At 72,000 feet the aircraft had reached maximum altitude. A few minutes later, I heard an unfamiliar noise—a muffled explosion. Engine revolutions per minute (RPM) rapidly spun down. Damn it! The engine had flamed out. Cockpit pressurization was instantly lost, my pressure suit inflated, and within seconds the interior of the canopy had frosted over. The good news was the pressure suit worked as advertised. The bad news was the frosted canopy prevented seeing anything outside the

185

cockpit. However, I was sure the frost would begin melting away once I restarted the engine again and the cockpit warmed up.

I turned south toward Laughlin, established optimum glide speed, and advised Laughlin that I was declaring an emergency because of the flameout. Upon descending through 35,000 feet, I would attempt the restart using the well-rehearsed procedure.

After descending through 35,000 feet and establishing the desired 180-knot indicated airspeed required for restart, the engine was windmilling at about 18 percent. With battery on, I opened the throttle and held the restart switch down for 20 seconds. Nothing happened—no relight. Soon, various "experts" in the tower offered suggestions. They probably were assuming I had screwed up the restart procedure. Descending through 30,000 feet, I tried again. No luck. More chatter from the tower. After trying unsuccessfully once more at 25,000, I told the tower to stop advising me. Bigger problems were on my mind. Where was Laughlin? Would I be able to see well enough to make a dead-stick landing with the canopy frosted over and restricting my vision?

Using my gloved left hand, I scraped some of the frost from the left side of the canopy during the descent from 25,000 feet. This small frost-free area provided limited visibility about the terrain off the left wing. After a few minutes, I spotted the Rio Grande and started a descending, circular turn to the left. At 8,000 feet, Laughlin came into view, not too far away. Keeping the airfield in sight off my left wing, I told the tower to keep the runway clear, that I could not see ahead of the aircraft and would enter traffic with a circular pattern turning to the left. I lowered the landing gear and flaps while turning final approach and used the parallel runway off the left wing to align the U-2 with the right-hand runway. Crossing the threshold, I looked left and estimated how high the aircraft was above the runway. Somehow it all worked out. The U-2 made a nice landing, and the flight ended without further mishap.

Col Nate Adams, wing vice-commander, climbed the cockpit ladder before the aircraft was towed off the runway. He congratulated me on saving the aircraft and said pieces of disintegrated turbine blades had penetrated the aircraft fuselage when the engine failed. That explained the noise prior to flameout and why it wouldn't relight.

After debriefing the test flight, filling out the usual paperwork, and removing the pressure suit, I took a shower. As I was starting to dry off, a sergeant ran into the shower room. "General McConnell wants to see you right away!" My response, "Let me get dressed first," was immediately overruled when a colonel opened the door. "Leavitt, grab a towel and get out here . . . right now! General McConnell wants to talk to you!"

I wrapped a towel around myself and walked barefoot to the next room. General McConnell, Second Air Force commander, had diverted his C-54 to Laughlin when he heard about the U-2 emergency and was standing there chatting with Hub Zempke. McConnell was six feet two, wearing a uniform, and had his hat on. Leavitt was five feet nine, barefoot, and buck naked, except for my impromptu "uniform"—a towel.

We shook hands. General McConnell was very complimentary about the successful emergency landing, and I appreciated his thoughtful visit and remarks. Later I received the Distinguished Flying Cross, first oak leaf cluster, for successfully handling this hazardous flight. Fortunately, McConnell didn't pin it on while I was wearing only a bath towel!

Capt Benedict A. LaCombe was returning from a night flight on 28 November when he was killed after losing control in the traffic pattern. LaCombe had been upgraded to lead crew on 24 July after serving as a U-2 combat crew member since 25 February and was acting as branch chief, U-2 Standardization Board, at the time of his death. The next morning, I was appointed as the board's branch chief.

That same afternoon, a telephone call from General Russell's executive officer surprised me. "General Russell invites you to his quarters for a drink about 5 o'clock. He'd like to talk to you about flying the U-2, since he has now started the checkout program." Russell had replaced Colonel Zempke a few days earlier. "Thank you, I look forward to our discussion," was a truthful reply.

After being greeted by the general and accepting his offer of a drink, I guessed this meeting was about business but did anticipate a pleasant chat. I sank back in a comfortable chair with drink in hand, eager to tell him about flying the U-2. He began by stating that standardization had an important function in every SAC wing, but it was critically important in the 4080th because of our difficult mission and poor accident record.

He then switched to asking a basic question about the U-2 traffic pattern. "I know the airspeed you should have on base leg and the airspeed on final approach, but how and when do you reduce the airspeed from base to final? I can't find the answer in the Lockheed manual." Forgetting that Bennie LaCombe had been killed the night before in the traffic pattern, I gave a rather casual answer. "Some guys bleed off airspeed on base leg and some guys lose 10 or 15 knots in the turn to final—it doesn't make much difference." Wrong answer! I'd just been sucker punched by the new wing commander.

"Captain Leavitt, I want you to return to your Standardization Board office and write a U-2 flight manual that meets Air Force standards. And don't ever give me an answer like that again!" Realizing the cocktail party was over, I straightened up in the chair, put my half-finished drink down, said "yes, sir" and "goodbye," and headed for the office. Instead of feeling put down by our new general, I respected him for waking me up to smell the coffee. Although Russell had commanded the wing for only a few days, he knew things were not going well and must change for the better.

In contrast to the business world, Air Force commanders seldom keep their job for more than two or three years. In my opinion, the Air Force profits from this turnover. Commanders are handed the responsibility for the care and maintenance of government property and the welfare, morale, and job performance of the personnel assigned. They are not stockholders, and they do not own the unit or air base. If the unit does well during his tenure, the commander's reward might be a medal, a promotion, or a new job with more responsibility—or under some circumstances, all three. If the unit does poorly, he may never be given another command, and his Air Force career could be limited.

Human nature being what it is, commanders who stay in one job too long are reluctant to correct weaknesses in their organization. Even some new commanders are reluctant to make changes until they have been with their unit for several months. Other new commanders believe in "sweeping clean with a new broom." In my opinion, a new commander has to look with "a fresh pair of eyes" the first few weeks in his unit. Waiting longer creates complacency, and long-standing deficiencies do not get corrected. Clearly, Russell was not going to wait.

After leaving Russell's quarters, I told Pat Halloran and Maj Richard "Steve" Heyser, members of the U-2 Standardization Branch, we had a big new task. We must write an official USAF flight manual to replace that very limited U-2 instruction book provided by Lockheed. Furthermore, we must get it done quickly. Two months later, we had revised all items affecting safety of flight.

Throughout my long Air Force career, I worked for, evaluated, and selected commanders and served many years as a commander myself. Commanders come in all sizes, colors, and genders, none of which matters. Instead, they are selected for command on the basis of their past performance and potential. The Air Force expects commanders to be ethical, possess good judgment, and be able to lead and improve their unit. Brig Gen Austin J. Russell exceeded all these expectations as commander of the 4080th Wing. At the end of the one year he commanded the wing, it had changed significantly for the better because of his strong leadership.

The progress made by the U-2 Standardization Branch during that year was cited on my annual OER written in July 1958. Without the cooperation, hard work, writing ability, advice, and technical know-how of the other U-2 officers who served in the branch, progress would not have been possible. My OER does not name these officers, but I credited their contributions on individual OERs. Excerpted are comments describing our accomplishments as written on my OER, endorsed by wing director of operations, Col Howard Shidal, and agreed by the wing CO, General Russell.

> When Major Leavitt was assigned as U-2 Branch Chief, the Standardization Division had just received an unsatisfactory rating by higher headquarters . . . records did not reflect the true status of personnel flying the U-2 . . . training directives needed complete overhauling . . . U-2 flight manual was inadequate . . . [and] local directives were sorely needed to supplement the flight manual and permit safe and efficient U-2 flight. . . . He immediately screened the records of all U-2 combat crews to determine the most highly qualified crews and requested they be assigned to the U-2 Branch . . . with his U-2 Branch crew-members, conceived and tested new procedures and techniques for safe flying operations . . .

changes were recommended and all were approved by higher headquarters for immediate use. . . . Prepared and coordinated additional manual procedures, other directives, and Wing Operations Memorandums . . . revised U-2 proficiency and emergency examinations to require greater knowledge for successful completion [and] made training recommendations to the Wing staff. . . . Many were accepted and resulted in a better U-2 training program. Subsequent higher headquarters inspection stated the Standardization Division was in excellent condition and all previously noted discrepancies were properly corrected. Major Leavitt's efforts contributed to a great degree to this excellent rating.

For the next two-and-one-half years, I served as chief, U-2 Standardization Branch. From time to time, U-2 standardization crews were replaced and returned to normal squadron duties. This rotation usually occurred in coordination with their assignment to one of the overseas detachments for approximately 90 days. The standardization crews who served during those years included Pat Halloran, who flew both the U-2 and SR-71 as an aircraft commander, commanded the SR-71 wing, served in several major staff positions, including the JCS, and retired as a major general in 1984; Steve Heyser, a high-time U-2 pilot who flew the first photo mission over Cuba in 1962, confirming the presence of Soviet ballistic missiles with pictures taken on his U-2 flight; Rudolf Anderson, who was killed by an SA-2 missile during the Cuban missile crisis and posthumously awarded the first Air Force Cross; and Roger Cooper, who made important contributions to the new U-2 flight manual. In March 1960, Roger saved a U-2 by successfully landing on a Canadian frozen lake after flaming out on a high-altitude nuclear sampling mission near the Arctic Circle.

When General LeMay was CINCSAC, he convinced Headquarters USAF that highly trained SAC aircrews should stay on aircrew duty as long as possible. In practice, this meant that many officers would be denied opportunities for career broadening, including overseas assignments, staff experience, and advanced education. A system was devised to make SAC aircrew duty attractive to career officers and Airmen.

Status and recognition were important. Each SAC aircrew was categorized as non-combat ready, combat ready, lead, or select. The categories provided a way to differentiate between aircrews performing the same basic tasks. The titles recognized job performance; for example, better to be a lead crew than a combat-ready crew. Select crews had an extra incentive. They were eligible for "spot" promotions, provided other eligibility criteria were met. A spot promotion from captain to major, for example, meant major's pay and rank during the time the crew member held the promotion. When the program began, time in grade with a spot promotion was counted toward eligibility for the next promotion. That feature was discontinued because it accelerated the promotion of SAC officers ahead of their contemporaries in other major commands.

On 20 June 1958, Joe King, Ray Haupt, Steve Heyser, Warren Boyd, Dick Atkins, Pat Halloran, and I became the first U-2 pilots to receive temporary USAF spot promotions. We were visiting my parents in Michigan when a telegram came announcing the unexpected promotion to major. Celebration was in order, so I went to the local liquor store to buy champagne. The clerk busted my balloon when she wouldn't serve me until I presented military ID showing this new major was over 21. She needed glasses—I was 29.

In June 1958, four RAF pilots came from Great Britain to Laughlin for U-2 training: Sqdrn Ldr Chris Walker, Flt Lt Mike Bradley, Flt Lt John MacArthur, and Flt Lt Dave Dowling. They were expected to arrive one Saturday morning at 0900, and the U-2 pilots had gathered at the Officers' Club to greet them. Several cups of coffee later, it was 1100, and they still hadn't arrived. One young lieutenant kept bugging me, "Where are they? Why are they late? What's taking them so long?" Finally I quieted him down. "They've been at language school in San Antonio this past week learning how to speak American. One guy didn't pass the final exam. They couldn't leave until he passed the reexam today." Satisfied, the gullible lieutenant nodded his head, and an understanding look spread over his face. Just then, in walked the RAF.

Scott Smith had arranged a cocktail party that night at his quarters in honor of our new RAF friends. After everyone was introduced, Scott invited them to his party. Chris Walker accepted the invitation for the RAF and wanted to know where, what time, and what to wear. Scott gave Chris a card with his home address and added, "Seven o'clock and don't dress—we're very informal in West Texas."

With our wives all atwitter, we had gathered in Scott's living room a few minutes before seven. Drinks in hand, we had prepared a rousing welcome for our newfound friends. The doorbell rang. Everyone stood for their grand entrance, prepared to yell "Welcome to Dragon Lady" or something similar but not quite sure how formal to be. Scott rushed to the door, opened it wide, and instantly forgot his welcoming speech.

There the four were . . . bowler hat, carrying an umbrella, white dress collar and black bow tie, highly polished black shoes, knee-length black socks held up by garters, . . . and wearing only the male equivalent of a bikini! A great entrance and what an icebreaker! Chris Walker capped the moment, "You said *don't dress!*"

The RAF pilots began their training immediately and by the Fourth of July weekend were beginning to fly the U-2. They were all experienced pilots and were eager to fly the U-2. They were also eager to tell us stories, especially one of the bachelors who recounted a romantic interlude with a famous Hollywood star who was making a movie in Africa when he was stationed there. We all received invitations for a large party they were throwing at the Officers' Club. They called it a "Colonial Day Celebration," and, as you might guess, the party date was July third.

On 7 July 1958, Dick Atkins, Capt Ed Emerling, and I flew three U-2s to Ramey AFB, Puerto Rico. We stopped at Ramey for crew rest and to refuel. Then we were to fly to Ezeiza Airport, Buenos Aires, Argentina, for three months' TDY.

On 8 July tragedy struck. We were notified that RAF squadron leader Chris Walker was killed on a high-altitude navigation training flight. The next day, we were notified that Captain Chapin was also killed on a training flight. The common link between the two deaths seemed to be a fault in the U-2 oxygen system. We were grounded at Ramey until further notice.

Assume a hypothetical example. A U-2 pilot is at maximum high altitude on a long-distance training flight. The throttle has been gradually retarded, and the engine is now at minimum fuel flow. Indicated airspeed is established in the very narrow range between Mach limit and stall. The aircraft is flying on autopilot, and the autopilot malfunctions. Airspeed increases and before the pilot realizes what has happened, the aircraft has exceeded the Mach limit and become uncontrollable. The pilot attempts to slow down by reducing the power further—the engine flames out. The cockpit decompresses, and his pressure suit inflates.

Meanwhile, the pressure-reducing valve in the gaseous oxygen system begins to freeze and restricts the flow of oxygen to his helmet. He becomes increasingly hypoxic as the lack of oxygen takes effect. Around 20,000 feet, he regains some degree of consciousness, enough to realize the out-of-control aircraft cannot be saved. Semiconscious, he cannot pull the ejection seat handle because of G-forces.

What caused the fatal accident? Was it the autopilot malfunction? Was it pilot error because the pilot let the aircraft exceed the Mach limit, although the margin for error was less than 10 knots? Was the engine too susceptible to flameouts, although careful throttle procedures and engine monitoring would prevent most flameouts? Was the gaseous oxygen system at fault because the pressure-reducing valve froze following cockpit decompression, although there was no direct evidence of ice in the valve when the crash was investigated on a warm July day?

Given all the unknowns, it was possible to fix two problems. The U-2 oxygen system was a high-pressure system that used gaseous oxygen. Gaseous oxygen can contain impurities, such as water droplets. When oxygen flows through a pressure-reducing valve, thermodynamic laws take over. As the pressure drops, volume rapidly increases, and the change in temperature at the reducer valve may turn water droplets to ice. If significant quantities form in the valve, the ice might prevent oxygen from flowing through the valve, and the pilot will be denied the oxygen necessary for survival. Tests were run at Laughlin on other U-2 aircraft. Water droplets were found in gaseous oxygen.

A liquid oxygen system is virtually pure of impurities. Changing from gaseous oxygen to liquid oxygen eliminated the problem of ice forming at the reducer valve. It seems evident that a pilot could have been suffering from hypoxia and partially regained consciousness at lower altitudes as the out-of-control U-2 descended. Realizing his plight, he might have survived if ejection seats were installed in this early U-2.

After being grounded for nearly a month, we flew back to Laughlin at low altitude. The aircraft were modified with the new oxygen system, and on 8 September we launched once again for Buenos Aires, first stopping at Ramey for fuel. On 12 September, we landed at Ezeiza Airport, Juan Peron's pride and joy. Peron had been overthrown and exiled three years earlier.

Dragon Lady Learns to Tango

September–November 1958

The 18-month period from July 1957 through December 1958 was called the International Geophysical Year (IGY). Sixty-six nations, including the United States and Argentina, agreed to study the earth and cosmic environment during the IGY. Coincidentally, nuclear testing in the atmosphere was being conducted by the United States, the Soviet Union, France, and Great Britain in the South Pacific prior to the first nuclear test ban taking effect in December 1958.

The nickname for the 4080th high-altitude sampling program (HASP) was Operation Crow Flight. The United States placed a very high priority on determining as much as possible from the nuclear tests. HASP was expected to provide data about weapon specifics as well as vital information about fallout patterns and radiation persistence.

The U-2 had proven its value collecting nuclear debris from nuclear explosions within the Northern Hemisphere. SAC's first U-2 "sampling" program was conducted by four U-2s simultaneously operating north and south from USAF air bases at Ramey AFB, Puerto Rico, and Plattsburg AFB, New York. Their total coverage extended nearly the entire distance from the equator to the Arctic Circle. Important conclusions from these flights were that: (1) debris from nuclear explosions in the Northern Hemisphere stayed in the northern latitudes, (2) debris tended to drift to the north and did not migrate to lower latitudes, (3) heavier particles carried by upper air winds became fallout over Scandinavia and other northern regions, and (4) lighter particles tended to dissipate in the tropopause, perhaps exiting into the stratosphere.

The lighter radioactive particles collected by U-2s in the tropopause were "pure"; that is, they did not include contaminated dust and debris resulting from the nuclear explosion. These minute particles were carefully examined for specific information about weapons design and construction. Remaining were at least two unanswered questions. How can we learn about thermonuclear weapons being exploded in the Southern Hemisphere? Where could we base U-2s to do nuclear sampling for the tests being run in the Southern Hemisphere?

From a geographic point of view, Buenos Aires was ideally located for the U-2 to test the atmosphere in the Southern Hemisphere. On a round-trip to the north from Buenos Aires, a U-2 could nearly reach the equator. Flying south on a round-trip from Buenos Aires, a U-2 could fly over the South Atlantic beyond the Falkland Islands and nearly reach Antarctica. Twice a week, U-2s flying from Plattsburg, Ramey, and Ezeiza would sample the atmosphere and tropopause from roughly the Arctic Circle to the Antarctic Circle. During these flights, air samples were collected in high-pressure storage bottles.

There was one fly in the ointment. Argentina had never allowed a foreign military unit to be stationed in Argentina. From 1944 to 1955, the dictator Juan Peron ruled Argentina. A military coup overthrew Peron in 1955. In 1958 a democratic government headed by Arturo Frondizi was elected. The United States immediately offered advice and badly needed financial aid to the Frondizi government. We also asked permission for the use of Ezeiza by U-2s during the IGY.

Frondizi had several good reasons to accommodate our request to use Ezeiza. Participation in the IGY was an excellent way to show the United States and other nations that Argentina would accept its international responsibilities. Also, Frondizi needed help to solve the financial crisis he inherited. The offer of American aid was a big carrot, providing an excellent reason not to ask difficult questions. Whatever the motivation, Frondizi's government reversed long-standing Argentine policy and allowed our U-2 detachment to become the first foreign military unit to be stationed in Argentina.

The eight-hour flight from Ramey AFB in Puerto Rico to Ezeiza Airport on the outskirts of Buenos Aires, Argentina, was an eye-opener. Looking down from high altitude and seeing the many-hued Caribbean far below was an unforgettable, beautiful experience. After passing over the South American coast near Trinidad, the course crossed the dense tropical rain forests of Brazil. The U-2 was cruise-climbing on its way to 70,000 feet. Looking ahead, a dense layer of clouds stretched across the horizon. Cloud tops appeared to be at my altitude. While flying over Texas during thunderstorm season, I had seen a cumulus cloud or two that high, but never an entire front.

Not eager to penetrate a thunderstorm over Brazil in a fragile U-2 without radar, I needed to know whether the U-2 would be higher than these dense clouds which might be thunderstorms. The tropopause is where the atmosphere becomes significantly more stable with altitude, thus separating the world's troposphere and the stratosphere. If the tropopause was near 70,000, chances are the clouds would be lower.

I did some quick "back of the envelope" computations using the outside air temperature gauge and the aircraft altimeter. The temperature gauge read around -100 degrees Celsius—the coldest I had ever seen. Based on my rough computations, the cloud tops were probably below the U-2's altitude. As it turned out, I crossed over the front at 70,000 feet, several hundred feet above the clouds. Lucky guess!

U-2 flights above the troposphere (the lower part of the atmosphere) and in the vicinity of the tropopause confirmed unexpected phenomena. The troposphere around the earth is not of uniform depth, and the earth is not a true sphere like a baseball. The depth of the troposphere is primarily caused by variations in the heating process with latitude, not the shape of the earth. Over the polar regions, the tropopause is usually 15,000–25,000 feet above the earth's surface. Over the central latitudes, the tropopause is usually 35,000–45,000 feet above the surface. And over equatorial latitudes, the tropopause usually occurs at 50,000–65,000 feet. Since air continues to cool in relation to the depth of the troposphere, the coldest air at high altitude in the troposphere is over the equator; the warmest is over polar regions.

This knowledge about Mother Earth was important when flying the U-2. True airspeeds are higher in the warmer Arctic air, but U-2s could not fly as high as in cold air. Neither could Soviet interceptors, so the U-2 relative altitude advantage was maintained.

The remainder of the flight to Buenos Aires was uneventful. The 4080th Wing had sent an advanced party to Ezeiza Airport before the flight, and the detachment was open for business when our three U-2s arrived. The detachment included maintenance, communications, operations, supply, purchasing, a flight surgeon, and parachute-rescue personnel. Mobile ground-controlled approach (GCA) radar from the USAF Communications Service was on the airport to assist during bad weather days. The operations section included pilots Dick Atkins, Ed Emerling, and myself and the staff navigator, Ray Reasoner.

To prepare the enlisted personnel for their TDY, a brief language course was given at Laughlin before departing for 90 days in Spanish-speaking Argentina. The language training had minimal payoff. Most NCOs had spent tours in Japan, Korea, or Germany. Their efforts to converse in Spanish were peppered with a strange mixture of English, Japanese, Korean, and German phrases. If not understood, they would turn up the volume. The Argentineans would listen with a puzzled look on their faces, nod their heads agreeably, and walk away without having a clue what the "Norte Americano" said.

Maj Hamilton Blackshear was our flight surgeon. "Ham" had a great personality. He sang, played the guitar, enjoyed the fine Argentine wine, told great stories, liked jumping out of airplanes, and was genuinely interested in the physiology of space medicine. His only drawback was that he did not like being around sick people—a fact Ham would readily admit. This flaw made little difference to us since we were all healthy anyway. After the American space program got going, Ham was transferred to Los Alamos where, among other responsibilities, he was in charge of the chimpanzees, our first astronauts. To readers who are old enough to remember, the first American in space was the chimp "Ham," named after our friend and doctor.

There were no living quarters for detachment personnel at Ezeiza Airport, so we lived at the Intercontinental Hotel in the center of Buenos Aires, overlooking the huge plaza where protests, demonstrations, and, occasionally, riots occurred. Dick Atkins and I were returning to the hotel late one afternoon in the embassy staff car when we saw a forbidding sight. Thousands of people were rioting in the plaza, and cars and buses had been overturned and a few were burning. We asked the embassy driver what was happening.

Our driver had been a taxicab driver in Brooklyn at one time and spoke English fairly well. "Don't worry. It's got nothing to do with you. The kids are fighting over Catholic schools versus public schools." Without waiting for our objections, he accelerated and headed into the mob, honking the horn to let the car pass.

The first few rioters saw our car and blocked passage. Our driver, showing his limited skills as a tactful, well-trained international diplomat, rolled down the window and yelled in Spanish something about, " . . . Norte Americanos!" I asked Atkins what he said. "Get out of the way for the North Americans!" was Dick's answer. As you might expect, the mob did not react kindly to the driver's demand.

Within seconds we were surrounded by angry young men rocking the car from side to side. Checking the size of the ashtray in the backseat, I realized there was no place to hide, and Atkins had already beaten me to the car floor. The driver suddenly shifted into reverse, shook off the car-shakers, and beat a hasty retreat from the plaza. We took another route to the Hotel Intercontinental and made it without further ado.

Our unusual status as an American military operation created a stir in Buenos Aires. People were both curious and friendly. The embassy suggested we have an open house to dispel rumors and potentially bad publicity. Working with the Argentine air force, we invited the public to Ezeiza one day. Dick Atkins gave a declassified briefing in Spanish about our IGY mission. A U-2 was on display within a roped-off area, pressure suits and survival gear were displayed and explained, pararescue NCOs made precision parachute jumps from our C-47, and the GCA radar van was opened to visitors.

A memorable sight in the 1950s was a U-2 making a maximum performance takeoff. We had parked a U-2 at the intersection of two runways with minimum fuel on board, pointed into the headwind. The fuel load was so light that the pogos, used for holding the wings off the runway, fell out of their wing sockets. Crew chiefs on each side held up the wings until I started the engine and the U-2 began to roll. The crew chiefs let go, and the U-2 was airborne in less than 500 feet. The steep climb angle of the nearly empty U-2 carried it to 10,000 feet or more before leaving airport boundaries. After continuing the maximum rate climb to 15,000 feet, I descended and circled the field once at low altitude before landing. Both the crowd and I enjoyed the brief flight!

HASP missions crossed the southeast coast of Argentina and continued over the South Atlantic. Once the U-2 passed beyond Bahia Blanca on the east coast of Argentina, no aviation facilities were within radio contact. A commercial frequency played a popular South American tune every 15 minutes for a station break. Without the station breaks to keep me company, it would have been a miserable, lonely eight-hour flight. The outbound course passed between Tierra del Fuego and the Falkland Islands. The course was reversed before reaching Antarctica, and the U-2 turned homeward bound for Ezeiza.

With only three U-2s at Ezeiza available to fly two long-range missions twice a week—Tuesdays and Thursdays—we needed to fix aircraft problems promptly. Serious problems required a test hop. One Wednesday two of our three aircraft were down for maintenance, but one was ready for test. I was not scheduled to fly a long mission on Thursday, so the obvious solution was for me to fly the test hop. There was a problem—a low-pressure area had settled over Buenos Aires, and the ceiling was less than 1,000 feet.

By this time, I was familiar with all the facilities at Ezeiza, had practiced several radar approaches with the USAF GCA assigned to support us, and was comfortable with bending the regulations a bit to have the U-2 ready for the next day. I took off with a light fuel load, climbed through the low deck of clouds, and headed east over the Atlantic to complete the routine tests. The aircraft was fine, and as I turned back to Ezeiza about 40 minutes later, the command post called on our squadron frequency. "Dragon Lady Test, we just received a phone call from Ezeiza Tower. An electrical power strike has been called in Buenos Aires, and all tower and navigation facilities are shutting down immediately and will remain down until further notice. Over. "

There was not enough fuel left to wait for the strike to end. With Buenos Aires radio off the air, I couldn't locate the base. I couldn't let down through the cloud deck without a known position because of the danger of hitting a building or some obstruction in Buenos Aires. I couldn't use our GCA to bring me back to Ezeiza because it had a limited search capability. Our command post suggested launching our C-47 and having it circle above the clouds over the end of the runway while it remained under surveillance by GCA. What a great idea! A few minutes later, our C-47 popped through the cloud deck about 10–15 miles away and began circling. We rendezvoused. GCA found my U-2, and uneventful approaches and landings were made a short time later by both aircraft. The strike ended a few hours later. Our two U-2s made on-time takeoffs on Thursday.

My Longest Day
16 September 1958

0415. The noisy phone ringing meant shave, shower, dress, and drive to Ezeiza.

0530. Ed Emerling and I were eating breakfast. Ed was flying south, and I was flying north to the middle of Brazil and back. The weather briefing looked OK. Two fronts were forming in southern Brazil and northern Paraguay, but I would be well above them. The Air-Sea Rescue C-54 was already airborne and would be ahead of my flight until Paraguay, where the U-2 would overtake the slower C-54. The briefer reminded me that a forced landing in Paraguay must avoid areas controlled by the Chaco Indians. Paraguayans would not go more than a few hundred yards from military posts to rescue anyone in Chaco territory. The staff navigator, Ray Reasoner, and I went over the route carefully and rechecked the preplotted celestial navigation plots on the map cards. There were no radio aids after reaching Paraguay; therefore, sun fixes and pilotage (reference to ground landmarks) would be the sources for correcting course errors.

0730. After recounting his activities last evening, Ham Blackshear gave me a quick medical check and cleared me for flight. The PE NCO helped me into the pressure suit and helmet. After he rechecked all connections, I was ready to start prebreathing.

0800. On schedule for a 1000 takeoff. When the mandatory one and one-half hour session of prebreathing 100 percent oxygen was completed, the PE NCO switched the pressure suit to a portable oxygen bottle, and we drove to the waiting U-2. The auxiliary power unit was already chugging away. Another U-2 pilot, today it was Dick Atkins, had inspected the aircraft. The pair helped me squeeze into the cockpit and transfer from the portable oxygen bottle to the aircraft oxygen system. After examining the Form 1 for discrepancies, pressure-testing the sealed faceplate, checking all the switches and instruments, and locking the canopy, I started the engine, turned on both cockpit seals, and called Ezeiza Tower for taxi and takeoff instructions.

1000. Takeoff and climb were routine. The flat green plains called the Argentine Pampas were soon far below. Off the right wing, I could see the Uruguay River forming the border between Argentina and Uruguay. The day was clear, and the wide Parana River that stretches 2,500 miles from Brazil through Paraguay to Argentina was soon visible off the left wing. I began collecting nuclear samples by turning on the equipment and wrote down the time—1100. Further along the route, I could see the Paraguay River flowing south on its 1,500 mile trek from western Brazil through Paraguay to Argentina, where it would join the Parana.

Clouds were forming in northern Paraguay and soon became broken to overcast. Periodically, I checked my position using the sextant to shoot sun lines. After being airborne for nearly three hours, a break in the clouds appeared. Looking down through the viewfinder, I could see the intersection of two large rivers. By 1300, the U-2 was over Brazil, and all that was visible in any direction was the dark tropical rain forest.

1345. Time to take the last celestial fix. The U-2 was approaching the equator, and the sun was nearly vertical overhead. I concentrated on tracking the sun with the sextant for a minute or two, but the sun seemed to be spinning. Wondering what-in-hell was happening, I stopped looking through the sextant and glanced at the instrument panel. The airplane had suffered a *complete* electrical failure (see fig. 2). The aircraft generator and inverter had failed, as well as the new nickel-cadmium battery—the only backup source of electricity in the U-2.

A strange emotion overcame me—one that I had never experienced before. I knew there was no way out of this emergency. I would soon die. Without navigation equipment except a magnetic compass, I would never find an airfield. Without a radio, I could not tell Air-Sea Rescue, or anyone else, what was happening. With three levels of jungle canopy stretching below in all directions and the nearest airfield a thousand miles away, I would not survive either a bailout or a crash. Without engine

Figure 2. My longest day. On a high-altitude sampling mission from Ezeiza Airport in Buenos Aires, Argentina, to the middle of Brazil, the U-2 had a *complete* electrical failure at 68,000 feet over the jungle.

instruments, I could not use normal descent procedures and get down from 68,000 feet. Without electrical power, I could not restart the engine if it flamed out. Without electrical power, my faceplate was fogging. Soon, I wouldn't be able to see anything. I prayed for help.

Remembering how Robert Seiker died at the Ranch, I hated to break the seal and open the faceplate, but I had to see. A flame-out and rapid decompression to 68,000 feet while the faceplate was open or incompletely sealed would be fatal. Choosing the lesser of two evils, I opened the sealed faceplate. Cockpit pressure was 28,000 feet. Without breathing, I quickly wiped off the moisture inside the faceplate and snapped it closed.

I focused on the instrument panel. What was working and what was inoperative? Hydraulic pressure, oil pressure, engine gas temperature, and fuel pressure gauges were inoperative, but the aircraft would fly without these gauges as long as the engine kept running and nothing else failed. The cockpit temperature control was stuck in its present position, but the windscreen would not frost over as long as the engine ran.

The electrically driven flight indicator was inoperative and couldn't show whether the U-2 was level, descending, climbing, or turning. The gyro compass was inoperative. I would have to rely on the magnetic compass for course headings; although not stabilized, it would point in approximately the right direction. The air-driven "needle and ball" could be used to turn while in clouds. Neither the airspeed indicator nor altimeter required electricity, so they were available. The autopilot became inoperative as soon as the electrical power failed. Autopilot failure would not be critical at lower altitude, but navigating out of this predicament at maximum altitude would require precise control over airspeed, altitude, and heading. Lacking an auto-pilot, navigation aids, most flight instruments, and an electrical system, I knew keeping the U-2 on course and flying for the next several hours would test my piloting skills to the utmost.

As the initial depression wore off, I analyzed the survival problem. The three biggest threats were (1) getting the U-2 down from altitude without flaming out, (2) finding a place away from the jungle where I could bail out or crash-land the U-2 without getting killed, and (3) flying with just the altimeter, airspeed indicator, and the needle and ball through the two weather fronts that were forecast. Far down my survival wish list was making it back to Ezeiza, 1,600 miles away. Using the needle and ball, I started a gradual turn and rolled out of it when the magnetic compass indicated south. I had been airborne nearly four hours.

Getting the U-2 Down to a Safer Altitude

The U-2 was flying near 68,000 feet when the failure occurred—in that narrow airspeed gap between Mach limit and stall we called "coffin corner." The throttle was nearly retarded to the minimum fuel flow position when the electrical failure occurred. Without engine gauges, I was not going to retard the throttle anymore for fear of an engine flameout, which could not be restarted without electrical power. For the next hour and one-half, I improvised a "get down" procedure. (1) Open the faceplate and wipe off the moisture so I could see. Close the faceplate. (2) Push the yoke slightly forward. Carefully watch the airspeed increase as the U-2 descends a few hundred feet. As the airspeed approaches the Mach limit, a burble will be felt. (3) Relax the yoke pressure and let the U-2 climb until the airspeed decreases to a safe number. (4) Repeat the procedure until the aircraft is below 45,000 feet. This was a painfully slow process, taking three or four minutes each cycle. I had to be very cautious not to exceed the airspeed limits.

At first, only 200 feet would be lost descending and 100 feet gained when the yoke was relaxed. Each time the procedure was repeated, more altitude was lost. Gradually, the airspeed margins spread, and I could lose more altitude each cycle.

1530. The U-2 was level at 45,000. There were three reasons for stopping the descent at that altitude. If the engine flamed out, I could survive the decompression without relying on the pressure suit working. The second reason was for fuel economy. I could squeeze more range out of the U-2 by remaining at 45,000 rather than descending to a lower altitude. The third reason was to stay above the weather.

Finding a Place to Bail out or Crash-Land

Survival prospects looked a little better at 45,000, but I was still over the jungle and did not know my exact location except that it was five or six hundred miles south of wherever the electrical system failed. A new problem emerged. The weather had deteriorated during the past three hours. I could not see the ground anymore, and high clouds were directly ahead. Hoping that the weather was not too rough, I flew through the clouds at 45,000 using the altimeter and needle, ball, and airspeed to keep the U-2 level and the magnetic compass on a southerly heading. After several minutes, I broke out of the clouds and could see the ground.

People who say it is better to be lucky than skilled were certainly right that day. Directly below the aircraft was the intersection of the same two rivers that I had noticed on the way north. The jungle was passed, the U-2 was apparently on course, and the engine was still running. A few minutes later, a second weather front loomed on the horizon. I flew through it, depending again on altimeter, needle, ball, and airspeed.

1645. The electrical failure had occurred nearly three hours before. The weather cleared, and I guessed Paraguay was below. Now all I had to worry about was crash-landing in Chaco Indian country.

Revising the Survival Plan

With a new surge of optimism, I changed my plan. After turning left about 20 degrees by referring to the magnetic compass, I thought it possible to find the Uruguay River. Following that river would lead to Argentina. But a new problem was on my mind. The totalizer showed that fuel was getting low. By nursing the remaining fuel, I might reach Buenos Aires or, in the worst case, be able to crash-land on the flat Pampas.

1730. I found the Uruguay River. It was my saving grace. By following it, I could find the Pampas. When they were in sight, I started a gradual letdown to save fuel.

1800. Buenos Aires was visible in the distance. The totalizer was showing minimal fuel, so I made a straight-in approach to Ezeiza. I hoped Ezeiza Tower would see my wings rocking to signal I had no radio. Ezeiza Tower signaled with a green light signifying I was cleared to land.

1825. The landing was uneventful. After stopping on the runway, two crew chiefs approached in a pickup truck at high speed and inserted the pogos. I taxied to our parking area, shut down the engine, and opened the canopy. The long nightmare was over. My crew chief ran up, climbed a ladder to the cockpit, helped me take off my helmet, and shook hands enthusiastically. "Major Leavitt! Air-Sea Rescue had given up hope when they didn't hear a radio signal for five hours. We all assumed that you were lost somewhere over the jungle. Welcome home!"

I signed off the Form 1. The aircraft had flown eight hours and 25 minutes. It was nearly out of fuel because so much of the flight was below optimum cruising altitude. Maintenance computed only 13 gallons of jet fuel were left in the tank when it was refueled the next day. It also found that the new NiCad battery had not been serviced with battery fluid, causing it to fail immediately when the generator failed. Apparently the instructions from Lockheed didn't state the battery had to be serviced before use.

A favorite saying of many experienced pilots is that "flying consists of hours and hours of boredom interrupted by a few minutes of stark terror!" In this case, the stark terror lasted considerably longer. In later years, I looked back on that flight as my most harrowing experience in an airplane—worse than any of my 252 combat missions or any other peacetime flight. Without exaggerating, it had been a very long, hard day!

Anne had arranged with her parents to take care of our two children while she joined me for a month in Argentina. Our Christmas present to each other was the round-trip fare for her visit. We had a delightful time in Buenos Aires and between missions enjoyed sightseeing and the nightlife in this cosmopolitan city.

When the TDY ended, the Argentine government awarded the U-2 pilots the Aviador Militar Honoris Causa Argentina—their military pilot wings—a nice gesture and greatly appreciated. Shortly afterwards, we returned to Laughlin. The interesting and sometimes exciting tour in Argentina was over, but it was nice to get back home again.

Black Cat Squadron

Spring 1959

After returning to Laughlin, we learned that General Russell was being reassigned. His year as our wing commander was time well spent. The wing had matured and was better organized, and most of the serious operational and maintenance problems were resolved. Russell was replaced in December 1958 by Col Andrew Bratton, another experienced and well-respected commander. Both Russell and Bratton knew how to "separate flyspecks from pepper." Other colonels of unusual competence were added to the wing staff, including Howard Shidal and T. J. Jackson as deputy commanders for operations (DO), John Harvey as base commander, and Ellsworth Powell as deputy commander for materiel.

By 1959 the 4028th was supporting the HASP with detachments at Plattsburgh AFB, New York; Ramey AFB, Puerto Rico; Ezeiza Airport, Argentina; and Eielson AFB, Alaska. Until 1958 training was focused on photographic intelligence. As the Air Force received more U-2s, pilot and maintenance training became more complicated. Modified U-2s were received with side-looking radar and with devices to collect signals intelligence and communications intelligence. The U-2 became a "high-altitude vacuum cleaner"—capable of picking up electronic signals from great distances and returning them for detailed analysis by intelligence experts. This capability has steadily improved for 50 years. The larger, technically advanced "S" series of U-2 lineage remain the most heavily tasked reconnaissance aircraft in the world.

That same spring, six experienced fighter pilots from the Republic of China (ROC) (Taiwan) reported for U-2 training. The U-2 Standardization Branch was responsible for their training and certifying their U-2 qualifications. As might be expected, language difficulties were a problem. To their credit, they studied hard and asked questions until they were satisfied before entering the flying phase in July. One ROC pilot crashed on his first takeoff. He was very distressed by his pilot error accident and the accompanying "loss of face." To avoid further humiliation when he would return to Taiwan, an arrangement was made to send him to Nellis AFB for F-100 training. With welcome assistance from instructors and navigators in the 4028th Squadron, the remaining five passed the standardization checks and graduated from training in September 1959.

A memorable incident was the first night training flight of ROC captain Mike Hua. After flying to Ogden, Utah, using celestial navigation, Mike headed back to Laughlin. Shortly later, the engine flamed out and would not restart. He knew he was over the Rocky Mountains but could not see the ground or the mountains below because of cloud cover. Later, he described the accident in an article about the Black Cat Squadron: "Suddenly, I saw lights at the eleven o'clock position. I had come out of the clouds to find that I was gliding along a narrow valley between tall mountains. . . . As I drew nearer to the lights, I saw an airport. . . . The landing gear did not extend fully. The belly scratched the pavement. The left wing tip struck the shoulder of the runway. The aircraft went into a ground loop and came to rest in one piece. I went into the only lighted building at the airport."[4]

The mountains he missed while descending through clouds into the valley were as high as 14,000 feet. The lights Hua first sighted were automobile lights on a highway leading to Cortez, Colorado. As Mike descended toward the highway, he spotted the only lighted airfield within several hundred miles. The flamed-out U-2 managed to reach the airport but not with enough altitude and airspeed remaining to land on the runway.

About 0500 the following morning, the 4080th Command Post called. I was to fly a T-33 to Cortez carrying a maintenance officer in the backseat, find out what happened, get security posted around the U-2, leave the maintenance officer in charge of the accident scene, and bring Hua back to Laughlin.

After landing at Cortez, I saw the damaged U-2 on the side of the runway. A policeman was keeping the curious away from the cockpit. No sign of Captain Hua. I asked the man sitting at the operations desk in base operations if he had been on duty when the accident occurred. He was still excited as he recounted the strange tale of last night's visit by the mysterious Chinese pilot from outer space. "I was typing a weather report. I heard the door open behind me and somebody walking in. Without turning around, I said 'Just a minute and I'll be with you.' When I turned around, here was this oriental-looking guy in a 'moon suit' saying, 'Maximum security! Maximum security!' I was shook up and typed for five more minutes without knowing what the hell I was typing!"

"Where's the pilot?" I asked the teletype operator. His response really got my attention. "The president of the Rotary

Club came down to see the accident about an hour or two ago, put him in his car, and took him to the Rotary Club luncheon in Cortez."

A local sheriff offered to drive me to the Rotary meeting to get Hua. Training the Chinese was a highly classified program, and I was worried about unwanted publicity linking the Republic of China Air Force (ROCAF) to the U-2 accident. I arrived just as the Rotarians were sitting down to lunch. Hua was seated to the Rotary president's right and was fully decked out in a cowboy shirt, hat, blue jeans, and belt they had given him! After introducing myself, the president invited me to sit on his left. He was obviously very curious about Hua, who had not explained why an Air Force pilot, apparently Chinese, was flying the U-2, or why he had crash-landed in Cortez. His first question was tough.

"He's an Air Force pilot. Is that true?" Answering yes, I bent the truth a bit. A minute later, a puzzled look came over the Rotarian's face, "If he's an American pilot, how come he doesn't speak English better?" My answer stretched the truth a little more, "He was raised in San Francisco's Chinatown and went to Chinese schools there before he entered the Air Force." This answer seemed to placate our host, as he munched a cracker. Before he could ask any more tough questions, the meeting was called to order, quizzing stopped, we finished lunch, and I thanked the Rotary Club for its hospitality to Hua and me. I flew back to Laughlin with Hua in the backseat that afternoon.

Months later, Hua was awarded an Air Force Distinguished Flying Cross for risking his life by descending through clouds that obscured the Rocky Mountains, finding Cortez at night, and successfully landing the flamed-out U-2 with relatively minor damage to the aircraft.

The five ROC pilots returned to Taiwan, but U-2 reconnaissance missions penetrating the Chinese mainland did not begin until 1962. These overflight missions by their Black Cat Squadron continued sporadically until September 1968. This was a joint intelligence operation by the United States and the Republic of China—American U-2s were painted with ROC insignia, ROC pilots were under the command of a ROCAF colonel, overflight missions were planned by Washington, and both countries were recipients of the intelligence gathered over the mainland. Americans in the detachment were said to be Lockheed employees.

ROC pilots flew 102 U-2 missions over denied areas in Communist China, North Korea, and North Vietnam (NVN) from 1962 to 1967. Hua flew 10 of the overflight missions against mainland China from 1962 to 1964. Overflights were stopped in 1967. The United States benefited from these dangerous missions in many ways. Aerial photography precisely located potential military targets within Communist China. We also learned of Chinese Communist (ChiCom) development of nuclear and thermonuclear weapons and located production facilities.

The ChiComs had integrated the Soviet SA-2 surface-to-air-missile (SAM) system into their air defense system by the time U-2 overflights began in 1962. The ChiComs vigorously opposed the overflights with both SAMs and MiG-21 fighters. The United States reacted by installing our latest electronic countermeasures (ECM) in the ROCAF U-2s. Under combat conditions, we were able to validate the effectiveness—and sometimes the ineffectiveness—of American countermeasures against Soviet equipment used by Communist China.

ROCAF pilots paid a steep price for their role in the joint US/ROC U-2 program. Twenty-eight ROCAF pilots entered U-2 training in the years from 1959 to 1973. Forty-three percent became casualties. Six were killed in U-2 accidents. Four were killed on reconnaissance missions. Two more were wounded after being shot down by SA-2 missiles. Both were captured and held by the ChiComs for 20 years.

Hua received the Outstanding Aerospace Engineer Award from Purdue, where he received his PhD after leaving the U-2 program in 1964. He went on to become a lieutenant general in the ROCAF and a key figure in the ROC aircraft industry. His *Air Power History* article gives a detailed explanation of the years the ROCAF U-2 pilots spent in the Black Cat Squadron. General Hua, a highly qualified aeronautical engineer and experienced U-2 pilot, also gave his estimate of the basic problem with U-2 accidents. "The U-2 designers emphasized mission success above safety and controllability."

Traveler's Delight—Siberia via Alaska
March–June 1960

The 4080th Wing received orders to send in early March 1960 a detachment of three U-2s to Eielson AFB, Alaska, to fly 11 photo reconnaissance missions. They would cover Anadyr and other Soviet installations opposite Alaska on the Chukotsky Peninsula, the northern coastline of Siberia as far east as Tiksi, and the eastern coastline of the Kamchatka Peninsula as far south as Petropavlovsk.

The detachment, called Congo Maiden, was commanded by Maj Joe Jackson. The pilots selected were Majors Edward Dixon, John McElveen, James Bedford, and myself. I was eager to go, but Anne, now four months pregnant with our third child, probably was not quite as enthusiastic. But, always the loyal Air Force wife, she accepted the upcoming three-month TDY in good spirits.

Congo Maiden resulted from an apparent compromise of the long-lasting argument between the CIA and Air Force over the control and responsibility for strategic reconnaissance. SAC needed Congo Maiden intelligence for planning because the shortest route for SAC bombers based in the United States to reach many USSR targets was over the Arctic. The Soviets realized this and were locating air bases, air defense radars, and SAMs in Siberia to protect their homeland. Finding "soft spots" in Siberia's air defense network was a vital aspect of SAC war planning.

The 1960 SAC U-2 missions were planned using the US definition of Soviet national airspace—an imaginary line extending only three nautical miles from the Soviet coastline. Flying this close to its coastline improved our chances for good photo coverage, and the United States could claim these flights were "legal." This was a classic example of optimism overcoming experience—the Soviet Union and the United States had no such agreement defining national airspace. Furthermore, there were numerous prior incidents during the Cold War when the USSR destroyed American aircraft flying on the periphery of the USSR or Eastern Europe. The UN Convention on the Law of the Sea, which attempted to define national airspace, did not enter into force until five years after the Cold War ended.

The U-2 pilots never doubted that Congo Maiden flights would be treated as hostile and that the Soviet Air Defense Force (PVO) would destroy, if it could, a U-2 in or near Soviet airspace. A well-publicized incident 23 years later confirmed our opinions. Korean Airlines flight 007 en route from Anchorage, Alaska, to Seoul, Korea, was shot down 200 miles from the Siberian coast by a Soviet interceptor on 1 September 1983. The worldwide reaction to this unwarranted shootdown of a Boeing 747 with 269 passengers convinced the Soviets to explain their justification for shooting down a civilian airliner. The Soviet response to the shootdown of flight 007 was not a mea culpa. To the contrary, the USSR stated the following violations by flight 007 caused the shootdown: flying in Soviet airspace, flying without lights, not responding to communication, and not contacting Soviet air traffic control.[5]

Assuming the Soviets used similar ROEs in earlier years, Congo Maiden flights in 1959 and 1960 would have certainly been considered fair game by the PVO. We flew in airspace claimed to be Soviet, flew both at night and in daytime without lights, maintained radio silence from takeoff until our return to Alaska, and did not file a flight plan or contact Soviet air traffic control.

When the U-2 was at maximum altitude, a Soviet interceptor pilot or GCI controller would have difficulty determining exactly where a U-2 was in relation to the Siberian coastline. It was also very difficult for the U-2 pilot flying 12 miles high to know whether he was within three miles of the ragged Siberian coast, particularly when clouds obscured the view. Whether or not the U-2 was actually in Soviet airspace was really a moot point. If the U-2 were shot down, the USSR would claim an airspace violation, and the United States would deny culpability with a cover story.

We flew our U-2s into Eielson from Laughlin on 11 March. The following two days were spent on orientation briefings and short, local area flights. Survival lectures were of high interest because of the nature of our mission. Several lectures were more relevant to big-game hunters than to U-2 pilots. For example, it was challenging to learn that any polar bear we happened to bump into would be difficult to kill with a powerful rifle, much less with our little .38 caliber pistol. We also were advised that the polar bear's liver was poisonous and eating it would be fatal. It left me wondering—how did I kill the bear in the first place?

What really captured our interest was how to survive a bail-out or crash landing without freezing to death. Our missions required flying over the Bering Sea, Arctic Ocean, frozen ice packs, and snow-covered terrain. We had a big problem: the U-2 survival kit was too small to contain both a parka and a rubber life raft. We could have our choice. Which did I want in my survival kit—parka or life raft?

The parka won. Sitting in a rubber raft in the Arctic Ocean with only a wet pressure suit to keep out the cold did not encourage any serious thinking about long-time longevity. On the other hand, a parka might be just the right thing to keep me warm on a frozen ice pack while I was fighting off hungry polar bears with my .38 pistol! More relevant was the possibility of being shot down or forced to crash-land in Siberia. The solution to surviving that unhappy situation was not promising.

Our three U-2s were parked and maintained in a large heated hangar. All maintenance was performed inside the heated hangar because touching the cold-soaked aluminum skin of the U-2 without wearing winter gloves in the sub-zero March weather was flirting with frostbite. March and early April missions took off at night to reach Siberia during the few hours of daylight. About 15 minutes prior to takeoff time, the U-2 with the pilot already in the cockpit was towed from the hangar to the taxiway nearest the end of the snow-packed runway. Congo Maiden missions required radio silence, so the only conversation with Eielson Tower was a discrete radio check. The tower signaled when it was OK to take off by blinking a green light. Takeoffs had to be on time for pre-computed celestial navigation plots to be accurate.

The missions over the Chukotsky Peninsula, Wrangel Island, and the Bering Sea coastline were accomplished without encountering serious problems. Soviet early warning radar picked up the U-2s before we crossed the Bering Straits, located between the United States and the USSR. SAC seldom informed pilots of mission results but on one occasion did send a translation of radio conversations between a Soviet pilot flying a YAK-28 and a GCI controller. The controller was vectoring the

YAK-28 pilot to intercept the U-2 flying along the Siberian coastline at about 65,000 feet. It went like this:

"Comrade pilot, your unidentified target is directly ahead flying at 10,000 meters [32,800 feet]. Advise when target is in sight. Continue to climb."

"Comrade GCI, pilot here. Level at 10,000 meters. I don't see the target."

"Comrade pilot, your target is now at 15,000 meters [nearly 50,000 feet]. Continue your climb. Advise when you have target in sight."

"Comrade GCI, pilot here. I'm level at 14,000 meters. No target in sight." [A few more minutes pass, both controller and pilot sound irritated.]

"Pilot! Target climbed to 17,000 meters [nearly 56,000 feet]. Target is directly ahead of you. Look sharp!"

[Pilot becomes frustrated as the YAK-28 struggles to climb higher.] "Damn it. I am looking sharp! There's no target ahead."

"Pilot, look sharp! Look sharp! He's right above you, maybe a little higher!"

[Pilot probably wonders what the penalty is to kill a GCI controller.] "I can't go any higher, and there is no target!"

[Then pilot breaks the tension in an excited voice.] "Wait! I have target in sight! It's way above me!"

Very excited, controller answers, "Quick! What kind of airplane is it?"

[Pilot's loud answer probably rang a few alarms at PVO HQ.] "I don't know, but it's a great big BOMBER!"

Judging from this conversation, the GCI controller and pilot knew nothing about U-2 operations. Apparently the information about U-2 border penetrations was closely held by the PVO commanders and not passed to subordinate units. Twenty-three U-2 flights by CIA pilots had overflown Soviet airspace by 30 April 1960. Soviet Air Defense Force commanders had been humiliated and chastised by Nikita Khrushchev and other Communist Party leaders for their failures to intercept and destroy these U-2s. Although information about U-2 overflights was withheld from the Soviet populace, protests were occasionally sent through diplomatic channels to the United States.

By 1960 Soviet leaders knew the U-2 was a reconnaissance aircraft and could collect valuable information about Soviet defense capabilities. This in itself was their sufficient reason to attack and destroy any U-2 flying over or near the Soviet Union. The United States response was to keep Congo Maiden flights highly classified and minimize Soviet chances to intercept and destroy the U-2s. Added secrecy was gained by taking off at night and keeping radio silence until back over Alaska.

In the 1950s and '60s, the Soviet Union was a tightly closed society and was hostile toward intruders, especially foreign aircraft. The Cold War history contains many hair-trigger responses by the Soviet PVO resulting in the destruction of unarmed military and civilian aircraft. The prevailing attitude on our side of the Iron Curtain recognized the danger. Eisenhower understood that U-2 operations against the USSR were provocative and was generally resistant to authorizing their use. John D. Eisenhower quoted from a 1958 Memorandum of Conference with his father. "Nothing would make me request the authority to declare war more quickly than violation of our airspace by Soviet aircraft."

The longest mission scheduled was to Tiksi on the Siberian north coast. In February I flew the preselected U-2 for the Tiksi mission on two practice flights in the United States. Both flights showed this U-2 was capable of making the round-trip from Eielson AFB, Alaska, to Tiksi with 10–15 gallons of fuel remaining on landing (1 percent of total fuel capacity, or about five minutes of flying time). In the event computations were incorrect and there was not enough fuel to reach Eielson, the alternative was an emergency landing at Nome, Alaska.

During the long Siberian winter, there is insufficient sunlight for a U-2 to photograph construction and other activities along the northern coastline. Even when the sun becomes visible for a few hours each day in late February and early March, it is so low on the horizon that good photography is not possible. SAC Global Weather predicted the first chance to complete a successful mission would occur in late March. SAC was reluctant to push the mission much later than March because fog and snowstorms are unpredictable during the Arctic spring and summer months.

The flight plan required grid navigation, augmented by celestial navigation, while flying across the Arctic Ocean to the flat Siberian coast. Navigating to Tiksi was further complicated by the difficulty in determining where the flat, snow-covered Arctic Ocean ends and the flat, snow-covered shore of northern Siberia begins.

The scheduled mission to Tiksi was cancelled several times because of poor weather in the target area. Cancellations were frustrating to say the least. Because the takeoff was scheduled for about 0600, wake-up was 0300. This meant going to bed about 1900 the previous night. After tossing and turning for a couple of hours, I would be awakened by a knock on the door about 0200. "Major Leavitt, sorry to wake you up, but SAC just called. The weather looks bad in the target area, and the mission has been rescheduled until tomorrow."

On 27 March the weather broke. Promptly at 0600 on a cold Alaskan morning, my U-2 was airborne. Everything went as planned until the U-2 reached the first checkpoint. I was a few minutes early, but the fuel reading was as predicted. By the time the U-2 crossed the Alaska coast outbound to Siberia, I was eight minutes ahead of schedule, and the aircraft was only at 63,000 feet and climbing slowly (see fig. 3).

Was a tailwind increasing the ground speed? Probably not—the winds were usually quite light at this altitude. Checking the outside air temperature gauge provided the answer. Arctic air at this altitude was significantly warmer than what we had planned. Warmer air means lighter air and accounted for the increase in true airspeed and the decrease in max altitude. The trade-off in fuel consumption was about even. By the time the sun began to rise above the horizon, another hour had passed.

The last celestial navigation preplots were based on sun lines. Since the aircraft was flying much faster than planned, the preplots were not much help but did confirm I was running ahead of schedule. Looking down through the viewfinder, there were no distinguishable features below—just miles of snow-covered ice in all directions.

I was briefed that a ridgeline of ice might separate the Siberian coast from the frozen ocean. Glare off the ice and snow was severely restricting visibility ahead of the aircraft, and I never saw a ridgeline. I was mentally cursing the SAC planners who had ordered this "mission impossible." Time was running out. Where were the New Siberian Islands, the Siberian coast, and the strait leading to Tiksi?

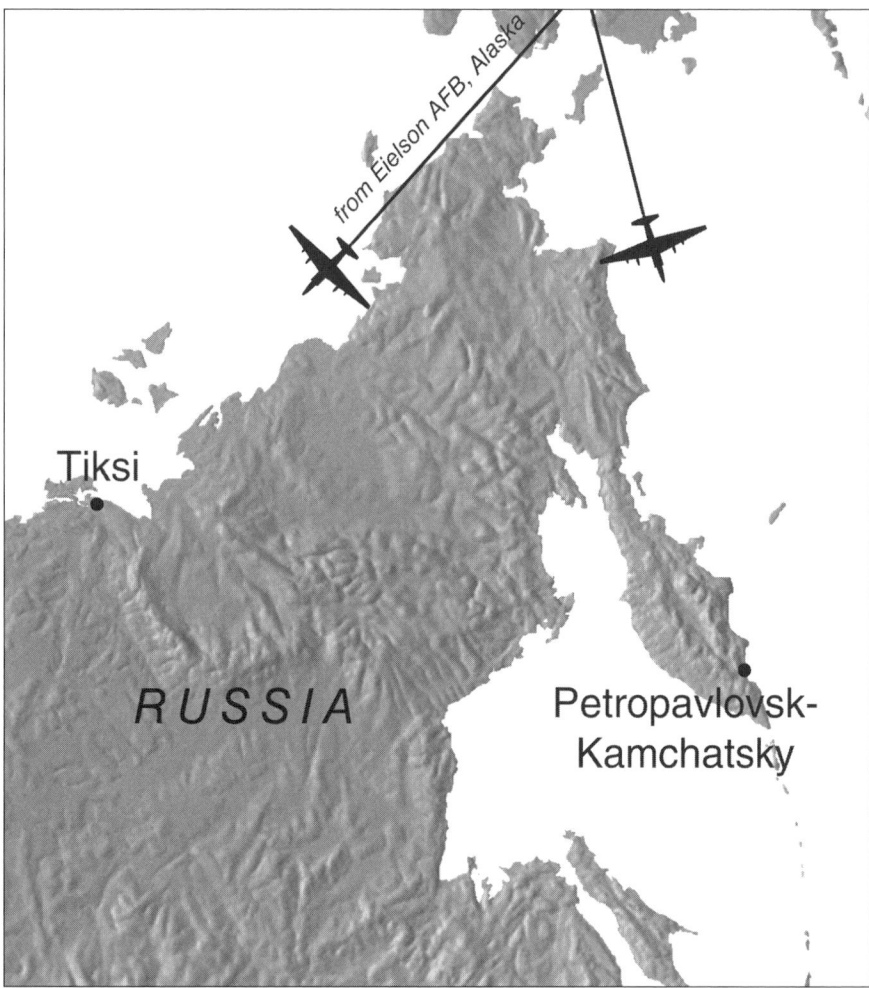

Figure 3. Eielson AFB to Tiksi and Petropavlovsk-Kamchatsky. Traveler's delight . . . Shown are two long reconnaissance missions Leavitt flew from Eielson AFB, Alaska. The first mission to Tiksi on the north coast of Siberia on 27 March 1960 was unsuccessful because of restricted visibility. The long mission on 30 April 1960 to Petropavlovsk-Kamchatsky was flown at the same time Gary Powers (on the other side of the international date line) was shot down over Sverdlovsk.

U-2 cameras were turned on. A few minutes later, I knew from the elapsed time that the U-2 must be over Siberia, but no landmarks were visible. I wasn't quite ready to admit failure and return to Eielson, so I flew ahead for three or four more minutes hoping to find some feature that would establish my location.

While taking one last look to my right rear and away from the reflecting sun rays, I could see the bay where Tiksi was located. I banked the U-2 toward Tiksi and flew by it a few minutes later before heading northeast and away from Siberia. After avoiding direct flight over the New Siberian Islands, I headed for Eielson, over four hours away.

The rapidly sinking sun left just enough twilight to see the desolate Siberian coast and mountain ridges to my right as the U-2 passed by the northeast side of the Chukotsky Peninsula. It was dark when the U-2 crossed the Bering Strait. Twinkling lights from little fishing villages along the Alaskan shoreline became visible. Those villages looked like Miami Beach compared to Siberia.

After landing, I completed the paperwork, debriefed the mission, and reported overflying Siberia for approximately 15-20 minutes. The Soviets either didn't notice or didn't want to admit another failure because they never filed a complaint. The mission had to be repeated because there was not enough sunlight to provide imagery. Ed Dixon repeated the mission three weeks later when there was more sunlight.

On the 15th of April, I flew a much shorter mission over Anadyr and the Chukotsky Peninsula. I saw some following contrails well below the U-2 but could not identify the type of interceptors. All the targets were photographed without any interference from clouds or fog. It was also a bright, clear day in Alaska, and the snow-covered peak of Mount McKinley, the tallest mountain in the United States, was a magnificent sight to see on the return to Eielson.

April is an astonishing month in central Alaska. The days rapidly grow longer, the snow-packed runway melts away, and by the end of the month, flowers are beginning to bloom. Now and then, the nighttime sky is lit with a startling display of Northern Lights. We were all acclimated to cold weather by this time. On sunny days with the temperature just above freezing, we enjoyed playing volleyball outside the big hangar—usually officers versus Airmen, or skins versus T-shirts.

There was one more long reconnaissance mission to fly. Petropavlovsk on the southern tip of the Kamchatka Peninsula was a major seaport, naval base, and military headquarters. SAC planners needed to know what was there and how it was defended. Unlike middle-of-the-night wake-ups, takeoff wasn't scheduled until 1100, so I slept until 0700, ate a leisurely breakfast, and went through the usual routines prior to takeoff. Three years earlier at the Ranch, these procedures had seemed strange. Now they were just part of a day's work. In my effectiveness report covering the period, the rating officer noted: "He has flown more in the unit aircraft [U-2] than any other pilot."

It was a very interesting flight. The weather was excellent across Alaska and down the Siberian coast and the Kamchatka Peninsula. I flew southwest more than 1,100 nautical miles photographing airfields and radar sites along the way. Cloud coverage over Petropavlovsk was scattered to broken. After circling Petropavlovsk seeking cloud-free camera angles, I headed back to the northeast along the coast. On the way home, Soviet fighters chased my U-2 for several hundred miles. Looking through the viewfinder, I could see their contrails and imagine them struggling to reach my altitude. As a flight ran low on fuel, another would replace it. I found their futile pursuit strangely exhilarating.

Weather was fairly clear when I crossed the Bering Strait again and flew the remaining 700 nautical miles to Eielson and landed that night with minimum fuel. The flight had lasted 9:10 hours and covered more than 3,800 nautical miles—the longest flight I made in a U-2. It was 2010 on 30 April 1960. It was also the last Congo Maiden mission flown for a reason we wouldn't know for another day or two.

A message arrived on Monday from SAC grounding our U-2 detachment until further notice. There was no explanation. Our speculations centered on the possibility of another U-2 accident. A day or two later, a radio broadcast said there was a missing U-2 that had gone down in Turkey near Lake Van. This was bad news; we all had friends flying with the CIA, and we knew where CIA detachments were located. It was possible that a friend had been killed in that accident. On 3 May, the true story began to unfold.

"Oh What a Tangled Web We Weave When First We Practice to Deceive"—Sir Walter Scott

In early 1960, President Eisenhower was under heavy pressure from the CIA to determine the status of Soviet ICBM development and deployment. Gen Thomas S. Power, CINCSAC, had raised serious questions about SAC being able to survive a Soviet ICBM attack. Power argued that the Soviets had more deployed ICBMs than the United States and that their advantage was increasing. The US reconnaissance satellite program in 1960 had not yet matured and could not provide sufficient coverage of the USSR to either prove or disprove Power's claim.

Under pressure, a reluctant President Eisenhower approved one more CIA U-2 flight to resolve the ICBM issue but set a revised flight deadline of not later than 1 May 1960 because of the Paris summit conference with the USSR beginning on 16 May. The unforeseen tragedy of the final CIA U-2 flight resulted in the grounding of our U-2s.

The first publicity about this ill-fated final flight came from a radio broadcast. It repeated a cover story that a NASA high-altitude weather reconnaissance aircraft with a civilian pilot on board flying from Turkey was missing near Lake Van. We knew all the CIA U-2 pilots based at Adana AB, Turkey, and were concerned about who was on board and missing.

We seriously doubted the circumstances described in the cover story prepared by the CIA and released by the White House on 3 May. This cover story stated that a NASA weather reconnaissance aircraft, piloted by a civilian, had inadvertently penetrated the Soviet Union after taking off from Adana. When the pilot became unconscious from lack of oxygen, the aircraft had continued to fly on autopilot, causing the inadvertent penetration. When this cover story was released, the CIA did not know exactly what had happened to the U-2 overflight mission flown on 1 May, except that it was missing without radio contact.

What was the truth? On 1 May, a U-2 piloted by Gary Francis Powers flying at 70,000 feet over Sverdlovsk in central Russia was shot down by an SA-2 missile. When NASA released this ill-advised cover story, the Soviets had already interrogated Powers, located the camera film and flight plan from the downed U-2, and knew the flight had originated in Pakistan, not Turkey. They knew the United States was lying about hypoxia being the cause of the overflight after capturing Powers. Aircraft equipment, the pilot's flight plan, and film recovered from the crash site proved the United States was lying about it being a NASA weather research aircraft. Clearly, it was a US military reconnaissance aircraft flown by a former military pilot working for the CIA.

Eisenhower had accepted the assertions of the CIA that the pilot could not survive if the U-2 were hit by a missile at high altitude. Why CIA director Allen Dulles and Richard Bissell, second in charge at the CIA, would make such an assertion to the president is difficult to understand. It was impossible to accurately predict whether a U-2 pilot would survive if his aircraft were shot down. The CIA must have previously considered the possibility that a U-2 pilot might be captured after being shot down, or it would not have made cyanide pills available to a pilot before a mission. Contrary to erroneous American press reports that emerged after the incident, U-2 pilots had no obligation to commit suicide rather than be captured. Pilots did not view suicide as an option unless repeated, extreme torture was unbearable.

Another factor the American press later exploited was the explosive charge on the right-hand canopy rail. Why did Powers not blow up the aircraft after the missile struck? I flew the U-2 well over 100 times. Each flight, I would look at that explosive device and wonder how a pilot wearing a pressure suit could leave an out-of-control U-2 in time after starting the firing sequence for the explosive charge. A design engineer drinking coffee and pulling only one G while sitting at his desk in Lockheed's Skunk Works might think this explosive device was practical—not me. Having fought to eject from an out-of-control F-84 in the Korean War, I had a hard time imagining how any pilot could be expected to focus on destroying the airplane rather than saving his own life during an out-of-control emergency.

Khrushchev, with the unwitting assistance of the CIA, had set a trap for President Eisenhower that became one of the most embarrassing diplomatic blunders in American history. The serious fallout from the incident traced back to events in 1959 when Khrushchev toured the United States with President Eisenhower. There seemed to be some relaxing of Cold War tensions when, after the tour, Khrushchev spoke of "peaceful coexistence" with the United States and its allies. Eisenhower and Khrushchev agreed to a major powers summit conference in Paris on 16 May 1960, with the goal of further reducing international tensions. The U-2 incident destroyed that opportunity, if it really existed, in 1960.

A series of notes and pronouncements were exchanged between the Soviet Union and the United States concerning the U-2 incident, summarized below.

- US Note to the USSR, 6 May 1960: "As announced on 3 May, an unarmed NASA weather research aircraft has been missing since 1 May. Civilian American pilot is Francis Gary Powers. Request Soviet Government provide facts of investigation and fate of pilot."

- Khrushchev speech to USSR Council of Ministers, 7 May 1960: "Data from the investigation leave no doubts with respect to the purpose of [the 1 May] flight. . . . This aircraft was specially equipped for reconnaissance [with] apparatus for aerial photography for detecting the Soviet radar network. . . . [There are] films of Soviet defense and industrial establishments [and] a tape recording of [Soviet radar] signals. . . . The pilot also stated that he served [in a program] under cover of [NASA which] is engaged in high altitude military reconnaissance. . . . [This] completely refuted the U.S. State Department's [absurd explanation]. . . . American authorities apparently seek to return . . . to the worst times of the 'cold war.'"

- Eisenhower's news conference, 11 May 1960:

  (1) There is a need for intelligence-gathering activities.

  (2) Intelligence-gathering activities have a "special and secret character."

  (3) Activity is "distasteful but a vital necessity"—the reason for "Open Skies" policy.

  (4) U-2 incident must not detract from whole range of East-West relations.

  "I will have nothing further to say about this matter."

- Eisenhower at Summit Conference opening on 16 May 1960: "The United States has made no threat [to continue overflights]. . . . These flights were suspended after the recent incident and are not to be resumed."

- Khrushchev at Summit Conference opening on 16 May 1960: The US government must "firstly, condemn the unpardonable provocative actions of the US Air Force in regard to the Soviet Union and, secondly, renounce continuing such actions and such a policy against the USSR in the future. . . . So that the present issues may simmer down . . . we feel that the best thing will be to postpone the Heads of Government conference for some six or eight months." [Khrushchev then walked out, and the conference ended in failure.]

The 16 May 1960 Paris Conference turned out to be a diplomatic disaster for the United States because of the U-2 loss on 1 May. The president of the United States was embarrassed in front of cooperative allies by having to admit to a program about which the details had been withheld. Furthermore, the huge amount of valuable intelligence gathered from the CIA U-2 program was overshadowed by the CIA cover story and misleading information provided the president following the shootdown.

Congo Maiden ended with my flight down the Kamchatka Peninsula. Someone noted the coincidence in dates between Powers's flight and mine. My takeoff was on 30 April in Alaska, but after crossing the international date line in the Bering Straits, it was 1 May in Siberia. About the time Powers was shot down, I was heading back to Alaska from Petropavlovsk.

When the president announced the end of U-2 reconnaissance against the Soviet Union, we all speculated about the future of the U-2 program. Before leaving for Alaska, a friendly colonel from HQ SAC told me that satellite reconnaissance was coming and would replace U-2 overflights. When we volunteered for U-2s, the verbal commitment was "three years and your choice of any flying job in the Air Force." With more than three years in the U-2, I decided to volunteer for a fighter assignment when we returned to Laughlin.

After standing down until 13 May, we began flying HASP missions—I flew five missions before the end of the month. On 8 June, we flew back to Laughlin via the Pacific Ocean. The Canadians would not give us permission to overfly Canada because the U-2 incident was such a touchy subject.

It was great to be home again. Since July last year, I had been TDY for six of the past 12 months. Even the dog thought I was a stranger. I called SAC Personnel and reminded the officer of the promise of three years in U-2s and having the choice of any flying job in the Air Force. "How about a fighter assignment in USAFE?" The personnel officer instantly corrected me. "The promise was three years in U-2s and *any flying job in SAC.*"

After a long pause and some rebellious thoughts, I asked, "What's the newest aircraft in SAC?" He said, "The B-52H is coming into the SAC inventory early next year at Wurtsmith AFB [Michigan], but you have never been in bombers." I asked, "What are the requirements to become a B-52H aircraft commander?" After a brief discussion, he conceded that I met the flying time requirements. "You'll have to convince the wing commander. He only wants experienced B-36 or B-47 aircraft commanders."

The next week, I took a T-33 cross-country to Wurtsmith AFB. The 379th Bomb Wing (Heavy) was just organizing, and B-52Hs would not arrive until winter. The timing was opportune; it left time to attend B-52 school. The DO colonel looked shocked after looking at my flight records. He saw I was an ex-fighter pilot. After a long pause, he said politely, "Captain Leavitt [I was no longer a 'spot' major], we're not taking anybody without B-47 or B-36 experience. You're not a bomber pilot and aren't qualified."

After advising him that SAC HQ said I met the qualifications, he said with emphasis, "You're not qualified. You should have called me before flying up here." We had reached an impasse. "Colonel, if you don't mind, let me talk to the wing commander." "OK," he said, "but Colonel Kunkel will tell you the same thing."

Deflated but persistent, I knocked on Col John Kunkel's door. We talked for a few minutes about why I wanted to be a B-52H aircraft commander. After looking over my flying records, he said, "Welcome aboard! We're glad to have you." I had passed the entrance exam and was on my way to flying "BUFFs"—Big Ugly Friendly Fellows.

Looking Back—The Early U-2 Program
1954–1960

President Eisenhower took office in 1953 and called for a "New Look" at our overall defense strategy. By then, the USSR had demonstrated a nuclear weapon capability, had publicly displayed long-range bombers, and had acquired the technology to build rockets. Our Cold War enemy was apparently building an offensive force capable of waging nuclear war. Eisenhower's response was to emphasize nuclear deterrence by increasing both our air defenses and strategic offensive forces. Although defending against bomber attacks would solve part of the problem, we needed enough offensive systems—bombers and missiles—to deter the USSR from attacking the United States.

How much strategic nuclear capability was enough? The United States had little definitive intelligence about USSR strategic forces. Needing answers, Eisenhower urged Khrushchev to accept an Open Skies policy that would allow both nations to overfly each other with reconnaissance aircraft. When Khrushchev turned down Eisenhower's Open Skies offer, the United States sought a very high-altitude reconnaissance aircraft that could safely overfly Soviet air defenses and photograph large swaths of the Soviet Union.

Eisenhower appointed James Killian, president of MIT, to chair his Technological Capabilities Panel (TCP). Killian appointed Edwin Land, of Polaroid camera fame, to head the intelligence subcommittee of the TCP. The U-2 program resulted from their findings and recommendations. Missing from the TCP committee were highly qualified senior Air Force officers with R&D and operational experience.

In his report to Allen Dulles dated 5 November 1954, Land reasoned the CIA, not the Air Force, should develop and operate the U-2. The principal reason seems to have been maintaining project secrecy. Convinced that Lockheed's Skunk Works design by aeronautical genius Kelly Johnson would answer the requirement, the secretary of state, secretary of defense, secretary of the Air Force, CIA director and deputy directors, and deputy chief of staff (DCS) for USAF R&D went to Eisenhower for program approval.

Whether the CIA and the other experts overstated the need for the CIA to develop the U-2 and operate the program remains a contentious issue. The National Security Act of 1947 and Executive Order 9877 were the "birth certificates" authorizing the USAF and the CIA. They assigned to the Air Force the responsibility for developing and acquiring systems that would support a variety of air operations. The CIA did not have responsibility for developing aircraft. Turning U-2 development over to the CIA represented a major departure from national policy. This decision in favor of the CIA was certainly a slap in the face to Air Force R&D and to SAC, where strategic reconnaissance had previously been assigned.

Were There Problems with the U-2 in the Early Years?

The biggest problem in the early years was the extremely high accident record. Lockheed's Skunk Works took the U-2 from blueprint to operational status in only 17 months and stayed within budget estimates. This commendable achievement in timing and pricing masked the fact that early-production U-2s had design deficiencies that resulted in too many accidents. Because no previous aircraft had sustained flight at 70,000 feet, unexpected problems developed. A few more months in development and a few more dollars might have corrected these flaws, saved lives, and cut aircraft losses.

In 1978, after becoming Vice-Commander in Chief, SAC, I attended a U-2 Accident Board briefing. With no personal involvement in U-2 operations after 1960, I had scant knowledge of the number of U-2 accidents from 1960 to 1978 or their causes. It was disturbing that this 1978 accident was a replay of U-2 accidents 20 years earlier. I asked, "What is the accident rate for the U-2 program?" No one could answer. USAF, SAC, and the CIA had never disclosed U-2 accident rates. A balanced appraisal of the contract between the government and Lockheed should acknowledge the many pilot fatalities and the many accidents that required replacement U-2s.

Was the CIA Emphasis on Secrecy Effective?

Eisenhower recognized the urgent need for better intelligence on Soviet Union activities but was resistant to any overflight program that could result in the shootdown of American military aircraft. Only after assurance from the "experts" that the USSR could not detect overflights, shoot down the U-2, and capture the pilot did Eisenhower award the project to the CIA.

Awarding the CIA a mandate to develop and operate the U-2 because only the agency could maintain the secrecy required by Eisenhower was wishful thinking. The CIA claimed *the de-*

velopment and introduction of the U-2 could be kept secret under its control. This claim was disproved by accidents and incidents in 1956 and 1957. The CIA claimed *U-2 overflights would not be detected by Soviet radar.* This claim was disproved in 1956 when the first few U-2 missions flew from Wiesbaden, Germany, over Eastern Europe. The CIA claimed that the *United States could deny involvement if a U-2 was ever shot down and the CIA pilot was captured.* This claim was emphatically disproved when CIA pilot Powers was shot down and captured on 1 May 1960. The CIA claimed *only the CIA could effectively manage this highly classified program.* This claim is even more obscure; the CIA used active duty Air Force personnel for training, detachment commanders, and USAF reserve officers for pilots (Powers et al.). The irony is the Soviets kept our U-2 program secret rather than disclose their own weaknesses.

Did the U-2 Resolve Questions Concerning USSR Preparedness?

The first few overflights of Soviet air bases and production facilities ended the allegations about a "bomber gap." SAC clearly possessed a much larger force of long-range bombers. Other U-2 flights disclosed the Soviet Union was developing ICBMs, but they were not yet operational in the mid-1950s. Powers's flight on 1 May 1960 would have provided more data on rocket and ICBM development. These early U-2 flights over the USSR and Eastern Europe gave the United States the necessary confidence to react, but not overreact, to the growing threat imposed by the USSR and its allies.

U-2 operations over the USSR and the other Warsaw Pact nations and U-2 peripheral missions around Soviet borders produced extensive intelligence about enemy air defenses—radars, command and control facilities, surface-to-air missiles, and fighter interceptors. Another important product of this reconnaissance for war planning was the exact location of key industrial targets, transportation facilities, power plants, military bases, seaports, and command centers.

Less publicity has focused on the contributions of the HASP. The HASP provided invaluable information about nuclear weapon development which remains classified today. A by-product of the

HASP is our knowledge of the final disposition of radioactive debris from nuclear explosions. Since atmospheric testing of nuclear weapons ceased in 1958, this data is irreplaceable.

Did Bureaucratic Rivalries and Personal Ambitions, Hidden under the Cloak of Extreme Secrecy, Create the Climate for Problems?

Distorting the many accomplishments of the early U-2 programs in the CIA and SAC is the unfortunate aftermath of Powers's flight on 1 May 1960. In my opinion, the blame for the diplomatic crisis, the collapse of the Paris conference, and the international embarrassment of President Eisenhower must be placed on high-ranking CIA officials.

The CIA knew the Soviets were reacting to the U-2 overflights. At some point during the four years from 1956 to 1960, someone responsible in the CIA should have asked this question: "If the USSR shoots down a U-2 on one of the overflights, don't you believe we should dump the old cover story and admit the United States did it with a military pilot and military aircraft because Khrushchev wouldn't go along with Ike's Open Skies offer?" Instead, after capturing Powers, Khrushchev exposed the CIA cover story as absurd and left Eisenhower and the State Department hanging out to dry.

In the final analysis, neither the CIA nor the USAF could have kept the program at the advertised level of secrecy. There were good reasons to classify at the highest level some aspects of the U-2 program, including aircraft design and performance, camera and other sensor technologies, operational plans, and mission results. Both the Air Force and the CIA were capable of protecting these kinds of data.

Has the SAC U-2 Program Been a Success, and Are U-2s Still Flying?

Five decades have passed since the U-2 first flew. With passing years, new U-2s arrived with better sensors and improved performance and maintainability. The U-2 still flies—not the grandfather anymore, not even the father (U-2R, briefly called the TR-1), but the grandson (U-2S). The U-2 is a veteran of the Cold War, high-altitude nuclear radiation sampling, the Cuban missile crisis, the Vietnam War, the invasion of Panama, Gulf War One, Kosovo, the wars to free Afghanistan and Iraq, and of countless other past crises. It earned the reputation as the most versatile and useful reconnaissance aircraft in the history of aviation. I am proud to have been part of that long line of officers, Airmen, and civilians that made it possible to fly a U-2 "toward the unknown."

Notes

1. From mid-1956 until September 1960, I was involved in the USAF U-2 program. First steps were acceptance and physical qualification, then U-2 training at Area 51, lead crew in the 4028th Squadron at Laughlin AFB, Texas, and nearly three years as Standardization chief, U-2 Branch. In November 1957, Brig Gen A. J. Russell, the newly assigned 4080th Wing commander, tasked me to write the U-2 flight manual. Pat Halloran, Steve Heyser, Rudy Anderson, and Mike Styer—U-2 pilots on the Standardization Board—all contributed to the finished new flight manual.

Chris Pocock, an aviation historian in the UK, has written two U-2 books—*The U-2 Spyplane: Toward the Unknown* and *50 Years of the U-2*. His books include the technical details concerning equipment, costs, aircraft design by Lockheed, program development, personnel involved, reconnaissance accomplished, and political disagreements between the CIA and USAF. Although I have an earlier background in the U-2 than Chris, I find his books to be excellent sources for both technical and historical details covering the long life of this amazing aircraft. As Chris and I have discussed, I do not agree with some of his comments about the early CIA management of the program vis-à-vis the USAF, particularly his negative references to General LeMay and other USAF generals at that time.

2. Trudy became quite a traveler. Born in Albany, Georgia, in 1956, she also lived in Little Rock, Arkansas; Del Rio, Texas; Oscoda, Michigan; McLean, Virginia; Bitburg AB, Germany; Wiesbaden AFB, Germany; and a second time in McLean, Virginia, where she died in 1971. She had nine puppies in Del Rio, Texas, which cured us forever of wanting to breed dogs.

3. Lt Col Joe M. Jackson (colonel, USAF, retired) was awarded the Medal of Honor for rescuing three combat controllers on 12 May 1968 who were left behind after their base in South Vietnam had evacuated and the enemy was closing in. One rescue attempt had already failed when Jackson landed his C-123 amid smoke and explosions from heavy mortar fire. Under heavy fire, he took off with the controllers and returned them safely.

4. Hua, "Black Cat Squadron," 7.

5. British Broadcasting Corporation (BBC), "1983: Korean Airliner 'Shot Down.'"

229

Chapter 6

B-52 Aircrew
Major—1960–62

Changing from the High to the Mighty
Deterrence—1960–62

Life at Laughlin was not dull. A few days before Mary was born, Anne used a garden hoe to kill an eight-foot rattler that curled up on our doorstep after shedding its skin! Aside from rattlesnakes, Del Rio was a friendly city, and we enjoyed our association with several civilian families and were active in the local Episcopal church. Across the Rio Grande was Ciudad Acuña with a bullring and "Ma" Crosby's Macarena restaurant. We always speculated about her excellent steaks—were they a by-product of today's bullfight? Only aircraft on official business could land at Laughlin AFB, so our visitors were limited. There were exceptions. One Friday afternoon John Wayne and his son Patrick came into our U-2 squadron operations and swapped stories with the pilots. The Waynes were filming *The Alamo* near Del Rio.

On 10 August, Mary was born. Shortly after leaving the hospital for home, Anne had a life-threatening hemorrhage. I knew nothing about the care and maintenance of a baby only three days old. Without asking for help, the phones began ringing. The next-door neighbor, a trained nurse, and another neighbor took turns taking care of Mary. Other wives brought food and watched the house and kids while I stayed near Anne at the hospital. Air Force doctors and nurses in the base hospital worked around the clock and saved Anne's life. Anne recuperated, and several days later life returned to normal. This emergency left an unforgettable impression on how fortunate we were to be an Air Force family. I am doubly thankful—saving Anne and giving us a wonderful daughter, Mary.

Transfer orders from the high-flying U-2 to the mighty B-52H came in September 1960. After 10 years flying alone in single-engine fighters and U-2s, strapping into the left seat of an eight-engine aircraft weighing a half-million pounds and depending upon five other crew members, B-52 crew duty promised to be a different flying experience. Offsetting the anticipation was apprehension. From a career viewpoint, flying B-52s was the mainstream of SAC business. But the colonel at Wurtsmith AFB had said, "You've never been in bombers before and aren't qualified to be an aircraft commander." What would happen if he were right?

After arriving at Wurtsmith AFB, we moved into the new family housing, and I reported for work. With no B-52s on the base, there was not much to do. They needed an instrument instructor pilot (IP), so after a local checkout, I gave instrument checks in the T-33 and flew as copilot in a KC-135 tanker. Gradually, other crew members and their families arrived from B-47 and B-36 bases around the country. Some viewed me as a "bastard at the family reunion" because of my lack of bomber experience, but all were generous in offering advice about SAC policies and procedures.

In November I drove to Castle AFB, California, for B-52 crew training (academic phase). The first few days were mind-boggling! Learning all the technical data and emergency procedures for an aircraft with eight engines, multiple hydraulic systems, a myriad of flight and engine instruments, complicated primary and secondary electrical buses, multiple generators and alternators, fuel systems that included air refueling, both upward and downward ejection seats, complex armament systems, ECM, radars, radios, and navigation aids—all tied together with circuit breakers and switches galore—was a challenge. Adding to the confusion was an unfamiliar nomenclature for some systems. As an example, hydraulic "pumps" had suddenly become hydraulic "packs."

Finally, it began to make sense. Before falling asleep one night, I visualized four F-84Fs fastened together in flight with one cockpit controlling everything. The B-52 did not look like this, but the image helped clarify the complexity. By the time the academic phase ended, I was ready for flight training.

During the Christmas holidays, the Air Force announced the annual promotion list for majors. The promotion board considered two categories of officers eligible for promotion. The "primary zone" category that year included captains with 12 or more years' service as a commissioned officer. The "below the zone" category included captains with 10 to 12 years' service as a commissioned officer. About 10 percent of the promotions to major were below the zone. I was fortunate to be included in that group.

B-52 training (flying phase and "H" difference) started in late January 1961 at Walker AFB, Roswell, New Mexico. Our newly formed B-52H crew included a helicopter pilot as copilot. An experienced B-47 radar navigator, Capt Jim Karpowicz, assumed the important responsibility for radar navigation and bombing. Two young lieutenants—Denny Smith and Bob Monsell—were assigned as navigator and ECM operator, respectively. Jim Karpowicz was exceptionally helpful in bringing the two younger officers to high levels of proficiency. The tail gunner, SSgt Larry Tobias, was a man with unique talents. He thoroughly enjoyed betting nonbelieving new gunners that he could flip a playing card over the top of our squadron operations building. The standard bet was a fifth of Jack Daniels. His trick seemed impossible, but Larry kept his bar stocked with "JD" bought by the nonbelievers.

When the Big Day, 31 January 1961, arrived for the first of our 10 training flights, we were ready. During my Air Force career, I flew more than 40 different kinds of Air Force aircraft. First flights were always interesting but not always memorable. My first flight in a B-52 was memorable. Taxi, takeoff, and climb went smoothly. The instructor pilot was visibly relaxed as we rendezvoused with a KC-97 tanker. Approaching the air-refueling boom, I was thinking, "What a piece of cake. I've air refueled many times in fighters. No sweat! This will show the IP what a smooth hookup really means."

I flew the B-52 into the refueling envelope. The boom made a nice "plunk" as it contacted our open air-refueling receptacle. Fuel started to flow. Everything was going well until the B-52 drifted a little left. Not a problem, I thought; I will just turn the yoke a little to the right for the necessary correction. Oops! The aircraft started moving left instead of right. That was unexpected, so I turned the yoke a little more to the right. Wow! Now, the airplane was moving too rapidly to the right. Within seconds, the boom operator signaled an outer limit disconnect. The IP looked perturbed,

"You have air refueled before, haven't you?" Properly humbled, I muttered, "Roger, but it's been awhile."

We left the tanker after several more frustrating attempts to air refuel and completed the other mission requirements. As we taxied to the parking area after making a good landing, the IP patiently explained that the B-52E had spoilers on each wing. The spoilers aid the airplane in turns by "spoiling" the lift on the down wing. The unexpected movement in the opposite direction begins when the yoke is first turned in the desired direction. As the spoiler starts to rise, it provides some lift and raises the wing. The extended spoiler quickly overcomes this lift with more drag, and the airplane turns in the same direction as the yoke. I was overcorrecting because of this effect.

After another flight, I had the spoiler situation under control, but a tough air-refueling requirement lay ahead. The aircraft commander had to refuel for 10 minutes without disconnecting and take on board 100,000 pounds of jet fuel. The mechanical controls on the B-52E were not power-boosted, and 10 minutes on the end of an air-refueling boom proved to be a wearisome task. After 10 minutes' refueling, I looked forward to the "H" model with power-boosted controls that would make air refueling much easier. All in all, I enjoyed flying the B-52E and felt very confident after completing the course—thanks to the excellent instruction by Captain Roberts.

Several of us usually ate our evening meals at the Walker AFB Officers' Club. One night, we found the main dining room doors closed. Behind the closed doors, a "special" meeting was under way, and we could not enter. It was the John Birch Society, a semisecret, extreme anticommunist organization with strong political overtones. Although military officers were overwhelmingly opposed to Communism, the John Birch Society was out of place in the Walker AFB Officers' Club. We ate our dinners in another room and exchanged opinions during dinner about the incident.

I believed then and continue to believe that Americans serving in the military must be able to exercise their right to vote but should not be subjected to political pressure on a military reservation or by persons senior in rank or position. The armed forces of the United States depend upon the continuing support of Congress and the president for preparedness.

Since political power shifts back and forth between our political parties, bipartisan support is required to equip and operate our military forces. History has not been kind to nations such as Nazi Germany, Fascist Italy, and Communist Russia that depended upon a tight alignment between dictators and their military leaders.

After B-52E flying training ended in March, our crew moved to Wurtsmith AFB, home of the 379th Bomb Wing. By the end of June, the wing authorization of 16 B-52Hs had arrived. Our crew began B-52H training 17 June 1961.

The New Guy in any military organization has to establish credibility and gain the confidence of both superiors and subordinates. As a B-52H aircraft commander with no bomber experience and no previous responsibility for an aircrew, I had to move quickly before the opportunity for acceptance was lost and negative opinions formed. It seemed there were several ways to do this, but most important were flying the B-52H safely and accomplishing the required aircrew training objectives professionally.

The B-52H initially had a serious technical problem. Eight turbojet engines hung in twin pods underneath the wings. A constant speed drive in each twin pod connected an engine to an alternating current (AC) generator. The four generators powered the AC electrical systems throughout the aircraft. One of the first B-52Hs delivered to Wurtsmith suffered serious damage when a driveshaft overheated, caught fire, and caused the engine to catch fire. Maj Bill Gramprie, the IP on the burning aircraft, landed 18 minutes later. The Wurtsmith Fire Department extinguished the fire before it expanded beyond the engine pod and saved the aircraft. The manufacturer later modified the constant speed drives.

On a night low-level simulated bombing mission over a radar bombing site (RBS) in Missouri, one of the four engines that furnish electrical power failed on our aircraft. Loss of one engine was not a serious problem. I called Wurtsmith Command Post and received approval to continue the training mission. Our second target was a low-level RBS in Mississippi. We flew further south, and after completing the bombing run in Mississippi, a second engine failed with subsequent loss of the AC electrical generator. I aborted the mission and headed for home.

After reaching cruising altitude near the SAC base at Blytheville, Arkansas, we lost a third engine and the third AC generator. At that point, I declared an emergency and landed at Blytheville without further incident. That was the only emergency or serious malfunction I experienced while flying a B-52H.

In three months that passed quickly, our crew flew over 100 hours and became combat ready. The crew did well except for the copilot with the helicopter background. After failing an instrument check in July, he was replaced by an excellent young pilot, Lt Don Milliken. October capped our training as a bomber crew. Crew R-12 went on alert for the first time on a beautiful fall day.

The northern woods surrounding Wurtsmith were changing to their autumnal colors. Lakes and rivers surrounded Wurtsmith AFB. The green pine and white birch trees along the riverbanks marked the way as the picturesque Au Sable finished its casual trip from the forestlands of north-central Michigan down through the small city of Oscoda and emptied into Lake Huron. Small whitecaps and two or three sailboats did little to disturb the otherwise tranquil waters of Lake Huron. Now and then, a B-52 or KC-135 taking off would break the silence. To my ears, USAF jet engine noise was always the Sound of Freedom.

SAC's strategic bombardment mission was the backbone of our national deterrence policy in 1961. Pres. John F. Kennedy had announced a new ground-alert policy: 50 percent of SAC's bombers and tankers would be on alert. To meet Kennedy's requirement, the number of aircrews increased to a ratio of 1.8 aircrews per assigned aircraft. By July 1961, SAC met the new goal. General Power, who had replaced General LeMay as CINCSAC in 1957, informed the press, "These planes are bombed up and they don't carry bows and arrows." He also announced to Congress an airborne alert capability. "We in the Strategic Air Command have developed a system known as airborne alert where we maintain airplanes in the air 24 hours a day, loaded with bombs, on station, ready to go to target. . . . We must impress Mr. Khrushchev that we have it, and that he cannot strike this country with impunity."[1]

The most important duty in an aircrew's life at Wurtsmith was alert duty. Approximately one-half of the B-52s and KC-135 tankers were always on alert. An APU attached to each aircraft provided electrical power. At any hour of the day or night, without warning, the Klaxon might ring. The crew chief and maintenance Airmen would then race to turn on the APU while the aircrew ran from the alert facility, boarded the B-52, started engines, radioed the command post, and prepared to taxi for takeoff. It was amazing to see how quickly these half-million pound aircraft could start, taxi, and be on the runway ready for takeoff. Only afterwards would the aircrews learn whether this was a practice alert or "the real McCoy."

After reporting for alert duty, we inspected our assigned B-52H and placed helmets and other personal equipment by our seats. The bomb bay was loaded with four thermonuclear bombs varying in mega tonnage. Two Hound Dogs (AGM-28 air-to-ground attack missiles), each with approximately one-megaton yield, hung on wing pylons. The atomic bombs dropped on Hiroshima and Nagasaki yielded around 20 kilotons each—equivalent to exploding *20 thousand tons* of TNT. A one-megaton yield is equivalent to exploding *one million tons* of TNT, or 50 times the yield of the bombs dropped on Hiroshima and Nagasaki. Although damage expectancies are not directly proportional to yield, the weapon loads carried on one B-52H above would cause immeasurable damage. Seeing these weapons made an indelible impression of the awesome responsibility assigned to a B-52H crew. Americans should be truly thankful that the Cold War ended without a nuclear exchange and without the loss of millions of lives on both sides of the Iron Curtain.

Aboard each alert aircraft were the mission folders and authentication documents required for positive control of the nuclear weapons. Weapons release documents remained in locked boxes. Both the aircraft commander in the front cockpit and the radar navigator in the rear cabin had to agree on message authentication and release authorization from higher authority before weapons release was possible. The bizarre behavior in the satirical movie *Doctor Strangelove or: How I Learned to Stop Worrying and Love the Bomb* was technically and physically impossible in the real world

Alert aircrews and maintenance personnel lived in a closely guarded alert facility next to the fully loaded B-52s and near the end of the takeoff runway. They ate, slept, studied, listened to briefings, watched TV, played cards and ping-pong, and exercised in the alert facility. Alert scheduling varied from time to time. Each bomb wing could control the duration of alert tours. For example, some wings preferred seven days, others four days on alert followed by three days off. Sgt Larry Tobias, our tail gunner, loved alert duty. Larry was an excellent poker player and enjoyed teaching the other sergeants the fine art of "when to hold 'em and when to fold 'em."

As a flight commander, I had supervisory responsibilities in the alert facility. The time spent on alert provided a great opportunity to learn about the details of SAC nuclear operations. Each crew studied and was tested on assigned wartime targets. Crews proved their understanding of procedures to authenticate messages and maintain positive control of nuclear weapons by passing frequent tests. Passing grade was 100 percent, no exceptions.

General Power began an aircrew recognition program in 1958 called "First Team." One aircrew from each SAC wing traveled to SAC headquarters for the occasion. I was the first U-2 pilot selected and was impressed by the eloquence of General Power when he addressed the attendees. His inspirational talk heightened my interest in the writings of Herman Kahn, Albert Wohlstetter, and others. By 1961 I understood the political and military consequences of nuclear deterrence and believed that a well-equipped, highly trained SAC was the best hope for peace.

While I was on alert in late 1961 or early 1962, General Power sent a SAC team to each bomb wing with a highly classified briefing intended for bomber aircrews on alert. The key briefing chart showed a graph with two lines curving upward from lower left to upper right. One line represented the rapidly increasing total number of Soviet ICBMs on hand and projected to be available in a few months. The second line represented the total number of SAC ICBMs on hand and projected to be available in a few months. When the curves crossed, the Soviets would have more ICBMs.

Power wanted the bomber crews to know that a Soviet nuclear attack was likely when the Soviets had more ICBMs than the United States. If that happened, we needed to be fully prepared to retaliate with our B-52s. I do not know whether Power favored a preemptive attack before the predicted date when the curves crossed. I do know Power had neither the authority nor the responsibility to order a preemptive attack.

That ICBM briefing destroyed the confidence I had in General Power. Perhaps the briefing was his way to motivate aircrews by purposely exaggerating the probability of a near-term Soviet attack. It seemed irrational to me that the USSR would initiate an attack against the United States because its ICBM force was only marginally larger than our ICBM force in 1962. For the USSR to choose that option in 1962, Khrushchev would have to believe that several hundred B-52 and B-47 bombers on alert and armed with thermonuclear weapons would never reach their targets. Furthermore, the Soviet missile attack would have to destroy our growing inventory of Atlas, Titan, and Minuteman ICBMs.

My belief then, and it remains today, is that weapon systems do not cause wars—national policies do. The United States needed strong strategic nuclear forces to support our deterrent policy. Successful deterrence meant the Soviet Union would not attack the United States with nuclear weapons because its leaders knew our *retaliatory* response would cause unacceptable damage to their own country.

Every year during the Cold War, Congress and the Defense Department struggled with the budget for strategic forces. Administrations varied widely—the extremes were Carter (procrastinate) and Reagan (build). Despite varying degrees of political support, the deterrent policy of the United States remained generally consistent throughout the Cold War. After more than four decades, the Cold War ended in our favor. Neither side had resorted to using nuclear weapons. Deterrence worked and served its purpose.

Six months after first flying the B-52H, I "made the team" and was no longer apprehensive about the career change. My annual OER by the squadron commander reflected this progress:

> In a short time attained combat ready status. . . . His crew was first to complete quarterly training requirements . . . first to fly a special mission subsequently flown by the other crews. His crew's performance was best . . . gratifying to have Major Leavitt as a flight commander, particularly on alert. Morale was higher, productivity increased and discipline was at its highest . . . supervised the squadron ground training

program, one of the best on the base . . . frequently selected to address civic groups.

The wing commander added to the OER: "This highly motivated officer is an asset to his organization and the USAF. I am pleased to have him as a member of the 379th Bombardment Wing."

I was no longer the unwanted fighter pilot and had earned my spurs as a B-52H aircraft commander. The entire R-12 crew had worked hard and performed its duties in a highly professional way that made progress possible. It became one of the first B-52H lead crews.

Crew Duty Ends

Two events ended my B-52H aircrew duty. First, Headquarters USAF asked me to volunteer for the X-20 Dyna-Soar space program. Dyna-Soar was an advanced experimental weapon system to be launched by a Titan II rocket that would glide around the earth in low orbits before landing on a skid at one of 10 airfields. I told Colonel Kunkel about the Dyna-Soar offer and asked his opinion. He expressed disappointment that I would leave the B-52 program after only one year and stated that in his opinion SecDef Robert McNamara would cancel the X-20 Dyna-Soar program. (Later events proved him to be correct.) Second, Kunkel said he wanted to replace the current chief, Training Operations Branch, and place me in charge of training B-52 and KC-135 aircrews.

I accepted the challenge Kunkel offered and declined Dyna-Soar. SAC had recently directed a new training policy for bomb wings called "wing centralized scheduling." By 1962 crew strength had doubled because of increased alert, and SAC personnel strength reached 282,723—the highest number in its history. Operational squadrons lacked the staffing necessary to schedule all flying, alert, and training activities. Monthly schedules were constantly changing because of unforeseen requirements, leaving aircrews and their families as the unhappy victims. Centralized Scheduling was to resolve the complex scheduling problem and introduce some stability into aircrew lives.

The new system required an unusual amount of coordination and communication. Approximately 300 people at Wurtsmith flew the B-52H and KC-135 aircraft. About 240 belonged to specific crews; the rest were command and staff members. The Training Operations Branch had four principal tasks: meet the alert requirements, train and maintain at combat-ready status the maximum number of aircrews, satisfy quarterly SAC training objectives for every combat-ready aircrew, and keep qualified command and staff personnel current in the B-52H or KC-135.

The 379th Wing had 16 B-52Hs and 20 KC-135s. Half were on alert and not available for training, and two or three of those remaining were usually undergoing maintenance or inspections. On a typical day we might have four or five B-52Hs available for flying—enough for two short three-hour sorties and four long 10- to 12-hour sorties. With 30 B-52 aircrews, the average was three or four sorties per month—about 30 flying hours.

Since the B-52H aircrew was composed of different specialties (pilot, copilot, radar navigator, navigator, electronic warfare officer, and gunner), each sortie had to be carefully planned to include individual training requirements. The devil was in the details, and there was little room for error. Unexpected sickness, bad weather, crew transfers, family emergencies, aircraft system malfunctions, cancelled air-refueling tankers, closed RBSs, ORIs, unplanned TDY, jammed 20 mm cannons—these unpredictable events could raise havoc with the monthly schedule. Compounding the problem were non-combat ready crews who needed more sorties than the combat ready. When any of these "bad news" events happened, our task was fixing them without tearing apart the entire monthly schedule. In 1962 computers were not yet available, so we had to do it the hard way—trial and error. An appropriate job description for our work was stuffing 10 pounds of potatoes into a five-pound bag.

Those who worked closely with Col John Kunkel, the 379th Wing commander, admired his leadership and devotion to duty. One night I spent with Colonel Kunkel illustrates the man's character. A late winter storm hit Wurtsmith with snow, sleet, and freezing rain. Kunkel personally directed the deicing operation in the alert area all night despite the miserable weather. His objective was to keep the B-52Hs free from ice so they could maintain alert. As ice began forming on an aircraft, maintenance trucks would spray anti-icing fluid on the wing and tail surfaces. Then, maintenance crews would sweep off the snow and slush. After several hours fighting the storm, we had no more anti-icing fluid. One by one, the "Buffs" iced over. By dawn, the storm won, and Kunkel sadly notified SAC that all our bombers were off alert.

On 27 April, a landing F-101 hit a deer on the runway and sheered the nose wheel, closing the runway for about 40 minutes until the debris was cleared. The wing DO and I were sitting in a staff car on a taxiway watching the cleanup activity. A B-52H that had been practicing landings was waiting on the taxiway. The aircraft commander saw our staff car and radioed for guidance on how to log the time spent waiting before he could take off again. I told him to log the normal allowance for ground operation and not count the additional wait as flying time.

In early May, the SAC Inspector General conducted an ORI of the 379th Bomb Wing. One inspector checked the tower times for takeoffs and landings and compared the result to the maintenance records for each aircraft. The B-52H on the taxiway had followed my instructions and logged 30 minutes less time than the tower recorded between his first takeoff and final landing.

The maintenance inspector, a colonel on the ORI team, visited my office the next day. "Why did you tell the aircraft commander not to log all the time the engines were running, in violation of maintenance tech orders?" My answer, based upon 12 years of flying, did not make the colonel happy. "I was never in maintenance, but in operations we could only log 10 minutes for taxi time."

A few days later, a Second Air Force special investigation board convened at Wurtsmith. Its job was to investigate issues the IG had raised in his ORI report. One issue was whether I had encouraged fraudulent record-keeping by telling the B-52 pilot to limit the amount of taxi time he logged in the Form 781. I was dismayed that SAC would consider punishing me for trying to do the right thing.

When the special investigation board convened, I was still hot under the collar. After reporting to the board, the president asked if I knew of the allegation and the charges. I told him, "Yes, sir, and I would like to make an opening statement." He nodded his head in agreement. "Colonel, I'm an operations officer and have never heard of this maintenance tech order that states an aircraft can stay on the ground with engines running for an indefinite period of time and then count all that ground time as flying time. The tech order is illogical. I believe when a pilot logs *flying time, that it is for flying*, not for sitting in an airplane on the ground with engines running! Under the same circumstances, I would do exactly the same thing again!"

The colonel raised his hand in protest, interrupted my little speech, and told the court reporter to turn off the recording machine. He then warned me to allow the hearing to proceed without any more outbursts. The next day, I learned the board had dropped the serious charge of "encouraging fraudulent record-keeping." On 1 June, instead of a court-martial, I received a letter of admonishment from the 40th AD commander stating, "You will, under all circumstances, avoid giving instructions to crews unless they are in compliance with pertinent directives and technical orders." I suppose the board had to take some action to answer the ORI report, but this was an example of swatting flies with a sledgehammer.

After the wing passed the ORI, Colonel Kunkel transferred to the Pentagon. He had commanded the newly formed 379th Bomb Wing, the first to be equipped with the new B-52H, on a newly built SAC base with a mix of personnel from all over SAC. He met the challenge, and the wing achieved combat-ready status in less than one year—a difficult task. I do not believe he ever received sufficient credit for his accomplishments.

Col Paul K. Carlton became the new 379th Wing commander. Colonel Carlton was a dynamic leader and quickly made his presence felt throughout the wing. He had a knack for solving tough problems by listening to different viewpoints throughout the staff before arriving at the solutions. The wing continued to improve under his leadership. General Carlton retired in 1977 after a long and distinguished career. His last assignment was commander, Military Airlift Command (MAC).

In August the Pentagon screened me for a classified job. War Plans wanted an operations officer with both U-2 and B-52 experience. I flew to Washington for an interview but learned very little about the new assignment. After returning to Wurtsmith, I learned the transfer to War Plans would occur in a few weeks. In the meantime, I was temporarily assigned to the 40th AD staff as the operations training officer. On 9 September 1962, I signed out from the 379th Bomb Wing and reported to Brig Gen (later Maj Gen) Harold E. "Buzz" Humfeld, 40th AD commander.

Planning and scheduling air training for the wing was a fascinating business. It provided an opportunity not available as a B-52H aircraft commander to learn about both bomber and tanker operations. Despite the lack of computer automation, the Training Operations Branch was able to stabilize the monthly and quarterly training programs. The DO noted this progress in my final OER at Wurtsmith, and Colonel Carlton added a very nice endorsement.

The air division's job was supervising four subordinate SAC wings. Its staff was small, and Buzz Humfeld kept an "open door" policy so that everyone knew what was going on. One morning around the middle of October, the SAC message traffic indicated SAC bombers were evacuating our Florida bases and relocating to northern SAC bases to avoid damage from hurricanes that were developing in the Caribbean. I checked the weather reports and did not see anything like a hurricane moving toward Florida. Being curious, I asked General Humfeld why SAC was evacuating Florida. He said a second B-52 wing—the 19th from Homestead AFB, Florida—would soon be operating from Wurtsmith, but the real problem was Cuba, not hurricanes.

Cuban Missile Crisis—Deterrence Plus
14 October–21 November 1962

The Cuban missile crisis occurred while the Leavitt family was busy packing for our move to Washington. Instead of moving, I was "frozen" in place, and the empty moving van went back to Toledo, Ohio. For several days, I had nothing to do but observe ongoing base activities, read message traffic concerning the crisis, and keep track of changing events. The chronology of the crisis follows and includes my observations at the time and in retrospect, as well as facts, explanations, and opinions from other sources.

July, August, and September 1962: CIA U-2 overflights of Cuba in late July provided evidence of increased Soviet military assistance to Cuba. Photography taken on 29 August confirmed the presence of SA-2 SAMs. On 9 October, it was determined

SAC commanders in 1961 prior to the Cuban crisis. *Left to right*: Lt Gen Archie Old, commander, Fifteenth Air Force; Lt Gen John McConnell, vice CINCSAC; General Power; Lt Gen Walter Sweeny, commander, Second Air Force. (Not shown, Lt Gen Hunter Harris, commander, Eighth Air Force.)

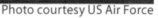

Photo courtesy US Air Force

U-2 pilot Maj Rudolph Anderson. SAC U-2 pilots during the first phase of the Cuban missile crisis confirmed the USSR was installing ballistic missile sites in Cuba. Anderson was killed when his U-2 was shot down by a Soviet SA-2 SAM fired from a Cuban missile site. He was posthumously awarded the first Air Force Cross.

Photo courtesy US Air Force

SAC airborne's best punch. During the Cuban missile crisis, SAC had 555 B-52s. One-eighth were airborne every hour from 22 October until the crisis ended on 21 November 1962. Seventy B-52 sorties were airborne at any one time, each nominally loaded with four nuclear weapons. B-52s flew 2,000 sorties, averaging 23 hours per sortie, during the crisis without incident.

KC-135 tanker. Most sorties had two air refuelings from KC-135 tankers.

Atlas **Titan**

ICBM order of battle during Cuban crisis. On a typical day during the crisis, SAC had 183 ICBMs on alert. The first Minuteman ICBM launch occurred on 28 September 1962, and several Minuteman ICBMs joined the alert force before the crisis ended. There were 56 Titan I and 119 Atlas D and E ICBMs available throughout the crisis. The JCS declassified data shows 80 Polaris submarine-launched ballistic missiles (SLBM) were also on alert during the crisis. The USSR was estimated to have less than 100 ICBMs at the time of the crisis, with 50–80 on alert.

SAC B-58. SAC had 76 supersonic B-58 medium bombers during the crisis. They did not fly airborne alert or deploy because of their short range without air refueling.

SAC B-47s. SAC had 675 B-47 medium bombers that were relocated to dispersal bases or placed on home alert. Bases not in the continental United States (CONUS) included Spain and Alaska.

that shipping crates on Soviet ships bound for Cuba contained IL-28 bombers.

12 October: Lacking was photo intelligence of the presence of Soviet offensive ballistic missiles. Presidential order assigned the high-altitude surveillance task to SAC.[2]

14 October: U-2s flown by SAC majors Anderson and Heyser photographed the San Cristobal area where the Soviets were building a site for medium-range ballistic missiles and possibly another site for intermediate-range ballistic missiles (IRBM). The Air Force rushed the photography from these missions to the White House. The president and his senior advisors now had confirmation of the potential threat.

16 October: CINCSAC, General Power, asks the JCS for approval to place one of every eight B-52s on airborne alert, to disperse SAC medium bombers, and to raise SAC's defense readiness condition (DEFCON) from 4 to 2. The JCS agreed that SAC should move to one-eighth airborne alert and disperse other SAC and North American Aerospace Defense Command (NORAD) aircraft carrying nuclear weapons.[3] Secretary of Defense McNamara, who was present at the meeting, later addressed the increased alert levels at a White House meeting and approved the increased airborne alert and DEFCON 2.[4]

17 October: JCS authorized SAC to begin moving SAC aircraft out of Florida. General Power discussed this with his staff and subordinate commanders.

18 October: SAC directed its units in Florida to relocate. The 19th Bomb Wing at Homestead AFB was to resume alert at Wurtsmith AFB. The 306th Bomb Wing at MacDill AFB, Florida, was to resume alert at Hunter AFB. CINCSAC directed implementation of one-eighth airborne alert, approximately 70 B-52s, to be in the air around the clock effective on 22 October at 1200 EST. CINCSAC further directed implementation of medium force dispersal to be effective 22 October at 1300 EST. B-47s were dispersed to 40 civilian airports and assumed alert. About 200 ICBMs became ready for launch.[5]

22 October: The president announced to the nation a strict quarantine on all offensive military equipment under shipment to Cuba and requested the Organization of American States (OAS) to endorse the quarantine.

23 October: When the endorsement from the OAS was given on October 23, the president issued Proclamation 3504 establishing the quarantine effective on 24 October and directed the secretary of defense to take appropriate measures.[6]

The JCS directed SAC to establish DEFCON 2 and generate all forces effective 1400Z on 24 October. The other US forces at DEFCON 5 moved to DEFCON 3.

During the crisis, tensions were high at Wurtsmith. With two wings of B-52H bombers and a squadron of KC-135 tankers, the base became a likely target for Soviet missiles from either the USSR or Cuba. The 379th Wing rented cars from local dealers for transportation for the newly arrived 19th Wing. Civil engineers began sandbagging the basement windows in base housing. If attacked, families were to take cover in their basements—not a realistic solution, but it convinced skeptics that the crisis was serious.

24 October: There was progress. Some Soviet ships responded to our quarantine and altered course away from Cuba. The same day, I was talking to General Humfeld when the red phone rang. General Power had an announcement for all SAC numbered air forces and division commanders. The National Command Authority (NCA) had moved SAC to DEFCON 2.[7] Power's voice message was sent in the "clear," meaning uncoded.

> This is General Power speaking. I am addressing you for the purpose of re-emphasizing the seriousness of the situation the nation faces. We are in an advanced state of readiness to meet any emergencies and I feel that we are well prepared. I expect each of you to maintain strict security and use calm judgment during this tense period. Our plans are well prepared and are being executed smoothly. If there are any questions concerning instructions, which by the nature of the situation deviate from the normal, use the telephone for clarification. Review your plans for further action to insure there will be no mistakes or confusion. I expect you to cut out all non-essentials and put yourself in a maximum readiness condition. If you are not sure what you should do in any situation, and if time permits, get in touch with us here.[8]

The Kennedy administration learned later of Power's phone call to his SAC commanders. Imbedded high in the Kennedy administration were several anti-SAC and antinuke critics who later accused General Power of violating security, trying to intimidate the Soviets, and exceeding his authority by implying the United States had decided to enter a nuclear war over Soviet missiles in Cuba. In my opinion, these "Monday morning quarterbacks" needed to take a deep breath before voicing their ill-advised criticisms that ignored three facts that General Power had to consider.

First, a presidential decision had placed SAC in DEFCON 2. General Power, as CINCSAC, was obligated to insure that all his subordinate commanders were fully aware of the serious situation facing our nation.

Second, SAC had over 282,000 personnel assigned at 43 CONUS and 14 overseas bases in 1962. Serving under the SAC numbered air forces were the operational units, including 59 aircraft wings and 33 missile squadrons. Size and distribution of SAC resources greatly increased the probability of communication error. Power's clear message to avoid errors encouraged subordinate commanders to use the telephone for clarification or if unsure what to do.

Third, no American commander wants to be the victim of another Pearl Harbor disaster. Power did everything possible to make sure his forces would not be destroyed because they were unprepared or uninformed.

Raymond Garthoff, Mac Bundy, and Scott Sagan were critical of Power in their books assessing the Cuban missile crisis because Power sent his message in the clear. In fact, Power adhered to federal policy of using unclassified means for announcing DEFCON changes. Not until 1972 was the policy changed to require the notification of DEFCON changes to be classified. If the Soviets were intimidated after intercepting Power's message, it probably strengthened our negotiating position. The purpose of deterrence was to avoid nuclear war. Letting the USSR know our nation was prepared and capable of retaliating with overwhelming strength to an attack remained a recurring US theme throughout the Cold War.

After retiring, I participated in a crisis management study while a visiting scholar at Cornell University. Former secretary of defense McNamara talked to our study group one day about the Cuban missile crisis. He surprised me by stating that SAC increased the B-52s on airborne alert without his knowledge or approval. During a coffee break, I told McNamara that perhaps I misunderstood his comment. He said that was his recollection of the incident. After returning to my home in California, I told General LeMay, CSAF during the Cuban missile crisis, about McNamara's recollection. LeMay took strong exception to McNamara's recollection of events. Supporting data from JCS notes and other sources discloses that LeMay was correct.

25 October: Kennedy warned the Soviets that "further action will be justified" if they continued putting offensive missiles in Cuba.

27 October: A Soviet SA-2 SAM shot down and killed my friend Maj Rudy Anderson while flying a U-2 reconnaissance mission over Cuba. Tragic circumstances surrounded Anderson's death. Rudy and Capt John Campbell were testing a new U-2 capability at Edwards AFB prior to the Cuban missile crisis. One night around midnight, the command post at Laughlin, Rudy's home base, received an emergency call from Edwards. A U-2 had just crashed, killing Anderson. Immediately, the Laughlin base chaplain and Rudy's commanders drove to the Anderson home, awakened his wife, and told Jane the distressing news.

An hour or so later, another officer hurried over to the Anderson home. Jane, grief-stricken and still in shock, learned that Edwards had made a tragic mistake. The U-2 pilot killed was John Campbell, not Anderson. When Rudy returned from Edwards, Jane pleaded with him to leave the U-2 program. Rudy had been flying the U-2 for five years and was more than eligible for a new assignment. Realizing the trauma that Jane had experienced, Rudy agreed that he would leave, but he had one more assignment to complete before transferring—one for which he had been training. Rudy's agreement with Jane was cancelled by a Cuban-manned SA-2 battery on 27 October.

Cuba returned Rudy's body to the United States after the missile crisis ended. Kennedy wanted to attend Rudy's funeral and present the Air Force Cross posthumously to Jane. She refused and another family member accepted the medal.

28 October: The day after the Cuban SA-2 shot down Anderson's U-2, President Kennedy's brother Robert notified Soviet ambassador Anatoly Dobrynin that the United States was ready to begin military action early the next week. The USSR reacted quickly. Radio Moscow broadcast that the dismantling of "arms which you described as offensive" would begin the next day.

For the next three weeks, SAC continued the full-scale airborne alert while USAF and Navy reconnaissance aircraft monitored the dismantling of Soviet missiles and their shipment back to Russia. Meanwhile, Kennedy and Khrushchev continued to negotiate a settlement to the crisis. The last piece of the puzzle fell in place on 20 November when Soviet cargo ships took 42 IL-28 bombers in crates back to the USSR.

November 21: The crisis ended, and SAC reverted to its normal alert status. The 42 ballistic missiles in Cuba were shipped back to the Soviet Union. Not until later did Americans learn that Khrushchev succeeded in negotiating a quid pro quo with Kennedy. After a face-saving delay of three months, Kennedy pulled our Thor IRBMs from the United Kingdom. A short time later, our Jupiter IRBMs in Turkey and Italy were also withdrawn.

The presence of 70 airborne B-52s at all times during the crisis—each loaded with thermonuclear weapons and orbiting within reach of the Soviet Union—sent a strong warning to Khrushchev. Nor could Khrushchev and Fidel Castro ignore the Army, Navy, and Air Force conventional forces massed for an invasion of Cuba. The combined strength of strategic and general purpose forces ended the crisis.

November 24: Aircraft dispersal ended.

November 25: SAC returned to DEFCON 4.

From 22 October until 21 November when the crisis ended, B-52s flew 2,000 airborne alert sorties. The effort totaled 47,000 hours—averaging more than 23 hours per sortie—all without an accident. The last sortie flew from Wurtsmith. After it landed, airborne alert fell back to peacetime requirements.

President Kennedy visited Headquarters SAC on 7 December 1962 and presented General Power with a plaque. He congratulated SAC for the extraordinary role it played in resolving the crisis and for the outstanding record in flight safety during airborne alert in the Cuban emergency. Among other comments, Kennedy said, "The airborne alert provided a strategic posture under which every United States force could operate with relative freedom of action."

After tensions eased, we moved to Washington, arriving in early November. While driving, I reflected on the past two years with B-52s and compared that experience with my prior flying assignments. To the best of my knowledge, in 1962 I was the only Air Force officer who had served in a combat crew in the Korean War and in F-84Gs, F-84Fs, U-2s, and B-52s. These years had been a great learning experience. One conclusion dominated my thoughts . . . the Air Force had come of age.

Notes

1. House, *Department of Defense Appropriations for 1960*, 381.
2. Department of Defense, *Annual Report for Fiscal Year 1963*, 4–8.
3. Notes taken from transcripts of meetings of the JCS, October–November 1962, dealing with the Cuban missile crisis, 3–6. Provided by SAC historian. Information is now declassified.
4. "Off the Record Meeting on Cuba, October 16, 1962, 6:30–7:55 PM," John F. Kennedy Papers, 9–10.
5. Message 10-049, SAC to JCS. Document is now declassified.
6. Ibid.
7. "A memorandum dated 11 Jan 2002 from the director of the Joint Staff communicated the decision by the Secretary of Defense that 'National Command Authorities (NCA)' no longer be used. 'President' or 'Secretary of Defense' or both should be used when appropriate. The term NCA formerly was used to signify constitutional authority to direct the Armed Forces in their execution of military action." "Joint Structure and Organization," www.dinfos .dma.mil/DinfosWeb/JSPAC/JointStructureandOrganization.pdf. However, *NCA* is used in this book because that is the correct terminology for the time frame the author recounts.
8. 14th Strategic Aerospace Division, *Cuban Missile Crisis Annex*, vol. 2, 3–4.

Chapter 7

Pentagon
Major–Lieutenant Colonel—1962–66

The Pentagon
November 1962

My youngest daughter, Mary, then two years old, enlivened our trip from Wurtsmith. A small stuffed dog, now worn and threadbare from frequent washing, had been with Mary most of her life. Appropriately named "Doggie Doggie" by Mary, they were inseparable. As we entered northern Virginia and met heavy traffic, Mary tossed Doggie-Doggie out the car window. Her cries of regret immediately followed. I pulled over to the side of the road and waited for a break in traffic. Her brother Trig then recovered Doggie Doggie, and a grateful Mary stopped crying—the joys of parenthood!

During my Pentagon job interview in August, I had met Maj Bert Brennan. Bert had been my platoon leader in Beast Barracks when I was a plebe at West Point and was now a staff officer in War Plans. We talked about where to live in the Washington area. He recommended a new development in McLean, Virginia, where he had purchased a home.[1]

McLean was a small town in 1962 but becoming well known because Bobby Kennedy and his large family lived there. I drove to McLean and liked the newly finished homes Bert had recommended. After surviving the sticker shock, I signed a contingency contract and took a brochure and blueprint back to Wurtsmith. Fortunately, Anne liked the house, and we lived in it for nearly five years.

Living in our new neighborhood was almost like living on an air base. Col Bud Rundell lived on one side and Col Jerry Brown on the other. Charlie Gabriel lived next to Rundell, and Bert Brennan lived next to Charlie. Scott Smith, a friend from U-2 days, moved next to Jerry Brown a few months later. Two other Air Force families and two Navy families had backyards that adjoined ours. Someone said our neighborhood only lacked a control tower and approach lights to complete the scene.

Working at FEAF headquarters in Tokyo had provided excellent training in how large staffs work. However, the Pentagon dwarfed FEAF headquarters. Approximately 32,000 people worked in this five-sided building built early in World War II. I reported to the offices for War Plans on the fourth floor. A courteous secretary provided the first surprise of the day. Although assigned to War Plans, the offices for the Air Battle Analysis Center (ABAC) were nearby in a Pentagon annex crudely called the "pickle factory." Fatalities from the European theater in World War II had been stored there in a cold room until moved to a national cemetery—thus the nickname.

By 10 o'clock, 12 of us were waiting in the ABAC conference room for our indoctrination briefing. Col Mel Slate, chief of the ABAC, welcomed us. After a long theatrical pause, Slate broke the silence. We were all carefully chosen to build *models*. Incredible! What possible use would I be building models? When everyone quit mumbling and quieted down, Slate explained what *models* meant.

SecDef McNamara and his Whiz Kids had introduced systems analysis into the Pentagon as part of the decision-making process. Judgments based solely upon the personal military experience of well-decorated senior military officers seemed to carry little influence with the Whiz Kids. The secretary and his staff leaned heavily on cost analysis and probability estimates to solve major defense issues. The Air Force needed a comparable staff that could analyze issues in ways that were compatible with the way the SecDef's staff resolved issues. The ABAC was given that responsibility. By using computers to conduct war games that created simulations of interactions between enemy and friendly weapon systems, the ABAC would provide the Air Staff with analytical data and the rationale for many USAF decisions and weapon system requests.

The ABAC doubled that day, from 12 to 24 officers and civilian analysts. When I left three years later, ABAC had become the Directorate of Studies and Analysis (S&A) with Maj Gen Howard Davis as director and several hundred people attached or assigned.

During that first afternoon, I met Col Gerald Adams, the chief of the War Games Division. Jerry was an exceptionally fine officer and supervisor, always helpful and understanding. We remained friends long after leaving our Pentagon duties. His last assignment before retirement was base commander, Warren AFB, Cheyenne, Wyoming.

The big project assigned to ABAC at that time was modeling the SAC war plan and then testing the model in a war game. The project had been under way for months and was a tedious task to say the least. The ABAC scenario described how the war started and provided key assumptions concerning the readiness of SAC. Estimates included the number of SAC aircraft that successfully launched and the number of aborts en route. Every bomber and tanker route from every SAC base, from every refueling point, and to every target was carefully plotted. Air Force intelligence provided the exact location of every target and every known defensive system. The ABAC computed a cumulative penetration probability and the probability of destroying targets for every bomber and a cumulative kill probability for every defensive system. When the ABAC finished the project in November, the massive report was several inches thick and gave precise answers to many questions. All it needed was a general's blessing before it went to the JCS for approval.

Maj Gen John Carpenter was director of plans and the approval authority. Carpenter was a very intelligent and experienced planner with a reputation for quickly separating the wheat from the chaff. He opened the thick study, read the foreword and key assumptions, closed the report, handed it back, and said he did not agree with the ABAC assumptions. Months of detailed work went down the drain!

I learned two important lessons from my brief experience working on that study. First, avoid finite answers to complex problems with many variables and unknowns. Aggregate whenever possible. If your job is estimating the distance between two points, accuracy does not improve because you guess the distance is 63,360 inches, or 5,280 feet, instead of one mile. Second, an analyst must understand that some events resist quantification because they are too complex and include too many unknowns. To illustrate this fact, assume that it is September 1939. Your project as an analyst on Hitler's staff is to estimate how many Germans will eventually die if the invasion of Poland starts World War II. An impossible task! Analysts are not soothsayers.

Several days after the war game fiasco, Colonel Slate came back from the morning DCS Plans and Operations staff meeting with a big surprise. I was to report immediately to Gen Maxwell Taylor, the CJCS. General Taylor and General LeMay, USAF chief of staff, had a heated exchange at the JCS meeting. Taylor doubted that tactical aircraft could live over the modern battlefield because an SA-2 shot down Rudy Anderson's U-2 over Cuba. LeMay strongly disagreed. As the only U-2 pilot in the Pentagon, I was to explain to Taylor why he was wrong.

General Taylor was alone in his office. I stood in front of his desk and introduced myself. He did not waste any time asking his question. "If a U-2 flying at 70,000 feet can be shot down with a SAM, what makes LeMay think that tactical aircraft can survive over the modern battlefield in a hostile SAM environment?"

I explained that the U-2 was flying straight and level, was not flying very fast (about 420 knots), was not very maneuverable, and was visible on both early warning and SAM radars for many miles before reaching SAM firing range. In contrast, most tactical aircraft were faster and more maneuverable and could often fly under radar coverage. Furthermore, because SAMs were getting better, the Air Force was developing electronic countermeasures to protect fighters and bombers. Taylor listened, gave no indication of agreeing or disagreeing, asked no other questions, and dismissed me.

When I returned to the ABAC, the chain of command wanted to know the details of my meeting with Taylor. A few days later, I became the project officer for a new study—the manned aircraft penetration study. The gut issue (Taylor's question) was the survivability of tactical aircraft in a hostile SAM environment. Two other pilots, a radar navigator, and a civilian analyst rounded out the study group. The study dominated my interest for the next three months and greatly increased my knowledge of friendly and enemy radars, antiradar missiles, friendly and enemy SAMs, antiaircraft guns, and ECM, including different ways to jam radars and use chaff.

One advantage to working in the Pentagon is the easy access to information. By the time the study was completed, we had a working knowledge of the systems mentioned in the previous paragraph. The R&D community had provided us necessary information about new and proposed systems, and various industry sources—smelling possible contracts—were knocking at the Air Force door with proposals for new systems. My OER in June 1963 stated, among other things:

> The study, when concluded, was distributed in report form and also briefed widely by the project officer throughout the Air Staff and the Joint Chiefs of Staff, and in the latter case, quite often to a hostile audience. Major Leavitt's presentation was superb and particularly his handling of questions from the hostile audiences. . . . The majority of every audience was convinced of the logic and technical truth of the presentation. This study was of tremendous value to the Air Force in presenting a case for the future manned aircraft's ability to survive in a hostile SAM environment.

The Pentagon is an interesting place to work. There are so many people involved in every aspect of Pentagon business that individual reputations are hard to establish. The study mentioned above apparently established my credentials in the Air Staff and the JCS. Following the survivability study mentioned above, the ABAC assigned me a related project—analyze the Army Mauler and HAWK weapon systems. The Air Force was searching for tactics and countermeasures that would work against comparable Soviet air defense systems. The Weapon Systems Evaluation Group incorporated the findings from this new analysis in its study "Project Duel."

Aircraft survivability was a hot issue in the Pentagon in 1963 and 1964. The Army was seeking more money for HAWK SAM missile batteries; the Redeye shoulder-fired, heat-seeking anti-aircraft missile; and rapid-firing cannons with high-kill probabilities to protect troops from air attack. The Navy wanted money for new radars, fire-control systems, and associated weapons to protect surface ships from enemy aircraft and missile attacks. At the same time, the Air Force was trying to convince anyone who would listen—especially McNamara's budget people—that despite the Army and Navy advocacies for their antiaircraft systems, Air Force fighter aircraft could survive in a hostile environment if given a few million bucks for countermeasures.

Maj Ed Chavarrie and I prepared a cost-effectiveness comparison of land- and carrier-based tactical operations that the SecDef used in his annual memorandum to the president on general purpose forces.[2] The Navy wanted to challenge our report in front of the joint chiefs. The agreed plan was to brief our report, and then the Navy would respond with its report. Ed and I worked long and hard preparing briefing slides for the Big Day. I briefed the Air Force study first. Surprisingly, there were few questions or comments following my briefing. General LeMay pointed at a chair directly behind his. I was to sit there while the Navy briefed its study.

The Navy briefer was a distinguished looking captain, recently the skipper of an aircraft carrier, and wore the Navy Cross, second only to the Medal of Honor. The Navy briefing was heavy on claims and light on facts. From time to time, I handed LeMay a note citing a weak spot. After the captain finished briefing, the chairman turned to LeMay and asked for his opinion. LeMay, never long on words, said, "It was as full of holes as a Swiss cheese." The chief of naval operations, after hearing LeMay's comment, said with flushed face that he would return with a rebuttal. He never did.

Life was getting busy again. In December I enrolled at George Washington University for a master's degree in government (public administration). The classes met at night and usually did not interfere with ABAC work. GW accepted my academic record from West Point but noted that I had no credits in American history. After losing my claim that the military history classes at West Point were really about American history, I joined the GW freshman class in American History 101. At age 34, I was twice as old as my youngest classmates, but I grudgingly admit it was an excellent course and well worth the time. Most subjects taken as part of the public administration curricula during the following two years were relevant to my work as an analyst in the Pentagon and my later career. After I received the master's degree in February 1965, my weekends became much more pleasant.

Quick Fix

Spring 1963

For nearly a month, President Kennedy and his principal advisors had wrestled with the emerging nuclear threat caused by Soviet missiles and IL-28 bombers in Cuba. An option considered was invading Cuba and forcefully removing the threat.

One can only conjecture how the Soviets would have reacted if we had invaded Cuba. One worrisome possibility: Khrushchev would create a crisis in Central Europe, where the military balance of power favored Warsaw Pact forces.

During Eisenhower's presidency, American forces in Europe expanded both inventory and means for delivering tactical nuclear weapons. The overriding NATO strategy was blunt—a major attack by the Warsaw Pact would result in NATO responding with nuclear weapons. The United States had signed Military Committee (MC) document 14/2, the NATO strategy document, thus agreeing to the immediate use of nuclear weapons in general war and ruling out limited war. The following are excerpts from MC 14/2.

> 14. In case of general war, therefore, NATO defense depends upon an immediate exploitation of our nuclear capability, whether or not the Soviets employ nuclear weapons.

> 19. NATO must also be prepared to respond quickly with nuclear weapons should the situation require it. . . . If the Soviets were involved in a local hostile action and sought to broaden the scope of such an incident or prolong it, the situation would call for the utilization of all weapons and forces at NATO's disposal. . . . In no case is there a NATO concept of limited war with the Soviets.[3]

Warsaw Pact plans indicated the routine use of nuclear weapons by both sides and Warsaw Pact confidence in winning despite the devastation caused by nuclear weapons. Gen Pyotr Ivashutin, chief of Soviet military intelligence, prepared a study in 1964 that stated

> NATO's defensive preparations were a sham. . . . A swift offensive operation could guarantee success for the Warsaw Pact. . . . The operation was feasible regardless of Europe's nuclear devastation.

> . . . Technically superior Soviet air defenses could destroy incoming NATO missiles before these could cause unacceptable damage. . . . The Soviet Union could prevail in a war because of the West's greater vulnerability to nuclear devastation.[4]

The inevitability of nuclear war became a major issue with the MC 14/2 strategy. Could NATO defenses be strengthened to the point where nuclear war could be avoided? The answer had to be yes, but it would take time, money, and persuasion to convince our NATO allies and ourselves. A major problem was the survivability of NATO's air forces. USAFE, operating from mostly unprotected air bases in 1963, was especially vulnerable to air attack.

Following World War II, several American air bases were located east of the Rhine River within easy range of air and ground forces belonging to the Soviet forces in Germany. As the Cold War intensified, our fighter wings moved to the Eifel area west of the Rhine River—the great natural barrier that runs from south to north through the Federal Republic of Germany (FRG). The relocated fighter wings at Bitburg, Ramstein, Hahn, and Spangdahlem were roughly 300 miles from East Germany and Czechoslovakia and near France, Luxembourg, and Belgium.

Gen Charles de Gaulle became president of France's Fifth Republic in January 1959. Over the next few years, it became increasingly difficult to plan on French participation in NATO. President de Gaulle eventually forced the United States to close its air bases in France and, in 1966, withdrew all French forces from the integrated military command of NATO. If enemy attacks destroyed USAFE facilities in Germany, the lack of French air bases would drastically affect all NATO air operations. USAFE air bases in the United Kingdom were unlikely to be overrun by a Soviet offensive in Central Europe, but they were vulnerable to air attack.

Since the early 1950s, the operational emphasis in USAFE was on delivering tactical nuclear weapons. USAFE fighter pilots and aircraft were on alert in much the same manner as SAC aircrews and aircraft. On the other hand, not well planned was their role in conventional war—a war without releasing nuclear weapons. To sustain conventional operations, USAFE and the other Allied air forces in the Central Region needed to survive Soviet air attacks.

USAF leaders knew our European air bases were vulnerable to air attack. They also knew that maintaining a strong tactical nuclear capability in USAFE already took a large bite from the annual Air Force budget. They placed higher priorities on increasing the number of Minuteman ICBMs, moving the supersonic B-70 from R&D to production status, and developing new fighters and munitions for TAC and Air Defense Command (ADC). An underlying factor, less obvious but present, was the resentment senior Air Force generals felt toward the SecDef's staff, particularly the so-called Whiz Kids who controlled the defense budget.

Sensing that the Air Force and Army would not lead the way toward improving the survivability of our forces in Europe, the defense comptroller, Assistant Secretary of Defense Charles Hitch, formed a study group to fix air defenses in Europe. The study was called "Quick Fix," and my name was "volunteered" to represent the Air Staff. A colonel experienced with the HAWK and other Army air defense systems represented the Army. A very bright analyst, a PhD in physics who belonged to Alan Enthoven's staff, assisted with the study and arranged support where needed.

Quick Fix proposed many changes to improve the air defenses of Central Europe. Despite the study's name, several proposals took years to complete. Army proposals included dual HAWK belts stretching across the Central Region and a battery of rapid-firing antiaircraft cannons protecting each air base from low-altitude, high-speed attacks. Air Force proposals included such relatively low-cost items as camouflaging key facilities. At the other end of the cost spectrum were rapid runway repair capabilities, individual concrete hangars for fighter aircraft, and dispersal bases for reinforcements.

Defense manufacturers occasionally learned about our study and offered their products to improve survivability. One prominent company was touting a mobile, fast-firing antiaircraft cannon mounted on a vehicle. The company approached Enthoven with the offer to brief the gun system. I had a chance to analyze the capabilities before the briefing. It was a good system, but the kill probability was highly exaggerated. During the briefing, the salesman claimed "a 95 percent probability of killing a fast-flying aircraft." Enthoven politely listened and then said the kill probability seemed too high.

After the briefing, the salesman came over to my office. "Major Leavitt, Dr. Enthoven seemed to think a 95 percent kill probability was too high. What do you think an acceptable kill probability would be?" My answer was not intended as guidance, just a way to placate his hurt feelings. "You would have to analyze the weapon performance, but I imagine something around 15 percent would be more reasonable." Guess what happened? Two or three weeks later, the briefer reappeared. This time his analysis "proved" a 15 percent kill probability! There were too many instances like this when systems analysis was king. It may have been that day I heard Enthoven pass his classic advice, "It is better to be approximately right than exactly wrong!"

When Quick Fix ended, one official in the comptroller's office asked me to take the study recommendations to the Air Force, along with a verbal message. The comptroller would support the recommendations with budget money but wanted the Air Force to first make the request. He wanted a senior Air Staff general to send him a letter asking for the funding. I went back to Colonel Slate who said it was above his pay grade and referred me to General Carpenter, the plans director. Carpenter later notified me that if the comptroller wanted to fund any of these programs, the Air Force would not object, but the Air Force would not initiate the action.

True to the comptroller's word, the next year's defense budget contained money for Quick Fix proposals. When I transferred to Germany in 1967, several Quick Fix proposals were in place. In 1976, when I became DCS for operations and intelligence for USAFE, the proposals were in full bloom, including individual concrete hangars for aircraft, a double belt of HAWK missiles, antiaircraft defenses, and dispersal bases.

Assistant Secretary of Defense Hitch sent a nice commendation letter through channels for my work on Quick Fix. I appreciated the letter and endorsements but often wondered what the SECAF and chief of staff really thought.

A flexible response strategy was articulated in 1968 via MC 14/3, which superseded NATO MC 14/2. By then, the Vietnam War had become the Pentagon's primary concern.

A Memorable Day

Air Force pilots assigned to the Pentagon stayed on flight status by flying administrative aircraft at Andrews AFB, Maryland. For three months after arriving, I flew the Cessna U-3B (no relation to the U-2), a small twin-engine prop aircraft nicknamed the "Blue Canoe." In April 1963, I upgraded to the T-39, the North American twin-engine business jet. The T-39 transported VIPs and other high-priority passengers to conferences, important meetings, and so forth.

On 21 November 1963, I flew Senator John C. Stennis to Houston, Texas. Stennis was an active supporter of military and space programs. During his long, distinguished career, he served as chairman of the Senate Appropriations Committee and replaced Sen Richard Russell, Jr., as chairman of the Senate Armed Services Committee after he retired. The aircraft carrier USS *John C. Stennis* is named in his honor. Senator Stennis visited the Houston Space Center that day and was returning to Washington the next day. President Kennedy was touring several Texas cities at the same time as the Stennis trip.

The copilot and I spent the night in Houston. At approximately 0830 CST, 22 November, we took off for Washington with Senator Stennis on board. The presidential aircraft headed for Dallas a few hours later. Our six-hour flight back to Andrews was uneventful except we noticed there was minimal radio chatter the last hour or two.

Andrews Tower ordered us to taxi to the VIP ramp after we landed at 1500 EST. I shut down the left engine, and the copilot opened the passenger door for Senator Stennis. He climbed down the cabin ladder just as an Air Force brigadier general approached the aircraft. I watched from the cockpit window while Stennis and the general talked. I told the copilot that Senator Stennis looked very distraught—maybe a death in his family. Stennis climbed back into the cabin and stood by the entrance to the cockpit where we were sitting. I will always remember what he said: "Gentlemen, I have sad, terrible news. The president of the United States was shot and killed in Dallas an hour and a half ago. The vice president, Lyndon Johnson, suffered a heart attack and has died. The new president of the United States is the Speaker of the House, John McCormick."

I shut down the right engine and stepped down from the T-39. Just then, an Air Force colonel came running toward us. Nearly out of breath, the colonel said to Stennis, "Senator, the report we heard earlier was incorrect. President Kennedy is dead, but the vice president did not have a heart attack. Lyndon Johnson has been sworn in as president of the United States."

The copilot and I climbed back in the T-39, started the engines, and taxied to the parking area. There was concern that the Kennedy shooting could be the first step in an attempt to overthrow the government. The base operations officer told us to remain available for another flight and not to leave without his permission. Base operations released us at 1800, and we went home. Camelot was history.

Vietnam War Rears Its Ugly Head

Historians often rate the Vietnam War as the low point of American twentieth century history. Whether one supported the war or was opposed to the war, the wound has been slow in healing. Rather than address the many opinions already expressed about America's experience in the Vietnam War, my comments will be restricted to events which either my associates or I witnessed after 1959. Even those of us who participated in the war often differ in our opinions of what went wrong.

In order for these different views to make sense, remember the American involvement in the war lasted a long time. There was ample time to err. Political decisions made long before the Gulf of Tonkin incident established the precedent for ambivalent military policies as the war dragged on and on.

The die was cast for future problems with Indochina when the principal World War II Allies—the United States, Soviet Union, and Great Britain—met at Potsdam in July 1945. The primary purpose of the conference was the settlement of postwar European issues. France was invited to participate as a signatory of the announced goals of the Potsdam Agreement. Without apparent objection, the principals agreed to return all the French prewar colonies in Indochina (Vietnam, Laos, and Cambodia) to France.

The Potsdam Conference split Vietnam into two parts. Ho Chi Minh and his troops occupied Hanoi after Japan surrendered. On 2 September 1945, he declared that North Vietnam was the Democratic Republic of Vietnam (DRVN), an independent country with himself as president. President Truman ignored Ho Chi Minh's request for recognition. France sent 35,000 troops to South Vietnam (SVN) in October. For the next eight years, the French—with covert American assistance—fought a losing war against Ho Chi Minh.

The Geneva Conference met in May 1954 with the Potsdam attendees plus representatives from North and South Vietnam, Laos, and Cambodia. The Geneva Accords split Vietnam at the

17th parallel and called for an election in two years to unify the country. Ho Chi Minh returned from exile as president of the DRVN. Ngo Dinh Diem became prime minister in SVN and later president. Nearly one million Catholics from the DRVN moved south, and 100,000 Communists from the Republic of Vietnam (RVN) moved north to the DRVN, leaving a cadre of about 10,000 undercover in SVN. The French army returned to France.

In 1955 two critical events occurred. The Soviet Union pledged military aid to the DRVN. Three months later, President Eisenhower pledged support and military aid to the RVN. The United States had successfully stopped the spread of Communism in Northeast Asia at the Korean 38th parallel in 1953. Eisenhower saw Southeast Asia as the next area threatened by Communist expansion. With Soviet support, Ho Chi Minh could turn Vietnam, Laos, and Cambodia into Communist states unless America intervened. Eisenhower's "domino theory"—Thailand and other Southeast Asia nations would fall like dominos if Vietnam fell—became the rationale for the US Vietnam involvement.

Another critical event occurred two years after the Geneva Accords were signed. Diem did not comply with the accords and failed to call for a free election to unify Vietnam. The United States backed Diem's decision because of our fear that Ho Chi Minh would win the election and turn Vietnam into a Communist state aligned with both the USSR and China. Ho Chi Minh reacted by beginning a terrorist campaign in SVN.

In 1957 we missed another opportunity to disengage. The Soviet Union proposed the permanent division of Vietnam into North and South. The United Nations would then admit both countries. The United States rejected the Soviet proposal because it did not want to recognize Communist NVN. In mid-1959, Ho Chi Minh called for overt action by the Viet Cong located in SVN to overthrow Diem.[5]

Most wars have a reasonably specific date for the beginning of hostilities. Not so for the Vietnam War, at least as far as American combat involvement was concerned. One possible date was in October 1959. Following Viet Cong attacks on RVN troops, President Eisenhower approved a significant increase in the size of the military assistance advisory group (MAAG) to the RVN. Its job was to train RVN troops and to determine weapon requirements. In the fall of 1960, the MAAG increased in size, and the United States gave a squadron of old AD-6 attack aircraft and several H-34 helicopters to the RVN air force.

In an early January 1961 speech, Khrushchev said that the USSR would support wars of national liberation in Algeria and Vietnam. Kennedy reacted to Khrushchev's speech by stepping up interest in counterinsurgency. A second possible date for the beginning of the war was 24 October 1961, when President Kennedy promised Diem that the United States was determined to help Vietnam preserve its independence.

In October 1961, the 507th Tactical Control Group began operations at Tan Son Nhut Air Base near Saigon. In rapid order, the 4400th Combat Crew Training Squadron (CCTS) went to Ben Hoa. Eight T-28B trainers modified for counterinsurgency activities and four RB-26 light bombers constituted the firepower for this group called Farm Gate. The early ROEs forbade combat unless a Vietnamese was in the aircraft. The ROEs gradually changed. Captain "Iwo" Kimes flew T-28B/C missions with the air commandos of the 4400th CCTS. Records indicate that Kimes flew the first USAF ordnance-delivering combat mission of the Vietnam War on 26 December 1961. The target was a Viet Cong camp in the jungle north of Saigon.[6]

In 1962 Air Force and Army advisors were already serving in the RVN, but there was little open discussion in the Pentagon of American involvement. It was common knowledge that the United States was supporting the Diem government with military assistance and advisors. In February Military Assistance Command, Vietnam (MACV) replaced the MAAG. The name change signaled the more active role the United States would assume in pacifying Vietnam.

Nineteen sixty-three was a bad year militarily and a disastrous year politically. Diem's corrupt government created massive resentment by repressing Buddhists and declaring martial law. Television news shocked the American public by showing Buddhist priests burning themselves to death in protest to Diem's persecution. The Kennedy administration dithered from August until November over whether to remove Diem with a coup. Finally, a coup led by Gen Duong Van Minh assassinated Diem on 2 November 1963.

By the end of 1963, more than 16,000 American military advisors were in South Vietnam. Among them was Volney Warner, then a major, later a four-star Army general. Warner became a province senior advisor in the Delta just after the coup removed Diem. He described the experience in a May 1986 ROTC graduation speech to Saint Anselm College in New Hampshire.

> At first I experienced the incredible feeling that I had joined a civilization in the Delta 100 years behind my own . . . a Peace Corps atmosphere prevailed (Peace Corps with side arms). . . . It began as a heady, self-satisfying experience. . . . Over time, possibly six months, the glow wore off, and by tour's end I concluded that had I been a Vietnamese in the Delta in 1963, I most assuredly would have been a Viet Cong. . . . Graft and corruption flourished everywhere. The cruelty was intolerable. Regard for the peasant was non-existent. The idea that Vietnamese peasants understood the difference between communism and capitalism was absurd. . . . Aid simply did not "trickle down" but instead fueled graft from the top.

> Convinced that we were losing, I was equally convinced the U.S. Advisory effort needed leverage in the form of money and the power of removal of the inefficient and ineffective Vietnamese in positions of authority. Further, that the Vietnamese were not as interested in their war as we were.

> For the U.S. to do what needed to be done politically in South Vietnam would have required its virtual colonialization . . . an effort for which the French had just been repudiated and driven from the country. . . . (I am not opposed personally to the U.S. attempting colonialization, just to being so clumsy and inefficient at it.)[7]

During late 1963, the ABAC began getting requests from USAF officers assigned to the JCS staff about air commando operations in South Vietnam. Usually they were technical questions such as "what ordnance can a T-28B/C carry?" or "what is the range of an A-1E fully loaded?" Then one day, a JCS colonel asked me to come to his J-3 office. He said the JCS was studying the possibility of sending several Army brigades to SVN. He wanted to know the appropriate number of USAF fighter squadrons that should accompany the Army brigades.

I could not find anyone in the Air Staff who wanted to answer this question. The Air Force normally sizes the force after determining the enemy threat and the mission objectives. In this case, neither threat nor objective was known. We finally decided that one USAF fighter squadron per Army brigade would answer the question from the JCS, but that was a strange way to allocate forces. What was the strategy?

Policy Shifts to Gradual Escalation

1964

President Johnson inherited Kennedy's foreign policy and defense team. The new president followed essentially the same approach to solving the Vietnam insurgency as did his predecessor. SecDef McNamara visited South Vietnam in March 1964, met with Gen Nguyen Khanh, the new leader of SVN, and committed the United States to providing whatever was required to defeat the Communists.

McNamara did not disclose what the administration really intended. It turned out to be a tightly restricted escalation policy that stabilized South Vietnam without aggravating the USSR and China. The administration believed a gradual escalation would minimize the loss of American lives, preserve the infrastructure of SVN, and pacify the insurgency without creating political crises with the two Communist powers. Overt tactical actions by the North Vietnamese or Viet Cong in South Vietnam would be met with decisive force but limited in scale to the specific occasion.

It was not clear what "decisive force" meant. Early in the war, the JCS asked the Air Staff what new developments would improve CAS effectiveness. Among other things, we recommended cluster bomb units (CBU)—small bomblets that increased the effectiveness of a general purpose bomb by spreading explosives designed over a larger area. The administration rejected using CBUs then but authorized their use two years later as the war continued. Were CBUs too large an escalation step one year and just right two years later? Such decisions led to the oft-repeated criticism, "We're fighting a war with one hand tied behind our back."

There was little support in 1964, outside of military circles, for attacking North Vietnam by invasion or by widespread bombing. Nor did the administration seriously consider closing the Ho Chi Minh Trail because it meant killing NVN soldiers as they wended their way south. Policy also forbade interdicting the trail as it passed through "neutral" Laos and Cambodia on its way to the South Vietnamese Delta region. There was no administration support for blockading Haiphong Harbor or bombing the railroad leading south from China to Hanoi. Although these actions would have stopped the flow of war materials to NVN, the administration feared they would aggravate relations with the USSR and China.

In August 1964, an alleged attack by North Vietnamese against two US Navy ships resulted in the Gulf of Tonkin Resolution. Whether the attack actually occurred in the manner described by the press became irrelevant when Congress passed the resolution giving the president authority to pursue this undeclared war.

It was no secret in 1964 that the USAF chief of staff, General LeMay, did not approve of the way the Vietnam situation was being handled. LeMay believed the gradual escalation policy was doomed to failure. Furthermore, the SecDef had cancelled several R&D projects that were high-priority USAF programs and strongly backed by LeMay. One morning, Colonel Slate handed me a sign-up roster. "At the Air Council meeting, General LeMay said that he wants to make sure that everyone votes in the coming presidential election." The roster listed every officer's name in the ABAC. Opposite each name were two columns with the headings "Are you a registered voter?" and "If not, do you intend to register for the 1964 election?"

I returned the sign-up roster without answering the questions. The next morning, Colonel Slate brought the roster back. "Dick, you are the only one in the ABAC who hasn't signed." I again declined to sign and instead gave him a personal memo written the previous day stating that voting, or not voting, was a right of citizenship and a private matter and that the Air Force had neither the right nor the need to know my intentions. The next morning, Colonel Slate came by once again. "Dick, you'll be pleased to learn the chief has withdrawn and destroyed the sign-up rosters!" My government course at George Washington University had raised my sensitivity to this issue!

By 1964 our policy in Vietnam was "tit for tat"—but light on any pushback. I made a computer model for War Plans to study the gradual escalation policy. The model's name was the Computer Analyzed Game of Escalation (CAGE). CAGE postulated a series of enemy escalation steps in Vietnam. We wanted high-ranking defense and state officials to play the role of "American policy maker." The purpose was to make them aware of the possible consequences of gradual escalation. For each step up the escalation ladder by NVN, the American policy maker could choose one of several responses. CAGE continued this back-and-forth process until reaching a stalemate or a violent conclusion. CAGE generated a lot of interest with research organizations belonging to the Army, Navy, and Air Force, as well as service staffs.

After hearing about CAGE, the USAF chief scientist asked to review the model and to act as the American policy maker. At one point in CAGE, he challenged the options that were available for him. I told him, "Doctor, all of these are logical responses." His curt answer taught me a well-deserved lesson. "Major Leavitt, what may seem logical to someone with 50 percent knowledge of the situation may be totally illogical to someone with 100 percent knowledge of the same situation!" The man was right. My access to the political side of the war placed me in the 50 percent category, but I learned from observing different officials react to CAGE that gradual escalation was no way to fight a war.

The Air Staff explored many options to improve the effectiveness of our bombing campaigns. At the low end of the spectrum was CAS in South Vietnam. Early in the war, there were few pitched battles. The enemy controlled the villages at night and kept a low profile in the daytime. CAS was effective where applied, but the opportunity for it to be decisive in this low-level war was not there. A large fraction of the remaining air effort was devoted to interdiction. There was no passion within the Johnson administration to interdict the flow of supplies by blockading NVN ports or by attacking railroads coming down from China. Instead, the interdiction campaign focused on the Ho Chi Minh Trail. Jungle and darkness hid much of the NVN operation. Despite our best efforts, the steady movement of supplies and reinforcements down the trail was enough to sustain the insurgency in South Vietnam. It was a difficult, low-payoff mission for fighter units and continued until the war ended.

A third task for the Air Force and Navy was bombing targets in or near NVN cities. There was no essential industrial base in North Vietnam that kept the war going. Instead, the sources for the NVN war materials were China and the USSR. Many military targets, including airfields and SAM sites, were off limits at this stage of the war. Instead, the bombing attacks focused on a few military targets and the transportation routes to the south including railroads and bridges. Knocking down bridges and destroying railroad tracks were costly and ineffective in the Korean War and were not any easier in the bombing campaign called Rolling Thunder. The administration stopped the bombing several times, primarily to entice the NVN into negotiations. This on-again, off-again aspect of Rolling Thunder, conducted mostly by fighter-bombers, had little effect on the war because of the paucity of high-priority NVN targets and logistical support by China and USSR.

At one point, the Air Staff asked SAC to examine the possibility of a major attack on the Hanoi-Haiphong area with B-52s. SAC responded with a briefing. Senior Air Staff officers attended as well as some lower-ranking staff like me. The briefing was positive in the sense that the mission could be accomplished but negative because the SAC staff estimated high B-52 losses—around 15 percent, as I recall.

Two decades later, in his book *A Bright Shining Lie*, Neil Sheehan wrote about the attitude of Ho Chi Minh and the NVN leadership toward bombing: "They could be physically destroyed and the will of their people broken if the United States turned its air power loose on the North without restraint, targeting the flood-control system of the Red River Delta and the population itself, killing millions as Curtis LeMay, the chief of staff of the Air Force wanted to do. 'Bomb 'em back into the Stone Age,'" he said.[8]

Sheehan took General LeMay's comment out of context. It is a fact that LeMay disagreed with the Johnson administration for entering the war without a clear objective of how we could win the war. He also disagreed with the "gradual escalation" policy favored by McNamara, Taylor, and others. LeMay's off-hand comment about bombing them back into the Stone Age was a dramatic way of describing our overwhelming power. He was not advocating killing millions of North Vietnamese with nuclear weapons as Sheehan and others have implied.

On 23 January 1973, nearly eight years after the SAC briefing, the war finally ended with a treaty signed in Paris to become effective on 28 January. American B-52s and tactical aircraft fought and won the concluding battle of the war—called

Linebacker II. This was the type of air campaign that LeMay had in mind in 1964–65.

The SAC commander, General Ellis, and I had several private discussions with General LeMay during the years 1978–81. My comments about LeMay are based upon these conversations as well as my Air Staff experience from 1962 to 1966. LeMay was the favorite whipping boy for some civilian executives in the Kennedy-Johnson administrations and their antimilitary advisors. They sought to destroy his reputation whenever possible but avoided direct confrontation. Their preferred weapons were innuendo and hearsay.

Saving Pilot Lives—Not Easy, Costs Money

The Air Force and Navy air strikes began in earnest in 1964. The USSR had equipped the North Vietnamese with EW, GCI, and tracking radars for antiaircraft guns. It was just a question of time before SAMs would become part of their air defense system. For two years, the ABAC had touted the requirement for equipping fighter aircraft with ECM carried in external pods to reduce aircraft losses. The R&D community in the Pentagon, working with industry, had several promising solutions. All we needed was program approval and budget money.

The Air Force had a formal process for approving requirements such as ECM equipment for fighters. Major air commands normally established requirements. For example, TAC, PACAF, and USAFE owned most of the fighters in the Air Force, so they would have primary interest in ECM pods for fighters. Assuming Air Force Systems Command (AFSC) could find a technical answer to a requirement, the Air Staff would review it. However, asking is not the same as receiving. Headquarters USAF had to establish priorities among all the major air commands for equipment due to budget constraints. Two Air Staff boards examined proposals. The first, the Air Staff Board, was composed largely of major general directors. The second, the Air Council, was composed of lieutenant general DCSs. The Air Force chief of staff or vice chief of staff chaired the Air Council. After the Air Force established its priority programs, McNamara's staff put its spin on the requirement by disapproving, delaying, or approving the request.

During the McNamara era, the Air Staff grew cynical about his staff's review and approval process. According to office gossip, a new system had to jump three hurdles before approval. First hurdle: "You don't need this new system, the old one works fine." Assuming the Air Force successfully proved the need, the second hurdle was higher. "OK, maybe you need a new system, but the one you're proposing won't work." After rounding up enough technical arguments to convince even the most skeptical review authority, the proposal might move on to the third hurdle. It was a very high hurdle and seldom jumped. "All right, maybe there is a need for the new system, and maybe it will work, but it costs way too much money."

When the Air Staff Board reviewed the requirement for fighter ECM pods, there was reason for optimism. Two years of analysis coupled with industry and Systems Command efforts were finally coming to fruition. Things were going well, and a practical, cost-effective ECM pod was within reach. After quickly reviewing the ECM pod data, the board chairman welcomed a well-known WWII fighter pilot recently returned from a year in Southeast Asia, where he had commanded a fighter wing. The highly decorated colonel reminded everyone of Steve Canyon, a comic strip hero of that era.

"Welcome home, Colonel. What can you tell the board about the status of our operations in Southeast Asia, particularly in Vietnam?" The colonel responded with an upbeat appraisal, modestly presented, but leaving the impression that this guy really knew what he was talking about. The board collectively leaned forward, hoping for one more drink from the wellspring of recent experience.

The board chairman could not let the moment pass. "Today we've been listening to a proposal for ECM pods to be carried on fighters. With all your experience, do you believe we need them?" His answer brought smiles of relief from several board members and tears of frustration to the eyes of those who had worked long and hard on the project. "No, sir, fighter pilots in combat don't need crap like that on their aircraft." Several heads nodded affirmatively; others looked around doubtfully. The meeting adjourned. We returned to our offices without a decision. The Air Staff Board put ECM pods on the back burner for several more weeks.

In March 1965, USAF and Navy aircraft began flying missions against both the Ho Chi Minh Trail and North Vietnam. Rolling Thunder was the operational plan for bombing NVN. It soon became obvious that the USSR had furnished NVN with a very effective air defense system. Radar coverage existed over the entire targeted area of North Vietnam. Many targets were well protected by concentrations of Soviet 37 mm and 57 mm antiaircraft guns, plus some larger 85 mm and 100 mm guns. These four gun systems were most effective from low through medium altitudes.

The SA-2 SAM was most effective at high altitude. A U-2 photographed the first SA-2 SAM site in April 1965, and many more sites were located by the end of the year. If the attack was planned at very low altitude below radar coverage, the aircrews were confronted by the highly effective Soviet ZSU-23-4 rapid-firing, multiple-barreled cannon. Although most losses were from antiaircraft fire, SAMs killed 11 aircraft in 1965—the first loss, on 24 July 1965, was an 8th FBW F-4C stationed at Ubon, Thailand.

Mounting fighter losses raised the awareness and necessity for ECM equipment. Because of past delays, there were no ECM pods and radar homing and warning (RHAW) systems. Finally, recognizing the need for protection from SAMs, the Department of Defense (DoD) authorized the Air Force to begin procuring jamming pods under Quick Reaction Certification (QRC) program authority. In January 1967, the first ECM pods, QRC-160s, arrived to equip F-4s. By the end of the Vietnam War, most fighter and reconnaissance aircraft were equipped with ECM pods and RHAW systems.

The battle for air superiority between SAMs and offensive aircraft has never ended. After our initial encounters with SAM defenses, the USAF developed Wild Weasel fighters that would locate SAM sites and destroy SAM radar with radar-homing missiles, like the early Shrike, or by direct attack by the fighter itself. As jamming and other ECM techniques have been developed and improved aircraft survivability, so have enemy SAM systems. The battle continues today with our stealthy (low-observable) fighters and bombers having the upper hand, at least temporarily.

Blue Dart

After spending most of two years analyzing enemy air defenses, advocating systems to protect tactical aircraft, and struggling to understand a poorly defined escalation policy, I began a new project. The SecDef had requested that USAF form a special study group, Blue Dart, to examine interrelationships between offensive and defensive forces. Study results could shape the size and composition of future forces. My duties were to war-game various weapon systems, prepare analytical studies using different strategic situations, and develop a method for comparing the results.

Defense studies at that time customarily started with a scenario. Typically, the scenario described an imaginary political-military crisis that led inevitably to war. In Blue Dart, the war was to be between the United States and the Soviet Union. Lacking a Tom Clancy in our study group, Maj George Sylvester and I were stuck with writing an imaginative yet plausible scenario that would start this all-out war.[9]

The more we wrote, the more obvious it became that no scenario would seem plausible to everyone reviewing the study. Writing scenarios reminded me of a pep rally before a football game. With due respect to the pep rally, how the football team performed would decide the game, not the miniskirted cheerleaders at the pep rally. In Blue Dart, the cost-effective analyses of weapon systems would point to the best composition of future forces. Blue Dart management agreed that the analyses of offensive and defensive systems would stand on their own and that the scenario would be bare bones. With scenario-writing no longer a hot item, the Blue Dart leader, Col John Germeraad, put me to work war-gaming various weapon systems, preparing analyses, and developing methods to compare results.

Among the weapon systems we studied in Blue Dart, three remained the subject of follow-on studies—the Minuteman ICBM, a new bomber called the advanced manned strategic aircraft (AMSA), and the F-12, a Mach 3 interceptor. All were controversial in one way or another.

In 1964 SAC had 142 Minuteman IA and 556 Minuteman IB ICBMs, each with a single reentry vehicle (RV)—the nuclear weapon. The newer and more capable Minuteman II, also with a single RV, would be operational in 1965. A new ICBM, Minuteman III, began development in the mid-1960s. Instead of carrying a single RV, the Minuteman III could carry three. The three RVs, called multiple independently targetable reentry vehicles (MIRV), were carried on a liquid-propelled, post-boost vehicle called a "bus." Because the bus passed over a fairly large area, the MIRVs could independently attack three different targets. The yield for each Minuteman III MIRV was less than the yield for a Minuteman I or II RV. However, improved accuracy and the opportunity to attack more targets made the MIRV an attractive trade-off for SAC planners. The first Minuteman III squadrons became operational in 1970. By 1976, 11 Minuteman III squadrons were on alert with 550 ICBMs. The total number of Minuteman RVs increased from 698 in 1964 to 2,100 in 1975, largely because of MIRV technology.[10]

After leaving Blue Dart, I learned that Secretary McNamara had decided to limit the number of Minutemen to 1,000 before asking the Air Force to conduct Blue Dart. A copy of his letter to the Air Force mysteriously appeared after the study ended. In the upper left-hand corner was McNamara's initialed comment that 1,000 Minuteman ICBMs were enough.

The DoD had cancelled the full development of the supersonic B-70 in 1959, and the new SecDef, Robert McNamara, reduced the prototype XB-70 program to three aircraft in 1961. McNamara also directed the phaseout of all B-47s by the end of September 1966. SAC had 626 B-52s at the time of the Blue Dart study. Within 10 years, the B-52 inventory would shrink to 420 aircraft as older models went to the boneyard. When the FB-111 became available, it would replace the B-58, but that process would not be complete until January 1970.

General LeMay was concerned not only about the lack of a long-range modern bomber to replace the aging B-52 but also with how to increase the shrinking bomber force. A team conducting a high-powered study led by Col David Jones, who later became the USAF chief of staff and CJCS, had been cloistered in Los Angeles where it had ready access to the aerospace industry.[11] After many weeks of intense study, the team proposed a new supersonic bomber called the AMSA. Eventually, the transformed AMSA became the B-1. Blue Dart studied the proposed AMSA as well as alternative force structures with B-52 and FB-111A bombers.

In April 1962, the Air Force first flew an astonishing new aircraft called the YF-12A. Lockheed designed and built the aircraft at Kelly Johnson's Skunk Works. It could fly faster and higher (Mach 3+ and 80,000 feet) than any other military aircraft in the world. With an advanced Doppler radar and air-to-air missiles, the F-12A theoretically could intercept and destroy any Soviet bomber before it could reach the CONUS. The YF-12 survived Blue Dart, but the program ended without the aircraft becoming an operational fighter interceptor. Instead, the YF-12 lived several other lives while morphing into the SR-71, a long-range Mach 3+ reconnaissance aircraft. SR-71 deliveries to SAC began in 1966.

As the SecDef had requested, Blue Dart compared offensive and defensive options available to the future Air Force. Although Blue Dart had no authority to resolve all the force structure problems facing the Air Force, it did focus Air Force thinking on what the principal issues would be. Colonel Germeraad credited me for authoring a major portion of the report and briefing the results, but his leadership made the study a success. In August 1964, as Blue Dart ended, I moved to the AMSA focal point office as a mission analyst.

Advanced Manned Strategic Aircraft—Tough Fights

The Air Staff has several fiefdoms, each headed by a lieutenant general DCS who reports to the USAF chief of staff. Each DCS has responsibility for an important area of related Air Force activities. One step down the pecking order is a major general director. Reporting to the director are divisions. Still further down the ladder is the branch. Each branch has action officers who do the research, write and coordinate staff papers, prepare and give briefings, and maintain contact with major air commands. The new assignment was under the DCS for programs and requirements and, more specifically, the director of operational requirements, Maj Gen Jack J. Catton.

On 1 May 1964, I reported to the new job in operational requirements. Col William R. MacDonald was the strategic division chief, and Lt Col Clyde Denniston was our aircraft branch chief. My job was to work with Lt Col Wallace Hynds preparing analyses, writing advocacy letters, and doing whatever else we could do to strengthen the case for AMSA.[12] After the first few days in the new job, it was apparent that MacDonald, Denniston, and Hynds were three exceptional staff officers—helpful, considerate, and knowledgeable.

Because the chief of staff made AMSA the top-priority Air Force development program, the focal point office was under a lot of pressure to make it happen. Every week, General LeMay expected a progress report that he could send to Secretary of the Air Force Eugene M. Zuckert. LeMay's objective was for Zuckert to pass this on to Secretary McNamara along with a strong recommendation for starting the development of AMSA. The times that we briefed Zuckert were disconcerting. He was always polite, paid attention to the briefing, nodded his head in the right direction at the right times, and said he would give it careful study before discussing it with the SecDef. He never committed to the program. After working there for a while, I realized that it would be a cold day in hell when Zuckert supported anything that McNamara opposed.

At one of our weekly séances with General LeMay, Wally Hynds sounded a little frustrated over our lack of progress with Zuckert. LeMay offered some advice that turned out to be true. "Don't let it get you down. Think of it like a wrestling match. Keep wrestling and one of these days we'll wear them down, and we'll get the new bomber." It turned out that LeMay was prophetic. Four presidents and 20 years later, the Air Force finally got the AMSA—known by then as the B-1B bomber.

After President Johnson's landslide election in November 1964, he invited the JCS and the SecDef to attend an informal breakfast meeting at his Texas ranch. When they finished eating, Johnson asked the chiefs to tell him the most important item each wanted in the forthcoming defense budget. Based on his seniority in the JCS, General LeMay was asked to speak first. "Mr. President, I need $10 million to start advanced development on AMSA, our proposed new bomber."

LeMay's words were hardly out of his mouth when McNamara banged his fist on the table. "He's not asking for $10 million. That's just his foot in the door. He's really asking for $100 million!"

LeMay flushed and before he could respond to McNamara's outburst, President Johnson intervened. "Gentlemen, let's not argue the point now. Curt, how about you sending an AMSA briefing to the White House so I can understand what you want?" LeMay agreed and the meeting moved on to other subjects.

When LeMay returned from Johnson's ranch, he told Catton about the breakfast meeting and that he needed a briefing and accompanying letter to send to the White House next week. Because of our AMSA responsibilities, General Catton felt Wally Hynds and I should know about the scene at Johnson's ranch. Whether the incident occurred exactly as Catton stated, General LeMay was clearly offended by the SecDef interrupting his response to the president. LeMay often disagreed with administration policies, but he did agree to delay retirement and remain chief of staff until January 1965. This was widely seen as a political bribe to keep LeMay from speaking out during the 1964 election campaign against the administration's conduct of the Vietnam War and other defense policies.

Wally Hinds and I burned the midnight oil and finished the briefing and accompanying letter on Thursday. The letter went to Catton for approval. Catton called a Saturday morning meeting in the conference room. About a dozen Air Force generals were around the conference table reading copies of the letter due to LeMay on Monday. After listening to all the changes and nitpicks suggested by the visiting generals, Catton said to rewrite the letter and have it ready for his approval by Monday morning.

I left the meeting disgusted. Changing the original letter to include all their suggestions would have created a literary monstrosity. Wally said not to worry and to take the rest of the weekend off, and he would fix the letter. Monday morning, I could hardly wait to see Wally's redo. Wally was not only smart as hell, he was gutsy. There were no changes in the letter when we took it to Catton for approval. I expected Catton to throw us out of his office. Instead, Catton read it, said "Great letter!" and sent it to LeMay for signature.

A week or so later, the White House notified us of the briefing time. Catton was the briefer, and Wally accompanied him to flip charts. After the briefing, President Johnson asked no questions and offered no opinion but thanked Catton for the briefing. We later learned that General LeMay, always the good soldier, had sent a copy of the letter and briefing to Secretary McNamara before the briefing date. We believed McNamara put his spin on the AMSA proposal before Johnson heard the briefing.

By December we had completed all the submissions necessary for the AMSA Advanced Development Program. I spent the next few weeks working on the FB-111A, a modification of the F-111. In January 1965, my temporary duty in operational requirements ended. It had been a challenging, enjoyable assignment and provided insight into Pentagon politics at a higher level than my previous assignments. Working for Jack Catton was especially worthwhile. The man exuded leadership, and his open-minded, enthusiastic approach to solving difficult issues inspired those who were fortunate to work for him. General Catton retired in September 1972 after three years of commanding MAC.

For nearly a year, I had not been in close contact with my former office. When I first reported to the Air Battle Analysis Center in 1962, the emphasis was on war gaming, not systems analysis. McNamara's Whiz Kids had made it clear—the USAF needed a more sophisticated approach to decision making to be competitive in the annual defense budget battles. The name changes over the three years from Air Battle Analysis Center to Air Battle Analysis Division to Studies and Analysis Directorate were not simply cosmetic. They reflected Air Force acceptance of the need for modern business management practices compatible with the SecDef's demands.

The first step in making better decisions requires studying the known and analyzing alternatives. Those important functions became the responsibility of the S&A Directorate. If S&A were objective, accurate, and thorough, Air Force leaders would have the necessary information available to make responsible decisions. Beefing up S&A to meet the challenge meant buying the latest computers, establishing contacts with RAND and other operations research organizations, and augmenting the S&A staff with varied disciplines and talents. In addition to Air

Force officers with operational experience, S&A hired civil servants and military people with educational backgrounds that included engineering, game theory, and statistics.

Maj Gen Howard A. Davis was the new director of Studies and Analysis. With a strong operational background and keen intellect, he was able to focus on the core issues facing our strategic, tactical, and airlift forces during the difficult years of the mid to late '60s. Not shy about selling his product, Davis made sure that the Air Staff, including the chief of staff, stayed informed about study findings and understood the analytical comparisons. On top of all this, he was a strong leader who quickly gained the respect of all the people in the directorate and his associates in the Air Staff.

A major study effort, Blue Lance, was under way in the Pentagon. The SecDef directed each service to study all strategic offensive and defensive forces. I was in charge of developing and directing the Air Force computer programs that would compare the cost-effectiveness of different combinations of air, land, and sea forces. With lots of help from expert computer programmers, we created two large programs. Force Option Ranking by Cost Effectiveness (FORCE) compared 2,800 combinations of offensive air, land, and sea forces in 69 different scenarios. Defense Evaluation through Effectiveness and Cost Techniques (DETECT) made a similar analysis for defensive systems. By the time we finished, we had a roomful of computer paper. The toughest part lay ahead—sorting through all the output to find those systems that were cost-effective in nearly every situation.

At the highest end of the conflict spectrum, ICBMs and sea launched ballistic missiles (SLBM) carrying MIRVs were the most cost-effective nuclear weapon systems. Silo-based Minuteman IIIs cost less to purchase and maintain than nuclear submarines equipped with Poseidon SLBMs. However, Minuteman silos were more vulnerable to a preemptive Soviet attack than nuclear submarines at sea. Command and control issues existed with the nuclear submarines, but their survivability tended to offset this disadvantage. The AMSA was more cost-effective than the aging B-52 force, primarily because of its better probability of penetrating Soviet defenses. In addition, bombers are effective in conventional wars, whereas ICBMs and SLBMs are not.

Blue Lance provided strong analytical support for the concept of a nuclear triad composed of ICBMs, SLBMs, and bombers. Subsequent studies throughout the Cold War confirmed the continuing need for the triad. All three legs of the triad were upgraded or replaced by similar systems during the '60s, '70s, and '80s, but the prime advantages of the triad remained the same:

- *Command and Control*, secure and fast, president to strategic forces;

- *Survivability*, under all foreseeable circumstances;

- *Scalability*, having an appropriate response for any nuclear crisis;

- *Verifiability*, required by arms control agreements now and in the future;

- *Safety*, against accidental, inadvertent, or unintentional release of nuclear weapons; and

- *Absolute Deterrent*, against any nation considering an attack on the United States

Our analysis of defensive systems offered no clear-cut winners. The glaring defensive weakness was the inability to counter an attack by Soviet ballistic missiles. The United States lacked a feasible antiballistic missile system in 1965, and none was on the horizon. Not until technology solved the complex problem of destroying ballistic missiles after launch and before impact could the United States defend itself against such an attack. The most useful defensive systems against ICBM and SLBM attacks were over-the-horizon radars and satellites with infrared sensors that could detect the launch of ballistic missiles. Detecting the launch of enemy ballistic missiles gave the president and SecDef enough time to authorize the launch of our own strategic nuclear forces. Since nuclear deterrence depended upon the Soviets knowing they could not attack the United States without suffering intolerable damage to their own country, our radar and satellites were also key systems in deterring nuclear war.

The Lockheed YF-12 had flown in April 1962. The air defense community was pushing hard to buy 72 of these advanced aircraft to protect the United States against Soviet bomber attacks. Blue Lance acknowledged the YF-12 performance but could not make cost-effectiveness comparisons without more data.

I returned to S&A once again after the study director submitted Blue Lance to the SecDef.

Great Air Battle—F-12 versus the Advanced Manned Strategic Aircraft

Studies and Analysis continued to grow in 1965. More than 100 people were now analyzing the theoretical battles between existing and future enemy and friendly weapon systems. After nearly three years of experience in major studies, I was a battle-scarred veteran, so to speak. When the USAF released the long-awaited promotion list to lieutenant colonel in early 1965, I had been wearing the oak leaves of a major for two years as a "spot" major and four more as a temporary major. The first promotions on a promotion list go to officers in the primary zone with more years of commissioned service. This meant waiting a few more months to pin on the new rank for those in the below-the-zone (BTZ) category. Waiting did not matter; it was good news to be selected BTZ.

From time to time, General Davis had me review in-house studies for quality. Some analysts tend to overstate claims, ignore realities, and quantify the immeasurable. A study suffering these defects cannot withstand careful scrutiny, and the Pentagon hierarchy would usually discount or ignore it. More dangerous are analysts who know the desired answer and cleverly invent data to prove it or hide data that disprove it. These analyses are often difficult to unravel. They sound like sweet music to the boss's ear. As they move up the chain of command, they accumulate supporters like fleas on a dog. During the McNamara years, when cost-effectiveness was king, all services became too skilled at submitting analyses that seemed factual but had hidden biases. We needed to improve the credibility of our studies.

Parametric analysis offered one way to avoid the "finite answer trap." There are limits to nearly everything we do. These limits are called "parameters," "boundaries," or "constraints."

Assume a friend asked, "What kind of gas mileage do you get?" If you answered, "About 18 miles per gallon around town; maybe 22 to 26 on the highway, depending on the traffic and how fast I'm driving," you provided parameters to your answer. You did not answer "exactly 21.5 miles per gallon" because you knew that driving habits, fast or slow traffic, low tire pressures, air conditioning, and other factors made "exactly 21.5 miles per gallon" misleading.

Without knowing the origin of parametric analysis, I became an advocate in S&A and briefed its merits to other organizations including ACSC and the Military Operations Research Society. By exploring the effects of different assumptions, a parametric study becomes a useful aid in decision making. It establishes likely parameters that comprise the range of outcomes. A finite answer to a complex, real-world problem like the performance of a future weapon system in a future war against an ill-defined enemy is unlikely to have only one answer. More important is finding the strengths and weaknesses of the future system by using different assumptions.

The methodology can also apply to combat decision making. A wise commander carefully examines the upside and downside before reaching an important decision. Consider a hypothetical case where an F-16 wing is tasked to destroy a high-priority, well-defended, hardened enemy command center. The wing commander asks the staff to plan the mission and compute the probability of success. The staff decides the strike force will be four F-16 aircraft, each carrying two 2,000-pound Paveway II laser-guided bombs (LGB) that have both laser and GPS guidance capabilities. Staff members also compute an 80 percent probability that the F-16s will destroy the hardened target using the eight bombs.

The wing commander realizes the need for more information and asks questions that might determine the success or failure of the mission. The questions require the staff to do more research—to find the parameters that will identify the risk and improve the probability the mission will succeed. For example, some questions that could be asked are as follows: What is the probability the F-16s can penetrate enemy defenses and reach the target? Will fighters from other units suppress enemy SAM and GCI sites before our attack? Will support jamming aircraft be available to jam enemy radars in the target area? What is the weather forecast in the target area? Are Paveway II LGBs available? If not, do we have 2,000-pound Joint Direct Attack Munitions? If we have to use bombs terminally guided by GPS, what is the damage expectancy? The question list grows as war and weapons increase in complexity.

If a staff understands all the parameters of a mission and presents accurate data, the commander is able to make a logical decision. In later assignments as a senior officer, briefing officers were often surprised when I asked detailed questions concerning the subject they were briefing. It was my way of determining whether they had considered all the pertinent facts and issues.

Dr. Harold Brown became secretary of the Air Force in October 1965 and remained in that position until the Nixon administration took office in 1969. Dr. Brown, a man of awesome intellect, served as defense director of Research and Engineering prior to becoming SECAF. He knew the advantages and disadvantages of existing and proposed Air Force weapon systems and understood the recent Blue Dart and Blue Lance studies.

One of Brown's first acts was to challenge a major procurement issue. The Air Force could no longer be on both sides of an important argument. One side was the Air Force claim that the AMSA (later renamed the B-1) could successfully penetrate every Soviet air defense system, including advanced systems with interceptors having F-12–like capabilities. The other side was that the F-12 could shoot down everything that flew, including advanced Soviet bombers like the AMSA. He wanted a thorough Air Force study to resolve the dilemma.

General Davis gave me the responsibility for this important study. Seven officers with different qualifications were added to the study group: a radar expert, a weather officer with a PhD in mathematics, the best S&A computer programmer, an aeronautical engineer, an intelligence officer with long Pentagon experience, an interceptor pilot from ADC, and a SAC B-52 radar navigator. The study group contacted AFSC on aircraft performance details, Air Staff Programs on budget issues, Lockheed on F-12 capabilities, Hughes on the ASG-18 fire-control system and GAR-9 (AIM-47A) air-to-air missile capabilities, Cornell Aeronautical Labs on terrain-following radar

(TFR) capabilities, North American Rockwell on AMSA capabilities, the lab at Wright-Patterson AFB for reducing aircraft radar cross sections (RCS), several companies who built defensive jamming equipment, and Air Force and SAC Intelligence for future Soviet air defenses.

Working against the F-12 were high procurement and operating costs. The unit cost of this largely titanium aircraft was at least twice as much as any previous fighter and probably more than an AMSA. Special fuel, pressure suits, and high-maintenance costs added to normal operating costs. ADC asked for 100 F-12s but later cut the requirement to 72. To offset the cost of F-12 procurement and operations, ADC offered to drawdown the remaining interceptor force.

The F-12 had some distinct advantages. It could fly higher and faster than any other aircraft in the world. Combat radius was 1,200 nautical miles. The ASG-18 fire-control system and AIM-47 missile on the F-12 had been successfully tested. The F-12 was an awesome threat to any penetrating bomber.

The study group had a theoretical bomber, the AMSA, with desired specifications but no actual test data to support the performance claims. From U-2, RB-57, and EC-135 experience and from satellite data, Air Force Intelligence knew how the Soviet air defense system functioned. We knew ways to degrade Soviet EW and GCI radars with jamming and direct attacks. We did not know how to degrade the look-down-shoot-down Doppler radar on the Red F-12. In our final analysis, the AMSA had to survive a one-on-one, head-on engagement with the Red F-12 in order to penetrate the USSR and attack assigned targets.

AMSA had several important advantages over contemporary bombers. The swing-wing AMSA could fly supersonically, although fuel consumption was much higher than during subsonic flight. This high-speed dash capability compressed the reaction time available to enemy air defenses. TFR allowed AMSA to fly close to the ground at high subsonic speeds, thus avoiding detection by flying under the coverage of EW and GCI radars. AMSA could carry roughly twice the weapons payload of the B-52. Included were as many as 24 short-range air-to-surface attack missiles (SRAM) with 200-kiloton nuclear warheads. The rocket-propelled SRAM, with a range of nearly 100 miles, could suppress or destroy EW and GCI radars as the AMSA approached the Soviet Union and penetrated coastal defenses.

The fire-control officer in the F-12 radar had to guide the AIM-47 all the way to the target in order to destroy it. The tests against drones showed how effective the F-12 could be if given enough time and distance to detect and track the target, fire the missile, and guide it to impact. We realized AMSA survival against the Red F-12 depended upon shrinking the time and distance for engagement and making the AIM-47 miss before it could explode near the AMSA.

Our analyses showed the biggest payoffs for the AMSA came from combining speed and stealth. Stealth was relatively new in 1966, and there was a great deal of skepticism surrounding the subject. Our study stressed the importance of reducing the RCS of the AMSA to delay detection and to avoid radar-guided missiles.

The principal advocate for the F-12 in DCS Plans and Operations was a general who was very critical of our crediting the AMSA with a significantly reduced RCS. He knew that the F-12 would be ineffective if it could not detect the AMSA in time to launch the AIM-47. We arranged a visit for the general to the Wright-Patterson AFB laboratory, which was developing ways to reduce radar cross sections. Upon his return, the general called from his office. "Leavitt, you have killed the F-12."

The distraught general gave radar reduction too much credit. There were other reasons for "killing" the F-12. Our primary national military policy was to deter nuclear war. The Soviet Union had concentrated on building ICBMs and SLBMs, not bombers, as its strategic weapon systems. The F-12 could not reduce the amount of damage caused by a Soviet ICBM/SLBM attack against the United States. Furthermore, it may not have been significantly more effective at destroying Soviet bombers than the F-106 interceptors in ADC.

The F-12 would have been difficult to keep on a quick-response alert because of certain aircraft characteristics and the physiological requirement for aircrews flying at high altitude to wear pressure suits. To add to its problems, the F-12 operational costs were far higher than any other fighter aircraft. When SAC acquired the SR-71, a derivative of the YF-12 designed for long-range, high-altitude strategic reconnaissance, the true cost per flying hour became a genuine concern.

America's deterrence policy depended upon answering any Soviet preemptive attack with an overwhelming response. The strategic triad of ICBMs, SLBMs, and bombers first needed to survive a Soviet attack and then retaliate. There was an aging problem—the bomber leg had grown old. Serious doubts arose about B-52s being able to penetrate Soviet airspace. They were particularly vulnerable to Soviet SAMs, a fact convincingly confirmed six years later over Hanoi when Soviet SA-2 missiles destroyed 15 B-52s during Linebacker II. Modern bombers in the triad would do more for deterrence than adding F-12s that offered only a marginal defensive payoff. When the study ended in 1966, we were ready to resolve Brown's dilemma.

The study was briefed to the Air Staff, chief of staff, director of defense research and engineering, SECAF, and CINCSAC. It became the principal input to the advanced bomber study submitted to the SecDef. The Office of the Secretary of Defense (OSD) indicated that the penetration data would be used in a memorandum to the president as the best information on this subject available in the country.

The culmination of the briefing schedule was speaking to 40 leaders of major defense industries. The USAF chief of staff, Gen John P. McConnell, introduced the briefing. He stated that he totally agreed with the study and conclusions. Furthermore, he expected industry support for the study conclusions and urged leaders to accept the study as a guidepost for future Air Force developments. He then introduced me as the study leader and briefer, turned around, and left the room. The audience was attentive, asked many questions, and was very complimentary of the study group's work.

All the team members made outstanding contributions to the project, and we were all appreciative of the support provided by General Davis and Lt Gen Keith Compton, DCS for operations and plans.

The SecDef discontinued development of the F-12 on 27 November 1967. The AMSA became an advanced development project called B-1. In 1970 the Air Force awarded development contracts for the B-1 to Rockwell International (airframe) and General Electric (F-101 engines).

Four years in Studies and Analysis was a great experience. Many officers and civilian employees had helped make the transition from cockpit to Pentagon desk successful. Along the way, I earned a master's degree by attending George Washington University at night and completed ACSC by correspondence. When the senior school selections for 1966–67 were released, my new assignment was as a student at the National War College at Fort McNair, Washington, DC. The future looked bright.

Broadening Horizons

The nation that makes a great distinction between its scholars and its warriors will have its thinking done by cowards and its fighting done by fools.

—Thucydides, Greek general and historian
Circa 460–400 BC

Prior to World War II, career officers had little exposure to foreign policy and international affairs. This lack of exposure stemmed from the long-standing American policy of avoiding entangling alliances. After World War I ended with the Versailles Treaty, the United States had reverted to isolationism once again. Defense policy was the sickly offspring of two parents— isolationism and hard times. The era of American isolationism ended when Germany and Italy declared war on the United States following the Pearl Harbor attack.

In his magnificent book *An Army at Dawn*, Rick Atkinson documents the growing pains our military forces suffered following the outbreak of World War II. In 1939 the Army could field only five divisions. Congress budgeted $9 billion for the Army in 1940, a sum exceeding the grand total of all Army budgets since 1920.[13] A year after the draft law passed in 1940, Army personnel had increased to 1,400,000. By the end of the war, 16,122,566 men and women had served in the armed forces.[14]

World War II challenged members of the officer corps of all services in ways that only a few farsighted officers anticipated but no one had experienced. They were often thrust into command and staff positions by circumstances beyond their control and, too often, beyond their competence. The rapid expansion of our military in WWII taught an important lesson. Future leaders of the armed forces must be better prepared for their wartime responsibilities. Serious mistakes made early in the war might have been avoided if staff officers had known the capabilities and limitations of the other services.

To increase interservice cooperation and understanding, in June 1943, the Army-Navy Staff College was established at Fort McNair in the District of Columbia as the first step toward correcting this problem. The upgraded National War College replaced it on 1 July 1946. The stated mission of the NWC is to "prepare future leaders of the Armed Forces, State Department, and other civilian agencies for high-level policy, command, and staff responsibilities. To do this, NWC conducts a senior-level course of study in national security policy and strategy for selected U.S. and foreign military officers and federal officials."[15]

I joined the NWC Class of 1967 on 2 August 1966. We were 140 experienced officers and civilians from all four military services, the State Department's Foreign Service, and other agencies of the executive department of the US government involved with national security matters. The first day, we met the faculty and our fellow students. Each class member introduced himself to the entire class and faculty by briefly reciting his background and experience. Several were Vietnam returnees, although this was just the summer of 1966.

The most decorated officer in the Army, winner of the Medal of Honor and Distinguished Service Cross during the Korean War, Lt Col Lloyd "Scooter" Burke had left the hospital a few days earlier after recovering from serious wounds in Vietnam. The Navy captain of the cruiser that intercepted the Soviet transport carrying nuclear weapons during the Cuban missile crisis provided us a firsthand insight to that historical event. Heisman Trophy winner and three-time All American, USAF lieutenant colonel Felix "Doc" Blanchard, joined Olympic star and future ambassador David Bolen in modestly introducing himself. After the introductions, I realized that an important part of the NWC education would include knowing these men of many talents and backgrounds.

A few weeks after entering, the commandant's office advised me to bring my wife to an award ceremony in his office the next day. The Air Force was awarding the Legion of Merit for "performance of outstanding service to the United States as Planning and Programming Officer . . . from 1 November 1962 to 1 July 1966." For a relatively new lieutenant colonel, this was an unusual and unexpected honor. To cap it off, General Compton, USAF DCS for plans and operations, and General Davis, USAF director of studies and analysis, attended the ceremony where Vice Adm Fitzhugh Lee, NWC commandant, pinned on the medal.

In my opinion, the learning experience at NWC was without exception the best our country could offer. Fundamental differences distinguished NWC from other civilian and military institutions that offered courses in national security policy and foreign relations. One difference was the method of instruction. Another was the access and availability to high-level decision makers gained by locating the college in Washington. The NWC nonattribution policy allowed guest speakers to express their opinions openly without fear of being misquoted by the press. The experienced faculty and student body makeup were other distinctions.

The principal method of instruction was exposing the students to major issues facing the United States in the implementation of our national security policy. Every school day, the class focused on a specific subject. NWC would invite the top authority in the nation on that subject to be the guest speaker. If he or she were unavailable, the faculty would pursue the next best. There were no "school solutions." There were no tests and no grades except for a final evaluation on a training report. The goal was to broaden the students' knowledge by studying the pros and cons of major issues.

A typical subject in 1966 was the Communist threat to the Sukarno government in Indonesia. On the day before this subject was the topic, each student received an abundance of reading materials for study. Typically, the reading materials presented the other side of the issue—not only the opinions expected from the guest lecturer, who in this case was the US ambassador to Indonesia. After the lecture, the speaker opened the session to questions. Several students (volunteers) joined the speaker for a private lunch. The last academic classes for the day were seminars for study groups of 10 to 15 students. By the time we adjourned for intramural athletics, everyone had acquired an understanding of the political-military situation in Indonesia.

National War College, Fort Lesley J. McNair, Washington, DC

Surprise presentation ceremony, National War College, 26 September 1966. *Left to right*: Major General Davis, director of USAF studies and analysis; Lieutenant General Compton, DCS for plans and operations, USAF; Lieutenant Colonel Obarski, AF Commendation Medal recipient; Lieutenant Colonel Leavitt, Legion of Merit recipient; Anne Leavitt; and Admiral Lee, commandant, NWC.

In 1966 the Vietnam War was front-page news. Public opinion was still generally supportive of our involvement. Not all was peaceful on the home front. Pickets and protestors regularly appeared at the Pentagon entrances, and college protests often went out of control. One senator who became a leading antiwar spokesman was William Fulbright from Arkansas. My father-in-law, Dabbs Sullivan, an investment banker from Little Rock, maintained a friendly, long-time relationship with Fulbright. I asked the NWC faculty members if they wanted Fulbright as a guest speaker, assuming Dabbs could arrange it. The NWC dean quickly agreed. I coordinated arrangements with the senator's office after Fulbright agreed. About a week or two before his scheduled appearance, Fulbright's administrative assistant called and cancelled the senator's appearance. We never knew why. Fulbright, the leader of the antiwar movement in the Senate, may have been unwilling to face questioning from a pro-military audience that included recent returnees from Southeast Asia. Or he may have felt disclosure of his appearance at the NWC would weaken his standing with the antiwar community.

There was constant discussion among NWC students about Vietnam policy. Although most officers believed we must intervene to stop the spread of Communism in Southeast Asia, there was no unanimity about the best strategy to accomplish that objective. Nearly all agreed that the administration's policy of gradual escalation was not getting the job done. Although we were winning on the battlefield, the enemy was elusive and seemingly immune to high casualties. Political progress in the South Vietnamese government was not apparent, and American casualties were rising with no end in sight.

General Taylor, former chairman of the JCS and the author of *Uncertain Trumpet*, had returned after being our ambassador to Vietnam for a year and would be a guest speaker. General Taylor was widely considered to be the principal advocate for our gradual escalation policy. Custom allowed each NWC student to pick one guest speaker during the year with whom to share a small group luncheon. I chose to have lunch with General Taylor. The big day came, and I could hardly contain myself waiting to question him about our escalation policy. If he defended the policy, I intended to debate the issue with him—in a polite way, of course. Finally my moment came.

295

"General Taylor, do you think gradual escalation has been successful and is the right way to fight this war?" His frank answer left me speechless. "No, it is a complete failure."

The class visited the State Department. After separating into smaller groups, each group visited Secretary of State Dean Rusk in his spacious office. Rusk perched informally on the front of his desk, casually smoking a cigarette as he answered our questions. The topic soon turned to the Vietnam War. The Soviet Union or China had supplied SA-2 SAMs to North Vietnam commencing in 1965. The ROEs in 1965 prohibited attacking these SA-2 sites. By the end of 1965, the SA-2s had destroyed 11 American fighters.

There seemed to be two reasons for this prohibition. First, the intelligence community believed either the Chinese or USSR military operated the SA-2 sites. The administration did not want to provoke either China or the USSR by killing their soldiers at the SA-2 sites. Second, some SA-2 sites were located in close proximity to the NVN civilian populace. The administration policy was to avoid any collateral damage that might kill North Vietnamese civilians. By 1967 the continuing SA-2 buildup provided SAM coverage beyond Hanoi and Haiphong nearly to the Chinese border.

An Air Force officer asked Rusk why we could not attack SA-2 sites around Hanoi or the railroad tracks leading north to China. Rusk answered, "If anyone told me that we could bomb within 30 miles of the Chinese border and not start World War III, I would say they were crazy."

Did Johnson, Rusk, and McNamara really believe that China or the USSR would enter into a hot war with the United States if we attacked SAM sites in North Vietnam? Probably not, but Rusk's answer was consistent with the administration's inadequate approach toward ending the Vietnam War. First, ignore the ever-increasing numbers of American casualties, and continue fighting a war of attrition in South Vietnam. Second, avoid any escalation strategy against NVN that conceivably could cause China or the Soviet Union to enter the war.

In 1967 the administration slightly relaxed the ROEs and allowed attacks against SA-2 sites not located inside a populated area where collateral damage might kill civilians. Probably the most difficult and dangerous mission associated with these on-again, off-again bombing campaigns over North Vietnam was attacking a SAM site. Although the Air Force suppressed or destroyed many SA-2 sites, we continued to lose aircraft to the SA-2 for the remainder of the war.[16]

In 1953 President Eisenhower settled the Korean War by threatening to escalate the level of hostilities. In 1962 President Kennedy ended the Cuban missile crisis by demonstrating with SAC and conventional forces that we would not tolerate Soviet missiles in Cuba. These forceful actions by Eisenhower and Kennedy sharply contrasted with Johnson's ineffective policy in Vietnam.

A high point for many of us was to hear former president Eisenhower address a joint session of the NWC and the Industrial College of the Armed Forces. He covered a wide range of subjects that reflected his unequalled military and political experience.

Officer Personnel used a "dream sheet" that officers were required to file periodically. The purpose was to keep it informed of your career objectives and requested assignments. After promotion to lieutenant colonel in 1965, I had requested duty as a fighter squadron commander in the Vietnam War. Officer Personnel notified me in late 1966 that my next assignment would be an F-105 squadron commander in Thailand operating against NVN and Laos targets.

The Air Force expanded quickly during the mid-'60s to meet the increased demands of the Vietnam War and NATO. An unexpected development was the 1967 Colonel Promotion Board that met early. I had only been a lieutenant colonel for 18 months and had no expectation of promotion. When the USAF released the promotion list, no one was more surprised than I to find his name on the list. The *Air Force Times* published my picture with a comment stating I was the youngest colonel. The Air Force is a competitive society. The unasked for notoriety was like having your picture posted on the local post office wall!

A few weeks after releasing the promotion list, the USAF colonels' branch cancelled my assignment to Southeast Asia as an F-105 squadron commander. Gen William Momyer, Seventh Air Force commander in Saigon, refused to accept colonels who were not currently qualified in the type of aircraft assigned to their tactical unit—the F-105 in my case. Disappointed, I headed for the colonels' branch in the Pentagon.

"Why don't you send me to combat crew training and let me get combat ready in the F-105 or F-4?" The major behind the desk answered quickly, "No colonels can go to combat crew training. All the slots are reserved for lieutenants through lieutenant colonels." (This policy changed later in the war.) "We're sending you to command a college ROTC unit."

"Like hell you are! There's a war on, I'm only 37 years old, in good shape, and want a flying assignment." We had reached an impasse. The major ended our meeting by saying there was nothing more he could do and he had an appointment with Colonel White, the personnel officer for USAFE who was visiting the Pentagon on business.

As I stood up and walked toward the door, Colonel White entered the office. Before the major could intervene, I introduced myself to White and told him I was desperately looking for a flying assignment. "Since Personnel will not send me to Southeast Asia, are there any openings in Europe?" White glanced at my records and made my day. "How would you like to go to the 36th Tactical Fighter Wing at Bitburg AFB, Germany, as the assistant deputy commander for operations?" I jumped at the offer. "Yes, sir! Thank you very much!" Colonel White pointed at the major's desk, "Tell him you are going to the 36th Wing."

The major had overheard my conversation with White. He warned me that the colonels' group did not approve of my asking White for a job without going through "proper channels" and that Personnel would not forget this incident. After having spent four years doing business in the Pentagon, I knew this was a hollow threat.

Before the academic year ended, the class split into smaller groups for the annual visits to Europe, Asia, Africa, and the Middle East. I chose the European trip because my next assignment would be in Germany. We visited Spain; France; West Germany, including East Berlin; Yugoslavia; and the UK.

On the first day in each country, the American Embassy told us its opinions on the political and military issues of current interest in the host country. The business day ended with a cocktail party and the opportunity to socialize with the ambassador and staff. The next day or two, the host government lectured on military capabilities, external threats to that nation, economic conditions, and relations with the United States.

Each visit usually included a visit to its ministry of defense and senior military college. After a free day for sightseeing, we traveled to the next country on our itinerary.

Two events stood out, although the entire trip was worthwhile and memorable. The Cold War was in full bloom in 1967. I had never been in a Communist country before and was anxious to visit Berlin, see the Berlin Wall, and go into East Berlin. A US Army bus drove us to Checkpoint Charlie, the exit/entry point to East Berlin. We were all in uniform. As the bus stopped, an East German army guard climbed on the bus armed with his automatic weapon. I was sitting in the front seat by the door next to Maj Gen Avelin Tacon, NWC assistant commandant. The guard stared at us and motioned to Tacon and me to hand over our American diplomatic passports.

The postwar agreements between the USSR and the Western Allies allowed military officials from the four occupying powers (USA, UK, France, and USSR) to travel between the occupied zones without forfeiting their passports to the East Germans. From a legal viewpoint, East Germany was in the Soviet zone, and the East German guard had no status with the American military. The American Embassy had warned, "Don't give an East German guard your passport!" The guard with his hand out to collect our passports stared belligerently at us for a minute or two. Tacon and I stared back, said nothing, and made no effort to show our diplomatic passports. The guard moved to the next row and tried again—same reaction from that row. Finally, the frustrated guard turned on his heel and left the bus, leaving behind a minor bureaucratic victory for the good guys! The bus drove into East Berlin where the mayor told us the joys of Communism, followed by a sightseeing tour of the city.

The visit to Belgrade, Yugoslavia, provided a closer look at a Communist nation. Yugoslavian president Josip Tito had recently relaxed some of the traditional Communist controls on the country's economy. Tito's chief economic planner, a London School of Economics graduate, gave a memorable lecture on the difficulties and failures in the Yugoslavian economy caused by centralized planning. He gave the examples of building an aluminum plant where there was no bauxite and an automobile plant where there was no skilled labor. By citing

Yugoslavia's many mistakes, he convinced Tito to loosen the economic reins and decentralize economic decision making.

The Yugoslav equivalent of our CJCS lectured on the military threat—"potential enemies are on seven Yugoslav borders," if I remember correctly. He denied that Yugoslavia had a military alliance with the Soviet Union or other Warsaw Pact nations.

A visit to the Military Museum disclosed a lopsided view of history. Displays emphasized Tito's military successes in WWII, but the long Serbian history of losing wars to aggressive neighbors was minimized. The museum gave ample credit to USSR assistance during the war against the Nazis but ignored the large amount of American military aid sent to Tito's armies in 1944–45. A visitor's book was available. I signed and added a comment recommending that the United States be credited for WWII aid.

We stayed at Belgrade's best international hotel. Although no students confirmed this observation from personal experience, the hotel seemed overrun with hookers. Old-fashioned free enterprise could apparently trump Communism. On our last day in Belgrade, we had a few hours for sightseeing. A Navy captain and I went window-shopping. First stop was a bookstore filled with Communist literature. At NWC we learned that a prominent dissident had written a book criticizing Tito and his regime. The very nervous clerk behind the counter breathlessly explained in his broken English that he had never heard of the book, and, not only that, he certainly would not sell it from his store.

Walking down the street, we noticed a well-dressed man stopped whenever we stopped, all the while staying a discrete distance behind us. We decided to have some fun with our "tail." In the next block was a large department store with escalators running to the upper floors. After letting the Yugoslav James Bond get closer, we both took the up escalator. The captain jumped off on the second floor, and I went on to the third. Looking back, we could see Bond was distraught and wondering whom to follow. My Navy friend and I had agreed to meet on the sidewalk outside the store and let Bond find us so he would not get in trouble. When Bond finally arrived, we enjoyed a good laugh and strolled back to the hotel with him in tow about 50 feet behind.

NWC was a great learning experience. My overall performance evaluation was "in the top 10% of the entire class of 140 students and the top 10% of the 35 Air Force students." A committee of members of the NWC faculty rated my individual research paper, "Necessity for a Systems Analysis Approach to our Conduct of International Affairs," as "outstanding." The paper was withdrawn from NWC for the use of HQ USAF, as noted in a commendation letter from the USAF chief of staff, General McConnell.

The NWC Class of 1967 included four military officers who years later would command their service before retiring: Adm Owen W. Siler, commandant, US Coast Guard, 1974–78; Adm Thomas B. Hayward, chief of naval operations, 1978–82; Gen Edward C. Meyer, chief of staff, US Army, 1979–83; and Gen John A. Wickham, chief of staff, US Army, 1983–87. The Air Force four-star was Gen Bennie L. Davis, Commander in Chief, SAC, 1981–85.

Thirty-five civilian officials from various branches of the federal government graduated from NWC in 1967. Seventeen were from the Department of State. Five became United States ambassadors: Hon. David B. Bolen, Hon. Pierre R. Graham, Hon. John W. McDonald, Jr., Hon. Frank V. Ortiz, Jr., and Hon. David T. Schneider. By the time all the civilian students had retired, 24 of the original 35 had reached civilian grades equivalent to general officers.

As June graduation approached, we said our goodbyes. The class was scattering to new assignments all over the world. This had been a great year. Now it was time to get back to work. I was eager to swap textbooks and lectures for an F-4 checklist, a G-suit, and the roar of jet engines!

Notes

1. Col Herbert O. Brennan was missing in action over NVN on 26 November 1967. His aircraft was carrying bombs with a new type of fusing. The bombs exploded prematurely when released, destroying his aircraft. Bert was an outstanding officer in every sense of the word, and his loss was deeply felt by all.

2. Lt Gen Edgar A. Chavarrie's long and distinguished Air Force career ended when he retired from the Air Force in August 1988. He now lives in Alexandria, Virginia.

3. Pedlow, MC 14/2 (Rev) (Final Decision)-23.5.1957, "Overall Strategic Concept for the Defense of the North Atlantic Treaty Organization Area," secs. 2 and 3, 9, 11.

4. Mastny, PHP—Parallel History Project on NATO and the Warsaw Pact, press release.

5. The RVN government called Communist insurgents in South Vietnam the "Viet Cong."

6. Col Ira Kimes retired from the Air Force in 1978. In addition to 63 combat missions during 1961–62, Kimes flew 100 combat missions in the Korean War, 54 combat missions in F-104s from Da Nang in 1965, and 162 combat missions from Cam Rahn Bay in 1969. His 379 combat missions were the most flown by any USAF officer in the West Point Class of 1950. US Military Academy, *Register of Graduates*.

7. His distinguished career included many other key assignments related to the Vietnam War, such as the International Policy Division, Department of the Army, where he worked on plans for Southeast Asia. In 1967 at the White House, he worked on the Vietnam Pacification Program. He returned to Vietnam in 1969 as commanding officer, 3d Brigade, 4th Infantry Division, and assistant chief of staff of the 11th Field Force. He then became executive officer and senior aide to General Westmoreland, Army chief of staff. General Warner retired from the Army on 1 August 1981 after serving as commander, US Readiness Command, and director of the Joint Deployment Agency.

8. Sheehan, *Bright Shining Lie*, 380.

9. Lt Gen George Sylvester retired from the Air Force in 1981. His last assignment was vice-commander, AFSC. In addition to his extensive background in test and evaluation and aircraft systems development and planning, Sylvester served as a fighter squadron commander and combat support group commander in Vietnam.

10. Hopkins, *Development of Strategic Air Command, 1946–1986*. There were 450 Minuteman IIs and 550 Minuteman IIIs in 1975 (ibid.).

11. USAF members of the study group included several future generals: Gen David C. Jones, Gen James R. Allen, Lt Gen George Sylvester, and Maj Gen Robert Lukeman.

12. Col Wallace G. Hynds, Jr., was KIA over NVN on 2 August 1967 while serving as deputy commander of operations, 432d Tactical Reconnaissance Fighter Wing. His career decorations included the Silver Star, Legion of Merit, Distinguished Flying Cross, five Air Medals, Commendation Medal, and Purple Heart. US Military Academy, *Register of Graduates*.

13. Atkinson, *Army at Dawn*, prologue, 1–18.

14. DoD, "Principal Wars in Which the United States Participated," table 2-23.

15. National War College, "Mission."

16. This material is based on discussions with Maj Gen James E. McInerney, USAF, retired. One of the most decorated officers in the Air Force, as a lieutenant colonel he earned the Air Force Cross, three Silver Stars, seven Distinguished Flying Crosses, the Bronze Star, and 15 Air Medals while commanding a "Wild Weasel" squadron assigned the extremely dangerous job of hunting and destroying SA-2 sites. His final assignment prior to retirement in 1980 was director of programs, Headquarters USAF. US Military Academy, *Register of Graduates*.

Chapter 8

USAFE
Colonel—1967–69

Back to Business

There is an old Army maxim: if you choose a military career, you must go where you can hear the sounds of gunfire. With that saying in mind, I volunteered to serve in Vietnam and was disappointed when Air Force Personnel said "not qualified." I needed a flying job to become "qualified."

USAFE offered that, plus the opportunity to play an active role in the Cold War. With bags packed, kids and dog on board, we drove to Maguire AFB, the aerial port of embarkation in New Jersey. The next day, we flew to Rhein-Main AB and began a three-year overseas tour in Germany.

We moved into a furnished apartment on Bitburg AB the day after arriving. A few days later, a shipment arrived with 2,000 pounds of our clothes, personal items, linen, silverware, and so forth. Our eighth grader, Lloyd, and second grader, Mary, joined their classes at Bitburg's school for military dependents. DoD schools for overseas dependents used the same textbooks as schools in Maryland and northern Virginia, making the transition easy for Lloyd and Mary. Once Lloyd learned where the nearest bratwurst stand was located, his cultural transition to Germany was complete. We had enrolled our oldest daughter, Chris, a junior in high school, in The American School in Switzerland (TASIS), before leaving McLean.

The 36th TFW in 1967 was one of the top fighter wings in the Air Force. The wing had five tactical squadrons. Three F-4D squadrons—the 22d Tactical Fighter Squadron (TFS), 23d TFS, and 53d TFS—had recently transitioned from F-105s. The 525th TFS flew F-102s in the important NATO air defense role. The 71st Missile Squadron maintained nuclear alert with the ground-launched, short-range Mace missile.

Col Charles C. "Buck" Pattillo commanded the 36th TFW. Buck had earned his well-deserved reputation throughout the Air Force as an outstanding officer who possessed exceptional skills as a fighter pilot.[1] The famous Pattillo twins, Buck and Bill, had been stationed together from World War II until 1965. In the early 1950s, they helped organize the Skyblazers, the aerial demonstration team in Europe, and flew in more than 250 air shows. In 1953 Buck and Bill were the original left and right wingmen on the famous USAF demonstration team, the Thunderbirds.

Pattillo and his deputy commander for operations, Col Jack Robinson, provided both the leadership and management skills required to make the 36th TFW a top-notch fighter wing. My boss, Jack, was a considerate, well-informed supervisor who always found time to answer questions and explain USAFE procedures and tactical doctrine despite his always busy schedule. He had a strong background in the fighter business and knew all aspects of tactical operations. It was a pleasure to work for him.

Although neither mentioned their concerns to me, Pattillo and Robinson must have been skeptical about Air Force Personnel assigning a new colonel to the 36th TFW who had not flown fighters since 1956 and had spent the interim years in U-2s, B-52s, the Pentagon, and NWC. In their shoes, I probably would have shared their skepticism. Anxious to put this competence issue to bed, I started F-4D training as soon as possible.

First step was "flying" the simulator for a few hours. Simulator training emphasized cockpit familiarization ("switchology" in pilot vernacular) and emergency procedures. Finally satisfied that my ignorance would not kill him, the instructor pilot strapped himself into the back cockpit of an F-4D, and we tried the real thing. The F-4 was big, fast, and—according to some—ugly, but it was a great fighter aircraft that I thoroughly enjoyed flying.[2] On the second flight with a "clean" F-4 (no external stores), I busted Mach 2 for the first time. After a local area check, I was ready for weapons training.

In 1967 USAFE maintained Wheelus AB near Tripoli, Libya, for bombing and gunnery training. The large expanse of desert with only a few nomadic tribes made the Wheelus ranges ideal for practicing bombing and gunnery. Except for occasional sandstorms that made flying impossible, the weather was excellent.

The Libyan air force shared Wheelus with USAFE and located its own fighter and transport squadrons there. Libya is an Islamic nation, and every morning the calls to prayer from a nearby minaret signaled the beginning of another day. Libyan air force pilots shared the Officers' Club with us. They kept to themselves but occasionally would converse. One memorable officer was the squadron commander, Maj Muammar Qaddafi. On 1 September 1969, Qaddafi became Libya's military dictator after leading the coup that overthrew King Idris.

The first gunnery mission at Wheelus called for a formation takeoff—my first in a long time. My takeoff position was on the flight leader's left wing. With afterburners roaring, the flight rapidly accelerated through 110 knots. As the F-4 nose started to lift and the aircraft wanted to fly, the controls did not feel right. I brought throttles out of afterburner and back to minimum power, lowered the nose, deployed the brake chute, and started braking. The instructor in the rear cockpit yelled, "What are you doing?"

"I'm aborting. It doesn't feel right," was my answer. "It was probably just downwash from lead's aircraft," he said. Doubts passed through my mind, but I said nothing as we taxied back to the flight line. He was probably right since this was my first formation takeoff in a long time. Maybe formation takeoffs in an F-4 felt different from other fighters? Worse yet, maybe I was too apprehensive and had overreacted?

After we climbed down from the cockpits, maintenance solved the problem. The aileron hydraulic actuator was disconnected from the left aileron. If we had not aborted, the loss of lateral control after takeoff would have been disastrous. An inexperienced crew chief had failed to notice the aileron disconnect during the pretakeoff check. A close call—for a change, the grateful instructor bought the drinks that night.

There is nothing quite like practicing bombing and gunnery in a modern fighter aircraft. Speeds rapidly change from below 300 to above 500 knots. The three-dimensional aspect of climbing, diving, and high-G turns while watching other aircraft in your flight, selecting the right weapons and switches, locating and lining up with the target, listening to the range control officer, checking the fuel and engine instruments, carefully aiming, firing the cannon or dropping a bomb, pulling up and away from the target, and readying for the next pass are challenging both mentally and physically.

After a flight or two on the gunnery range, I felt reassured. The fighter business was coming back relatively fast. To prove the point, I challenged the other pilots by betting on best score for each event. Fighter pilots never change. They could not wait to show me how hot they were. Most times someone else would win; now and then, I would—good for the ego! Gunnery practice reminded me of playing golf—lots to talk about, plenty of opportunities to brag or make excuses, but true lovers of the game always look forward to playing the next round.

After returning from Wheelus, Jack Robinson attached me to the 53d TFS for flying, ably commanded by Lt Col William E. "Earl" Brown, Jr. Earl was an F-86 pilot in the Korean War with 125 combat missions and had recently returned from a combat tour with the 8th TFW at Ubon, Thailand. Earl and his wife, Gloria, were an ideal Air Force couple—a strong, considerate commander respected by all and a wife who devoted her time and many talents to helping her husband and the young families in his squadron.[3]

Earl and I had long, friendly conversations. One day he told me of the best thing that happened to him in his 17-year Air Force career. The Air Force had transferred Earl, his wife, and children several times from one air base to another. Moving across the United States was difficult for a black family during the 1950s and early '60s. Before starting the trip, the Browns had to plan carefully each stop along the route. Were there friends with whom they could stay while en route? Restaurants where they could they eat? Who would help them in an emergency?

Shortly after the 1964 Civil Rights Act passed, Earl transferred again. For the first time, his family experienced the freedom to travel that most Americans had enjoyed since birth. Hotels and restaurants accepted them, and the sad history of racial discrimination was legally over. No American family should suffer such humiliation.

The winter months in Germany are not very severe. Nevertheless, the Eifel region of Germany is frequently overcast with restricted visibility. Clouds are not as turbulent as in the American Midwest, although an occasional thunderstorm shakes things up a bit. While letting down from a local flight one winter day, I encountered heavier clouds than normal. Suddenly, a bright flash, jolt, and loud noise caught my attention. Lightning had hit the left wing, leaving a small hole, and the electrical shock knocked out some instruments. Three years later in Southeast Asia, a bolt of lightning cracked the cockpit windscreen. These two incidents satisfied any curiosity I had about lightning striking an aircraft in flight.

My primary attention shifted to the daily operations and routine problems of the 36th TFW. A familiar aircrew issue fell into my lap. The aircrews were complaining about too many alerts, not enough free weekends, and too many additional duties. One young pilot answered our sampling questionnaire by stating he was working 143 hours a week! Using his numbers, that left only a little over three hours a day for eating, sleeping, watching TV, and doing the other things a newly married lieutenant must do. His response was not factual, of course, but was indicative of a genuine morale problem.

These aircrew complaints were reminiscent of the problems encountered at Wurtsmith with B-52 and KC-135 scheduling. Solving the problem at Wurtsmith boiled down to stabilizing the schedule and leveling the workload as much as possible. By working with the squadron operations officers, we were able to resolve most of the scheduling and workload problems at Bitburg. In 1967 computers were available, and we developed a program to incorporate operations scheduling and training accomplishments.

There was an important leadership lesson embedded in the solutions to both the Wurtsmith and Bitburg problems. The military is by nature a structured organization—roughly a pyramid. Military law stipulates that the people at lower levels in the pyramid must follow the orders and policies established by people at higher levels in the pyramid. In exchange for complying with these orders and policies, the people at the lower levels expect the higher levels to treat them fairly and, within their power, insure their well-being. This is hardly a new concept; most successful officers and noncommissioned officers have always accepted these responsibilities. To paraphrase the famous tribute to George Washington's leadership: "First in war, first in peace, and last in the chow line!"

Another morale problem was not easy to correct. The 36th Wing had recently converted from the single-cockpit F-105 to the two-cockpit F-4D. Headquarters USAF was convinced that only pilots should be in the F-4D cockpits. The inference that a real, honest-to-God fighter pilot needed another pilot in the aircraft was a tough pill to swallow for former F-105 pilots. When the 36th Wing received young graduates from pilot training to fill the rear cockpits, too many older pilots treated them as extraneous. This partially corrected itself as the former F-105 pilots began rotating to Vietnam.

The replacements for the outgoing F-105 pilots were F-4 pilots who had already completed a combat tour in Southeast Asia. This changed the faces but did not solve the problem. Vietnam War returnees had volunteered for Germany to be F-4 aircraft commanders. They expected USAFE to honor this commitment. On the other hand, USAF tasked USAFE to train the young "guy in back" (GIB) so he could rotate to Southeast Asia as an F-4 aircraft commander.

We found a compromise by creating dual-capable aircrews. The aircraft commander and GIB took turns flying in the front and rear cockpits. Aircraft commanders flew 60 percent of the time in the front cockpit and 40 percent in the rear. The compromise was a modest success. By the time a GIB left for Vietnam, he was a trained aircraft commander. Meanwhile, aircraft commanders became more familiar with weapons system management, radar, and the other electronic systems controlled from the rear cockpit. The Air Force ultimately solved the problem by training navigators to be GIBs.

NATO Changes to Flexible Response

By the late 1960s, the simultaneous threats of China-sponsored Communism in Southeast Asia and USSR-sponsored Communism in Europe were stretching thin the US containment policy. During the previous two decades, the USSR had greatly strengthened its military as well as the military forces of its satellite states in Eastern Europe. Whether the USSR would use this military advantage to expand Communism in Europe became the overarching issue. Based upon the post–World War II conduct of the USSR, there was reason for serious concern in the Western democracies.

When the Federal Republic of Germany (West Germany) rearmed and became a key member of NATO, Khrushchev saw the need for closer military control over Eastern European Communist countries and formed the Warsaw Pact in 1955. Member nations were Albania, Bulgaria, Czechoslovakia, the German Democratic Republic (GDR) (East Germany), Hungary, Poland, Romania, and the USSR. At the beginning, the non-Soviet Warsaw Pact (NSWP) nations retained a significant degree of control over their armed forces while accepting USSR leadership in planning and equipment.

Two events in 1956 caused Khrushchev to tighten control over the Eastern European armies. Polish students and workers in Poznan rioted against the Communist government and the Soviet domination of Poland. Concerned that the Polish army would resist Soviet intervention, Khrushchev kept Poland as a Warsaw Pact ally while reducing the presence of the Soviet army in Poland. In October, Wladyslaw Gomulko restored many of the freedoms lost during the Soviet dominance of Poland but managed to keep close ties with the USSR. On 23 October, an anticommunist civil war broke out in Hungary between the Communist government and student-led dissidents. Premier Imre Nagy declared Hungary neutral and withdrew from the Warsaw Pact. The Soviet army immediately intervened and brutally crushed the revolution by 4 November 1956.

By 1968 well-equipped, much larger forces belonging to the Warsaw Pact now confronted NATO. The USSR had 33 army division equivalents stationed in East Germany, Poland, Czechoslovakia, and Hungary. Another 66 USSR division equivalents were located in the Western military districts of the USSR within a few hundred miles of East Germany. NSWP nations had 58 division equivalents located in East Germany, Poland, Czechoslovakia, Hungary, Romania, and Bulgaria. NATO forces in Central Europe, including France and Italy, totaled 48 division equivalents. Similar numerical advantages in tanks and artillery—roughly 2.5 to 1—favored the Warsaw Pact. Defining the Warsaw Pact numerical advantage in tactical aircraft was difficult because NATO reinforcements could arrive quickly from the United States and UK.

Why did the Warsaw Pact not attack NATO while it had this military advantage? The primary reason was the US support for the European democracies, underwritten by our announced policy to contain Communism. The Truman Doctrine, Berlin

Airlift, Korean War, support for Taiwan, and commitments made to NATO provided ample proof that the United States would not allow a Warsaw Pact attack on a NATO nation. Although the European press had often scoffed at the idea that the United States would sacrifice New York to save Berlin, or any other NATO city, Khrushchev and his military leaders knew an attack on NATO was a high-risk venture that might result in nuclear war.

These same leaders learned a lesson or two from the Cuban missile crisis about US nuclear weapon policies. By greatly increasing the alert status of our long-range bombers, nuclear submarines, and silo-based ICBMs, we signaled that an attack by a Cuba-based ballistic missile would result in immediate US retaliation against the USSR. Our general purpose forces in position to invade Cuba signaled that we would invade Cuba before the missiles could become a nuclear threat. The crisis demonstrated that nuclear deterrence was effective in avoiding nuclear war between the United States and USSR. Less clear is whether our containment policy was completely effective. Khrushchev did remove the missiles, but Castro's Communist government stayed in place. The less publicized quid pro quo: a few months later President Kennedy removed Thor and Jupiter IRBMs from the UK, Turkey, and Italy.

When I worked on the OSD study Quick Fix in 1963, it was apparent the Kennedy administration wanted to back away from dependency on nuclear weapons and find a way to defend Western Europe as long as possible with conventional weapons. Changes take place slowly in NATO. Not until 16 January 1968 did the new strategy, MC 14/3, a flexible response strategy, become effective and replace MC 14/2.[4]

The United States was now committed to a flexible response to support our containment policy, rather than automatically responding with nuclear weapons as stated in MC 14/2. Assuming the USSR learned from all these lessons, its best opportunity for expansion in Europe would now depend upon fast-moving, hard-hitting conventional forces seizing limited objectives and then calling for negotiations before NATO could intervene militarily. This USSR scenario depended upon America's allies offering little resistance and the United States negotiating rather than using tactical nuclear weapons.

In 1967 the deputy chief of staff for operations in USAFE was Maj Gen David C. Jones.[5] He had recently supervised the forced withdrawal of USAFE units from France in 1966 and their relocation to the UK and Germany. At a conference I attended with other wing mobility officers, General Jones expressed his concern about the vulnerability of USAFE air bases to Warsaw Pact air attacks. Operational units had to be able to move to an alternate air base and quickly resume combat air operations.

The mobility plan for moving a modern fighter wing to an austere base involves a process akin to medical triage following a natural disaster. What goes and what stays? Who flies and who drives? Moving aircraft and some aircrews is the easy part—every flyable aircraft goes with an aircrew. Everything else is located, prioritized, packed, and made ready to move in a specified sequence by either ground or air transportation. Support squadrons, such as maintenance, munitions, communications, avionics, security police, medical, and civil engineering, have to decide what goes and what stays. Every crate and box that goes must have a list of contents and specify total weight.

After two or three practice exercises, the 36th was ready to execute our mobility plan. Everyone knew the rules of the game, and the last practice exercise had been very successful. A week or two later, the USAFE Inspector General, Brig Gen William MacDonald, accompanied by his ORI inspection team, flew to Bitburg for a no-notice mobility exercise. Planning and practice paid off. Within a few hours, each squadron had completed packing and moving its equipment in crates and boxes to its designated spots on the flight ramp.

When the squadrons finished, there were hundreds of crates and boxes on the ramp. The IG complimented me on how quickly we were ready. Proud of the 36th Wing's performance, I said, "Open any crate, General. You will find the number of parts in the crate exactly match the contents list that is fastened on the outside of the crate."

"OK, let's open that one," he said, pointing at a large crate not far away that belonged to one of our best units. I handed him the contents list that described the avionics test equipment in the crate. After confidently opening the crate, I stared in disbelief. Rocks filled the crate!

The IG laughed, easing my embarrassment a bit. His inspectors checked the rest of the crates and boxes. They were all correct—no more rocks. Gen John "Black Jack" Pershing, commander of US Army forces in the First World War, once said, "Planning is 10 percent, execution 90 percent." A fighter pilot expression seemed more descriptive of the results of this mobility exercise: "S--- happens!"

Shortly after the mobility inspection, I arranged for Earl Brown's squadron to have a practice deployment to the Norwegian fighter base at Bodo, near the northern tip of the Scandinavian Peninsula and only a short distance from the USSR. We were intercepted by Royal Norwegian Air Force (RNAF) fighters as we entered Norway's airspace and were escorted the rest of the way to Bodo.

We toured Bodo with the group commander. Aircraft hangars were tunneled deeply into the mountainside with huge antiblast doors at each opening. The temperature inside was approximately 50 degrees Fahrenheit, an ideal climate to do maintenance. The F-5 fighters were in pristine condition. The group commander invited me to attend a flight briefing the next morning. A Norwegian captain started briefing an aerial gunnery flight in English. I leaned over and quietly told the group commander, "Colonel, please don't feel the briefing has to be in English. I've flown many gunnery missions and will understand enough of the briefing if the briefer speaks Norwegian to his pilots."

The colonel's answer straightened things out in a hurry. "He's not speaking English because you are here. All our briefings, tower instructions, and all radio transmissions are in English. As you know, English is the international language for aviation. Besides, we save money in our defense budget by not having to translate flight and maintenance manuals, etcetera, from English into Norwegian." (He did not mention that three versions of Norwegian exist in this small nation of five million people.) The RNAF operation at Bodo was convincing proof that Norway had a first-class air force.

The unexpected occurred upon returning from Norway. USAFE needed a replacement to be the director of ORIs. The IG called me to USAFE headquarters at Wiesbaden for an interview. The ORI assignment would be a big jump in responsibility for a junior colonel. The ORI team tested the combat readiness of all USAFE units. ORI results strongly influenced USAFE training and the future assignments for commanders at all levels. The balance between nuclear and conventional readiness had to become compatible with MC 14/3. The ORI team would play a major role in making the transition. I looked forward to assuming this new responsibility in a few months, not knowing that the assignment would be changed because of a dispute over an Accident Board report.

On 12 December 1967, an RF-4C belonging to the 26th Tactical Reconnaissance Wing (TRW) at Ramstein AB, Germany, crashed in Spain. The 26th TRW kept a training detachment at Moron AB. USAF investigates serious accidents by appointing accident investigating boards, usually from units not involved in the accident. Seventeenth Air Force appointed me board president for this accident.

After the board members arrived in Spain, we surveyed the accident scene before beginning deliberations. The wreckage pattern indicated the aircraft struck the ground with a nearly vertical impact angle. A careful examination of the wreckage confirmed the engines were running and the aircraft was intact until the crash. Before the crash, the pilot had lost control of the aircraft and ordered the navigator to eject. Both crew members safely ejected. There were no radio calls concerning aircraft malfunctions.

The aircraft commander, a recent graduate from combat crew training, was new in the theater and had never flown from Moron before the night of the accident. It was a dark, overcast night, and Operations deleted part of the preplanned mission because of poor weather. It seemed to be a classic "pilot error" accident caused by inexperience. Records indicated that the pilot was physically qualified. No emotional, family, or other problems had surfaced prior to the accident.

The board's attention then turned to the circumstances preceding the flight. After a hard look at training procedures at Moron, the board found convincing evidence that poor supervision from the training detachment contributed to the accident.

The Accident Board report went to Headquarters Seventeenth Air Force. Several weeks later, a senior colonel at Seventeenth Air Force called. He recommended deleting the contributing cause regarding poor supervision. I told him the president could not change a finding approved by the board. A few days later, the same colonel warned that it was in my best interests to delete the contributing cause. Besides, the wing commander had assured him that he had corrected the poor supervisory situation at Moron. I told him that was good news but did not alter the fact that poor supervision contributed to the accident.

More time passed. The next call came from the chief of safety at Headquarters USAFE. According to him, Gen Maurice A. Preston, USAFE commander, wanted the reference to supervisory error deleted. I told him that General Preston could certainly add his objection or recommendation to the report, but in good conscience, I could not change the board findings.

A few days later, USAFE cancelled my assignment to be the ORI director. Some cynic once said, "No good deed goes unpunished." Years later, a search of the archives showed the findings were not changed by USAFE headquarters, despite complaints.

A highly qualified officer, Col James Breedlove, deputy commander for operations for the 81st TFW, became the ORI director, and I became his chief of the Operations Division of ORIs for the next year. Jim was a pleasure to work for and a great boss. He transferred to Thailand in June 1969 and became the 388th Wing commander in December 1969. Maj Gen James Breedlove retired in 1977. His last assignment was deputy Commander in Chief, US Southern Command.

Deep Furrow 68

A Troubled Time

Because NATO nations are democracies to varying degrees, political changes at home can upset long-standing agreements. The worst example occurred in 1966, when France withdrew from military participation in NATO. Good examples were Greece and Turkey, which continued to honor their NATO obligations despite conflicts in Cyprus that threatened to drag the two nations into war.

The Supreme Allied Commander in Europe (SACEUR) maintains an acceptable level of military readiness by holding large-scale exercises with forces from his three major regional commands: Allied Forces Northern Europe, Allied Forces Central

Europe (AFCENT), and Allied Forces Southern Europe (AFSOUTH). These NATO commands are subordinate to the SACEUR—in 1968, Gen Lyman Lemnitzer, US Army. AFSOUTH was host for the large NATO exercise Deep Furrow 68. Participants were air, sea, and land forces from the United States, Greece, and Turkey. A joint task force (JTF) was organized to weld together the US and Hellenic (Greek) components of the exercise. The location of the JTF was Elefsis Royal Hellenic AFB near Athens. Brig Gen Bill MacDonald was JTF commander, and I was JTF chief of staff. Our first priority was establishing a complete JTF command post.

After a few weeks, the JTF completed the planning and coordination for the exercise. This included preparing a drop zone for the airborne assault by the 82d Airborne Division; invasion beaches for the amphibious assault from the Mediterranean; artillery ranges; operational airfields for NATO aircraft; maneuver areas for the ground troops from Greece, Turkey, and the United States; and observer teams for monitoring the exercise.

Deep Furrow 68 went well. One highlight was the airdrop. Forty-five C-141 transports flew from the United States with an 82d Airborne brigade and made the longest airdrop in history up to that time. Another highlight was the amphibious assault on the Aegean coast.

Deep Furrow had a beneficial effect on relations between Greece and Turkey. The new government in Greece was attempting to tone down intercommunal fighting in Cyprus between Greek and Turk Cypriots. While working together during the exercise, senior military leaders from both countries focused on NATO matters, not Cyprus.

The grand finale of Deep Furrow was a long parade through the ancient city of Drama. Thousands of Greek citizens lined both sides of the parade route waiting for the troops to pass. When Gen Georgios Papadopoulos, standing in an open jeep, passed the bystanders, a roar of approval greeted him—loud enough to drown any lingering doubts about his current popularity.

Living in Greece during this time of political turmoil was a novel experience. I enjoyed working with the Greek military, and the Greek civilians were generally friendly to us. Despite the enthusiastic crowd at Drama, I still wondered whether the

United States made a bargain with the devil by supporting General Papadopoulos and the coup.

The political situation in Greece in 1968 was tense. On 21 April 1967, a coup had overthrown the monarchial government. The coup leaders—called the "junta of colonels"—were led by General Papadopoulos. They cited an imminent Communist takeover as their reason for changing the government. After the coup, they held secret talks with Turkey over Cyprus. The Turks backed off from their threat to invade Cyprus, and Papadopoulos withdrew excess Greek troops from Cyprus.

On 31 January 1968, the European Council expelled Greece because of the military coup. Greece adopted a new constitution by an overwhelming popular vote in 1968. The new constitution included a list of rights similar in context to our Bill of Rights. Unfortunately, Papadopoulos reneged on preelection promises by withholding several important individual rights.

The base commander at Elefsis was promoted from captain to colonel in recognition of his role in the coup. One night at Elefsis, we discussed the dissension caused by Papadopoulos withholding important constitutional rights, such as freedom of the press and political freedom. Because of this, I maintained Greece was not a true democracy. The colonel angrily replied, "Don't talk to me about democracy in Greece! Greece was a democracy two thousand years before there was a United States."

My answer would probably not win the Nobel Prize for diplomacy. "Greek citizens are living today, not two thousand years ago. Papadopoulos must prove Greece today is a democracy by restoring the basic freedoms in your new constitution, or you are not a truly democratic government." We ended our conversation, shook hands, and went home.

The United States recognized and supported the Papadopoulos government as an effective counter to Communism—a compromise with democracy the United States believed necessary under the existing circumstances. The junta of colonels continued in power. Under pressure in 1973, they gradually legitimized the lost freedoms and became a limited democracy.

For several weeks preceding Deep Furrow 68, Czechoslovakia was in turmoil. Student-led demonstrations against Pres. Antonin Novotny, a hard-line Stalinist, began in 1967 and seriously strained relations between the USSR and Czechoslovakia. The world press called it the "Prague Spring." Alexander Dubcek, a Communist who supported Khrushchev's policies, replaced Novotny in January 1968. Dubcek sponsored a popular reform program that increased political freedom, lifted censorship, and used the media for sponsoring the reforms that would democratize Communism.

The anticommunist movement moved too quickly for the USSR. A Warsaw Pact conference met in July without inviting Czechoslovakian participation. Conference members feared Czechoslovakia would leave the Warsaw Pact and the liberalization movement would spread to other Pact nations. Pact leaders insisted on a hard-line approach and sent an ultimatum to Dubcek. The Czechoslovakian Presidium rejected the ultimatum. Dubcek then unsuccessfully tried to buy time through negotiations.

Before General Lemnitzer left for Belgium, Papadopoulos hosted an elaborate formal dinner at the King George Hotel in Athens where Lemnitzer stayed. In the early morning of 21 August 1968, I received a call from the JTF command post at Elefsis. Supreme Headquarters Allied Powers, Europe (SHAPE) wanted General Lemnitzer to know that Warsaw Pact tanks and troops were invading Czechoslovakia. I called Lemnitzer and passed the message that he needed to discuss the situation with SHAPE. Secure telephones were available in our JTF command post at Elefsis. Lemnitzer said it would take too long to get to Elefsis, so we went to a nearby telephone booth with a pay phone. Using the commercial line, he finally contacted the SHAPE command post. While standing 20 feet away from the phone booth, I could still hear Lemnitzer's voice.

"This is General Lemnitzer. I need to talk to the duty officer right away." Long pause on the other end. "Tell me all you know about the Soviet invasion." Another long pause, "No, this is not a secure line. I'm using a public telephone." Seconds later and much louder, "Damn it, I know this is classified; now, tell me what's going on!"

After several minutes, a calmer General Lemnitzer left the phone booth. Apparently, the SHAPE duty officer had finally realized that he was not going to win a debate over telephone security with his agitated four-star boss. Lemnitzer flew back to Brussels that morning. I never knew whether NATO expected the invasion or was surprised because of an intelligence failure. NATO forces made no effort to intervene, and Czechoslovakia offered no serious military resistance to the sudden invasion.

The Warsaw Pact invasion of Czechoslovakia in August was a forceful reminder of the ever-present Communist threat. Was the USSR tightening its grip on Eastern Europe as a prelude to invading Western Europe? We maintained military forces in the CONUS that were dual-based. Their purpose was to reinforce NATO if a political crisis developed between East and West. What would be the USSR reaction if we reinforced NATO at this time by sending our dual-based forces to Europe? The war was heating up in Vietnam. Did the Johnson administration realize reinforcing Western Europe could overcommit our military? What if the USSR misread our reaction and started a war against NATO? Fortunately, as the crisis passed, nothing happened.

The Leavitt family had moved to Wiesbaden before I left for Greece. Wiesbaden is a beautiful city, one of the few large cities in Germany not bombed during World War II. We lived in a multistory apartment house owned by the Air Force that overlooked the city and had a bird's-eye view of the weekly fireworks displays. Anne and my two daughters joined me in Athens during the last weeks of Deep Furrow. They enjoyed sightseeing in and around historic Athens.

The new job as chief of the Operations Inspections Division began. My previous experience with ORIs was from the receiving end, not the giving end. SAC prided itself on tough ORIs, and USAFE seemed just as tough. Why are ORIs so important and so tough? In a nutshell, an ORI is the measuring stick used to determine whether the combat unit is maintaining standards and is capable of meeting wartime commitments.

The purpose for having ORIs is to prevent systemic failures such as America experienced at the beginning of World War II. Although the ORI is only one link in the chain of events that keeps USAF combat ready, it is an important one. The ORI focuses on the lower levels of command that control the resources necessary to fight or to support combat. In USAFE, that level was usually an air base with a wing equipped with fighter, reconnaissance, or transport aircraft. We also inspected nuclear weapon storage sites that supported USAFE and our NATO allies.

The American public may not understand the emphasis the Air Force places on ORIs. Perhaps a historical simile may be helpful. Quality standards were low in the automobile industry following World War II. Nevertheless, every car they could build could be sold. America needed cars, and their quality was not a major issue. Only after major sales losses to high-quality foreign competitors in the sixties and seventies did our automobile industry pay attention to improving quality. The reputation for poor quality in American cars was finally overcome, but not before our automobile industry had suffered irreversible losses in sales to foreign competition.

The problems cited about the automobile industry can, and will, occur in any organization that ignores competition, has low standards, fails to invest in the future, does not rigorously examine internal operations, and lacks effective leadership. When a business suffers these faults, it will lose money and probably fail. When a military organization suffers these faults, it will be ineffective in war, suffer heavy losses, and jeopardize our nation's well-being.

The American military performed poorly at the outbreak of WWII. Causes were similar to the causes in the postwar automobile industry. America knew of the increasing capability of our future enemies but did not react. Congress was unconvinced that substantial changes were necessary until war was on our doorstep. Military leaders were often too old and too set in their parochial ways. Training was poor for most military personnel. Our equipment (tanks, guns, aircraft, communications, etc.) was largely obsolete. The internal inspection system lacked realistic tests of readiness. Only after getting America's nose bloodied at Pearl Harbor and again in North Africa did we realize how far we had fallen and did we make the necessary corrections.

USAFE commanders realized the ORI team served as their "eyes and ears" and allowed the IG to recruit top-notch people from the USAFE wings located in Third, Seventeenth, and Sixteenth Air Forces. Experienced inspectors who knew the business made my transition easy. The fighter pilots assigned were combat veterans, experienced in USAFE operations, and graduates of the Fighter Weapons School at Nellis AFB, Nevada. The Plans officer, Maj "Serge" Demchuk, was one of the most competent officers I have ever met. Maj Bob Ledford and Capt Ron

Hatchett served overlapping tours as intelligence experts. Ron later received his doctorate and represented the SecDef in arms control negotiations in Europe for several years. Capt Frank Black, a recent returnee from Southeast Asia, was our reconnaissance expert. Experienced officers and NCOs with expertise in supply, maintenance, communications, disaster control, and security rounded out the team.

Our ORIs were no-notice inspections that lasted from five to eight days depending upon the size of the inspected unit. Simultaneous with the arrival of the ORI team chief, the wing command post (WCP) would receive a scenario message describing a political-military crisis that had been developing in Europe that called for a higher state of readiness. As the inspection progressed, the wing would receive more scenario messages updating the crisis and calling for certain actions. Each action triggered one or more evaluations by the ORI team.

For example, did the command post process the message traffic properly, have a complete knowledge of its responsibilities, and notify the appropriate personnel in the wing? Was the wing commander effective in managing the senior wing staff and insuring all necessary actions were under way? Did the wing generate the required number of combat-ready aircraft and load these aircraft with wartime munitions in the allotted time? Were the aircrews totally familiar with launch control procedures and the mission folders for their assigned targets? Were bombing and gunnery scores satisfactory for the aircrews that flew bombing and gunnery sorties during the ORI?

The ORI team also evaluated the response of all support organizations on the air base. We learned whether base supply could manually find and deliver aircraft parts by ruling its computers inoperative because of electrical outage. Using simulated casualties with mock wounds, the base hospital had to demonstrate its triage plan for processing wounded personnel. Inspectors carefully checked mobility plans and emergency evacuation plans for civilian dependents. Realistic disaster exercises tested base security and the fire department.

After the final exercise, the ORI team would meet and discuss the strengths and weaknesses of the wing. Each inspector then prepared a written report that went through several stages of review before becoming final. One outstanding fighter pilot and operations inspector took a lot of good-natured kidding because he was always the last to finish typing his report. A copy of the cartoon showing Snoopy stuck for words after typing "'twas a dark and stormy night" was mysteriously pinned to Bill's typewriter when the writing began after every inspection.

The last step was preparing the outbriefing to be given on exit day. The outbriefing used colored slides for rating every aspect of the ORI: blue for excellent, green for satisfactory, yellow for marginal, and red for unsatisfactory. A few months later, we added moving pictures of the exercises to the outbriefing. Those long, hard days of report preparation seldom ended before midnight.

As a courtesy just before the outbriefing, I held a private preview for the wing commander. The typical wing commander stayed in close touch with his unit during the ORI, so the outbriefing contained few surprises. Even in the best wings, our inspectors would find discrepancies that required corrective action. The wing commander needed to understand these discrepancies. After fixing the discrepancies, the wing was required to report the corrective actions to USAFE. Acceptance by USAFE closed the ORI. Telling a wing commander his unit failed or was marginal never went down easily. They all knew that poor results could end a promising career. After the ORI ended and all reports were completed, the ORI team would return to Wiesbaden.

Switching Priorities—Nuke to Conventional

An engineering adage warns, "If it ain't broke, don't fix it." Government and private organizations have used the adage as an excuse for not making changes. Our military may have a tendency to resist change because of past successes. Blame some of that on experience, not ignorance. However, Congress is usually the prime source of resistance because of the high cost of transformation. In reality, the military does business somewhere between repeating past practices and preparing for future successes.

Given all of that, American military history is replete with examples of obsolete technology being replaced by new—carrier pigeons by wireless, single-shot rifles by machine guns,

321

horse cavalry by tanks, battleships by aircraft carriers, piston-powered aircraft by jets, dumb bombs by smart bombs—the list is endless. Equally important causes for change are the political and military realities at a particular moment in history.

Bombing Hiroshima was one of those moments. It began a new era when our dominance in nuclear weapons underwrote all US defense policy. NATO was formed in 1949 with our guarantee that US nuclear dominance would protect our treaty allies from Soviet aggression.

By 1962 the USSR had major nuclear forces, and both the United States and the USSR faced unimaginable damage if the Cuban missile crisis had ended with a thermonuclear exchange. In the aftermath of the crisis, reality set in. Nuclear dominance was not an *optimum* weapon, although it might be the *ultimate* weapon. The prime reason for large strategic forces equipped with thermonuclear weapons was to *deter* Soviet attacks on the United States and our NATO allies. Another post-Cuba realization was that defending NATO with the automatic tactical nuclear response described in NATO strategy document MC 14/2 was a high-risk plan for both the United States and its NATO allies.

The replacement NATO strategy document, MC 14/3, relied on a flexible response strategy with conventional forces resisting Warsaw Pact aggression but not ruling out the use of tactical nuclear weapons if circumstances demanded. USAFE was particularly involved in the policy change because our tactical fighter wings were "dual purpose." They were capable of delivering both nuclear and conventional weapons.

Conventional weapon readiness, especially planning, had taken a backseat to nuclear readiness under MC 14/2. Now priorities had to change to accommodate to MC 14/3. During my first ORI, it became clear to me that the significant shift from a nuclear to a flexible response had not filtered down to the USAFE wings. Their primary emphasis and training was still on nuclear readiness.

We needed to revise the ORI to force change. For example, could the WCP respond to conventional tasking orders? How long did it take maintenance to generate combat-ready aircraft? Could munitions load conventional weapons quickly and safely? Could the wing mobility officer demonstrate an effective mobility plan? Were flight briefings professional and oriented to tactics with conventional weapons?

The revised ORI would affect 16 fighter and reconnaissance bases and eight support bases. Our usual inspection schedule was a week preparing at Wiesbaden and a week giving the ORI. Because of the significant changes proposed, we spent an extra week at Wiesbaden coordinating the ORI changes within USAFE headquarters and the numbered air forces. Then we advised all bases of the new ORI criteria.

The first few new ORIs had mixed results. Two commanders understood the new policies, and their wings were working hard to meet the new criteria. Another wing commander had been in command for more than two years and chose to ignore the directed change. His wing failed, and USAFE transferred him to a dead-end assignment. The fourth wing commander paid lip service to the change but accomplished little. We gave his wing the benefit of a recheck, and it passed a few months later. ORI results always traveled quickly among the wings and numbered air forces. Consequently, succeeding ORIs showed steady improvement as commanders accepted the new reality.

Making necessary corrections is a continuing task for the military. On 23 January 1968, our well-trained, well-equipped military with experienced leadership suffered an unnecessary and embarrassing defeat. North Korean patrol boats boarded and seized the USS *Pueblo*, a Navy intelligence ship in international waters off Wonsan, North Korea. The captain surrendered and did not scuttle the ship. North Korean gunfire killed one Sailor as the captain stalled for time while trying to destroy classified material. The 82-man crew was imprisoned, and North Korea kept the ship.

There was no effort to protect the *Pueblo* while it gathered intelligence. No Navy or Air Force aircraft were on alert with munitions loaded and within range of Wonsan. If a flight had been scrambled at the first sign of trouble, the North Korean patrol boats could have been attacked and the *Pueblo* probably saved. This flagrant oversight pointed to poor coordination in the Pacific Command between Intelligence and Plans. Apparently, Intelligence believed North Korea would not attack the *Pueblo* in international waters and did not require an operations plan that would provide protective coverage.

The postincident reaction smacked of closing the barn door after the horse escaped. Over the next five days, the USAF deployed nearly 100 tactical aircraft from the United States to the Pacific in response to the *Pueblo* Incident. The USAF also activated 13 Air Force Reserve and Air National Guard units in the United States. Despite this increased capability, President Johnson ruled out any plans to destroy the captured ship or otherwise intervene with military action. Nearly a year later, the United States signed an apology and falsely admitted violating North Korean waters. North Korea then released the POW but kept the *Pueblo*.

USAFE recognized the potential for a "*Pueblo*-like" incident in Europe, possibly in the surrounding waters or on land from terrorists. With the approval of the USAFE commander, we notified all the fighter wings of a new requirement and explained the evaluation criteria that would apply for future ORIs. Reactions to this and other new ORI changes varied. They varied from the inevitable "We've always done it this way; why change now?" to the positive "It's about time NATO got off this nuke-only business."

The WCP is the center for decision making in an ORI. The wing commander and staff receive orders and reports from higher headquarters in the WCP and respond by directing the flow of activity on the air base. Wing commanders are under heavy stress during an ORI. If they have accomplished their jobs and been effective leaders, they will handle the stress well. As tasking messages arrived at the WCP, my job was to observe and evaluate the decision-making process being led by the wing commander and staff.

Watching more than 30 ORIs provided a case study with 30 examples of executive leadership under stress. Any preconceptions I held about "the perfect leader" soon disappeared. They came in all sizes and shapes. Some looked like they walked off a Hollywood set. Others looked like an unmade bed. Some were authoritarian by nature, and others were participative. The majority knew exactly what to do and used their staff to get it done. A few did not know what to do and could not separate good staff advice from bad. The best commanders shared three common characteristics. First, they knew the strengths and weaknesses of every subordinate unit and worked especially hard to correct the weaknesses without ignoring the strengths. Second, they communicated frequently with subordinate commanders, including NCOs, so everyone knew goals and accomplishments. Third, they were long on carrots and short on sticks.

One case stands out in my memory. In late 1968, we gave an F-100 wing an ORI. Nearly everything in this wing was rated "excellent." The wing commander's eyes filled with joyous tears of relief as he gave his last hurrah to his assembled wing. Before leaving for his new assignment, he introduced his highly qualified replacement, a colonel who had just returned from Vietnam where he commanded a fighter wing.

Nearly a year later, this same F-100 wing was scheduled to transition to F-4Ds. Transitioning to new aircraft is always a difficult task for a wing and usually takes many months to gain full combat readiness. After reviewing the impending delay, Gen Joseph Holzapple, USAFE commander, decided two years was too long between ORIs. He ordered an ORI before the wing began transitioning to F-4Ds.

I flew to the F-100 base early one Sunday morning with ORI staff members and began the no-notice inspection. The WCP was receiving the first few ORI messages as we entered. The vice wing commander was in charge, as the wing commander had driven to a sports car race several hundred miles away. One of the first ORI messages received in the command post had a classified nickname.

I stood behind the vice-commander while he read the message and then watched him put it aside without taking any action. I picked up the message and handed it back to him—an unusual act of kindness on my part—and suggested he read it carefully. He handed the message to a senior NCO who explained the message to him. It was the beginning of a weeklong nightmare. The wing commander finally was located and arrived back at the air base. By the time he arrived, the wing had failed every major exercise and inspection.

The outbriefing was painful. Nearly a year earlier, this wing could claim it was the best in USAFE. Now it was unsatisfactory. USAFE removed the wing commander immediately and transferred him to a staff job in Headquarters USAFE. A few months later, he came by my office and began to talk. "At first, I couldn't accept the results of the ORI and blamed you and your ORI team for an unfair inspection. Then after reading the report and studying the discrepancies, I realized they were factual and fair. After I took over the wing last year and began to notice some problems, supervisors would always say, 'We have always done it that way,' or 'We got an excellent rating from the ORI team last year,' or some similar excuse for not correcting a problem. I realize now that it was my fault for not correcting the problems before they became too serious."

The colonel was a gentleman to apologize and offer his explanation for failure. His mistake was not making corrections while they were fresh in his mind. As my career progressed and I addressed officers becoming squadron, group, and wing commanders, I cautioned them, "You are exceptionally well qualified to be a commander. The Air Force has confidence in your judgment. Although you may be in this assignment for two or three years, the first few weeks are critical. You will have the opportunity to look at everything with a fresh pair of eyes. Isolate the good from the bad and from the unknown. Do not fail to make a change when you believe change is needed. If you wait too long, you will become comfortable with the status quo, and your command will not progress."

One of the most interesting and dramatic inspections involved special operations forces (SOF). It was a genuine eye-opener to witness the skill displayed in all phases of their ORI. I flew with a SOF crew on a night mission planned by the ORI team. The scenario called for picking up agents operating behind enemy lines. The rendezvous point was an abandoned airstrip in Bavaria. To get there required the modified C-130 to fly at low level through the Alps using terrain-following radar. Timing had to be precise—within one minute of the agreed pickup time at the airstrip. As the C-130 approached, a discrete signal would flash only one time. The signal would clear the C-130 for a short-field, lights-out landing. After stopping in minimum distance, the C-130 spun around with cargo doors open, pulled the "agents" on board, made a maximum power takeoff, and returned home by the same route. The crew completed every part of the mission successfully. I was proud to be in the same Air Force as those SOF professionals.

USAFE announced that Brig Gen Devol "Rocky" Brett, commander of the 81st TFW at RAF Bentwaters, England, would replace Ben Edwards as the new IG.[6] We had scheduled an ORI for the 81st prior to the announcement of Rocky's new job. The ORI team invested a lot of work and planning in each ORI, so I asked General Holzapple if we could go ahead with the scheduled date. He reminded me that General Brett would soon be my new boss but that if I still wanted to go, he would approve the date.

Our practice was to maintain very carefully the no-notice aspect of each ORI. If there were no "leaks," we could better evaluate wing performance as it moved from routine daily operations to wartime status. When secrecy held, the wing reaction was often surprising. We hit the 81st TFW at about 1800 (6:00 p.m.) on a Saturday evening. The timing could not have been worse. We were unaware that the 81st had scheduled a basewide farewell party for the Bretts beginning at 1900 that same evening. As you might expect, there were many irate people at Bentwaters when the ORI cancelled their party. Rocky took this unexpected development in his usual good humor, but his lovely wife Mimi believed I was the "inspector from hell!" We pulled no punches during the ORI, and the 81st TFW did very well despite the unfortunate timing. Rocky saw an ORI from both receiving and giving viewpoints, which benefited our team later.

After Rocky arrived at Headquarters USAFE, we both agreed that the change from MC 14/2 to MC 14/3 was going well, and the recent inspections reflected progress in combat capability. Now it was time to make another significant change in the ORIs. Without detriment to the examination of basic combat capability, we began examining in depth many aspects of management, particularly in the support organizations, such as supply, quality control, and maintenance. The change recognized that combat capability and wing support functions were joined at the hip.

ORIs routinely checked the wing mobility plan at each air base. Clearly, the emphasis on mobility started by General Jones two years earlier had progressed to the point where a larger exercise was in order. I kicked around an idea within the ORI team for a complex bare-base mobility exercise. Would a composite wing with three fighter squadrons from different bases and a provisional wing headquarters be able to operate effectively from an air base several hundred miles away? We found an abandoned World War II air base, Falconara, on the east coast of Italy that seemed to meet bare-base criteria for a realistic mobility exercise—poor facilities, limited ramp area, no barracks, one runway, an old control tower, and located off commercial airways.

Our visit to the proposed base in Italy disclosed other requirements for the exercise. USAFE civil engineers would have to build a ramp using pierced-steel planking for parking three squadrons of fighters. A WCP equipped with extensive mobile communications would be critical to the success of the mission. A small medical dispensary with a flight surgeon, a weather detachment, security police, a veterinarian (food and sanitation), storage areas for mobility boxes and supplies, several flight line vehicles, and personnel tents would round out the requirements.

After completing the preliminary planning, one big problem remained. Fighters could fly from their bases in Germany and the UK to Italy, but how would they move personnel, materials, PSP, and supplies to Italy in a timely manner? I went to Rhein-Main and discussed the problem with the general in charge of intratheater airlift. He liked the concept, but the problem was funding. To protect the airlift system from abuse, customers paid from their budget for hours used. The only exception for customer funding was the hours allocated for training the airlifters. We struck a deal. If USAFE could find $100,000, the general would fund the remaining expense from his C-130 training budget.

Next stop for approval was Lt Gen George B. Simler, vice-commander, USAFE. Simler liked the concept but said, "$100,000 is the absolute maximum. If you spend more, Leavitt, your butt will be hanging from the nearest flagpole!" His somewhat less than enthusiastic endorsement sealed the deal. Simler's bark was always worse than his bite, but I did note the flagpole height outside headquarters.

Mobility exercise "Creek Kitty" ran for three weeks in December 1969. Airlift carried civil engineers and other support personnel to Italy. Three days after arrival, the PSP parking ramp, command post, tents, and other essentials were ready. When the fighter squadrons arrived, Mother Nature ceased cooperating. Heavy winter rains made each day miserable, reminiscent of WWII cartoons with Willie and Joe slogging through European mud. The PSP ramp became very slippery. Ground crews used muscle to stop the fighters from sliding off PSP into the mud. Despite bad weather, the Composite Group flew all the planned sorties without an abort and met all training objectives.

We completed the mobility exercise within the budget, thanks to the airlifters who flew over 130 sorties. The USAFE staff heard our briefing on exercise results and recommendations. Generals Brett and Simler favorably commented about the exercise on my annual OER. I included similar remarks in the OERs of my staff who planned and prepared the exercise.

After returning to Wiesbaden, Col Ken Tallman called from USAF Personnel and said he would become the next 8th Wing commander at Ubon, Thailand. Ken asked if I wanted to be his vice wing commander. My instant reply, "Yes!" signaled I would finally be in the Vietnam War. Directing ORIs was the best practical learning I experienced in my career. I worked for three exceptional leaders—Jim Breedlove, Ben Edwards, and Rocky Brett. They had all recommended me for command of a fighter wing in Southeast Asia. Tallman's offer made that one step closer.

Mobility exercise—Falconara, Italy. *Above*: Two F-4D squadrons and one F-100 squad-ron formed the Composite Exercise Group. All parked on the PSP ramp built by USAFE civil engineers when the exercise began. Despite stormy weather and a slippery ramp, all scheduled sorties were flown without incident. *Below*: Over 100 C-130 sorties by USAFE-based aircraft made the exercise both possible and realistic.

East Berlin during the Cold War. The historic Brandenburg Gate in East Berlin bordered Communist East Germany (German Democratic Republic) and democratic West Germany (Federal Republic of Germany). The picture was taken in the GDR looking toward the FRG.

East Berlin memorial. The final USSR WWII campaign began 16 April and ended 7 May 1945 with Germany's surrender. The USSR lost approximately 50,000 troops taking Berlin in this last major battle against Nazi Germany. The memorial in East Berlin commemorates its sacrifice and is where the Soviet dead are interned.

Notes

1. Lt Gen Charles C. "Buck" Pattillo retired 1 June 1981. A fighter pilot in Eighth Air Force in World War II, he earned the Distinguished Flying Cross and three Air Medals. After a series of staff and command assignments, Buck commanded the 36th TFW before rotating to Southeast Asia where he commanded the 8th TFW in the Vietnam War. Following general officer assignments in Air Materiel Command, the JCS staff, Air Training Command, and PACAF, he became a lieutenant general in 1979 and deputy CINC, US Readiness Command. Decorations include two Distinguished Service Medals, four Legions of Merit, two Distinguished Flying Crosses, 11 Air Medals, and the Army Commendation Medal. His twin brother, Maj Gen Cuthbert "Bill" Pattillo, retired the same year, and they live near each other in Florida. US Air Force, "Biographies: Lieutenant General Charles C. Pattillo."

2. Originally designed and procured for the Navy, McDonnell built over 5,200 F-4s and RF-4s for the United States and friendly foreign nations. The biggest user, the USAF, procured 2,800 F-4s and RF-4s.

3. Lt Gen William E. Brown, Jr., retired 1 December 1984. His last assignment was commander of Allied Air Forces Southern Europe. His military awards included the Defense Distinguished Service Medal, two Air Force Distinguished Service Medals, three Legions of Merit, two Distinguished Flying Crosses, five Air Medals, two Air Force Commendation Medals, and the Purple Heart. Pennsylvania State University awarded him its highest recognition, the Distinguished Alumni Award. US Air Force, "Biographies: Lieutenant General William E. Brown Jr."

4. "In case of general war, therefore, NATO defense depends upon an immediate exploitation of our nuclear capability, whether or not the Soviets employ nuclear weapons." Pedlow, MC 14/2 (Rev) (Final Decision)-23.5.1957, "Overall Strategic Concept for the Defense of the North Atlantic Treaty Organization Area," sec. 2, 9.

5. General Jones's illustrious career included commander, USAFE, 1971–74; USAF chief of staff, 1974–78; and CJCS, 1978–82.

6. Lieutenant General Brett retired in 1980 after an exemplary 35-year career. His decorations include the Defense Distinguished Service Medal, two Air Force Distinguished Service Medals, the Silver Star, four Legions of Merit, three Distinguished Flying Crosses, the Bronze Star Medal, nine Air Medals, the Purple Heart, and both the Army and the Air Force Commendation Medal. His final assignment was commander, NATO Allied Air Forces South. US Military Academy, *Register of Graduates.*

Chapter 9

Vietnam War
Colonel—1970–71

Alligators, Snow, and Snakes

January 1970 was a busy month. It began with notification that Ken Tallman would not be the 8th TFW commander at Ubon. The brigadier general promotion board had selected Ken for promotion, and USAF policy during the war avoided assigning generals as fighter wing commanders. Ken's replacement and my future boss would be Col David Schmerbeck, a senior officer from Headquarters SAC.

By the end of January, we had moved to McLean, bought a new home, reentered our two younger children in McLean's excellent school system, and bought a standard poodle pup that Anne named GIB, the acronym for an F-4 backseater—guy-in-back. His name was a courtesy to our old boxer dog, Trudy, who with 12 years of loyal service certainly ranked GIB and deserved the front seat!

Survival training occupied the lion's share of my time for the next two months. Improved enemy air defenses had caused growing numbers of destroyed USAF aircraft, aircrew fatalities, and POWs. Knowing that losses are the inevitable by-product of an air war, the USAF developed extensive training programs to improve an aircrew's chances for survival. Training for aircrews bound for Southeast Asia centered on instilling confidence by training them how to survive a shootdown or accident, how to evade the enemy, and what to expect and how to conduct themselves as POWs in a North Vietnamese prison camp.

First stop was Homestead AFB, Florida, for water survival training. The South China Sea forms the eastern border of Vietnam, and the Gulf of Thailand forms the southern and western borders of Thailand and Cambodia. The Mekong River flows southward through the Indochina Peninsula. Countless smaller rivers and tributaries run through Vietnam's delta region. All

333

this water suggests a fair probability that an aircrew will get wet feet after ejecting from an aircraft.

Training began immediately after arriving at Homestead. During the next several days, the instructors thoroughly trained us on air-sea rescue procedures and the proper way to use the survival gear we carried on each combat mission. They also discussed water hazards, for example, the very poisonous sea snakes found in the South China Sea. The high point of water survival training was parasailing off the aft deck of a Navy ship. As the senior officer in our class, I had the dubious honor of being first to go. Floating on Biscayne Bay that afternoon until rescued by a helicopter ended the training and left a pleasant memory of water survival school.

Next stop was escape and evasion training at Fairchild AFB, Washington. A heavy winter snow was starting to melt when survival training began in late February—quite a climatic difference from what we would encounter in Southeast Asia. Classrooms and a simulated North Vietnamese prison camp were on the air base. Rugged foothills near Fairchild provided a challenging environment for winter survival and for hiking through hilly, wooded terrain covered with ankle- to knee-deep wet snow.

Instructors carefully briefed our class about the physical dangers, particularly hypothermia—subnormal body temperature from exposure that can cause death. The previous class suffered a fatality during the three-day evasion exercise. A sergeant climbed into his sleeping bag one night wearing a sopping wet flight suit and jacket. Although warned not to wear wet clothes in his sleeping bag, he ignored the advice and apparently froze to death around midnight. His death resulted in a major shake-up of the supervisory staff in the escape and evasion school. Nearly a year later, an autopsy report from Wilford Hall Medical Center stated the cause of death was actually an overdose of anticold pills he swallowed that evening.[1]

The climax of the evasion exercise involved treating the students as POWs. USAF NCOs and junior officers permanently assigned to the survival school and wearing North Vietnamese army uniforms acted as prison guards. After interrogation by a team of "NVN intelligence officers," guards put me in a dark, cold cell behind locked door and steel bars. They ordered me to remain standing and stay awake. At random intervals, guards banged their nightsticks against the bars and inspected the cell to make sure I was not lying down or asleep.

On the final day of confinement, guards rousted me from the cell. Since I was the senior POW, the "NVN commandant" wanted me in his office immediately. Three lieutenant colonels and I stood at attention in front of his desk as the make-believe commandant ranted and raved about our alleged misbehavior. Without warning, the lieutenant colonel standing on my right fainted. His chin caught the edge of the commandant's desk, and he fell to the floor unconscious and bleeding from his chin. A concussion under some circumstances can terminate a pilot's flying career. When I dropped to my knees to help, the NVN commandant screamed, "Stand at attention!"

My response was instant and emphatic, "I'm giving you a direct order, *sergeant* (guessing his actual USAF rank)! This exercise is over. Call the hospital immediately. Tell them we need an ambulance to take an injured officer to the hospital." When he started to assume the NVN commandant role again, I said, "Do what I told you to do! Call your commanding officer right now. Tell him that Colonel Leavitt has discontinued this exercise because an officer is seriously injured, and I want an ambulance here immediately." A young lieutenant arrived shortly and relieved the "commandant" from his role. The ambulance followed the lieutenant with siren blowing and took the injured lieutenant colonel to the hospital. Within minutes, an NCO arrived with a note stating the survival school commander wanted to see me in his office immediately.

I arrived at the colonel's office not knowing what to expect but ready to raise hell. Instead of a confrontation, the colonel quickly apologized for what had happened and thanked me for interceding. He then explained at some length the psychological difficulties Airmen experience when they play "bad guy" every day. Some abuse their families when off duty; others start fights or drink to excess. He believed that no one should serve more than a year as an NVN POW guard, but the USAF had lengthened their tours from one to two years because of personnel shortages. I agreed with the colonel and hoped the Air Force would solve the problem. Later, the USAF reduced the tours back to one year. Today, television allows supervisors to monitor all simulated POW interrogations.

On 7 April 1970, I left the United States for a one-year tour in Southeast Asia. Before continuing on to Thailand, I spent about a week at Clark AB in the Philippines attending Jungle Survival School and visiting Thirteenth Air Force headquarters. Jungle Survival School was a fascinating adventure. After two days of academics concerning jungle flora and fauna, we left early in the morning for two days in the jungle. I wrote Anne:

> Our guide was a little Negrito, formerly a real headhunter, now "on our side," according to the instructors. They are really primitive—amazingly so in this day and age. We spent the afternoon in the jungle learning about water trees, edible plants, etc. That night we made tents out of a poncho and mosquito net and "slept outside." The next day we took a helicopter to our escape point where the evasion problem began. But first, the Negrito cooked us a meal of jungle plants (taro, tapioca, yams, and palm hearts) pressure cooked in a bamboo pole—very interesting. Food was not exactly scrumptious, but was OK.

A very poisonous snake interrupted training that afternoon by biting a pilot who was leaning against a tropical tree. A nearby helicopter landed after the instructor radioed for help and rushed the pilot to the Air Force hospital at Clark AB. He arrived in time for the antivenom medicine to save his life. About six weeks later, the pilot joined the 8th TFW at Ubon. I asked him about the incident. He said, "After the snake bit me in the back, I felt like the top of my head had been blown off!" Anne's letter continued:

> Then we split for the evasion problem. I crawled into some thick, cruddy looking undergrowth and tried to disappear. Most of the night, I spent trying to stay awake so the damn jungle rats wouldn't bite me. One rat nibbled on my combat boot, but I kicked him loose before he could bite. About midnight, a Negrito found my trail and crawled in after me. Supposedly, they can smell us. I was glad to see dawn finally come. A "Jolly Green Giant" (chopper) then came in and dropped a jungle penetrator. After hauling me on board, the course training ended.

Thirteenth Air Force, under the command of Lt Gen Marvin L. McNickle, supported all USAF tactical units in Thailand. Operational control of these units remained with Seventh Air Force headquarters in Saigon, South Vietnam. During my visit, Thirteenth Air Force Intelligence disclosed the way POWs commu-

Jungle survival. Drinking water from a jungle vine—survival method shared with monkeys?

Arrival at Ubon. Colonel Druen, 8th TFW deputy commander for operations, was a friend from Pentagon days. The stars represent the MiG-21s shot down by the 8th TFW.

nicated with each other and other important information about POW status. For example, in case of capture, I learned that Col John Flynn had been promoted to brigadier general while he was a POW in the "Hanoi Hilton." John was now the senior Air Force POW. To spare him from further NVN abuse and torture, his promotion was not publicized.

On 16 April, a T-39 flew me to the Ubon Royal Thai Air Force Base (RTAFB) in Thailand, the home of the 8th TFW. At long last, my little odyssey to get into the Vietnam War was over. Ubon was a pleasant contrast to K-2 during the Korean War.

Eighth Wing—Test Bed for the Future

My new "home away from home" was a house trailer shared with a friend from Pentagon days, Col Dan Druen.[2] Dan was the deputy commander for operations and nearing the end of his combat tour. Later that day, I met the wing commander, Col "Skip" Stanfield, whom Colonel Schmerbeck would replace within a few days, and the other key staff and unit commanders.

Because time was short before the change-of-command ceremony for Stanfield and Schmerbeck, the goal was to become combat ready quickly and knowledgeable about the wing capabilities and problems. Besides listening to many briefings and visiting every organization at Ubon, I flew one local area checkout and nine combat missions in F-4Ds in the first 11 days on base.

Wolf Pack, the 8th Wing call sign, had capabilities not found in other fighter wings during the Vietnam War, with four F-4D squadrons and an AC-130 gunship squadron. One fighter squadron, the 433d TFS, was the first unit to use laser-guided bombs in combat. Dubbed "smart bombs" because of their greatly improved accuracy, these 2,000-pound LGBs began the evolution to the precision-guided munitions (PGM) that underwrite Air Force capabilities in the twenty-first century

In 1970, to guide an LGB to the target, the flight leader circled at a lower altitude while the backseater kept the laser sight aimed at the target. After identifying the target, a second F-4 carrying an LGB began a high-speed dive bomb run from higher altitude. After bomb release, sensors in the nose of the LGB homed on the reflected laser beam and began steering the bomb through the tail fin mechanism. The 2,000-pound bomb usually exploded within 20 feet of the target—several times more accurate than other methods of aerial bombing. I flew 40 or 50 missions with these early LGBs and remained an outspoken advocate of smart bombs for the rest of my Air Force career.

This advocacy was soon tested. Gen Joseph Nazzaro, the four-star commander of PACAF, and his staff visited Ubon about once a quarter.[3] Because Colonel Stanfield would be gone, I had to brief the PACAF staff. Nazzaro was no neophyte to Ubon. He had commanded PACAF for over two years and visited Ubon several times. In stark contrast, I had been at Ubon less than two weeks.

Aerial photos showed the target damage from laser-bombing missions. By taking measurements from the photos, experts from Air Force Systems Command computed the circular error probability for each bomb expended. Armed with this newfound knowledge, I decided to "enlighten" Nazzaro by telling him how great the 8th Wing was doing with laser bombs.

The subject did not really capture his attention. "You wing commanders are all the same; you extol the virtues of how accurately you can bomb. I'll hear the same thing over at Korat and Udorn with their F-4s." Since neither Korat nor Udorn had laser bombs, his comment hurt. I knew that most conventional bombs missed, not hit, their target. For that reason, high damage expectancy required multiple attacks and many bombs. Unwanted collateral damage was a politically important side effect. The LGB could reliably destroy a target while minimizing collateral damage.

The aircraft in the second squadron of F-4Ds, the 25th TFS, was equipped with long-range aid to navigation (LORAN)-D systems. The primary mission of the 25th TFS was dropping sensors and fragmentary bombs along the Ho Chi Minh Trail (see fig. 4). When the sensors hit the ground, they became a key part of the high-tech Igloo White Program, called the "McNamara Line" by skeptics. The sensors detected vehicle movement and sent LORAN time difference (TD) coordinates of the vehicle location to the Igloo White Information Surveillance Center. The center plotted the data and relayed these LORAN TDs to the Tactical Air Control Center that, in turn, authorized the 25th TFS to bomb the target using these LORAN coordinates.

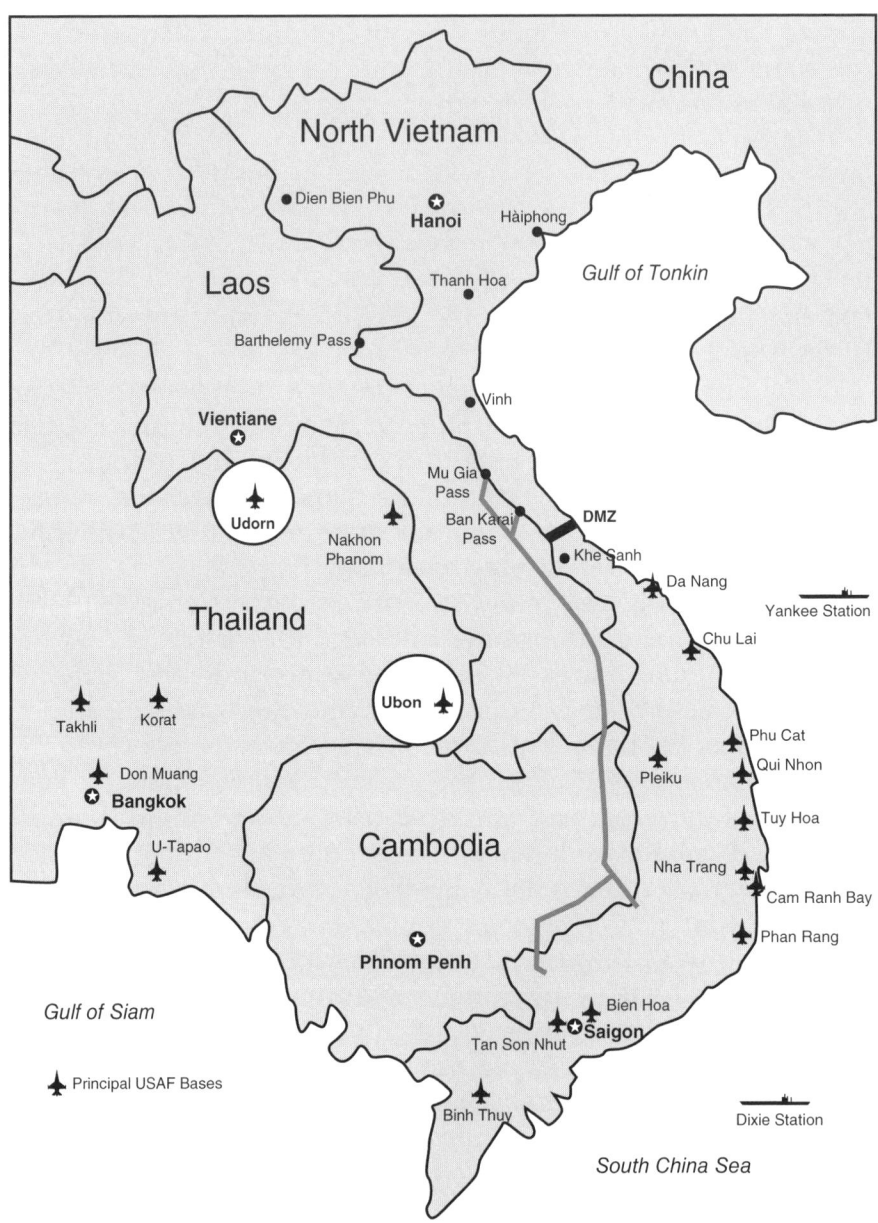

Figure 4. Southeast Asia. Ubon RTAFB was home for the 8th TFW, located near Cambodia west of the Laos border (*circled on the map*). Udorn RTAFB was home for the 432d Tactical Reconnaissance Wing (TRW) located near Vientiane, Laos (*circled on the map*).

On paper, Igloo White promised to be a giant step forward in disrupting the movement of supplies from North Vietnam down the trail to South Vietnam. In actuality, it suffered from major weaknesses. Probably the most serious error was assuming that LORAN-D was an extremely accurate navigation system. Although LORAN-D was generally more accurate than radar navigation, it was not akin to the GPS that came along a decade later. When LORAN-equipped aircraft dropped sensors along the Ho Chi Minh Trail, the true location of traffic detected by these sensors was typically not accurate enough for precision bombing. This initial inaccuracy compounded when F-4Ds equipped with LORAN-D bombed using LORAN TDs the Intelligence Surveillance Center provided. By the time the center sent the TDs back, the truck targets would have moved, thus causing inaccuracies.

Other problems existed with Igloo White. Accurate delivery of sensors required high-speed straight and level flight at low altitude. The elapsed time from detection to strike also created errors. How far did NVN trucks move after sensors detected their movement and F-4s arrived with munitions and began their attacks? If the NVN parked trucks in jungle areas, dense foliage protected the trucks from bombing attacks. Was it sensible to risk an aircraft and crew for such a marginal return? In my opinion, Igloo White could never pass a reasonable cost-effectiveness test.

The 497th TFS flew night missions against supplies entering South Vietnam through the mountainous passes connecting Laos and Vietnam—a difficult, dangerous job. The NVN needed to keep the passes open and defended them with large numbers of antiaircraft guns. The combination of antiaircraft fire, nighttime, and seasonal bad weather made these missions both difficult and dangerous. The 497th TFS also escorted AC-130 gunships at night. The reason for escorting AC-130s was to suppress antiaircraft guns and SAMs.

The AC-130 "Spectre" gunships belonging to the 16th Special Operations Squadron (SOS) were awesome truck-killing machines that specialized in night operations. Equipped with the latest infrared and ultraviolet technology, a 105 mm howitzer, and 20 mm Gatling guns, Spectre killed more trucks per mission than any other system in the war. According to the

AC-130 gunship. The AC-130 gunship was the most effective night weapon system used during the Vietnam War. It has a crew of 14—five officers and nine enlisted. The AC-130 continues to be effective in low-threat areas such as Iraq and Afghanistan. Collateral damage is minimized because of the accuracy of its fire control systems. A 25 mm Gatling gun, a 40 mm Bofors cannon, and a 105 mm howitzer are all mounted on the left side, as shown in these photographs.

16th SOS history, Spectre destroyed or damaged over 10,000 trucks along the Ho Chi Minh Trail and flew 1,327 consecutive on-time combat missions.

One night I flew a mission with the 16th SOS to gain firsthand knowledge of AC-130 capabilities. During the mission, the crew discovered several trucks driving down the Ho Chi Minh Trail. The trucks could not see our black Spectre aircraft flying on this dark night at medium altitude. The infrared and ultraviolet sensors in Spectre picked up the trucks with amazing clarity. The computer-assisted aiming system for the 105 mm howitzer was highly accurate. Nearly every time the 105 mm howitzer fired, a few seconds later the display screen flared as the shell hit, and the truck exploded. After an hour or two along the Ho Chi Minh Trail, the C-130 airborne battlefield command and control center (ABCCC) diverted our AC-130 to another area in Laos.

The new mission was to support an infiltration team of special operations forces surrounded and under fire in Laos. Spectre quickly established radio contact with the SOF team. The SOF team leader *whispered* over his radio that the NVN soldiers had encircled his team and were closing in. During their withdrawal under heavy fire, the NVN had wounded every member of this team. Spectre began circling the area over the firefight. For the next several hours, the team leader *whispered* directions to the Spectre crew. For example, "Bring your fire support one hundred yards closer on our north flank!" And, "That's just right. Now, shift it 50 yards to the left. We can see 'Gomers' moving through the trees over there." As dawn approached, Spectre contacted the ABCCC and requested F-4 support from the 8th TFW. When Wolf Pack arrived, Spectre handed over the mission to the F-4s and returned to Ubon. By mid-morning, the SOF infiltration team was rescued, and our medics were treating the wounded.

Because the 8th flew both day and night missions, the bars in the Officers' Club and NCO Club were open most of the time. They stayed open so the aircrews could unwind after a combat mission, relax, and enjoy the camaraderie that exists among those who fly combat. Certain practices grow into customs. Some were local, and other customs applied at clubs throughout the Air Force. For example, it was generally unacceptable to wear a hat in an Air Force bar. Violators, depending upon the club, were expected to buy everyone in the bar a drink. Such was the custom at Ubon.

One morning, an Air Force T-39 brought four congressmen to Ubon, accompanied by a very senior Air Force general. After their short flight from Bangkok, they were hungry and wanted breakfast. I took them to the Officers' Club because the kitchen was open. The club was empty except for two AC-130 crews that had landed two hours earlier, finished breakfast, and were drinking beer.

One congressman wore his hat after entering the club. A loud bell behind the bar rang, followed shortly by a Thai waitress. She handed a bar check for eight beers to the offending congressman. He was not a happy camper. "Why are they drinking beer at 8 o'clock in the morning, Colonel? Why do I have to buy them a round of drinks?" I explained to him they were AC-130 crews, had just returned from eight-hour combat missions, and local custom required that anyone wearing a hat in the bar had to buy drinks. He grudgingly reached for his wallet after the other three congressmen kidded him into submission. After the VIPs left, I went back to the club, found the two crews, and shared a good laugh.

One of the most difficult tasks a commander has in a combat environment is drawing the line on off-duty behavior between what is tolerable and what is not. Three incidents occurred at Ubon that illustrate my point. The first incident involved a floor show touring the USAF air bases in Thailand. As usual, several scantily clad Thai dancers were performing risqué dances that created intense interest among the young fighter pilots. Suddenly, a lieutenant jumped on the stage and simulated performing a sex act on one too-willing dancer. I told his squadron commander to get the lieutenant off the stage and bring him to my office in the morning. The next morning, I explained to the chagrined lieutenant that his conduct was unacceptable and beneath any reasonable standard for an Air Force officer. After banning him from the club for a month, the word spread, and the fighter pilots calmed down a bit. "Calming down a bit" is a relative term, not to be confused with a church lawn social or a visit to the public library, but more like the "Black Hole" (area of the stadium where the team's rowdiest fans congregate) at a Raiders football game with the Raiders winning 21-0!

The second incident occurred at the NCO Club. A Thai waitress was talking to a young black sergeant. A big white sergeant waited until the black sergeant left the club. He accosted the black sergeant for talking to the waitress and then beat him up. The black sergeant picked himself off the ground after the beating, found a 44-inch metal pipe, followed the white sergeant to the movie theater, and hit him over the head with the pipe. The security police immediately arrested the black sergeant and locked him up.

In 1970 racial tensions were high, and serious incidents had occurred at several Air Force bases. The next day, Colonel Schmerbeck called my office around noon. "Dick, the NCO Club is surrounded by a ring of black NCOs. Nobody can enter the club. Go over there and find out what's going on." I walked over to the club. Sure enough, 40 or 50 black NCOs surrounded the club and allowed no one to enter. The senior NCOs were bunched near the front entrance. I approached a senior master sergeant I knew well and respected as a tolerant individual.

"What's going on, Sergeant?" Immediately, a dozen or more angry NCOs clustered around. "They arrested the wrong man last night, Colonel. That 'redneck' SOB has been beating up every young black Airman who even talks to one of the waitresses. We have had enough. You do something about it, or we will!"

After patiently listening to their indignant complaints, I told them an investigation was already under way. "I promise you the sergeant you call a 'redneck' will be severely punished, if what you say is true. However, remember this. No one can hit another man over the head with a metal pipe and get away with it. Two wrongs do not make a right. I understand why you have protested. Now go back to work, and let the system take care of this. I am going to walk up the street to my quarters. When I get there and turn around, I expect you all to be gone!"

They moved aside. I began walking up the street. Unanswered questions passed through my mind. What would I do if they continued their protest? Did they trust me to follow through on my promise? After opening the front door to my quarters, I forced myself to turn around and look. Thank God, they were all gone! The protest was over. In following days, further investigation confirmed the white sergeant had assaulted several other black Airmen. He was court-martialed, found guilty of all charges, reduced to Airman basic, and given a bad-conduct discharge. The young black sergeant's court-martial found him guilty of an assault and awarded lesser punishment commensurate with the circumstances surrounding the incident.

A third problem stemmed from young fighter pilots having limited off-duty recreation. They flew approximately every other day, but unless they had an additional duty in the squadron or wing, the nonflying days were open. One day, a junior officer confided to me that something strange was going on in the Thai city of Ubon. Several pilots who were former college athletes had started a contest in the local slaughterhouse. The test was being able to knock out the animal with one blow from a sledgehammer before the Thai workers slaughtered it. The participants were all high-potential young officers. Their "contest," although probably legal, was hardly "conduct befitting an officer and gentleman." Remembering my own days as a junior officer, I knew that additional duties provide something constructive to do during off days from flying.

Security at Ubon was a problem. NVN had penetrated our perimeter defenses and destroyed aircraft. Another penetration attempt ended recently when security police killed two saboteurs as they cut through our perimeter fence. Every night, SP patrolled the local city because of drug traffic in the local bars. I asked for volunteers from these young pilots to augment the security police. Several volunteered, seemed to enjoy the opportunity, and did a good job. Included in my OER, Maj Gen James Kirkendall wrote: "Colonel Leavitt instituted a revolutionary program which utilizes outstanding young aircrews as officer augmentees in the security police field. The results were marked improvement of the security of the wing as well as broadened education for aspiring young officers."

Life was never dull. During July more than 20 inches of rain fell. After one very heavy rain, water two feet deep flooded a locked maintenance building filled with classified equipment. I drove down the taxiway to estimate the damage with the chief of maintenance. We passed a Thai worker carrying his shoes. He was wading through standing water, when suddenly he screamed. A cobra had bitten him on the bottom of his foot. We put him in the staff car, radioed the command post to alert the base hospital, and raced to the hospital. A doctor was ready.

He cleaned the wound on the heavily calloused foot where the cobra had bitten, gave him a tetanus shot, and sent him back to work. Lesson learned: poisonous snakes do not always release venom when they strike. Returning to the maintenance building later, two angry cobras floated by when we unlocked the door. A security policeman shot them. I had a snake-filled dream that night!

Tough Times for Military Dependents

When my family left the United States for Germany in 1967, the antiwar movement was just picking up steam. We lived on USAFE air bases during our three years in Germany. Both Trig and Mary attended DoD schools, and most of their classmates were military dependents. The majority of their friends had fathers who were either coming from or going to Southeast Asia. Upon returning to McLean, Virginia, in early 1970, my family experienced for the first time the riots, vitriolic press, burning campuses, and widespread antiwar movement that seemed to dominate public interest in the United States.

My daughter Chris, then a freshman at the University of Colorado, took a double dose of the antiwar hysteria. Chris had chosen the University of Colorado because she wanted to continue skiing—a sport in which she excelled. Her academic interest was social science, particularly Eastern European history. When the Social Science Department turned out to be a hotbed for Marxism, she sought a different field. Not only was Chris strongly anticommunist, but the college radicals knew her father was an "Air Force colonel who was bombing innocent women and children in Vietnam."

My 15-year-old son, Trig, played both baseball and football at Langley High School and was an excellent student. A baseball teammate's father was a publicity-hunting antiwar congressman from northern California who was prone to make unwarranted accusations such as "genocide" about the military in general and the Air Force in particular. Anne had shielded me from whatever dirty looks and discourtesies she received when some civilians learned she was married to an Air Force colonel. When Trig became aware of these unwarranted charges, he wrote that he would like to know what a typical combat mission was like. The following letter written on 20 May 1970 attempted to resolve these issues.

Dear Trig,

Enjoyed your letter and the snapshots of you and Mary! I now have 18 missions and have not flown quite as much lately because the new Wing Commander keeps me busy on other projects. However, I am now leading flights regularly instead of being a wingman. You asked about combat, so I will describe a typical mission.

Get up about 0500, dress in one of our new fireproof flying suits, put on jungle boots, shave and head for a quick breakfast at the club. Start briefing at 0600. We get a rundown on the weather, run over the Rules of Engagement, note special instructions, listen to the latest intelligence, and see where the flak guns have been firing most. Then we study the target for a while. After that the flight briefing starts. We discuss all the details—radio communication procedures, type of attack, air refueling and weapon delivery procedures, and whatever else is necessary to make a successful mission.

A few minutes later, I put on my "G" suit; grab a couple of baby bottles filled with ice water that I slip in my pocket; then strap on my pistol, knife and survival vest. After checking my emergency radio, I pick up maps, helmet and head for the F-4 in my staff car. (I leave it on the flight line so the GI's will know that I'm flying.) After talking to the crew chief, I walk around the aircraft for the pre-flight check. The GIB checks the bombs, fuses and guns. We then climb aboard, strap in and start the engines. The flight taxis to the arming area where the munitions crew arms our bombs and missiles.

About that time, I am sweating real good and hoping to get airborne where it's a lot cooler. Finally, we pull out on the runway, check over each of the "birds," go into afterburner and takeoff. About a half-hour after takeoff, we usually meet a KC-135 tanker. We join up on him and fill 'er up with Esso Extra, or whatever brand of jet fuel they're pumping that day.

After filling her up, we "cross the fence" into enemy territory, move into combat formation and start talking to various controllers. They talk to us about our mission and tell us sometimes to meet a FAC (an airborne controller who will show us exactly where to bomb, if it is not too "hot" an area for the FAC). We start looking for the FAC and after finding him, we compare notes about where the target is. Sometimes the target is very hard to find because of camouflage and jungle canopy.

The FAC usually marks the target by firing a smoke rocket near where the bombs are supposed to hit. We then start rolling in on dive bomb runs, or high-speed, low level attacks, if necessary. You really get moving on a dive bomb run; put the airplane at just the right dive angle and airspeed, center the pipper—then "bombs away," suck in your gut and feel the G's build up as you pull out and start jinking. Sometimes you can see the Gomers shooting their guns, but mostly you can't. Sometimes they fire quite a bit of flak, but many times there is little or no reaction. Then you wheel around and see where your bombs hit. The FAC decides whether you go back and hit again, or whether one pass did the job, We have some real smart laser bombs, like "Fat Albert," so frequently we get passed on to another FAC because we destroyed the target.

After bombing, we either head for home, or refuel again and find some more targets. After shooting a letdown and GCA back at Ubon, we land, taxi in, and tell the maintenance people how our aircraft performed. Then we debrief Intelligence and tell them how things went. After taking a shower and having lunch, I return to the office for my other duties.

The missions are interesting and challenging. We try to keep all the odds in our favor and still do our job. The "Gomers" are pretty smart, however, and have proven to be a very resourceful enemy. We spend a lot of time, money and effort trying not to do any unnecessary damage or kill any innocent people. Do not believe what some of our radicals are saying that we are indiscriminately killing a lot of innocent people—we are doing our job the hard way for us, in order to not do unnecessary destruction. And that's really the way it is.

Hope you will do well on your exams. Take care of yourself and write me again.

Love,
Dad

A June letter to Trig emphasized that our targets were military, not civilian:

Dear Trig,

I took off yesterday in a monsoon rainstorm leading a three-ship flight. Each F-4 had two 2,000-pound LGBs (laser guided bombs) and three 500-pound area bombs. Our mission was to knock out NVN flak guns discovered yesterday morning by a FAC. After rendezvousing with a tanker in the clouds, we refueled and headed for the target in Laos. Weather improved near the target area and we found the FAC who was flying an OV-10 Bronco.

The FAC fired a smoke rocket at the first gun position. Wolf Three rolled in on the target my GIB was lasing, dropped one LGB and damaged the gun. FAC then spotted the second gun with another smoke rocket. Wolf Three dropped his second LGB despite some moderately heavy flak and destroyed the gun—big secondary explosion! I sent Wolf Three home. FAC moved along and found another gun. This time, Wolf Two rolled in, dropped one bomb—direct hit—scratch another gun. FAC found a fourth gun. Wolf Two nailed it with his last 2,000-pound laser followed by another secondary explosion.

It was my turn to bomb. Wolf Two took over the lasing job. FAC found gun number 5. I rolled in, got a bull's eye plus a secondary explosion. FAC said the bomb hit right in the gun barrel—scratch number 5. We were getting low on fuel when the FAC found gun number 6. I nailed it with my last LGB. Score: six LGBs dropped; five guns destroyed, one damaged, three secondary explosions.

Hillsboro called and asked if we had any bombs left. Between 75–125 NVN troops were attacking a friendly position. Wolf Two was out of bombs; I had three cluster bombs remaining. We scrounged a tanker and the FAC and I worked the target. He smoked the target and I put three good ones right in their lap. The FAC was ecstatic—we had broken up the NVN attack! By then it was quite dark and we headed for home and an uneventful landing.

Hope you are meeting new friends and having a fine summer. Write soon.

Love,
Dad

IG Again

Vice wing commanders served as the local inspector generals in PACAF. There is a temptation for wing commanders to focus most of their time and energy on the flying operation. After all, combat is where "the rubber hits the road." Overdoing this will inevitably cause the support organizations—maintenance, supply, munitions, SP, personnel, civil engineering, hospital—to go their separate ways. The IG has to make sure this does not happen.

The IG had another important responsibility. He sought solutions to complaints, grievances, and personal problems not resolved at unit level. Problems ranged from financial, to marital, to racial, to job dissatisfaction, to discomfort (too hot), to haircuts, to Thai girlfriends, to almost everything and anything. Too often, they stemmed from the failures of junior officers and NCOs to take care of and communicate with their people.

One day, the Munitions Maintenance Squadron commander asked if I would talk to a sergeant who was one of his best team leaders. The sergeant wanted to be discharged as a conscientious objector. After the sergeant came to my office and sat down, I reminded him that he was highly thought of by all who worked with him and that his team needed his leadership. With this behind us, I asked and he answered several questions.

"Did you know about the Vietnam War when you enlisted in the Air Force?" "Yes, sir, I watched it on television and read about it in newspapers and magazines." "Were you trying to avoid combat in the Army?" "No, sir, I just liked the Air Force better." "Did you want to be trained as a munitions specialist?" "Yes, sir, it's a tough job, but I like it." "Then why do you want to become a conscientious objector?" "Sir, I received a letter from my sister at Kent State. In May, she saw the National Guard shoot the antiwar students, and she thinks the war is wrong and I should get out."

I shifted the conversation. "Do you know who Senator Fulbright is?" "Yes, sir, he is an important senator who is against the war." I asked, "Did you know that Senator Fulbright votes for appropriation bills that we need to continue fighting the war? He does that because he is a loyal American, and his duty as a senator is to provide the material that is necessary to fight the war, even if he disagrees with the war. When you joined the Air Force and took the oath to obey the lawful orders of your superior officers, you did not say, 'except when I disagree.' I know you are a good, honest man. Why not live up to your oath, just like Senator Fulbright does, and go back to work?"

He thought for a moment, nodded his head, stood up, saluted, and went back to loading bombs on F-4s. A month later, I saw him busily loading bombs on an F-4. It was a miserably hot day, and the loading crew was sweating profusely. He saw my staff car and waved. I stopped. He yelled over to the car with a big smile on his face, "Hey, Colonel Leavitt, how about telling me that stuff about Senator Fulbright again?" We both laughed. I drove off. He finished his tour—a good American in many ways.

Another Airman's job was delivering parts from maintenance control to the flight line. This was hot work but necessary. He had graduated from Georgetown University with a degree in international relations before joining the Air Force. His father was a Foreign Service officer in the State Department. He decided just before the monsoon season began that he was a conscientious objector and proposed working in the hospital until we approved his discharge. This interview took a different turn. "With your educational and family background, you must have discussed the war many times. Why did you enlist in the Air Force?" His answer was frank, "I did not want to be drafted into the Army. I was afraid they might put me in the infantry and I might get killed." Next question, "Why did you not go to Canada and hide like other antiwar protestors?" Another frank answer, "Because I knew my future career in the State Department might be at risk." My final comment, "You are presently performing in a job that has only an indirect connection to killing people or fighting the enemy. Your answers have nothing to do with being a conscientious objector. You want to work in the only air-conditioned workplace on the base—the hospital. Forget it. Now get your butt back to work, and do the job you were trained to do!" With a sheepish look on his face, he left the office. His squadron commander said later that the issue did not rise again.

My experience with ORIs in USAFE was helpful in inspecting the subordinate 8th Wing units. I started with the flying end of the business—operations. The 8th Wing had a strong, experienced Operations and Plans staff, well led by the deputy commander of operations, Col (later Lt Gen) Dan Druen. It included Lt Col Jack L. Gregory, who supervised mission planning; 15 years later, General Gregory commanded PACAF. Another young fighter pilot, Capt John G. Lorber, became General Lorber and commanded PACAF from 1994 until 1997.

The Maintenance and Supply Group had a difficult job. The R&D programs—laser and electro-optical bombs, LORAN-D, and AC-130 gunships—brought exciting new capabilities. The downside was too many out-of-commission aircraft and in-flight malfunctions. During May and June, I spent long hours walking the flight line and visiting the maintenance shops and correcting things. General Kirkendall noted these efforts. "His supervisory talents led to identification of discrepancies and improved standards on the flight line, in maintenance shops—particularly AGE [aerospace ground equipment], propulsion and NDL [national desired ground zero list]—and in munitions loading. This culminated in the 8th TFW achieving the highest MSET [Maintenance Standardization and Evaluation Team] rating in PACAF." Kirkendall's comments were appreciated, but the maintenance supervisors and Airmen who worked to improve their areas really earned the high rating.

The air base group had important tasks. Base security was a constant concern because of Ubon's close proximity to Laos. Twice during my tour at Ubon, NVN saboteurs attacked. The first time, they reached the transient aircraft parking ramp and destroyed a support aircraft. The next time, SP opened fire on two intruders at the base perimeter, hit the explosives strapped to their bodies, and blew them to bits.

The air base group purchased some food served in the dining halls from the local Thai economy. We kept costs down by competitively bidding contracts for fruit, vegetables, bread, and other commodities. One day, the Thai district governor, a major general, sent a message to all USAF air bases in northern Thailand. From now on, a centralized purchasing office working for the governor would perform all local procurement. We would provide our "shopping list," it would do the buying, and we would pay his purchasing office upon delivery of the commodities.

This procurement scheme offered no benefit to the Air Force, hurt local merchants, and was a wonderful opportunity for graft. I spoke to the other Thai bases, told the Thirteenth Air Force commander what I intended to do, and then called the governor. "If you make us buy food through your office, I will order all our food from the Philippines. Not only Ubon but all our air bases in your district will do the same thing. Do you want all the merchants around the air bases angry with you?" He answered, I'll call you back." Fifteen minutes later, he called. "Big misunderstanding; I am rescinding the message."

Thai tailor shops near the USAF air bases did a thriving business. Entrepreneurs from India owned most of the shops and sold clothes to air base personnel. Prices were low, so business was good. One favorite item was the "party suit," a brightly colored, tightly tailored replica of the flight suit (a green, one-piece coverall). Party suits added color and spirit to wing and squadron parties. Each squadron had party suits that matched its squadron color, with creative additions more common than not.

Adorning the suits were sew-on patches of various sizes and shapes, also made at the tailor shops. Originality counted. The Ho Chi Minh Trail passed through the mountainous Mu Gia Pass into Laos from Vietnam. We bombed Mu Gia repeatedly, and the NVN defended it vigorously with antiaircraft fire. One whimsical patch, Visit Vietnam: Ski Mu Gia Pass, displayed the appropriate amount of fighter pilot irony. Other patches were risqué or carried a message, especially those referring to a certain female movie star who patronized the NVN and posed behind enemy antiaircraft guns. The one thing a party suit was *not* good for was flying combat. The cloth was not fire retardant, and the colors would never pass for camouflage in an escape and evasion situation.

One day I was strapping on my survival equipment in the locker room prior to a combat mission. As I looked up, a young officer was also getting ready for a mission. To my amazement, he was wearing a bright-colored party suit! (To protect the innocent, let me call him "Larry.") "Larry, what the hell are you doing? Where is your flight suit?" His answer, "Today is my last combat mission before going home on leave. I'm celebrating!" He looked indignant, but he changed into his flight suit.

Larry was an outstanding young fighter pilot. Upon graduation from flight training, he went directly to the front seat of an F-4. During his tours at Ubon, he performed exceptionally well. Larry was the flight leader on this last mission before his leave. On the mission, antiaircraft fire severely damaged his F-4 during an attack against an antiaircraft battery. Larry and his GIB successfully ejected over the South China Sea. Air-Sea Rescue picked them up and returned them to Ubon that afternoon.

Whenever a rescued aircrew landed, custom called for everyone available to welcome them home. A crowd surrounded the chopper as Larry emerged. He spotted me in the crowd. "Colonel Leavitt, I wish I had my party suit on when they rescued me!" I answered, "Yeah, Larry. Then we could have gone to the Pentagon together and explained to the chief of staff what's happened to discipline in the 8th Wing!"

This incident made me reflect. Our combat loss rate was low—much lower than in the Korean War and much lower than when fighters were flying against the well-defended Hanoi-Haiphong complex. Nevertheless, we did suffer casualties. We need fighter pilots with spirit, but Larry's attempt to wear a party suit was long on "every man a tiger" and short on aerial discipline. Shakespeare wrote it best, "All's well that ends well." Larry became one of the top fighter pilots in the Air Force and a very successful commander before retiring with more than 30 years of exceptional service.

In the final analysis, The Great Party Suit Caper had a happy ending. We lost an F-4, but the aircrew was saved.

Cambodia Complicates the War

For several years, the heavily forested areas along the border between Cambodia and South Vietnam had been a "safe haven" for NVN troops and supplies moving down the Ho Chi Minh Trail. There were 14 major NVN army bases located in Cambodia within 35 miles of Saigon, the capital of SVN.[4] Nixon's decision was to help the Lon Nol government in Cambodia and the Vietnamization of the war by invading Cambodia with American and RVN troops. The two-month long incursion would reduce the serious military threat to SVN caused by NVN forces in Cambodia, help Lon Nol against the Khmer Rouge and NVN, and improve our negotiating position in Paris with the NVN.

The incursion, Operation Toan Thang 43, began in May 1970 and lasted two months. The attacking ground force was comprised of the US 1st Cavalry Division, 11th Armored Cavalry Regiment, 25th Infantry Division, and several RVN Army units.

Pres. Richard Nixon wrote in his memoir that Operation Toan Thang 43 had been the most successful operation of the Vietnam War because it destroyed the enemy bases nearest Saigon, bought time for Vietnamization, frustrated the North's potential for a spring offensive, and permitted the survival of the Lon Nol regime.[5] USAF officers and Airmen in Southeast Asia gladly noted Nixon was finally taking an aggressive approach to breaking the long, stalemated war. We had difficulty understanding why the Cambodian incursion incited riots in the United States, closed colleges, and caused violent antiwar protests.

When the NVN were forced to retreat from their camps on the Cambodian border, they moved to the interior of Cambodia near the capital, Phnom Penh. I flew a few missions in Cambodia, two of which stand out in my memory. The first happened in late June with the 433d Squadron commander flying as the only wingman. Our target was a small bridge near the Cambodia-SVN border that I missed on a previous mission. Destroying the bridge was part of a campaign to prevent the NVN from returning to their border camps. This time, I knocked the bridge down with my second bomb.

As we pulled off the bridge target, "Hillsboro," the ABCCC aircraft called, "Wolf Pack Lead, NVN troops have captured buildings on the outskirts of Angkor Wat. They are in a fierce firefight with Lon Nol's troops [friendlies] who have surrounded the area. If you have any ordnance remaining, can you help?"

Angkor Wat, the world famous Buddhist temple complex, is often listed as one of the Seven Wonders of the Ancient World and has immense historical value to the Cambodian people. "Roger, Hillsboro, we have eight Mark 82s, but need fuel to reach Angkor Wat." Minutes later, a KC-135 tanker appeared, and we refueled and headed west. Approaching Angkor Wat, we could see a low cloud deck covering the area. The local tower at the large commercial airfield near Angkor Wat said the clouds went down to about 700–800 feet with good visibility underneath. I decided to make low-level bomb runs below the clouds. The eight Mark 82 bombs were "Snake-eyes" with high-drag fins used to slow the bombs after release. Snake-eyes improved low-level bombing accuracy and descended slowly enough to keep the aircraft ahead of the bomb blast.

NVN troops occupied two long buildings outside the moat that surrounded the Angkor Wat complex. We each made two passes, dropping two bombs per each pass. The eight bombs all hit the targets—four bombs in each building. We knew we had clobbered the target and headed for home. Two days later, we learned this CAS mission turned out better than we expected. The "good guys" moved into the area and counted more than 100 "Gomers" killed by air.

Later, I flew in an OV-10 Bronco with a FAC on a Cambodian CAS mission. The OV-10 flew about 1,000–1,500 feet above the terrain and between 120–150 knots airspeed. The FAC had instructions to contact a controller with Cambodian army troops. The controller on the ground spoke both French and English. We made radio contact near a north-south road with no villages nearby.

"Bronco, this is Pierre. We want to cross this road, but a machine gun fired from the other side when we started to cross yesterday. Would you cross the road and see if you can see a machine gun position?" Bronco acknowledged the request and five minutes later called back, "Nothing there, Pierre, it looks OK to cross the road." Pierre was not one to throw caution to the winds. "Bronco, this is Pierre. Would you please fly south down the road about two kilometers near the wat [Buddhist temple] and see if any machine guns are located there?" Bronco acknowledged Pierre's request and once again called back, "Nothing there, Pierre. We will check to the north." (Sensing Pierre's reluctance, we had anticipated his next request before he could ask.) We flew north on the road for a few kilometers, then returned. Bronco called Pierre again. "Pierre, it looks OK in all directions for you to cross the road." After a long pause, Pierre answered, "Thank you Bronco. Maybe we will try to cross the road tomorrow."

We returned to Ubon. The four-hour mission provided a depressing perspective on the war in Cambodia. By the time the OV-10 landed, I realized there was a huge motivational gap existing between Lon Nol's Cambodian forces and the way American forces fight wars. Unless Lon Nol's army changed and was willing to fight for its country, it seemed inevitable the Khmer Rouge with NVN assistance would win. Nixon won a *tactical* advantage with the incursion, as stated in his memoirs. However, the incursion lacked a *strategic* advantage unless the United States committed to fighting a civil war in Cambodia with ground forces. Since the Nixon Doctrine rejected fighting a war with American "boots on the ground," the incursion had no strategic future and, in fact, added fuel to the antiwar fire in the United States.

Postwar note: the Khmer Rouge continued to grow in strength and overthrew Lon Nol's government in 1975. Pol Pot, the Khmer Rouge leader, then destroyed Cambodian society with a forced agrarian movement that included assassinating 1.5 to 2 million Cambodians representing the educated, business, and leadership classes of their society.

The Khmer Rouge consisted of only a few thousand troops in 1970. One cannot help wondering that if the Cambodian army had fought hard and won in 1970–71, would the Khmer Rouge have been defeated and more than a million Cambodian lives been saved later?

Ups and Downs
Summer 1970

For the past 20 years, I witnessed the Air Force change from being the junior offspring of the World War II armed forces into a mature, well-equipped organization led by experienced officers and NCOs. By 1970 nearly all officers were college graduates, and a significant percentage had postgraduate degrees. Roughly 80 percent of the Air Force were enlisted personnel; half of these were NCOs—staff sergeants or above.

The Air Force has always taken great pride in the experienced, well-trained NCOs who form the backbone of our technical service. NCOs accomplish the lion's share of "hands on" leadership in the Air Force. They are the product of selective enlistment policies, excellent technical training, and years of experience. Air Force recruits prior to 1967 were high school graduates, or equivalent, with Armed Forces Qualification Test (AFQT) scores in the top three of five aptitude categories.[6] These three categories included only aptitudes ranging from average to high. With few exceptions, recruits responded to training, obeyed the rules, and sharpened their skills during their first enlistment. About half reenlisted and became career NCOs.

SecDef McNamara threw a severe challenge at military leadership by imposing Project 100,000 in December 1966. As part of the "War on Poverty," McNamara ordered a combined total of 100,000 Category IV recruits each year. Average reading ability was at the sixth grade level, with 13 percent below the fourth grade level. Data reported to Congress shows the Air Force took approximately 42,000 of the total 354,000 Category IV recruits accepted by all the services from 1967 through 1971. At any one time, this amounted to nearly one-quarter of the 177,000 lower three enlisted grades in the USAF.[7] The Category IV recruits constituted a disproportionate number of discipline problems, military offenses, mistakes on the job, and accidents.

"Project 100,000" Airmen often had two strikes against them before they entered the Air Force—the Air Force gave some a third. A squadron commander brought a young black Airman to my office, recommending an administrative discharge. His commander said the Airman seemed unable to comply with our rather easy regulations. Most recently, he bought a pistol in a

Thai pawnshop and attempted to smuggle it on base. The Airman said that he enlisted after completing three years at Fordham University and really wanted to stay in the Air Force. He admitted buying the pistol but said he did not know it was against the rules.

I knew an attempt to get him a security clearance had been rejected. The security investigation had disclosed that three years at "Fordham University" were really three years in a New York juvenile detention facility. The security clearance investigation uncovered the details. He had killed his father by stabbing him repeatedly when he found him beating his mother. The judge had sealed his juvenile criminal record upon his release from juvenile detention.

After reading his superiors' reports and the psychiatrist's opinion, I mulled over all his problems. Society had failed him before he joined the Air Force. The officers and NCOs in our wing who tried to teach him had failed. I wished there had been some way to straighten him out and make him a useful citizen, but his presence in the wing was a continuing distraction from our primary mission. Sadly, I signed the paperwork recommending an administrative discharge. In December 1971, Nixon finally ended Project 100,000, but the 1971 recruits remained in the Air Force until 1974.

A Senate committee traveling to the military bases in Vietnam and Thailand visited the 8th Wing. They were trying to resolve a serious question. Why was the Army in Vietnam having such a serious problem with marijuana usage, "fragging" (the intentional killing of officers by their own troops), desertion, and other discipline problems, whereas the Air Force did not seem to be having similar problems? We first discussed marijuana. It was cheap and readily available in Ubon Ratchathani, the Thai city next to the air base. SP patrolled the bars and other known locations where marijuana could be purchased or smoked. We punished Airmen caught smoking or possessing marijuana, and businesses and other locations that ignored our marijuana avoidance policy were placed off limits. This economic pressure served as a deterrent to both sales and usage. Yes, there were violators—mostly young Airmen—but marijuana was not a major problem.

The committee asked for more discussion about the behavior differences between Army enlisted personnel in Vietnam and Air Force enlisted personnel in Thailand. There was the obvious difference between serving in peaceful Thailand or wartorn Vietnam. There were also leadership and demographic differences. In 1970 the average Air Force NCO was older, more career oriented, and had more experience than the typical Army NCO. Repeated combat tours to Vietnam had drained the Army of experienced NCOs.

Even well educated professionals occasionally caused problems. Young Air Force doctors during the Vietnam War were usually products of the Berry Plan. In exchange for draft deferment and the government paying for their medical education, the Berry Plan required three years in one of the military services. The Air Force granted captain commissions to doctors after they completed medical school and internship. Although most had no intention to remain in the Air Force, it was a rare event when a Berry Plan doctor failed or refused to perform his duties.

For that reason, it came as a surprise when a young doctor came into my office in August for an hour or two of IG "séance time." He had decided "not to get involved in anything anymore because the other doctors do not like me!" Lacking a psychiatrist's couch, I had to listen to his self-pitying complaint while he was sitting across the desk. Running through my mind was the realization that maybe the TV comedy *M*A*S*H* was not too bad an exaggeration. He was acting like a 14-year-old adolescent with a girlfriend who said she no longer loved him. After mixing all the patience, sympathy, and encouragement I could muster into a "Buck up, Doctor" speech, he left my office promising to mend professional relationships and try harder.

A far more serious incident occurred in mid-August. A Jolly Green Giant rescue helicopter radioed "Mayday" before crashing into the jungle north of Ubon. Because the crash site was not far from the Laos border, we could not rule out that the NVN may have shot down the chopper. The 8th Command Post immediately called the hospital for a doctor to accompany a rescue team to the crash site. The chief flight surgeon did not respond because he was "busy packing his household goods." The doctor on standby for emergencies refused to go. I intervened and gave him a direct order to go with the rescue team. He refused to go to the jungle crash site whether or not people were injured and stated, "I did not join the Air Force to get killed." What happened to his Hippocratic Oath? Finally, an off-duty doctor volunteered. His team rescued the downed helicopter crew.

I attempted to court-martial the cowardly doctor who refused to go, but the case never went to court before he was discharged because of a legal technicality. The replacement chief flight surgeon arrived a week later. An ex-fighter pilot with 4,000 hours of flying time, he was a welcome addition to our hospital staff.

No one becomes accustomed or indifferent to losing a friend or acquaintance, whether in a peacetime accident or in combat. Military tradition calls for the commander to express condolences in a letter to the immediate family. Deaths also occur overseas that are unrelated to combat. One morning, I was shocked to learn that a senior NCO in our headquarters had been murdered—stabbed in the heart with a knife by his Thai girlfriend. How do you write a letter explaining the circumstances of his death to his wife and four children?

The PACAF commander, General Nazzaro, visited Ubon again in late summer. By this time, I was no longer a "new guy" and could answer his questions with more credibility than during his last visit in April. He asked Colonel Schmerbeck if he recommended me to be the wing commander of the 432d TRW at Udorn RTAFB when Col David Mellish, the present 432d Wing commander, left in November. Schmerbeck agreed. The move would be an opportunity for me because Schmerbeck, 8th TFW commander, would not rotate home until after I left next April.

Then a telephone call from Air Force Personnel asked if I would be willing to leave the 8th TFW now and extend my Asian tour for a year to command a fighter wing in Korea. The year in Korea would be unaccompanied by family. I turned this opportunity down for two reasons: it meant nearly a two-year separation from my family, and I would not be able to finish this combat tour.

A few days later, Maj Gen O. B. Johnson, 313th Air Division commander, called from his headquarters at Kadena AB, Okinawa. "Obie" had been the director of operational requirements at FEAF headquarters, Tokyo, where I worked 17 years earlier. "Would you like to command the 18th TFW after you finish your combat tour? Kadena is a two-year tour, and you can bring your family." Obie made my day. "Yes, sir, I would really like that!" When Anne heard the news, she accepted it in good spirits but reminded me that Trig and Mary would have to change to overseas schools again after only a year and one-half in McLean, Virginia.

The AC-130 Spectre gunships assigned to the 16th SOS were creating intense interest in the Pentagon. These powerful gunships had earned their reputation for being the most effective weapon system against NVN trucks traveling down the Ho Chi Minh Trail at night. PACAF sent me to Wright-Patterson AFB and the Pentagon to discuss AC-130E improvements that AFSC and the 16th SOS had proposed. Meanwhile, the 8th Wing began acquiring a new squadron of multisensor B-57Gs for night interdiction. This version of the B-57 series had more capability than the earlier B-57s, but the AC-130E gunship remained top "truck killer" on the Ho Chi Minh Trail.

Thirteenth Air Force Personnel called about 1 August, after I returned from the Pentagon. General Nazzaro decided that I would replace Colonel Mellish as the 432d TRFW commander at Udorn RTAFB. Before the transfer, I would command the 8th TFW while Dave Schmerbeck took 30 days of leave in September. When Dave returned from leave, I could take a two-week leave in October before reporting to Udorn.

It was surprising to me that these "job offers" all came in a short time period. Later that month, the 8th Wing personnel officer said Personnel was bringing my records up to date for the PACAF Brigadier General Selection Board meeting on 7 September. A letter to Anne was realistic about this news: "I'm interested, but not expectant. If the B.G. board met six months from now, I would be in much better position. Maybe, since they are giving me a wing out here, they will forward my file to the Central Board anyway."

I looked forward to commanding a wing. USAF policy assigns the overall responsibility to wing commanders for the flying and nonflying assets in their wing. Doctrine, regulations, manuals, and customs provide detailed instructions and guidance. In theory, all should go well if you simply complied with the instructions and guidance.

In reality, managing a wing in combat is not that simple. Suppose a friend said, "You want to be a champion golfer? Just read *How to Shoot Par*, buy some clubs, practice once a week, and you will win the club championship in two months." You would cast a skeptical look at your friend. Unforeseen and unpredictable factors will affect your golf score. They will also affect your performance as a wing commander.

There are differences between wings that only meet minimum standards and wings that exceed expectations. The significant difference is leadership and morale at all levels from colonels to junior NCOs. The conductor in a large symphony orchestra does not write the music, train the musicians, repair the instruments, or play the French horn. Instead, he insures these tasks run smoothly, or the symphony becomes discordant. Like the conductor, the wing commander's most important role is building and maintaining a team that performs tasks smoothly and successfully accomplishes the wing mission.

I had spent 13 years working in wings, inspecting wings, and being a vice wing commander. Soon it would be my turn to command one. Until then, Wolf Pack would be very busy. Monsoons were ending, and improved weather meant more combat activity.

One F-4 bombing mission I led into Laos was especially memorable. The F-4s were heavily loaded with bombs and fuel. For safety reasons, our standard procedure was to make individual takeoffs. Each J-79 engine in the F-4D had an afterburner. Together, they added about 50 percent more thrust—from 20,000 of pounds thrust to over 30,000. This extra push made takeoffs faster and safer. After becoming safely airborne, the flight leader would turn away from the traffic pattern, shut off his afterburners, and establish climb speed. The other aircraft would join on the flight leader after becoming safely airborne. After join-up, the flight would head for the target or for an air-refueling tanker.

After taking off, I banked to the right, turned off both afterburners, and established join-up speed. My wingman, Wolf Two, was a new squadron commander but an experienced fighter pilot. I watched him closing smoothly off my right wing. When he was about 100 yards away, he called, "Wolf Lead, Wolf Two here. Your right afterburner is still on." I checked both throttle positions. "Negative, Wolf Two. Both afterburners are off." At that point, his F-4 stopped closing on mine, and, as he slid off to the right, he calmly reported, "Well, Wolf Lead, if your afterburner is not on, you are on fire."

Bad news! I quickly stopcocked the right engine, turned away from the city of Ubon Ratchathani, and headed for the nearby river. If we had to bail out, I did not want the bomb-loaded F-4 to crash into the crowded city. Right engine RPM was dropping to windmill speed. No fire warning lights glowed on the instrument panel. Hopefully, the fire would go out now that the engine was stopcocked. I called the wingman again, "Wolf Two, I stopcocked the right engine. Is the fire out now?" His answer raised a new set of problems and really got my attention. "Negative, Wolf Lead, you are still burning."

Aircrews fear fire in an aircraft, and I am no exception. The GIB and I talked over the emergency as we approached the river. He was very calm and professional about the ejection possibility. I waited a few seconds and called again. "Wolf Two, let me know if the fire goes out. We are heading for the Mekong. We will jettison the bombs and eject over the river if the fire is still burning." Seconds passed.

We leveled off over the river and were getting ready to jettison the bombs when Wolf Two called again. "Wolf Lead, the fire just went out!" We were near the air base. I found a place to jettison the bombs without killing any Thais and made an emergency single-engine landing. The 8th Command Post had another F-4 ready to go. We grabbed it and rejoined our flight. The rest of our flight had air-refueled while waiting for us.

Although the aborted F-4 had no visual external damage, the fire caused a major accident. One or more of the short-petal afterburner nozzles had reversed, causing the afterburner flame to flow upward into the titanium plate that shielded the fuel tanks. The intense flame burned through three-quarters of the titanium shield before the fire went out. If the wingman had not warned me, the aircraft would have exploded in a few more seconds. Sometimes flying is more exciting than other times. Thanks, Wolf Two!

Life at Ubon was not all work and no play. The district governor occasionally invited me to play golf with him. He called it, "Our new custom—Sunday morning golf!" He had carved an 18-hole golf course from the jungle using prisoner labor from his military stockade. Three "ball watchers," located on each side of the fairway at 50-yard intervals, made sure the governor never lost a ball and always had a good lie. The governor always won, and the scorecard was not subject to review. A great host and fun to play with, the governor provided a pleasant break in my usual routine.

Dave Schmerbeck left for the states on leave, and I assumed command of the 8th Wing. September passed quickly. Improved weather resulted in more missions that were effective. By the end of September, my total combat missions at Ubon exceeded 80.

When Dave returned, my bags were packed, and I was ready to go on leave before reporting to Udorn. Dave had a local F-4D flight that afternoon to reacquaint himself in the aircraft. After taxiing into the parking area, he did not respond to the crew chief's signal to shut off engines. The crew chief climbed the ladder to the cockpit assuming there was a problem with the aircraft. Dave was unconscious and died early that evening from a heart attack despite the best efforts of the hospital staff to revive him. Dave Schmerbeck was a true gentleman and good friend. I deeply regretted his untimely passing.

The Seventh/Thirteenth Air Force commander called later that evening, cancelled my move to Udorn, and said I should stay at Ubon as 8th Wing commander. About 0200 the following day, General Nazzaro called from PACAF and said to continue with his plan and go to Udorn as 432d Wing commander after returning from leave. Col Larry Killpack would assume command of the Wolf Pack before I left for leave.

Back to Work

After Larry Killpack had assumed command of the Wolf Pack, I packed a suitcase and caught the C-130 shuttle to Bangkok for the first leg of a long trip home. One measure of progress in the military has been the recognition that families really do matter. During World War II, many Army Air Force personnel were separated from their families for long periods of time—two or three year separations were common for those sent overseas in 1942 and 1943. Two complementary changes improved the family separation problem during the Vietnam War. One was the rapid development and availability of commercial jet aircraft during the 1960s. Jet transports cut in half the time it took piston-powered aircraft to fly from Saigon to California. The second change was Defense Department support for the R&R program. As its name implies, R&R gave a welcome break from the routine of combat and made it possible for brief family reunions.

After boarding the aircraft at Dulles International for the first leg of the flight back to Thailand from my R&R, my thoughts returned to the two weeks spent at home. Anne had "assumed command" of the family in my absence, and everything was well planned, organized, and under control. In addition to her family responsibilities, Anne was a part-time bookkeeper for a contractor. Trig and Mary were doing well in school. Anne's overall competence and loving support never failed to amaze me.

October was "Time for Football!" We saw Trig, a linebacker at Langley High School, play in two Friday night games. One Saturday, we drove to West Point for an Army game. After attending church services on both Sunday mornings at St. Dunstan's, where I had been a lay reader and member of the vestry, we joined our old gang at two Washington Redskins home games. Between football games, we enjoyed partying with our many friends in McLean.

The long flight back to Thailand left plenty of time to think. Seven months in combat reminded me of playing slot machines in Las Vegas. Now and then, a good mission would have a nice payoff. Most of the time, mission results did not match the investment. We had the best aircraft, aircrews, and weapons the world had ever seen, but we were pounding tacks with a sledgehammer. The good news in 1970 was that we were losing fewer aircrews and aircraft when compared to pre-1969 losses. Our containment policy had been mishandled in this Southeast Asian war, and a vocal minority of Americans was ready to "throw in the towel."

Ever since the Kent State incident, antiwar rhetoric had increased and was front-page headlines and featured on television news. In June 1970, the Senate repealed the Gulf of Tonkin Resolution that had authorized American military involvement against NVN. In October, the biennial election in the United States was only a month away. The Vietnam War seemed to be the foremost election issue in both the House and Senate races.

Our failure to end the war before Nixon replaced Johnson in 1969 traced to our unwillingness to risk war with China and/or the USSR. The Johnson cabinet believed that one or both nations would enter the war against the United States if the United States escalated beyond a very limited war. "Limited" meant no invasion of North Vietnam, no blockade of North Vietnam ports, no destruction of railroads connecting China to North Vietnam, no major bombing campaign against North Vietnam cities, no destruction of North Vietnam infrastructure including dikes, no invasion of Cambodia or Laos to close the Ho Chi Minh Trail, and no overt action to stop mistreatment of American POWs.

In April 1970, Nixon had announced the United States would withdraw 150,000 Americans from the Vietnam War during the following year. The Army of the Republic of Vietnam (ARVN), trained by American advisors, equipped with American arms, and supported by American logistics, would become responsible for ground operations. US Air Force and Navy forces would continue to provide support for South Vietnam in the air and at sea. By keeping this pressure on North Vietnam, Nixon expected to be able to negotiate an honorable peace treaty with the North Vietnamese, thus ending the war. In October 1970, Nixon proposed to the NVN a cease-fire until the warring governments signed a peace agreement. The NVN failed to respond to Nixon's proposal by the time my R&R ended.

Serious military questions would inevitably arise and need answering before the United States and SVN could negotiate a successful peace treaty. If Nixon moved away from "US boots on the ground" to a policy that favored "SVN boots on the ground," would he relax the political restrictions imposed on Air Force and Navy operations? If US Army and Marine troops withdrew, was the SVN army strong enough to hold off the NVN army? How much continuing support would SVN require from USAF airpower and US Navy air and sea power?

There were no clear answers to these questions because we had accepted an expensive, long-lasting stalemate as the least painful way to preserve South Vietnam. The Nixon administration now seemed to be moving away from the stalemate. I was cautiously optimistic, but it was difficult to see the path ahead.

367

The long trip back was over as the C-130 landed at Udorn, and the remainder of my combat tour began.

Col David Mellish, outgoing 432d Wing commander, arranged a welcoming party of commanders and staff to greet me. One of the best rewards for being in the Air Force for several years is finding old friends wherever you transfer. Among those present were Col Steve Heyser, the U-2 pilot who first photographed the Soviet missiles in Cuba, now a staff officer in the Seventh/Thirteenth Air Force headquarters at Udorn, and Col Ted Katz from the "Deep Furrow" NATO exercise in Greece, now the 432d Air Base Group commander. One fighter squadron commander was Lt Col Andy Merrick, a B-52H aircraft commander at Wurtsmith. Friends from Germany included F-4 pilot O. B. Baird from the 36th Wing and RF-4C pilot Dick Greenlee from Headquarters USAFE at Wiesbaden.

Big Challenge at Udorn

Udorn was an exceptionally busy air base. It was the closest USAF base to Hanoi and only a few miles south of the Laotian Plain of Jars where the major battles for control of that war-torn country occurred. Udorn's base population was around 10,000. The operational side of the 432d Wing included two squadrons of F-4Ds (13th and 555th TFSs), two squadrons of RF-4Cs (11th and 14th Tactical Reconnaissance Squadrons [TRS]), a reconnaissance technical squadron, and the Seventh Airborne Command and Control Squadron flying C-130Es. Also assigned to Udorn were about 700 personnel from Military Airlift Command operating HH-53 rescue helicopters. Training Lao T-28 pilots was an ongoing activity under Air America supervision.

Supporting the operational squadrons were the maintenance, supply, munitions, civil engineer, transportation, and SP squadrons. The 1974th Communications Group was responsible for all USAF communications activities in Thailand. USAF relationships to other tenant units on the base, especially Air America, were somewhat ambivalent. However, the 432d Wing inherited the support problems for the tenants, such as housing, feeding, and supplying. The air base group, commanded by Colonel Katz, performed the important roles of feeding, housing, and providing recreation facilities for all the USAF personnel at Udorn.

The 432d Hospital Group manned a busy 100-bed hospital. Whenever an aircraft was lost from enemy action in northern Laos or crashed near Udorn, the 40th Aerospace Rescue and Recovery Squadron (ARRS) flying HH-53 Jolly Green Giant helicopters would bring the downed Airmen to this hospital.

Without any publicity, the hospital staff also treated Thai volunteers and Lao soldiers wounded during battles against the NVN and Pathet Lao in Laos. After one particularly fierce battle, the hospital received several hundred Thai and Lao wounded. The hospital commander, Col Walter Hein, placed the overflow of the soldiers in tents next to the hospital building. Although many had suffered serious injuries, only one of the several hundred died after entering our hospital. Medics found this Lao soldier lying on the ground two days after the battle ended. Gangrene had already infected his intestinal wound. He eventually died despite several operations and a heroic struggle on his part. When the hospital settled back to normal, the young doctors, one at a time, told me about our wonderful surgeon, Dr. Hein, and how many lives he had saved. They appreciated that Walt had enhanced their own surgical skills from working with him during many operations.

General Nazzaro and the PACAF senior staff visited Udorn shortly after I returned from R&R. I asked Nazzaro privately why he went ahead with my transfer to Udorn after Dave Schmerbeck died. He explained his reasoning. The 432d Wing at Udorn included both fighter and reconnaissance F-4s. Because of my recent fighter background and earlier reconnaissance experience in U-2s, Nazzaro believed that I could manage both operations. The other reason traced to the difficult morale and management problems at Udorn. He did not want a new commander whom he had not observed.

Nazzaro said major problems at Udorn needed fixing quickly. Operational effectiveness was the lowest of the PACAF F-4 wings. There were too many aborted and ineffective missions. Bombing effectiveness was below the other Thai-based fighter wings. Morale was poor, judging from the number of IG complaints and military offenses. The reenlistment rate was the lowest in PACAF.

Although I had only been at Udorn for a short time and was not yet the wing commander, Nazzaro's observations coincided with my own. Correcting the problems would require time—not much time, provided he would give me a free hand and some help with badly needed money. The enlisted barracks were in sad shape. Before leaving, he agreed to find some money for improving the enlisted barracks. We had a rocky start when I first met General Nazzaro six months earlier at Ubon, so his supportive attitude was a welcome change and really appreciated.

Shortly after he departed, USAF Personnel sent a message rejecting General Nazzaro's request to transfer me to Okinawa as the 18th TFW commander after completing the tour at Udorn. Instead, I would become director of strike forces, DCS plans and operations, HQ USAF, in the Pentagon, reporting in May. This meant that I had only five months remaining to make changes where needed at Udorn. It was time to act.

Col Dave Mellish, the outgoing wing commander, was exceptionally helpful during the time our assignments overlapped. Although I was technically the vice wing commander until the formal change of command occurred, Dave handed over most of his wing commander responsibilities after I arrived. He carefully explained the command relationships within the 432d and was frank about his being an unpopular commander. He believed that PACAF sent him to Udorn to restore discipline and operational effectiveness and to improve the appearance and facilities of the air base. He discussed all the steps that he had taken. Despite good intentions, several of his initiatives had backfired. The 432d was clearly an unhappy organization with marginal operational performance compared to other Thai-based tactical wings.

After hearing complaints whenever I met officers and Airmen, I realized that with this much smoke, there had to be fire. Too many aircrews, junior officers, and NCOs resented Dave's efforts, perhaps through misunderstanding or a lack of communication. A confirmation of poor morale was the first-term reenlistment rate—only 10 percent for the previous six months—the lowest in PACAF. I decided to focus on improving morale as the first order of business.

Twenty years in the Air Force was long enough for me to know that only a few people will maintain high personal standards in their jobs regardless of their boss, work environment, the pay, the climate, or whatever else bothers other people. At the opposite extreme are only a few people who will gripe from the time they get up in the morning until they fall asleep at night, yet somehow do their job. Most Air Force people are between these extremes. The majority will work better when they are mostly satisfied with conditions and not so good when they are mostly dissatisfied with conditions.

A successful commander carefully spends his time and energy while working with these three kinds of people assigned by the Air Force personnel system. He will allocate some time and energy to encouraging and rewarding the top percentile who set and maintain high standards. He will not spend unnecessary time and energy into making chronic gripers into happy warriors. Instead, he will allocate most of his time and energy on the majority of people in his unit who will perform their jobs better if they are satisfied with conditions.

The dictionary defines *morale* as "an emotional or mental condition with respect to confidence, zeal, etc., especially in the face of opposition, hardship, etc." *Esprit de corps* is defined as "a sense of unity and common purpose among the members of a group." Morale seems to be more an individual characteristic, while esprit de corps is a group characteristic. Applying these definitions to a wing in combat is appropriate but raises questions. Can most individuals have low morale if the wing has high esprit de corps? In my opinion, the answer is no, that is an unstable situation.

Improving aircrew morale was important. The typical aircrew flew a combat mission every other day. The air war remained a dangerous business. Most of the 432d combat missions were flown over Laos. Unless they were rescued by the Jolly Green Giant helicopters after being shot down, none shot down in Laos during my tour made it home after the war. Without exception, the 432d aircrews accepted the risks willingly. Whatever morale problems had came from other issues, not exposure to combat.

A commander quickly loses credibility by imposing petty rules and restrictions. I experienced such a restriction on one of my first nights at Udorn. My favorite drink in those days was a vodka and tonic. I asked the bartender for one, and he answered, "Sorry, Colonel, we do not carry tonic." This seemed strange. "What's the problem? They have tonic at the other Thai bases." His answer baffled me. "The commander read that tonic water was brain degenerative and told us not to buy it anymore." (Looking back over several years of vodka and tonic drinking, I now had the perfect excuse for failing to write home yesterday!) Stopping the consumption of tonic was the wrong way to motivate people, particularly combat aircrews with more serious life-threatening concerns than drinking tonic water.

A more damaging example of a well-intentioned policy that backfired was the wing regulation for off-duty aircrews. In a previous assignment, Dave Mellish served on a naval aircraft carrier as an Air Force exchange officer. The carrier's policy was to control shore leave equitably by using the first letter of the Sailor's last name. On odd-numbered days, last names beginning with "A, C, E" and so forth could go ashore. On even-numbered days, names beginning with "B, D, F" and so forth could go ashore. Dave remembered his Navy experience and had established the alphabetical procedure for 432d Wing aircrews leaving the base.

A common occurrence illustrates one problem with the wing regulation for off-duty aircrews. Assume F-4 pilot Adams and his navigator Brown flew a combat mission on an alphabetically "odd" day and they were not scheduled for the following "even" day. They decided to leave the base for dinner at a Thai restaurant, but the policy would not allow Brown to go. Crew integrity is violated in this Adams/Brown example. Discriminating against aircrews is a poor way to build esprit de corps.

Dave put teeth into his wing regulation for off-duty aircrews by having SP spot-check the names of officers leaving or entering the main gate. It did not require Sherlock Holmes to know that an officer with an "A" name on a "B" night was violating the regulation. Officers who violated the regulation could expect an Article 15 for punishment. The *Uniform Code of Military Justice* (*UCMJ*) allows Article 15s to be awarded for nonjudicial punishment (not a court-martial), but Article 15s are still bad news for an officer's future career.

I found approximately 40 unprocessed Article 15s in the left-hand desk drawer of my predecessor resulting from violations of the wing regulation for off-duty aircrews. This was a far higher percentage of Article 15s than a relatively small number of officers should experience. The aircrews waiting punishment were very angry. This problem was easy to fix. First, I deleted the off-duty aircrew regulation and told squadron commanders they were responsible for controlling when their aircrews could leave the air base. Second, I took the unprocessed Article 15s and threw them in the wastebasket. The *UCMJ* grants the successor commander the authority to do this.[8]

Japanese motorcycles were for sale in the city of Udorn. Base regulations forbade owning motorcycles or driving motorcycles on the air base. Some GIs ignored the regulation and purchased them regardless. They paid a Thai to register the motorcycle, then "rented" it back from the new Thai "owner." Meanwhile, off-base motorcycle accidents had killed or seriously injured several Airmen who owned these motorcycles. None of the dead or injured had taken motorcycle training. I called a meeting for all motorcycle owners. "Would you attend and pass a motorcycle training course on base if you could drive and keep your motorcycle on base?" The response was a unanimous, "Yes, sir!"

I ate most of my meals in the Officers' Club. The club had two dining rooms; one was for colonels and visiting VIPs, and the other was for all other officers. The first day at Udorn, my escort officer took me to the colonels' dining room. Although the menu was the same in both dining rooms, colonels had better service because there was an extra waitress for the approximately 10 colonels who regularly ate there. After that first day, I chose to eat in the main dining room. By joining different officers for each meal, I quickly learned the names and faces of many officers. Once their shyness disappeared, they talked about flying, their jobs on the base, and a new complaint. "Why do colonels eating in their room get better service than we do when we pay the same for club membership and meals?" "Good question—let me work on it."

Other morale issues kept popping up. Seventh/Thirteenth Air Force had imposed a nighttime curfew on base personnel visiting adjacent Thai cities. It was difficult to enforce, and statistics showed the curfew did little to reduce incidents.

Another issue affected retention. A significant number of officers and NCOs wanted to extend their tours in Thailand. If they wanted to extend and their commander concurred, I believed in approving extensions, except for married men. Some married men established marriage-threatening relationships with Thai women. Too many times these semipermanent relationships ended in disaster, including broken marriages, suicides, and an occasional murder.

Another source for poor morale at Udorn was the enlisted barracks. Enlisted personnel lived in old two-story, open-bay barracks without air-conditioning, fans, window screens, modern latrines, or recent painting. I was determined to rejuvenate the barracks with whatever money we could find and hoped to hold General Nazzaro to his commitment about sending barracks rehabilitation money from PACAF.

A problem for both the officers and enlisted personnel was the seven-day workweek. The war went on every day, and the seven-day week was necessary from an operational viewpoint. The wing could not declare Sunday, for example, a nonwork day and ignore our tasking from higher headquarters. However, working day after day with no break in the routine was not conducive to either good morale or good performance. The solution to this dilemma was for the squadrons to schedule every officer and Airman for one day off per week—not the same day for everyone, but one day a week they could count on for their personal use.

When a combat wing is on a downhill slide, the temptation is to blame the wing commander. He sets the pace but is seldom the whole problem. After living with the 8th Wing for six months and the 432d Wing for only a few weeks, I knew that the 432d had more problems, but both wings shared a weakness. Commanders and senior NCOs were not communicating enough with their subordinates. This was particularly true of squadron commanders who overfocused on their own combat missions and did not spend enough time with the officers and NCOs who did the "heavy lifting" before and after the combat missions.

I was ready for action when the change of command ceremony ended. For the 432d Wing to progress, there had to be far more activity than just changing wing commanders. I met with the senior wing staff, group commanders, and the new vice wing commander, Col Lyle Mann, and outlined my proposed improvement plan. Job One was to improve morale and internal communications. Modest improvements in morale would occur quickly with several policy changes, such as insuring that everyone in the wing had an off-duty day each week. Substantial improvements would take longer and depend upon their individual leadership and the cooperation of their subordinates—squadron commanders, section heads, junior officers, and NCOs. Gaining and maintaining cooperation depended upon good communications up and down the chain of command. These leaders needed to actively pursue these objectives and accept the responsibility for their unit's performance. We would meet once a week and discuss progress, or lack thereof.

I released a revised set of wing directives and policies the next day, then ate lunch in the colonels' dining room at the Officers' Club. Only three or four colonels were eating lunch. During lunch, I explained that other club members complained about their club dues being spent on extra waitresses for the colonels' dining room. Starting now, only one waitress would serve, and there had to be enough business to keep the colonels' dining room open. Two Seventh/Thirteenth Air Force staff colonels at lunch were unhappy about this change.

As I walked into my office after lunch, the wing executive officer handed me a note. Maj Gen Andrew Evans wanted to see me in his office—right away! Udorn was also the home for the Seventh and Thirteenth Air Force headquarters. General Evans commanded all PACAF forces in Thailand and was my immediate supervisor.[9] Evans had replaced General Kirkendall in mid-October, and I had only met Evans socially.

Word travels fast. Someone had already briefed him on the revised 432d Wing regulations. Without wasting any time and looking perturbed, he asked what was going on. I told him that poor morale was hurting 432d Wing performance and that all the changes were necessary and needed immediately. He listened quietly, but his response included a veiled threat. "Colonel Leavitt, I'm going to hold you responsible for everything that happens in the 432d." My response, "I would expect that, General, and I wouldn't want it any other way." I saluted and left. After that shaky start, we got along well. It was a pleasure to know and work for General Evans, an experienced fighter pilot and veteran of both World War II and Korea.

When I walked into the Officers' Club for dinner that evening, several aircrews were standing by the bar. They asked me to join them. It was a setup. Even the bartender was smiling. Before I could order, the bartender slid a vodka and tonic across the bar at me. Everyone laughed. The Tonic Water Battle was only a small victory but symbolic of better times ahead. I went to bed that evening feeling good about the day's activities but realizing it was time to focus on other important issues.

General Nazzaro said the most pressing operational problem was improving combat effectiveness. The 432d had unique capabilities. Our RF-4s could photograph potential targets, and within minutes after landing, photos were available to photo interpreters and intelligence officers. Unfortunately, Seventh Air Force was not fully exploiting this capability. I needed the Seventh Air Force deputy for operations to decentralize some controls that would allow faster response to targets of opportunity.

Before leaving Ubon for Udorn, the Seventh Air Force operations staff told me the 432d reputation for bombing accuracy was not good, based on bomb damage assessment reports from the FACs and from aerial photography. Our operational effectiveness depended upon aircrews destroying targets. I decided to appeal to the professional pride of the fighter aircrews.

The aircrews convened one evening in the Officers' Club patio. Hors d'oeuvres and beer or soft drinks created a receptive mood for our first large meeting. We discussed the new policy changes that were in effect, and they voiced their strong support for the changes. Then I renewed a tradition that was dear to their hearts. Starting the next day, they could have the traditional end-of-tour flyby. Aircrews completing their last mission saw the flyby as closure for their part in the war.

The talk switched to correcting the wing reputation for poor bombing accuracy. After having flown several combat missions with the 432d fighter squadrons, I knew they were capable of doing better. They just needed a dose of "style"—another way to describe professionalism in combat. I asked everyone to live by eight simple rules. If they did, I promised the 432d would become "Best in PACAF."

1. Know and adhere to the ROEs.

2. Study the weather, intelligence, and aerial photos of the target.

3. Carefully plan tactics. Take advantage of sun, terrain, and prevailing winds.

4. Know your weapons and optimum delivery techniques for all munitions.

5. The flight leader is in charge. Advise him of problems and unexpected developments. Keep mouths shut and eyes open.

6. Listen carefully to the FAC. Know exactly where to bomb. Take great pride in bombing accurately.

7. Kill the target with one pass. Repeated passes raise the chance of being hit by flak. No single enemy target is worth your life.

8. Make enemy defenses guess by jinking in random patterns.

I ended the meeting on a personal note. "Here's a challenge to anyone flying a mission with me. If you can bomb better than me, bet a drink on it—payable after the mission!" This fighter pilot braggadocio brought smiles—and a few shouts like, "You are going to be buying me drinks, Colonel!" Exactly the gung ho responses I wanted. When I lost the bet, this Old Man (42 last week) was glad to lose to a young tiger. It did not take long to find improvement. I wrote Anne, "Had a really good mission two days ago. Today it came back through channels as 'one of the most outstanding examples ever seen in the Southeast Asia air war.' The FAC was a romanticist probably, but we all appreciated the accolade. We were dropping high-drag bombs (low-altitude delivery) and just could not seem to miss— not always the case!"

Number One Concern became the low sortie rate for assigned aircraft. As the Vietnam War developed, the USAF assigned enough tactical aircraft to Southeast Asia to support routine operations. By 1970 "routine" meant no major bombing campaign against North Vietnam, no major offensive against South Vietnam by the NVN army, and no South Vietnamese invasion of Laos. Given enough time, hundreds of reinforcement aircraft and supporting personnel could fly from the CONUS. Nevertheless, if the military situation called for *immediate* help, reinforcements from the states could not be there in time. PACAF would have to play the game with the cards it had been dealt. For that reason, tactical wings must be able to step up the pace and generate more sorties with on-hand aircraft, personnel, and supplies.

A rough way to measure the operational readiness of a fighter wing in combat is to determine the daily sortie rate per assigned aircraft. For example, if a typical fighter wing with 72 assigned aircraft averaged 72 sorties a day, its daily sortie rate per assigned aircraft would be 1.0. All other factors being equal, higher sortie rates mean a wing is more efficient and can inflict more damage on the enemy. A key factor in raising the sortie rate is reducing "turnaround time" between sorties—the time an aircraft spends between landing from one combat sortie and taking off on another combat sortie.

During my USAFE tour giving ORIs, I watched many fighter wings turn around aircraft. An F-4 wing flying two sorties per day per aircraft was exceptional. In sharp contrast, USAFE air defense squadrons were masters at turning around F-102s. To be effective, air defense interceptors have to "scramble"—get airborne in a hurry, intercept enemy aircraft, fire missiles, land, refuel, load munitions, preflight the aircraft, and scramble again. F-102 squadrons turned aircraft in less than an hour by prepositioning munitions, fuel, and support personnel. Their turnarounds worked like well-oiled machines.

My goal at Udorn was to comply with all safety regulations and flight manual checklists but turn an operational F-4 in about 30 minutes by amplifying the techniques used by F-102 squadrons. I discussed this with operations, maintenance, and munitions supervisors. As expected, there was skepticism, "Colonel, we've always done it the way we're doing it now." (This kind of reaction reminded me of Einstein's observation that making the same mistake over and over again was a sure sign of insanity.) When the meeting ended, they gave me the benefit of the doubt and agreed to try the new way. The credibility I gained the previous few days was now at risk.

We built the Quick Turn area near munitions storage and easily accessible to fuel trucks. Pilots returning from combat missions called the command post when 100 miles from Udorn and stated whether their F-4s were in commission.

In-commission F-4s taxied to Quick Turn immediately after landing. Replacement aircrews were standing by, already briefed for their next mission. Munitions maintenance prepositioned the required munitions. Two munitions loading teams were standing by in their bright red T-shirts and baseball caps—special recognition for their key role in Quick Turn. One team loaded the portside pylons, the other the starboard. The F-4 crew chief and a maintenance NCO debriefed the landing aircrew and performed the required preflight inspections while the new aircrew strapped into ejection seats and prepared to start engines. The control tower expedited taxi and takeoff instructions after the pilot started engines. Every step by each participant complied with operation and maintenance checklists.

Quick Turn worked like a charm. The Air Force IG, Lt Gen Selmon Wells, flew to Udorn to make sure we were following safety regulations. He watched while an F-4D with a typical bomb load turned in 19 minutes from landing until takeoff. Wells was very complimentary, saying that Quick Turn was a smooth operation and complied with all regulations.

The policy changes made in November had an immediate effect on morale and improved the sortie rate. I firmly believe leaders must provide short-term goals to motivate people. It is not a short-term goal to tell a crew chief, "Good work! Six months from now when you rotate home, I'll put you in for a Commendation Medal." A short-term goal is a better motivator. "Good work! If your 'bird' goes through periodic inspection without major write-ups, you get a trip and two days off in Bangkok."

I later told the Seventh Air Force commander, Gen Lucius Clay, we could drop 1,200 MK-82 500-pound bombs against targets in the Plain of Jars in one day. With 12 bombs per aircraft, that meant approximately 100 sorties, or about 2.5 sorties per aircraft in the two F-4D squadrons. By 3:00 p.m. on evaluation day, two squadrons had dropped 1,000 MK-82s. The 1,200 goal was easily within reach when the Seventh Air Force director for materiel called. "Stop! You are running out of bombs. A shipment will not arrive by train until tomorrow. You proved your point."

Son Tay Heartbreaker

The deputy director of operations for Seventh Air Force visited Udorn in mid-November. In private conversation, he asked if I wanted to join a highly classified project. Volunteering meant no more combat missions for me until the project ended. As the new wing commander, I was reluctant to stop flying combat missions. Enemy activity had increased significantly with the end of the monsoon season. The annual battle for control of northern Laos created many more significant targets than during our interdiction efforts against the Ho Chi Minh Trail. Therefore, I declined joining the project after explaining my need for combat experience in the Plain of Jars. Before leaving, he named several 432d F-4 crews who were already in the project. Until the project ended, the 432d could not schedule them for combat missions. The following summary is partially based upon personal observations and conversations with Col Arthur J. "Bull" Simons, US Army, at Udorn at the time, and with Lt Gen Leroy J. Manor in 1974.

On 20 November 1970, a special operations force of 56 highly trained Army special forces volunteers led by Colonel Simons departed Takhli RTAFB and landed at Udorn RTAFB. Five hours before takeoff, Simons told his men:

> We are going to rescue 70 American prisoners of war, maybe more, from a camp called Son Tay. This is something American prisoners have a right to expect from their fellow soldiers. The target is 23 miles west of Hanoi. You are to let nothing interfere with the operation. Our mission is to rescue prisoners, not take prisoners. And if we walk into a trap, if they know that we are coming, don't dream about walking out of North Vietnam—unless you've got wings on your feet. We'll be 100 miles from Laos; it's the wrong part of the world for a big retrograde movement. If there's been a leak, we'll know it as soon as the second or third chopper sets down; that's when they'll cream us. If it happens, I want to keep this force together. We will back up to the Song Cong River and, [expletive deleted], let them come across that . . . damn open ground. We'll make them pay for every foot across the [SOB].[10]

Not until the Son Tay Raiders landed at Udorn the afternoon of the 21st did I learn of their mission. Our wing command post prepared for a busy night. As departure time approached, I walked with Bull Simon and his men to the ramp area where their helicopters waited. Never had I seen more determined, tough, dedicated, brave men. If success were possible, they would succeed. Watching these courageous Soldiers climb on board the "choppers" filled my heart with pride in being an American and my mind with prayer for their success. At 11:18 p.m. on 21 November 1970, they took off for Son Tay.

It was a clear night with partial moon. To divert NVN attention from the rescue attempt, Navy carrier forces attacked the port of Haiphong, and Air Force Wild Weasel F-105s attacked SAM sites near Hanoi and Haiphong. Ten F-4s, including six from Udorn, flew combat air patrols, screening the Raiders from MiG interference.

About 90 minutes later, the command post began to pick up broken radio transmissions coming from the Raider choppers. First indications were the raid was successful. The command post broke into cheers. As the choppers drew nearer, it became evident they had not rescued any POWs. When they landed, I met Bull Simons as he left his chopper. Walking along with an unlit cigar in his mouth, Bull was very much the Humphrey Bogart type—cool and terse. He masked his disappointment and explained there were no POWs in the prison. I changed the subject. "Was it like the Son Tay prison mock-up where you trained in Florida?" "Yeah, pretty much, except the rice paddy ditches were deeper than at Eglin. I fell into one. When I looked up, a Gomer jumped into the ditch with me. I killed the SOB with my .357."

The press speculated, often critically, about attacking an empty prison with no POWs to rescue. Why did we not know there were no POWs there? After the POW release in 1973, we learned the NVN had transferred the POWs to Dong Hoi in July 1970. An intelligence leak did not cause the transfer. The NVN moved the POWs because the well in the compound dried up and the nearby Song Cong River overflowed its banks, threatening to flood the prison. In retrospect, there were two indications that Son Tay was an inactive prison. In July an SR-71 photo mission characterized Son Tay as less active than usual. On 3 October, another SR-71 mission showed little signs of life. Whether lacking positive evidence of POW presence was sufficient cause to cancel the raid remains a matter of opinion.

From a tactical viewpoint, the raid was successful. No Americans died in the raid; one broken ankle was the only serious injury. The Raiders killed approximately 200 NVN soldiers in and around the prison compound. However, the antiwar doves in Congress were vocal and critical. I wrote Anne, "I got so damn mad at the Senate doves who screamed about the Raid. A lot of really brave guys did something that shows our Country still cares, and then the Fulbrights, et al., carp and criticize. I'll tell you; around here there weren't any critics—just heartbroken people when the planes came back empty."

The POWs returned to the United States in early 1973 and talked about the positive results of the raid. When the raid was in progress, the POWs at Dong Hoi, 15 miles east of Son Tay, could hear the noise and quickly realized what was happening. America had made a serious attempt to set them free. The raid uplifted morale. The NVN moved all POWs at Dong Hoi and other outlying prison camps to Hanoi after the raid. They joined the other American prisoners and were no longer alone in cells. The treatment of POWs seemed to improve. The raid did serve a useful purpose after all.

Bull Simons, after his retirement, conducted a rescue operation in Iran in 1979 that freed two of Ross Perot's Electronic Data Systems Corporation employees held as hostages. Simons arranged their escape, and they safely returned to the United States. Colonel Simons, US Army, retired, died three months later from heart complications.[11]

Recce Bird Shot Down and the Aftermath

When President Johnson stopped the bombing campaign against North Vietnam in 1968, most photo reconnaissance coverage of NVN ended as well. Although infrequent high-altitude flights by the Mach 3+ A-11 and its successor the SR-71 provided strategic intelligence of the Hanoi-Haiphong area, they did not monitor areas near the border to South Vietnam where supplies and NVN troops would be located prior to invading SVN. A successful surprise NVN attack against Hue, other coastal cities, and the large American base at Da Nang would add fuel to the antiwar fire in the United States and set back negotiations to end the war.

For insurance against such an attack, MACV needed continuing proof that such a buildup was not under way. When the

Change-of-command ceremony, Udorn RTAFB, Thailand, 1970. General Evans changes command of the 432d Wing from Colonel Mellish to General Leavitt.

bombing stopped, North Vietnam agreed that one unarmed reconnaissance aircraft flying at low altitude could periodically photograph the area in North Vietnam where a buildup might occur. One escort fighter could accompany each reconnaissance aircraft. Seventh Air Force assigned these missions to the 432d because we had both RF-4s and F-4s.

A lieutenant colonel pilot, experienced in the RF-4, joined the 432d in early November. He was to become the squadron commander after the present RF-4 squadron commander returned to the United States. On 11 November, the newly assigned pilot flew an authorized low-level reconnaissance mission over NVN. These missions were not usually dangerous because the NVN had agreed not to fire at the single reconnaissance aircraft and the escort. Ignoring the agreement, the NVN shot down the RF-4. There were no chutes or beepers. The pilot and navigator were killed.

MAC commander visit. General Catton, MAC commander, visited the 40th ARRS Squadron at Udorn. It was equipped with HH-53C helicopters and rescued many downed aircrews. *Right*: The commander of the Jolly Green Giants, Lieutenant Colonel Modeca.

Adm Thomas Moorer, JCS chairman, visits Udorn. General Evans (*far left*) introduces General Leavitt (*far right*) to Admiral Moorer. Ambassador to Laos, G. McMurtrie Godley, exits the T-39. Colonel Rogers, vice-commander of the Seventeenth and Thirteen Air Forces, stands next to Evans.

Melvin Laird, the SecDef, reacted promptly after learning the NVN had broken their agreement. Laird announced the United States would retaliate. The newly arrived Seventh Air Force deputy for operations took charge of the planning. He withheld the date for retaliation and the designated enemy targets from the tactical wings that would fly the combat missions. Meanwhile, the assistant DO continued managing Seventh Air Force assets supporting the highly classified Son Tay Raid. Then the unimaginable happened.

The new DO did not know about the Son Tay Raid. The retaliation raid was to be a "max" effort, with takeoff times set for early on 22 November—only a few hours after the Son Tay Raid took off! Since Thai-based wings were supporting the Son Tay Raid, we did not know about the retaliation raid until a long message began coming into our command post from Seventh

Photo courtesy US Air Force

Admiral Moorer congratulates a MAC HHC-53 air rescue crew for saving an RF-4 aircrew shot down in Laos

Air Force. The Son Tay raiders and our supporting fighters began landing around 0130 (1:30 a.m.).

For the past three weeks, Dave Mellish had allowed me to be the de facto wing commander. This night proved to be an unexpected final exam before the official change-of-command ceremony. Teletypes were painfully slow in the Vietnam War. When we saw it was a max effort, our maintenance and munitions people rushed to get as many aircraft ready as possible. All squadron commanders and aircrews assembled in the wing briefing room in the predawn hours. I told them the targets were in North Vietnam, but I didn't know where. The raid was in retaliation for shooting down our Falcon (432d) aircrew. When I asked for volunteers, every man in the room enthusiastically volunteered. It reminded me, once again, how great these

VIP visitors are good for morale. A sergeant explains the RF-4 camera system to Admiral Moorer and his staff. This sergeant could write home that he did a fine job briefing the CJCS!

General Nazzaro, Commander in Chief, PACAF

Gen John D. Ryan, chief of staff, USAF

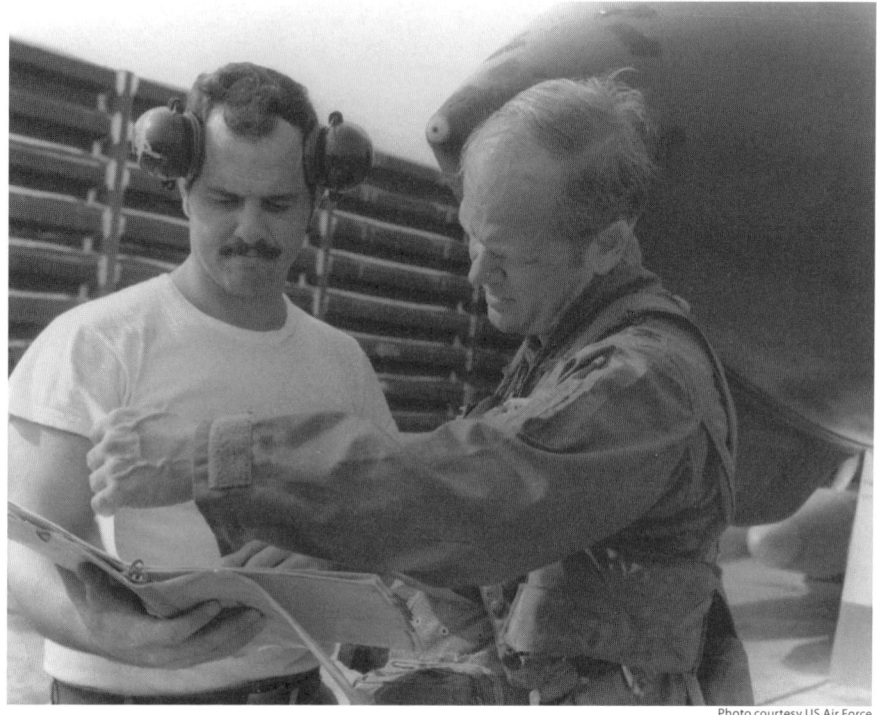

Working with guys who "keep 'em flying." Checking the aircraft Form 1 with the crew chief for discrepancies before takeoff.

young warriors were and how proud all Americans would be if they could only see them.

Maintenance turned enough aircraft from the earlier Son Tay support missions, and we met the tasking requirements from Seventh Air Force. Operations assigned aircrews to flights, briefed the ROEs, air refueling arrangements, and weather, but we still did not know the targets—the long message was still coming in a few bits at a time. As takeoff time drew near, we went to the aircraft and prepared to start engines. Still lacking targets, I told the intelligence officers to recall all crews to the briefing room as soon as target data arrived. At the last possible moment before start engines time, the targets arrived. After spending a few minutes studying targets, we launched on time. I led the raid. We air refueled on the way and bombed our assigned NVN targets, and the 432d came home without a loss.

Photo courtesy US Air Force

Congratulating several munitions maintenance Airmen for their outstanding work.
Their squadron commander and section leader watch. Weather is hot and humid.

The *Bangkok Post* reported that NVN called the raid "an extremely serious act of war." Secretary Laird said, "We are conducting limited-duration protective reaction air strikes against missile and antiaircraft gun sites and related facilities in North Vietnam, south of the 19th parallel." The North Vietnamese were probably confused since the Son Tay Raid and the retaliation raid nearly overlapped. The American press named it the "One Day War."

The 432d received accolades for our performance during the One Day War. Seventh Air Force singled out the 432d as the "best-performing wing." They called to say that we "did particularly well in a hard day's work." Because of the lack of preparation time and related factors, other wings were unable to respond with the required number of fighters. In addition, several KC-135 refueling aircraft failed to reach their orbits in time to refuel the fighters. In my opinion, the officers and Airmen in the 432d deserved these accolades from Seventh Air Force. I am also thankful that nothing went wrong after we launched. All our aircrews and aircraft returned safely despite the "hurry up" circumstances.

Seventh Air Force operations had set the stage for a near fiasco. Sending a multipage tasking order by a slow teletype machine that arrived just in time for takeoff was ample cause for failure. Allowing two major operations to proceed at approximately the same time without alerting the wing commanders or coordinating within the Seventh Air Force staff was inexcusable. These staff failures resulted in the removal of the newly assigned deputy for operations. He was replaced by Maj Gen Joe Wilson, an experienced fighter pilot and tactician.

December—Lots of War and a Little Love

The fighting in Laos near NVN surged in December. The winter weather dries the terrain in northern Laos and provides ideal conditions for an attacking army. NVN needed this part of Laos for the Ho Chi Minh Trail. The inept Pathet Lao provided political cover for seasoned, tough NVN troops who did most of the serious fighting. Because both the Johnson and Nixon administrations feared the political consequences of invading Laos with American troops, the CIA and Air Force did the fighting in Laos, while the government kept our involvement secret.

This subterfuge had a wider impact than one might expect. In December, Cong. Gillespie "Sonny" Montgomery (D-MS) visited Udorn. He was on his way to Vientiane, Laos, to drop off a petition at the North Vietnamese Embassy requesting better treatment for our POWs in North Vietnam. We discussed the progress of the war in some detail. Montgomery was a decent, responsible congressman; however, he seemed surprised to see we were still fighting a war here. When even Congress does not know what is happening during a war, one can imagine how the American media can distort reality.

The increased operations tempo resulted in what Intelligence calls "a target-rich environment"—shorthand for lots of things to bomb. As the month wore on, the intensity increased, as described in several letters to Anne.

12 December

The last couple of days have been tough ones. Yesterday morning we had an F-4 hit on a bomb run. The pilot pulled off, was checked over by his flight leader, looked OK, went back in and as he released his bombs, the aircraft pitched up and down violently. The GIB, apparently thinking they were hit, punched out—right in the middle of a large number of Gomers. Meanwhile, the aircraft commander recovered and returned the aircraft safely to Udorn.

We established contact on the ground with the GIB and with other USAF units flew bombing and strafing sorties all afternoon to get him out. After three missed attempts due to hostile fire, we were finally able to get a PJ (pararescue jumper) down to him and brought him into the Jolly Green Giant. However, he had been killed from a head shot and so all the effort failed. The GIs, pilots and everyone else felt badly because everyone had tried so hard to save him. Right in the middle of the rescue attempt, I'm sitting in Wing Command Post trying to generate more aircraft and crews, and a letter addressed to me as the Wing Commander came from some Peacenik telling me how horrible we all are persecuting the poor innocent North Vietnamese. Made me want to throw up.

17 December

Spending a different kind of night sitting in a C-130 Airborne Command and Control Center watching the nightly battle for truck-killing on the Ho Chi Minh Trail. The squadron of these C-130Es in the Wing has an important role in the air war. There is a big capsule in the cargo compartment with extensive radios, wall maps and seats for controllers keeping track of FACs, strike aircraft, gunships, B-52s and what-not. We'll be on the scene until tomorrow morning—12 hours. I flew an F-4 sortie this morning, so I'm really earning my flight pay today.

19 December

We lost an F-4 today, but thank God the crew was recovered in good shape. Things have been considerably more "exciting" the last few weeks. I flew to Ton Son Nhut for business with Seventh Air Force on Monday. While there, the generals had some kind words about how the Wing has improved.

23 December

We lost another aircraft on Monday, but the crew was recovered in good shape. . . . Christmas is now only two days away. Otherwise, business as usual.

25 December

Christmas Day was back to reality. I led a mission to the PDJ [Plaine des Jarres]. As we neared the target area, an A-1E flight leader called for help. His wingman's aircraft was hit and the pilot was going to eject. He asked if we would fly top cover until rescue helicopters arrived. I "Rogered" the request and turned quickly towards his location. We soon spotted the flight leader's aircraft circling a parachute that was floating downward. Then the flight leader made a sickening radio call. "Aggie One, don't bother. The seat ejected OK and the parachute opened, but there is no one in the chute."

The Yankee ejection system in the A-1E automatically opens the parachute and extracts the pilot from the seat after the seat ejects. The pilot had changed aircraft just before takeoff and had not properly secured himself in the seat. Every Christmas Day, I still remember that empty parachute floating downward in Laos with no one in it.

Despite this tragic incident, the letter written home on Christmas Day included an upbeat note.

Last night—Christmas Eve—was different. The Deputy for Materiel had a nice cocktail party and dinner. Then the Junior Officer's Council went around the base on a big flatbed truck and sang carols. I visited every guard walking the perimeter fence with his sentry dog and wished them a "Merry Christmas"—dogs, too. There was a good band, plus singer at the Club. Everyone was in a party mood with squadrons taking turns singing carols amidst the champagne.

On 30 December 1970 my letter home said:

I was proud of how well the Wing performed today. We were given a lot bigger "frag" than would normally be our share and the guys did it without even a late takeoff. We were helping rescue a downed FAC and when the word gets around that an aircrew has been shot down, the troops really produce. There are a heluva lot of dedicated and worthwhile young Americans still around despite what the newspapers say and what campus radicals do.

I'm looking forward to '71. I have no regrets about the time spent over here. I have tried to do my best, flying and otherwise—now it will be nice to walk away from it. I can already see that you cannot walk away without leaving something behind; too many friends and too many experiences where you would like to have done just a little bit better. Nevertheless, enough is enough. After awhile, you start thinking nothing can happen to you, and that is not a real healthy attitude in combat.

New Year's Eve came and went. The club was colorful because all of the squadrons appeared in their brightly hued "party suits." Jane Fonda's conduct in North Vietnam was very much on the disapproving minds of everyone present. After losing aircraft and friends to NVN antiaircraft fire recently and having other friends suffering as tortured POWs in the Hanoi Hilton and other POW compounds, no one condoned this American actress posing with an antiaircraft gun and NVN crew.

New Year's Day about 0800, the hospital commander, Col Walt Hein, called my office. "I'm missing the hospitalized pilot who was rescued. Also, the nurse assigned to his ward. Do you have any idea where they are?" My mind flashed back to the New Year's Eve party. One young nurse epitomized the anti-Fonda mood. Sewed on the back of her party suit was a patch referring to Fonda. The three-word expression on the patch was sexually explicit as to what should happen to Jane Fonda. I remembered seeing the nurse earlier in the evening, but not after midnight. When Walt confirmed she was the missing nurse, I told him, "Walt, send another nurse over to her quarters and see if she and maybe the pilot are there."

We solved the mysterious disappearances. They overslept. After the rescue, the young bachelor pilot had been hospitalized with minor injuries. The missing nurse was in charge of his ward. She left her post without permission, although from the pilot's viewpoint, the evening activities improved his morale and expedited his recovery. Walt Hein, a great hospital commander and surgeon, took a different stance. He asked me to press charges against both the pilot and nurse.

I really struggled with Walt's request. On one hand, all the aircrews would sympathize with the fighter pilot, recently "snatched from the jaws of death," as the newspaper might write. They would argue it was practically the duty of any red-blooded young American, especially a bachelor pilot, to leap from his sickbed into the arms of a willing young nurse on New Year's Eve. Indeed, in their minds, she might be said to be a modern-day Florence Nightingale taking care of her patient's needs on a 24-hour-a-day basis!

On the other hand, Walt could not allow a nurse in charge of a ward to disregard her responsibility to her patients in the middle of the night and leave them unattended. Nor could he allow patients to leave the hospital without permission. He was correct on both counts, of course. What a dilemma! Aircrew morale was high now, and the fighting in Laos had intensified. The wing needed the full support of the aircrews. There was no way the aircrews would understand punishing a pilot who was shot down in combat, rescued from the jungle, and hospitalized for injuries.

I told Walt that under these extenuating circumstances, I would not charge the pilot. If he believed it was necessary to punish the nurse as an example to others, then he should process an Article 15. I realized this was uneven punishment for a discipline problem, but, as Sherman said, "War is hell!" The story ended with the nurse receiving an Article 15 and a fine. The pilot got a Purple Heart for his injuries—plus a chewing-out from his squadron commander.

Out of the Doghouse

Daily 30-minute "stand-up" staff meetings serve important purposes: avoiding unpleasant surprises and prioritizing problems. Every Friday morning I held a more rigorous meeting for 432d group and squadron commanders. They had to bring charts or analyses showing how they were doing. An unprepared commander, or one ignoring an important area, could expect a rough time. Commanders quickly learned to expect the third degree and nicknamed it the "Weekly Bleed"! After nearly everyone "bled" a few times, peer pressure had a healthy effect on their preparation for these meetings. The 13th TFS commander, Lt Col James Light, was always prepared and on top of things in his squadron. Eight years later, Major General Light became SAC DCS for materiel and later commanded Fifteenth Air Force as a lieutenant general before retiring in 1988.

Winter weather and increased activity in the Plain of Jars gave both fighter and reconnaissance aircrews renewed purpose. The bomb damage assessments were the best in three months, there were no serious incidents, and morale seemed very high.

A 6 January letter to Anne noted our improved bombing: "Flew #106 today. The FAC complimented us on our bombing and said our Wing was doing a lot better 'since we'd got the sermon.' I told him, 'Thanks a lot, but I was the preacher!' We all had a good laugh over that."

Another January letter to Anne indicated the war was still going on: "Today they got lucky and dinged me a couple times, nothing serious, just an external fuel tank. First time in 107 missions—I'll be more careful next time."

Morale, work performance, and discipline had improved due to the policy changes that had been implemented. The quality of work on the flight line and in maintenance shops was noticeably higher. The Quick Turn policy created a lot of interest and, at the same time, resulted in increased sortie production. The wing went 11 straight days without a mission lost or aborted because of maintenance. Discipline noticeably improved with only two military offenses in December. Morale got a further boost when General Nazzaro loosened the purse strings and provided repair money for Airmen barracks. Colonel Katz and his engineers squeezed the dollars hard and made significant barracks improvements. Reenlistment rates jumped above the PACAF standard—from 12 percent the previous quarter (worst in PACAF) to 32 percent for October through December. January reenlistments were already off to a fast start.

The Thirteenth Air Force IG inspected in early January, and the 432d came out clean overall. While digging into the Officers' Club, the auditor discovered an embezzlement scheme concocted by two Thai employees—the bookkeeper at the club and a key employee at the base finance office. They stole about $25,000 from cash spent on slot machines. We fired the two employees. I reported the crime to the governor, hoping he would help us recover the money. He told me the bookkeeper had purchased an apartment house and given the house to her mother. I asked the governor to make her sell the house and return the money. He said, "Since she gave the house to her family, we do not consider that a criminal offense in Thailand and should not prosecute." My next question was, "How do we get our money back?" His answer reminded me that not all nations share the same understanding of crime and punishment. "Why not hire her back, Colonel, and deduct the money from her paychecks?" Negotiations ended when I responded, "No thanks, Governor!"

In early January 1971, PACAF advised that the USAF IG Team, headed by General Wells, would inspect the 432d later in the month. I wrote Anne after the IG inspection led by General Wells ended, "He dug into things a lot deeper than the 13th AF IG, particularly in maintenance. I stayed right with him for three days, including meals, drinks and reading *Stars & Stripes*. Anyhow, it came out quite well. They said we had the best operation and maintenance of the bases they had looked at over here. Wells's final words were, 'You are doing good work. Keep it up!' Now we can get back to war again."

The successful IG inspection, improvements in aircraft readiness, reduction in incidents and disciplinary offenses, higher reenlistment rate, notable increase in troop morale, and improved bombing results soon came to the attention of higher headquarters. Thirteenth Air Force hosted a commanders' conference at Clark AB in the Philippines. Word was traveling fast that the 432d Wing was doing very well. General McNickle and his staff let me know they were pleased with the rapid progress.

All the services were under pressure to remove "irritants," and the 432d was leading PACAF in that regard. We began receiving at least three and as many as five VIP visits each week. In one short period, Admiral Moorer, JCS chairman; General Ryan, USAF chief of staff; Gen William Momyer, TAC commander; Gen Jack Catton, MAC commander; Lt Gen John D. Lavelle, PACAF vice-commander; and General McNickle, Thirteenth Air Force commander, visited the 432d. These VIP visitors often boosted morale, especially when they chatted with officers and Airmen and displayed interest in their jobs.

Two VIP visits stood out in my mind. Admiral Moorer spent considerable time looking at our munitions and special capabilities. We had a short private conversation about how to attack NVN targets if the president authorized bombing North Vietnam. Not foreseen was that 20 months later I would be a member of Admiral Moorer's JCS staff, working for the J-3, Vice Adm Jerome King, and planning the final bombing of the Vietnam War, Linebacker II, often called the "Christmas Bombing Campaign."

General Ryan was a great officer whom I admired very much. Walking through our command post, Ryan stopped by a wall chart listing the number of combat missions flown by each crew. I had about 120 at the time. After a long pause, he said, "You are flying too much, Colonel Leavitt." I mumbled something about how a fighter wing commander needed to fly in order to check performance and spot problems. He ended the discussion by saying, "Two or three missions a month are all

396

you need." Since he did not give me a direct order to stop, I interpreted his comment as "advisory," bit my tongue, and continued to fly combat missions, reaching 152 before leaving in April. Later, I learned Ryan had already made the decision that I would come to the Pentagon and not command the 18th Wing at Kadena as Johnson and Nazzaro had asked.

An excellent young information officer, Capt Tim Talbert, was working closely with the editor of the base newspaper, Sgt Bob Clark, in publicizing exceptional performance by individuals, particularly NCOs and young Airmen. Both Tim and Bob played important roles in keeping an upbeat attitude in the wing. The movie *Easy Rider* was a smash hit with the 18- to 25-year-olds at that time, so Talbert and Clark wanted to rename the base newspaper *Easy Flyer*. I went along with their suggestion.

The 432d was gaining more reenlistments but needed to keep working the issue. The USAF is a technical service. Roughly 70 percent of the enlisted personnel must be experienced in their career field for the Air Force to function properly. Every year thousands of experienced NCOs retire and must be replaced. Replacing lost experience is a long process that begins by having first- and second-term Airmen choose an Air Force career.

A name with a derogatory tone crept into the GI lexicon during the Vietnam War that hurt reenlistment. NCO supervisors were often referred to as "lifers," mostly by younger Airmen who saw themselves as civilians wearing uniforms. I wrote the following commentary, "Famous Lifers," for *Easy Flyer*. Other base newspapers and *Airman* magazine reprinted it.

There's a new label in the Air Force these days—"Lifer." It flashes back to Class B movies with George Raft shuffling endlessly through cold prison corridors. It insinuates that the career Airman has taken a life sentence just like three time losers at Sing Sing. It's a word that can easily be shouted by some guy standing on the street corner throwing rocks at school buses. It bugs me. Why? Because I'm a lifer and one who doesn't like to be cut low by prejudicial words.

None of us were born lifers. We acquired it one-step at a time. Along the way, civilian life frequently beckoned. The grass often looked greener in the neighbor's back yard. "Peacetime" years were not always very peaceful—Korea, China Straits, Lebanon and Berlin Crises, Cuban Missiles and then Vietnam. We sweated out housing, pay raises, ORIs, long TDYs, alert duty and frequent moves. Somehow, the years passed and our sense of belonging grew. Good outfits, good guys, and good memories outweighed the bad. So, we became lifers.

On second thought, maybe the word is not all bad. Most people who accomplish anything in this world are lifers. They concentrate on their vocation until they do it better than the average bear. We may march to the beat of different drums, but the doctor who brought us into the world was a lifer, too. So was our favorite teacher, and so were Vince Lombardi, Franklin Roosevelt, "Satchmo" Armstrong, Pope John, Billy Graham, Henry Ford and George Patton. Unfortunately, so were Karl Marx, Ho Chi Minh, Mao Tse Tung, and most of those who are trying to upset our apple cart. That's why we need professionals in the military today and in the future.

So, we are not going to get hung up over the "lifer" label. We spent too many years earning it . . . and we're in good company.

Policy changes helped, improved communications helped, and higher operational effectiveness helped. The wing reenlistment rate for first-term Airmen went from 10 percent in September 1970, the lowest in PACAF, to 59 percent in February 1971, the highest in PACAF.

General Lavelle Visits Udorn

The vice-commander of PACAF, Lieutenant General Lavelle, visited Udorn in early February. From 1964 to 1966, Lavelle, then a major general, served as director of programs, Headquarters USAF. My job during those earlier years involved briefing him periodically. We got along well, and I looked forward to seeing him again. Lavelle's aircraft arrived late on National Prayer Breakfast day, and the several hundred attendees were already eating breakfast. As Lavelle walked into the large dining hall, I pointed to his empty reserved seat at the head table. He waved, said to go ahead with the program, and sat down in an empty chair by several NCOs.

As the service was ending, Lavelle walked forward, complimented the chaplain, and shook hands with all the senior officers standing there. He mentioned that he enjoyed the service and was particularly impressed with the nice master sergeant sitting next to him. "What a great guy!" It was difficult to keep a straight face as I later explained who the "great guy" was. General Lavelle looked aghast as the story unfolded.

A year earlier, a Thai court convicted the sergeant of killing his adopted Thai child. The court found that after killing the child, he hid the evidence by dissecting the body and flushing the body parts down a toilet. The sergeant pleaded not guilty, denying any responsibility for the crime. The Thai judge sentenced him to 14 years in prison.

Protesting his innocence, the sergeant filed an appeal. While the appeal was pending, the Thai governor allowed him to post bail and return to his job in the base hospital as long as he signed in every hour at our wing headquarters. For several months, the sergeant continued protesting his innocence and never attempted to escape. The frequent signing-in routine was a nuisance to us. I asked the governor if the sergeant could sign in only twice a day.

The governor agreed and reduced the bail bond to $25. Another month passed without incident. The governor called again and expressed surprise (probably disappointment) that the sergeant had not left Thailand since the bond was only $25. I explained that the sergeant insisted he was innocent and had filed the appeal to clear his name. The governor offered a solution that would make King Solomon proud. "California has a Thai prisoner in San Quentin. Let's exchange prisoners. Put the sergeant in San Quentin, and I will put the Thai in our prison." As gently as possible, I explained to my governor friend that international prisoner swaps were beyond my pay grade. When I left Udorn, the sergeant was still waiting for his appeal.

Usually the VIP and staff did not stay overnight at Udorn. If the VIP stayed, the opportunity arose to break away from the ritual of prepared briefings. The wing commander's hootch at Udorn had a kitchenette, small living room with a bar, two bathrooms, and two small bedrooms—one for the VIP, the other mine. An outdoor patio with barbecue pit completed the scene and made outdoor entertaining easy during the balmy winter evenings. Conversations with VIPs provided feedback as to how the wing was doing, what was going on in the Pentagon and other headquarters, what to expect in coming months, and, sometimes, an informal report card on the wing commander.

In late December 1970, the USAF released the promotion list to brigadier general. Prior to the list being published, several PACAF generals had leaked that I was nominated by PACAF. As it turned out, only one colonel from my year group was pro-moted—Lincoln D. Faurer, a West Point classmate and good friend. "Link" was highly qualified for selection. He continued his outstanding performance in a succession of high-level posi-tions. In 1981 Lieutenant General Faurer became director of the National Security Agency, a position he held until retiring in 1985.

Because of this "near miss" in 1970, it seemed important to hold a career-enhancing position after leaving Udorn. In my mind, commanding the 18th Fighter Wing at Kadena would be just such a job. Lavelle's visit clarified the issue. Lavelle said that Nazzaro could not swing the Kadena job because the Pen-tagon maintained that the job at Headquarters USAF was more important. Both he and Nazzaro disagreed but said if Pentagon generals really believed that, it was important to go there.

I wrote Anne two days after General Lavelle left:

> The personnel colonel traveling with Lavelle told me that Lavelle told Nazzaro I was the best commander in the Pacific—nice flattering words! Apparently all the other Wing Commanders griped to Lavelle about General Wells's IG inspection. Since the 432d did quite well (Wells told 13th Air Force, the 432d was the best wing he had seen over here), Lavelle wanted to know what I thought.

> I told him that General Wells's inspection and the preparation for it had helped this Wing—and Lavelle really got mad. We had some rather heated words over this subject; he obviously does not like Wells, but I stuck with my opinion. Otherwise, things went quite well and he liked the Wing's progress.

> Last night we lost an F-4 on GCA final, 11 miles out from Udorn. No radio transmissions, no problems up to that point; the first accident in the 432d in more than a year. The aircraft commander had 311 mis-sions (two tours in this war), was an Air Force Academy grad, and had just been picked as our Junior Officer of the Year—a really great young guy. The navigator was less experienced, but a fine young officer. Both were killed.

John D. Lavelle was promoted to general and assumed com-mand of Seventh Air Force on 29 July 1971. In 1972 the USAF chief of staff, General Ryan, fired General Lavelle for conduct-ing an unauthorized bombing campaign against NVN targets. Lavelle was retired at his permanent grade of major general and died 10 July 1979. The 432d Wing at Udorn, at that time commanded by Col Charles Gabriel, future USAF chief of staff, performed the unauthorized bombing campaign.

A year later, when I was assigned to the JCS, the JCS director asked me to investigate the unauthorized bombing and write a white paper explaining how this happened. I read the correspondence sent by the JCS prior to the bombing and interviewed participants of a meeting in Hawaii.

The JCS had sent a representative to meet in Hawaii with Lavelle prior to the beginning of the unauthorized bombing. Apparently their meeting failed to clarify how much latitude Seventh Air Force really had in reacting to NVN air defenses. I concluded the white paper by stating the new ROEs were too loose and subject to various interpretations. Since I was not privy to the conversation in the chief's office when he called Lavelle back to Washington and fired him, it was difficult to find all the facts that led to Lavelle's overstepping his directions from higher authority.

Lam Son 719

On 9 February 1971, Secretary of Defense Laird announced the reasons for the stepped-up action in Laos, which the ARVN named Lam Son 719. Excerpts from his address to the Senate and House Armed Service Committees follow.

> I conferred at length with President Thieu, Ambassador Bunker, General Abrams, and others about the situation facing allied forces in the current dry season. We agreed that the military aspects of Vietnamization had progressed so well that the armed forces of the Republic of Vietnam (ARVN) now were capable of conducting multi-Corps operations against enemy-occupied sanctuaries along the borders of South Vietnam, without US ground forces or US advisors.

> Our assessment made clear the fact that, as a result of the advantages gained following last year's Cambodian operations, the enemy was now being forced to place much greater reliance on the "Ho Chi Minh Trail" and its related sanctuaries in southern Laos. . . . I agreed with President Thieu and other South Vietnamese leaders that operations against sanctuaries in the southern Laos panhandle would contribute . . . to the security of the Republic of South Vietnam, and . . . would save additional American lives and enhance the security of the remaining US forces inside South Vietnam and set the stage for bringing home additional thousands of Americans in coming months.

It was the unanimous conclusion of the Commander in Chief, the Secretary of State, and myself that we should use whatever airpower is
necessary to assist the South Vietnamese in their ground operations
against sanctuary areas in both Cambodia and Laos, while at the same
time precluding the use of American ground combat troops or advisors
in these operations.

By using the ARVN, assisted by "whatever airpower is necessary," the Nixon administration could deny that the United
States was violating the Geneva Treaty. Laird and others may
have sincerely believed the Vietnamization program had progressed to the point where South Vietnam could defend itself
after American ground forces went home. Regardless of their
reasoning, the agreed goal was worthwhile. Whether the goal
was achievable would depend largely upon ARVN planning,
preparation, and execution. An unanswerable question hung
over Lam Son 719. Would the ARVN operate effectively without
American assistance and guidance?

I flew to I Corps headquarters in the northernmost region of
South Vietnam for a briefing on Lam Son 719. The objectives were
to disrupt the flow of materials down the trail, destroy enemy
supply bases, seize the key logistics center at Tchepone, Laos,
and then withdraw to South Vietnam. American airpower would
support the ARVN. The 432d would support the ARVN by providing CAS, suppressing antiaircraft fire, and flying reconnaissance missions. Although the briefing did not offer many details about coordinating air strikes with the ARVN, I returned to
Udorn convinced Lam Son 719 was a long-overdue operation.
The 432d would make a maximum effort with all its resources.

After briefing the 432d unit commanders and wing staff
about our role in Lam Son 719, I assembled the top three NCO
grades in our outdoor theater. The success of our efforts would
depend upon the total support of all our officers and enlisted
personnel. Following a practice I had started earlier, all the top
three NCO grades received the same briefings given the staff
and commanders. By the end of the day, the entire 432d team
knew we were committed to Lam Son 719—we called it Big
Push 71.

Phase I of Lam Son 719 began on 29 January when US
ground forces opened Route 9 to the Laotian border. On 8 February, the ARVN started phase 2 by extending the attack into

Laos. The 432d began an intensive air campaign supporting the ARVN.

The emphasis during Lam Son 719 was "bombs on target." This meant hard work for aircrews, crew chiefs, munitions loaders, maintenance and supply personnel, and all support organizations. Quick Turn really paid off. One F-4D (tail number OY 800) flew six sorties one day, as described by Talbert. "To say that 800 had a busy day is putting it mildly. . . . It flew more missions, six, and carried more bombs, 108, than any F-4 in Southeast Asia during a 24-hour period. Two crew chiefs kept 800 flying during this period. SSgt Luther Kelley worked during the day—TSgt Charles J. Campbell at night. Actually, 800 flew six-and-a-half missions—airborne at midnight, it flew 45 minutes into the new day."

My letter to Anne on 13 February was upbeat:

> Otis Moore came in today to fly in the back seat of an RF-4. Glad to have him visit us—he's a really nice guy. He's the new Chief of Staff for Seventh AF.[12] It was a pleasure having him attend the morning "stand up" briefing. We have been flying our socks off the last few days and the airplanes/guys are really hanging in there. One F-4 from midnight to midnight flew six and one-half combat sorties—it was airborne at midnight! It dropped more than 100 bombs in six sorties. I'll bet that's some kind of 24 hour record for fighters—we're putting the ground crew in for an award.

And on 14 February, I wrote Anne:

> Big Push 71 is still on; we're trying to generate more sorties/bombs than ever before and the Wing is all keyed up for it. We have taken clerks, cooks, civil engineers, etc. and have them unloading bombs, driving tugs, etc. Also flushed out the "old soldiers" from behind their desks in maintenance and they are now fixing airplanes. Also, I canceled temporarily the One-Day-a-Week-Off policy, so everyone is working. Morale is high. There is a lot of desire here and we will do whatever is expected.

F-4 aircrews reported some difficulties in the target areas. They were accustomed to working with FACs who had a good grasp of the tactical situation and knew where and how to direct our bombing attacks. Too often, FACs in Lam Son 719 worked with US Army helicopters flying at low altitudes and ignored USAF fighters orbiting above them. Despite these problems, we were able to destroy many targets in support of the ARVN.

I had asked General Nazzaro during an earlier staff visit to swap 12 F-4Ds equipped with the LORAN-D navigation system belonging to the 8th Wing at Ubon for 12 standard F4-Ds from the 432d. I beat down the usual objections from PACAF and the 8th Wing by citing the minimal cost and overall gain to Seventh Air Force. General Nazzaro finally ordered the transfer. LORAN-D improved our capability for locating targets, particularly at night. We assigned LORAN-D aircraft to flight leaders on most missions.

On 12 March, I wrote Anne about interesting VIP visits: "We had an interesting DV today, Dr. Pracha, the Chief Information Officer for Thailand. Educated at Yale and Oxford, fortyish, very sharp guy. Yesterday, the King and Queen were here; she is a really beautiful Thai. The King is also US-educated—MIT and has a daughter there now."

Discussions with the king and Dr. Pracha focused on the press being restricted from reporting on USAF operations in Thailand. It was common knowledge in the world press that USAF aircraft were flying combat missions from Thailand. Nevertheless, the press was not allowed on Thai bases to observe USAF operations or to interview USAF personnel. In 1964 censorship might have been reasonable. In 1971 it was unreasonable. The king agreed with my view. He turned to the American ambassador accompanying the royal party and asked, "Why is there such a restriction?" The ambassador said that he did not know but would look into the problem. To the best of my knowledge, this censorship lasted until 1973 when the war ended.

The 17 March letter I wrote Anne included some good news: "At 0630, 5 April, my plane is supposed to arrive at Travis AFB via Bangkok and Yakota. That's 19 days from today! General Nazzaro arrives Friday for his final swing through Southeast Asia. There are many things to show him; for example, our barracks renovation. All the hootches are painted now and look much better. The troops like the two-man rooms. Things have returned to normal. *Easy Flyer* published a congratulatory statement I wrote for all the people in the Wing."

The ARVN air assault on Tchepone was successful, thus achieving a major objective of Lam Son 719. Then the NVN struck back with tanks reinforcing their infantry. We continued to support the ARVN after the final phase of Lam Son 719 began on 16 March. The withdrawal from Tchepone and retreat to

South Vietnam was a costly fight for the ARVN and for Army helicopter aircrews. According to after-action reports and post-war analyses, Army helicopter pilots were unaccustomed to the intense antiaircraft fire. During Lam Son 719, the Army had 728 helicopters damaged or destroyed.

After Lam Son 719 ended, I wrote a congratulatory editorial. One paragraph is quoted.

> For this, we all worked like hell. The 432d Wing loaded more bombs and flew more sorties than ever before in a comparable period. It wasn't easy. Augmentees hustled bombs, drove AGE and worked long hours in unfamiliar jobs. "Sierra Hotel" took on new meaning. Flight Line Angels eased the strain with sun tan oil, lemonade and smiles. We sweated, cussed and scrambled. But we did it and then we asked for more. The war isn't over. We will be called again. But if someone mentions Tchepone, or Big Push '71—tell 'em you were there, friend—you and the rest of the 432d.

The antiwar movement and media in the United States, however, had already labeled Lam Son 719 a defeat by the time it ended on 6 April 1971. Media criticism focused on the ARVN withdrawing from Tchepone, ARVN casualties, and US Army helicopter losses. The media ignored three important facts. First, occupying Tchepone permanently was not an objective. Cutting supply lines and destroying the logistics system and supplies stockpiled in Tchepone were the objectives. Second, the ARVN and US airpower scored a decisive victory over the best NVN troops before the ARVN withdrew from Tchepone. Third, severing the Ho Chi Minh Trail cost NVN for nearly a year the supplies and the logistical means to attack SVN. This allowed the continuing withdrawal of American troops from South Vietnam, the goal Laird had emphasized to Congress.

General Nazzaro visited Udorn for the last time on 18 March. He was the first four-star general that I knew quite well. We had a rough start a year earlier at Ubon when I tried to extol the virtues of laser bombing, and he was skeptical. Our relations improved, thanks to his staff members who said nice things to him about my performance. Nazzaro liked straight-forward answers. If he did not agree, he would say so. He was constantly evaluating my decision making and performance—sometimes in an offbeat way.

I looked forward to General Nazzaro's staff visits. As the wing's performance improved, he became more responsive to our requests. For example, when he understood the need for improving the enlisted barracks, he had PACAF send us self-help money. He was always responsive to suggestions for improving operations. When he understood how the 432d would use F-4Ds with LORAN-D, he arranged the transfer of several LORAN-D aircraft from Ubon. He tried several times to keep me in PACAF after my tour ended at Udorn to be 18th Wing commander at Kadena AB, Okinawa. The Pentagon overrode each request. After he retired in 1971, we never met again. Gen Joseph J. Nazzaro died in 1990—a true gentleman, patriot, and great leader.

On 23 March, I wrote Anne again: "Yesterday we lost an F-4 from the Wing, first loss in quite a while. Air Rescue picked up the crew this morning, which made everyone happy as hell. I'm going to fly my last mission on 2 April. Flying combat has its moments—kind of grows on you. I'll miss the challenge of doing my best under sometimes tough circumstances. At the same time, it will be a relief to quit worrying about getting hacked down by some 'Golden B-B.' "

On 28 March 1971, I wrote the last Vietnam War letter to Anne: "One of the things that made this year pass so quickly, and relatively painlessly for me, has been your letter writing. Twelve thousand miles is a long, long way, but knowing that nearly every day, I would get a cheerful, newsy letter from you, Anne, made it seem a lot closer. The fact that you never complained or burdened me with the many problems that must have arisen is just one more testimony to the great person you are. Thank you for being wife, mother and business manager in my absence."

Sawadee Udorn

The date of expected return from overseas service (DEROS) finally arrived on 3 April 1971. It was time to go home. The American public was tired of the war, and returning veterans were a nonevent. That did not matter to me. The opportunity during the past year to work with thousands of splendid young Americans was an ample reward. Emotions about

F-4D loaded for Lam Son 719. Triple Nickel's (555th TFS) F-4D loaded for a CAS mission. Seven MK-82 500-pound bombs and four BLU-27 750-pound napalm bombs were a typical load for CAS.

Fellow crew members. *Left*: Maj Bill Roberts, F-4D weapon systems officer on most of my missions and also wing executive officer. Bill was very talented both in the air and on the ground. *Far right*: SMSgt Burton was line chief—an extraordinary NCO who was a great leader and highly competent.

The people and the places in "Big Push '71"

TOTAL SORTIES

SORTIES TODAY

BIG PUSH '71

Photo courtesy US Air Force

The people and the places in "Big Push '71." To energize the wing during the six weeks of Lam Son 719, Captain Talbert, the base information officer, publicized the individual efforts of many people. A full page (half is shown) appeared in our newspaper. A montage showed aircrews, maintenance personnel, bomb loaders, and supervisors. SMSgt Burton (*headband*) was line chief and kept things moving. Nurses did their bit by talking to the men during breaks and driving a lemonade truck in the 100-degree, humid weather.

leaving the 432d Wing surfaced in my final *Easy Flyer* editorial, "Going Home":

> DEROS—a word sexier than Raquel Welch, tastier than a T-bone medium rare, more satisfying than a cold beer on a hot day. DEROS—a paid-in-full, one-year, GI contract for services rendered in Southeast Asia. A year starting with misty-eyed goodbyes and ending with laughing hellos. A changing, mixed-up year that finds us returning to the World older but younger, richer but poorer, happier but sadder. Older by 365 days, but younger because of close association with today's fresh ideas. Richer realizing that much has been gained through our collective efforts, but poorer because too many brave men will never return. Happier because fortune smiled and we return safely, but sadder knowing the task remains, the war goes on. Before leaving let me state a couple of impressions. . . .

Air war is teamwork with a gallon of sweat on the ground for a drop of sweat in the air. The linebackers in this ball game pump fuel, the safety walks a canine through the dark night, the offensive line fixes telephones, repairs airplanes, loads 500-pounders, cooks meals, orders parts, and shuffles papers. The coach sits at 25 thousand in Hillsboro orbit. And the quarterback drops bombs instead of throwing them. We don't have any breakaway runners—no one can do it alone.

Because of this teamwork, you are the best in SEA—a fact confirmed by past inspections, maintenance records, flying safety awards, supply effectiveness, sortie rates, spirit, morale and discipline. For you, no task is too hard—no job is too small. You take care of each other and are tough, smart and responsive. The Falcon call sign that your aircrews proudly use means precision bombing and anywhere/anytime picture taking. You will continue to set the example because you are confident of your ability and your past successes breed future successes.

I am proud to have served with you. Good luck!

Aggie One

The last combat mission for an aircrew was a traditional cause for celebration. By the time the Vietnam War came along, the celebrations were full-blown and memorable. It began with people assembling around the aircraft while aircrew members did their last preflight. An unusual number of reconnaissance aircrews had joined the fighter aircrews, NCOs, headquarters staff, and commanders standing around my bomb-loaded aircraft. I waved at the crowd, tried to look professional, started the walk-around at the left wing, checked the 2,000- and 500-pound bombs, and looked for fuel and hydraulic leaks.

Everybody watched silently as I completed circling the aircraft. Before climbing into the cockpit, I asked the crew chief for the aircraft forms. Pappy Hayes, the wing DO, yelled, "Gotcha!" The crowd broke into loud laughter. What the hell was so funny? Then the crew chief pointed at the window over camera station three, and it hit me! The plane was an RF-4 reconnaissance aircraft, not an F-4 fighter, and I did not notice! They had painted the tail with fighter markings and moved it into the fighter ramp area after hanging bombs on the pylons. It was a great practical joke—and I bit! At my *Sawadee*—farewell roast—party, the 14th TRS presented a picture of that RF-4 dressed like an F-4. The nameplate on the picture frame was a gentle dig that nearly

Photo courtesy US Air Force

Last combat mission in Vietnam. A crowd had gathered around my aircraft, and an Airman was set to fire the toy cannon we used on special days—unusual, but nice of them to wish me luck on number 152.

Photo courtesy US Air Force

Mistaken identity. 14th TRS members had prepared a big practical joke for the occasion. They had hung bombs on an RF-4C, painted the tail with F-4D markings, and towed it to the fighter ramp area. I thought it was an F-4D when I started the walk-around inspection.

Practical joke. Everyone was laughing. . . . I did not know why until Col Pappy Hayes stopped me from climbing into the cockpit. He pointed at the camera window. I realized it was an "RF" (reconnaissance Phantom), not a fighter. I enjoyed their practical joke.

Sawadee **Udorn**. Colonel Gabriel, incoming vice-commander, passed the champagne.

432d key staff joins in final picture together. *Left to right*: Colonel Hayes, Operations; Colonel Mann, vice-commander and my replacement as new wing commander; Col Bill Musick, Maintenance and Engineering; and Colonel Katz, Combat Support Group. That evening, the *Sawadee* party capped a great assignment with wonderful people.

all of my combat missions were in F-4s, not RF-4s: "Colonel Leavitt: Next time, don't put all your eggs in one basket!"

After landing from the last mission—number 152—a wave of nostalgia hit. This mission closed the book on 20 years of climbing in and out of cockpits as an aircrew. My longtime goal to command a fighter wing in combat was accomplished. I was thankful for surviving the war and deeply regretted every loss we suffered. The *Sawadee* that evening was fun and memorable, with many nice speeches. One tribute I especially treasure was from Sgt Bob Clark and appeared in the 1 April 1971 *Easy Flyer*:

Lifer: A First Termer and a Lifer He Has Known

This "lifer" made the guys under him (and their number was considerable) work like hell. But the guys didn't seem to mind it much. In fact when they did their share, they asked for more. Why? Because this guy was out there with them telling them why they were working their heads off. Because of him, "Big Push," "Sierra Hotel" and "Press On" became terms you worked by—and loved it.

Our friend the lifer really got down with the troops and told them "what was going on." He might have broken the chain of command a time or two, but ask any enlisted troop if a word of encouragement and a pat on the back from one of the "big guys" doesn't make him feel good.

This guy won the respect of not just this first termer, but every first termer who would leave narrow minds in the scrap pile and listen to what he was saying. He was saying that the troop who is left alone to do his job and not be harassed would do the job and do it well. He wasn't saying forget about regulations, tech manuals and respect for others. His rules were fair and easy to swallow.

This lifer didn't sell every one of us on a 30-year career. You can be sure he changed a lot of minds. As for the rest of us that were set on another walk of life, he gave us a healthy respect for the Air Force that we shall never lose.

This lifer left a lasting impression on the young guys on his team. All of us are extremely proud to have served on that team.

Win Quickly—America Is Impatient

America's military history is replete with good and bad examples of "How to Fight Wars." Good examples emphasized fast-moving offensive campaigns that achieved objectives quickly and decisively. Bad examples were defensive campaigns that slowly, or never, achieved their political objectives. The good examples maintained public support and patriotic enthusiasm despite severe American casualties. The bad examples eventually lost public support, created political problems, and increased widespread antiwar sentiment that focused on American casualties. As a general rule, quick and decisive victories resulted in fewer casualties, cost less, and led to improved political relations between warring nations after the war ended.

By 1971 the Vietnam War had dragged on for more than seven years—the fighting had been neither quick nor decisive. Antiwar sentiment was now high in the United States. The American public had no clear understanding of the on-and-off negotiations in Paris. President Johnson chose not to run for a second term, mostly because of the unpopular war. President Nixon believed American participation in the war could end by training and equipping the ARVN to do the fighting. American troop withdrawals began despite doubts concerning the effectiveness of Vietnamization.

At the time of the Tonkin Gulf Resolution in 1964, the United States had strong conventional forces and the largest nuclear deterrent in the world. We had a huge asymmetrical advantage over North Vietnam in sea power and airpower. Instead of seizing the offensive advantage and using our asymmetrical advantages against NVN, both the Johnson and Nixon administrations chose to defend SVN, primarily with ground forces supported by American airpower. Our complex objective was to contain Communism in Southeast Asia by fighting the NVN invasion of South Vietnam without drawing the USSR or PRC into the war. The strategy may have been compatible with our political objective but was slow-maturing and resulted in over 58,000 American dead. I privately disagreed, as did many associates, with this limited strategy.

Crushing NVN quickly and decisively early in the war with *offensive* actions would have contained the spread of Communism and restored the Geneva Treaty boundaries. For those who believe the USSR and China would have entered the war, convincing evidence says otherwise. Neither the USSR nor Communist China entered war in 1972 when the US Navy blockaded and mined the harbors of North Vietnam and USAF and Navy aircraft bombed the Haiphong-Hanoi complex and forced NVN into signing the peace treaty.

Men and women in our armed forces fight with the expectation that their country has noble objectives and their efforts will mean one more step on the path to victory. The battles fought in the Vietnam War certainly did not approach the size or importance of the major campaigns of WWII. Nevertheless, the procedures that influence fast and decisive action are important in all wars—large or small. Active duty officers are obligated to do their duty to the best of their ability. Within the constraints imposed by the president or his national security advisor, I focused on improving procedures involved in fighting the air war.

Fast and decisive action is the primary responsibility of the highest command that plans and authorizes specific military action. In the Vietnam War, Seventh Air Force had the responsibility for air operations after the battle for Khe San. The execution of Seventh Air Force plans depended upon subordinate commands—wings and squadrons. These subordinate commands provided the resources and detailed instructions, for example, aircrews, aircraft, weapons, and intelligence briefings.

Reaction times for USAF aircraft during the Vietnam War depended upon roughly the same factors encountered in World War II and the Korean War. However, political guidance in the Vietnam War was more detailed than in the two previous wars. Before anyone squeezed a trigger or dropped a bomb in a proposed attack, Seventh Air Force scrutinized the mission proposal to insure compliance with the ROEs and to avoid expanding the war by attacking target systems not approved by higher authority.

A sequential chain of events occurs in every combat operation, large or small. In tactical warfare, targets move. Enemy aircraft, troops, trucks, supply dumps, antiaircraft guns, and field headquarters all move. The name of the game in the air war is to find and destroy these targets before they can move. In Vietnam air operations, the following sequence applied: *Discovered + Analyzed + Decided + Communicated = Action.*

Discovered targets came from aerial photography, pilot reports, friendly ground forces, FACs, POWs, natives, and other sources. The air tactical operations center (ATOC) at HQ Seventh Air Force *analyzed* the discovered target and *decided* when to attack. The ATOC prepared the "frag"—fragmentary operations order—and communicated the frag by teletype with the wings selected for the mission. The wings selected aircrews, prepared crew briefings, loaded munitions, launched aircraft, and attacked targets. If everything went quickly and smoothly, the result was *timely action.*

Unfortunately, the process from *discovery* to *timely action* often took too long. Wing commanders used different approaches to speed the process. In my previous assignment, the 8th TFW used fast-mover FACs—single F-4s flying at low level to locate targets. The hope was that an experienced fast-mover FAC could spot targets and quickly direct other F-4s to these targets. Becoming a fast-mover FAC was a macho thing for a young fighter pilot. Other than personal gratification, the fast-mover FAC program did not provide much useful information compared to reconnaissance aircraft. Disadvantages were the number of sorties used daily by the fast-mover FAC program and high loss rates. Postwar analyses disclosed a loss rate much higher than other fighter missions.

I asked for and received General Clay's permission to develop a procedure that combined the reconnaissance and fighter capabilities of the 432d Wing. We placed F-4s loaded with munitions on 10-minute alert. Returning RF-4s from reconnaissance missions contacted the 432d command post before landing and advised whether they photographed enemy activity. With an affirmative answer, we launched an F-4 flight toward a KC-135 tanker rendezvous. Immediately after the RF-4 landed, a technician rushed the exposed film to the reconnaissance technical squadron light table. As soon as the photo interpreter identified target(s) and determined coordinates, our command post informed the ATOC. Upon receiving ATOC approval, the command post passed target description and coordinates to the F-4 flight leader. Meanwhile, the ATOC notified the ABCCC C-130E that the mission was approved and airborne. This procedure dramatically cut the elapsed time from discovering to killing a target. Frequently, we destroyed targets within one hour of discovery.

During the seven years of fighting, technology and combat experience had improved our military effectiveness, particularly in the application of airpower. Although ending the war quickly was by now a missed opportunity, a "cut and run" departure in 1971 was not an acceptable way to end this long-running war. We entered the war to contain the spread of Communism into Southeast Asia. The mission was not yet accomplished. Although South Vietnam was the well-publicized battleground, covert activities by North Vietnam showed their intentions to install Communist governments elsewhere in Southeast Asia. In 1971 Laos and Cambodia were in the NVN crosshairs and teetered on the edge of takeover.

Thailand had good reason to worry about the intentions of the PRC. A major highway leading from China through northwest Laos and pointing toward Thailand was under construction. Was the highway a probable invasion route for the PRC army? During my tour in Thailand, our ROEs did not allow USAF aircraft to fly across this "Chinese Road" in northwest Laos. The political reasoning behind this ROE was apparently to avoid any direct contact between PRC and US military forces.

NVN and PRC activities were the two primary reasons for the Thai government allowing United States bases in Thailand. First, American forces based in Thailand gave it an insurance policy against invasion by the PRC. Second, these bases supported efforts to keep pro-democratic governments in Laos and Cambodia. Thai "volunteers" fighting against Pathet Lao and NVN troops in Laos gave further evidence of Thailand's commitment to resist Communism.

In 1971, it seemed to me the rationale for entering the war remained valid—containing Communism in Southeast Asia. The war had lasted too long because our political leaders overrated or misunderstood the historical relationship between China and Vietnam. In reality, the two nations had a long history of border clashes and racial enmity. They had become Communist rivals—both seeking hegemony in Southeast Asia. An old saying that "the enemy of my enemy is my friend" probably explains why the PRC and USSR supplied NVN the war materials necessary to offset our intervention as an ally of South Vietnam. Our political leaders also assumed the PRC and USSR were close enough allies to fight the United States if we expanded the war to NVN. In reality, the USSR and PRC had grown apart after the Korean War. Consequently, we missed the opportunity to end the war before 1971. The war was still winnable if the American people and their elected officials would recognize the progress made in SVN and allow the Navy and Air Force to take the war to North Vietnam.

Notes

1. CMSgt Robert Moran, USAF, retired, telephonic interview by the author, spring 2006. Chief Moran was an experienced survival instructor at Fairchild at the time of this incident.

2. Lt Gen Walter D. Druen, Jr., retired on 1 August 1982. After graduating from Virginia Polytechnic Institute, he entered the aviation cadet program and received his pilot wings and commission in December 1951. During the Korean War, he flew 100 combat missions in F-86s and during the Vietnam War, 173 combat missions in F-4s. His last assignment was commander of Allied Air Forces, Southern Europe, and Deputy Commander in Chief, USAFE, Southern Area. Military decorations and awards include two Distinguished Service Medals, the Silver Star, two Legions of Merit, three Distinguished Flying Crosses, Meritorious Service Medal, 15 Air Medals, and two Air Force Commendation Medals. US Air Force, "Biographies: Lieutenant General Walter D. Druen Jr."

3. Gen Joseph J. Nazzaro retired from active duty in 1971 and died in 1990. He graduated from West Point in 1936. Nazzaro commanded a bomb

group in Europe during World War II, and his distinguished career was high-lighted by commanding SAC from 1967 to 1968 and PACAF from 1968 to 1971. Decorations include three Distinguished Service Medals, the Silver Star, four Legions of Merit, the Distinguished Flying Cross, and two Air Medals. US Military Academy, *Register of Graduates*.

4. Palmer, *Summons of the Trumpet*, 229.

5. The context of the above paragraphs follows Cerami's excellent article, "Presidential Decision Making and Vietnam," 71–73.

6. Statement of Dr. Wayne Sellman, director of accession policy, OSD, to House Committee on Veterans Affairs, *Project 100,000*, 101st Cong., 2d sess., 28 February 1990. The five categories separated a continuum. The first two categories included above average aptitudes, with Category I scores ranging from 100 to 93 and Category II from 92 to 65. Category III recruits had average aptitudes, with scores ranging from 64 to 31. Category IV included recruits with below average aptitudes, scoring from 30 to 10. Congressional law prohibited the services from enlisting persons in Category V, which included aptitudes below the 10th percentile (ibid., 231).

7. Approximately 630,000 enlisted personnel were in the Air Force in 1970. Approximately 177,000 were in the lower three grades. Approximately 42,000, or 24 percent, were "Project 100,000" Airmen.

8. *Uniform Code of Military Justice*, 10 US Code, subtitle A, pt. 2, chap. 47, subchap. 3, sec. 815, Art. 15 (d). "The officer who imposes the punishment authorized in subsection (b), or his successor in command, may, at any time, . . . set aside in whole or in part the punishment, whether executed or unexecuted."

9. Maj Gen Andrew J. Evans, Jr., served in WWII, Korea, and Vietnam. A 1941 West Point graduate, he flew 129 missions as a fighter pilot in WWII and shot down eight enemy aircraft. In Korea, as deputy commander, 49th FBG, he flew 67 missions. Decorations included the Distinguished Service Medal, Silver Star, Legion of Merit, Distinguished Flying Cross with two oak leaf clusters, Air Medal with 12 oak leaf clusters, the Army Commendation Medal, Purple Heart, French Croix de Guerre, and Korean Ulchi. His last assignment was commander of US Military Assistance Command, Thailand. He died 25 December 2001. US Military Academy, *Register of Graduates*.

10. "Son Tay Raid," Son Tay Association.

11. For more detail on this interesting project, see ibid.

12. Maj Gen Otis C. Moore retired in 1977 after 29 years service. A 1948 graduate of West Point, General Moore earned three Distinguished Service Medals, the Legion of Merit, two Air Medals, and three Commendation Medals during his distinguished career. After leaving Vietnam, General Moore commanded Fourteenth Air Force. His final assignment was assistant DCS for plans and operations, HQ USAF. He died in 2008. US Military Academy, *Register of Graduates*.

Chapter 10

USAF Headquarters
Colonel—1971-72

Small Fish, Big Pond, Smart Bomb

After a few days spent traveling from the West Coast to the East Coast, Anne and I were home in McLean. The cherry trees along the Potomac were in bloom and a pleasant diversion as I drove down the parkway for my first day at work. After walking into the Pentagon, I headed for the basement where the Air Force Command Center under the deputy for operations, Maj Gen Carlos M. "Tote" Talbott, did business.[1] After a warm welcome, Talbott introduced Brig Gen John Baer, the officer I would replace as deputy director of strike forces after he retired.[2]

Strike forces served as the operations interface between HQ USAF and all the operational commands. Strike forces included tactical, aerospace defense, strategic, airlift, special ops, reconnaissance, and tactical control divisions. Each division had a colonel in charge and a supporting staff. PACAF, because of the war in Southeast Asia, received constant attention. My day would begin by reviewing the daily briefing that would wend its way to the USAF chief of staff and his deputy chiefs. The first stop after Tote Talbott was his boss, Lt Gen George Eade, the recently appointed DCS for plans and operations.[3]

General Eade had extensive experience in SAC after joining the command in 1946. His assignments included B-29 pilot, squadron commander, operations officer at several command levels, wing commander of two bomber wings, chief of the Safety Division, chief of the Control Division, director of Operations Plans, DCS Plans, DCS Operations, and chief of the Single Integrated Operational Plan Division, Joint Strategic Target Planning Staff of the JCS. To say General Eade knew something about SAC and nuclear planning would be like saying Henry Ford knew something about cars!

General Eade was a "quick study" and rapidly assimilated information on tactical operations. I soon learned that Eade wanted to understand all aspects of our tactical operations in Southeast Asia and was particularly interested in LGBs and electro-optical bombs because of their accuracy and effectiveness. In early 1971, I was the only senior officer in Plans and Operations having combat experience with both of these weapons. I was determined to persuade the Air Staff to accelerate development and acquisition of these new weapons. Systemic to any bureaucracy are disbelief and rejection, often having disguised meanings; the Pentagon is no exception. For example, when I asked Air Staff agencies to expand rapidly the purchase of PGMs, initial responses went something like the following.

R&D answered: "That's interesting, but we have a new approach to bombing that is even better." (Meaning: we are on top of everything, so mind your own business.) War Plans answered: "I have never dropped LGBs myself, but my bomb wing won the SAC bombing competition with great radar bombing." (Meaning: my vast experience and high rank tell me you are peddling B.S.) Programs answered: "It costs too much to replace our existing inventory with these new, expensive bombs." (Meaning: you are new in the Pentagon and do not know how hard it is to get funding. Come back next year.) Others answered: "Maybe they worked in Southeast Asia, but the Warsaw Pact has better defenses. They would not work in Europe." (Meaning: you Vietnam War guys do not understand how tough air defenses are in Europe.) These and similar responses can have a chilling effect on new ideas and programs.

General Eade's advocacy would be critical if the PGM programs were going to move from test and evaluation into large-scale production. We needed a dramatic success with PGMs to tear down this bureaucratic resistance to change. I had one in mind. Everyone familiar with past events in the war knew how difficult, costly, and ineffective our many attempts to destroy the Thanh Hoa and Paul Doumer bridges with unguided bombs in NVN had been. To emphasize this point, 873 sorties carrying unguided bombs had attacked the Thanh Hoa Bridge in previous years and caused only minor damage. Eleven attacking aircraft were lost.

The bridges were key links between the Hanoi-Haiphong area and the invasion staging areas in the southern part of NVN. Stopping the southward flow of men and supplies across these bridges would seriously disrupt whatever plans the NVN might have to invade SVN. The 8th TFW at Ubon was the only F-4 wing equipped with LGB and EO weapons. I knew the 8th TFW could destroy the two bridges with 2,000-pound LGBs. The 8th had few EOs and less confidence in their effectiveness.

General Talbott approved the strike plan to use LGBs against the Paul Doumer and Thanh Hoa bridges. After a thorough discussion, General Eade sent the proposed plan to Seventh Air Force, realizing that without authorization to bomb that far north, it could not implement the plan. However, when authorization was approved, he wanted Seventh Air Force to be ready to bomb.

Higher authority finally sent the long-awaited authorization. On 10 May 1972, the 8th Wing F-4Ds knocked the Paul Doumer Bridge near Hanoi out of commission with LGBs. The F-4 flight carrying EOs on the same mission apparently released out of range and was ineffective. Three days later, 8th Wing F-4Ds successfully destroyed key segments of the Thanh Hoa Bridge with eight LGBs. No F-4s were lost in either raid. Seventh Air Force had provided our needed dramatic demonstration of LGB effectiveness.

PGM development continued after the Vietnam War. Most important was the need for a self-contained system that would allow bomb-carrying fighters to acquire a target, release the bomb, and turn away from the direction of flight while the laser designator continued to illuminate the target. Industry developed an external pod for fighter aircraft that provided this much improved delivery capability. By the time the Gulf War began in 1991, the Air Force was well equipped with PGMs. PGM flexibility and accuracy have steadily improved by integrating other features including GPS guidance and airborne insertion of GPS target data.

Battling the Chip with Ravens

The evolution of electronics during the twentieth century changed the way nations fight wars. Nearly every phase of offensive and defensive operations today depends upon the performance of systems that use electronic components. From satellites to guided munitions, from electronic fuel controls to glass cockpit displays, from decision makers studying faraway screens to fighter pilots taking instructions over secure radios, from electronic warfare officers in our bombers staring at RHAW gear to enemy SAM operators watching acquisition radars—in every situation, success and survival depend upon the digital chip, the cornerstone of modern electronic warfare.

For the USAF to perform its assigned combat missions in wartime, our aircraft must be able to survive in enemy airspace. However, gaining and maintaining air superiority has become an increasingly difficult and complex problem because of electronics.

In 1971 the Air Staff was struggling with the requirement for improving electronic warfare in support of tactical systems. The deputy chief of staff for R&D had assigned the responsibility to the director of requirements, who had considered many separate proposals but failed to produce an overall program. General Ryan, USAF chief of staff, then reassigned the project to operations with instructions to examine the issues, prepare a study with recommendations—and do it promptly.

I was selected to head the study. Before beginning the tactical electronic warfare (TEW) study, we reviewed past, current, and proposed programs dealing with electronic measures.

The expanded use of radar in World War II force-fed the development of electronic warfare. Radar allowed defensive systems to operate effectively for the first time at night or in bad weather. Ground-based radar systems gave both antiaircraft artillery and air defense fighters an advantage over attacking aircraft.

In World War II, the Army Air Forces flew more than 2.3 million sorties and lost 23,000 aircraft, or about a 1 percent loss rate per sortie. Could we learn from the worst examples of losses? From 1 August 1943 until 6 March 1944, Eighth Air Force flew many combat missions against German targets. There were seven large missions when Eighth Air Force suffered its highest losses. Eighth Air Force launched 3,622 sorties from England that crossed the European coast during that period; 12 percent were lost. German air defenses were much less effective later in the war, primarily because the Luftwaffe had a sharp drop in experience from pilot losses on the Russian Front and from our long-range P-51 and P-47 fighters.

Our Cold War enemy positioned large, well-equipped offensive and defensive forces along the periphery of Western Europe. If the Warsaw Pact attacked NATO, the USAF might have enough warning time to reinforce our European bases with aircraft and personnel from TAC, AFR, and ANG. The total number of combat and combat-support aircraft in the inventory was approximately 5,000. Assuming adequate warning, perhaps 3,500 USAF tactical aircraft could support NATO at the outbreak of hostilities. Meanwhile, the USSR could have 1,260 tactical bombers, 4,325 tactical fighters, and 2,650 manned interceptors—roughly a 2.3:1 advantage over the USAF. Further complicating our task would be Soviet SAMs, estimated to be 10,000. If we suffered a 12 percent loss rate like Eighth Air Force experienced at one point, the enemy would destroy one-half of our tactical air forces in two or three days of combat. The message was clear. The USAF must find ways to avoid high loss rates per sortie.

The USAF had fought Soviet systems in both the Korean and Vietnam wars. During the Vietnam War, the USAF flew 1,399,225 *attack* sorties against targets in North Vietnam, South Vietnam, Laos, and Cambodia. Our average loss rate per attack sortie was 0.117 percent, nine times lower than the 1.0 percent WWII average loss rate and 100 times lower than the worst losses of Eighth Air Force. Why were losses so much lower in the Vietnam War?

Most attack sorties in the Vietnam War went to areas where the air defenses were light to moderate. Only 13 percent of the attack missions flew against the most highly defended area—North Vietnam. Forty-seven percent of attack missions were against moderately defended targets in Laos and Cambodia. The remaining 40 percent were against the lighter air defenses encountered in South Vietnam.

North Vietnam air defenses included many of the same defensive systems that the USAF would encounter in Europe—large concentrations of antiaircraft guns around key locations, SA-2 surface-to-air missile defenses, high-performance Soviet fighters operating under GCI control, and an integrated command and control system. This defensive order of battle was responsible for higher USAF losses per sortie over NVN.

The primary killer was flak—antiaircraft artillery. In March 1968, 1,158 antiaircraft sites were located in North Vietnam. Nearly 5,800 guns were at these sites: 83 percent were 37 and 57 mm rapid-firing cannons. The remainder was comprised of radar-controlled 85 and 100 mm guns that threatened intruders flying at medium and high altitudes. The ZSU-23-4, a lightly armored Soviet vehicle, began protecting SA-2 sites in 1967. With four 23 mm cannons mounted in the turret and 2,000 rounds of ammunition, this radar-controlled weapon was very effective against low-flying aircraft. Flak was also a serious threat over Laos and a somewhat lesser threat over South Vietnam.

Another familiar enemy was the MiG family of USSR fighter interceptors. MiGs did not engage USAF aircraft over Laos, Cambodia, and South Vietnam but were a serious concern over NVN where they operated with early warning and GCI radar coverage.

In 1965, when the SA-2 SAM system began appearing in large numbers in NVN, the USAF countered the SA-2s by modifying fighter aircraft with radar homing and warning sensors and missile jamming pods. The first ECM pods arrived in 1965. SA-2s destroyed 54 aircraft through 1968, a loss ratio per sortie of only 0.039% for the 140,000 attack sorties flown over North Vietnam, before Johnson halted the bombing campaign. By 1972 nearly all USAF fighter aircraft were equipped with RHAW gear and pods.

The fourth area of concern was the command and control system established throughout NVN. It netted together EW radars, SAM sites, AAA sites, GCI radars, and communications, giving NVN defenses a distinct advantage over our attacking aircraft.

The overall loss rate of 0.117% for 10 years in the Vietnam War was not an applicable planning factor against USSR and Warsaw Pact air defenses. Warsaw Pact defenses were tougher than anything in Southeast Asia, except possibly defenses in the Hanoi-Haiphong area. Their hostile environment included SAMs, GCI-controlled enemy fighters carrying radar-controlled and heat-seeking missiles, radar-controlled antiaircraft guns, and airborne- and ground-based jamming devices to interfere with our communications, navigation, and weapons delivery.

The objective of the TEW study was to find ways and means that USAF tactical forces could operate against these sophisticated air defense systems without suffering severe losses. Negating the effectiveness of all enemy systems using electronics was not possible—not in a war limited to conventional weapons. For that reason, we focused our TEW study efforts on radar and communications.

Both offense and defense depend upon radar for mission accomplishment. An abbreviated list of offensive uses includes rendezvousing with air-refueling tankers, navigating at low level with TFR, detecting and tracking enemy fighters, guiding air-to-air missiles, and all-weather bombing (GPS was not available in the seventies). Defense uses radar to detect incoming attacks, acquire individual targets, control defensive interceptors, steer SAMs, and guide air-to-air missiles.

Defensive Warsaw Pact commanders must prioritize NATO offensive attacks and promptly allocate defensive forces against the attacks. This process requires fast, accurate decision making and reliable communications between the defensive commander and subordinate defensive units. Without timely communications to all defensive units, the commander cannot optimally manage the air battle.

To minimize Warsaw Pact defenses, we examined many types of advanced jamming systems and techniques, expendable and recoverable jamming drones, decoys, and proposals for new jamming aircraft. We spent several weeks sorting through all the countermeasures to radars and communications known within the defense industry and the military R&D community. Countermeasures evaluated had at least one of four capabilities: confuse, saturate, kill, or jam radars.

Two countermeasures with a World War II history were decoys and chaff. Decoys may draw the attention of enemy radars, but to be truly effective decoys must *confuse* the defense by approximating the speed and radar signature of tactical fighters. Decoys that are fighter look-alikes have a high procurement hurdle to jump because of their cost. Chaff can clutter radar screens, thus distracting the radar operator from the real target. To be effective, chaff has to match specific frequencies of threat radars. Because chaff falls slowly when dispensed from an aircraft, modern Doppler radars can eliminate chaff from their radar screen. Drones carrying radar jammers could *saturate* an air defense sector with false targets as well as provide support jamming for our attacking fighters and bombers. This dual capability would make drones more useful than decoys. If enemy SAMs or interceptors engaged the drone instead of our attacking aircraft, or if the jamming from the drones protected our attacking aircraft, the drones would serve a useful purpose. Plausible war plans that included radar-jamming drones probably would be limited to special high-priority targets. For example, radar-jamming drones might have cut B-52 and fighter losses during Linebacker II, the large-scale bombing campaign against Hanoi-Haiphong in December 1972. The drone's major drawback is high cost.

TEW carefully examined drone costs. In WWII, the German V-1 "buzz bombs" used against England were drones that carried explosives, not jammers. Germany built the V-1 for under $500 each, a cost validated after WWII by an English automobile manufacturer reverse engineering the V-1. Unfortunately, by the early 1970s production costs had risen dramatically. Adding a jamming system to the basic drone multiplied the 1970 costs and complexity many times over. When a support system with personnel, maintenance, and storage facilities was included in the price tag, jammer drones became very expensive countermeasures.

The ultimate way to downgrade air defenses is to *kill* the capability by attacking enemy radars, fighter bases, SAM sites, and command centers. This task is easier said than done. The enemy knows these assets are high on our target lists and will defend them vigorously. Antiaircraft artillery and interceptors protect EW and GCI radar sites. Command centers are often hardened, underground, and camouflaged. SAM sites may be visible but are a hotbed of defensive fire from SAMs, automatic weapons, and antiaircraft artillery. Other SAM systems can be mobile and difficult to locate. To answer this requirement, the USAF had procured a variety of weapons capable of killing air defense systems, including the standoff weapon, a guided weapon launched several miles from target; the antiradiation missile, a weapon that homes on radar; PGMs, laser, or EO weapons (GPS in the '90s); the F-15, the world's best air-to-air fighter to counter enemy fighters (after mid-'70s); and the Wild Weasel, a two-place fighter configured to kill SAM sites.

Another way to neutralize radar is to *jam* it. Effective jamming allows fighters to bomb high-value targets by reducing fighter losses from local air defenses protecting these targets. Jamming helps the planner solve one trade-off dilemma—the main bombing effort can be against high-value targets, not enemy air defenses. Jamming can improve the survival odds for fighters, but there are no guarantees.

The Vietnam War identified a large gap in USAF jamming capabilities. Although the small ECM jamming pods carried by USAF fighters gave some protection against radar-guided missiles and airborne radars, they could not counter the signal strength of land-based EW, GCI, and SAM radars. One might ask, why not build a larger pod with much more output power for the fighter? The answer lies in the size, weight, and power requirements for the bigger pod. It meant adding at least 6,000–8,000 pounds of equipment in a large external pod, new radomes, and an electronic warfare officer to operate the complex system. These changes were not feasible in tactical fighters dedicated to air-to-air and air-to-ground combat missions. It became clear to the study group that a fighter-type aircraft could either carry ordnance or an advanced ECM jamming package, but not both.

The Navy led the way to solving the Air Force problem when it acquired the Grumman EA-6B Prowler. The EA-6B's ECM package featured the ALQ-99, a powerful set of jamming systems that rapidly detect enemy transmissions and jam over a wide range of frequencies. Although the ALQ-99 was truly state of the art, the EA-6B airframe with four crew members was not. The study group wanted the powerful ALQ-99 jamming system installed in USAF aircraft capable of escorting our latest fighters through hostile defenses.

The subsonic EA-6B with a top speed of 500 knots and a much slower cruise speed was a mismatch for the new F-111, F-15, and F-16 fighters. All three had cruise speeds 100–200 knots faster than the EA-6B, and all were capable of supersonic speeds. Although the EA-6B could perform support jamming for USAF fighters while orbiting out of the range of defensive weapons, it could not perform escort jamming. We wanted one type of jamming aircraft for both escort and support.

After the study group did some head-scratching, we found our solution. The OSD had reduced the total number of F-111 tactical wings to four. The USAF chose to keep the improved F-111D and F-111F models coming from production with new avionics and other improvements rather than retrofit all the older F-111A models. This program reduction forced the USAF to deactivate 42 F-111A aircraft. The twin-engine, two-seat F-111A had successfully demonstrated in Vietnam its high-speed, low-altitude, and long-range capabilities. It seemed likely that if the F-111A had ALQ-99 jamming systems on board, it could provide escort jamming for our fast tactical fighters. It could also orbit as a standoff jammer and protect support aircraft from enemy air attack for several hours without air refueling. Modifying F-111As with ALQ-99s and associated ECM gear would be far less expensive than building a new jamming aircraft.

When the TEW study ended, General Eade arranged a briefing schedule. I briefed the TEW study and program proposal two or three times a week for the next month or two. General Ryan approved the new EF-111A program in early 1972. It then became a USAF R&D program in the OSD Five-Year Defense Plan. Northrop Grumman received evaluation contracts in 1972. Grumman won the prototype contract in January 1975, and the first prototype flew in March 1977.

The first EF-111A Ravens in combat supported the successful raid on Libya in April 1986. Ravens served with distinction in the 1990–91 Gulf War. In May 1998, Ravens were retired as a cost sav-

Photo courtesy US Air Force

EF-111A Raven

ing in favor of a joint program that shares upgraded Navy EA-6Bs with Navy and Air Force crew members.

1972—Year of Decision

The Vietnamization program made genuine progress after Gen Creighton Abrams assumed command of MACV in 1968. Abrams shifted the emphasis to pacification of the villages, development of the South Vietnamese economy, and building a trained, well-equipped army supported by organized local reserves and police forces. By 1972 the political-military situation in South Vietnam had changed. The homegrown Viet Cong insurgents never recovered from their heavy losses during the 1968 Tet Offensive—a fact ignored by the American media. The 1970 incursion into Cambodia and into Laos with Lam Son 719, plus air interdiction along the Ho Chi Minh Trail, had seriously depleted NVN supply stockpiles along the border areas of SVN. American ground forces had mostly gone home as Nixon promised, while our Air Force and Navy remained.

Developments had changed South Vietnam since 1968. Topping the list was Abrams's successful pacification program. Pres. Nguyen Van Thieu, a popular leader, had been reelected in October 1971. The economy had flourished, and peaceful travel between villages and cities was now commonplace. Large Viet Cong losses had eliminated any prospect that NVN could stage another insurrection like the 1968 Tet Offensive.

NVN leaders knew the ARVN had grown stronger with better training and new American weapons replacing obsolete leftovers from the Korean War. Nevertheless, they interpreted the disorganized ARVN withdrawal from Lam Son 719 as a major NVN victory and proof of their continued superiority in battle. The enemy knew from bitter experience at Khe Sanh and elsewhere that massive close air support could decide a battle. It also knew we had withdrawn many tactical fighters and B-52s from Southeast Asia. The enemy ruled out the United States destroying North Vietnam with massive air attacks. Our politically constrained attacks against NVN prior to stopping the bombing in 1968 had given NVN leaders a false sense of security against the threat posed by airpower. They believed heavy cloud cover over North Vietnam would restrict the number of days for bombing. If we did bomb, they believed concentrations of SA-2 missiles and MiG-21 interceptors would protect Hanoi and Haiphong. They did not understand that LGBs were available in larger numbers and could destroy key bridges and other high-value targets. All in all, the NVN badly underestimated what an all-out bombing campaign, coupled with mining Haiphong Harbor, would do to their logistics system, command and control infrastructure, and civilian economy.

The stage was set by 1972, a presidential election year, to end the war. Nixon was fighting hard for a second term and was determined not to allow the Vietnam War to stand in his way. Although polls showed strong support for his Vietnam policies, he knew America was war-weary. Antiwar activists were focusing on the upcoming fall elections as the political means to oust Nixon and end America's role in the war.

NVN leaders underestimated Nixon's determination. His narrow victory over Hubert Humphrey in the 1968 election convinced Nixon to change Johnson's Vietnam policies. The real problem was finding a way to achieve "peace with honor"—Nixon's campaign slogan. After a few months in office, Nixon had announced his new policy: support the pacification of South Vietnam with money and advisors, continue air and naval support, and withdraw Army and Marine troops. By the end of April 1972, there would be less than 70,000 US troops in Vietnam. The troop withdrawals led to a sharp decline in American casualties. Army and Marine deaths during 1968 and 1969 totaled 26,524. Army and Marine deaths during 1971 and 1972 totaled 2,603, of which 391 were in 1972—a 90 percent decline for the two-year period.[4]

Despite ARVN progress in South Vietnam, NVN leaders had reason to believe 1972 was the right year for a war-ending offensive. Knowing the political sentiment in the United States, the NVN ruled out the possibility that American ground forces would ever return to Vietnam. This belief was confirmed when NVN rejected Nixon's peace plan in Paris, yet US troop withdrawals continued with the imminent loss of the 101st Airborne Division.

The NVN leadership had good reason to be skeptical about the quality of the relatively untested senior ARVN leadership. Senior NVN generals had two decades of combat experience against the French and the American armies. Many ARVN generals were political appointees with little combat experience, and few had led large-scale operations. NVN leaders believed the ARVN could not win after the American Army and Marines withdrew. They planned an invasion to collapse the Thieu government and consolidate all of Vietnam under Communist rule.

Intelligence reports during early 1972 indicated that NVN was building up forces along the demilitarized zone (DMZ) separating the two Vietnams. Although reconnaissance flights confirmed the buildup, the JCS lacked authorization to attack these NVN positions. At the same time, the peace treaty talks were not going well in Paris. Probably sensing the upcoming crisis from the intelligence reports, Nixon withdrew Henry Kissinger from the talks on 23 March.

The NVN Eastertide Offensive started on 30 March 1972 with an all-out attack in Quang Tri province (see fig. 5). It was the first phase of a three-pronged, large-scale offensive involving an estimated 200,000 NVN soldiers. The second phase began on 12 April with an attack on Kontum near the borders of Laos and Cambodia. After Kontum fell, they could take Pleiku and effectively split South Vietnam in half. The third phase began on 19 April with attacks on An Loc, 60 miles from Saigon near the Cambodian border.

On 2 April, Nixon authorized US Navy carrier aircraft to attack NVN invasion troops around the DMZ. Two days later, he gave SAC B-52s permission to bomb NVN targets and Seventh Air Force permission to attack invading NVN troops. The Pentagon was buzzing with activity, particularly the Air Force and Navy staffs. We knew the outcome of the Eastertide Offensive would prove, or disprove, Nixon's policy and probably the outcome of the war. The decision would depend upon whether the ARVN could successfully defend South Vietnam with US air and naval support.

Shortly after the NVN attack, General Ryan called Maj Gen Bill Evans and me to his office. Evans was the new assistant deputy chief of staff for R&D.[5] Ryan wanted us to select new developments in equipment that could help Seventh Air Force operations in Vietnam. As soon as possible, I was to take working samples of the new equipment, fly to Saigon, and explain to Gen John Vogt, Seventh Air Force commander, how this equipment would be useful and when it would become available.

A few days later, I was on my way to Vietnam with an assortment of equipment items that had not yet been combat tested

431

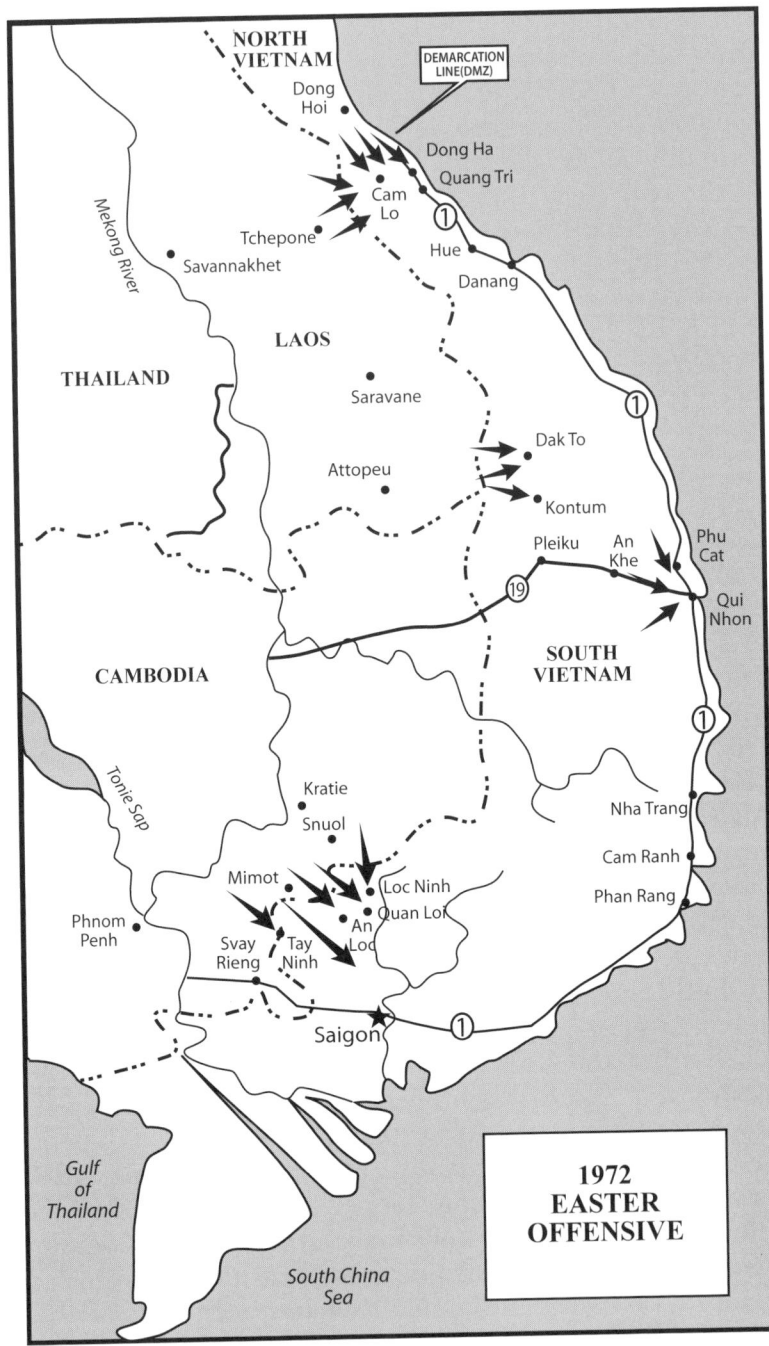

Figure 5. NVN provides major test for ARVN

but looked promising. After landing at Tan Son Nhut, I briefed General Vogt and his assembled staff. Probably dating back to the Roman Empire, commanders in the field do not appreciate uninvited "out of town guys" telling them how to do better. Since General Vogt knew that the Air Force chief of staff had sent me, he politely listened. He suggested that I also visit his other bases during my trip.

First stop was Da Nang where the 366th TFW was located and only about 60 miles from Quang Tri City where the NVN and ARVN were locked in a fierce battle. After discussing the uses for the new equipment with 366th TFW Operations, I watched MAC unloading Army main battle tanks from new C-5 Galaxy transports—one big tank per one big transport.

Next stop was Udorn where Charlie Gabriel commanded the 432d Wing that I had commanded a year earlier. When I arrived, Charlie was reviewing a tough mission flown that day with his deputy for operations, Col Joe Kittinger.[6] The intense activity evident at both Da Nang and Udorn confirmed that the air campaign, named Freedom Train by the JCS, was already in high gear. B-52s and fighters were no longer constrained from bombing many targets in NVN. The early results looked good.

After returning to the Pentagon, I learned the intensity of both the air and ground war had increased. The ARVN had lost Quang Tri to the NVN after nearly a month of fierce fighting. On 24 April, a NVN tank-led assault on Tan Canh routed the ARVN and opened the door to capturing Kontum. NVN troops fired Soviet wire-guided Sagger missiles against ARVN tanks for the first time in the war. They were highly effective and caught the ARVN and its American advisors by surprise. Then the NVN made a classic mistake. Instead of pursuing the routed ARVN troops and seizing Kontum and Pleiku, they stopped for 20 days to plan their next advance. During the 20-day pause, John Paul Vann, the senior American in the Central Region, restored ARVN defenses and arranged with MACV for extensive air support, particularly from B-52s.[7]

General Abrams was in a race with time. He had to stop the NVN with the air resources on hand, particularly the limited number of B-52 sorties available daily in April and May. He rotated the entire B-52 effort every day during the peak period of Eastertide. On its designated day, each military region under attack (MR-1 at Quang Tri, MR-2 at Kontum, and MR-3 at An Loc) received three B-52 sorties every hour for 24 hours—night and day, good or bad weather. The three B-52s arriving every hour flew in a tactical formation that maximized the effective coverage in the target zone. Each B-52D carried 108 bombs—60 in the bomb bay weighing 500 pounds each and 48 externally weighing 750 pounds each. The target zone for dropping the bombs was a rectangle about 3,000 feet wide and 10,000 feet long. Every hour, 324 high-explosive bombs would detonate in rapid succession in the target zone.[8] Abrams wanted this maximum effort to go against enemy infantry and supporting artillery, not against logistics. The effect of this bombing on unprotected troops was catastrophic and crushed the NVN attacks.

To avoid bombing friendly troops, target zones were normally a mile or more away from our forces. The USAF had developed a portable radar beacon for ground troops to use when calling for CAS. If the tactical situation required, by using the radar beacon the target zone could be located closer than one mile. At Kontum, it was located as close as 700 yards. The portable radar beacons were included in the package prepared for General Ryan and used at Kontum to direct the B-52s.[9] The final NVN efforts at Kontum ended on 27 May, and the enemy began to withdraw.

On 8 May 1972, President Nixon authorized Linebacker I. Although the NVN invasions had not succeeded in completely breaking through the ARVN defenses, the battles in South Vietnam were not going well for the ARVN. American advisors remained with their ARVN units, but American support would have to come from the USAF and USN. By 11 May, an additional eight squadrons of F-4s and one squadron of F-105G Wild Weasels were at USAF air bases in Thailand. One additional F-4 squadron was in South Vietnam. By 23 May, SAC had moved 124 B-52s to Andersen AFB, Guam, totaling 209 B-52s available for Linebacker I operations. USAF arrivals in September would include three A-7 squadrons and two F-111 squadrons. The USN recalled the *Saratoga* and *Midway* from port, and they joined the other four carriers off the Vietnam coast.

Linebacker I had two complementary purposes. First, provide air support for the ARVN, which was having an extremely difficult time contending with the three-pronged NVN invasion. Second, shift the attention of NVN leaders to their own backyard by attacking NVN bridges, airfields, power plants, military facilities, and railroads.

Laser bombs knocked out Hanoi's electrical power plant on 8 May and the Paul Doumer Bridge on 10 May. Bombing stopped all rail traffic moving south from Hanoi. On 9 May, Navy aircraft mined seven NVN harbors, most importantly Haiphong. No cargo ships arrived or left Haiphong after the mining until the USN swept the mines in the spring of 1973 after the war ended. This interdiction campaign eventually reduced to a trickle the supplies headed down the Ho Chi Minh Trail. However, the NVN fighting in South Vietnam suffered no serious shortages until June or July.

During the siege at An Loc, the ARVN endured constant bombardment from NVN artillery. Close proximity to Cambodia and to its storage sites along the Ho Chi Minh Trail gave the NVN attackers access to large stockpiles of munitions. May was the peak month. Supported by artillery fire, three NVN divisions repeatedly attacked with infantry and tanks. An Loc received 47,000 inbound artillery rounds. On the worst day, 10 May, the NVN fired 7,600 artillery rounds. B-52 attacks on 11 May authorized by Abrams broke the back of the NVN offensive. By the end of May, the NVN offensive had peaked. Lt Gen James Hollingsworth was the senior advisor at An Loc. After receiving the increased B-52 allocation, he told Abrams, "By God, it just saved us, that's all. And I'll say that your intelligence department must be awfully damn good—that you knew that it was time to go. We just couldn't hit her any better on this one."

After the war, the NVN acknowledged the impact of the B-52 bombing. "The enemy mobilized a large number of B-52 sorties to viciously attack our campaign rear areas. . . . Three waves of [our] assaults . . . were all unsuccessful. Our units suffered heavy casualties and over half the tanks we used in the battle were destroyed. On 15 May, after 32 days of ferocious combat, our troops ended the attack on Binh Long City."[10] (NVN knew An Loc as Binh Long City.)

The first Eastertide NVN attacks sought a rapid breakthrough in Quang Tri Province and then moved south from Quang Tri City down the coast to Hue. After losing Quang Tri City in April, ARVN resistance stiffened in June, aided by US tactical aircraft, Navy gunfire, and B-52s. Before June ended, an ARVN offensive was under way. On 16 September 1972, the ARVN recaptured Quang Tri City.

The NVN Eastertide Offensive failed at all three invasion points—Quang Tri, Kontum, and An Loc. The ARVN had passed a very tough exam, but not with high grades. When properly led by qualified, brave Vietnamese, it did well. At other times, American advisors had to assume control in order to save the day. Eastertide not only built confidence in the ARVN but also exposed the weak commanders who would be replaced. Most estimates state the NVN lost approximately 100,000 of the 200,000 troops who started the offensive. ARVN losses were 40,000 killed.

Looking back at the victory experienced by the ARVN, with major assistance provided by US Army advisors and USAF and USN forces, certain facts seem evident. First, there is ample evidence that senior battle-tested US Army and civilian advisors (e.g., John Vann) successfully overcame the shortage of experienced, capable ARVN generals. Second, the impressive use of USAF and Navy tactical airpower to disrupt the flow of NVN logistics to its forces made NVN realize there was no way it could continue an aggressive offensive. Third, General Abrams focused on B-52 bombing. When he authorized the concentration of B-52 bombing at An Loc for 24 hours, 72 B-52 sorties dropped 7,776 bombs in a target strip 3,000 feet wide and 10,000 feet long. This saturation would theoretically have a killing or disabling bomb explosion twice a day in every square foot in the target zone. Any enemy soldier caught in this onslaught probably became a casualty.

The USAF released the promotion list to brigadier general in December 1971. I was on the list. Congress limits the number of brigadiers to one-half of the total number of all generals. As retirements and promotions occur in the general ranks, new brigadiers fill the vacancies based upon their date of rank as a colonel. After waiting seven months for promotion, my career took a sharp turn. On 20 July 1972, I became deputy director, J-3 (Regional Operations), JCS—a great job with many challenges. Because the JCS required a brigadier general (or rear admiral) for the job and I was still a colonel, General Ryan "frocked" me. I could wear the uniform and use the title of a brigadier general but was paid as a colonel until officially promoted on 1 September 1972.

Promotion to brigadier general. Lieutenant General (later General) Eade, deputy chief of staff for USAF Plans and Operations, and Anne each pin on a star.

USAF C-5 cargo aircraft airlifted tanks to reinforce the ARVN. Photo taken during General Leavitt's trip to Vietnam during NVN Eastertide Offensive.

The Pentagon

J-3 senior staff, JCS. *Bottom row, left to right*: General Leavitt, assistant J-3, Vice Admiral King, and deputy directors. Standing are division chiefs.

Notes

1. Lieutenant General Talbott retired in 1974 as Vice-Commander in Chief of PACAF. A West Point graduate in January 1943, he served in the 368th Fighter Group in Europe, earning the Distinguished Service Cross, Distinguished Flying Cross, Purple Heart, and 16 Air Medals. He later served in tactical units, staff, and high-level commands, earning four Distinguished Service Medals, another Distinguished Flying Cross, and two Legions of Merit. US Military Academy, *Register of Graduates*.

2. Brigadier General Baer retired in 1972 following an impressive career in tactical aviation and high-level staffs. A West Point graduate in the Class of 1943, he served in the 368th Fighter Group in Europe. Awards include the Silver Star, Legion of Merit, Distinguished Flying Cross, and 20 Air Medals. Ibid.

3. General Eade retired in 1975 after serving two years as Deputy Commander in Chief of US European Command. Commissioned in September 1942, he flew 37 combat missions in the European theater of operations. His many awards include the Defense Distinguished Service Medal, Air Force Distinguished Service Medal, Legion of Merit, and four Commendation Medals. US Air Force, "Biographies: General George J. Eade."

4. Data source is Vietnam War Memorial, Washington, DC.

5. General Evans, a 1946 West Point graduate, was a fighter pilot in the Korean War and fighter wing commander in the Vietnam War. He commanded AFSC from 1975 to 1977 and USAFE from 1977 to 1978. His numerous awards include the Distinguished Service Medal, Silver Star, Legion of Merit, four Distinguished Flying Crosses, Bronze Star Medal, 24 Air Medals, and two Commendation Medals. General Evans died 12 December 2000. US Military Academy, *Register of Graduates*.

6. Colonel Kittinger, world-famous balloon pilot and holder of many international ballooning awards, was shot down on 11 May 1972 over NVN. POW Kittinger was released in March 1973.

7. Sheehan, *Bright Shining Lie*, 756–81. Sheehan summarizes the important battle for Kontum and the impact the B-52s had on the NVN offensive.

8. If a different flight of three B-52Ds bombs every hour, and each B-52D drops 108 bombs, then in 24 hours 72 B-52s will drop 7,776 bombs. If one exploding bomb kills or disables anyone within 50 feet, then one bomb is effective over an area of 7,850 square feet, and the total effective coverage for all 7,776 bombs is 61,041,600 square feet. A 3,000-foot wide and 10,000-foot long target zone covers 30,000,000 square feet. Theoretically, in this example, a killing or disabling bomb explosion would occur twice a day in every square foot in the target zone. These computations exaggerate effectiveness because the bombs drop over a 24-hour period and are not uniformly distributed. Nevertheless, the target zone would look like the face of the moon, and probably anyone caught in the onslaught would become a casualty.

9. Sheehan, *Bright Shining Lie*, 781. The Army apparently called the new radar beacon "Combat Skyspot," the name previously assigned a larger 1965 system.

10. Sorley, *Better War*, 334–35. Quotations are from this brilliant history of the last years of American involvement in Vietnam. Sorley thoroughly documents the major defeat NVN suffered by SVN during the Eastertide Offensive. The NVN quote is from the Military History Institute of Vietnam, *Victory in Vietnam*, vol. 2, *Coming of Age of the People's Army of Vietnam*, 389ff.

Chapter 11

Joint Chiefs of Staff
Brigadier General—1972–74

Moorer Changes the War

The past six years spent in the National War College, NATO, PACAF, and HQ USAF provided an excellent background for my new responsibilities as deputy director for regional operations (J-3). Regional operations included all US military operations and exercises outside the United States. Despite these other responsibilities, the lion's share of regional operations activity still involved the Vietnam War.

During the 1960s, all three JCS chairmen were Army generals —Lemnitzer, Taylor, and Earle Wheeler. When Admiral Moorer became chairman in 1970, more than the color of the chairman's uniform changed.[1] Moorer believed that the United States had not exploited our large asymmetrical advantages over NVN in sea power and airpower. Instead of winning a war, we had simply contained the NVN invasion of South Vietnam with "boots on the ground," supported by airpower. Moorer advocated a more comprehensive strategy. For example, he persistently advocated the Navy mining the harbors of North Vietnam to stop the flow of supplies from China and the USSR.

The responsibilities of the JCS in 1972 differed from their current responsibilities. In 1972 the chairman attended the National Security Council meetings and was the president's principal military advisor. However, he could not issue orders to the unified and specified commanders without approval of the SecDef unless it was an operational emergency. In addition, the service chiefs retained command authority over their own service components in the unified and specified commands. Under Goldwater-Nichols congressional legislation passed in 1986, the JCS chairman and the commanders of the unified and specified commands gained operational control over these commands at the expense of the service chiefs, who retained control over training, logistics, R&D, recruiting, and so forth. During the acrimonious debates over Goldwater-Nichols, Admiral Moorer, by then retired, fought hard to keep the previous system plus a strengthened position for the chairman. He lost. Time will tell whether Moorer was right.

The J-3, Vice Adm Jerome H. King, was the only vice admiral who was not an Annapolis graduate, a singular achievement in those days. After graduating from Yale and receiving a reserve commission through the Navy ROTC program, he served on a cruiser for a few months prior to Pearl Harbor. During World War II, he progressed rapidly, accepted a regular commission, and served with distinction in the major Pacific naval battles. King was a "black shoe," meaning an officer from the surface fleet, not carriers or submarines. Prior to becoming J-3, he commanded the Navy forces in Vietnam during 1970–71 and joined the Navy staff as deputy chief of naval operations for surface warfare.

Jerry King had an interesting work ethic. He was a dynamic individual who worked while standing at a vertical desk. His earlier years as a communications officer left him with an eagle's eye for incomplete or improper addresses. I soon realized the man had a great sense of humor that complemented his keen mind. Although we crossed swords a few times, Jerry gave me some wonderful assignments during the two years he was my boss. We became close friends after retirement found us both in California.

By mid-summer 1972, the Army and Marines had nearly completed their scheduled troop withdrawals from Vietnam. In sharp contrast, Navy and Air Force units were busier during Linebacker I operations than any previous time during the long Vietnam War. Two Navy aircraft carriers, each accompanied by five or six support ships, joined the four carriers already on station. Fifteen USAF and five Marine fighter squadrons augmented the existing tactical aircraft in South Vietnam and Thailand. SAC raised the number of B-52s in the Pacific to 209. By July the Eastertide Offensive had stalled. When the Paris peace talks resumed in July, it seemed the war might finally end.

Meanwhile, Admiral Moorer negotiated a new strategy with the White House. If NVN broke off the peace talks, he proposed a full-scale bombing campaign using all the assets assembled for Linebacker I. Probably the most important difference in the new campaign was the target selection process. The White House had selected and deselected targets in the previous air campaigns, such as Rolling Thunder. This time the JCS and the subordinate commands would select targets and run the air campaign.

After the chairman had given his approval to go ahead with the planning, my staff in J-3 chose targets and prepared the overall plan for Linebacker II. NVN targets included everything of significant military value that our experienced planners and the Defense Intelligence Agency recommended. Infrastructure targets that supported the NVN military were also included, such as electrical power, port facilities, radio stations, and railroad facilities.

We expected complaints about collateral damage from the press because NVN commingled military and support facilities with civilian communities. However, attacks on military targets where civilians might be living or working are in compliance with the laws of war.[2] Linebacker II avoided bombing facilities that had no military significance, and planners further minimized civilian casualties by carefully selecting bombing aimpoints.

SAC B-52s and USAF tactical aircraft would attack targets in and around Hanoi and later Haiphong. Navy and Marine aircraft flying from the six carriers on station in the Gulf of Tonkin would attack targets in and around Haiphong and continue laying mines off NVN ports. CINCSAC; the Commander in Chief, Pacific Command (CINCPAC); and MACV would receive the plan and approved targets with instructions to develop appropriate tactics and logistics planning but do nothing more until given release by Admiral Moorer.

For eight years, the NVN had used a "bait and switch" foreign policy. Whenever we got tough, they talked peace. After we took the bait, they switched back to war. This time it would be different. In the JCS, we expected the new campaign called Linebacker II to be the knockout punch that would end the war by forcing NVN to complete negotiations.

Our *primary political* objective was to force NVN to return to the peace talks and accept the terms and compromises already negotiated. The *secondary political* objective was to limit collateral damage to the civilian population, thereby partially avoiding the inevitable criticism we expected from antiwar elements in the United States and from the press. To avoid religious concerns, Christmas Day would have no bombing.[3]

The *primary military* objective was to destroy NVN's capability to renew fighting if peace treaty negotiations stalled again. The *secondary military* objective was to minimize our losses by suppressing NVN air defenses in the area of Hanoi-Haiphong.

Attacking night and day, every day, regardless of weather, was a major departure from past bombing campaigns against NVN. Therefore, the major role in Linebacker II would fall to aircraft capable of all-weather bombing. For the Air Force, this meant B-52s, F-111s, and F-4s with LORAN-D. The Navy would bomb with A-6s, A-7s, and F-4s. Navy EA-6Bs would support Navy attack aircraft with jamming.

The overall objectives hung on B-52s surviving and doing their job. It would not be a milk run. B-52s had to destroy their targets, survive the concentrated enemy air defenses, and fly hundreds of sorties through well-defended areas of NVN. As it turned out, in 11 days the B-52s flew 729 sorties through the extensive NVN air defenses. Intelligence knew approximately how many SA-2 sites and SA-2 missiles were included in the NVN air defenses. We expected NVN to fire hundreds of its SA-2 missiles and to use MiGs to intercept B-52s both before and after its bomb runs.

After Linebacker II ended, SAC estimated NVN actually launched 1,082 SA-2s during Linebacker II; 890 were launched at B-52s and the remainder at tactical aircraft. If B-52 losses became intolerable, Linebacker II would fail. Therefore, tactical aircraft had the responsibility of protecting the B-52s as they flew their night bombing missions. They would provide MiG combat air patrols, destroy SAM sites, drop chaff, and jam radars. The detailed planning and execution for suppression of enemy air defenses remained the responsibility of Air Force and Navy commanders in the Pacific during Linebacker II.

A controversy developed within J-3 after we completed the plan. An Air Force general objected to the "night and day, every day" aspect of the plan as not feasible for tactical aircraft. I knew the winter weather in North Vietnam was so poor that waiting for "blue sky" days would ruin our best chance to strike a war-ending blow. Weather forecasts indicated that only 25 to

30 percent of the time would visual attacks be possible. Admiral King supported my position. Because King was not an aviator, he had Admiral Moorer settle the issue. After listening to my reasoning, Admiral Moorer unhesitatingly agreed with the plan as written.

After the Linebacker II planning ended, Admiral King called me to his office. The Navy had recalled to active status an *Iowa*-class battleship. During Linebacker I, the battleship steamed across the Pacific. When it arrived off the coast of North Vietnam in a few days, it would begin shelling coastal targets with powerful 16-inch guns firing 2,000-pound shells. These big guns had a reputation for accuracy. They could hit a target the size of a football field from 15 to 20 miles away. My experience in Vietnam with laser-guided bombing was that an F-4 could drop a 2,000-pound LGB and hit the hot dog stand, men's room, ticket office, or visiting team's locker room at that same football field—take your choice. Biting my Air Force tongue, I resisted the temptation to tell him my parochial views.

Admiral King asked me to arrange for an RF-4C to overfly the target area after the shelling stopped and to film the damage. Seventh Air Force responded. The film showed no shell holes and no damage. King called me to his office after seeing the report. After exchanging the usual polite amenities, his conversational tone shifted to serious business. After I firmly denied any interservice chicanery, he said, "OK, there is another offshore firing mission tomorrow. An SR-71 will overfly the area. Have the SR-71 film brought back to the NPIC [National Photographic Intelligence Center]. Send me the results."

Two or three days later, the latest photo report was ready. The results were the same—no shell holes and no damage in the target area. When I showed Jerry King the new report, there were no recriminations. "OK, I believe you. Get with the Navy staff and find out what went wrong." After staff members explained how they measured the distance and azimuth from the battleship to the target, I knew the solution to their accuracy problem. The gunnery officer used nautical charts to locate the position of the battleship. He located target coordinates by measuring their latitude and longitude from a map of the coastal areas. The nautical charts did not correlate with the shore map. Big mistake! The maps of North Vietnam prepared by French cartographers before World War II were notoriously inaccurate. Measurements could easily be in error by several hundred yards. The battleship returned home after Linebacker II. King had not supported bringing the battleship to Vietnam and did not regret that it went back for decommissioning.

Jerry King was an innovative J-3 and quick to recognize the value of better technology. The leadership he provided in developing the Worldwide Military Command and Control System illustrated King's ability to think well beyond current capabilities and match future requirements with advancing technology.

When the Air Force proposed the Global Positioning System for JCS approval, Jerry strongly advocated that all the services provide its development and funding. The Air Force wanted financial commitments from the other services before going ahead with full-scale development. The Army balked, the Navy was lukewarm, and the Air Force refused to finance the entire bill since all services would benefit from GPS. This foot-dragging delayed completing the first operational GPS satellites until the late '80s.

Every morning at 0800, the JCS generals and flag officers (admirals) met for a briefing that covered the principal military happenings in the world. Now and then, newspaper headlines or pictures relevant to current service activities would flash on the briefing screen. One morning the briefing team set a little trap for the chairman. A new Navy policy allowed female Sailors to serve on board ship. When Admiral Moorer took his seat, the briefer—without further ado—flashed a headline on the screen from the *Philadelphia Inquirer*, "First Female Sailor on Board Navy Ship Becomes Pregnant!" The briefing room was hushed, everyone leaning forward while we waited expectantly for Admiral Moorer's reaction. His whimsical, nautical comment hit the nail on the head, "There's been some friggin' in the riggin'!" After everyone had a good laugh, we got down to more serious business.

Linebacker II

Linebacker I ended on 22 October 1972. There was reason to be optimistic about a peace treaty. NVN's failed Eastertide Offensive and the drubbing it suffered from Linebacker I shifted the solution to the war from the Vietnamese battlefield to the Paris conference where Le Duc Tho bargained shrewdly for NVN. He knew there was weak political support in the United States for continuing the war and that Nixon wanted Kissinger to wrap up the war before the upcoming US presidential election. He was also aware that by agreeing to unimportant and unenforceable compromises, he could win the most important issues for North Vietnam. As might be expected, the compromised treaty reached during the secret talks between Le Duc Tho and Kissinger was anything but equitable.

Among their few important concessions, the North Vietnamese agreed that President Thieu could remain in office—a reality they knew the United States could not change. By agreeing to release all POWs, the proposed treaty satisfied an important emotional issue in America. The other concessions that the North Vietnamese made were largely unenforceable unless the United States strongly intervened at some future date. The fatal flaw in the proposed treaty was our agreeing to a cease-fire in place, thus allowing NVN to occupy major portions of South Vietnam. The NVN army could now remain and establish a lasting presence in areas of South Vietnam adjacent to Laos and Cambodia as well as keep its existing positions in South Vietnam below the DMZ.

President Thieu reviewed the peace treaty as proposed and refused to sign. He publicly demanded numerous changes on 24 October 1972. Thieu was upsetting Nixon's applecart just two weeks before the presidential elections. Ignoring the rift, Kissinger held a press conference a week before the election, claiming that an agreement was within reach. After he won the election, Nixon attempted to placate Thieu by promising retaliation if NVN violated the proposed peace treaty—a promise he later could not keep after the Watergate scandal doomed his presidency.

Kissinger went back to Paris and proposed numerous changes that reflected Thieu's concerns. The NVN delegation walked out because of these proposed changes. Nixon then sent an ultimatum giving NVN 72 hours to resume negotiations. When NVN leaders ignored his ultimatum, Nixon ordered Linebacker II to commence.

The JCS message, dated 17 December, ordered the commencement of Linebacker II on 18 December and stated it would be a three-day maximum effort against targets in the Hanoi-Haiphong area. The message alerted the subordinate commands to prepare for operations past three days. The first missions flew on 18 December 1972.

The Air Force was not operating alone during Linebacker II. In accordance with the JCS Linebacker II plan, USN tactical aircraft attacked targets along the coastal areas and Haiphong. As expected, chronic bad weather in December hampered the tactical aircraft of both the Navy and Air Force, thus reducing the number of daytime sorties for both services. Despite bad weather conditions, Navy and Marine aircraft struck 119 targets with 505 sorties in the first five days of Linebacker II. Their targets included air defense locations, NVN Army barracks, petroleum storage areas, Haiphong shipyards, the NVN naval base, railroads, and truck depots. Navy and Marine aircraft flew 277 night support sorties, and Navy aircraft also reseeded the minefields laid off NVN ports during Linebacker I. Naval losses were two A-7s, two A-6s, one RA-5, and one F-4.[4]

Attacking NVN was a dangerous task. A complex network of defenses included 21 SA-2 SAM sites in the region of Hanoi and Haiphong, 145 MiGs under GCI control, and numerous radar-directed antiaircraft batteries. Protecting Hanoi was the highest concentration of defense systems the USAF had ever encountered. Although B-52s did the heavy lifting, they share credit with USAF and naval tactical aircraft for their successes. Unsung heroes were KC-135 tanker crews who made Linebacker II possible.

B-52D sorties originated from two SAC bases in the Pacific. Forty-six B-52Ds flew from U-Tapao RTAFB in Thailand, and 53 B-52Ds flew from Andersen AFB, Guam. Earlier in the Vietnam War, B-52Ds had the "Big Belly" modification. Each fully loaded B-52D from U-Tapao carried 48 MK-117 bombs externally and 60 MK-82 bombs in the bomb bay for a total bomb weight of approximately 60,000 pounds. A B-52D flying from Andersen carried a lesser bomb load of 35,000 pounds. A heavier load would require two air refuelings for the 12-hour round-trip to NVN.

SAC's 99 B-52Gs in the Pacific flew 219 sorties from Andersen, each carrying approximately 21,000 pounds of bombs.[5] In addition to the differences in payload, all B-52Ds had the newest ECM equipment, whereas only 45 of the 99 B-52Gs had the new equipment. SAC had attempted to complete the installation in all G models, but both maintenance and logistic sources ran out of stock before Linebacker II.

On 18 December 1972, the first night of Linebacker II, 129 B-52s dropped 2,400 *tons* of high-explosive bombs in the Hanoi high-threat area. This constituted the largest attack by bomber aircraft and highest tonnage dropped on a single raid since 334 B-29s bombed Tokyo on 9 March 1945. The Tokyo raid dropped 2,000 *tons* of firebombs and blackened one-quarter of Tokyo. Fourteen B-29s were lost on the Tokyo raid, and three B-52s were lost on the Hanoi raid. The firestorm in Tokyo resulting from the B-29 raid killed 84,000 people. The North Vietnamese reported after Linebacker II ended that the entire *11-day bombing campaign killed 1,318 civilians* in North Vietnam.

This careful, accurate bombing and avoidance of civilian casualties for 11 nights of intense activity met the *secondary political* objective of Linebacker II—limit collateral damage to the civilian population. Factual reports from NVN did not deter extreme antiwar critics at home and abroad from exaggerating claims about collateral damage.

The *secondary military* objective of Linebacker II was to minimize our own aircraft losses—for both bombers and fighters. The primary battle was waged between B-52s and SA-2 sites. SA-2 kills depended upon experienced NVN operators, who fired 890 missiles at B-52s.[6] Linebacker II had ways to minimize SA-2 effectiveness. The important role assigned to supporting tactical forces was to suppress air defenses, particularly the SA-2. Realizing that suppressing all the NVN air defenses was not likely, SAC also depended upon tactics, ECM, and avoidance to protect B-52s.

Tactics

SAC determined that a stream of B-52s in three waves passing through the NVN defensive complex centered on Hanoi and Haiphong would saturate the NVN command and control system. Each wave contained several "cells." The three B-52s in each cell provided mutual jamming support against the SA-2 radars. As Linebacker progressed, MiGs flying at high altitude above the bomber stream called NVN control centers as to the location, heading, and altitude of the attacking B-52s waves and cells. This unusual defensive tactic—using MiGs to supplement ground-based radars—suggests that both SAC's saturation and cell tactics were effective.

Critics of Linebacker II bomber tactics focused on two issues. The first was the route flown by succeeding waves as they attacked Hanoi. For the first three days, the waves of bombers entering NVN headed toward Hanoi on approximately the same routes. This repetitious attack pattern may have sacrificed surprise in the NVN control centers. SAC planners believed the advantages outweighed the disadvantages. The chosen routes avoided most SA-2 sites until reaching the high-threat area surrounding Hanoi. The routes also provided the best radar imagery of the targets. Selecting the best offset aimpoints for radar bombing maximized damage expectancies and minimized collateral damage.

The second issue pertained to the exit procedure after bomb release. The plan required B-52s to turn westward and exit over North Vietnam toward Laos into a 100-knot headwind instead of exiting southeast over Haiphong and the Gulf of Tonkin. There were reasons for exiting to the west after bomb release. One was to avoid flying over SA-2 sites located to the east and south of Hanoi. Second was to avoid interfering with Navy night attacks around Haiphong. A third reason was to get the B-52s quickly out of the Hanoi high-threat area. Beginning on the fourth night, SAC authorized some waves to exit over the Gulf of Tonkin.

Electronic Countermeasures

Not known when SAC planned the tactics was that B-52Gs without new ECM equipment would be particularly vulnerable in the banked turn after bomb release. Effective jamming decreased while banking because the focus direction of the jamming transmitters changed. Compounding the ECM problem was the difficulty pilots experienced in keeping three B-52s in relatively close formation at night while banking with numerous missiles streaking by their formation and with explosions lighting the sky nearby. Fighter pilots often avoided SA-2 missiles by jinking—rapidly changing the altitude and heading of their maneuverable aircraft. A pilot flying a loaded B-52 weighing several hundred thousand pounds does not have jinking in his bag of tricks!

Avoidance

The obvious way any attacking aircraft can avoid surface-to-air missiles is to stay away from SAM sites and outside their missile range. During Linebacker II, the probability of B-52s being hit by SA-2 missiles was greater on missions that flew within the range of eight SA-2 sites, such as defended downtown Hanoi, than when flying within the range of one SA-2 site, such as located near remote MiG bases. This assumption became reality during the 11 days of Linebacker II. An analysis of routes flown during Linebacker II reveals routes that minimized exposure to SA-2 sites had much lower loss rates. The North Vietnamese apparently intended that their 145 MiGs would defend most areas away from Hanoi and Haiphong.

Suppression attacks on MiG bases and F-4 counterair patrols sharply reduced the MiG threat during Linebacker II. The first three nights of Linebacker II taught lessons that were useful on succeeding nights.

First Night—Target: Hanoi—Threat Rating: Very High. One hundred and two fighter sorties protected B-52s during this night raid—17 suppressed air defenses, 63 flew counterair patrols, and 22 laid chaff corridors to clutter the radar screens defending Hanoi. SAC planners separated 129 B-52s attacking Hanoi on 18 December into three waves. NVN fired 164 SA-2 missiles at the B-52s, destroying one B-52G before bomb release. One B-52D and another B-52G were destroyed turning after bomb release where jamming became less effective. Neither B-52G had new ECM equipment.

There were several reasons why the old ECM equipment provided less protection. SA-2 sites depended upon the downlink from missile to launch site for missile course corrections. B-52G downlink jammers with only two transmitters may not have had sufficient power to jam SA-2 downlink signals. This old ECM equipment also lacked sufficient power to prevent radar "burn-through" when within missile range. One B-52D was lost in the post-target turn where jamming was less effective.

Second Night—Target: Hanoi Area—Threat Rating: High. Ninety-three B-52 sorties (30 Ds from U-Tapao and 27 Ds and 36 Gs from Andersen) attacked targets in the high-threat area using slightly modified tactics. NVN launched 182 SA-2 missiles. Although no B-52s were lost, missiles damaged one B-52D and one B-52G in the second wave. They were within range of three SA-2 sites. After this successful night, JCS extended Linebacker II indefinitely and added MiG bases and SA-2 sites to the target list.

Third Night—Target: Hanoi—Threat Rating: Very High. The most violent night of the air war occurred the third night, 20 December. SAC scheduled 93 B-52 sorties. Both waves one and three had targets near the center of Hanoi protected by eight SA-2 sites (see figs. 6 and 7). Targets included the Hanoi rail yards, located only 2.5 miles from the center of Hanoi. Wave two targets were north of Hanoi, and that route avoided all but one SA-2 site. Before the night was over, the NVN fired 221 SA-2 missiles, destroying four B-52Gs and two B-52Ds and damaging a third B-52D.

In the first wave, one B-52G aborted before reaching the high-threat area. With reduced mutual jamming support in that cell, SA-2s destroyed one of the remaining two B-52Gs. While the second wave was still en route, SAC learned that SA-2s had destroyed the two B-52Gs and one B-52D in the first wave. The B-52D was hit in the post-target turn and may have had degraded ECM equipment. Two cells of B-52Gs (six aircraft) were in the second wave of 10 cells en route to their target—Hanoi rail yards, located only 2.5 miles from the center of Hanoi. Gen John C. Meyer, CINCSAC, recalled these two cells of B-52Gs. After that, if one B-52 in a cell aborted the mission, the remaining two would join another cell. The resulting five-aircraft cell could sustain a higher level of mutual ECM support.

SAC explained the recall: "In view of the losses taken by the first wave on this date, the relatively light weight of effort provided by these six aircraft, and the fact that the succeeding wave would provide a substantial weight of effort in the Hanoi area, a decision was made by CINCSAC to withhold IVORY and RUST cells." Meanwhile, the third wave continued to the target, and SA-2s shot down two more B-52Gs with old ECM equipment. After this night, no more B-52Gs flew sorties into the Hanoi high-threat area.

A procedural problem may have influenced the loss rate. Tactics could not change immediately. Approximately 50 hours elapsed from mission planning until the last time over target. Thirty-six hours went to planning the overall mission at Headquarters SAC, then planning and coordinating the mission at Eighth Air Force, and finally preparing mission folders and briefing all crews. The remaining 14 hours elapsed from start engines at Guam until "bombs away" in NVN. Staffs were finalizing missions scheduled for 20 December when the last B-52 was dropping its bombs on 18 December.

From 18 through 20 December, SAC flew 315 B-52 sorties into high-threat areas. SA-2 missiles destroyed nine B-52s— three B-52Ds and six B-52Gs. *None of the six destroyed B-52 Gs had new ECM equipment.* B-52Gs did not fly again in Linebacker II until after the Christmas stand-down and only bombed targets in lower-threat areas during the last four nights of Linebacker II. They flew 93 sorties without losses from 26 to 29 December.

The new ECM equipment proved to be a lifesaver during Linebacker II. During the first three nights, 65 B-52G sorties *without* new ECM suffered six losses—a 9.2 percent loss rate per sortie. During those same three nights, 250 B-52s sorties *with* new ECM suffered three losses—a 1.2 percent loss rate per sortie.

The Chiefs Meet

While SAC, Eighth Air Force, and Seventh Air Force were reviewing tactics and the high number of B-52 losses, an extraordinary meeting occurred on 23 December in the JCS situation room where we monitored the daily progress of Linebacker II. Admiral Moorer and the service chiefs attended the meeting. The only other persons in the room were Col (later Brig Gen) Clifford Schoeffler and I—the senior J-3 action officers for Linebacker II. Moorer began by saying that a senior Air Force general had contacted him stating that it might be best to stop Linebacker II because of high B-52 losses. Moorer did not name the general, but everyone seemed to know the contact. Moorer then turned to the chiefs and asked for their individual opinions.

Adm Elmo Zumwalt, chief of naval operations, said the Navy losses were not excessive and the Navy would continue. General Abrams, Army chief of staff, deferred to General Ryan, the Air Force chief of staff. Ryan said he talked to General Meyer (CINCSAC) before the meeting. Meyer told Ryan that SAC did not want to stop; B-52s were doing a great job, and SAC had changed some tactics to reduce losses. Meyer also said if SAC backed down, it would be a blow to our nuclear deterrent policy. General Ryan disagreed with the unnamed senior general who had suggested we stop. Instead, Ryan emphatically supported Meyer and said the Air Force would continue Linebacker II. Admiral Moorer thanked the chiefs for their opinions and said he too agreed that Linebacker II must continue. Schoeffler and I breathed a sigh of relief.

Linebacker II Ends

On the morning of 28 December, Washington time, I took another Linebacker II extension message into Admiral Moorer. Things had been going well, and I knew that in a few more days Linebacker II would cause a total collapse of all NVN resistance. He read the message, looked up and said, "Dick, we are not going to start Linebacker II up again. I cannot send this message."

I was astonished at his response and reminded him of how well things were going. Although the North Vietnamese took advantage of our Christmas stand-down by replenishing their supply of SA-2 missiles, our aircraft losses had been light since Christmas. The first two nights after Christmas, we lost two B-52Ds each night, but none the last three nights. Intelligence reported that the North Vietnamese were nearly out of SA-2 missiles and several known SA-2 sites had been destroyed by our Wild Weasel aircraft. The flow of war materials by rail from China had stopped, and bombing had destroyed two major rail yards. All of North Vietnam's ports had been mined again, and no supplies were coming in by sea. Bombing had destroyed its primary petroleum, oil, and lubricant storage and supply depots. Key bridges were down and Hanoi radio destroyed. More than 150 B-52 sorties had destroyed its two principal military

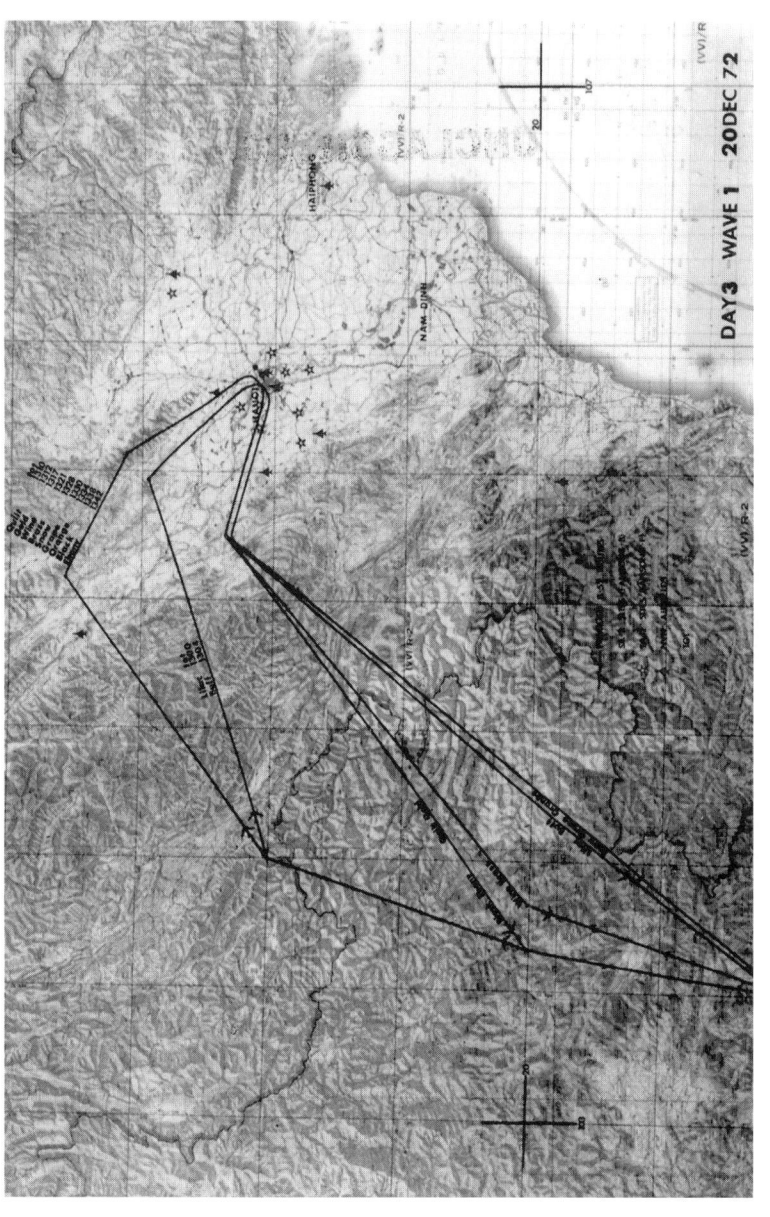

Figure 6. Wave one, 20 December 1972. Nine cells of a total of 27 B–52s attacked Yen Vien rail yards and adjacent warehouses. The eight stars on the map near Hanoi represent SA-2 SAM sites with Fansong F radars. Three more SA-2 sites with Fansong B radars were between 10 and 40 miles northeast of Hanoi, and another SA-2 site with Fansong B radar was 30 miles south. The aircraft profiles on the map are MiG–21 air bases, the most commonly used NVN interceptor.

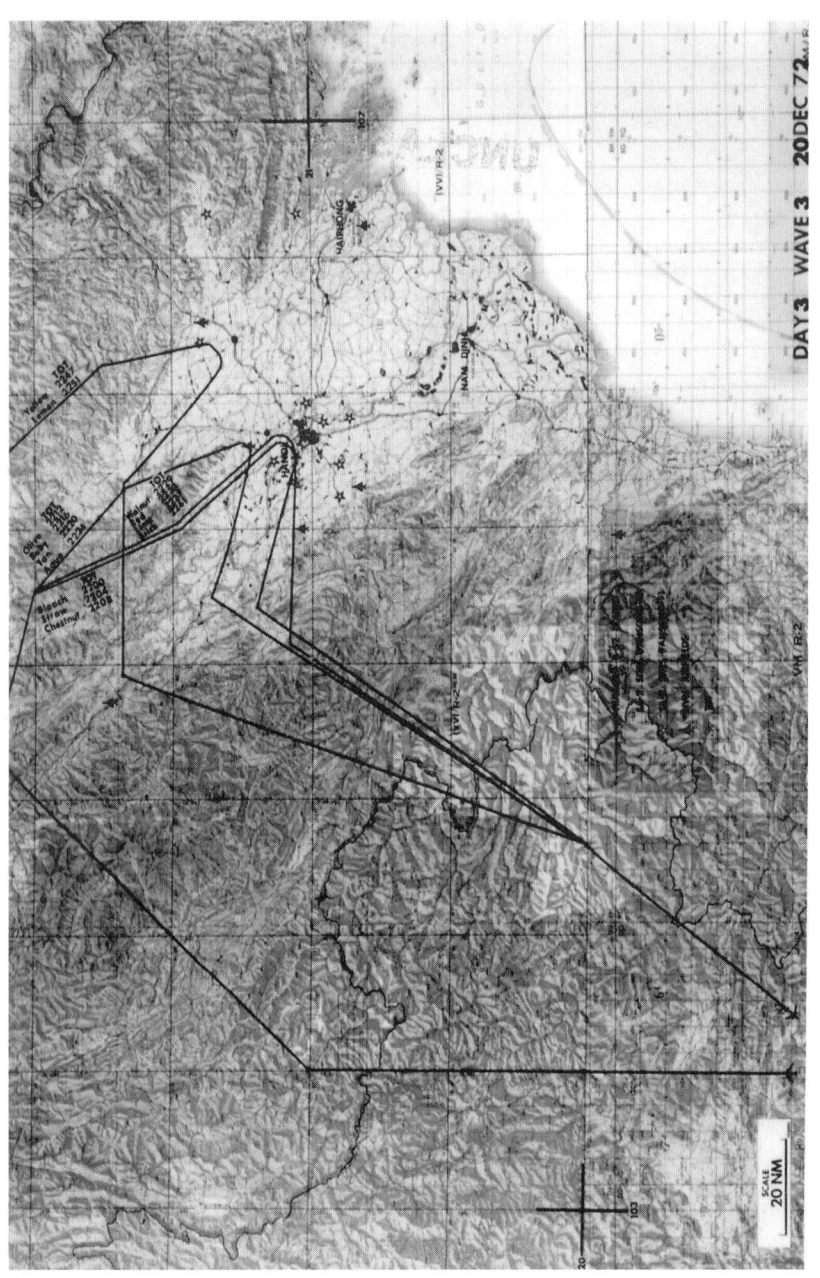

Figure 7. Wave three, 20 December 1972. When the third night ended, it had become obvious that the older ECM equipment in G models was not providing enough protection against the SA-2 SAM missiles.

The "Big Belly" B-52D. Loading 108 bombs one at a time in the B-52D bomb bay would be a long, difficult process. Clip-in loaders carrying 28 bombs each greatly simplified the task.

B-52D dropping some of its 108 mix of 500- and 750-pound general purpose bombs. B-52Ds stationed at U-Tapao, Thailand, dropped a major portion of all bombs expended during the 10 nights of Linebacker II.

complexes. Command and control centers lost effective military contact with their forces stranded in South Vietnam. Admiral Moorer listened patiently, nodding his head in agreement. Then I asked him why we were stopping. His answer cleared the air. "I received a call from Kissinger from Paris this morning. He said the North Vietnamese agreed to our terms. Stop Linebacker II—the war is over."

I left Admiral Moorer's office with conflicting thoughts running through my head. From the early days in the Pentagon in 1963 until 1973, the Vietnam War had seldom left my mind. Moorer had confirmed that Nixon and Kissinger were satisfied Linebacker II had accomplished its *political* and *military* objectives. All our intelligence sources, including photo reconnaissance, confirmed the enemy had neither the resources nor military infrastructure to renew fighting if the peace treaty negotiations stalled again. This was later confirmed by the NVN military leader, Gen Vo Nguyen Giap. His memoirs, available in Hanoi's Vietnam War Memorial, state, "What we still don't understand is why you Americans stopped the bombing of Hanoi. You had us on the ropes. If you had pressed us a little harder, just for another day or two, we were ready to surrender!" Giap goes on to describe how the American media helped the NVN cause by causing more disruption in America than NVN could on the battlefields.

The remaining issue was not military; it was *political*. Clearly, the South Vietnam government was dissatisfied with the peace treaty. It left NVN troops occupying significant areas within South Vietnam. It did not disarm NVN. It left South Vietnam dependent upon unenforceable promises of a weakened American president to intervene if NVN broke the treaty. It was signed in Paris, not Hanoi, thus ignoring the historical and psychological advantages gained when the defeated Japanese were forced to surrender in Tokyo Bay on the USS *Missouri*. Yes, our POWs would return several months after the bombing stopped, but not until we met the 31 March deadline for minesweeping NVN ports. Linebacker II left NVN no longer able to fight. Whether it would renew fighting later would depend upon our willingness to enforce the peace treaty.

The Price We Paid

During the 11-night campaign, 671 B-52 sorties *with* new ECM equipment suffered nine losses for a loss rate of 1.34 percent per sortie. Prior to Linebacker II, the loss rate to SA-2s was 2.09 percent for USAF tactical aircraft. With B-52G sorties included in the Linebacker II total, loss rate per sortie was 2.06 percent. We had achieved the *secondary military* objective of Linebacker II—minimizing losses against the most heavily defended targets the USAF had ever encountered. SAC B-52s flew another 393 combat sorties during Linebacker II, principally in South Vietnam, without a loss.

It is important to put a face on these numbers. SAC suffered 66 casualties resulting from the shootdown of 15 B-52s. Eight were killed in action; 25 were MIA and later declared dead. The remaining 33 became POWs and returned to the United States before April 1973. Tactical aircraft lost were three F-4s, two F-111s, two A-7s, two A-6s, one EB-66, one HH-53, and one RA-5C.

The Most Important Battle of the Vietnam War

Linebacker II, a classic example of force application by air and naval power, was led by a combat-seasoned chain of command. Admiral Moorer, JCS chairman, and Adm Noel Gaylor, CINCPAC, were Navy fighter pilots in WWII and Korea. General Meyer was a fighter ace with 24 WWII victories, plus two more in the Korean War. Lt Gen Gerald Johnson, Eighth Air Force commander, was a WWII fighter ace with 16 victories. General Vogt, commander of Seventh Air Force, was a WWII fighter ace with eight victories.

Some chroniclers of the war contend that Linebacker II turned the tide toward the United States. Lewis Sorley's book *A Better War* notes that historian George Herring called the situation at the end of Linebacker II "the ultimate irony . . . the U.S. position in South Vietnam was stronger at the end of 1972 than at any previous point in the war."[7] Longtime observer of the war Sir Robert Thompson thought the United States could at this point have dictated the terms and that "the war could have been won, in that a real and enforceable peace could have been obtained."[8] Thompson also said, "In my view, on December 30, 1972, after eleven days of those B-52 attacks on the Hanoi area, you had won the war. It was over!"[9]

Linebacker II, the final major battle of the Vietnam War, was probably the last time heavy bombers and supporting fighters would fly in large formations to bomb highly defended targets. There are economic and practical reasons for no more Linebackers. The economic reasons are daunting. In 1972 SAC had 400 B-52 heavy bombers. Today, the total B-52 and B-1B bomber inventory is approximately 100 aircraft. Despite their limitations, the large payloads and long endurance of the B-52 and B-1B are useful against targets in low-threat areas. Today, stealthy B-2 and F-22 aircraft and cruise missiles can successfully penetrate modern air defenses and destroy their targets with precision-guided munitions. In the future, these capabilities will merge into long-range, hypersonic delivery systems— manned and unmanned—capable of destroying any target anywhere in the world.

International Reaction and Legal Aspects Attendant to the Linebacker II Campaign

As expected, certain elements of the media—foreign and domestic—viewed the bombing with critical eyes and accused the United States of committing war crimes and other serious offenses. W. Hays Parks (BA, JD) discusses and refutes these allegations in an excellent, knowledgeable article, "Linebacker and the Law of War," published in *Air University Review* in 1983. Parks was chief, International Law Branch, International Affairs Division, in the Office of the Judge Advocate General of the Army at that time.

During the Johnson presidency, the use of airpower was greatly restricted. In a broad sense, our tactical aircraft—USAF, Navy, and Marine—were limited to supporting friendly ground forces in South Vietnam. Our primary strategic bomber, the B-52, was used as an airborne artillery piece by Gen William Westmoreland and his successor General Abrams. They both realized a battle zone could be saturated with hundreds of bombs from well-directed B-52D sorties. By limiting air attacks to South Vietnam and those sections of the Ho Chi Minh Trail adjacent to South Vietnam, the United States accepted a "no win" policy against a resolute enemy with untouchable supply lines connecting NVN by rail and sea to China and the USSR.

Rolling Thunder, the nickname for the previous very limited air campaign against NVN, was stopped in October 1968. The ROEs for Rolling Thunder were so restrictive that NVN was not intimidated despite the courageous efforts of USAF, Navy, and Marine aircrews.

After Nixon became president in 1969, the demands of public opinion forced change in the prosecution of this seemingly endless war. Under Abrams, Vietnamization had made genuine progress. Therefore, Nixon accepted the risk of withdrawing American ground forces over the following two years, our casualties dropped dramatically, and the stage was set for Nixon's reelection in 1972.

The North Vietnamese lit the fuse for change when they launched their full-scale offensive against South Vietnam at Easter time in 1972. It failed, primarily because of the massive intervention of US air and naval forces and the improved performance of the ARVN guided by American advisors. Linebacker II ended the fighting.

Parks emphasizes in his article that the charges made by unfriendly critics after the bombing stopped were incorrect and disingenuous. As explained earlier, the target selection process was heavily weighted in favor of avoiding collateral damage. The approval to choose targets did not rest upon the broad shoulders of either SAC or the theater commanders. Those decisions remained with the JCS staff, supported by the Defense Intelligence Agency and other departments.

Perhaps the most important decision I made in my military career was to insist that Linebacker II had to be an all-weather bombing campaign despite objections by at least one superior in the JCS. The outgoing JCS message to SAC and CINCPAC on 17 December 1972 stated: "A. Utilize visual as well as all weather bombing capabilities."

With personal knowledge of fighters, B-52s, and winter weather in Vietnam, I knew the campaign would drag on and have unforeseen consequences otherwise. As it turned out, the weather was only good enough for visual bombing for two days during the period from 18 December until the campaign was terminated on 28 December.

History Lessons from Vietnam

Because the Vietnam War lasted too long, politicians often characterize the war as a quagmire. A closer analogy is probably quicksand—the more we struggled without finding a way out, the deeper we sank. President Truman ignored Ho Chi Minh and allowed the French to regain their colonial empire in Indochina in 1945. President Eisenhower increased American aid and military assistance to the South Vietnamese government in 1953. President Kennedy sent air commandos to "train" the South Vietnamese air force in 1961 and increased our uniformed military advisors to 16,000. President Johnson greatly increased our involvement following the Gulf of Tonkin Incident in 1964.

In the context of the Cold War, these presidential decisions may have seemed logical. Truman placed a higher priority on securing Western Europe by having France join NATO than on freeing Indochina from colonialism. Eisenhower ended the Korean War by forcing an armistice on the Chinese-backed North Korean government but had no illusions about the continuing threat Communism posed to Southeast Asia. Eisenhower founded the Southeast Asia Treaty Organization in 1954 to keep Communism at bay in that part of Asia.[10]

When Kennedy took office, he had recently converted to the importance of Asia. In October 1962, the Laos Accords became effective and called for the USSR to guarantee that NVN would not transit Laos and Cambodia in order to support the Viet Cong insurgency in South Vietnam. The Cuban missile crisis, also in October 1962, turned Kennedy's attention away from Southeast Asia. For the next 13 years, North Vietnam brazenly used the Ho Chi Minh Trail in Laos as its logistics sanctuary for military operations in South Vietnam. During that time, the USSR continued to ignore its guarantee. The Ho Chi Minh Trail ultimately cost South Vietnam its freedom. In a September 1963 interview, Kennedy told Walter Cronkite that "in the final analysis it is the people and the Government [of South Vietnam] itself who have to win or lose this struggle. All we can do is help, and we are making it very clear. But I don't agree with those who say we should withdraw. That would be a great mistake."[11]

Things were not going well in Southeast Asia after Lyndon Johnson took office. The year of 1965 was particularly threatening because of Communist activities. NVN had moved regular army troops into South Vietnam. The National Intelligence Estimate stated the Indonesian Communist Party (PKI) was "by far the best organized and most dynamic entity in Indonesia."[12] The United States provided support to the Indonesian army in the civil war, and it crushed the PKI. The number of Indonesian and Chinese casualties in the civil war ranged from 300,000 to 800,000. Our successful intervention in Indonesia probably influenced Johnson to stay the course in Vietnam.

Although General Westmoreland, Ambassador Taylor, and other advisors recognized the need to close down the Ho Chi Minh Trail and deny the NVN a logistics sanctuary, President Johnson turned down their advice in April 1967.[13] His principal advisors and the growing antiwar movement believed that expanding the war beyond South Vietnam would bring China and possibly the USSR into the war on behalf of NVN if the United States took offensive actions against NVN. A more perceptive analysis of the historical relationships between China and Vietnam would have discredited this view. American support for a democratic government in South Vietnam did not seriously threaten the vital interests of either China or the USSR. They would not have risked a major war by directly engaging American forces in combat. When we heavily bombed NVN and mined its seaports during Linebacker I and II, neither the PRC nor USSR intervened. What is past is past, but a question lingers. Would a land-sea-air offensive against NVN in 1966, 1967, or 1968 have ended the war and saved both American and Vietnamese lives?

Nixon realized the need for a change when he assumed office. General Abrams, Westmoreland's replacement, pursued a successful proactive strategy that concentrated on the Vietnamization program from 1969 to 1972. By 1970 the pacification of South Vietnam was proceeding well, and the withdrawal of American Soldiers and Marines had begun. We had finally escaped the quicksand.

After NVN signed the Paris Peace Treaty in 1973, there was less concern about Thailand, the Philippines, Singapore, and Malaysia becoming Communist. Remaining at risk were South Vietnam, Cambodia, and Laos. In 1973 and 1974, Congress ruled out further support for South Vietnam. When Watergate ended Nixon's presidency, Vietnam disappeared from the radar screen. Two years after we left, North Vietnam again invaded South Vietnam. Without our air and naval support and desperately short of war materials because of punitive legislation by our Congress, South Vietnam was quickly conquered. For the next several years, the people in South Vietnam, Laos, and Cambodia paid a terrible price for depending upon American promises.

Congressional partisanship meant more than our promises, more than wartime victories, and more than the sacrifice of 50,000 American lives. When NVN broke the peace treaty in 1975 and invaded SVN with an army rebuilt by the USSR and PRC, the United States turned its back on its wartime ally.

Many military historians now concede that we may have won on the battlefield but lost the important battle for public opinion. One-sided reporting since 1975 has made it easy for the American public to forget. Most Americans have seen on television that helicopter evacuation of the American Embassy in Saigon *two years after American forces left Vietnam*. In their minds, the forced evacuation serves as positive proof that we lost the war.

Americans have also forgotten that four consecutive American presidents approved the "domino theory" to stop the spread of Communism beyond Indochina throughout the rest of Southeast Asia. After adding up the score, the outcome tends to support their presidential decisions. Yes, Communist NVN conquered SVN, and Cambodia suffered terribly under the Khmer Rouge. Laos retained a small degree of independence. The remainder of Southeast Asia remains independent today. Our Soldiers, Sailors, Marines, and Airmen made their freedom possible.

Once war becomes a political football and the politicians and public choose sides, with the media acting as cheerleaders, maintaining a consistent military strategy is increasingly difficult. This is a painful lesson that future military and political leaders should remember from the Vietnam War. To avoid this trap, I believe the following:

- The United States should not enter a war unless we intend to win. What constitutes "winning" must be thoroughly analyzed and agreed beforehand. A declaration of war may be appropriate under special circumstances.

- Speed wins wars. Our military strategy should avoid gradual escalation.

- Win before the next presidential election—or sooner. Political campaigns during wartime inevitably weaken the public's support for the war.

- Do not fight a war against a nation that is supported by another nation(s) that serves as a logistics sanctuary. If special circumstances force such a war, the president and SecDef should agree beforehand that if diplomacy fails to neutralize the sanctuary, then we must attack the sanctuary nation until it stops supporting our enemy.

- Maximize use of our asymmetrical advantages in space, air, and sea power. Our technology-based services equipped with precision-guided munitions—connected by space assets that provide instantaneous command, control, communications, reconnaissance, and intelligence—are the best in the world and are likely to remain that way.

- Avoid strategies primarily dependent upon American "boots on the ground." Soldiers and Marines suffer the highest number of casualties. The media and American public quickly lose confidence when American casualty lists grow.

- Do not sacrifice American lives to avoid collateral damage. If the enemy collocates legitimate military targets with the civilian population, destroy these targets and acknowledge the reason for collateral damage. Senior commanders should make these sensitive combat decisions, not military lawyers.

- Avoid ambiguous slogans about "winning the hearts and minds" of the enemy populace. War is a nasty business and not the preferred way to win friends. After the war ends, there will inevitably be resentment on the losing side. Japan and Germany suffered defeats beyond imagination in today's world, and resentment remained in some quar-

465

ters after the war ended. Nevertheless, both nations became strong allies during the postwar era. Vietnam today welcomes American trade and tourists. Time and money heal most wounds.

Picking Up the Pieces

The principal terms of the Paris Peace Treaty included withdrawing all American forces from South Vietnam, resupplying South Vietnam with weapons and munitions, and clearing mines from Haiphong and other North Vietnamese ports. March 31st was the deadline for completion. Admiral King assigned the staff responsibility for several of these tasks to regional operations.

Probably the most dangerous task following the end of the war was sweeping Haiphong and other North Vietnamese harbors of mines. We had one Navy officer in regional operations with the qualifications to monitor the minesweeping operation. Working on the scene with the North Vietnamese and the Navy minesweepers, he made frequent reports on the ongoing operation. The minesweeping was completed without incident in compliance with our agreement. Great work, Navy!

The Paris Peace Treaty terms also included repatriating American POWs within 100 days. Maj Gen "Chappie" James was deputy assistant secretary of defense (public affairs).[14] POW repatriation was one of his major projects. Chappie knew my interest in POWs and in late March invited me to his office to read the complete list of POWs being repatriated.

More than two years had passed since a bizarre incident at Ubon had occurred. At that time, a very excited lieutenant ran into my office. "Colonel Leavitt, an airplane has just been hijacked!" He immediately captured my total attention. Had someone stolen an F-4? The adrenalin stopped pumping a few minutes later as the lieutenant's story unfolded. An American civilian, Bobby Joe Keesee, posing as a newspaper photographer, rented a light aircraft flown by a Thai pilot. His alleged purpose was to take aerial photos of Ubon RTAFB. Although the Thais had only a few airplanes on the air base, the 8th Wing was the tenant and had no control over Thai operations.

Immediately after takeoff, Keesee put a gun to the Thai pilot's head. "Cross Laos, head for North Vietnam, and land on the ocean beach near Vinh. Let me out there, and you can fly back to Thailand. If you don't do as I say, I'll kill you!" The pilot followed orders and landed on the beach. Keesee jumped from the aircraft and ran for the nearby jungle. The pilot took off under fire from the NVN and made it back to Ubon.

To my surprise and horror, Keesee's name was on the list of POWs arriving from Hanoi. The POWs were to receive a hero's reception at Clark AB in the Philippines as they disembarked from the transport aircraft. I told Chappie about Keesee hijacking the Thai airplane.

"Dick, it's too late to do anything about it. The reception is already planned, and Keesee will be getting off the plane with the POWs." My response got Chappie's attention. "If you don't back off, I'm going to the SecDef and tell him that Keesee is not a hero—he's just a damn crook. He should not be honored as one of the POWs!"

An hour or two later, Chappie called again. "OK, Dick. We will keep him on the airplane until all the POWs are gone. Then security police will put him in a jeep, drive to downtown Manila, and dump him there. The crime was in Thailand, and there is no extradition agreement between Thailand and the Philippines, so that's all we can do."

Most POWs had no recollection of Keesee until near their time of release. The North Vietnamese had isolated Keesee from the American POWs in the Hanoi Hilton. Keesee was a one-man crime wave. In 1962 he hijacked an airliner and flew to Cuba. Castro sent him back to the United States, where Keesee spent the next two years in a federal prison. In 1964 a US federal court convicted Keesee of stealing government parachutes. He perpetrated many other frauds over the years. In 1974 Keesee received a 20-year sentence for conspiring in the murder of a US diplomat in Mexico. In March 2000, a US district court sentenced Keesee to two life terms without parole for admitting to the murder of Harry M. Christensen.

A sensitive issue for the JCS to decide was whether Air Force wings or Navy carriers would return first to the United States. Air Staff reasoned that wings sent from TAC during the 1972 NVN Eastertide Offensive had been on temporary duty in Vietnam and Thailand longer than the additional aircraft carriers that went on station. Therefore, let those TAC fighter wings go home first.

Navy staff did not agree. Navy policy was to assign aircrews to specific aircraft carriers in the Atlantic, Mediterranean, or Pacific Fleets. Aircrews generally did not move from fleet to fleet or from carrier to carrier. Because of this policy, most aircrews assigned to the Pacific Fleet had flown several combat tours in the Vietnam War, whereas Air Force aircrews had generally returned to noncombat assignments after completing a year in Vietnam or Thailand.

It seemed to me there was a logical solution. Leave the same aircraft carriers in the Pacific. Replace their aircrews with qualified aircrews from the Mediterranean and Atlantic Fleets. For example, an F-4 aircrew flying off a carrier in the Med for the past several years could replace an F-4 aircrew flying off a carrier in the Gulf of Tonkin. Not feasible, said the Navy staff. The issue escalated from me to the J-3 to Admiral Moorer, who decided Navy aircraft carriers had priority. TAC wings stayed in Thailand.

Because timely communication between ship and shore was often difficult or impossible, the US Navy entrusted the ship's captain or the commander of several ships at sea to make decisions at sea that on land would have required approval by higher authority. For example, assume the admiral commanding Task Force XX decided that he could not follow a Commander in Chief, Atlantic Command (CINCLANT), operations plan because something unforeseen had occurred. The admiral might have changed course and sent CINCLANT a message. "UNODIR [Unless Otherwise Directed] Task Force XX will proceed to Point Limbo instead of Guantanamo Bay." Because there was no immediate response to the contrary, the admiral assumed approval and headed for Point Limbo.

UNODIR messages can serve a useful purpose as long as the commanders use good judgment. When a commander misuses UNODIR authority, he can cause serious problems. Misuse happened in September 1973.

One responsibility of regional operations was gaining approval for military exercises outside the United States. A Navy flotilla commanded by a rear admiral had JCS and State Department approval for a "goodwill cruise" around South America.

The flotilla would make port calls in major seaports and participate in sea exercises with several South American navies. The
plan listed the US Navy exercises approved for each nation visited
on the goodwill cruise, including exercises with the Chilean navy.

Chile in 1970 had elected Salvador Allende, a Marxist, as its
head of state. In 1973, unknown to the JCS, the Chilean military
planned a coup against Allende. As the flotilla approached Chile,
the JCS received a message from higher authority to cancel the
specific exercises dealing with the Chilean navy. A succinct, high-
priority JCS message went to the admiral commanding the flotilla. The message deleted the exercises with the Chilean navy.

The admiral answered the JCS order with a routine message
sent through Navy channels before reaching the JCS. Using
the UNODIR protocol, the admiral substituted new, unapproved
exercises with the Chilean navy for the deleted exercises. Several days later, when his UNODIR message finally reached the
JCS, his flotilla had already completed the *unapproved* exercises with the Chilean navy he added in the UNODIR message.
By then, the coup was over and Allende had committed suicide.

The world press blamed the United States for backing the coup.
I do not know whether the United States covertly backed the coup.
I know the admiral added fuel to the fire by exercising with the
Chilean navy during the coup. He retired after this incident.

The Watergate scandal increasingly dominated the interests of
the executive branch throughout 1973 and affected Pentagon civilian leadership. Melvin Laird had resigned on 29 January 1973
after serving as secretary of defense during the final four years of
the Vietnam War. President Nixon then selected Elliot Richardson
to become the new SecDef. When Watergate caused the resigna-
tion of Attorney General Richard Kleindienst on 30 April 1973,
Nixon selected Richardson to be the new attorney general after
serving only four months as secretary of defense. James R.
Schlesinger replaced Richardson as SecDef on 2 July 1973.

Notes

1. Adm Thomas H. Moorer, a 1933 graduate of Annapolis, was a fighter
pilot at Pearl Harbor on 7 December 1941. He served in the Pacific during
World War II earning the Silver Star, Distinguished Flying Cross, and Purple
Heart. After attending the Naval War College, he held a series of important

staff and command assignments. In 1962 he commanded the Seventh Fleet, in 1964 he took charge of the Pacific Fleet, and in 1965 he took command of NATO's Atlantic Command and the US Atlantic Fleet. He became chief of naval operations in 1967 and CJCS in 1970. Upon retirement in 1974, Admiral Moorer was the first person to be awarded a second Defense Distinguished Service Medal. He died in 2004 at age 91. Department of the Navy, "Biographies in Naval History: Admiral Thomas Hinman Moorer, USN (Ret.)."

2. A discussion of this issue appears in Parks, "Linebacker and the Law of War," 2–30.

3. The bombing pause on Christmas Day had an ironic twist. Linebacker II was nicknamed the "Christmas Bombing Campaign" by the world. Histories of the Vietnam War continue using that misnomer.

4. Department of the Navy, "Naval Aviation Chronology, 1970–1980."

5. These and other statistics pertaining to Linebacker II were extracted from formerly classified Linebacker statistics and other SAC studies in August and September 2006.

6. Ibid. SAC estimates NVN launched 1,082 SA-2 missiles in Linebacker II—890 were launched at B-52s.

7. Sorley, *Better War*, 356. Quoted from George C. Herring, "The Nixon Strategy in Vietnam," in Peter Braestrup, ed., *Vietnam as History: Ten Years after the Paris Peace Accords* (Washington, DC: University Press of America, 1984), 57.

8. Ibid. Quoted from Sir Robert Grainger Ker Thompson, *Peace Is Not at Hand* (New York: David McKay, 1974), 35.

9. Ibid. Sir Thompson as quoted in W. Scott Thompson and Donaldson D. Frizzell, eds., *The Lessons of Vietnam* (New York: Crane, Russak & Co., 1977), 105.

10. Rostow, "Case for the Vietnam War," 41.

11. University of California, Santa Barbara, "John F. Kennedy: Transcript of Broadcast with Walter Cronkite."

12. Fernandes, "Indonesia 1965."

13. Ibid.

14. Gen Daniel "Chappie" James became the first African-American promoted to USAF four-star general on 1 September 1975. His Air Force career began at Tuskegee Institute where he was commissioned in 1943. He flew 101 combat missions in F-51s and F-80s during the Korean War. Following several peacetime assignments as a fighter pilot, he was assigned as vice wing commander, 8th TFW, and flew 78 combat missions over North Vietnam. He was widely known for his eloquent speeches on Americanism and patriotism. In addition to his many military decorations, General James received the George Washington Freedom Foundation Medal in 1967 and again in 1968. From 1 September 1975 until 5 December 1977, he was Commander in Chief, NORAD. His final assignment was as special assistant to the chief of staff, USAF. He retired 1 February 1978 and died later that month. US Air Force, "Biographies: General Daniel James Jr."

Chapter 12

Yom Kippur War
Brigadier General—1973–74

Storm Clouds Rising

The potential for another Arab-Israeli conflict never went away after the 1967 Six-Day War.[1] Israeli spoils of war included Egyptian land in the Sinai on the eastern side of the Suez Canal and the Gaza Strip. Israel also kept the Golan Heights because of its commanding view of southwest Syria. Egyptian president Gamal Abdel Nasser unsuccessfully fought the low-level War of Attrition with Israel to force the Israelis to return the land taken in the Six-Day War. During those years, the USSR began increasing the capabilities of the Egyptian and Syrian armed forces with modern weapons and military advisors. The USSR had correctly analyzed the Six-Day War results, and its military aid to Egypt and Syria featured advanced air defense and anti-tank weapons, particularly missiles.

After Nasser died in 1970, Egyptian president Anwar Sadat gave diplomacy a chance while the United States intervened to resolve the Egyptian land issue. The Israelis would not budge. When our diplomatic efforts failed, Sadat planned for war. Israel's other traditional enemy was Syria, now under its new leader, Pres. Hafez al-Assad. Among other issues, Assad believed the Israeli occupation of the Golan Heights overlooking Syria was a strategic threat to his country. Sadat and Assad secretly planned simultaneous invasions to defeat Israel. They chose Yom Kippur on 6 October 1973, the most sacred Hebrew religious holiday, as the ideal time for their surprise attacks.

Crediting the Israeli poor initial response to the Arab attacks to "surprise" is a political excuse and not factual. The average Israeli citizen may have been surprised, but not Golda Meir's cabinet. Israel had both strategic and tactical warnings leading up to and including the attacks on 6 October. Meir and her closest cabinet members chose not to mobilize reserves and not

471

to preempt the imminent attack despite multiple warnings.[2] Both the chief of the Israel Defense Forces (IDF), Gen David Elazar, and the Israeli air force (IAF) chief, Maj Gen Bennie Peled, urged mobilization and a preemptive Israeli air attack when the evidence of Egyptian-Syrian attacks became overwhelming.

By the evening of 5 October, intercepted intelligence convinced Peled that war was imminent. He ordered the IAF to upload air-to-ground munitions on attack aircraft and prepare for preemptive strikes against Syrian and Egyptian targets. Early in the morning on 6 October, Peled asked Meir for permission to launch preemptive strikes. Meir declined Peled's request after stating that friendly nations, as well as Israel's enemies, would accuse Israel of starting the war if the IAF attacked first.[3]

Peled returned to his office and ordered the IAF to download air-to-ground munitions and to begin uploading air-to-air munitions. His new goal was to gain air superiority as soon as the war began by defeating the Syrian air force before turning IAF attention to the Egyptian front (see fig. 8). Because of the delayed mobilization, most of the recalled Israeli army reserves had not reached their units by the time Syria attacked the northern front on 6 October. The Syrians overran several Israeli army positions that lacked reserve reinforcements. Peled decided the Syrian army posed the highest threat to Israel at that moment. He canceled the upload of air-to-air munitions and began uploading air-to-ground munitions for close air support missions. This change in readiness meant that gaining air superiority would no longer be the top priority mission for the IAF.

Effective CAS depends upon trained aircrews, proper munitions, and forward air controllers to direct friendly aircraft. The IAF had highly proficient aircrews, especially for air-to-air combat. Reservists typically filled the cockpits of the older attack aircraft used for CAS. When the first army reserve officers who were FACs reported for duty, the army quickly sent them to the Syrian front where the fighting was fierce. This "first in, first out" practice resulted in many army units receiving FACs that had never trained with their newly assigned units, a factor degrading CAS performance.

In a world replete with high- and low-altitude SAMs, radar-controlled antiaircraft artillery, and enemy fighters, effective CAS depends upon defense suppression and ECM. The IAF

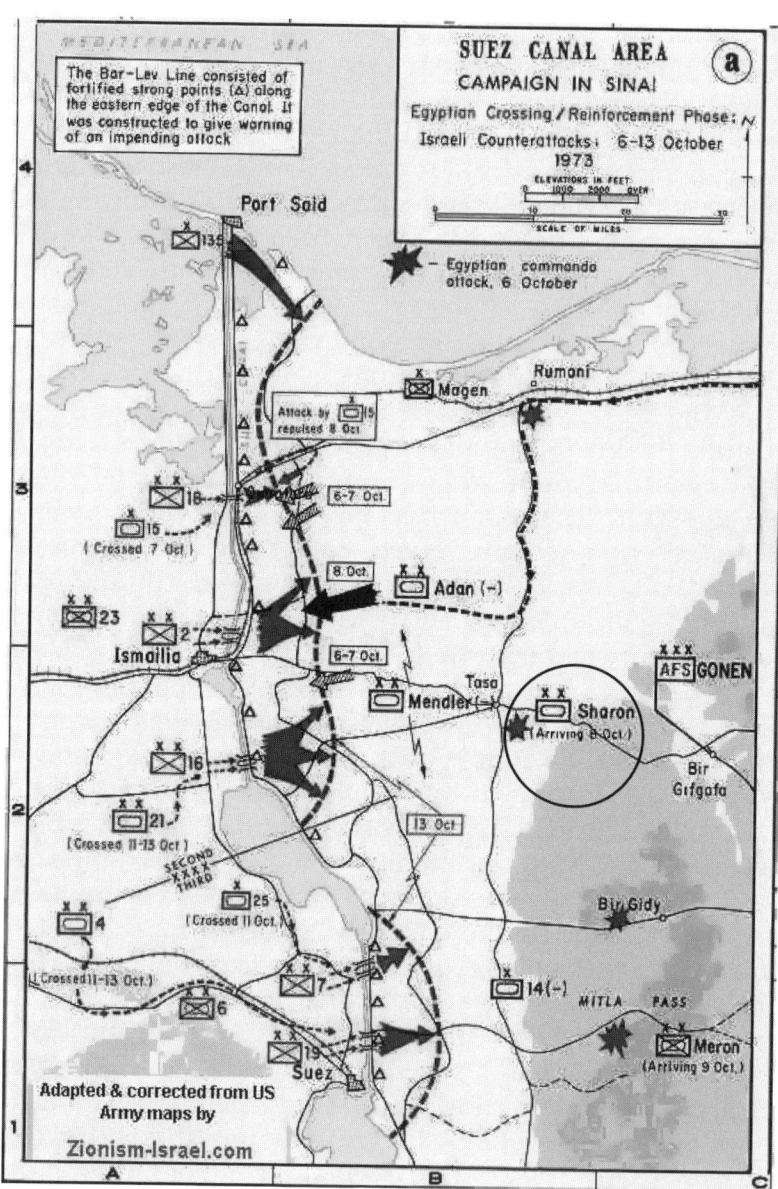

Figure 8. Egyptian front—Yom Kippur War. The Bar-Lev Line along the east side of the Suez Canal was to give warning of an Egyptian attack. The outposts were too far apart to provide significant mutual support. The Israelis had planned on protecting the outposts with close air support. After failing to suppress the Egyptian SAM sites, the IAF lost too many aircraft in a vain effort to drive off the Egyptian army. Without tanks, aircraft, and artillery support, the Bar-Lev Line was destroyed—with many casualties. Circled is Ariel Sharon's headquarters when the war started.

made no timely effort to suppress Syrian or Egyptian air defenses—a holdover from its success in the 1967 Six-Day War. Adding to the problem, IAF pilots had not been thoroughly trained in the use of ECM, and many chose not to turn on the jamming pods received from the USAF. Neglecting defense suppression was the major IAF error in the war. Ground-based air defense systems supplied by the USSR shot down 79 Israeli aircraft the first three days of the war and another 18 aircraft before the war ended.

IAF prewar plans called for suppressing air defenses along the Egyptian side of the Suez Canal as a first order of business. Instead, the IAF focused on the Syrian front in the first several days and did not accomplish the defense suppression task against Egypt. Egyptian forces overran the poorly defended Israeli outposts on the east banks of the Suez Canal on 6 October. This well-planned and rehearsed Egyptian attack met all of its objectives before halting in the Sinai about 10 miles east of the canal. Egyptians shielded their advancing army by moving air defenses forward with their advance.

Early Saturday morning on 6 October, the Pentagon learned about the Arab attacks. Although military intelligence analysts had not ruled out a renewed war against Israel, their collective judgment was prejudiced by Israel's quick victory in the Six-Day War. When Arab attacks on 6 October nearly defeated Israel, it was a rude shock to our intelligence experts, particularly the head of USAF Intelligence, Maj Gen George Keegan. Despite mounting evidence to the contrary, Keegan insisted the Yom Kippur War was a replay of the 1967 Six-Day War, with the IAF having the decisive role.

The IDF slowed both the Syrian and Egyptian attacks and restored a semblance of order after three days, but a major problem confronted its continuing operations: the IDF was running out of critical supplies, particularly munitions. Before the MAC airlift began, El Al, the national airline of Israel, took 80 Sidewinder missiles back to Israel from the naval air station at Oceana, Virginia. The Sidewinder, a heat-seeking air-to-air missile, was already in short supply after the initial air battles between the Israeli and Arab air forces. This was one of the first clues that the Yom Kippur War would not be the one-sided affair experienced in the 1967 Six-Day War. We answered an urgent

Israeli request for air-to-air missiles by allowing El Al to pick them up in the United States and carry them back to Israel. El Al transports were people-carriers, not cargo-carriers. The continued use of El Al for moving heavy loads of munitions and other materials not only would waste time and money but also would not satisfy the urgent and growing Israeli need for munitions.

Hard feelings still existed within the State Department and Congress because Golda Meir in 1972 torpedoed the US compromise plan to return part of the Sinai to Egypt. Nevertheless, a compelling argument for airlifting supplies traced to our special relationship with Israel. In 1948 the United States was the first nation to recognize Israel, and in 1973 Israel remained the only true democracy in the Middle East. Many American Jewish families kept close ties with Israel, and their considerable influence in the American media and Congress helped persuade Congress and the administration to act.

Golda Meir hinted through her Washington contacts that if Israel could no longer defend itself with conventional munitions, Israel would attack Egypt and Syria with nuclear weapons. The Nixon administration knew that Israel possessed several nuclear weapons. Meir might be bluffing, but the United States could not gamble with the chance of a nuclear war engulfing the Middle East. The stakes were too high. Sending enough conventional munitions to Israel would take Meir's nuclear threat off the table.

Israeli historians report that the American response to Meir's request for aid was not immediate. Since the United States was not a belligerent in Israel's war, the expression "not immediate" is correct. One reason for the delay was a credibility problem about Israel that existed in the US government. The Israelis had a well-publicized image of being invincible in battle. "Common knowledge" concluded that the Israelis may have been surprised on 6 October by incompetent Arab armies but that the IDF would quickly recover and win. It took several days before Washington and the rest of America fully understood their peril. The Israelis were truly fighting for survival this time against well-prepared, well-armed, and brave Arab armies.

Admiral Moorer alerted the J-3 and J-4 about the possible requirement for airlifting supplies to Israel. The J-3, Jerry King, told me to inform the Air Force but to emphasize that no final

475

decision had been made. I discussed the airlift possibility with Lt Gen "Dutch" Huyser, the USAF deputy chief of staff for plans and operations. He agreed to keep the planning low-key until we had direction from the SecDef. Huyser informed Gen George S. Brown, USAF chief of staff, and Gen Paul "P. K." Carlton, commander of Military Airlift Command. General Carlton had anticipated that an airlift might be required, but there was a problem. Until MAC received approval for the airlift from the president and SecDef, Carlton could not recall the MAC fleet from its worldwide, high-priority missions.

By day's end, J-3 established a command post in regional operations to serve as the JCS focal point for an airlift. Our job would be keeping the SecDef, JCS chairman, and the services informed, as well as directing the flow of supplies to Israel. Maj Gen Maurice "Moe" Casey, director of transportation in J-4, provided supply and airlift experts to our command post while he personally maintained direct contact with General Carlton at MAC headquarters. After the Vietnam War ended earlier in 1973, we left a large inventory of our war materials in South Vietnam. MAC was busy moving these to our depleted stockpiles in the United States and Europe. Nickel Grass, as the airlift operation would be called, would interrupt that operation. Our military was cautious about reducing the already depleted stockpiles of munitions and other war materials.

Diplomatic efforts to end the war failed on 9 October when Egypt refused to stop fighting, although Syria was willing. The Egyptian refusal cleared the last political obstacle to the airlift. Approving an airlift was a difficult decision but a correct one.

The first complications were international. Soviet aid and advisors had rebuilt the Egyptian and Syrian militaries with equipment and advisors after the Six-Day War. A Soviet airlift continued this support after the Yom Kippur War began. An American airlift to help Israel fight two Soviet client states could conceivably lead to another crisis with the USSR. Premier Leonid Brezhnev seemed interested in some form of détente. Would Brezhnev sacrifice détente if he thought our airlift to Israel was a challenge to the USSR?

A second set of complications involved US economics and politics. The Arab world knew of our strong ties to its enemy Israel. Would it punish American intervention by cutting oil production? The Israeli government had rejected our proposed resolution of borders. Could the present crisis be resolved diplomatically by our insisting that Israel must compromise the border issue? Watergate had weakened Nixon but strengthened cabinet rivals. Would Kissinger with his extensive background in international relations and national security prevail, or would Secretary James Schlesinger prevail with his more conservative approach to crisis management? In the end, they reached a balance point, with Kissinger being "good cop" and Schlesinger being "bad cop."[4]

IAF losses continued to mount, and the SecDef recognized its urgent plea for more F-4E fighters. He authorized 48 F-4Es from the USAFE inventory in Germany to be transferred to Israel. The Air Staff asked if I could arrange for the SecDef to modify his decision. TAC had 48 of the latest versions of the F-4E with the tank-killing Maverick missile capability and other major improvements. TAC wanted 24 sent to the IAF for a realistic combat evaluation. After Admiral Moorer agreed, we approached the SecDef. Schlesinger explained that he chose USAFE for the 48 aircraft because it would demonstrate the advantage of forward deployment. I explained the technical advantages of the latest F-4Es and the need for a combat evaluation. Schlesinger then approved taking 24 offered by TAC and the other 24 from USAFE.

Every JCS operational plan has a nickname. Not a day had passed before the fighter pilots in regional operations recommended the airlift be nicknamed "Nickel Grass." It struck a fond memory in my mind. The fighter pilot's song from WWII and Korea, "Throw a nickel on the grass, save a fighter pilot's ass! Oh, Hallelujah! Hallelujah! Throw a nickel on the grass and you'll be saved!" How appropriate. "Nickel" was airlift, and the "fighter pilot" was Israel. Jerry King approved after I explained the meaning. Weeks later, Jerry good-naturedly chided me. Apparently everyone except Jerry and I knew that "flower children" in that era called a five-ounce bag of marijuana "nickel grass"!

While waiting for presidential approval to begin the airlift, the State Department, National Security Council, and Pentagon resolved serious issues associated with a military airlift to Israel. Our European and Asian allies had refused to help Israel because they feared the economic consequences of an Arab oil embargo. Without European airspace, air bases, and support facilities, Nickel Grass became a very complex operation. Loaded C-141 and C-5 transports in 1973 could not reach Israel without refueling. The best alternative to a Western Europe air base was Lajes Airport in the Portuguese Azores. Lajes was roughly halfway to Israel and had supported USAF deployments to Europe for many years. When Portuguese authorities in the Azores refused to allow MAC transports to refuel at Lajes, aggressive diplomacy changed their minds. According to a Pentagon rumor, Kissinger offered the Portuguese a choice: approve MAC transports landing at Lajes, or fight a Marine expeditionary force that would land and take over the base. Whether this threat rumor was true or not, the Portuguese changed their minds and allowed MAC to use Lajes.

The 1973 War Powers Act became law about the time the Yom Kippur War began. The act would prevent MAC from overflying war zones or flying into hostile areas without presidential notification followed by congressional approval. Watergate had Nixon cornered in October 1973, and he was not in a position to challenge Congress. To avoid confrontation, Nickel Grass flight plans complied with the War Powers Act by flying over the Straits of Gibraltar, threading a needle through the Mediterranean, and avoiding Libya's exaggerated claim of territorial waters far off the Libyan coast. To defend against Egyptian or Libyan fighters, two USN aircraft carriers in the Mediterranean patrolled the route leading to Lod, the airport at Tel Aviv, Israel.

My recollection is that higher authority ordered the JCS to get ready to comply with an airlift two or three days after Golda Meir's request. In regional operations, we staffed a 24-hour command post to handle all the activity associated with the proposed airlift. The JCS J-4 located the war materials at military depots and other installations and fed that information to our command post. The Air Staff provided us pickup and delivery schedules for the proposed airlift. After these necessary steps were completed, we waited for an execution order for Nickel Grass from the SecDef.

Secretary Schlesinger called for a progress report on the preparation for Nickel Grass. Moe Casey and I accompanied Admiral Moorer to the SecDef's office. We explained that the military supplies were located at various depots in the United

States and were ready for pickup. MAC had prepared flight plans and whatever else might be required to begin operations. While awaiting orders, MAC was continuing normal operations. Schlesinger then asked, "How long will a flight to Israel take?" My response was, "About 13 hours' flying time, Mr. Secretary, from Dover, Delaware, to Tel Aviv. Aircraft will stop en route at Lajes for refueling and crew change before proceeding to Tel Aviv." He seemed satisfied, and this explanation ended the briefing.

The next day, Secretary Schlesinger called us again to his office. "Has the first MAC transport landed in Israel yet? You told me yesterday it would take 13 hours." Four-star Moorer looked at two-star Casey, and then both turned around and looked at one-star Leavitt for the answer. For a few seconds, I collected my thoughts. This was a huge misunderstanding between the JCS and SecDef. I would have to tell him the bad news. "Mr. Secretary, the MAC aircraft are still at their home bases and have not picked up supplies from the depots yet. Thirteen hours was the flight time from Dover. MAC and the other commands have not received an execution order to start Nickel Grass."

Dr. Schlesinger often smoked a pipe. For a moment, I thought he would bite the pipe stem off the pipe. Then he took the pipe from his mouth and emphatically told Admiral Moorer to start the MAC airlift *immediately*. We all left his office in a hurry. Since the JCS had waited for several days for permission from the SecDef to start the airlift, I was unhappy about becoming the fall guy for the delay. Admiral Moorer put his arm around my shoulder as we walked down the Pentagon corridor. "Dick, you've got to understand. They never gave us approval to send the execution order to MAC or anyone else. But when these guys pull the trigger, they expect a bullet to come out the end of the gun!" Admiral Moorer's remark lightened my load.

I heard after the war that Kissinger demanded an investigation of the delay. Perhaps Kissinger did this to embarrass Schlesinger, since managing the airlift was the SecDef's responsibility. Perhaps Schlesinger, who was new in the job, did not realize the need for an execution order and never told Admiral Moorer to send one. Perhaps Kissinger deliberately caused the delay for diplomatic reasons and blamed the delay on the lack of an execution as a convenient excuse for foot-dragging. As Sir William

Gilbert said, "Things are seldom what they seem, skim milk masquerades as cream." When the fighting ended, the two-day delay had not changed the outcome of the war.

On 9 October, the IDF began winning fiercely contested battles with the Syrians. Despite heavy losses in the air and on the ground, the IDF blunted the Syrian offensive and was now retaking lost territory. Syrian dictator Assad did not know that Sadat had told Kissinger that Egypt's goal was limited to restoring the 1967 prewar boundaries east of the Suez Canal. When Syria's Egyptian allies refused to continue advancing into the Sinai, Assad wanted a cease-fire. By 14 October, the IDF had stabilized the Syrian front roughly along prewar boundaries. Although Damascus was now visible from forward IDF positions, the IDF made no effort to take the Syrian capital. General Elazar's gamble to take the offensive against Syria before tackling Egypt had paid off.

Prior to 14 October when the airlift began, the IDF had reached dangerously low inventories of ammunition, fighter aircraft, and other war materials. Israel's prewar inventories could no longer support the extremely high expenditure rates experienced in the past eight days of desperate fighting. Consequently, the IDF restrained offensive operations against Egypt until the United States assured Israel we would replenish all future expenditures. According to Israeli sources, Kissinger told Israeli ambassador Simcha Dinitz on 10 October, "The IDF must attack with all its strength, as if it had another forty aircraft in hand, and not stint on ammunition or aircraft, because the United States will supply everything."[5] With that commitment, Israel's confidence rebounded, and its renewed optimism was confirmed when Nickel Grass began on 14 October. Without detracting from the courageous IDF performance in fighting and winning a war while badly outnumbered, it seems fair to state that Nickel Grass resolved this major concern for Elazar and his generals in the field. It allowed the IDF to take the offensive against Egypt and not worry about the ongoing Soviet airlift to Egypt.

By the time another week passed, the IDF had won decisive battles in the Sinai, crossed the Suez Canal, and encircled the Egyptian Third Army. In the process, the opposing armies fought the largest tank battle since World War II at the "Chinese Farm" east of the Suez Canal. The Egyptians tried to isolate Israeli forces that had crossed the canal into Egypt. For two nights and a day, the fierce battle continued before the Israelis finally won. This battle protected future prime minister Ariel "Arik" Sharon's flank and ultimately sealed the fate of the Egyptian Third Army.

After the two divisions commanded by Sharon and Maj Gen Avraham Adan successfully crossed the Suez Canal on 16–18 October, they split. Adan turned south toward Suez City, and Sharon headed north toward Ismailiya and Cairo. Adan soon had the Egyptian Third Army trapped on the east side of the Suez Canal without reinforcements and short of supplies. Sharon's division blocked any relief the Egyptians could bring from the north to spring the trap that was rapidly enveloping their Third Army.

Brezhnev recognized the plight of the Egyptian forces and sent a message to Nixon requesting that Kissinger immediately fly to Moscow for consultations leading to a joint US-USSR cease-fire proposal. Nixon was overwhelmed by domestic events. Beleaguered by Watergate and fighting to avoid impeachment, he lacked a vice president after Agnew resigned. His cabinet was destroyed by the Saturday Night Massacre. Performing erratically under all this stress, Nixon passed his presidential foreign policy responsibilities to Kissinger. Kissinger delayed the Moscow trip for three days. During the delay, the IDF took full advantage of the tactical situation by continuing offensive actions, completely encircling the desperate Egyptian Third Army, and denying Egyptian resupply efforts.

Kissinger saw direct contact with the USSR as an opportunity to switch Egypt to our side, isolate Soviet adventurism in the Middle East, and end the war with the IDF, thereby restoring prewar boundaries in the Sinai. The United States and USSR asked the UN Security Council for a cease-fire. Resolution 338 unanimously passed on 22 October and became effective that night.

Despite the cease-fire, both armies continued to fight throughout the night and into the next day. The IDF offensive reached the point where the Egyptian army was in desperate shape, with growing shortages of food and water. Brezhnev saw the continuing fighting as an Israeli effort to capitalize on the cease-fire, gain new boundaries, and destroy the remnants of the Egyptian Third Army. He sent Nixon a letter proposing a joint operation with Soviet and American troops enforcing the UN cease-fire. According to several sources, Brezhnev threatened to take unilateral action if the United States did not join the USSR in enforcing the cease-fire.[6]

Back in the Pentagon, the mood was upbeat. The IDF had won a major victory and trapped the Egyptian Third Army. Nickel Grass had worked well for Israel, and the UN cease-fire seemed the timely way to end the war. Then a major new crisis suddenly erupted during the evening of 23 October. Brezhnev was frustrated by being unable to get Nixon's attention and resolve the plight of the Egyptian Third Army. The USSR was mobilizing airborne troops to intervene in the Sinai and save the Egyptian Third Army!

DEFCON 3

It had been another long day in the Pentagon spent answering questions about the future of Nickel Grass, monitoring developments following the UN cease-fire, speculating about reopening the Suez Canal with American assistance, and considering the possible JCS requirement for a "lessons learned" team. After I had finished a late dinner at home, the phone rang. The JCS Command Post ordered me to report to the director of the Joint Staff, Lt Gen George Seignious, as quickly as possible.

I arrived in his office within the hour. Seignious got right to the point. The Egyptians had asked the Soviets for help because Israel had ignored the cease-fire and was destroying the Egyptian army. Brezhnev sent Nixon a message asking for US and Soviet forces to act jointly to enforce the cease-fire. Brezhnev had already alerted several Soviet airborne divisions as well as Soviet marines in the Mediterranean. He threatened to act unilaterally if we did not participate. Unless the Soviet Union backed off, we could be in a war: Egypt and the USSR against Israel and the United States—a situation neither superpower could conceivably want.

The order from the president and SecDef was to assume DEFCON 3 as soon as possible. My job was to select the appropriate DEFCON 3 alert measures, to prepare messages for the appropriate commands directing these alert measures, and to be ready within three or four hours for Admiral Moorer and the SecDef to approve, or disapprove, the messages. I chose alert measures that seemed appropriate under the circumstances outlined by Seignious. They were ready for approval when the SecDef, CJCS, and service chiefs assembled in the JCS command center.

By 1973 a rough parity existed between the two Cold War nations in terms of nuclear weapons development and the size of strategic forces. Only the highest levels in each government could authorize the use of nuclear weapons. Both nations understood the concept of nuclear deterrence and carefully avoided actions after the Cuban missile crisis that might lead to nuclear war. DEFCON 3 was a major change in the readiness of our military forces. Although ordering DEFCON 3 was in no sense a declaration of war, it served notice that we were prepared for war because of a threat to our national interests.

When Shakespeare wrote *Henry V*, Act I, at the end of the sixteenth century, he unknowingly described the twentieth century DEFCON system developed by the United States.

> In peace there's nothing so becomes a man
> As modest stillness and humility;
> But when the blast of war blows in our ears,
> Stiffen the sinews, summon up the blood.
> Then imitate the action of the tiger.

Five conditions of defense readiness describe our system. DEFCON 5 and DEFCON 4 are assumed with "modest stillness and humility." DEFCON 5 is the peacetime status of our armed forces. During the Cold War, the United States generally stayed at DEFCON 4—a posture that maintained some forces on alert but did not put the remaining forces, or the civilian economy, on a wartime footing. The last three lines of Shakespeare's verse describe DEFCON 3: "But when the blast of war blows in our ears, Stiffen the sinews, summon up the blood. Then imitate the action of the tiger."

Selected military forces are placed in a very high state of readiness, and other necessary actions are taken that will prepare the United States for imminent hostilities. Only twice during my Air Force career was DEFCON 3 ordered: the Cuban missile crisis on 23 October 1962 and the Yom Kippur War on 24 October 1973.

Setting the scene for the DEFCON 3 scenario were IDF victories that threatened the total destruction of a trapped Egyptian army. The reasons for moving to DEFCON 3 were not self-evident. They had something to do with our sending war materials to Israel and the Soviet Union sending war materials to Egypt. They had something to do with the Watergate scandal and Saturday Night Massacre on 21 October that incapacitated Nixon. They had something to do with the threatening tone of Brezhnev's letter to Nixon. They had something to do with Secretary of State Kissinger, who had assumed certain presidential responsibilities on top of his diplomatic responsibilities. They had something to do with White House chief of staff Al Haig who apparently isolated Nixon from the decision-making process. These reasons converging at the same time led to a dangerous situation.

SecDef Schlesinger, JCS chairman Moorer, and the service chiefs assembled in the JCS briefing room before 0600, 24 October. Moorer briefly reviewed events of the last few hours and explained why we were declaring DEFCON 3. The chiefs asked few questions. Sitting behind Admiral Moorer, I handed him one by one the messages my staff prepared for specific alert measures. The View Graph projector flashed each message on the screen for all to see. There was very little discussion. After everyone had a chance to read the message, Moorer would turn to the SecDef and say, "I recommend you approve this measure, Mr. Secretary." After Schlesinger approved, the message went to all addressees. The United States was in DEFCON 3 a few hours after the White House decision.

Years later, I read that one of the White House principals stated that SAC went to DEFCON 2. I knew this was not true. General Meyer, CINCSAC, had followed the SecDef directive and assumed DEFCON 3. Prior to writing this account, I asked the SAC historian to research this point. After carefully researching all records, he confirmed that SAC did not assume DEFCON 2.

DEFCON 3 ultimately served a useful purpose. Our reaction astonished the Soviets when they quickly learned of the increase, according to Israeli sources. Premier Alexei Kosygin said, "It is not reasonable to become engaged in a war with the United States because of Egypt and Syria."[7] Within 24 hours, our intelligence sources confirmed that the crisis with the USSR was winding down. On 28 October, messages went to most US commands reducing readiness to DEFCON 4, and the rest followed shortly thereafter.

I believe moving to DEFCON 3 was a bluff that worked, but there was a potentially severe downside. What if the Soviets had ignored our DEFCON 3 and entered the war in order to save the Egyptian army? Would we have challenged the Soviet-Egyptian forces by aligning ourselves with Israel and sent American troops into battle? No one knows the answers; the unknown remains unknown.

War Ends—Fact-Finding Begins

A few days after the war ended, wearing civilian clothes and carrying a diplomatic passport, I was on my way to Tel Aviv in an El Al 747. The United States had invested heavily in the Israeli victory. The quid pro quo was an opportunity to study the war up close before the inevitable "spin" could occur. Dr. Kissinger had arranged through the Israeli ambassador for a JCS team with representatives and technicians from all the services to perform this mission. I was appointed team leader.

At Heathrow Airport near London, the security surrounding El Al passengers was very tight. An armed guard stood at the door of the room where passengers bound for Tel Aviv waited. Another guard accompanied those who needed to use a restroom, but only one passenger at a time could leave the waiting room. When we finally boarded the 747, the flight attendant took me to a single seat in the upper deck. After an hour or two, the aircraft reached cruising altitude, flying southeast toward Israel, when it banked steeply to the right. A thought raced through my mind, "Are we being skyjacked despite all the precautions made at Heathrow?"

The flight attendant looked like his job involved more than carrying bagels, lox, or gefilte fish to passengers. Instead, he looked as if he might be the middleweight wrestling champion of Israel. I caught his attention. "Please find out why we are so abruptly changing course. If the aircraft is being skyjacked, I've got a lot of eating to do [pointing at the classified material in my briefcase]." He understood my concern and immediately went down to the lower deck. A few minutes later, he returned with both good and sad news. "No skyjacking. The crew was heading for a hospital in Switzerland because an elderly man suffered a heart attack. Doctors on board tried to revive him, but he died before they could get there. Now we are heading for Tel Aviv."

After landing, clearing customs, and checking in at the hotel, the American ambassador took me to a reception at Moshe Dayan's home. The reception was under way in the backyard of Dayan's home when we arrived. Dayan had an established reputation as an archeologist. The collection of antiquities that he had collected in the Sinai and other areas adjacent to Israel would be a welcome addition to any world-class museum. After an introduction by the ambassador, Dayan extended a warm welcome and said all Israelis deeply appreciated the timely support provided by the United States. He said the IDF would cooperate in every way with our fact-finding mission. At 0800 tomorrow morning at the Defense Ministry, the deputy defense minister would meet with me and arrange our itinerary with the IDF.

At 0800 the following morning, I met Dayan's deputy accompanied by IDF major general Rehavam Zeevi, the chief of the Department of Staff. After we made introductions and exchanged a few pleasantries while sitting around a coffee table, the deputy asked if I had an itinerary for our team visit. I extracted copies of our proposed itinerary from the briefcase and handed one to each Israeli. General Zeevi, who had been quiet up to this point, read the itinerary and slammed his fist down on the table. "We shed Israeli blood for America in this war. You are not going anywhere until the IDF has visited all these places first and written our own lessons learned!"

My response probably was not diplomatic but reflected an honest reaction. "Don't tell me that, General! You shed Israeli blood for Israel, not for America. You asked for supply support, and America gave it with the understanding that when the war ended, we could have a lessons learned team on the scene, free to examine everything that happened. If you don't honor our agreement, I will call Kissinger and ask him to stop sending anymore supplies immediately!"

486

They probably did not know whether I could call Kissinger and do this—and neither did I. However, this threat was the best card I could play. The deputy defense secretary intervened at this point. "General Leavitt, please come back tomorrow morning at 0800. We will have studied your request by then and will have an answer." I agreed; General Zeevi looked angry but said nothing.

The following morning we reconvened. Zeevi was silent. The deputy handed over the newly approved itinerary. It was exactly what we had requested. (Dropping Kissinger's name had worked.) The deputy also assigned an Army brigadier general to assist our team by answering requests for information and arranging transportation. The brigadier did an excellent job throughout the remainder of our visit.

The Yom Kippur War had not lasted long, but it included intense ground, air, and sea battles between opposing forces equipped with state-of-the-art Cold War weapons. The Soviet Union had armed and trained Egyptian and Syrian forces. IDF armaments came primarily from the United States, the UK, and factories in Israel. The lessons our team could learn would strengthen NATO as well as other American forces worldwide.

About two weeks later, General Zeevi telephoned me. "General Leavitt, I invite you and some of your colonels to come to my house for cocktails next Friday evening." We arrived at the specified time on Friday. After introductions, General Zeevi made a surprise announcement. "I want to apologize for what I said two weeks ago when we first met. Reports from the field say that your lessons learned team has been very helpful. They say the American team sees things with 'fresh eyes.' The IDF is learning things that probably would have been overlooked if your team had not been here."

General Zeevi and I became friends and remained in contact for a year or two. He began his involvement in Israeli politics after the war by consulting for Prime Minister Yitzhak Rabin's cabinet. In following years, he actively involved himself in right-wing Israeli politics. After forming the National Union Party in 1999, Zeevi became Sharon's tourism minister on 7 March 2001. Four Palestinian gunmen assassinated Rehavam Zeevi in an upstairs hallway of the Jerusalem Hyatt Hotel on 17 October 2001.

Learning lessons from Yom Kippur War. Major General Sharon is pointing across the Suez Canal and explaining his tactical success in splitting the Egyptian armies. The "civilians" are US officers and technicians on our joint team. General Leavitt is standing on Sharon's left.

Soviet BTR-60 armored personnel carrier. The Israeli army captured large numbers of Soviet tanks, armored personnel carriers, and artillery pieces. Our group had ample opportunity to examine the Soviet equipment in detail as well as to evaluate the performance of US weapons operated by Israeli defense forces.

Stouthearted Men

The history of warfare between nations is a recitation of increasing complexity that runs parallel to advances in technology. The best proof of that relationship during the Cold War era occurred when modern, well-prepared Egyptian and Syrian armies attacked Israel. The ever-increasing lethality of weapons; the interaction of air, ground, and naval systems; the importance of logistics; the dependence on comprehensive planning, reliable communications, and intelligence; and the rapidity with which things can happen all contributed to the complexity of war in October 1973.

Battles fought between the Arabs and Israelis provided data about weapon system effectiveness that were unattainable in even the best designed peacetime tests. With the cooperation of the IDF, technicians on our team tackled their job with enthusiasm. They searched for combat-generated data, analyzed their findings, and reported the strengths and weaknesses of most major weapon systems used during the war.

What has not changed over centuries of warfare is the requirement for skilled leadership and courageous warriors drawn from a populace that willingly makes sacrifices in order to save their nation. Israel made many mistakes before and during the war that could have meant a costly, perhaps fatal, defeat. The entire nation knew it was in a life-or-death struggle. What tipped the scales in favor of the IDF was its determination and resourcefulness—from senior commanders down to young draftees. The Egyptian and Syrian militaries were courageous, but there was a difference in motivation and leadership between the Arab forces and the IDF.

The Egyptian army—aided by Soviet advisors—planned, rehearsed, and executed the 6 October invasion across the Suez Canal. Plans included such details as the locations for unit flags after the army's invasion halted in the Sinai. The Egyptian attack was a brilliant success and quickly overran the Israeli forts along the canal. However, when confronted with the requirement to change tactics, the Egyptians were far less flexible than the Israelis.

An important battle in the Sinai demonstrated how the Egyptian army lacked flexibility. One day in November, I visited the

489

tank brigade commander in the Sinai who had played a key role in stopping the second Egyptian offensive. To protect his tanks from Sagger missiles, they were dug in on a sandy desert ridge overlooking a wadi, similar to the dry lake beds found in our Southwest. The Egyptian army had halted on the other side of the wadi after crossing the Suez Canal. An umbrella of SAM defenses and MiGs protected the Egyptians from Israeli air attacks.

When the Egyptians renewed their offensive into the Sinai, this outnumbered Israeli brigade stood in their way. On the first day, the Egyptian attack began with the sound of bugles blowing across the wadi. Soon, about 100 Soviet-built tanks became visible. Accompanying the tanks were 2,000 or 3,000 Egyptian infantry moving along with the tanks. The brigade commander focused his primary tank fire on the leading enemy tanks. One by one, his brigade destroyed the slow-moving Egyptian tanks and then shifted its fire against the Egyptian infantry. The attackers finally retreated after losing more than half of their tanks and hundreds of infantrymen.

Counterfire from the Egyptian tanks during the battle damaged several of the partially buried Israeli tanks. The Israeli brigade commander used the hours of darkness to replace his damaged tanks. Specialized vehicles carried them back to a repair facility. By morning, Israeli replacement tanks had arrived and were dug in.

The second and third days of the Egyptian assault repeated the pattern of the first day. By the end of three days of fighting, this brigade had destroyed or damaged several hundred Egyptian tanks and killed or wounded several thousand Egyptian soldiers. The Israeli brigade commander told me that the Egyptians could have overrun his outnumbered brigade on any of the three days by rapidly enveloping his position with fast-moving tanks, followed by attacking infantry. The inflexible tactics probably resulted from the refusal of high-ranking Egyptian officers to delegate authority to their field commanders. In stark contrast, Israeli field commanders accepted the responsibility for changing tactics whenever change seemed necessary.

Although the independence of Israeli commanders sometimes bordered on insubordination and occasionally resulted in recriminations after the war, the IDF tradition of "leading from the front" was a key factor in Israeli victories.

In November I visited Arik Sharon in his division headquarters near the canal. He was a gracious host and did not hesitate to elaborate on his role in the war or to answer questions. He first showed me where his command breached the huge earthen embankment on the east side of the Suez Canal. Sharon explained that he had preplanned this point of ingress and had deliberately weakened the embankment when he commanded the Southern Command. Red bricks identified the weak point. When he was ready to cross the canal, the weakened embankment quickly collapsed and opened the way for troops crossing into Egypt. Later, Sharon was accused by other senior generals of acting prematurely by crossing the canal without permission and leaving his flank exposed.

We crossed into Egypt and visited several company-size units deployed along the canal. Sharon had stopped the advance about 60 miles from Cairo. I asked, "Did you intend to take Cairo, knowing that most of the Egyptian army was deployed on the east side of the canal and would not be able to defend Cairo?" His answer was direct and made without hesitation. "No. There was no way my division of 8,000 Israeli troops could occupy and control Cairo, a city of five million people. My purpose in moving north along the canal was to destroy SAM sites and cut off any Egyptian efforts to resupply their forces trapped on the east bank in the Sinai." In later years, I have read books by Israeli authors stating Sharon wanted to take Cairo. I doubt it.

After eating lunch in a huge tent used for a mess hall and served by female Israeli soldiers, we drove from unit to unit followed by a small convoy from Sharon's staff. At every stop, soldiers appeared from nowhere shouting, "Arik! Arik!" Sharon would climb from the jeep and walk over to the troops, with the division photographer following close behind. The troops would crowd around Sharon before forming a semicircle with Sharon in the middle of the front row. The photographer would do his duty while Sharon shook hands and spoke briefly to the troops. There was no doubt in my mind after watching this scene repeated several times that Sharon was not only popular with his troops but had a strong political future. It was a memorable experience in many ways.

The Egyptians tried to isolate Israeli forces that had crossed the Suez Canal into Egypt. The opposing armies fought the largest tank battle since World War II east of the canal at an experimental Japanese farm, misnamed the Chinese Farm. For two nights and a day, a fierce battle raged, which the Israelis finally won. This battle protected Sharon's flank and ultimately sealed the fate of the Egyptian Third Army.

About two weeks after the battle ended, I walked the battlefield accompanied by an Israeli army colonel. Hundreds of destroyed tanks, armored vehicles, and artillery pieces painted with Israeli or Egyptian markings, never more than a few yards apart, cluttered the ground amidst the shell holes and other debris resulting from intense ground combat. Seeing the burned-out tank hulls and incredible destruction in this relatively small area left a lasting recollection of the horrors of war.

Another aspect of that battleground sticks in my mind. The USSR provided Sagger antitank missiles to destroy Israeli tanks. Wire-controlled Saggers, fired by Egyptian infantry, could penetrate tank armor using a shaped charge explosive. After penetrating, the molten hot metal traveling at extremely high speed ricocheted inside the tank, killing or severely burning the tank crew and often catching the tank interior on fire. Judaism requires that recoverable body parts be buried with the deceased. IDF rabbis had the solemn responsibility of searching through destroyed tanks and other vehicles in order to recover remains before repairs could begin on the tank.

Despite its heroic performance in combat, not all went well for the IDF. When Golda Meir decided to let the Arabs strike first, despite adequate warning, the war started badly. Blaming early defeats on the "surprise attack" provided political cover for less publicized prewar strategic errors. Probably the most serious prewar error was underestimating the impact that the Soviet SAMs and other air defense systems would have on both air and ground combat. The Israeli army expected the Israeli air force would gain and maintain absolute air superiority over the battlefield and enemy airspace, as it did in the 1967 Six-Day War. That did not happen in 1973.

The IAF had earned its well-deserved reputation for excellence. Top fighter aircrews, flying late-model F-4s and Mirages, were more than a match for Egyptian and Syrian aircrews in air-to-air combat. Because Israel is a small country, mainte-nance and repair facilities were usually collocated with opera-tional units. There, IAF aircraft were maintained in first-class shape. The United States kept the IAF abreast of our current technology, and our aid program made it possible for Israel to purchase state-of-the-art equipment. With all these positive factors, what caused the IAF to be less effective than in the Six-Day War?

Near the end of our visit, I spent nearly two days with Maj Gen Benjamin Peled, IAF chief commander. By then, nearly everyone in Israel agreed that the IAF had not met prewar ex-pectations. Our team had conducted interviews with IAF air-crews, studied aircraft loss rates, and analyzed battle damage reports. Those we interviewed were hesitant to point fingers at their leaders, but there was consensus that the IAF had failed to gain and maintain air superiority early in the war. Because the IAF failed, the Egyptians were able to cross the Suez Canal and advance without serious opposition into the Sinai. Because many IAF aircraft were lost or were ineffective while providing close air support on the northern front, the Syrian army came perilously close to Tel Aviv.

I wanted to hear Peled's explanations as to why Israel failed to gain air superiority early in the war. Peled knew the Soviet Union had replaced Egyptian and Syrian air defenses with modern systems after the 1967 Six-Day War. He knew the lo-cation of enemy early warning and GCI radars. He knew the location of the high-altitude SA-2 SAM sites and the medium-altitude SA-3 SAM sites. He had planned to destroy these systems as a first order of business. He knew that the Soviet ZSU-23-4, a low-altitude mobile system with four radar-controlled, rapid-firing cannons, was a formidable weapon, but he underestimated its lethality in combat. He also knew that the enemies pos-sessed the mobile SA-6 radar-controlled SAM system but knew little about its capabilities, and neither did the USAF. He knew that the Soviet SA-7, a heat-seeking, shoulder-fired missile, could be effective at low altitudes against slower aircraft, and he knew that the IAF lacked effective infrared countermeasures on all aircraft.

Peled correctly interpreted the available intelligence on 5 Oc-tober and knew that the Arabs would attack the following day.

493

He seized the initiative and ordered the IAF to load munitions for a preemptive attack. The IAF had a well-developed and rehearsed plan to attack the known air defenses of the Arab nations. Peled made a big mistake. He assumed Golda Meir would react to the ominous intelligence and authorize his preemptive attack. When Meir denied approval for the preemptive attack, Peled had to abandon his plan to gain air superiority.

Within the first few hours of the war, the Syrian attack overwhelmed many Israeli positions, and the Egyptians successfully crossed the Suez Canal. During our interview, Peled rationalized that the urgent need for CAS outweighed the necessity for air defense suppression. There were several reasons why his decision was questionable. The most important reason was that the IAF underestimated the lethality of the air defense systems supplied by the Soviets to Egypt and Syria. The IAF lost 79 aircraft, mostly to SAMs, in the first three days.

By 1972 the United States had been fighting the Soviet SA-2, SA-7, and ZSU-23-4 for several years in Vietnam. The total US investment in defense suppression was several billion dollars. Along with countermeasures, we developed special tactics for fighting in a high-threat environment. During the Vietnam War, we informed Israel of the necessity to protect its air forces from Soviet-supplied air defense systems. In fairness, IAF leaders recognized the serious SAM threat but had a belated interest in buying countermeasures. They did acquire some jamming pods for their fighters, and we provided additional pods during Nickel Grass. Several pilots reported they did not use them because of a rumor that SAMs could home in on the pod's jamming signal. The IAF had a particularly bad experience attacking a Syrian armor column protected by ZSU-23-4 mobile antiaircraft guns. It lost several aircraft in a low-level attack while flying down the length of the armor column.

The situation on the southern front differed from early battles between Israeli and Egyptian forces. The Egyptian army maintained an umbrella of SAM systems overhead while crossing the Suez Canal and invading the Sinai. The Egyptian army remained relatively immune from IAF air attacks because the IAF had not suppressed air defenses. Not until 14 October when the Egyptians began a new offensive and outran the protective SAM umbrella could the IAF provide CAS in the Sinai.

As the team neared the end of our visit, we still had not determined how our 24 newest F-4E models with Maverick missiles performed in combat. Every time evaluators had approached the F-4E issue, the IAF had shifted them off to another subject. None of the Israeli aircrews seemed to have any knowledge of the subject and did not offer any advice. I knew the USAF wanted an answer, and my plea to the SecDef for permission to send the new F-4Es to Israel hung over my head. Finally, frustrated at the IAF's stalling, I called Peled's office and asked for help. Two days later, we received permission to visit the air base with the new F-4Es.

The base commander apologized for the delay but explained that the IAF wanted to make a few minor modifications in the throttle quadrant and stiffen the wing a bit with a patch before using the F-4Es in combat. These "minor" changes had taken a little longer than expected, so "only a few of the new F-4Es saw combat." He said they did have film of a Soviet T-62 tank destroyed by a Maverick missile fired from an F-4E in combat. I took the film and had an intelligence analyst and photo interpreter examine it.

After the examination, the charade ended. Yes, there was a hole in the tank—probably caused by a Maverick missile. There was one problem. We had photographed this same destroyed tank several weeks earlier. Our earlier photo showed no Maverick hole but plenty of other holes. Because we kept inquiring about F-4E and Maverick combat results, the IAF flew a peacetime sortie against the dead tank and "killed" it again.

I confronted the IAF director of operations with the new facts. He apologized and admitted the IAF never flew the new F-4Es in combat because it had not finished the "minor" modifications before the war ended. I believe this incident was the only time the IDF tried to deceive us when we asked for information. Apparently the "urgent need" for replacement F-4s was no longer urgent when our latest model F-4Es arrived in Israel.

Before finishing our conclusions about IAF performance in the war, I needed frank conversations with IAF chief commander Ben Peled. After nearly two days' discussion, he reluctantly acknowledged that failing to suppress air defenses was a serious mistake and that the resulting lack of air superiority in the first three days nearly cost Israel the war. In my opinion, other senior

Israeli officials deserved the lion's share of the blame, especially Prime Minister Meir; Minister of Defense Dayan; and the director of intelligence, Maj Gen Eli Zeira. The Israeli commission that investigated the war treated Peled lightly. He remained IAF chief commander. Meir, Dayan, Zeira, Elazar, and others left office.

Ben Peled was a fine officer, and we became good friends. He visited my home in McLean after our return from Israel. Anne arranged a cocktail party in his honor. Three black limousines stopped in front of our house at the appointed hour. When the limo doors opened, Peled and his embassy escort entered the front door while their Israeli bodyguards guarded the limos and the house. I could see from the look on Anne's face that she had not suspected such security in our quiet neighborhood.

Ben Peled remained as the IAF chief commander after the war ended. He played a major role in the 1976 Entebbe Raid rescue of the Olympic hostages. An outspoken Zionist, he became bitter in later years. On his deathbed, 13 July 2002, with his family gathered near, he asked for a cigarette and a glass of wine. According to widely distributed reports in the Israeli press, his last words were "when I die, go out in the street and ring a big bell. When the neighbors will [sic] ask what happened, tell them that now dies a Jew that believed the Jews are able to create an independent state, and was wrong."[8]

I retired from the Air Force before the Israelis invaded Lebanon in 1982. Gen Charlie Gabriel, USAF chief of staff, sent me a brief note after the invasion: "Dick, they listened to what you said. This time they suppressed defenses first—no IAF losses. Charlie."

Although it was the smallest service in the IDF, the Israeli navy had an important role to play in the Yom Kippur War. Its job was stopping any infiltration of enemy forces or terrorists from the waters surrounding Israel and keeping shipping lanes open for the vital supplies arriving at Israeli ports. The navy was well prepared to fight a modern war at sea. Following the Six-Day War, the navy acquired small, fast missile boats equipped with the Israeli-built Gabriel missile. Both the Egyptian and Syrian navies equipped their missile boats with the longer-range Soviet Styx missile.

On 7 October, the Israelis engaged the Syrians off the Syrian port of Latakia. It was the first missile-to-missile battle in naval history. Although the Styx missiles had an advantage in range, the Israelis used ECM and avoided them. After the Syrians had expended all their missiles, the Israelis moved closer until the Syrian boats were within range of Gabriel missiles. They sunk four Syrian boats with no Israeli losses. The Syrian navy stayed in port for the rest of the war. A battle with the Egyptian navy off Damiette produced similar results. Gabriel missiles sank three Egyptian boats with no Israeli losses.

After completing our study effort in Israel, I briefed General Elazar and his staff on our findings. I asked Elazar if there were any surprises, particularly in new weapons or technology, which we missed or needed to know. His answer was illuminating. "There were no real surprises in weapons, technology, or tactics. The IDF lacked experience fighting against the new Soviet weapons such as the Sagger antitank missiles and SA-6 surface-to-air missiles, but we knew about their capabilities. *The only true surprise was the velocity of modern war.* We badly underestimated logistic requirements—how quickly ammunition would be depleted, how quickly so many guns, tanks, and aircraft would be destroyed or damaged, how many casualties would result in such a short time."

The team returned to the United States after briefing Elazar and his staff. Israel provided a unique learning experience for all of us, regardless of the color of our uniforms. It is difficult for Americans to grasp the impact that war has on such a small nation. Nearly every city block in Tel Aviv had a family with a son wounded or killed in the three-week war. Israel in 1973 had five million people. A rough equivalence for the United States would be 150,000 killed and 300,000 wounded in three weeks.

At the end of any war, you expect (or at least hope) for a permanent peace treaty. A disappointing aspect of the ending of the Yom Kippur War was the lack of any regional agreement. It seemed to me then, and seems to me now, that the differences between Israel and its Moslem neighbors are irreconcilable. Israel survives as a nation because it is stronger economically, politically, and militarily than its neighbors and has the support of the United States. If these factors change, in my opinion, Israel will have to depend upon nuclear deterrence and its abundant nuclear stockpile for survival.

Aftermath

When we returned to the Pentagon, there were numerous requests for briefings on survey team findings. The Army and Air Force staffs expressed highest interest because the major activity involved Israeli army and air force equipment and people. The first briefing I presented to the Air Staff generated numerous questions. From the tone of staff members' questions, it was clear our conclusions were contrary to their expectations about IAF performance during the war. When I returned to my J-3 office, a message from the Air Force chief of intelligence (DI) asked me to come to his office as soon as possible.

The DI, a clearly agitated major general, was sitting at his desk when I entered. He was a prolific writer with a history of strong opinions and controversial predictions. About 95 percent of the time, his soothsaying turned out to be correct. The remaining 5 percent was often embarrassing. He wasted no time getting to the point. "Dick, I want you to change your briefing and bring it into agreement with mine."

I knew why he wanted this. During the war, the DI had briefed the Air Staff on his analysis of events as they progressed. The DI's briefings on the Yom Kippur War fell into his 5 percent category. They amounted to a rehash of the 1967 Six-Day War, when the IAF had walked off with all the honors. The DI briefing ignored the difficulties that hampered IAF performance in the Yom Kippur War and downplayed the important army victories that stopped the Syrian invasion in the first three days and defeated the Egyptians later. My response was to the point. "General, as you know, I am assigned to the JCS, not the Air Staff. Our briefing reflected the interviews and data collected under our charter as the US Military Operational Survey Team. Our mission was to provide an objective after-action report on our visit to the Israeli Defense Forces. The survey team included well-qualified experts from all the services including the Air Force. I am satisfied the briefing accurately portrays what really happened during the Yom Kippur War. The war was certainly not a redo of the 1967 war for the IAF. USAF should study our after-action report and avoid the mistakes made by the IAF. The briefing stands as is, General." The meeting ended at that point. He never spoke to me again.

A few days later, my secretary said the Air Force chief of staff wanted to see me in his office. I had never met General Brown, the new chief. He commanded Seventh Air Force for more than two years during the Vietnam War and also had an extensive background in R&D.[9] Gen Richard Ellis, vice chief of staff, was talking to General Brown when I entered the chief's office not knowing what the subject was.

General Brown had a memo in his hand written by a major in Air Force Operations and forwarded by General Gabriel. Charlie replaced me in the Air Staff when I went to the JCS in 1972, and he was now the deputy director of operations. The memo alleged that our after-action report criticized the A-10—a new USAF R&D program scheduled to begin production in 1974.

General Brown said, "I understand you are opposed to the A-10 program and that your report backs that position." I told General Brown that in my role in the JCS I had no position on the A-10 program. There was no mention of the A-10 in the after-action report. The Air Staff had extrapolated data about Israeli A-4 battle damage and losses and concluded that if the SA-7 could damage or destroy the slower A-4, it could damage or destroy the A-10.

My answer was, "I can't disguise the data. That is a lesson that came out of the war about Israeli A-4s and should be viewed that way." The operational survey team had collected data on all IAF destroyed and damaged aircraft. The after-action report included an analysis of aircraft vulnerability to the Soviet-built SA-7, a shoulder-fired, heat-seeking missile. The IAF flew two models of the Douglas A-4 on ground attack missions. The newer models flew about 50 knots faster than the older when attacking targets. Statistics indicated that the added 50 knots reduced A-4 vulnerability against the SA-7, since a disproportionate number of the older, slower A-4s were lost or suffered battle damage from SA-7s.

General Brown had reason to be concerned about a critic misquoting, or a staff officer taking out of context, the A-4 data in our report. This was a tough financial year for the Air Force. Several "big ticket" items were in advanced development or early stages of deployment, including the F-15, B-1, F-16, EF-111, Minuteman III, and A-10.

The A-10 ("A" for attack) program responded to the need for an Air Force aircraft capable of providing CAS, tank busting, and other tactical missions at low altitude. The principal A-10 weapon is a 30 mm cannon that can rapidly fire depleted uranium (DU) rounds. When these heavy DU rounds strike a target, the impact is many times the destructive force of standard 30 mm rounds. The damage usually devastates armored vehicles. However, one characteristic of the A-10 created controversy. It was much slower than our jet fighters. Critics questioned whether the A-10 could survive at low altitude against enemy targets protected by modern air defense systems.

All military aircraft result from a series of compromises, such as range, speed, maneuverability, armament, survivability, weight, and cost. One design does not fit all purposes. Although air defenses have more time to shoot at slower aircraft, the slower aircraft can generally fly longer, carry more munitions, and see targets better—important virtues on a CAS sortie. The designers knew that a slower aircraft would be more vulnerable, so they compensated by making the A-10 an exceptionally rugged aircraft. The design had many survivability features, including a titanium "bathtub" cockpit to protect the pilot from shrapnel and small arms fire, both engines mounted above the wings to protect the engines and to reduce infrared exposure, and fuel tanks with fire suppressors.

General Brown did not take my explanation adversely, as near as I could tell. Three years later, I worked for General Ellis in USAFE. He told me that General Brown said after I left, "You know, I'm not sure that I agree with Leavitt about the conclusions that could be drawn from this, but I do respect his right to make that kind of a statement, and I think he told it straightforward."

A few days after General Brown's meeting, Gen Robert Dixon wanted to hear the briefing. Dixon had recently assumed command of TAC after serving as deputy chief of staff for personnel. I first met him in 1962 when he was a colonel in War Plans, and our paths had crossed several times in the interim. Dixon had a reputation for being caustic at times and very demanding of subordinates, but he was intelligent, forward-thinking, and generally objective. Although I liked Dixon very much and looked forward to briefing him, I expected that sparks might fly over the A-10 issue.

The briefing at Headquarters TAC went well. His staff asked a few questions, as did Dixon. Then he complimented me on the briefing and told me to come to his office. After the door shut, he said with an angry look on his face, "Leavitt, are you trying to piss off every four-star general in the Air Force? The major general promotion board meets in two weeks. How in hell do you expect to be promoted under these circumstances?"

Dixon's remarks discouraged me. During the past two years on the JCS staff, I always tried to be evenhanded with the services and did not expect the Air Force would want it any other way. The survey team report was no exception. Did a senior Air Force general and A-10 advocate complain about the A-4 findings to General Brown and other four-star generals? Was I going to become the sacrificial goat? "General Dixon, I have been doing my best. If that is not good enough for the Air Force, I suppose I'll have to find something else to do." With that, the meeting ended, and I returned to the Pentagon.

A few weeks later, the Air Force published the names of the 14 brigadier generals selected for promotion to major general that year. The board president was General Dixon. I ranked third on the list and first in my year group—a pleasant surprise that ended my paranoia over the A-10 flap.

A few days later, Lt Gen John Roberts, the Air Force chief of personnel, called with congratulations and a question. "Dick, what kind of job do you want for your next assignment—staff or command?" Without hesitation, I answered, "Command!" His answer was encouraging, "I thought you might say that. I'll see what we can do."

Diego Garcia

The Suez Canal remained closed to shipping after the war ended. Israeli and Egyptian mines, unexploded bombs, and other munitions had made passage extremely dangerous. Regional operations tasked the Navy to sweep mines and the Army to recover and demolish munitions dumped in the canal during the war. These dangerous tasks were finished without an accident or injury. A US Navy ship became the first to pass safely through the canal. Several weeks later, commercial shipping resumed. This operation was also a reminder that war in the Middle East could close the Suez Canal to shipping.

Arab oil nations flexed their muscles during the Yom Kippur War by reducing oil production as a protest against our aiding Israel. Their embargo taught an important lesson; our economy was too dependent upon Middle Eastern oil. If radical Arab regimes endangered our economic interests, would our military be able to intervene?

Although the powerful US Sixth Fleet dominated the Mediterranean, the distance from the Mediterranean to likely targets in the Middle East exceeded the normal range of carrier aircraft. Cold War requirements largely determined where we located our military forces. For that reason, the US Navy maintained only a small presence in the Persian Gulf and Arabian Sea. A US carrier from the Pacific Fleet would on occasion steam through the Indian Ocean and remain for a short time in the Arabian Sea. We lacked a deep water port in the Indian Ocean and a location for monitoring communications in that volatile part of the world that included India, Pakistan, and northeast Africa.

In 1966 a treaty between the UK and United States called the Anglo-American Exchange of Notes made the Chagos Archipelago, which included the atoll of Diego Garcia, available for defense purposes. The United States wanted an unpopulated island for security reasons, so the UK relocated the population and avoided UN sanctions by stating that the relocated people were workers, not natives. In 1970 a second US-UK treaty allowed the United States to build a naval facility for communications on Diego Garcia under a lease that expires in 2016.

The closest major Asian nation to Diego Garcia is India, about 1,000 miles to the north. One issue that particularly bothered the Indian government was the American naval base on Diego Garcia. Its stated objection centered on keeping the Indian Ocean as a nonmilitarized zone. Since India, Pakistan, Indonesia, and other nations bordering the Indian Ocean already had substantial military forces, its objection had a rather hollow ring.

Pres. Gerald Ford appointed the intellectual and very competent Daniel Patrick Moynihan as our ambassador to India. Moynihan, who later served four terms as the Democratic senator for New York, frequently lit up the State Department and

Pentagon with his witty, sometimes sarcastic, and always inci-sive reports. He stressed, among other things, that our com-munications with the Indian government must improve.

Rather than challenging the Indian government himself, Moynihan asked the JCS to send a representative to New Delhi. The JCS representative would meet with senior Indian military officials and address the Indian equivalent of our National War College. His primary objective was to explain that our Navy in-stallation on Diego Garcia would not threaten India. It would serve only as a communications and logistics link between American forces located on both sides of the Indian Ocean.

When Vice Adm Jerry King, J-3, said that I would leave for India in a few days, it was unexpected. From reading the message traffic back and forth from New Delhi to Washington, I realized the political atmosphere would probably be anti-American and perhaps even hostile. Jerry told me to report to Admiral Moorer, CJCS, who would explain the background and objectives. Moorer thoroughly explained the purpose of the trip. When he finished, out of curiosity I asked him, "Admiral, Diego Garcia is a Navy base; why not send a Navy admiral instead of an Air Force general?"

After nearly two years of experience on his JCS staff, I knew that he was not only a superb leader but had a great sense of humor. As I was getting up to leave, he answered my question with a big smile on his face. "You don't understand, Dick. The Navy can't afford to lose an admiral!" I laughed and went back to prepare for the trip.

The India trip was unexpectedly pleasant. The American Em-bassy scheduled background briefings with our embassy staff, followed by meetings with Indian military officials. The Indian general officers were friendly, engaged in frank discussions, and eager to have closer relations with the US military. They discussed the pros and cons of their own equipment while showing no desire to remain solely dependent upon the Soviet Union for military equipment or for anything else. The air force chief knew about our newest fighter aircraft and was clearly envious, except for the price. The generals seemed to accept our reasons for using Diego Garcia. I left with the impression that Diego Garcia was simply an issue raised by certain politicians to improve their public image—reminiscent of political arguments in the US Congress.

The student population at the war college included lieutenant colonels and colonels from India and many other countries in the Middle East and Southeast Asia. I talked about our foreign policy as it affected the US military, our Cold War concerns, and other obligations. The students wore uniforms and identified themselves by name, rank, and nationality during the question and answer session that followed. Questions were friendly and spoken in polite terms. After answering several questions, I realized they knew little about America's obligations and objectives as one of two superpowers.

The unfriendly exception was an officer in the front row. My presentation and answers to questions had clearly agitated this officer. When handed the microphone, he announced he was an Air Force colonel from Syria—or Iraq, I do not remember which. He launched into a tirade about American foreign policy in the Middle East, our support for Israel during the Yom Kippur War, and our capitalistic exploitation of smaller nations. The other students were not reacting positively to his outburst, so I thanked him for his opinions and turned to another student. The positive reaction by the other students and faculty suggested that the Pentagon should schedule more such visits to other nations.

The Navy base at Diego Garcia continued to grow in size and importance in the 1970s. In 1974 the UK and the United States agreed to expand the roles and missions of the base. During the three Middle East wars the United States has since fought— the first Gulf War liberating Kuwait beginning in 1990, liberation of Afghanistan from the Taliban beginning in 2001, and the Second Iraq War beginning in 2003—Diego Garcia has been a key base for port facilities, communications, logistics, and our long-range bombers. Today, Diego Garcia is one of our largest and most important overseas bases (see fig. 9).

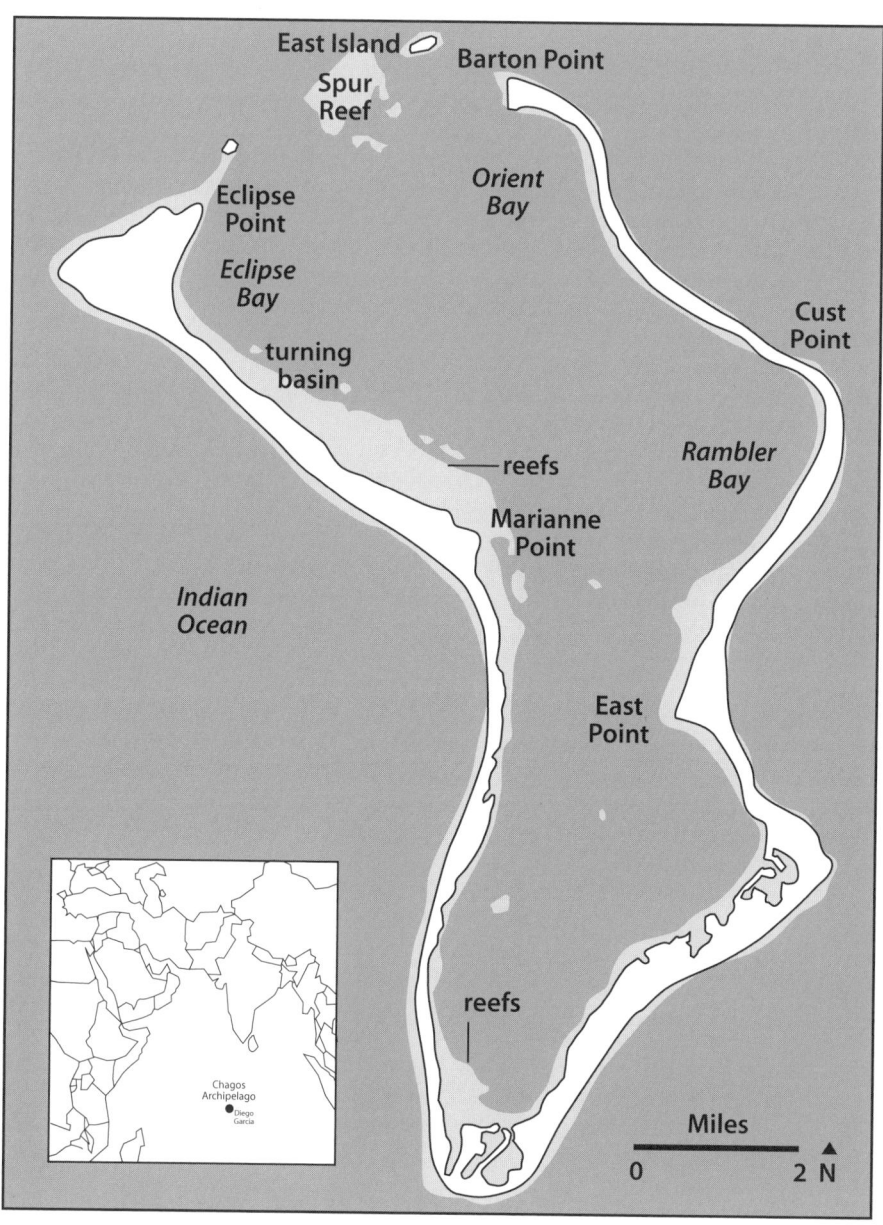

Figure 9. Map of Diego Garcia. Diego Garcia is an atoll in the Chagos Archipelago approximately 1,000 miles south of India in the Mid-Indian Basin. Diego Garcia–based aircraft can reach points of interest in the Middle East, West Africa, Southeast Asia, Australia, Thailand, and Indonesia.

Notes

1. Author's note: As the J-3, deputy director for regional operations, in the JCS, I was directly involved in monitoring the early stages of the Yom Kippur War; in preparing Nickel Grass, the massive airlift to Israel; and in raising the DEFCON on 20 October. As the war ended, I went to Israel as the head of the joint service team composed of Army, Navy, and Air Force personnel. Our tasks were to analyze the campaign strategies and tactics, study equipment strengths and weaknesses, and write the lessons learned report for the JCS. If there is a historical advantage to the following recital, it traces to my opportunity to see the war from two different perspectives: first, explaining the actions taken by the Pentagon, and second, explaining the actions taken by Israel during the war.

2. Buckwalter, "1973 Arab-Israeli War," 121–26. The author details the period of Israeli indecision leading to a near catastrophe for Israel and describes the excuses offered by Meir.

3. The comments in this and four succeeding paragraphs are summarized from personal discussions with Major General Peled in Tel Aviv during my fact-finding mission in November and December 1973.

4. An insight provided by Gen John Wickham, former chief of staff, US Army. During the Yom Kippur War, (then) Brigadier General Wickham served as the military assistant to the SecDef. A 1950 West Point graduate, he received two master's degrees from Harvard and graduated from the Army Command and General Staff College and the National War College. During the Vietnam War, he commanded a battalion in the 1st Air Cavalry Division, earning two Silver Stars, the Legion of Merit, a Bronze Star Medal with valor, 11 Air Medals, a Purple Heart, and the Combat Infantryman Badge. In a series of important assignments over the next two decades, General Wickham was awarded three Defense Distinguished Service Medals, four Distinguished Service Medals from the services, and two Legions of Merit. General Wickham retired in 1987. He received the West Point Distinguished Graduate Award in 2005. US Military Academy, *Register of Graduates*.

5. Morris, *Righteous Victims*, 434.

6. Rabinovich, *Yom Kippur War*, 465–79.

7. Ibid., 484.

8. Peled's widely quoted deathbed statement may have reflected his concerns that increasing numbers of orthodox Jews in the Likud (parliament) would jeopardize Israel's image as the heritage home for all Jews.

9. General Brown graduated from West Point in 1941 and served in the Eighth Air Force during WWII, earning the Distinguished Service Cross, Silver Star, two Distinguished Flying Crosses, and six Air Medals. During the Korean War, he served at Fifth Air Force, earning the Legion of Merit and Bronze Star Medal before returning to the United States for a series of staff and command assignments of ever-increasing importance. During the Vietnam War, he was deputy commander of MACV and commander of Seventh Air Force from 1968 to 1970, earning the Distinguished Service Medal. He commanded Air Force Systems Command from 1970 to 1973 and became chief of staff, USAF, in 1973 and chairman, JCS, in 1974, serving until 1978. General Brown died on 5 December 1978. US Air Force, "Biographies: General George Scratchley Brown."

Chapter 13

Commanding Chanute
Major General—1974-76

Training Young Airmen

A few weeks later, Lt Gen John Roberts, chief of Air Force Personnel, called again. "Do you still want a command?" I answered, "Yes sir, and do not care where." Roberts then said, "That's good because you are going to command the large technical training center at Chanute Air Force Base, Illinois." Although an Air Training Command assignment had not occurred to me, I looked forward to going to Chanute after my two-year JCS tour ended in July.

The JCS assignment provided a unique education in how high-level White House and Defense and State Department officials operate in times of crisis. The leaders in my chain of command—JCS chairman Adm Thomas Moorer; JCS director Lt Gen George Seignious; and J-3 director Vice Adm Jerry King—were exceptional men who contributed their experience, effort, and wisdom to solving America's serious problems from the ending of the Vietnam War through the aftermath of the Yom Kippur War.

Before leaving for Chanute, I received the Distinguished Service Medal (DSM) for my work on the JCS. The DSM is our highest military noncombat award. Although the DSM had my name on the citation, the talented officers and enlisted personnel from the Army, Navy, Marines, and Air Force serving in Regional Operations made it happen. Led by highly trained and experienced colonels and Navy captains, each branch of Regional Operations had produced outstanding advice and staff work. Too often, we may overlook the important work performed by the civil service staff. I will never forget my secretary, Diane Crumley, who kept paperwork flowing, knew all about JCS procedures, corrected my misspelled words, and deciphered my incoherent dictation. Thanks, Diane!

We spent three weeks on leave in Michigan and Arkansas before reporting to Chanute. The highways from Michigan to Arkansas pass through central Illinois, so we stopped in Rantoul for a quick, incognito visit to Chanute AFB. Chanute was the third oldest air base in the Air Force, named for Octave Chanute, an early pioneer in aviation history and credited for inventing ailerons. Thousands of technicians and aircrews in the Army Air Forces during World War II trained at Chanute. Renamed in 1972, the USAF School of Applied Aerospace Sciences (USAF-SAAS) at Chanute trained about 25,000 personnel each year with a faculty of 1,600 civilian and military instructors.

As I drove slowly through the base wearing civilian clothes, my first impression was disappointment. Chanute looked bad. It lacked the well-kept military appearance of most USAF installations. Without prompting, Anne interrupted my thoughts. "What have you done wrong that they sent you here?" I told her to ignore first impressions. After we resumed driving, my mind focused on Chanute and the challenges ahead.

We returned to Chanute for the change-of-command ceremony on 27 July 1974. The presiding officer was Lt Gen William V. McBride, ATC commander. (One month later, McBride pinned on his fourth star and became commander, Air Force Logistics Command.) After the ceremony, he explained why the USAF assigned me to Chanute. ATC training centers had a reputation for being the last stop before retirement for older major generals. General McBride was changing that reputation by placing younger major generals in command who could better relate to the people in training and who would probably progress further in their own Air Force careers. In a press interview after the ceremony, he made laudatory remarks about my Air Force career that helped community leaders in Rantoul and Champaign-Urbana understand the change.

My predecessor, Maj Gen Frank W. Elliot, left a lasting, favorable impression on the citizens of Rantoul. Good commanders focus on problems that need attention. Following the Kent State shootings in May 1970, University of Illinois students and other activists had disrupted traffic leading to Chanute and picketed the base. In the minds of many local leaders, the center commander at that time overreacted. When Frank Elliot replaced him in August 1972, the anti–Vietnam War movement was still active. Within a year, Frank gained "the hearts and minds" of the leaders in Rantoul and surrounding communities. Whatever rancor and ill feeling that existed were gone. Following the change-of-command ceremony and reception, we spent the rest of the day moving our furniture and clothes into our quarters on base. The house was nice with a big backyard that our two dogs appreciated. After the last bag was unpacked and Trig brought us dinner from some fast-food restaurant, I went to bed thinking about the meetings scheduled for the next day. An hour or two later, the red phone rang. The security police reported a fight in the student dormitory between two Airmen— one black, the other white. An hour or two later, the phone rang again. Someone rang the fire alarm in the large dormitory where the female Airmen lived. It proved to be a false alarm but forced all the women to evacuate the dormitory. These middle-of-the-night phone calls about incidents occurred every night before I found solutions.

Before the change of command, I drove carefully around the base photographing areas that needed "bucking up." At the end of the first meeting with the center staff and commanders, I flashed these photos on the screen with their location. Their excuses were interesting. "We don't have enough civil engineers to mow the grass." "The squadron commanders are busy with student problems and should not be responsible for base appearance." "The barracks are old and hard to keep clean." "Most Airmen just finished basic training and are adjusting to the real Air Force." The litany of excuses continued, but I had heard enough.

Before the first staff meeting ended, I asked all of the colonels to schedule a tour through their areas of responsibility. They should be ready to answer detailed questions and provide a thorough briefing before the tour ended. I needed to know the "good and the bad"—the successes and major problems in everyone's area of responsibility. Accompanying me would be Chanute's vice-commander, Col (later Brig Gen) Dennis B. Sullivan, who provided invaluable advice and suggestions during this orientation tour, as well as afterwards, until reassigned in July 1975.[1]

After completing the orientation tours, I had a much better appreciation of Chanute's mission and people. In area, population, and facilities, Chanute was similar to many medium-sized colleges in the Midwest: located on 2,125 acres of rich Illinois farmland, it accommodated numerous buildings filled with classrooms and training aids; library, gymnasium, baseball fields, swimming pools, tennis courts, golf course, and a movie theater; officer, NCO, and Airmen clubs; a commissary and base exchange; housing for 1,230 families and dormitories for several thousand students; a 35-bed hospital; an airfield for light planes; and a base population of about 12,000 during working hours.

With multiple roles in air and space, the Air Force demands are high for technically qualified personnel. Applicants must be at least high school graduates or equivalent, and many will have a year or more of college. The Air Force tests for aptitudes before applicants enlist, and those who show ability for a particular career field can select it. Recruits enter with the grade of Airman basic and must complete basic training before progressing to technical training.

Chanute taught over 100 courses including Aircraft Maintenance, Missile and Space Systems Maintenance, Transportation and Vehicle Maintenance, Fuels, Firefighting, Precision Measurement, Aircrew Personal Equipment, and Weather. The Aircraft Maintenance Officer Course (AMOC) trained junior and middle-grade officers to be aircraft maintenance officers. The length of courses varied but averaged four or five months. Approximately 120 foreign students from Iran and Saudi Arabia were also in training.

Airmen who successfully complete technical training are qualified as "3-level" technicians, equivalent to apprentices in civilian life. In their next assignment, NCOs will train and supervise them in "OJT"—on-the-job training. After gaining experience and passing written examinations, they will become "5-level" technicians, equivalent to journeymen in civilian life. Chanute also taught advanced courses to upgrade career NCOs from 5-level so they could become 7-level supervisors.

The USAF chief of staff called a few days after the change-of-command ceremony. He was concerned about reports by our local Office of Special Investigations (OSI) that stated Chanute had a serious, growing problem with race relations. The chief said that I had a good reputation with minorities and that I should resolve this problem. My first nights at Chanute had already made me aware of fighting between blacks and whites. The chief's comments strengthened my resolution to act quickly.

After serious disturbances occurred at several Air Force bases, Headquarters USAF created a new staff agency on each air base called Social Actions. The staff's job was listening to racial and other complaints involving discrimination, investigating the complaints, and finding solutions. A white captain, a black sergeant, and two civilian employees staffed Social Actions at Chanute.

The sergeant in Social Actions arranged an appointment with me. Personnel provided the sergeant's records before the meeting. After he introduced himself, I asked the sergeant to sit down and tell me what was on his mind. He was very articulate and clearly confident of his position. "General, first of all, you should know that I represent all the blacks on Chanute and speak for them. Second, I am warning you there is going to be a riot at Rantoul High School between blacks and whites. The racial situation is bad there, and the riot may start today or tomorrow!"

My response may not have been what he expected. "Sergeant, you are a 32-year-old tech sergeant who has been in the Air Force for 13 years and has a college degree. The black 18-year-old Airman, fresh out of basic, has little in common with you except skin color. You do not represent or speak for all the blacks on Chanute. . . . That is my job. I represent and speak for all Chanute personnel, regardless of color. You and your captain in Social Actions have important jobs. Working together, we can solve many problems. Next time you want to talk, make sure you come together. After you leave today, I'll call Rantoul High and get the principal's opinion about the impending riot."

I called the principal about the possibility of a riot in Rantoul High, where my daughter Mary was a freshman. After he discussed the possibility of a race riot with his staff and talked to student leaders, the principal called back and denied any possibility of a race riot. I called Social Actions and told the captain and the sergeant there was no riot impending. After this rough beginning, the sergeant and I got along well. He was really a highly qualified and effective NCO. A year later, I helped him enter Officer Candidate School at Lackland and earn a commission as a second lieutenant.

A young second lieutenant prepared the weekly OSI reports. His recent reports were long on assumption and hearsay and short on facts. He built ominous warnings largely from one-on-one fights in the barracks. After reading these "sky is falling down" reports, I understood the chief of staff's concern. We changed the local OSI policy: I would review the lieutenant's reports before they went to OSI headquarters.

Strict discipline and close supervision in basic training kept racial strife under control. Instructors stressed that pejorative words such as "nigger" and "honky" were not permissible and were racial insults. Basic training also taught recruits about the *Uniform Code of Military Justice* and obeying lawful orders. Recruits learned that Airmen with less than six months' service were effectively on probation and could be discharged for failing to meet Air Force standards and regulations. The typical Airman in training at Chanute had less than six months' service, and I had the authority to administer those convenience-of-the-government discharges.

Chanute's objective was to prepare Airmen for their next job in an operational USAF squadron. For that reason, Airmen were given more freedom so they could mature in ways that would enhance their value to themselves and to their new unit. Despite our good intentions, a few Airmen in technical training reverted to old habits while working or socializing with Airmen of a different race or national origin.

Security Police reported racial fights nearly every night. They were ignoring warnings by their chain of command to stop this fighting. Realizing this, I announced a tough new policy. The policy's success depended upon a major assumption: recruits are volunteers who completed basic training and will want to stay in the Air Force. Therefore, they will comply with the new policy.

Every squadron commander announced the new policy in squadron meetings for two days. Students signed statements verifying that they understood the policy. The meetings stressed that racial epithets and fighting must stop. Furthermore, participants in an interracial fight would report to my office at 0800 the following morning. I would interview each fight participant and ask what caused the fight. After listening to both, I would determine who caused the fight and administratively discharge the instigator. The first sergeant would escort the individual from the base by 1700 that same day.

A few days later, two Airmen were waiting outside my office at 0800. SP reported that they started fighting over a pool game in their squadron recreation room. I interviewed Jones, a black Airman, first. "The SP report says you hit Smith and started the fight. Why did you hit him?" His answer, "General, he was cheating and when I caught him, he got mad and called me 'nigger.' That's why I hit him. I'm sorry."

I told Jones to leave and interviewed Smith. "General, I wasn't cheating and got mad because he looked like he might hit me. I lost my temper and called him 'nigger,' and that's when he hit me." I asked Smith, "Did you learn in basic training not to use racial epithets? Did you get briefed by your squadron commander here about racial sensitivity, not calling names, and not fighting?" Smith said he had to answer yes to both my questions. "Airman Smith, report to your first sergeant and collect your belongings. I am administratively discharging you. Leave Chanute by 1700 today—dismissed."

After Smith left, Jones knocked at my door. He told me that Smith was a good friend of his and that he did not want to see him discharged. "That's too bad, Airman Jones. When you go back to the squadron, tell your friends that I mean business; no more fighting, and no more racial name-calling."

Two days later, a similar incident occurred. This time, I discharged the black Airman who caused the fight. The word spread, and the fighting stopped. Although this tough policy calmed things down, there were other serious racial problems at Chanute.

Rantoul and Chanute were figuratively joined at the hip—walk out the front gate of Chanute and you are in Rantoul. A community racial problem traced to the Order of Moose, a fraternal organization in Rantoul. Moose membership provided a social venue beyond what was available on the air base. Moose membership also included a substantial number of Chanute's white NCOs. Black NCOs who tried to join were not accepted. Minority officers and NCOs resented this discriminatory Moose practice and brought it to my attention. The senior Airmen advisor on my staff was an outstanding white NCO named Chief Master Sergeant McLaren. Chief McLaren, not a Moose member, tried to convince Chanute NCOs who were Moose members to change their discriminatory policy. Despite his efforts, nothing changed. I discussed this issue with several civic leaders. They sympathized but saw no way to change the Moose policy.

The Air Force was pushing hard for affirmative action. Broadening the base for racial minorities and women in management positions was an Air Force goal. One weapon used was the performance report for officers and Airmen. A mandatory comment in every performance report was whether the individual supported equal opportunity. This mandatory comment provided the muscle I needed to force the Moose to change.

The chain of command went to work. Group and squadron commanders told Chanute NCOs belonging to the Order of Moose they had three choices: their best choice, change the Moose membership policy and accept minority members; second best, resign their Moose membership in protest against the discriminatory policy; worst choice, receive a performance report stating they do not support equal opportunity.

Before long, the local head Moose wanted a meeting in my office. He stated "whites only" was a national Moose tradition. If my policy made the active duty NCOs quit, the loss of income would close the local lodge. My reply was unsympathetic. "Get your national headquarters to allow the change, or go out of business—your choice."

After this meeting, I asked a black chief master sergeant if he would apply for Moose membership. The head Moose quietly invited him to become a member, thereby "proving" that the Moose members were not prejudiced. The chief accepted membership on one condition—all minorities could join without regard to race. The Moose finally desegregated their lodge rather than have their NCO members suffer career damage.

Racial tension lessened after removing discriminatory practices, but gender discrimination still existed. Congress authorized Women in the Air Force (WAF) in June 1948. During the two years that I commanded Chanute, the separate status of the WAF still legally existed. Despite the official difference in status, WAFs and males trained side by side at Chanute in common courses.

There were problems. Because WAFs lived in a separate dormitory, male Airmen would hang around the sidewalks surrounding the WAF dormitory and harass the women entering and leaving. Setting fire alarms to go off in the middle of the night at the WAF dorm was a favorite male sport. A bigger problem was the number of WAFs eliminated from technical training for academic failure.

The average WAF scored higher in most categories of the AFQT, was a year older than the average male, and often had a year or more of college or junior college before enlisting. Despite these better qualifications, WAF eliminations ran approximately 50 percent higher than those for male Airmen—5 to 6 percent were male and 9 to 10 percent female. I believed the quality of WAF training suffered in comparison to male training and caused higher WAF attrition.

Chanute assigned males to squadrons by their specialty. For example, jet engine mechanics lived together, marched to school together, attended classes taught by the same instructors, trained on the same jet engines, and exercised, ate meals, and studied together. They lived and breathed jet engines from the time they arrived at Chanute until they left for an operational unit. Chanute did not assign the 400–500 WAFs to training squadrons by specialty. Instead, they lived in a separate female dormitory because there were too few WAFs available in any career field to form separate female squadrons.

Thirty years later, the answer seems obvious: integrate women and male Airmen into the same training squadrons. In 1974, when I first proposed doing this, it raised eyebrows. Before going any further, I tested the WAF reaction at Chanute to integrating. They assembled in the base theater to listen to the proposed change. There were two critical issues. First, did they want to be in the same school squadrons as men? Second, would they agree to living in the same barracks as men, although on a separate floor guarded from male access? After the briefing and questions ended, I asked for a yes or no vote. More than 90 percent voted yes on both issues.

While the staff worked on necessary details to accomplish the merger, letters arrived from concerned parents. "Is my daughter safe living in the same barracks as men?" I wrote back assuring them their daughters would be safe and protected from attack. When plans were completed, we had a second meeting in the auditorium. I briefed all the details before asking for a vote. The WAFs voted 97 percent for the final integration plan.

It was time to ask Lt Gen George McKee, ATC commander, to let Chanute be the test case for integrating WAFs into the real Air Force. McKee was a very progressive commander and a great boss. His thoughtful response was to go ahead with the test, quantify the results, and keep him informed. As months passed, the collected data showed significant improvements in academics. Washout rates dropped for both sexes and were now approximately equal at 4 to 5 percent. Incident rates such as AWOL, Article 15s, venereal disease, unmarried pregnancies, and drug arrests were all down. I attributed the overall success to integrating men and women in training. American society does not normally isolate the sexes, particularly in public school systems. It was not surprising that Air Force training improved after integrating.

General McKee and his successor, Lt Gen John Roberts, subsequently approved our program for the other technical training bases and led the way to integrating women in the USAF. Congress discontinued the WAF in June 1976, and women finally became equal in the Air Force. This was a major accomplishment during my time at Chanute.

One day the new ATC commander, General Roberts, called. "Dick, I received a call from the State Department with a strange request. An important Saudi prince is arriving next week for your AMOC. There is one problem. A husband can bring only one wife into the United States on his visa. The prince will not come unless he can bring both his wives. Since State does not want to offend the Saudis and the prince is a rising star in the Saudi Air Force, State wants us to overlook this little problem in international 'affairs.' [We both laughed.] The prince agreed not to appear in public with both wives. Keep this low key and out of the press."

The prince arrived on the appointed day. Protocol prepared our best guest quarters for his visit, and all seemed to be going well. That night, Anne and I went to the Officers' Club for dinner. Surprise! The prince was sitting at a nearby table with both wives . . . never mind the State Department agreement. The local media never noticed during his training that both wives were with him, so the Two Wives Caper became a nonevent.

The largest contingent of foreign students came from Iran. The Shah, Mohammad Reza Pahlavi, was building a modern tactical air force with the aid of American industry and USAF advisors. To fill the technical requirements, he drafted college graduates with engineering degrees. Their rank in the Iranian air force was roughly equivalent to the US rank of warrant officer. More than 100 were always at Chanute attending aircraft maintenance courses.

After completing training, graduates went to air bases in Iran as maintenance technicians. Although the Iranian students did not openly complain about their status in the Shah's new air force, a Saudi captain assigned to Chanute told me the Iranian students were not happy with their status. They accepted the draft but objected to their indefinite status with no separation date for returning to civilian life.

The Shah's autocratic regime and the behavior of his family and followers created widespread resentment. Following the revolution, the Shah fled Iran on 16 January 1979. Gen "Dutch" Huyser, Pres. Jimmy Carter's envoy, was sent to Tehran in a last-ditch effort to keep Iran democratic. Huyser told Gen Dick Ellis and me in 1980 that disgruntled warrant officers led the rebellion at Iranian air bases.

Chanute Gets Haircut and Shave

Technical training is the bridge between basic training and the "real" Air Force. Impressions formed during technical training—good and bad—influence students' attitudes about their Air Force future. Mentioned earlier was the poor appearance of Chanute. I wanted the young men and women in training at Chanute to understand that the Air Force is all about high standards. When they left Chanute, they needed to know that high standards extended beyond work and included the air base community where they would live.

Chanute was the primary source for training maintenance technicians for SAC bombers, tankers, and ICBMs. During the Cold War, deterrence remained the highest priority mission assigned to the Department of Defense. Deterrence depended upon SAC maintaining enough in-commission aircraft and missiles necessary to retaliate against any Soviet nuclear attack. Because of its nuclear responsibilities, SAC maintained the highest stan-

ATC Commanders' Conference, HQ ATC, Randolph AFB, Texas, 1975. *Left to right, front row*: Maj Gen Winfield W. Scott, Jr., Keesler Technical Training Center; Maj Gen Lloyd Leavitt, Chanute Technical Training Center; Maj Gen John Flynn, Air Force Military Training Center, Randolph AFB; Lt Gen Roberts, commander, ATC: Maj Gen Larry Killpack, vice-commander, ATC.

Greeting President Ford. President Ford attended the retirement ceremony for Cong. Les Arends, his longtime friend and Minority Whip.

Parade for Cong. Les Arends at his retirement ceremony, May 1975. *Left to right*:
Congressman Arends, General Leavitt, Captain Triplett (aide).

**Congressman Arends and General Leavitt shared a good laugh after the parade
ended.**

Political VIP visits Chanute. When Gov. Daniel Walker of Illinois visited on Armed Forces Day, he had a thorough tour of the facilities in the technical training center. General Leavitt is explaining the jet engine lab.

More VIP visits. This informal meeting at the Chanute Officers' Club included (*left*) the chairman of the House Armed Services Committee, Mel Price, and (*right*) the 24th Congressional District representative, Edward Madigan. Maybe I was laughing because Democrat Price and Republican Madigan were getting along so well that Price promised the money for a badly needed new 1,000-man dormitory at Chanute.

A different Air Force life at Chanute. Chanute AFB was the largest employer in Rantoul. Maintaining good relations was an important responsibility. After we arrived, the Rantoul press interviewed our family and ran an in-depth article with this family picture. Mary (*left*) was a freshman at Rantoul High. Lloyd ("Trig"), a freshman at the University of Virginia, and Chris Whitmyre, our 23-year-old newlywed, complete the family scene.

1976 New Year's Day reception. The line included the new center vice-commander, Col John Rollston, and (*far left*) his wife, Dee. John was subsequently promoted to brigadier in 1976.

Christmas. My young friend paid close attention while I talked to Santa on our hotline to the North Pole.

Shah's birthday. The Iranian students celebrated the Shah's birthday. Their officer in charge, an Iranian captain, is greeting Anne.

Photo courtesy US Air Force

General McKee. Lt Gen George McKee was commander of ATC from September 1974 until September 1975. A strong, supportive leader, he is shown above during a staff visit.

Photo courtesy US Air Force

Mathies Hall. The much-needed 1,000-man dorm was named after Sgt Archibald Mathies, a WWII Medal of Honor winner and a Chanute graduate. The CMSgt of the Air Force, Thomas Barnes, gave the commemoration speech.

dards of discipline and performance. Raising standards at Chanute would help our graduates adapt to SAC standards.

Three roadblocks stood in the way of improving student performance and base appearance. School policy prevented using student labor for base projects. Leadership in the school squadrons was entrusted to young lieutenants who lacked experience. The civil engineering budget was inadequate. School policy was the easiest roadblock to change. Our new policy assigned each group commander an area of responsibility. Group commanders then subdivided their area into squadron areas. Each squadron commander was given a list of tasks to be regularly accomplished. Although students had busy training schedules, several hours each day were unscheduled. Prorating this unscheduled time among the entire squadron for housekeeping and maintenance kept any student from being tasked too heavily. Within a few days after the new policy was announced, weeds were cut, lawns mowed, trash picked up, and so forth. Chanute began looking "GI" again, and each month the "best appearance" squadron was honored.

Squadron leadership was a more complex problem. There were two chains of command over the students. One was the USAFSAAS chain of command under the school commander, a senior colonel. It included the department heads, school staff, instructors, training aides, and curriculum developers. Two outstanding officers served in that capacity while I was center commander—Col Clinton G. Gillespie the first year and Col Robert K. McCutchen the second year. Clint and Bob had impressive records and were smart, experienced leaders.

The other chain of command was responsible for military training, discipline, housekeeping, and personnel functions. A lieutenant colonel commanded the student group, and lieutenants usually served as squadron commanders. Squadron leadership badly needed fixing. Many lieutenants could not keep up with all the personal, discipline, and family problems; schedule changes; and so on that complicated a squadron commander's life. Missing from these squadrons were the NCOs who taught classes but had no responsibility to students after they left the classroom.

I called Gen Russell Dougherty, Commander in Chief of SAC. After explaining the problem we had with squadron commanders, I asked, "Would SAC transfer several captains from ICBM crews and aircrews to become squadron commanders at Chanute? It would be a career broadening experience for the captains and be a great help for technical training. At the end of a year or two, they could return to SAC." General Dougherty, always cooperative and willing to listen to suggestions, saw merit in this proposal.

Within a few months, several of these new squadron commanders were in place. They quickly sensed how they could help the students. By speaking from their personal experience about the requirement for technically trained personnel and their important tasks, they motivated the students and became successful squadron commanders. In later years, several contacted me. They stated that being a squadron commander at Chanute was a rewarding experience that prepared them for future command positions.

Students also needed experienced NCOs in these training squadrons for providing guidance and for setting standards by example. This important NCO leadership was missing in the training squadrons in 1974. For example, an E-6 (technical sergeant) teaching B-52 aircraft maintenance had no association outside the classroom with students in a B-52 training squadron. Likewise, first sergeants and administrative staff in a B-52 training squadron lacked B-52 hands-on experience. This "blind leading the blind" situation contrasted with USAF operational squadrons where officers, NCOs, and Airmen work together in support of a common function.

An organizational change was needed that would merge the school faculty into training squadrons. This change was difficult to sell. NCOs assigned to teach school enjoyed the regular hours and classroom atmosphere. They did not want the headaches and responsibilities that accompany the NCO leadership role in a squadron. After listening to their complaints and explaining the benefits of the merger, I knew it was decision time. General McKee, ATC commander, gave permission to run a six-month test beginning in January 1975. The primary objectives were improving student performance, reducing incidents, and raising student morale. Important secondary objectives were reducing support manning and managerial costs.

All the realigned responsibilities for student training were placed under the commander, USAFSAAS (Colonel Gillespie, later Colonel McCutchen). A new resources group was formed and given the responsibility for logistics planning, procurement, transportation, supply, and finance. This left the air base group with security police, civil engineering, special services, personnel, chaplain, disaster preparedness, and the USAF Band of the Midwest. The base hospital did not change. The air base group, resources group, and hospital reported to the center commander, as did the commander, USAFSAAS. The center commander's staff included social actions, judge advocate, safety, information, contingency plans, and the operations center.

By mid-1975, field reports showed that the students coming from Chanute were better trained. There was also good news at Chanute. The AWOL rate had dropped 50 percent, and Chanute had the lowest percentage of student drug offenders in ATC. Support manning costs dropped $1.3 million in six months. The student attrition rate had dropped greatly in the past year, partly attributable to this reorganization and partly to better recruiting. General McKee directed the other technical training centers to reorganize like Chanute.

Chanute required huge amounts of typewritten material—especially for the school, where several hundred courses were taught, requiring updating manuals, revising tests, writing lessons, and so forth. Each major course and department required several typists. Centralized typing would improve efficiency, and word processing would save both time and labor. IBM helped develop our system. Offices were connected to the new Word Processing Center by telephone. With dictating equipment, magnetic cartridges, and the new electric typewriters, the written product was delivered the same day. IBM called it the most advanced program it had installed in a federal facility. By not replacing typists who retired or left, we were able to eliminate 30 salaried typists and secretaries. The USAF named the supervisor, Delores James, as the outstanding support person for 1975.

The civil engineering (CE) budget was inadequate in 1974 for this large air base. Most barracks, roads, utilities, and support facilities at Chanute were constructed at the beginning of World War II or early in the Korean War. The inflation rate grew by leaps and bounds in 1974—reaching 11 percent over the previous year—and jumped another 9 percent in 1975. Over the same two years, the defense budget increased at only half the inflation rate.[2] Inflation played havoc with the CE budget for items such as building and road maintenance and repair, electrical utilities, coal, and natural gas. Missing was money needed for dormitories, recreational facilities, and modern NCO and enlisted clubs.

The ATC civil engineer was Brig Gen Charles Lamb, a knowledgeable and imaginative officer. With his help at ATC headquarters, Chanute made significant progress despite the shortage of funds. The first step was rearranging priorities to meet our local needs. With the extraordinary cooperation of General Lamb and close budget controls locally, we came up with an unforeseen $1.8 million for things such as upgrading the electric distribution system, correcting drainage problems, modernizing the heating plant, and improving roads.

A problem that would not go away was the lack of adequate housing for students. A 1,000-person dormitory for NCOs on temporary duty for training had been approved earlier by Congress but was delayed because of the money crunch. Denny Sullivan and I thought renovating several Korean War barracks might be a practical solution to the housing shortage. We asked ATC for permission to remodel one as a test case.

The USAF has an extraordinary number of talented NCOs. Topping the list are chief master sergeants—E-9s.[3] CMSgt Pete Velez was a superb example. When Velez learned that we might remodel a Korean War barracks, he volunteered his time and talent to the project. A highly skilled draftsman and architect, he did the planning necessary for the project. After establishing that the 23-year-old building was structurally sound, the barracks were successfully upgraded to modern standards using local contractors.

Despite the success of this effort, no more Korean War barracks were renovated. The chairman of the House Armed Services Committee, Cong. Mel Price, visited Chanute in November 1975. While touring the base, he became convinced of our need for new dormitories. After Price returned to Washington, Congress "unexpectedly" approved a third 1,000-person dormitory for 1976 construction.

The successful barracks renovation inspired several other projects, made possible by the talented CMSgt Velez and our civil engineers. An unused hangar was made into a gym with two basketball courts, locker rooms, two racquetball courts, and a volleyball court. A roller rink was built inside an old storage building, and six lanes were added to the bowling alley. After a new base exchange (BX) was built with nonappropriated funds, the old BX was converted to an Airmen's club with a capacity of 650, called the "Pit and Ping." When a new commissary was built with nonappropriated funds, the renovated old commissary became a community center for families.

The University of Illinois was always cooperative with Chanute. Particularly helpful was Chancellor Jack Peltason. He introduced us to several faculty members with whom we shared interests. For example, the U-of-I had developed a system called PLATO (Programmed Logic for Automatic Teaching Operations). It was the first generalized computer-assisted instruction system wherein students interacted with a specific computer program for individualized instruction. Could Chanute serve as a PLATO test bed for training students on technical subjects?

Vehicle maintenance was an ideal course for testing PLATO. It was unclassified as well as shorter and simpler than others. Chanute NCOs and U-of-I programmers wrote the test program. A classroom was set aside with learning carousels. Each carousel held one computer and one student. Instructors were present but did not lecture. Students could proceed at their own pace through each lesson. After viewing the entire lesson, the program tested the student. Passing the test meant the student could begin the next lesson.

Although results were academically positive, there were problems. Many Airmen accelerated their schooling and graduated early with higher scores than before PLATO. Whether they would retain the course knowledge could not be readily determined. NCO instructors generally objected to being replaced by a computer. Another problem was the time and difficulty involved in writing an effective PLATO program. We decided not to pursue PLATO technology further until these problems were resolved.

Officers' clubs on military bases are no longer subsidized with appropriated (money from taxes) funds. Instead, each club has to support itself with profits from food and drink sales and from special events. The fact that Chanute had a relatively small officer population to support a large club partially explained why the club looked old and shabby. The club served important purposes by providing meals for officers and their guests and by hosting visiting dignitaries. Fixing it meant more than just "putting lipstick on the pig." We needed a lot of free labor for two days: Saturday one for gardens and surrounding lawns; Saturday two for interior cleaning and painting.

I asked for officer volunteers and their families to do the work. We made a picnic of the event each Saturday, with the club furnishing soft drinks, hot dogs, and potato chips. The owner of the flower nursery in Rantoul heard about the project. He remembered where the Civilian Conservation Corps had planted the flower beds and shrubbery before World War II and directed the restoration of the beautiful lawns around the club. The families worked hard, and everyone seemed to have a good time.

The club looked much better afterwards, but the main reception room—the Hunt Room—still looked old and tired. Honorary club members and concerned citizens donated the money and materials for the remodeling of the Hunt Room. It was renamed the "Bicentennial Room" to commemorate our nation's birthday. Nearly a year passed before the renovation was complete, but the end product was worth the wait, thanks to the generosity of Rantoul citizens.

Marijuana, Sex, Law, and Order

A significant responsibility of commanders that never goes away is maintaining good order and discipline. The larger the command, the more likely this will occupy a significant portion of their time. Commanders have many assets to help them meet these responsibilities, but their most important assets are strong, reliable commanders of subordinate units. Successful commanders also avoid trouble by communicating through base newspapers, meeting with base councils, using hotlines, talking to local media, working the Public Affairs office, and using all other forms of communication to keep everyone informed. If everyone knows and does his or her job, not much will go wrong. When things do go awry, the commander has security police, a legal staff, the base hospital, chaplains, and other professionals to enforce the law and to pick up the pieces.

The following describes incidents I encountered at Chanute and how they were resolved.

Both federal law and the *UCMJ* forbid the illegal sale and use of marijuana and other narcotics. During the 1970s, the armed forces struggled with the problem of illegal drugs. Too many service members returning from the Vietnam War brought their drug habits back with them. Many young recruits, fresh from civilian life, were casual users of marijuana, and a few were heavy users. Nevertheless, fearing a drop in enlistments and in retention, the political appointees in the Department of Defense avoided policy changes that would have severely cracked down on illegal drugs.

This policy vacuum left Air Force commanders with two big headaches: limiting access to illegal drugs and punishing users who were caught. There was an informal consensus that users of hard drugs—heroin and cocaine, for example—would meet a court-martial and, if found guilty, be discharged or otherwise punished. On the other hand, the first time an Airman was caught using marijuana, he or she was lightly punished under the less severe provisions of Article 15 of the *UCMJ*.

It seems obvious that officers and Airmen working with aircraft and missiles must be drug free. Mistakes can damage or destroy multimillion-dollar weapon systems as well as jeopardize the lives of aircrew members and missile support personnel. Our responsibilities at Chanute included sending drug-free Airmen into an Air Force that depended upon their reliable performance.

Unfortunately, the state of Illinois and the village of Rantoul viewed the drug problem at Chanute as an Air Force problem, not theirs. Illinois law allowed head shops where water pipes and paraphernalia associated with marijuana and other drugs were openly advertised and sold. Chanute Airmen caught with marijuana in their possession informed us that head shops either sold them marijuana or directed them to where marijuana was sold. One head shop existed in Rantoul only a few hundred feet from the main gate and was owned by a retired master sergeant.

This shop sold large psychedelic wall posters as well as drug apparatus. The Airmen living in barracks were allowed to mount these posters on the walls of their rooms. Since the posters sold for more than a dollar and there were more than a thousand rooms with lots of wall space, the sergeant had a high-profit sideline to his drug paraphernalia business.

I asked the mayor to revoke head shop licenses as a public nuisance. He stated it was beyond his jurisdiction. Next, our judge advocate general (JAG) invited the head shop owner to meet in my office. Appealing to his status as a retired NCO, I asked for help on a major discipline problem—marijuana use. After explaining that Airmen confessed that they located marijuana sources through his head shop, I asked him to stop selling drug paraphernalia to Airmen. He declined, as expected. I then told him the bad news. Effective tomorrow, Airmen could no longer decorate the walls in their rooms with posters.

Red in the face, he stalked out of the office stating there was no way I could shut him down. He was partially correct; I could not stop him from selling paraphernalia once the Airmen entered the head shop. The next day, his lawyer contacted our JAG and offered a deal. Let him sell the stock of psychedelic posters, and he would not order any more. After listening to his offer, I said he could sell posters to whoever wanted one. They still would not be allowed on the walls of our barracks.

The conversation shifted to selling paraphernalia, and I fired my best shot. Every day after student duty hours, a security policeman would walk up and down the sidewalk between the main gate and the head shop. The SP would not stop anyone from going into the head shop, but his presence on the sidewalk would obviously have a chilling effect on most young Airmen. When the head shop stopped selling paraphernalia, the sidewalk patrolling would stop.

The plan worked. Within a week, the lawyer and the retired NCO wanted another meeting. This time, they offered to stop selling paraphernalia if we would give them a month to sell their inventory and would stop the SP patrol. I gave them a week but kept the SP on the sidewalk until an off-duty NCO could browse through the shop and verify that the paraphernalia was all gone. Our little drug interdiction program was not as tough as bombing the Ho Chi Minh Trail in Laos, but it did shut at least this one source down.

The student populations at Chanute and the nearby University of Illinois in Champaign-Urbana attracted drug dealers like bees to honey. Squadron commanders, the OSI, security police, informers, and trained dogs at Chanute worked to keep a lid on the problem. Their efforts reduced the drug incident rate, but marijuana remained a problem. Among the 25,000 Airmen trained between October 1974 and October 1975, several hundred had faced drug charges—mostly for using marijuana. A command issue was what to do with these young Airmen.

Airmen claiming to be "first time" (their usual excuse) users, had usually been given Article 15s and allowed to remain in technical training. I decided we needed a stronger, more lasting approach and started a drug rehabilitation program. With their squadron commander's recommendation, Airmen apprehended for using marijuana could volunteer for drug rehabilitation. Nonvolunteers were discharged. The Menninger Clinic trained two senior Chanute NCOs to be drug counselors. An isolated, open-bay, two-story barracks became school for the six-week rehab course for up to 60 Airmen in each class. They were inspected twice daily and had no access to outside sources of drugs. Rehab blended military discipline and training, physical conditioning, motivational lectures, and one-on-one counseling. Program objectives were to strengthen interest in an Air Force career, understand personal responsibilities in the Air Force, and change attitudes toward drugs.

Upon successful completion of drug rehabilitation, Airmen reentered training with the next class in their career field. The results were excellent. Individual academic scores were higher and washout rates minimal. Squadron commanders were pleased with the appearance and conduct of the Airmen back from rehab. The recidivism rate was very low. The Air Force had gained a productive Airman. After becoming Vice-Commander in Chief of SAC in 1978, I started a similar program SAC-wide. It too was successful but was discontinued in 1982 when the Defense Department toughened the rules, authorized random urinalysis testing, and discharged all drug users. The services finally gained control of illegal drug usage at that time.

The nonpolitical leadership's reaction in Rantoul toward our efforts to curtail drugs was very positive. The citizens did not want Rantoul to be a wide-open city. Although Chanute was the largest employer, the prosperous farms and associated agriculture enterprises in central Illinois really defined their economy.

The famous Midwest work ethic carried over into civic pride. The "movers and shakers" in Rantoul included automobile dealer and banker Earnie Rogers, banker Jack Frost, Chamber of Commerce president Bob Green, newspaper publisher Glenn Hansen, businessman Bob Mathis, and many others who were strong supporters of my efforts to enhance Chanute's image and the USAF reputation in Illinois.

Airmen fresh from basic training averaged about 19 years old. Their top priorities boiled down to school, the opposite sex, and partying. Our task was keeping the other two priorities from interfering with school. We had some advantages. Most of the time, we knew where students were and what they were supposed to be doing. If they worked hard, we rewarded them. If they got out of line, we tightened the reins. If they got *way* out of line, we punished them. If they were uncontrollable, we sent them back home. Fortunately, the large majority managed their lives quite well and progressed through training without difficulty. The exceptions were memorable.

Occasional suicides, attempted or accomplished, are an unfortunate fact of life among large groups in their teens or early twenties. Roommates and NCO supervisors were our early warning line for preventing suicide. A depressed individual who might be suicidal was quickly sent to the hospital for counseling and treatment by professionals. Frustrated love affairs were a common cause for threatening suicide, especially among female Airmen. Cutting a wrist in the presence of a roommate or ex-lover seemed to be the preferred way to attempt suicide, gain attention, and *not* die.

Sometimes, the suicidal person did not think about unexpected consequences. One young woman jumped from the window of her second-story barracks—feet first. After falling 15 feet into a flower bed and landing on her feet, she suffered two broken ankles and was medically discharged after the casts were removed. A far more tragic case was the young male who left his room one night, climbed to the top of a water tower 100 feet high, and jumped. His body was found at the base of the water tower the next morning. He left no note or explanation for his suicide.

The Supreme Court ruled that abortions were legal with the 1973 *Roe v. Wade* decision. In 1974 the DoD required military hospitals to perform abortions when requested by dependent wives or female service members. The abortion issue was controversial at that time and remains controversial today, but the DoD orders were in compliance with the new Supreme Court decision.

A few months had passed when my executive officer reported some disturbing news. The Catholic Ladies Guild scheduled a protest meeting that evening and insisted that I attend. The subject was abortion. Before the meeting, I asked the hospital commander for an update, including statistics. When I entered the meeting, there were more than 100 women present, and emotions were running high. The chairwoman wasted no time getting my attention. She stated that the base hospital had performed "several thousand abortions" and demanded that I stop "the murdering of innocent unborn children immediately."

I always admired Harry Truman for his famous "the buck stops here" reference to accepting responsibility. As the senior military authority at Chanute, I kept Truman's comment in mind and normally chose to face contentious issues. I explained to the ladies present that the DoD directed all military hospitals to perform abortions. The base hospital had performed abortions but fewer than a hundred in nearly a year. The reference to "several thousands" was a gross exaggeration. Furthermore, no woman was given an abortion until she had been counseled by the medical staff and had carefully considered her alternatives. And no doctors were ordered to administer an abortion if they were ethically and professionally opposed.

During the meeting, I avoided expressing my personal views about *Roe v. Wade* because they were irrelevant to the issue at hand. The ladies needed to know that I lacked the authority to stop abortions at the base hospital. When the meeting opened for questions, the tone of the questioning had changed, and emotions had calmed. Three decades later, abortion remains an emotional and a political hot button.

Another difficult social issue was homosexuality in the military. When an officer or Airman was reported or accused of engaging in homosexual activity, the allegation was investigated as a violation of Article 125 of the *UCMJ*. If evidence confirmed the homosexual allegation, the individual was discharged. Conflicting state laws, changing public attitudes, and pressure from the American Civil Liberties Union and other activist organizations caused the military to modify its approach to punishing homosexuals. Although homosexual conduct was a punishable offense under the military Code of Conduct, homosexuals generally received administrative discharges instead of bad-conduct or dishonorable discharges.

With the large military population at Chanute, it was inevitable that both overt and covert homosexual activity would occur. Overt incidents involving males often began in a bar. An actual example based upon several allegations went like this. Sergeant "A" spots young Airman "B" drinking alone. A introduces himself to B and joins him at the bar. A buys B several drinks and offers to drive B back to the barracks. A stops the car and assaults B who is too drunk to resist. The next day, B reports the assault to his first sergeant. The OSI investigates and finds similar allegations by other Airmen against A. Offered an administrative discharge in lieu of court-martial, A accepts the discharge.

An infamous case occurred in the female enlisted dormitory. Three female sergeants processed new arrivals. After spotting an "interesting" prospect, they would invite her to a shower room meeting where they would describe social life in central Illinois. The meeting was really a screening process for lesbians. New arrivals that resisted were physically threatened or abused. The OSI investigation began after receiving complaints from several frightened new arrivals from basic training.

For weeks the OSI gathered evidence, including photos of lesbian activities, detailed love letters, pictures, and mock marriages. When the facts were gathered and the females all identified, the JAG advised them of their rights. Evidence was overwhelming, and approximately 20 women were discharged on the same day. One woman later protested to her father that she was innocent. He initiated a congressional inquiry, cited the Freedom of Information Act, and wanted our proof for her being discharged. I answered that she was protected under the Privacy Act, but I would gladly provide the proof if she would waive the Privacy Act. That ended the congressional inquiry.

The base commissary plays an important role in the life of military families. It is convenient to those who live on or near the base, and food prices are competitive with those of large supermarket chains. Commissaries operate without taxpayer expense by using centralized purchasing and small markups. All was going well in Chanute's commissary until an audit disclosed that the meat department was losing money. Suspicions arose that one or more employees were stealing approximately $400 of meat once or twice a week. I authorized the use of infrared cameras near the exits to catch the thief.

Two nights later, the cameras photographed a female employee loading steaks, hams, and other items into the trunk of her car after closing. For a number of very good security reasons, any vehicle entering or leaving a military base is subject to search. When she drove to the main gate, the SPs stopped the car, asked her to open the trunk, and found about $400 of meat stashed in the trunk (worth about $1,600 in 2009). The next day, the JAG filed charges against her in the federal district court, and she was fired from her commissary job.

A month passed. The JAG called the federal district attorney and asked how her case was progressing. The news was not encouraging. The DA said he was too busy chasing drug dealers to pursue this small case and had dropped the charges. A few days later, the president of the American Federation of Government Employees called. He insisted that I must rehire the woman because she was not guilty of any crime.

I asked for his full name and position and then responded. "Mr. X, how would you like the *Chicago Tribune* to print the pictures we have of your union employee stealing a large amount of food from an Air Force commissary? Accompanying the photos will be an interview with me stating that as the president of the union, you insisted I rehire this thief even though we caught her red-handed. Do you want that kind of publicity?" After a long pause, he answered. "No, General, I guess we will accept your decision and let this one go. Thanks for your time." We did not rehire her.

One Saturday afternoon, while driving with my daughter Mary, the portable phone (appropriately nicknamed "the brick" for its size and weight) rang. The command post reported that an Airman's wife fired a shot through the roof of her apartment in family housing. Her husband ran to a neighbor's apartment when she fired the shot. When the security police knocked on her front door, she would not open the glass storm door, waved a pistol at them, and threatened to kill her little daughter if they did not leave her alone. The command post said she apparently was drunk and mad at her husband for losing his government driver's license. SPs had blocked off the street and backed away from the apartment. What did I want them to do?

After stopping my car in front of the apartment house, I talked to the SP sergeant who had attempted to enter her apartment. Possibly, she was frightened by an armed SP knocking at her door, so I decided to try talking to her. The SPs stayed in the street behind their patrol cars. I walked up the sidewalk and rang the doorbell. The main door opened. A large black woman wearing a housecoat stood behind the glass storm door with a pistol pointed my way. "What do you want?" she said. Because I was wearing civilian clothes, I showed her my ID, said I was Chanute's commander, and asked if I could come in the house and talk to her. "Go away!" She slammed the main door shut.

I waited a minute or two and then rang again. When she appeared again, I said, "Can we please talk things over? I will help you and your husband, and I'll send the SPs away." It worked. She opened the door, led me into the living room, and sat down on the couch. Her four-year-old daughter stood by the table looking scared to death. A half-empty bottle of Jack Daniels was on the table in front of the couch. Hoping she might put the gun down, I told her Jack Daniels was my favorite whiskey. "Could I please have a JD and water while we talk?" She went to the kitchen for a glass. Unfortunately, the gun went with her. When she returned, I told her if she would give me the gun, I would send the SPs away and that we could drive to the base hospital with her husband. She finally agreed. I called the SP sergeant to the front door, gave him her pistol, and told him to call the emergency room at the hospital, put her husband in my car, and keep the SPs away.

Back in my seat by the couch, I asked "Why don't you get dressed in something else if we are driving to the base hospital with your husband and my daughter?" She nodded her head and went upstairs to change clothes. Her daughter relaxed a bit. When she came downstairs, she was dressed, but said she wanted to put the Jack Daniels back in the kitchen. I followed closely behind her. Suddenly, she reached for a big carving knife on the counter. I grabbed it before she could. Then she walked quietly to my car where her husband and Mary were sitting.

When everyone was in the car, I looked over at Mary. She was sitting in the right front seat with a What-Have-I-Gotten-Into look on her face. Pushing the speed limit, I headed for the base hospital. About halfway there, a commotion occurred in the backseat. The woman was trying to open the door and jump out. Child restraint locks prevented the rear doors from opening, and we made it to the hospital without further ado. The emergency team took her from the car and immediately strapped her down on a gurney. That was the last time I saw her . . . for several months.

Before leaving Chanute for my next assignment, the NCOs had a nice farewell party for Anne and me. When the evening ended, they formed a double line leaving the NCO Club—NCOs on one side, wives on the other. Halfway down the aisle, one wife waved to draw my attention. It was my JD-drinking, gun-toting, knife-grabbing "friend." She said, "General Leavitt, thanks for getting my husband's license back and for taking me to the hospital. I'm fine now!" I said, "Glad to hear things are going well. Take care of yourself!" I did *not* say what was on the tip of my tongue—"Thanks for not shooting me!"

Tough, Trim, and Talented

When the Vietnam War ended, the USAF included many Airmen who had enlisted to avoid being drafted into the other services. Depending upon their enlistment dates, these Airmen began leaving after the war. During 1973 and 1974, USAF recruiters had a difficult task filling their places with the draft no longer a motivating factor.

In my mind, three steps were needed to make significant improvements in USAF technical training. Step One: recruit good people to join the Air Force. By mid-1975, the recruiting situation had improved. Recruits were scoring better on the AFQT and were more amenable to discipline and training. Despite these facts, getting our NCOs to acknowledge any improvement in recruits was difficult. In their minds, the recruits were "never as good as they used to be." I could only conclude that these NCOs must have all joined the Air Force when "they used to be"!

Step Two: reorganize the officers and NCOs at squadron and group level in early 1975 to improve leadership at all levels. Merge men and women into training squadrons to improve the performance and behavior of both sexes. The number of students eliminated from training dropped significantly after these changes took hold.

Step Three: motivate the students so they will do well, not only in training but also after they join operational units. Tying together things like tightening up military personnel and base appearance, improving housing, enforcing drug policies, removing racial tension, and building better recreational facilities helped motivate students toward an Air Force career. Still missing were two important individual characteristics shared by successful career Airmen. We needed to instill confidence and pride in students who could become outstanding Airmen. I chose a slogan and a program to accomplish this objective and called it Tough, Trim, and Talented.

Tough students could withstand physical and mental pressures and come back for more. *Trim* students met all physical standards, including weight and general appearance. *Talented* students learned everything required so that in their next assignments they could excel on the job. When they graduated from Chanute, a certificate of accomplishment went to those who were indeed Tough, Trim, and Talented.

Airmen arrived at Chanute in good physical condition after completing basic training. Once they settled into technical training, good food in our dining halls and the lack of a rigorous physical training schedule had an adverse effect. Too many could no longer meet the *Trim* goal. A basewide physical training program went into effect in early 1976. Not everyone was ecstatic about it. One complainer wrote: "It's not legal to require me to exercise. I'll write my congressman if you don't stop!" (He had a strange misconception of his Air Force responsibilities.) Another said that physical training was hard on his morale. I told him, "After you get in shape, you will feel better because of your improved physical condition, and your morale will improve. If not, grin and bear it."

As months passed, official visitors to Chanute seemed pleased with what they saw in professional attitudes, morale, and discipline. Tough, Trim, and Talented was serving a useful purpose. VIP visits during that time included President Ford to honor retiring Congressman Arends; Illinois governor Walker; Congressmen Price and Madigan; ATC commanders Lieutenant Generals McKee and Roberts; Vice Admiral King, USN, retired; vice-commander of the USAF Military Personnel Center, Maj Gen Bennie Davis; USAF chief of chaplains, Maj Gen Henry Meade; CMSgt of the Air Force Barnes; the Thunderbirds, who attracted a crowd of 72,000; and many VIPs from central Illinois.

In early April, the deputy chief of staff for personnel, Lt Gen Ken Tallman, called. I was being reassigned in June to HQ USAFE as deputy chief of staff for operations and intelligence, a great job in the Cold War. I was anxious to get current in the flying business again. Tallman arranged for refresher and familiarization training at Luke AFB, Arizona, flying the F-4, F-5, and F-15.

The nearly two years spent at Chanute were memorable, pleasant, and challenging. Anne and I made many lasting friends in Rantoul and Champaign-Urbana. Before the change-of-command ceremony, the Champaign-Urbana *News Gazette* wrote some nice words about my two years at Chanute . . . "solid list of accomplishments . . . concentrated on reorganization . . . improvements in physical plants, living quarters and recreational facilities . . . men and women were integrated in student squadrons . . . results that were commended and followed throughout the Air Training Command." What the newspaper failed to credit was the outstanding support from Vice-Commanders Denny Sullivan and John Rollston, who came to Chanute as colonels and later became brigadier generals.[4] Colonels Clint Gillespie and Bob McCutchen excelled in their leadership roles as SAAS commanders. Col Monty Ballew was a great air base group commander. Working closely with me were Lt Col Tom Fincher, center executive officer, and my most helpful aide, Capt Hank Triplett.

A long-standing military tradition is the change-of-command ceremony. While serving a useful purpose by clearly showing everyone there is a new boss, the act itself is a sentimental mixture of "Auld Lang Syne," New Year's Eve, and "hail to the king; the king is dead!" General Roberts presented a second Distinguished Service Medal for my accomplishments at Chanute and for the Air Training Command. The symbolic passing of the flag from the outgoing commander to the incoming commander left no doubts in my mind about Chanute being in good hands. Maj Gen Edwin Robertson II, a highly decorated officer with extensive combat experience in both the Korean and Vietnam Wars, was the new center commander. Ed was returning from USAFE where he had commanded the 36th TFW at Bitburg before becoming vice-commander of Sixteenth Air Force in Spain.

Immediately following the ceremony, I flew to Maguire AFB at Dover, Delaware, and on to Rhein-Main AB, Germany. Anne and Mary stayed in Illinois for two or three more weeks awaiting travel orders by military air. After the "human dependents" were authorized to travel, we paid Pan American (Pan Am) to fly Gib and Paddy, our black standard poodles, to Rhein-Main. I picked up Anne and Mary at the military side of Rhein-Main and then crossed over to the freight area on the civilian side of the airport for the dogs. Surprise! Pan Am handed me the leashes for two *white* standard poodles, insisting they were "*Amerikanischer Hunde.*" After several minutes of debate, the freight manager conceded they were not my dogs. A few days later, Pan Am finally located our dogs in Karachi, Pakistan, and flew them back to Rhein-Main. We had a happy family reunion that night, human and canine—"all present and accounted for!"

Notes

1. Brigadier General Sullivan, a 1950 Annapolis graduate, received pilot wings with Class 51-E and flew 100 F-80 combat missions in the Korean War. He joined the high-altitude A-12 and SR-71 Mach 3+ programs and later became vice-commander of the 9th SRW. After Chanute, he commanded the USAF navigator-training wing and SAC's 12th Air Division. A National War College graduate, he gained an MA in international affairs and graduated from the Advanced Management Program at Carnegie-Mellon University. Decorations include the Legion of Merit with oak leaf cluster, Distinguished Flying Cross with oak leaf cluster, the Meritorious Service Medal, and Air Medal with two oak leaf clusters. US Air Force, "Biographies: Brigadier General Dennis B. Sullivan."

2. Based upon data from the Congressional Budget Office, *Budget and Economic Outlook: Fiscal Years 2001–2010*, 330.

3. E-1, Airman basic; E-2, Airman; E-3, Airman first class; E-4, senior Airman; E-5, staff sergeant; E-6, technical sergeant; E-7, master sergeant; E-8, senior master sergeant; E-9, chief master sergeant. Only 1 percent of the enlisted force are E-9s.

4. Brig Gen John Rollston, a 1952 West Point graduate, received pilot wings in 1953 and served in the Vietnam War, earning a Distinguished Flying Cross, Bronze Star Medal, Joint Service Commendation Medal, and eight Air Medals. He received an MS in engineering management from Rensselaer Polytechnic Institute, commanded two flying training wings, was awarded the Legion of Merit, became the ATC IG, and received the Distinguished Service Medal. He retired in 1980. US Military Academy, *Register of Graduates.*

Chapter 14

USAFE Operations and Intelligence
Major General—1976–78

Time to Reflect

The long flight from McGuire AFB, New Jersey, to Rhein-Main AB left plenty of time to reflect on past events and to wonder about the future. Twenty-six years had passed since reporting for pilot training at Goodfellow AFB. During those years, our country had endured the Cold War, the Korean War, the Vietnam War, the Cuban missile crisis, the Pueblo Incident, DEFCON 3 twice, and been led by six different presidents. It was now the summer of 1976, and America was once again shifting its attention to the upcoming presidential election.

During the past 26 years, I had military assignments in Texas, Arizona, Nevada, Japan, Korea, Georgia, Arkansas, the Azores, England, Alabama, Puerto Rico, New York, Argentina, Alaska, California, New Mexico, Michigan, Kansas, Virginia, Germany, Greece, Washington State, Florida, the Philippines, Thailand, Israel, and Illinois. Along the way, I had flown 262 combat missions in two wars, been a SAC fighter pilot for three years and U-2 pilot for nearly four, a B-52 aircraft commander for two more, and served in ATC, FEAF, SAC, PACAF, USAFE, the Air Staff (HQ USAF), and the JCS. I brought with me to the new assignment four important personal beliefs from these previous assignments.

Most importantly, we live in a republic where elected and appointed civilian officials control domestic, foreign, and military policy. The USSR, our principal Cold War enemy, was a communist dictatorship wherein all resources necessary to execute domestic, foreign, and military policy were controlled by a small group of Communist Party officials. Given that circumstance, the Soviet dictatorship could move faster, take risks, and subject its people to hardships not tolerable in a modern democracy.

543

Secondly, the media in a modern democracy has more influence on national policy than anything that has happened or will happen in battle. The risk of media distortion is highest when covering ground combat. The media coverage of the 1968 Viet Cong Tet Offensive in 1968 is a classic example of media distortion influencing national policy.

Thirdly, the lopsided US advantage in strategic and tactical nuclear weapons for the first two decades of the Cold War served two important purposes. First, it limited expansion of the Korean War beyond China's participation and finally ended it with Eisenhower's threat. Second, the nuclear advantage served as a protective shield against Soviet aggression during NATO's formative years. The superpowers reached rough equivalence in nuclear weapons in the mid- to late sixties. When that happened, both nations realized their society could not survive a massive exchange of nuclear weapons.

Conventional (nonnuclear) war remained an option, especially between clients of the two superpowers. The Korean, Vietnam, and Yom Kippur wars were fought between client states. The USSR and China aided their clients North Korea and North Vietnam against the US clients South Korea and South Vietnam. In the Yom Kippur War, the USSR aided clients Syria and Egypt against the United States and its client Israel.

Finally, receiving too little notice was the rapid buildup of Soviet strategic and conventional forces. Western Europeans had begun to question our nuclear commitment after the USSR reached rough equivalence with US strategic and tactical nuclear forces. Would the United States really risk losing New York City in order to save London or Brussels?

The United States answered this hypothetical question about our resolve by strengthening our conventional forces in Europe after the Vietnam War ended. I believed we were entering a dangerous time for NATO if the USSR misread our commitment to NATO. The aggressive foreign policies of the USSR were twice confirmed when they suppressed revolts in Hungary and Czechoslovakia. Would lightning strike again if Poland attempted to break free from communist control?

The long flight finally ended at Rhein-Main, where a staff car was waiting for the short trip to HQ USAFE at Ramstein AB in the Federal Republic of Germany near Kaiserslautern. Six years had passed between the end of my first tour in Germany and the beginning of my second. The political-military balance between the United States and USSR had shifted during those six years. The greatest friction and potential for war was now in Europe where NATO borders touched the Warsaw Pact nations.

A greater danger from war existed by 1975 for reasons that did not exist during earlier crises. Western Europe had recovered economically, whereas the controlled economies of Eastern Europe were lagging far behind. The USSR, realizing Europe was a powerful magnet to Eastern Europeans, had slammed shut whatever doors were open for commerce between East and West. The Berlin Wall best exemplified this regressive policy. Threatening the economic advantages enjoyed by NATO was the rapid buildup of all Warsaw Pact military forces. By 1975 the USSR had 500 more ICBMs than the United States and approximately the same number of SLBMs. The Soviet advantage in ICBMs was growing with the introduction of the mammoth SS-18 carrying 10 MIRV warheads per missile.[1]

After the Cold War, American tourists returning from conducted tours in Russia often concluded the Soviet war machine could not have been effective with such a depressed economy. Their presumptions ignored the centralized planning that controlled the Soviet economy. The Soviets sacrificed civilian needs in order to create an immense military establishment, explore space, build satellites, develop nuclear power, design and build aircraft, and expand the coal, metal mining, oil, and heavy machinery industries. Perhaps the best explanation lies in statistical comparisons. In 1976 per capita manufacturing output in the USSR was 752 pounds; US per capita output was 586 pounds. At the same time, per capita consumption in the USSR as a percentage of the gross domestic product (GDP) was only 53 percent, whereas in the United States it was 78 percent.[2]

How did we know the size and strength of the Warsaw Pact forces in 1976? The larger, well-equipped Warsaw Pact air forces were only minutes away, and USAFE intelligence monitored their training and exercises. USAF reconnaissance aircraft and satellites located and quantified the Warsaw Pact forces. Our agents and Warsaw Pact defectors confirmed estimates. We tested Soviet military equipment acquired from various forces and understood its strengths and weaknesses. Arms control agreements between the East and West removed much of the secrecy that previously surrounded Warsaw Pact exercises, troop movements, and USSR nuclear tests.

My new assignment as DCS for operations and intelligence in USAFE included two important responsibilities directly related to the imposing Warsaw Pact threat. First, seek and maintain a high level of objectivity and awareness within the intelligence community. Second, seek and maintain USAFE combat units at the highest possible level of combat readiness with their assigned assets. I looked forward to the task.

Deterrence Fades, Containment Gains

In 1976 the American public shifted its attention to the upcoming presidential election between Pres. Gerald Ford and the relatively unknown governor of Georgia, Jimmy Carter. The fighting in Vietnam had ended on 30 April 1975 after the rebuilt and reequipped North Vietnamese army captured Saigon. The Yom Kippur War was over, and the high gas prices caused by the Arab oil embargo were receding to normal. Receiving little notice, except in the Pentagon and NATO, was the rapid buildup of Soviet strategic and conventional forces. Ignoring this ominous fact, the US defense budget for 1976 (in billions of constant FY01 dollars) was the lowest for any of the years from 1962 to 2001.

The term "Cold War," as differentiated from other wars, aptly describes the near-frozen diplomatic relationships between the alliances led by the USSR and the alliances led by the United States. The greatest friction in the Cold War was on the European continent, where the USSR-led Warsaw Pact faced the US-led NATO. Boundaries created at the end of World War II separated the two blocs. The eastern borders of NATO stretched from the northern tip of Norway to Denmark, the Federal Republic of Germany, Italy, then across the Adriatic Sea to Greece, and to Turkey on the Black Sea. The UK, France, Belgium, Iceland, and Luxembourg did not adjoin Warsaw Pact nations but were NATO members. France did not actively participate in NATO military planning after 1966.

During the first two decades after NATO was formed, Western Europe was still recovering from World War II. Stalin and

Khrushchev kept Western Europe hostage during those years with large Warsaw Pact forces in Eastern Europe. The aggressive foreign policies of the USSR were twice confirmed when it suppressed revolts in Hungary and Czechoslovakia.

Basing American forces in Europe after World War II accomplished three objectives: verified our commitment to NATO, provided protective cover while NATO rearmed, and forced the USSR to realize that attacking NATO-based American forces would lead to nuclear war. NATO forces were equipped with tactical nuclear weapons and backed by the overwhelming US advantage in strategic bombers, ICBMs, and SLBMs. Starting a war against NATO during the '50s and '60s was too high a risk for the USSR despite its large advantage in conventional forces.

The USSR buildup that continued throughout the Cold War forced NATO defense policies to change. From 1948 to 1955, defending NATO depended primarily upon US *strategic nuclear* forces to deter the USSR. From 1956 to 1967, although NATO rebuilt conventional forces, NATO Strategy Document MC 14/2 called for the prompt release of *tactical nuclear* weapons for deterrence. When NATO Strategy Document 14/3 became effective 16 January 1968, it called on conventional forces to resist Warsaw Pact aggression but did not rule out using tactical nuclear weapons.

When the United States and USSR reached approximate parity in strategic nuclear weapons, a catchy media acronym, "MAD," entered the discussion. MAD meant mutually assured destruction. Antinuclear "experts" argued that the use of nuclear weapons by either the USSR or the United States would result in instant retaliation by the other side—thus "mutual." They presumed that both sides would use thousands of strategic nuclear weapons—thus "assured destruction." War planners knew that MAD ignored many important realities and avoided using the term. Nevertheless, there was general agreement among military and political leaders that reasonable limits on strategic nuclear weapons on both sides would be acceptable.

The first Strategic Arms Limitations Talks, called SALT I, began during Nixon's first term in 1969 and ended in May 1972. As is the usual case with treaty writing, the participants soon realized that the devil is in the details. During the three years of SALT I negotiations, the USSR increased the number of ICBMs from 1,050 to 1,550. The United States compensated by adding three MIRVs to most of the 550 SAC Minuteman III ICBMs.

While failing to limit offensive weapons, SALT I did produce an agreement signed by Nixon and Brezhnev to limit antiballistic missile systems. This agreement was weakened by including the right for either nation to withdraw after giving six months' notice. There was one important outcome from the three-year SALT I effort. Both nations agreed not to interfere with the verification procedures used to monitor strategic weapon development and basing.

SALT II was a long-running show that began after SALT I was signed and never became law, although both sides generally adhered to the memorandum agreed between Ford and Brezhnev at Vladivostok in 1974. After Carter took office in 1977, he wanted bigger cuts, but the Soviets insisted on the limits proposed at Vladivostok. SALT II negotiations were not completed until mid-1979 when Carter and Brezhnev signed a modified treaty that was never approved by the Senate. Nevertheless, the United States and USSR generally complied with the SALT II terms.

The sum and substance of NATO defense policy changes, of USSR achieving parity with US strategic nuclear forces, and of SALT II was that NATO must have strong conventional forces capable of containing USSR aggression. Failure could lead to a nuclear war devastating to Eastern and Western Europe, the USSR, and the United States.

Ellis Seeks New War Plan

Gen Richard H. Ellis was commander of USAFE as well as commander of Allied Air Forces Central Europe (AAFCE). He was the most decorated officer I served under during my USAF career. His combat awards included the Distinguished Service Cross, Silver Star, Distinguished Flying Cross, Air Medals, and Purple Heart. Noncombat awards included the Defense Distinguished Service Medal, Distinguished Service Medal (AF) with three oak leaf clusters, Legion of Merit with two oak leaf clusters, and numerous foreign awards and decorations.

Aviation cadet Ellis joined the Army Air Corps in 1941 and ended the war as Colonel Ellis. In 1945 he reverted to reserve status and remained in the reserve until recalled by the Korean

War. During the interim years, Ellis obtained a law degree from Dickinson Law School. After the Korean War, he moved through a succession of high-level assignments in Europe and the United States, including vice chief of staff, USAF, before being selected as Commander in Chief USAFE and commander AAFCE. In 1977 General Ellis became Commander in Chief, SAC, and served until retiring in 1981. He was appointed an ambassador on arms control issues after retirement and died in 1989.[3]

I was replacing the retiring deputy chief of staff for operations and intelligence, Maj Gen Jesse Allen. Until Allen left, General Ellis told me to become familiar with the commanders and the operations and intelligence staffs of the numbered Air Forces and visit their principal air bases. USAFE consisted of three numbered air forces: Third Air Force in the UK, Seventeenth Air Force in Central Europe, and Sixteenth Air Force in southern Europe. My previous assignment as director of readiness inspections from 1968 to 1970 provided a benchmark for the visits.

After I returned to Ramstein AB, General Ellis and I had a long talk. We discussed the sum and substance of NATO defense policy changes. Our conversation included how the USSR achieved parity with US strategic nuclear forces and why NATO must have strong conventional forces capable of containing USSR aggression. Another issue was how failure could lead to a devastating nuclear war involving Eastern and Western Europe, the USSR, and the United States.

USAFE Readiness

During the 1976 air base visits, I saw tangible evidence of increased combat readiness throughout USAFE—a credit to the efforts of USAFE commanders from 1971 to 1976: Generals David Jones, John Vogt, and Richard Ellis. When Ellis asked for my impressions after visiting so many USAFE organizations, I gave an overall appraisal of USAFE readiness. A key consideration in my appraisal was the present location of the Warsaw Pact air forces which threatened NATO defenses.

The USSR learned an important lesson about airpower in the last two years of WWII. In order to support its attacking ground forces with more airpower, it improved coordination between senior air and ground commanders. Fighters and bombers were then massed into "air armies" that improved concentration and effectiveness of their firepower. To make support from the air army effective and timely, the Soviets built or occupied airfields close to the launch point for their attacking "ground army." By being closer to the front, Soviet fighters and bombers could spend more time in the target area and be more effective before reaching fuel minimums.

The map below has a solid line that defines the boundary between NATO and Warsaw Pact countries (see fig. 10). (The line begins at the Baltic and runs southward between West Germany and East Germany down to Turkey.) Each dot represents an airfield either in use by military aircraft or capable of being used by military aircraft. The preponderance of air bases

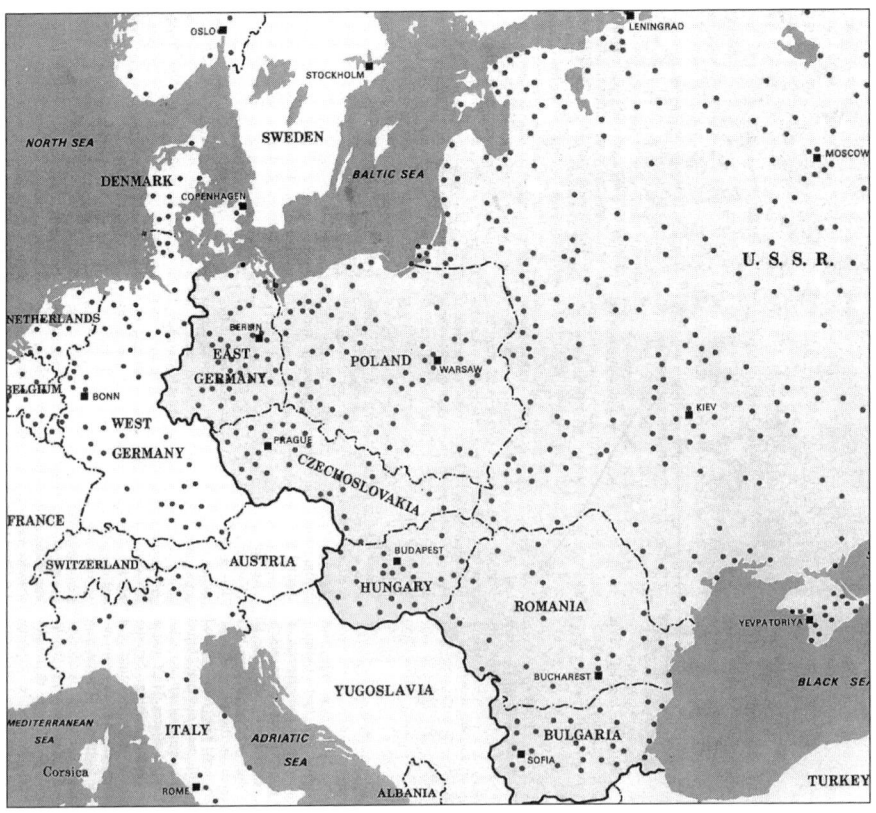

Figure 10. Cold War airfields and boundaries circa 1976

in East Germany, Czechoslovakia, and Poland are located where they could support a Warsaw Pact attack against NATO. NATO bases are normally back from their eastern border—located for air defense and far fewer in number. This Warsaw Pact positioning of air bases constituted one of the many strategic warnings the USSR gave NATO during the Cold War.

USAFE Air Bases. Tactical aircraft routinely operated out of individual concrete shelters which would resist anything except a direct hit by a high-explosive bomb. Belts of US Army HAWK surface-to-air missiles stretched north to south along the eastern border of the central region and reduced our air bases' vulnerability to air attack. The US Army also protected the approaches to our air bases with fast-firing Vulcan cannons mounted on mobile vehicles. Dummy control towers and camouflage at several air bases would confuse any Warsaw Pact pilot attempting to bomb or strafe. Runways could be quickly repaired.

Command and Control. The nearly completed Borfink Bunker would soon give the entire central region a secure underground capability from which to conduct air operations. Alternate command posts at each air base provided communications redundancy. When the new Airborne Warning and Control System (AWACS) aircraft began arriving, NATO would see a major improvement in air defense operations.

Commanders. Every squadron and wing commander I met was a Vietnam veteran with combat experience. Several had also fought in the Korean War.

Aircrews. Captains and majors were all combat experienced from flying in the Vietnam War. Typically, they had been flying high-performance jets for six to 15 years. I doubt if a more qualified crew force existed in any tactical air force, including WWII or the Korean War—certainly not in the Warsaw Pact.

Aircraft. The F-4E was the standard fighter aircraft in USAFE. The versatile F-4 series had been steadily improved since the USAF formed the first two F-4 wings in 1963. A rugged, versatile fighter, the latest model F-4E could kill tanks with the Maverick missile—an important factor since NATO was confronted by Soviet tank armies. USAFE was in the process of receiving the new F-15 fighter with outstanding air-to-air capabilities. Needed was a wartime commitment from SAC

551

for KC-135 tankers. Also needed was the EF-111, still under development but vulnerable to funding delays by presidential candidate Carter.

Maintenance and Support. NCO experience and high morale made these critical areas very strong.

Munitions. Stockpiles of conventional munitions on hand in Europe were too low. The USAF dragged its feet procuring LGBs. Part of the problem was the belief they could not be used in Europe because of clouds, low ceilings, and Warsaw Pact air defenses. Another factor was funding; they cost more than "dumb" bombs. Third was the progress under way in the weapons labs with new precision-guided munitions.

Conventional War Planning. The lack of conventional war planning was a deficiency everywhere I visited. After thoroughly discussing this deficiency then and later, Ellis authorized me to form a combat operations directorate and develop a concept plan for wartime operations in AFCENT.

The lack of conventional war planning was not a new issue to me. While serving on the JCS staff, I was chairman of the operations planner group for Exercise High Heels in 1973 and the J-3 for a similar exercise in 1974. These JCS exercises involved US commands in Europe. The JCS provided a scenario for each exercise that tested the US commands' understanding of plans and policies. In both exercises, US commands quickly sought JCS approval to use tactical nuclear weapons. A fault of the scenarios was that neither exercise adequately tested the USAF's complete understanding or compliance with NATO MC 14/3. Unless their subordinate headquarters had specific operational plans calling for conventional weapons, the US commands could not realistically respond to the JCS scenarios beyond a munitions loading exercise.

Support Plans. There were plans to reinforce USAFE during a crisis with Tactical Air Command, the Air National Guard, and Air Force Reserve units from the United States. An extensive structure of dual basing and collocated operating bases was near completion for bedding down reinforcements. When to deploy reinforcements to USAFE remained an unsettled issue.

Based on these factors, my overall assessment was that USAFE was strong—particularly against enemy air attacks.

Working with the other NATO air forces in the central region and with timely support from the United States, we could overcome the numerical advantages of the Warsaw Pact air forces, but not unless we gained and maintained air superiority.

Warsaw Pact Air Forces versus USAFE

How did the Warsaw Pact air forces compare to USAFE? What were the weaknesses of Warsaw Pact air forces? How could we offset their numerical advantages by exploiting the weaknesses? Could we gain air superiority over central Europe and maintain it over the land battle?

Years of collecting intelligence on the Warsaw Pact air forces gave USAFE intelligence a very clear understanding of their strengths and weaknesses. Fighting the MiG-15 in Korea and the MiG-21 in Vietnam taught us to be properly respectful of the air-to-air capabilities of modern Soviet fighters under GCI control. The payoff from suppressing Soviet-built air defenses was demonstrated in Linebacker II over Hanoi. The penalty for not suppressing Soviet-built air defenses was paid by the Israelis in the Yom Kippur War. The Yom Kippur War also confirmed Soviet SAM effectiveness against fighters unprotected by ECM.

The following explores four advantages and one disadvantage of USAFE in comparison to Warsaw Pact air forces.

Warsaw Pact Combat Experience. The first advantage belonging to USAFE was the reservoir of combat experience gained from three years of fighting in Korea and eight more years in Vietnam. We knew how to conduct successful *offensive* air operations. In contrast, whatever experience the Soviets gained from their limited involvement in Korea and Vietnam accrued from *defensive* air operations by their surrogates—North Korea and North Vietnam.

Warsaw Pact Aircrew Training. The second advantage belonging to USAFE was the quantity and quality of aircrew training. The typical USAFE fighter aircrew flew roughly twice the number of hours in one year than the typical Warsaw Pact aircrew. Mission planning in USAFE was decentralized, giving our aircrews a more thorough understanding of their tasks. USAFE training flights were led by a flight commander, whereas Warsaw Pact training flights were rigidly controlled by the ground-based command and control network.

Warsaw Pact Aircrew Loyalty. The third advantage for all NATO air forces was the questionable loyalty of some Warsaw Pact air forces. Poland, Czechoslovakia, and Hungary had bad histories under the Soviet Union and might be reluctant participants in a war against democratic Western Europe. In the Cold War, there had been few defections by Warsaw Pact aircrews, probably for several reasons. They normally flew in flights and were seldom alone, fuel on board limited their range from home bases, they were under constant radar control while airborne, pilots had high status in their downtrodden society, and the pilot's family served as a hostage against his defection.

Warsaw Pact Equipment. The fourth advantage for USAFE was in equipment. The Soviets made large numbers of excellent rugged, high-performance aircraft. Nevertheless, they tended to trail US manufacturers in both performance and versatility. The success of Soviet aircraft in the Jet Age has been very limited, even when surrogates fought in their own airspace with radar coverage. Whether Warsaw Pact aircraft could operate successfully over Western Europe without assistance from EW and GCI radars is at least doubtful.

Warsaw Pact Numerical Advantage. The Soviets had one important advantage: many more combat aircraft. The Soviets demonstrated in WWII their willingness to accept severe losses in exchange for long-term gains. Unless TAC, ANG, and AFR tactical aircraft reinforced before hostilities, USAFE would be outnumbered by four, five, or six to one by Soviet aircraft. Technology advantages we might have over Soviet aircraft would disappear against those odds. Every commander—air, ground, or sea—needs enough weight in the battle to win. We would probably lose air superiority unless reinforced.

The USAF chief of staff, General Jones, and General Ellis discussed these issues several times. When General Jones agreed to reinforce USAFE during a period of tension and use the expanded base structure of dual basing and COBs for the reinforcing squadrons, it allowed USAFE to plan offensive operations, as well as defensive. Once agreement was reached, the newly formed combat operations directorate began developing a conceptual war plan for the central region called "Counterplan." It addressed the first few days of a war, included a concept of operations to tie everything together, and assigned strategic and tactical objectives to units.

For example, offensive operations included suppressing enemy air defense systems so our fighters could attack targets such as command and control centers, airfields, and supply dumps and gain and maintain air superiority. Suppressing enemy defenses during Linebacker II kept B-52 losses at a tolerable level. In contrast, the Israelis ignored defense suppression in the early stages of the Yom Kippur War and paid a heavy penalty in both combat effectiveness and aircraft losses. NATO armies would pay a heavy penalty to a Warsaw Pact tank-led offensive unless we controlled the air over the battlefield and could provide close air support.

Another critical element of the plan was air refueling support. General Ellis and General Dougherty, CINCSAC, were able to secure a commitment for SAC KC-135 tankers to support the new plan. With SAC KC-135 tankers committed, Counterplan included designated orbit points for air refueling fighters. Among other advantages, air refueling allowed our new F-15s to spend more time on counterair patrol against Warsaw Pact air attacks. The new E-3 AWACS supplemented existing NATO EW and GCI radars and gave a major boost to the air defenses of Western Europe.

After General Ellis approved Counterplan, we briefed our NATO allies and convinced them of the necessity of having an integrated plan for the central region. The essentials were later adopted by NATO, and it morphed into the Central Region Plan for Conventional Operations. In the meantime, General Dixon, commander TAC, asked to be briefed on Counterplan. TAC fighter wings played an important role in USAFE as reinforcements, and Dixon needed to know the concept of operations and understand the tasks expected of TAC units. I flew to Langley AFB and briefed General Dixon and his key staff members. After the briefing, Dixon called me to his office. Through years of experience with Dixon, I expected some caustic comments. Instead, he surprised me. "Dick, that was the best briefing I have ever heard on air operations and a great plan!"

A week or so later, General Ellis said the chief of staff, General Jones, and General Dixon were coming to Ramstein. The chief wanted to hear the Counterplan briefing with only Ellis, Dixon, and himself in the room. I viewed this "command appearance" with some trepidation, although I was confident it would turn out well because of the strong support expressed by Ellis and Dixon.

Small Dogs Should Not Bite Big Dogs!

After briefing the first two or three slides, I could see the chief was upset. He turned to General Dixon for his opinion after stating that we would lose too many aircraft in defense suppression attacks. Dixon said something politic like, "I think you are right, Chief." General Ellis continued smoking his pipe and said nothing.

That afternoon, the four of us played golf on the challenging Ramstein AB course. Dixon's flip-flop during the Counterplan briefing occupied my thoughts. Dixon and I shared the same golf cart. While driving down the first fairway, I asked, "How could you tell Ellis and me one thing last week and then tell the chief the opposite today?" He answered, "You don't understand. I'm your friend and was trying to help you." My final comment showed my frustration, "With friends like you, who needs enemies."

Ellis told me the next day that he still supported Counterplan and to continue briefing our NATO allies. I was in the uncomfortable position of being involved in a policy disagreement between two senior four-star generals. Both Jones and Ellis were experienced commanders with extensive service in Europe. Both had strong opinions about USAFE based upon their own experience. General Jones commanded USAFE for nearly three years before becoming USAF chief of staff in June 1974. He had been the USAFE DCS for operations in the mid-sixties. During his USAFE assignments, he made many innovative changes that improved the combat readiness of this important command.

General Ellis served as the USAF vice chief of staff from 1973 to 1975 before assuming command of USAFE. Ellis had earlier served as vice-commander of USAFE from 1970 to 1971, commander of the 6th Allied Tactical Air Force from 1971 to 1972, and commander of Allied Air Forces, Southern Europe, from 1972 to 1973. With this broad NATO background, Ellis fully understood Europe and the political and military implications of our activities there. In his position as commander of AAFCE, he was able to persuade the other NATO commanders that a more aggressive approach to planning and integration was needed.

In my lifetime, the United States has fought in five significant wars: WWII, Korea, Vietnam, Gulf War I, and, as this is being written, Iraq-Afghanistan. In every war, there have been major disagreements between the principals *on our side* of the conflict. We look back on WWII with rose-colored glasses, but the intramural battles between Eisenhower and Sir Alan Brooke, George Marshall and Winston Churchill, Nimitz and MacArthur, Patton and Gen Sir Bernard Montgomery, and others created controversy and jeopardized wartime operations. These WWII adversaries were competent, experienced leaders who *knew* they were right. Most disagreements centered on strategies, plans, and priorities.

Several administrations in the United States since WWII have tried to codify by law the responsibilities of the senior civilian and military leaders, thereby eliminating friction and improving effectiveness. To simplify the military pecking order, picture a professional football team. The owner pays the players and staff, buys uniforms, hires the manager, and so forth. The manager arranges schedules, drafts players, finds transportation, and chooses the coaching staff. The coach designs the plays, trains the players, makes the game plan, and directs the game.

The "owners" in the military are Congress and the president. The "managers" are the secretary of defense, JCS chairman, service secretaries, and chiefs of the Army, Navy, Air Force, and Marines. The "coaches" are the commanders of the operational commands, such as US European, Central, Pacific, and Southern Commands. The team often has a losing season if the "owner" tells the "coach" what plays to call or the "coach" can't control the players and blames the "manager."

In the Vietnam War, the chain of command for planning and operational control of USAF forces began with what was then known as the National Command Authorities—president, national security advisor, and secretary of defense—and passed down the chain of command through the JCS chairman to CINCPAC, CINCSAC, and the MACV commander. For example, the Air Force chief of staff could advise, but not direct, the combat operations of PACAF or SAC. The secretary of the Air Force had no role in war planning or operations—a policy later changed by the Goldwater-Nichols Defense Reorganization Act of 1986.

Gen Al Haig was the Supreme Allied Commander, Europe, as well as US Commander in Chief, Europe. General Ellis was commander of AAFCE, as well as Commander in Chief of USAFE. If NATO went to war, Haig would inherit Eisenhower's WWII responsibilities, and Ellis would be in charge of NATO air forces in the central region. Ellis's other boss was General Jones, USAF chief of staff. Jones was "manager" of the entire USAF team, along with the SecDef, CJCS, and Air Force secretary. Although it did not control NATO planning and operations, the Pentagon did control most resources, equipage, manning, training, transportation, and other forms of support necessary for wartime success.

The issue of planning wartime air operations in Europe surfaced before USAFE developed Counterplan. General Jones had formed a study group in the Pentagon working on USAFE concepts of operations. It included officers in the Air Staff who had previously served in USAFE. As might be expected, their knowledge gradually became outdated because of the change from MC 14/2 to MC 14/3, the rapid buildup of Warsaw Pact forces in the mid-seventies, and the technological improvements in our own Air Force and in the air forces of our NATO allies. The Air Staff product was called "Checkmate" and included a European war game. USAFE was not asked to participate in its effort. After receiving the finished Checkmate, the USAFE staff determined that it was interesting but lacked depth and contained major errors.

On 31 July 1977, General Ellis left USAFE to become CINCSAC. Gen William "Bill" Evans, recent commander of Air Force Systems Command, replaced Ellis. I worked with General Evans in the Pentagon during the early '70s and had great respect for his abilities. A fighter pilot with extensive combat and command experience in both Korea and Vietnam, he was very knowledgeable about the newest advances in military aviation. The day after Evans arrived, he asked for the Counterplan briefing. He said afterwards, "By the way, the last thing General Jones said when I left his office was, 'First thing you should do is fire Leavitt!'"

Then he said, "Dick, I like the Counterplan and agree with the concept. Continue working with our allies and bring them into the plan." It was a pleasure working for General Evans.

Busy at Work

Gen David Jones merged operations and intelligence under one deputy chief of staff when he commanded USAFE from 1971 to 1974. Jones's experience as vice-commander of Seventh Air Force during the Vietnam War had convinced him that the two functions needed to work closer together. The merger created a complex and challenging job for one deputy, but his thesis was correct. My days began early in the morning by reading intelligence reports that focused on any changes in the status of Warsaw Pact forces. After a day filled with operational issues, staff meetings, visitors, telephone calls, reviewing correspondence, and listening to briefings, I would carry a briefcase full of paperwork to finish in my quarters after dinner.

On 27 March 1977 in the early evening, the phone rang from the USAFE Command Post. A terrible accident at Tenerife's Los Rodeos Airport in the Canary Islands had just occurred. Two Boeing 747s full of tourists had collided, one belonging to KLM and the other to Pan Am. They had been diverted earlier to Los Rodeos because a terrorist's bomb had exploded in the passenger terminal at Las Palmas.

The early report stated there were survivors from Pan Am 747. Not knowing the quality of medical care in the Canary Islands, I asked the command post to locate a medical evacuation aircraft for a possible flight to Los Rodeos. Then I called the American Embassy in Madrid (Canary Islands belong to Spain) and advised that we could quickly arrange to evacuate injured people to Spain or to any other major trauma center for burn patients in Europe. Since an American airline was involved, I also offered to send trained aircraft investigators from USAFE to help. An hour or so later, the embassy called back. The Spanish had declined all our offers of assistance.

This accident became the *single most deadly accident in aviation history* with 583 people killed. There were many contributing factors to this accident. Heavy fog obscured the taxiways and runway. Neither aircrew was familiar with the airfield. The tower operator did not give clear taxi and takeoff instructions. The KLM pilot attempted takeoff without being cleared; all on board were killed. The Pan Am pilot missed the intended taxiway for turning off and blocked the takeoff runway where the KLM 747 was taking off. Seventy persons on the Pan Am aircraft survived and were hospitalized. Nine of the 70 died from their injuries. Whether our medical evacuation would have saved their lives is problematic.

One morning, while reading the daily International Criminal Police Organization (INTERPOL) report, an item caught my attention. The French police reported that Carlos, the notorious terrorist fictionalized in *The Day of the Jackal*, was driving from Italy to Yugoslavia and would cross the border at Trieste at a certain time. The car was a Mercedes with a known license plate. I immediately called General Ellis and suggested the Italians should pick him up. Ellis passed the information to General Haig, SACEUR. About an hour later, Ellis called back with the bad news. Haig said that the Italians declined. They were not looking for trouble and would not interfere with Carlos leaving Italy.

During the '70s, the USSR began allowing a limited number of its Jewish citizens, including several well-known dissidents, to emigrate from Russia. The majority sought permanent residence in Israel and the United States. While waiting for approval and documentation, they were temporarily detained in West Germany. If emigrants were willing, our Russian-speaking intelligence personnel interviewed them. Of special interest were those who had served recently in the Soviet armed forces. There was no coercion—if they did not want to talk about their prior assignments in the Soviet military, the interview ended. Those who would talk usually provided only basic information about training, discipline, and morale. There were exceptions. One former NCO drew a detailed sketch of a new SAM site including measurements, types of equipment, and technical details. All in all, the interviews provided a broad picture of present-day life and morale in the Soviet armed forces.

General Ellis wore two hats—CINCUSAFE and commander, Allied Air Forces Central Europe. Headquarters USAFE and Headquarters AAFCE shared the same building at Ramstein AB. Ellis could walk down the hall from his USAFE office and be in his AAFCE office in a minute or two. Periodically, USAFE would participate in a large-scale exercise involving the national air forces assigned to NATO. The alert notices for one of these AAFCE exercises were sent early one morning to the command post for each of the national air forces.

After the exercise had been under way for awhile, each national headquarters reported its state of readiness. Ellis asked me to monitor the USAFE responses while he watched the other national responses. Everything was going well; all the national air forces were meeting their commitments except one—the First Canadian Air Group at CDB Lahr, Germany, had not responded.

General Ellis returned to his USAFE office and used the secure phone to call Lahr. The Canadian group commander, a brigadier general, was called to the phone. After identifying himself as the AAFCE commander, Ellis asked, "General, why has your group not responded to the NATO exercise?" Ellis listened for a moment, looked like he might break the phone in two, then said, "We will see about that!" and hung up. I worked for General Ellis for five years. He was a remarkably calm man—never raised his voice, always polite and courteous—even when he disagreed. That day was one of the two times when I ever saw him truly angry.

After waiting a moment for him to cool off, curiosity forced me to ask Ellis what the Canadian said that disturbed him. Ellis told me the Canadian brigadier said, "I don't have to take orders from you. I am Canadian!"

Events moved quickly after their brief conversation. The Canadian government removed the brigadier from command that day, returned him to Canada the next day, and retired him. This incident was an unusual exception to the good working relations that existed between the AAFCE commander and all the subordinate NATO commanders. Ellis was right in demanding action against the insubordinate brigadier. NATO could only be effective in crisis, or in wartime, by all nations clinging to their "all for one and one for all" commitment and complying with orders from the NATO chain of command.

Borfink Bunker was a large, secure underground facility intended to be the command and control center for the central region during periods of tension and in wartime. When General Jones commanded AAFCE, he was able to move Borfink from the concept phase to construction. In 1976, as the project entered the final phases of construction, USAFE began losing control. Experts in communications were not talking to the engineers who were constructing it, manning became an issue, the interior arrangements created disagreements, and personnel from other central region nations delayed making important decisions. The situation called for corrective action.

I supervised a new management group called Deep Look that met once a week. It amounted to a progress review for the Borfink Bunker. Each weekly meeting had a specific agenda, but there were many submeetings during the week to thrash out the details. Deep Look acted as a forum where all the agencies involved met, talked out their differences, and made agreements. With technical assistance from Air Force Systems Command, we overcame the foot-dragging, and Borfink became operational in late 1977.

One of my most important tasks in USAFE was working with the commanders and operational staffs of our NATO allies. The Royal Air Force and German Luftwaffe were next in size to USAFE, but smaller air forces belonging to the Netherlands, Belgium, Denmark, and Canada also had important roles to play in the central region. The large French air force, with excellent aircraft, well-trained aircrews, and modern air bases, did not participate and remained an enigma.

France joined NATO in April 1949. After Gen Charles de Gaulle became president in 1958, he started a phased withdrawal from the NATO integrated military structure. De Gaulle's principal objection seemed to be having all NATO forces under a US commander. In 1966, after the French had developed their own nuclear capability, de Gaulle announced their final withdrawal from the integrated military structure. American bases in France closed, and NATO headquarters moved to Belgium. France remained a member of the North Atlantic Council—the highest political authority in NATO.

While General Lemnitzer was SACEUR, agreements were made with the French to fight alongside allied forces in the event of war if the French chose to participate. Hoping they might choose to fight alongside us, we kept them abreast of our intentions and capabilities. I twice briefed senior French generals on how the French air force would fit into AAFCE war plans.

Although their immediate reactions to both briefings were very positive, I knew that the only response from Paris would be a thank-you note.

NATO air commanders in the UK and central region were generally friendly, interested, and willing to learn from USAF experience in Vietnam and other places. They lacked the more sophisticated USAF capabilities, such as PGMs, AWACS, and advanced ECM, but understood how these new capabilities would change the way Airmen fight wars. A special relationship existed between the RAF and USAF that traced back to WWII. Despite this bank of goodwill, USAFE and the RAF never agreed on all the command and control mechanisms in the central region.

General Haig pushed hard to have common communications systems with our NATO allies. "Interoperability" was the buzzword for describing this sensible objective. Imagine two army divisions, one German and the other US, fighting side by side against a Soviet attack through the Fulda Gap but unable to communicate with each other. Or RAF fighters engaged in a massive air battle with Soviet MiGs but unable to call USAFE fighters flying nearby. There was no simple solution because of technical limitations and high costs. Defense Department procurement policies chose interoperability between the US Navy, Marine Corps, Army, and Air Force over interoperability with NATO.

Air Show in Iran

The Shah of Iran had a strong interest in making the Imperial Iranian Air Force (IIAF) the best air force in the Middle East. His role model was the USAF. Iran purchased whatever first-line equipment the United States would allow for export. During the late '60s and early '70s, the IIAF bought more than 200 F-4s, mostly E models, and one squadron of RF-4s. The Shah's interests in military aviation did not stop with equipment. The Shah's young son was in the midst of USAF pilot training when the 1979 revolution occurred.

The Shah requested that USAFE send a squadron of F-4Es in the spring of 1977 to Iran, where US aircrews would join the IIAF in a training exercise. Iran would pay all expenses, including fuel, in exchange for USAFE F-4E aircrews instructing IIAF aircrews in fighter tactics and weapons delivery. Each flight of four aircraft would have two Iranian and two American crews—an American would lead the flight, the other American would lead the element, and two IIAF crews would be wingmen.

Iran prepared Shiraz Air Base for a firepower demonstration. Destroying targets on the airfield with F-4s delivering live munitions would be the climax of the training exercise. The Shah, American ambassador William H. Sullivan, and other high-ranking VIPs would witness the demonstration from a viewing stand near the runway.

General Ellis sent me to Iran to observe USAFE performance and to handle another sensitive issue. The Shah knew the USAF had developed new ECM pods for jamming Soviet air defense and SAM radars. The IIAF commander was pressing hard to get this equipment for the Iranian F-4Es. At the time, the political stability of the Shah's government was becoming an issue, and the USAF could not risk compromising our newest ECM equipment. I was to defuse the ECM issue by explaining to the Shah and Gen Amir Hossein Rabbi, IIAF commander, that shortages of the new equipment did not permit export.

Maj Gen Ken Miles, the chief of the military assistance advisory group, met me at Tehran's airport. Concern had reached the point where Americans serving as military advisors took special precautions in traveling to and from work because of rising unrest. Ken described life in Tehran as a series of contrasts between the haves and have-nots and the increasing political unrest between the Khomeini-led Shia mullahs and the Shah's government.

I traveled to Shiraz on exercise day. The Shah and Iranian and American VIPs were seated in a large briefing room. The building was T-shaped. The Shah sat at the head of the T in front of the briefing podium. One arm of the T led to a new radar simulator; the other arm led to offices and restrooms. An IIAF colonel speaking English described the agenda for the exercise. The colonel finished the briefing by telling the Shah that he could visit the radar simulator by walking down the center aisle and turning left. The Shah left his seat, walked down the aisle, and started to turn right. The colonel blurted out, "No! No! Turn left!" The Shah stopped, glanced back, and turned left. As the words left his mouth, the colonel turned pale. He looked like a rope had been placed around his neck, or he heard a firing squad say, "Ready . . . Aim . . . ."

After reassembling in the VIP reviewing stand, the firepower demonstration started. Maverick missiles, six-barreled Gatling guns firing 20 mm shells, and napalm and conventional bombs impressively destroyed all the targets. At one point, a Boeing 747 with an air-refueling capability flew by with four F-4Es in tow. This was an unusual sight since USAF KC-135 tankers were modifications of the much smaller Boeing 707.

During a halftime break, Sullivan, the US ambassador, introduced me to the Shah, who was sitting on an elevated seat in front of us. After shaking hands, I told the Shah that we had met years ago when he visited West Point. Rufus Smith and I were demonstrating plebe wrestling when he stopped to observe. I explained to the Shah why the USAF could not sell Iran the advanced ECM jammers at this time. He called General Rabbi to come over while we were talking. Whenever Rabbi spoke, he stood at attention and held his salute while talking. Since I was standing at ease and speaking in a conversational tone to the Shah, I felt compassion for Rabbi.

The Shah suggested that it would be better for us to discuss the details in Rabbi's office in Tehran. We made an appointment and met there later. Without much discussion of ECM pods, Rabbi and I talked of other matters. I quickly understood why Amir Rabbi was highly respected by the American officers in TAC and the Air Staff who knew him.

My first exposure to the Shah's ambitious program for the IIAF was at Chanute where we trained Iranian maintenance personnel. During this short trip to Iran, I learned these *homofar*—warrant officer equivalents—had provided the technical know-how required to keep the IIAF combat ready. That solved one problem, but they created another. The *homofar* were very dissatisfied with their status. They were college graduates with engineering degrees and had been drafted for an indefinite period of time. The first signs of insurrection leading to the revolution occurred at the IIAF air bases. The leaders of the revolt were the *homofar*, according to US sources.

In 1978 events began spinning out of control in Iran. The Shah took desperate steps to reduce the violent outbreaks.

The Shah departed Iran on 16 January 1979 for treatment of cancer and appointed a regency council to rule in his absence. The council failed to stop the dissidence. President Carter's efforts to stem the revolution were too late. In a last-ditch, ill-conceived effort, Gen "Dutch" Huyser went to Tehran and met with the Iranian equivalent of our JCS. Huyser's presence stirred up more trouble.

Huyser told Ellis and me in 1980 that we would never have an experience like his. The day before he left, 100,000 Iranians stood in front of his hotel screaming, "Kill Huyser!" During his meeting with the Iranian chiefs before leaving, Huyser asked each one to pledge he would stay and keep Iran from becoming a communist or radical Islamist government. The chiefs individually promised to stay. General Rabbi—with his hand slapped over his pistol holster—said if they did not stay, he would kill them himself.

The revolution continued. Many senior military officials were executed, including Gen Amir Rabbi, friend of America. When President Carter allowed the Shah to enter a cancer clinic in New York in early November 1979, an irate mob stormed the American Embassy and kept 55 American male prisoners for the next 444 days. Not until Inauguration Day for newly elected President Reagan were the Americans released. The American romance with Iran was over.

Time Heals Old Wounds

My two tours in Germany were roughly a decade apart. During the sixties, Germany still had scars from WWII, and the typical German veteran seemed to be in denial about his role in the war, at least when talking to an American. The WWII Luftwaffe pilots that I met at that time usually claimed to have fought only on the Russian Front, never against Americans. By the late seventies, Germany had changed, its economy had prospered, and its reluctance to discuss fighting against Americans had disappeared. Now a NATO member, the new, democratic Germany greatly strengthened our alliance.

Lt Gen Bernhardt, a Luftwaffe officer, was deputy commander of AAFCE. General Bernhardt's father had been a pilot in the First World War, was shot down over Russia, and captured.

After the Russian Revolution, he managed to escape and spent the next three years evading capture, finally making it back to Germany in the early twenties. The elder Bernhardt stayed in the German army, became a general, and fought on the Russian Front during WWII. After the war, the Soviets executed him along with several hundred other German generals who had surrendered.

His son flew FW-190 fighters during WWII. During the last few days of the war, Captain Bernhardt flew from an air base in southwestern Germany against the US Eighth and Ninth Air Forces. On his last day in combat, he landed low on fuel and out of ammunition. The air base had no ammunition and could only give him enough fuel to reach another air base near Munich. He flew to that air base. Personnel there told him they were out of both fuel and ammunition and that the Americans were rapidly approaching. Bernhardt decided he would avoid capture by walking up the mountain toward Berchtesgaden where Berghof, Hitler's home, was located.

Bernhardt began walking through the woods and up the mountain wearing his flight suit. SS troops making a last-ditch stand fired at him. Better to be captured by Americans than killed by Germans, he started back down the mountain. A squad of American GIs appeared. He surrendered to them. They told him to keep walking; they did not want any prisoners. After this happened several times, he decided to walk to Munich where his mother lived. After hiding there until the war officially ended, Bernhardt became a professional photographer. When the Federal Republic of Germany started the new Luftwaffe, he was asked to join and by 1976 had been promoted to lieutenant general.

My major general friend, the Luftwaffe deputy for operations, was a 13-year-old Hitler Youth near the end of the war. As Patton's armored columns breached the German fortifications near the Luxembourg-German border, his Hitler Youth group was given rifles, taken to a ditch near a bridge, and told to stop the Americans from crossing it. They hid in the ditch and waited for action. A short while later, one of Patton's tanks approached the bridge and started to cross. The turret gun swung toward the ditch where they were hiding. Suddenly, the tank stopped, and the hatch opened. A tough-looking old sergeant appeared.

"You kids! Drop your rifles and get the hell out of here before I shoot you all!" They scrambled from the ditch, leaving their rifles, and went back home. Their war was over.

Cake Cutting in Potsdam

The winter and spring of 1977 were grim times for American forces in NATO and elsewhere. On the other side of the Iron Curtain, the buildup of both conventional and nuclear armaments continued at a rapid pace. Despite intelligence confirming the Warsaw Pact buildup, newly elected President Carter's actions indicated there would be significant cuts in defense spending. Shortly after his inauguration, President Carter cancelled the B-1 bomber program except for four test aircraft already produced. The FY 1977 defense budget dropped below 5 percent of the GDP for the first time during the Cold War. The FY 1978 defense budget was even lower, while inflation was rapidly rising to historic highs.

My corollary in the German air force was a young major general, trained to fly in the United States, who was well on his way to becoming its chief of staff. In one of our frequent conversations, he disclosed it was building another large underground bunker. Since Boerfink Bunker served as the command and control center for all NATO air forces in the central region and was nearing completion, I asked him the purpose of this new underground bunker. He explained it was for logistics support and invited me to visit the bunker in the near future when it was completed.

Some gratuitous remarks by key officials in the new Carter administration implied our commitment to NATO was not as strong as it had been. The German military reacted to these remarks by cautiously withdrawing from the frank and open discussions that we had held in the past. Whenever I asked afterwards about visiting the new bunker, my friend managed to find an excuse to postpone the promised visit. General Ellis shared my opinion that the Germans had decided not "to put all their eggs in one basket" and were preparing to fight alone if the United States defaulted on the NATO commitment.

The Warsaw Pact and NATO showed official concern about the arms race in Central Europe by beginning the Mutual and

Balanced Force Reduction (MBFR) talks in 1973. The Warsaw Pact had 925,000 ground troops, and NATO had 777,000. The Warsaw Pact also had 15,500 tanks and 2,770 tactical aircraft versus 6,000 NATO tanks and 1,220 tactical aircraft in the region. These talks were intended to reduce the disparity between the size of NATO and Warsaw Pact forces, thus abating the possibility of war. MBFR made little progress because both sides had excluded strategic and tactical nuclear weapons from the talks.

To hold their numerical advantages, Warsaw Pact nations agreed at Helsinki in August 1975 to adopt several confidence-building measures that would eliminate the causes for tension in Europe. They would provide prior notification of major military maneuvers in Europe and, if applicable, the adjoining sea area and airspace. They also agreed voluntarily to invite observers to attend their military maneuvers. Additionally, they would give prior notification of major troop movements, at their own discretion. This was important because the USSR brought 100,000 troops into East Germany every spring as replacements. We needed to know if another 100,000 troops rotated back to the USSR.

The unforeseen Soviet invasion of Czechoslovakia in 1968 showed how quickly USSR tank armies could move and achieve a political objective. The disparity in force structures between NATO and the Warsaw Pact forced NATO to be always alert to the possibility of attack. For that reason, USAFE intelligence constantly monitored Warsaw Pact activities. One way to spot trouble before it happened was to daily plot its activities, establish a norm, and then look for deviations from the norm. In the winter and spring of 1977, there were some alarming deviations in these indicators.

For example, we had difficulty determining whether the normal rotation of troops had occurred. The USSR brought in 100,000 fresh troops, but were another 100,000 sent back to the USSR? Recent large Warsaw Pact exercises involving land, sea, and air forces were most disconcerting. After assessing these threatening actions, General Ellis asked for permission to keep one-third of our fighters loaded and on alert. Lacking guidance to the contrary, he placed one-third of our tactical aircraft on ground alert. A short time later, USAFE received notice to stand down all tactical aircraft until further notice. Ellis asked Haig what was happening. Haig told Ellis he did not know the reason for the stand-down.

In Berlin several key intelligence supervisors from another agency returned to West Germany and were replaced by their assistants. I learned later that a number of intelligence officers at Ramstein had quietly loaded emergency provisions in the family car and warned their wives about a possible evacuation. After several days, USAFE was told to resume normal operations. I never learned the reason for the stand-down. General Ellis supposed it was a way to make the Warsaw Pact aware of our concerns.

The US CINC, European Command, decided that meeting with the commanders of the Soviet Forces in Germany might shed light on the unusual pattern of Soviet activities. Facing them with a military agenda would be an intrusion on State Department or NSC prerogatives. On the other hand, an informal social gathering might not step on the toes of Washington bureaucrats and might decrease tensions in Germany.

An anachronism from World War II was an agreement allowing the Soviet Union to have a chateau in West Germany and the United States to have one in East Germany at Potsdam, a suburb of Berlin. The US Army's Berlin Brigade maintained the palatial old building with East German servants. We were warned that the Potsdam chateau was bugged and the servants were Soviet agents, so it was seldom used for official business.

On 7 May 1945, one of the last days of World War II, American and Soviet armies met on the Elbe River. Why not honor that anniversary by inviting the top Soviet commanders in Germany to join their American corollaries at the American chateau in Potsdam? The Soviets agreed and invited US Army commanders to their chateau in Frankfurt on that date.

General Ellis selected me to represent USAFE at the anniversary party in Potsdam. We talked about what could be gained from this meeting and determined two objectives. First, make the Russians aware that we watched them closely and knew what they were doing. Second, find out why they were not responding to the mutual agreements about simultaneous exercises, stand-downs, and reinforcements.

It was twilight on 7 May 1977 when the T-39 landed at Berlin's Tempelhof airfield. An Army staff car drove us through Checkpoint Charlie at the Berlin Wall and into East Berlin. As darkness descended, the contrast between brightly lighted, prosperous West Berlin and rundown, dismal East Berlin became overwhelming. With single lightbulbs hanging from bare ceilings, no traffic on the streets, the sidewalks empty of people, neighborhood stores dark, and an occasional dimly lit bar, East Berlin looked like a throwback to the mid-1800s.

Nearing Potsdam, we passed a large Soviet barracks with a high concrete wall surrounding the buildings. Then our headlights spotted a Soviet soldier dashing across the street, leaping up, grasping the top of the wall, and swinging himself over the wall into the barracks courtyard. The driver said the Russian troops could not be alone in the city and usually stayed in the barracks. When they were allowed out, they stayed in squad-sized groups for sightseeing. We speculated our "fence jumper" was a buck sergeant who risked losing a stripe in order to visit a local Fräulein.

US Army, European Command (USAREUR) made all the arrangements for the celebration. General Blanchard, CINCUSAREUR, was the host and brought several senior Army staff officers with him. The commanding general of the Soviet Forces in Germany, Blanchard's corollary, brought his staff. I represented USAFE. My corollary was a Russian major general who was director of operations for the Soviet tactical air forces in Germany. He brought along an English-speaking translator.

After introductions, we went to the bar, where both groups were cautiously assembling. I asked the translator what the general would like to drink. He responded, "Vodka and water, please." After the general took one sip, he handed it back. The translator said, "Too strong." A mild second drink apparently met his standards. We then went through a very elaborate buffet line. He wanted to follow me and was obviously nervous about making a social faux pas. Everything I took and ate, he took and ate—this guy was taking no chances!

We exchanged a few pleasantries before getting down to business. I wanted him to realize that we knew what they were doing. In an exercise, the general had landed a MiG-21 on the autobahn leading to Berlin a day or two earlier. I told the translator, "The general landed a MiG-21 on the Berlin autobahn two days ago. Ask him if it was hard to do." Looking like he might choke, the general finally answered, "Nyet, OK."

After dinner, I joined a British general who was talking to two Russians. One of the English-speaking Russians asked if I had ever seen the Soviet Union. I answered, "Yes, but only from above. I was a U-2 pilot." The Brit looked indignant, "I say old boy, you shouldn't say that!" I ignored the Brit, who may have thought this was still highly classified information, but the Russians looked impressed as the subject changed to a less controversial item.

Gen George Blanchard and the Soviet commanding general brought everyone together for a cake-cutting ceremony in the large, ornate dining room. With big smiles all around, they theatrically used a saber to cut the big cake. While this was ending, I approached the number two Soviet general, a tall

Photo courtesy US Air Force

General Blanchard and Soviet general cutting cake

man who had been an Olympic athlete in earlier days and spoke English. I asked him if we could talk privately in another room. He agreed.

I mentioned one by one the unusual activities that we had observed in the last few months, including the recent simultaneous land, sea, and air exercises. "General, could you explain why the Soviet forces in Germany are doing this instead of honoring the Helsinki principles?" His answer left me cold. "General, I don't know anything about these things." He turned on his heel and walked away. I stood still for a minute, thinking this man wore the real face of our enemy. I flew back to Ramstein that night. Not a happy day, but it showed whom we were up against.

Auf Wiedersehen, USAFE

Late in the afternoon of 27 September 1977, I was scheduled to fly an F-4E to a meeting in the UK and to return that evening. I usually piloted a T-39 to meetings within USAFE but occasionally took an F-4E to stay current in our primary business. The F-4E was parked in a concrete shelter built to protect combat aircraft from air attack. The crew chief and the backseater were standing by the F-4E awaiting my arrival.

In northern Europe, darkness comes early in the fall. After strapping into the front seat and putting on my helmet—reality struck! There was not enough light in the hangar. I could not read the gauges. I swallowed my pride and called the crew chief. "Sergeant, please get a tug and pull the aircraft forward so I can see the gauges." After the F-4 moved, I started engines. With gauges and switches now visible, I took off and headed for the UK. On the return flight, I came to grips with my problem. After flying fighters for over 27 years, my eyes were not good enough to fly alone in a fighter anymore. My 49th birthday was still a few weeks away, but I already felt my youth was gone!

In October 1977 Brig Gen Clyde Garner, assistant deputy chief of staff for operations and intelligence, finished his three-year tour. Clyde had commanded the 50th TFW at Hahn prior to his promotion to brigadier and subsequent transfer to Headquarters USAFE. Clyde was a personable, well-liked officer who seemed to know everyone in USAFE. His background knowledge and advice had made my job much easier during the past year.

General Ellis, now CINCSAC, chose Clyde to command SAC's 57th Air Division with the headquarters at Minot AFB, North Dakota. As a long-time fighter pilot, Clyde was surprised when he found his new command included four large air bases—two with both B-52Hs and KC-135s and two with 150 Minuteman III missiles assigned to each. Clyde retired in 1980. He suffered from multiple brain tumors and died shortly after retiring to his home in Texas.

When he left, General Ellis asked me if I would like to return to SAC. The lieutenant general commanding Fifteenth Air Force was retiring in a few months, and I would replace him. Until then, I would be SAC's chief of staff. I enjoyed working for General Evans but looked forward to the opportunity for a command in SAC. So I thanked Ellis and waited for orders. They arrived in November with a January 1978 reporting date.

Maj Gen Robert W. "Bill" Clement replaced Clyde at USAFE. A "star man" in the 1950 class from West Point, Bill had an unusually versatile and successful USAF career. In the '50s, he flew 100 combat missions in the Korean War, ferried fighters across the Atlantic to NATO, earned a graduate degree, taught math at the Air Force Academy, and was chief of computer programming at the Air Force Intelligence Center.

In the sixties, Bill flew F-100s and F-4s in USAFE, graduated from the Army War College, was executive assistant to the MACV commander, became an operations officer in the 8th TFW at Ubon, and joined J-3, JCS, as an operations staff officer.

In the seventies, Bill was vice-commander, 81st TFW in the UK; commander, 432d TFW at Udorn; base commander, Wright-Patterson AFB; commander, 35th TFW at George AFB, CA; and vice-commander, Twelfth Air Force, before coming to Ramstein.[4] Bill was a great asset to the USAFE staff. He replaced me in January when I left for SAC.

Notes

1. Soviet estimates are from Cline, *World Power Assessment*, 57. SAC data is from Hopkins and Goldberg, *Development of Strategic Air Command, 1946–1986*.
2. Central Intelligence Agency, *Handbook of Economic Statistics*, 62, 63, 65.
3. US Air Force, "Biographies: General Richard H. Ellis."
4. US Military Academy, *Register of Graduates*.

Chapter 15

HQ SAC
Lieutenant General—1978–81

New Job—SAC

By mid-January 1978, I was working at my new job as chief of staff, HQ SAC, at Offutt AFB, Nebraska. General Ellis, my boss in USAFE, had become CINCSAC when his predecessor, General Dougherty, retired in August 1977. In June 1978, I became Vice-Commander in Chief of SAC and was promoted to lieutenant general. As such, I served as commander in the absence of General Ellis, supervised the functions of HQ SAC, chaired several boards and special projects, and worked sensitive problems and issues not resolved at subordinate SAC commands.

Photo courtesy US Air Force

Headquarters SAC, circa 1980

SAC was the largest major air command in 1978 with more than 118,000 officers, Airmen, and civilians located on 25 air bases in the CONUS and Guam (see table 1). Principal subordinate commands were Eighth Air Force located at Barksdale AFB and Fifteenth Air Force located at March AFB. Each air force was commanded by a lieutenant general. Subordinate to the two air forces were air divisions, normally commanded by brigadier generals. A typical air division included B-52/KC-135 wings and an ICBM wing located at two or more air bases.

Table 1. SAC statistics 1979–80

Command Leadership	
Commander in Chief	Gen Richard H. Ellis
Vice-Commander in Chief	Lt Gen Lloyd R. Leavitt, Jr.
Chief of staff	Maj Gen Earl G. Peck
Personnel	
Officers	18,575
Airmen	85,401
Civilians	14,217
Total	118,193
Air Order of Battle	
Bombers	80 B-52Ds 270 B-52G/Hs 68 FB-111As
Tankers	485 KC-135s 128 KC-135s ANG/AFR
Reconnaissance	22 U-2s 18 SR-71s 15 RC-135s
ICBMs	54 Titan IIs 450 Minuteman IIs 550 Minuteman IIIs
Attack missiles	1,383 SRAMs
Command aircraft	4 E-4A/B national emergency airborne command post 15 EC-135 airborne command post

Source: J. C. Hopkins and Sheldon A. Goldberg, *The Development of Strategic Air Command, 1946–1986: The Fortieth Anniversary History* (Omaha, NE: Office of the Historian, Headquarters SAC, Offutt AFB, 1986).

During the Vietnam War era, tactical air forces had received the lion's share of the Air Force budget. No new bombers were being produced for SAC; the last B-52 and B-58 bombers were delivered in October 1962. The last KC-135 tanker was delivered in January 1965. The phaseout of B-47 bombers and KC-97 tankers was accelerated the same year. In December 1965, SecDef McNamara called for the retirement of all B-58 bombers and the older B-52s by the end of June 1971. He also announced that 210 FB-111s would replace the older bombers, but only 66 FB-111s were acquired before production ended.[1]

President Carter took office in January 1977, and it soon became clear that his administration would severely curtail defense spending. Initially, this meant there would be no new strategic programs. First on the chopping block was the B-1 bomber, and Carter canceled production shortly after his inauguration. Instead, the new administration turned to developing cruise missiles. Next to be cut was the McDonnell-Douglas advanced tanker/cargo aircraft. The 91 KC-10s approved by President Ford were reduced to 20.

Guidance from the civilian secretaries in the Defense Department forced Ellis to abandon SAC's advocacy for the strategic modernization required to regain dominance over the USSR—a military advantage the United States had held until this point in the Cold War. Ellis now testified that the US strategic objective would be to maintain "essential equivalence" with the USSR. Theoretically, with strategic nuclear forces in balance, both the USSR and the United States would be deterred from nuclear war. Our major challenge in HQ SAC was keeping alive the need for SAC modernization with HQ USAF, the SecDef, and Congress within the constraints imposed by "essential equivalence."

In several respects, SAC in 1978 was similar to a very large American corporation. Money is the most common denominator shared by private industry and the military. With a strong product and good sales, money becomes plentiful. If not, factories close, jobs are lost, and stock plummets. In the USAF, insufficient money causes aircraft and missiles to be difficult to maintain and less capable air base installations to deteriorate, pay to stagnate, and morale and retention to decline.

Three related economic factors caused SAC to have severe financial problems in fiscal years 1977, 1978, and 1979: (1) the high inflation rate, as measured by the consumer price index (CPI) during both the Ford and Carter presidencies; (2) the federal budget outlay for defense as a percentage of the GDP declined during the Carter presidency below 5 percent for the first time since the Korean War; and (3) SAC's pro rata share of the defense budget was reduced by approximately 25 percent during the first three years of the Carter presidency (see table 2—Carter years are displayed in italics).

Table 2. SAC defense budget 1975–80

Fiscal Year	Defense % of GDP	Defense Budget (Billions)	SAC Share of FY Budget (Billions)	SAC % of Defense Budget	CPI Inflation
1975	5.6%	$87.6	$2.6	2.96%	9.1%
1976	5.2%	$89.9	$3.2	3.55%	5.8%
1977	4.9%	$97.5	$2.4	2.46%	6.5%
1978	4.7%	$104.6	$2.4	2.29%	7.6%
1979	4.7%	$116.8	$2.5	2.14%	11.3%
1980	4.9%	$134.6	$3.3	2.45%	13.5%

Source: Office of the Historian, Headquarters SAC

Rampant inflation ran well ahead of the annual pay for both officers and enlisted personnel. The negative effect of inflation on reenlistment rates and officer retention became obvious by FY80. Congress attempted to offset the impact of runaway inflation by increasing pay and allowances each year. For example in FY77, the pay for a married sergeant with over six years of service was $8,546 annually including the housing allowance. In FY80, it was $10,335—an increase of 20.9 percent in four years. However, the cost of living increased 44.7 percent over the same four years.

The airlines were expanding rapidly in the '70s. Prime sources for filling their vacancies for well-trained, jet-qualified pilots were the USAF, Navy, and Marine Corps. A familiar sight outside the front gate of SAC air bases during this time was one or more parked motor homes used by major airlines for recruiting. They enticed pilots to join their airline with pay, location, retirement benefits, and free time that SAC could not equal. The loss of trained pilots became a major SAC concern.

Our typical SAC pilot was a married captain with 10 years' service. His annual pay in FY77 was $22,401, including allowance for quarters and flight pay. In FY80, his annual pay had increased to $26,462—an increase of 18.1 percent. However, the 44.7 percent cost-of-living increase over the three years left a larger gap in spendable income.

Pilot retention was not just a SAC problem. All the operational commands were hurt; TAC actually lost a higher percentage of pilots than SAC. We spent a lot of time in 1978–79 trying to stop the bleeding. Among other changes, we minimized additional duties, giving aircrews more free time when not on alert and not flying. When appropriate committees from the Senate and House of Representatives visited our headquarters, we emphasized the seriousness of the pilot retention problem. The pilot retention problem was not resolved until the '80s during the Reagan presidency.

SALT I and II

The United States' large advantage in nuclear weapon systems over the Soviet Union disappeared in the 1970s. Both nations now had the capability to destroy the other's economy, kill an untold number of people, decapitate the opposing government, decimate each other's military, and end civilized society in their opponent's part of the world.

The Soviet Union had pursued a program to increase nuclear armaments since the early '60s with the apparent intent to gain nuclear superiority over the United States. In the mid-seventies, it was well on its way to reaching that goal. SAC had 1,054 ICBMs, while the USSR had approximately 1,500 ICBMs and was adding 200 a year. The US Navy had 41 SLBM nuclear submarines, and the USSR had 62 SLBM submarines. SAC had 350 B-52 and 60 FB-111 bombers. The USSR had 150 intercontinental bombers and was building the supersonic Backfire, a bomber it said lacked intercontinental range.

Comparing USSR and US strategic nuclear capabilities was like comparing apples and oranges. USSR ICBMs were more numerous and could carry a bigger payload than SAC ICBMs. To offset those numerical and throw-weight advantages, the United States had developed the multiple independent reentry vehicle (each MIRV contained a nuclear warhead). Minuteman III carried three MIRVs each, thus increasing the maximum number of warheads on our ICBMs to 2,154. The USSR countered our Minuteman III increase with 10 MIRVs on each huge SS-18 ICBM that was rapidly entering service.

579

In the '50s and '60s, when the United States had several times the strategic nuclear capability of the Soviet Union, conceivably the United States could have survived nuclear war by attacking first and destroying the vulnerable Soviet nuclear forces. Whatever Soviet nuclear forces survived our first strike would be severely degraded. The notion that the United States would launch a first strike against the USSR was never credible to my knowledge and certainly not credible while I was vice CINCSAC.

A preemptive attack has roughly the same objectives as a first strike but would be used only when the president and defense secretary (then called the National Command Authority) had absolute knowledge that an enemy attack was planned and perhaps was under way. If Roosevelt had ordered the Navy to attack the Japanese carriers as they were steaming across the Pacific toward Pearl Harbor, our attack would have been preemptive. The possibility that an unforeseen and totally unacceptable action by the USSR could result in our launching a preemptive strike probably served as an added deterrent to nuclear war.

A variation of damage-limiting was a counterforce attack where only the enemy's strategic nuclear forces and other military targets would be attacked, with the expectation that the USSR would then spare our urban-industrial areas from destruction. Whether nuclear war between superpowers could be constrained remains unknown.

The peacetime status of the US strategic nuclear triad included submarines at sea carrying SLBMs, dispersed intercontinental bombers on alert carrying multiple bombs and missiles, and ICBMs on alert in hardened, dispersed silos. All were tied into an elaborate command and control network that included redundant communications, radars, and satellites. Confirmed evidence of an enemy attack on the United States could immediately initiate an appropriate response from the National Command Authority to our strategic forces.

The time from launching a Soviet ICBM until it impacted in the United States was about 30 minutes—less for a Soviet SLBM launched from a submarine near our coast. During the 30 minutes or less, the inbound missiles had to be discovered by our warning systems, decisions had to be made by the proper authority (normally the president), and orders had to be sent to the appropriate command centers. Do we ride out the attack and risk losing our ICBM force, with our bombers not airborne and submarines in port? Or do we launch on warning before the Soviet ICBMs and SLBMs can impact and destroy our forces? The fate of millions of American and Soviet citizens would depend on the president's decision.

As both nuclear arsenals grew larger, it became more difficult to visualize a nuclear exchange that could be limited to military targets without escalating to attacks against government facilities and other urban-industrial targets. Both the United States and USSR had created redundant capabilities, each capability having a different vulnerability. The aggregate survivability for both US and Soviet strategic nuclear forces was very high. Adding strategic weapons to either side would not significantly change that conclusion.

Both the United States and USSR saw economic, political, and military advantages in capping the arms race if rough parity could be achieved and maintained. From November 1969 until May 1972, the United States and the Soviet Union negotiated limits and constraints on intercontinental nuclear weapon systems. These first Strategic Arms Limitation Talks froze the force levels of long-range bombers, nuclear submarines with SLBMs, and land-based ICBMs. Although SALT I was a step in the right direction, the strategic forces were neither even nor symmetrical when President Nixon and General Secretary Brezhnev signed the Interim Agreement on 26 May 1972.

SALT II negotiations began in November 1972. Freezing the force levels in SALT I gave SALT II a chance to progress in other fundamental and important technical issues. After two years, President Ford and General Secretary Brezhnev met at Vladivostok in November 1974 and agreed on most issues. The State Department released the elements of the Aide-Memoire which recorded the SALT II agreement. It provided for

—an equal aggregate limit on the number of strategic nuclear delivery vehicles—ICBM and SLBM launchers, heavy bombers, and air-to-surface ballistic missiles (ASBMs). Initially, this ceiling would have been 2,400 as agreed at Vladivostok;

—an equal aggregate limit of 1,320 on the total number of launchers of MIRVed ballistic missiles and heavy bombers with long-range cruise missiles;

—an equal aggregate limit of 1,200 on the total number of launchers of MIRVed ballistic missiles; and

—an equal aggregate limit of 820 on launchers of MIRVed ICBMs.[2]

SALT II was signed by President Carter and General Secretary Brezhnev in Vienna on 18 June 1979. Although the Senate would not ratify the treaty after the Soviets invaded Afghanistan in December 1979, both sides said they would comply with the provisions as long as the other side reciprocated.

The SALT II limits described above limited the growth of strategic nuclear forces but left unresolved fundamental disagreements over two issues. The United States was developing air launched cruise missiles (ALCM) with nuclear warheads to be carried externally on B-52s. Was the short-range ALCM truly an intercontinental weapon? While this issue remained unresolved, the United States continued development of the ALCM.

The second disagreement concerned the Backfire bomber. The USSR insisted it lacked enough range to be counted as an intercontinental weapons system. The United States presented a technical analysis by a prominent American aircraft manufacturer that concluded the Backfire could reach the United States and was "intercontinental." After retiring, I visited a Russian air base while attending an arms control conference. The Russian commander allowed me to inspect a Backfire. In my opinion, the Backfire contained approximately the same technology as our FB-111, was larger, and could reach targets in the United States. Whether it would be a one-way mission, or round-trip, would probably depend upon the availability of air refueling and location of the target.

Both SALT I and II recognized the importance of verification by reliable and cooperative methods using national technical means (NTM). Satellite photography reduced the possibility that clandestine efforts could violate treaty limits. Testing of new systems was monitored several ways, including collecting electronic signals from telemetry. When the Soviets detected an

American violation, they were quick to complain. One day a severe winter storm hit a Minuteman silo under construction. Engineers stretched a canopy over the silo hole to keep snow from accumulating in the unfinished silo. Snow soon covered the canopy, obscuring the silo location. The next day, the USSR complained through the Standing Consultative Commission that we were obstructing verification from NTM. We quickly removed the canopy.

SALT II answered justifiable concerns about verification. The USSR was testing the feasibility of deploying mobile ICBM launchers. The United States maintained that mobile ICBMs would violate the fundamental SALT principle of verification. If their ICBMs were mobile, how could they be located and verified? The USSR raised similar objections to US cruise missiles. In the protocol accompanying the agreement which would expire in 1981, the treaty specifically allowed the deployment of both mobile ICBMs and cruise missiles after 1981.

Although SALT II limited the growth in the total numbers of strategic nuclear weapons, it did not close the door on research and development programs. SAC needed two new systems: (1) a heavy ICBM capable of carrying 10 MIRVs to offset the USSR SS-18 advantages and (2) a long-range, modern bomber capable of successfully penetrating USSR air defenses. Convincing the Carter administration to meet these two requirements proved to be a frustrating task.

The Air Force began developing a large ICBM, nicknamed MX, in the 1960s in anticipation of the requirement to match the rapid Soviet growth. Harold Brown, Carter's SecDef, asked Congress for full-scale engineering development in January 1979, stating that "various factors—silo vulnerability, block obsolescence, and advances in strategic defense capability—require action to prevent the deterioration of our currently effective forces into a force with undue reliance on one or two components."

By the mid-70s, advanced ICBM technology threatened the survivability of silo-based ICBMs for two reasons. First, with SS-18s carrying 10 MIRVs, the USSR could assign multiple warheads against each silo. Second, improvements in guidance technology raised the probability that a single MIRV could destroy a silo.

MX Snipe Hunt

SALT II allowed the United States to add a large, new missile with 10 MIRVs to our strategic inventory. SAC's first priority in strategic force modernization had to be the MX missile, a position supported by HQ USAF. The MX offered hard-target kill capability and parallelism with the Soviet SS-18 that did not exist with either Minuteman II or III. Before going into production, the DoD encouraged the Air Force in 1978 to solve the difficult problem of basing the MX. The objective was to base the missiles in such a manner they would survive a Soviet ICBM attack.

The USAF spent the last years of the Carter administration trying to compromise the strong beliefs of civilians in the DoD with the realities of survivability and the demands of command and control. Compounding the basing problem was the reluctance of civilian authorities in remote locations to have MX based in their area. Their "not in my backyard" attitudes and the new environmental impact laws further delayed MX basing.

When I was a Cub Scout in northeastern Michigan, a favorite con game used by our Scout leaders with the youngest scouts was to schedule a "snipe hunt" at twilight. The fact that there were no "snipe" in Michigan did not discourage those unsuspecting Cubs who wanted to hunt the elusive snipe the next night after failing to catch any the first time. Similarly, SAC, AFSC, and the Air Staff went on a three-year snipe hunt trying to find a survivable basing mode for MX missiles that would satisfy all parties.

The MX operational base site selection study was completed in June 1980 by HQ SAC. The study assumed one base would be located in Nevada and the other base in Utah. Possible locations in Nevada were Ely and Coyote Spring. Utah possibilities were Beryl, Milford, and Delta. The study was comprehensive and included such disparate issues as quality of life, cluster proximity (how many missile clusters fell within a 55-mile radius of the base), airfield operation, water availability, constructability, weather, logistics (access to road and rail transportation), and physical security. Beryl, Utah, and Ely, Nevada, were the preferred locations in the study as first and second bases.

Within a few weeks after the study was released, there was a storm of protest from various environmental activists, led by the local press in Nevada, objecting to the acquisition of public land. In a presidential election year, this became a sensitive issue. The Air Force had spent three frustrating years struggling with the Defense Department, Government Accountability Office, Bureau of Land Management, local politicians, and the press trying to find a way to base the needed MX missile. One outcome became clear in 1980. There would be no final resolution of MX basing until after the presidential election dust had settled.

After winning the 1980 election, President Reagan formed the Commission on Strategic Forces to restructure the ICBM modernization efforts. In April 1983, it recommended deploying 100 Peacekeeper missiles (formerly termed MX) in existing Minuteman silos. The Senate limited the number to 50 missiles and tied additional procurement to approval of another basing mode. The 50 were deployed in former Minuteman silos at Warren AFB, Wyoming. A "survivable basing mode" was never approved. When the Cold War ended—so did the snipe hunt.

Chicago Crash Jeopardizes KC-10 Buy

In January 1977, President Ford in one of his last official acts approved the acquisition of 91 advanced tanker/cargo aircraft (ATCA). These large aircraft would be especially useful on the overseas deployments of tactical fighter squadrons. The ATCA could carry deploying personnel and mobility cargo, as well as refuel the fighter aircraft en route. In July 1977, Harold Brown, President Carter's new secretary of defense, reduced the buy to 20 aircraft. On 19 December 1977, the USAF awarded this smaller contract to McDonnell-Douglas for the commercially available DC-10. The first six KC-10 Extenders would arrive in 1981.

On 25 May 1979, American Airlines Flight 191 crashed shortly after taking off from Chicago O'Hare International Airport. Two hundred and seventy-one persons on board the aircraft and two more persons on the ground were killed. Under normal circumstances, the Air Force would not be an interested party in this unfortunate accident. However, with the first deliveries of the KC-10A to SAC scheduled to arrive in a few months, SAC was vitally concerned about the safety of the aircraft.

The National Transportation Board determined that improper maintenance procedures led to the failure of the pylon structure supporting the left engine. During takeoff rotation, the left engine pylon and a small section of the leading edge fell off the aircraft. After the aircraft climbed to about 325 feet, it began to roll to the left. The aircraft suffered an asymmetrical stall and did not recover.

Most accidents are not caused by a single failure. Instead, one failure leads to another and yet another until the failures become unmanageable and result in a crash. The puzzling factor was the loss of control after successfully climbing to 325 feet. In this accident, the left outboard slats retracted when the hydraulic lines to the slats were severed. This caused lift to be reduced on the left wing and increased the stall speed to 159 knots. The "accepted" airline procedure was to climb at V2 (153 knots) until reaching an 800-foot altitude, then lower the nose and gain airspeed. In this damaged aircraft, V2 became 159 knots. When the aircraft slowed down below 159 knots while attempting to climb to 800 feet, stall was inevitable, and the accident occurred.

As part of the accident investigation, 13 qualified pilots flew 70 takeoff profiles in a DC-10 simulator. Everyone who flew the exact profile described above "crashed." All who increased their airspeed above 168 knots saved the aircraft. Speed is your friend. From the first time I had a malfunction in a jet that could cause loss of control, I knew the safest way to avoid an accident was to keep airspeed well above stall speed until the aircraft was on the landing runway. We checked the flight manuals for all types of SAC aircraft to see if there were any misleading instructions. Only one type had to be changed.

After describing all this to General Ellis, he asked me to fly a DC-10 with a Douglas test pilot and "wring it out." The Douglas plant at Long Beach, California, picked a JAL DC-10 for the test flight. Several engineers sat in the passenger section. I flew the aircraft from the left seat, and the test pilot talked me through every conceivable emergency from the right seat. We deliberately did "dumb" things; each time the DC-10 recovered safely. The engineers in back looked very pale, but thankful, as they exited the airplane. After two hours of pushing the limits, I was convinced this large aircraft was safe and

SAC heavyweights. In 1961 Boeing delivered the first B-52H. At 156 feet high and 41 feet wide, with a wingspan of 185 feet and eight turbofan engines, the B-52H dwarfed men and vehicles. With 20,000 pounds of weapons, the combat radius was 4,600 miles without refueling.

Four modified Boeing 747s became National Emergency Airborne Command Post aircraft and were designated E-4A/B. On alert, they insured connectivity between US strategic forces and the commander in chief if the United States were attacked.

Fifty-nine three-engine Douglas DC-10 transports were modified and became KC-10 tankers. KC-10s can carry personnel and pallets as well as refuel other aircraft.

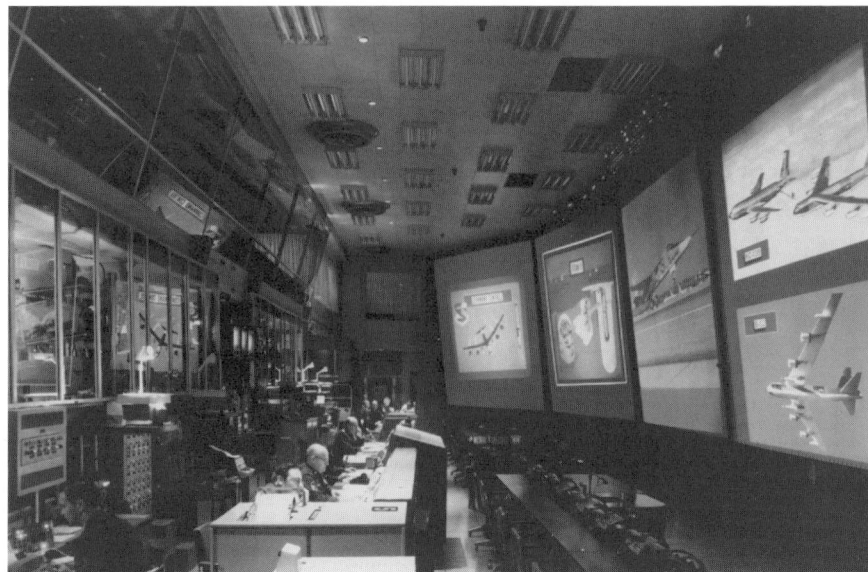

SAC underground command post. During exercises, alerts, and emergencies, the battle staff sits in the upper left balcony overlooking main floor action and from where all screens are visible.

Promotion day to lieutenant general. General Ellis presents the flag. General Leavitt's daughter Mary and son, Lloyd ("Trig"), do the heavy lifting. His wife, Anne, helps to celebrate the occasion.

reported that to Ellis. SAC owned 59 KC-10s by the time the purchase program ended.

SAC Grows—Air Defense Command Shrinks

A long-standing arrangement about nuclear war responsibilities was changed by Headquarters USAF in October 1979. Air Defense Command was reorganized and the management of its resources divided between SAC, TAC, and the Air Force Communications Service. SAC became responsible for managing ADC space surveillance and missile warning systems, although NORAD retained operational control. SAC acquired Peterson AFB, Colorado; Thule and Sondrestrom Air Bases in Greenland; and Clear AFS, Alaska, in the revised arrangement.

Our long-standing national policy was to separate the responsibility for determining whether the United States was under attack from the responsibility for responding to the attack. This reasoning prevailed during the Cold War. The "nightmare scenario" dreamed in Hollywood and enhanced by antinuke critics was that placing both offense and defense under one command would allow a demented or incompetent commander to start a nuclear war. At first glance, this reorganization seemed to trespass on the separation principle. A closer analysis disclosed the new arrangement carefully separated "operational control" from "resource management." A rough analogy: SAC owned the fire trucks and fire station, but NORAD would ring the fire alarm.

Aerospace Defense Command forces that SAC gained included those responsible for ICBM and SLBM warning, space surveillance, communications, and support. A first order of business for SAC was gaining familiarity with the more remote locations, so I visited Thule Air Base on the west coast of Greenland just north of the Arctic Circle. Greenland had been a colony of Denmark until Nazi Germany occupied Denmark in 1940. The Danes then gave autonomous rule to the approximately 50,000 inhabitants—largely Inuit and Danish fisherman. My interests during the visit would be the ballistic missile early warning system on a mountain near the airfield and the facilities for 3,000 personnel stationed at Thule.

It was a crystal clear arctic day when the EC-135 with the SAC staff aboard let down to Thule. The air base stood in sharp contrast to the desolate terrain and pristine, blue water in Baffin Bay, where an iceberg floated a mile or so off shore. The word "austere" gained special meaning as I taxied by buildings leading to base operations.

A large, red-bearded Dane—who immediately reminded me of the famous Viking "Eric the Red"—met our aircraft. He managed Danish interests and the contract Danish workers who ran and maintained base support facilities. The Thule workforce had become a community for homosexual Danes. "Eric" enforced an agreement that kept USAF personnel "off limits" to these workers. Violations meant contract termination.

Eric had converted a WWII Quonset hut into his handsome wooden-paneled home where VIPs stayed. Featured was a well-stocked wooden bar, 30 feet long, at which he regaled visitors with stories about life in the arctic. He once bet a visiting ship's captain that he could dive under the iceberg in the harbor and surface on the other side. A photograph by a bottle of scotch apparently confirmed this hard-to-believe exploit.

After two days, SAC staff members had learned what they needed to know about Thule. Strong crosswinds were already building, so we had to leave or be stranded. I held the yoke fully clockwise on a takeoff roll while the IP steered with the rudders. It was a very "sporty" takeoff, but otherwise the flight back to Offutt was uneventful.

Tinkering with SAC Structure

SAC was organized in 1946 as one of the three major commands of the Army Air Forces. SAC's original mission statement was to "be prepared to conduct long-range offensive operations in any part of the world . . . , [sustain] combat operations employing the latest and most advanced weapons; [and] to perform such special missions as the Commanding General Army Air Forces may direct."[3]

In 1960, although most nuclear weapons in terms of striking power were still under the control of SAC bombers and ICBMs, increasing numbers of Navy ballistic missiles were deployed on submarines at sea. Furthermore, tactical forces overseas controlled hundreds of tactical nuclear weapons. The need to coordinate target planning became obvious with the proliferation of all these weapons under different commands. The Joint Strategic Targeting and Planning Staff (JSTPS) was created to perform that important task. The JSTPS was collocated with HQ SAC at Offutt AFB. SAC was no longer responsible for target planning and allocation of weapons, but interaction was continuous and necessary between the SAC and JSTPS staffs. Many SAC staff members were "dual hatted," meaning they worked for both SAC and the JSTPS.

While commanding USAFE, General Ellis recognized that SAC should have other specific commitments in support of NATO. General Dougherty, CINCSAC until 1977, agreed with Ellis. They convinced the JCS to allocate a specific number of SAC KC-135 tankers to the operational control of USAFE in the event of NATO-Warsaw Pact hostilities. Aided by air refueling and controlled by the new E-3 AWACS, tactical fighters became more survivable and effective.

Although the B-52 would be severely challenged by Warsaw Pact air defenses, there were many targets where the large conventional bomb loads of the B-52 could be decisive. To improve its command and control, SAC reactivated the 7th AD with headquarters at Ramstein AB, Germany, on 1 July 1978.

SAC had extensive experience in conventional operations during the Vietnam War. After the war ended, the SAC staff had shifted its attention to the growing Soviet nuclear threat and the ongoing struggle for MX and a new bomber. Lacking in SAC headquarters was a focal point for conventional operations.

With the approval of General Ellis, I formed the Consolidated Contingency Steering Group (CCSG) for planning and coordinating conventional warfare operations in SAC. Assigned under the deputy chief of staff for operations plans, it included members from DCS/Operations, DCS/Logistics, and DCS/Intelligence. They worked under the eye of the experienced and highly motivated Colonel Robertson in an area affectionately called "contingency country."

The CCSG created the Strategic Projection Force (SPF) with the main bomber and tanker force coming from the 57th AD commanded by Brig Gen John Shaud. Reconnaissance aircraft consisted of SAC U-2, SR-71, and RC-135 aircraft. TAC supported the SPF with the E-3A AWACS aircraft. Three SPF deployments during 1980–81 were successful.[4] In 1980 the JCS developed the Rapid Deployment Joint Task Force (RDJTF) composed from all services. SPF became SAC's contribution to the RDJTF.

Connectivity—Key to Command and Control

Being able to send, receive, and execute orders is fundamental to fighting a successful war. Before the twentieth century, sharp eyes, good ears, and a loud voice were physical qualities demanded of effective commanders. Even the best leaders could not see beyond hills or in darkness, could not listen to their own commanders in the midst of battle, and could not give orders if their troops were beyond shouting distance. Modern technology has changed the way we send, receive, and execute orders. With satellites, broadband communications, high-speed computers, and highly trained staffs, present-day commanders have access to an abundance of timely information that enables them to make prompt decisions, even on events happening thousands of miles away. There is an important condition: connectivity must be reliable and stay that way under severe stress. Anyone ever frustrated while using e-mail knows the importance of maintaining "connectivity."

The most severe conditions imaginable would be imposed in nuclear war. Severity is magnified if the enemy attacks first with ballistic missiles. During the brief time provided by our warning systems, many things had to happen. NORAD warning systems had to detect the attack and, if possible, determine the number of attacking missiles. The National Command Authority had to be notified with enough confirmed detail to retaliate. At the same time, SAC and other nuclear weapon commands had to be alerted and prepared to launch. Without a reliable command and control system that would survive under attack, the United States could not depend on deterring nuclear war.

In the seventies, the reliability of communications became a subject of concern. One concern was the disabling effects on electronic equipment caused by the electromagnetic pulse (EMP) emitted by high-altitude nuclear explosions. Multiple tests showed that unprotected satellites, microwave UHF and

VHF radios, and telephone relay centers were among the systems most vulnerable to EMP.

SecDef Harold Brown visited SAC in 1977 and received a short briefing on the vulnerability of the E-4, the president's airborne command post, to EMP. After the briefing, Brown directed the CJCS, Gen George Brown, to conduct a strategic connectivity study. One year later, SAC briefed the study to President Carter. One of the principals at the briefing and throughout the following years of connectivity improvement, Al Buckles, said Carter's instructions were, "Fix it!"

On 1 July 1980, the Joint Strategic Connectivity Staff (JSCS), a specialized JCS agency, was created at Headquarters SAC. General Ellis was the director of the new agency, and Rear Adm Paul Tomb was vice director. The JSCS was to analyze and recommend improvements to the strategic command and control systems linking the NCA, commanders of the nuclear forces, and the nuclear forces. Fixing connectivity in SAC involved more than protecting the president's E-4 from EMP. Sixteen EC-135 aircraft were on alert and dispersed at different bases in the United States. The dispersed EC-135s raised the probability that one or more airborne command posts would survive a nuclear attack.

An important link in the connectivity chain was the extensive long-distance commercial telephone system in the United States. Two major corporations, AT&T and ITT, dominated the long-distance telephone business in the '70s and '80s. Their practice at that time was to consolidate relay stations, thus gaining economies of scale. The downside of this practice occurred if one or more of these central locations were destroyed. If that happened, long-distance telephone communications throughout major portions of the United States would end. The strategic command and control system needed a redundant long-distance system with more relay stations, located far enough apart so they would not to be destroyed by the same nuclear blast.

Charles Brown, AT&T chairman, and Rand Araskog, ITT president and chairman, worked with General Ellis and the JSCS to resolve the vulnerability problem for long-distance telephones. While this was happening, Brown was under pressure from Congress and the Justice Department to break up

AT&T into the so-called Baby Bells. Brown agreed to the breakup in 1982, but not before new relay stations were dispersed and the system became far less vulnerable to nuclear attack.

President Reagan saw a short briefing after assuming office that gave the terms of reference for strategic force connectivity. His administration continued to fund necessary connectivity improvements during his years as president. During those years, much was learned about technical ways to avoid catastrophic failures from EMP. By the end of his second term, about $60 billion had been spent on strategic force connectivity. As a result, our strategic forces were more capable of responding to a Soviet attack. If either superpower had inadvertently started a nuclear war, a surviving command and control system would also improve chances of stopping the war before both societies were destroyed. This factor strengthened our confidence in subsequent arms control agreements.

An incident occurred on 30 March 1981. As I walked by our outer office, TV news interrupted their program. A criminally insane man had just shot President Reagan. The president's status was unknown. I told the senior controller to recall the alert forces to their alert areas. The press tried to make an issue of this by suggesting SAC had raised the DEFCON. The allegation was not true. SAC policy allowed a fraction of the alert force to leave the alert facility for visits to well-defined places on the base, such as the BX. While away from the alert facility, force members remained in contact by radio and could be recalled on a moment's notice. Without knowing the circumstances surrounding the assassination attempt, I felt the prudent thing was to bring the alert force back to its duty location. The next day, Casper Weinberger, the new SecDef, called and asked for details. After our talk, he thanked me for taking appropriate action.

After retiring, I consulted on arms control issues. Many misinformed but well-meaning "experts" have written about accidental or unintentional nuclear war. Few have actual knowledge of nuclear weapons, their safeguards, or the associated command and control systems. As vice CINCSAC, I gained a great deal of confidence and knowledge about the command and control of nuclear weapons, probably exceeded by few people in the United States at that time. The US system for command and control of nuclear weapons was carefully designed, frequently tested for reliability, highly redundant, and manned by personnel who were periodically screened and held to high standards. The entire system had many checks and balances. The release of nuclear weapons was deliberately not tied to the DEFCON system.

Alerts Serve a Purpose

The dictionary defines *alert* as "fully aware and attentive; wide-awake." That definition applies reasonably well to a military alert and does not mean "going to war." The US DEFCON system defines military alerts as conditions of readiness varying from peacetime to wartime. They range from DEFCON 5, a normal peacetime situation, to DEFCON 1, maximum readiness and at war. During the Cold War, the US military was usually in DEFCON 4. This status required strengthened security and more emphasis on training but was not war. While in DEFCON 4, SAC emphasized training the bomber and ICBM forces using practice alerts that simulated higher states of readiness.

The CINCSAC and the other unified and specified commanders have sufficient latitude within the DEFCON system to bring their forces to a point where they are "fully aware and attentive; wide-awake." At Pearl Harbor on 7 December 1941, the necessity for being alert was learned the hard way. In tactical emergencies such as Pearl Harbor and New York City on 9/11, first responders—military and civilian—must be ready.

An incident with serious command and control implications occurred on 6 June 1980. The red phone rang during the morning staff meeting. The SAC senior controller said that NORAD was reporting 1,000 Soviet ICBMs launched and heading toward the United States. With no international incidents raising political temperatures and no crisis brewing, I was more than half-convinced that the NORAD alert was a false alarm. Nevertheless, I hurried to the underground SAC Command Post with many thoughts running through my mind. The senior controller, an experienced colonel, was already waiting at the door. "We have checked all other sources, General Leavitt. There is no attack under way."

While we were talking, NORAD called. Failure of a computer chip had allowed a NORAD training tape to be broadcast. SAC forces returned to their normal posture within 18 minutes of the initial alert.

This incident stirred widespread interest in the press, Congress, and Carter administration. Gen David Jones, JCS chairman, personally made a thorough investigation of the false NORAD warning. General Jones knew the warning and alert systems thoroughly and also knew the various ways that an attack could be confirmed. He visited both SAC headquarters and NORAD to confirm that the incident and causes had been accurately reported. During his visit to SAC, he questioned me carefully and was apparently satisfied that SAC had not only reacted to the NORAD alert promptly but that the NORAD alert warning was not confirmed by other technical means and that no attack was under way. Although no one wants to see a malfunction in any part of the warning system, there is some consolation in knowing that the many redundancies in the system prevented an unintended result.

Highest and Fastest

The first time I flew was in an old Ford trimotor transport from Alpena to Detroit. I was about 14. An early memory was sitting in a rattan seat behind a big steel beam that ran across the center aisle from left wing to right. To get in the seat, you had to gingerly step over the beam. It was not an exciting first flight. While I was at West Point, cadets flew on WWII transports to Army and Air Force bases for summer training—more boring than exciting. One summer, I scrounged a ride in a WWII B-25 from New York to California. One of the pilots, an English instructor at West Point, felt sorry for me sitting in the noisy rear compartment. He invited me to the cockpit and let me control the old bomber—that was exciting.

During my last summer leave from West Point, I took a private flying lesson at the Alpena airport—Phelps Collins Field—named after a local pilot killed in the First World War. The lesson cost $14 an hour. My mother, who had never flown, cautioned me not to fly too fast! Her concern was unnecessary in the old Piper Cub. It became really unnecessary when the instructor, a WWII Navy pilot, demonstrated how to fly but landed without ever letting me touch the controls!

Those early tastes of flying destroyed whatever interests I had in old airplanes. During my flying career in fighters, reconnaissance aircraft, and bombers, I wanted to fly the newest, highest flying, and fastest aircraft. Why? Because their military application was my primary interest. Flying memory firsts that stick include the first time landing a jet, pulling six Gs, dive-bombing an enemy target, dogfighting with MiGs, flying at 70,000 feet, onloading 100,000 pounds while air refueling a B-52, breaking Mach 1 and Mach 2, landing an E-4 (USAF version of the Boeing 747), and flying an F-15.

Brig Gen Patrick Halloran was assigned to the SAC staff in June 1977 as the inspector general. Pat was one of the first pilots to fly the SR-71 and had 600 hours in the aircraft. When Pat received his second star and moved to the JCS staff, we had no general officers at the headquarters with SR-71 experience. By 1980 the only SAC aircraft that I had not flown was the SR-71 Blackbird. General Ellis agreed that it would be useful if I became familiar with the aircraft and SR-71 operations at Beale AFB.

Nearly four years flying the U-2 made the high-altitude aspect of SR-71 flight seem very familiar. The modern full-pressure suits and helmets were a giant step more comfortable and safer than our U-2 partial-pressure suits. After a day or two of ground training, a thorough briefing by the instructor pilot, and SR-71 simulator time, I was ready for a front-seat ride in the world's fastest and highest flying aircraft.

The IP mentioned the SR-71 had an occasional problem called an "inlet unstart." Normally, a pointed, moveable cone in each engine inlet kept the airflow to the engine compressor at Mach 0.5. The spike had to move backward as the speed increased. This movement was essential for Mach 3.2 flight. If the inlet failed to operate properly, airflow to the engine compressor would stop. Asymmetrical thrust from the other engine would cause a violent yaw, a cannon-like noise, and some bouncing around in the cockpit. When that happened, the pilot could "unstart" both engines, which moved both spikes out where the engines could be restarted, and the flight continued.

As we unloaded from the van in front of the parked SR-71, I was struck by the appearance of this futuristic, big, black machine. The SR-71 flew combat sorties over Southeast Asia from Kadena AB, Okinawa, during the Vietnam War. Because of its ominous appearance, the Okinawa natives nicknamed the SR-71 "Habu," a pit viper with a large head common to Okinawa. The nickname stuck. The SR-71 was 18.5 feet tall and 107 feet long, and the delta wing had a span of 56 feet. "Chines" running along the fuselage from front to back gave additional lift and a manta ray–like appearance. Under the aircraft in the hangar were small puddles caused by dripping fuel. As airspeed increased during the climb to altitude, aircraft skin temperatures would raise causing metal-to-metal joints to close, and the fuel would stop leaking.

After being strapped in the front cockpit and hooked to the aircraft oxygen supply, we checked radios, and the IP gave last minute taxi instructions. Few things are as exciting as your first flight in a new supersonic aircraft. This flight was no exception. However, my major concern was whether, at 51 years old, I could fly as well as I did in my thirties and forties. As vice CINCSAC, this seemed important. No screwups, please.

The two powerful J-58 engines soon had us racing down the runway, breaking ground, and climbing to our rendezvous with a KC-135 carrying the special jet fuel used for the SR-71. Air refueling was noneventful. We resumed climbing to cruise altitude. As we passed through 60,000 feet, a loud bang followed by a sharp yaw to the left made me remember the briefing about "unstart." The IP quickly reminded me what to do. After restart, we resumed climbing to 80,000 feet and accelerating to Mach 3+.

It was a clear, blue-sky day with only a few clouds below as we headed for Denver. From 16 miles above the earth, one can see a long, long way. The most obvious difference between flying the U-2 at 70,000 feet and the SR-71 at 80,000 was watching geographical points come and go so quickly. The U-2 covered about *eight* miles per minute; the SR-71, about *36* miles per minute. An hour later, we turned from Denver and headed back to Beale. I made two or three touch-and-go landings before the final landing. Ben Rich from Lockheed Skunk Works was waiting on the ramp with the wing commander. I congratu-

SR-71 flight—very high and very fast. The USAF was under pressure from the Carter administration to reduce or retire SAC's 18 SR-71s because of high operational expenses. General Ellis asked Leavitt to become familiar with the program and pilot the SR-71.

The full-pressure suit was a great improvement over the partial-pressure suits worn in the early U-2 days. Flying at 80,000 feet was better than at 70,000, and speeds over 2,000 mph were four times faster than a U-2.

lated Ben for building such an amazing aircraft, and then thanked the IP, wing commander, crew chief, and his ground crew. The T-39 flight back to Offutt later in the day at eight miles per minute seemed endless!

After returning from Beale, I was better prepared to discuss SR-71 problems. Only nine SR-71s were in the SAC inventory. The primary issue with the SR-71 program was its high cost. Not only were asset costs high but so were operations and maintenance costs. The second problem revolved around satellite reconnaissance versus SR-71 reconnaissance. Most members of Congress and too many USAF generals did not understand orbital mechanics or why reconnaissance satellites could not photograph a potential military target 24 hours a day.

The reality is that a reconnaissance satellite may circle the globe every 90 minutes, but its orbital path is constantly moving in relation to the rotation of the earth underneath. Since the enemy can compute when the satellite will be overhead, it can also disguise activity during that period. In contrast, SR-71 flights can be scheduled to overfly targets whenever reconnaissance is required.

While the Cold War lasted, SAC was able to defend keeping the SR-71. In 1989 the argument was lost, and the remaining SR-71 aircraft were retired. The CINCSAC at that time was forced to make the difficult choice of losing a B-52 wing or the SR-71s. In 1995 three SR-71s were reactivated. The three were retired again in 1999, thus closing the book on the fastest, highest flying military aircraft in aviation history.

Skunk Works, Stealth, and the B-1A

In 1965 I led a study directed by Dr. Harold Brown, then the secretary of the Air Force. Brown challenged the Air Force to solve a dilemma: could the AMSA (the B-1) penetrate an air defense system that included the F-12 with a lookdown, shootdown capability? In our study, the AMSA "won," primarily because its radar cross section was reduced to the point where the F-12 radar could not acquire it in time to kill the AMSA with the AIM-47 missile. Four B-1A prototype bombers were built during the Ford administration. Their radar cross section was reduced but not to the point where they could be classified as "stealthy."

President Carter stopped further B-1 production after assuming office in 1977. At a 30 June 1977 presidential news conference, he stated that "the existing testing and development now under way on the B-1 should continue to provide us with the needed technical base in the unlikely event that more cost-effective alternative systems should run into difficulty. . . . In the meantime, we should begin deployment of cruise missiles using air-launched platforms, such as our B-52's, modernized as necessary."

Thirteen years after the 1965 study, SAC still lacked a new bomber. While we were in USAFE, General Ellis briefed me on Have Blue, a secret test demonstrator aircraft using modern stealth technology. Lockheed Skunk Works had a test program for Have Blue that ran from 1975 to 1978. Both Lockheed and Northrop now indicated their interest and confidence in building a stealth bomber. Stealth was a logical development to incorporate in the design of any new SAC bomber.

In early 1979, I visited Ben Rich, manager of the Lockheed Skunk Works in Burbank, California. My objective was to learn more about the practicality of building SAC bombers and cruise missiles with stealthy characteristics. The Skunk Works was developing the F-117 Nighthawk, an attack fighter that benefited from the Have Blue experiment. At the time of my visit, the F-117 was only a wooden mockup with bits and pieces of the production aircraft being manufactured on the factory floor.

"Stealthy" commonly referred to minimizing the detection and tracking of an aircraft by radar. The more comprehensive term is "low observable." This means the aircraft cannot be effectively tracked by radar, not easily seen nor heard, nor successfully attacked with heat-seeking missiles. Low observable also means that the aircraft does not emit signals from radars or radios that could be tracked by ground-based sensors. One caution: low observable does not mean "invisible." As air defense technology improves, so must low-observable technology.

The black F-117 Nighthawk set the new standard for low observables. It flew at night, avoided electronic detection by not depending upon radar for navigation or bombing, included the latest technology in absorbing or reflecting radar signals, and

601

obstructed infrared emissions coming from both engine exhausts. The F-117 proved its worth in the first Gulf War by bombing heavily defended downtown Baghdad. No F-117s were lost.

Next, I visited the remote test facility where accurate, scientific measurements were made in the ongoing battle between various enemy radars and our aircraft—current and future. The test facility allowed new designs and concepts to be tested before committing to production of new aircraft or modifying existing aircraft.

After returning to HQ SAC, I talked to General Ellis about the bomber issue and the importance of selecting a survivable replacement for the aging B-52 fleet. We agreed upon several key issues.

1. The Carter administration would not restart B-1 production. Its decision was not all bad. Although the B-1 was fast and could carry a large bomb load over long distances, it lacked the ability to penetrate and survive against advanced air defense systems already in being. There was no way to "glue on" a low-observable capability. Also, we had no ECM answer to the "lookdown, shootdown" capability the USSR was developing for air defense fighters.

2. The B-52H should be converted to cruise missile carriers as the missiles became available.

3. The elapsed time from project approval for a new bomber to operational readiness was at least 10 years and perhaps 20. SAC should seek development of a new low-observable bomber without further delay.

4. Many nations, in addition to members of the Warsaw Pact, bought USSR air defense systems, including China, India, Libya, Iraq, Syria, Cuba, North Korea, Vietnam, Yugoslavia, and Iran. To bolster foreign sales, the USSR continually upgraded the radars used for EW, GCI, antiaircraft guns, SAMs, and air defense fighters for these nations. Linebacker II bombing raids against Hanoi and Haiphong demonstrated how difficult a future regional war might be for SAC against these defenses.

B-1A flight. Only four B-1As were built before President Carter terminated the program. The USAF was given minimal funding to continue testing for aerodynamic issues but not for developing the weapon systems important in a future bomber, for example advanced ECM equipment.

Leavitt with SAC test crew. When President Reagan authorized production of the B-1B, it was a long way from becoming a combat-ready strategic bomber. This fact was obvious when I flew the B-1A with the SAC test crew.

Not since the 1962 Cuban missile crisis had I flown in a B-52. During SAC staff visits to B-52 bases, I occasionally had the opportunity to fly a training mission with a combat-ready crew. These flights refreshed my memories of B-52 aircrew duty and its rigorous training requirements. Little did I realize then that the B-52H would still be flying 47 years after the first one— "State of Michigan"—arrived at Wurtsmith in 1961! The flights also served as a reference point for comparing the B-52H to the B-1A prototype located at the Air Force Flight Test Center at Edwards AFB, California.

In early January 1980, I arrived at Edwards AFB to fly the B-1A. The four prototype aircraft authorized by President Carter were parked on the ramp by the office occupied by the SAC test and evaluation team and Rockwell. Only enough funding was provided to keep the number four prototype in flying condition. After a short briefing by the SAC detachment commander, we approached number four. It looked like it was on life support. External tubes and cables were connected to many aircraft orifices. I climbed into the left seat, and the test pilot led me through the starting procedure. He warned that flight instruments might fail during takeoff but would come back after a few moments.

Sure enough! As soon as I broke ground and started to climb, the flight instruments failed. They reappeared after a few minutes. The rest of the 3.8 hour flight went very well. The B-1A handled well at high and low speeds and all altitudes. Performance on long, low-level runs at Mach .85 about 200 feet above the ground was the best I had ever experienced. Air refueling was easy, as were the traffic pattern and landing. Since the prototype aircraft were not allowed to be equipped as bombers, a bomb-navigation system and electronic countermeasures were not installed. My overall evaluation of this fine aircraft was that it was 20 years too late for high-intensity warfare.

Election Night 1980

It was Christmas Eve 1979 when the red phone rang in my quarters. The National Military Command Center was advising the unified and specified commanders that Soviet airborne troops were loading on aircraft near the Afghanistan border. I asked the SAC duty officer to call me when the invasion actually began. At 6:30 a.m., I called the duty officer. He explained that bad weather over Afghanistan had forced the airdrop to abort. After the invasion took place the next day, the press badgered President Carter. He denied having prior knowledge of the invasion. It was hard for me to believe that military commanders would be informed before the invasion, but not the president.

With the Soviet army in Afghanistan, 1980 began as a tough political year for the Carter administration. The failed attempt to free Americans held by Iran finally jolted the administration out of its complacent attitude about defense requirements. Despite setbacks, 1980 was better for the military than the previous three years. The overdue debates over MX basing and a new bomber renewed interest in strategic weapon systems. Candidate Reagan's constant criticism of military readiness added fuel to the fire in this election year. Congress passed legislation before the end of 1980 that raised the FY 1981 defense budget by 6.1 percent in constant dollars.

On Election Day, before the polls opened, I had a private breakfast with a Democratic senator who was a key member of the Senate Armed Services Committee. He had visited SAC several times during the past three years and was well aware of our money and modernization problems. I greatly respected his objectivity and extensive knowledge of defense issues and foreign affairs.

It was an open secret that the active duty military was very dissatisfied with the Carter administration. This dissatisfaction was shared by many Democrats in the House and Senate, especially veterans of WWII and Korea. Our conversation turned to the election. I asked, "Who's going to win today, Senator?" He answered, "Here, read this, Dick," and handed me a letter from his coat pocket. The letter was addressed, "Dear President-Elect Reagan." After congratulatory remarks addressed to Reagan, his letter was a plea for bipartisan support on matters related to defense and foreign relations.

Senior officers in the military seldom express their political views except among close friends. They know that in the long term, the military establishment depends upon the goodwill and support of both political parties. Personal opinions were traditionally confined to voting, not to electioneering.

For that election evening, the dozen or so generals at Offutt and their wives had planned a potluck dinner in Quarters 13 to watch election returns. When the TV was turned on at 6:00 p.m., Reagan was winning in a landslide! The room filled with cheers and smiles. These generals had worked hard to field the badly needed MX yet could never satisfy the Carter appointees in the Department of Defense; they had seen the B-1 pushed aside with no replacement bomber in sight; they had watched hundreds of officers and NCOs leave the service because their pay never kept up with rampant inflation; and they had been embarrassed by the fiasco that failed to rescue American prisoners held in Iran. Their smiles that night reflected their personal mood changes more than partisan reactions. They were happy to serve under a new president who promised to rebuild the armed forces and restore pride in being an American service member.

Titan Trouble in Arkansas

In 1980 the SAC ICBM force consisted of six Titan II squadrons with nine missiles in each squadron, nine Minuteman II squadrons with 50 single-warhead missiles in each squadron, and 11 Minuteman III squadrons with 50 MIRV missiles each and three nuclear weapons in each MIRV. When all 1,054 ICBMs were on alert and in commission, SAC had 2,154 nuclear weapons carried on silo-based ICBMs under positive control and ready to launch when ordered by the NCA.

The first US ICBM to reach operational status was the Atlas D, a liquid-propelled missile that became operational in 1960. The liquid-propelled Titan I became operational in 1962. Neither Atlas D nor Titan I was silo-based. The much improved Titan II began replacing Titan I in 1963, and 54 of these large ICBMs were in silos by 1967. With a range of thousands of miles and a multimegaton Mk-6 warhead, the accurate, powerful Titan II was quickly labeled by the press as a "city buster."

In a rough sense, the military value of an ICBM depends upon several factors. Can it be safely maintained at a reasonable cost while on alert in peacetime? Does it have a high probability of surviving an attack by enemy ICBMs while in its silo? Can it be integrated into the existing command and control system?

Can it be launched quickly when ordered? Does it have high reliability during launch and accuracy in flight? Does it have a high-yield warhead that will insure hard-target kill probability?

While the Titan II answered most of these questions with high grades, there was a safety problem. The liquid propellant rocket was composed of highly toxic ingredients that had to be carefully contained until rocket ignition. If spilled during refueling or otherwise, this evaporating fuel could be fatal to those working near the missile and dangerous to persons downstream from the evaporating gases. In August 1978, propellant spillage at a launch complex in Kansas damaged the Titan II. A $4.8 million contract was awarded on 5 September 1980 to restore the launch complex to operational status.

On 18 September 1980, General Ellis was TDY. Around 6:00 p.m., I received an emergency call to report to the SAC Command Post. A dangerous situation was developing rapidly at a Titan II missile site near Damascus, Arkansas. An Airman performing maintenance on the inside of the silo had accidentally dropped a wrench. The wrench fell approximately 80 feet down from where he was working and penetrated the missile fuel tank. The Airman left the silo without reporting his error. The pressure rose in the silo as the liquid propellant turned to gas.

An underground, heavily reinforced launch control facility (LCF) housed four Titan combat crew members on alert. The LCF was connected by a long tunnel to the silo with a blast lock between to protect the combat crew in the LCF from a surface explosion of a nuclear weapon or from a Titan explosion within the silo. The alert crew notified the 308th Strategic Missile Wing at Little Rock AFB of the rapidly rising silo pressure. The wing ordered the crew to evacuate the LCF because of the life-threatening emergency. After the LCF was evacuated, there was no other place where conditions inside the silo could be monitored. The 308th then notified the local sheriff for Damascus, and residents within a one-mile radius of the Titan site were evacuated.

The key SAC staff assembled in the command post and quickly established contact with the missile manufacturer and other Titan experts. After discussing the situation, I concluded there were three courses of action. None were promising.

1. Slide open the 740-ton cover on top of the silo. Toxic gas would escape and lower the pressure inside the silo. This might save the missile and avoid an explosion. Drawbacks: Large quantities of toxic gas would release when the door opened and drift over the local area, endangering local citizens. Also, an explosion in the open silo might launch the partially fueled Titan to impact somewhere in the United States.

2. Keep the silo cover closed. Do nothing else and hope the water already dumped inside the silo reduced the overpressure. Also, hope that no electrical short would cause the gas to explode. Drawback: With no way to measure the pressure rise and no way to stop an explosion, this course of action was surrendering to a possible disaster without exhausting all potential alternatives.

3. Reenter the LCF wearing protective gear. Read the instrumentation and determine whether pressure was decreasing and whether the LCF was too contaminated to occupy. Find a way to draw the toxic gas from the entire facility. Drawback: Very dangerous to the volunteers, even in protective gear. Insure they not turn on anything electrical. This seemed to be the best way to resolve the crisis. After I consulted with the missile wing, the SAC experts agreed, and I authorized this course of action.

I called the governor's office in Little Rock about 8:00 p.m. It located the governor in Hot Springs. After I explained to him the dangerous situation and our plan, he thanked me and said to keep him apprised of developments.

Around 9:00 p.m., two volunteer Airmen from the missile maintenance squadron donned protective clothing and attempted to enter the LCF. They quickly returned. The LCF was too obscured with toxic gas to read the instruments. After discussion, we chose to wait for two hours before trying again. Two more Airmen volunteered to enter the LCF. They were given permission to investigate but ordered not to turn on anything electrical. I called the governor again and informed him of our status.

The new volunteers reported that conditions seemed improved. One telephoned that he was standing near a switch next to an exhaust duct. He thought the exhaust fan would draw toxic fumes from the tunnel. The wing command post ordered him not to turn the switch. Approximately one minute later, a huge explosion destroyed the facility. One Airman who was blown into the perimeter fence survived, although injured. The Airman near the exhaust duct was killed. Accident investigators found the switch turned on.

I arrived at the site the next morning. A warhead lay on a public road several hundred yards from the destroyed silo. It was protected by security police until nuclear experts removed it. The silo was nothing but a huge hole surrounded by rubble. Large concrete pieces of the silo cover were blown a quarter mile from the silo. That afternoon the national media assembled for a press conference. Their questions centered on the warhead lying in the road, questions that defense policy did not allow me to answer. I told them repeatedly that I could not answer warhead questions. The next day, I called SecDef Harold Brown and suggested the policy should allow exceptions.

The *Arkansas Democrat-Gazette* reported that the Air Force had not given the governor prior warning of the Titan emergency. I had my exec call the governor's exec and inform him the SAC Command Post had taped our conversations, if his memory needed refreshing. No response was received from the governor's office.

This accident was the beginning of the end for the Titan II ICBM force. The last Titan II wing was deactivated on 31 July 1984.

New SAC Bomber

The Vietnam War finally was ended with the Linebacker II bombing of Hanoi and Haiphong. SAC B-52s caused most of the damage during the 11-day campaign. To preclude heavy B-52 losses in Linebacker I, hundreds of supporting sorties were flown by USAF and Navy tactical aircraft. Two important lessons for the future were provided by Linebacker II—one positive, one negative. The positive lesson was that a well-executed bombing campaign can strongly influence the ending of a war and, at the same time, minimize civilian casualties. The negative lesson from Linebacker II was that B-52s would suffer unsustainable losses attempting to penetrate the vastly improved Soviet air defense system of the 1980s and later.

After canceling the B-1 in 1977, the Carter administration dodged the bomber survival issue by developing the air launched cruise missile. I represented SAC on the ALCM selection board. ALCMs could be launched as far as 1,500 miles from targets protected by air defenses. With terrain clearance capability and low radar cross section, ALCMs could avoid radar detection by flying close to the ground and strike targets with reasonable accuracy. On the other hand, ALCMs lacked the flexibility and versatility of manned bombers, attributes particularly important in conventional warfare.

In 1980 President Carter announced the United States would comply with the unsigned SALT II Treaty as long as the USSR complied. Each nation was limited to an aggregate of 2,250 strategic nuclear delivery vehicles (ICBMs, SLBMs, and heavy bombers) at the end of 1981. The United States was in compliance in all categories. After retiring the remaining 75 B-52D models starting in 1982, there was room under SALT II for the new Peacekeeper ICBM and approximately 100 new bombers to replace B-52s.

Although SAC's major Cold War responsibility was deterring nuclear war, SAC had fought in two major wars following WWII—Korea and Vietnam—using only conventional, not nuclear, weapons. During the 1970s, SAC committed B-52s to support USAFE if war began in Western Europe between NATO and the Warsaw Pact. B-52s dropping large numbers of conventional bombs might be effective, but serious doubts arose about B-52 survival rates against the integrated Warsaw Pact radars, fighter interceptors, and SAMs. B-52 defensive avionics and countermeasures had been improved after the Vietnam War ended, but it was not much of an exaggeration to state the improvements were like "putting lipstick on a pig" when encountering an array of advanced Soviet air defenses.

Meanwhile, a high-ranking Russian in the Soviet hierarchy became disillusioned with the direction in which Brezhnev and his associates were leading their country. At great risk to his own life, he provided the United States data in the late 1970s on Soviet development programs, including air defense fighters. To minimize the risk of disclosure, only a very few senior

Air Force officers had access to the information. In SAC, only General Ellis, the director of plans and requirements, and I had access to the information. Presumably, SAC was kept informed because these future Soviet defenses threatened our bombers in the Single Integrated Operational Plan (SIOP). In order to read this intelligence, I had to fly to the Pentagon, enter a well-guarded and protected area, sign in and out, and take no notes. Back in HQ SAC, I would discuss what I learned with General Ellis.

The CINCSAC and staff generally understood the military requirement for a new bomber better than most political appointees in the DoD. One exception was Dr. Harold Brown, SecDef during the Carter years and a brilliant man with an encyclopedic knowledge of defense issues. After his exposure to the B-1 development from the time it was an AMSA in 1961, Brown also knew that the B-1 was a missed opportunity and the Air Force should seek more advanced technology.

Another exceptional appointee was Dr. Hans Mark. Trained as a physicist, he served as undersecretary and later secretary of the Air Force from 1977 to 1981. Mark was interested in the requirement for a new bomber, perhaps more from a technical than from an operational viewpoint, although he did not hesitate to express his operational views.

After the B-1 was cancelled, neither General Ellis nor I wanted to continue fighting the Carter administration for the B-1. Nevertheless, we believed that bomber modernization was imperative as long as Soviet air defenses continued to improve. General Ellis encouraged the SAC staff to seek an interim bomber that would fill the gap, while we pursued an advanced bomber based on stealth technology.

SAC experience with the FB-111A had been excellent from a performance viewpoint, except for range and payload. General Dynamics proposed as the interim bomber an enlarged FB-111A called the FB-111H. Selling points for the FB-111H were availability and low program costs. When neither Air Force Systems Command nor the Air Staff supported the FB-111H, General Dynamics withdrew its proposal.

The most important advancement in these new generation Soviet fighters was a radar and missile system with lookdown, shootdown capability, similar to the system tested in the mid-

'60s for the F-12—the fighter version of the SR-71. To the best of my knowledge, at that time there were only three ways to counter a lookdown, shootdown capability: stay out of radar coverage, neutralize the enemy radar by jamming, or fly a stealth bomber the radar could not track. The first way was usually not feasible, the second way had not yet been developed, and the third way required a stealthy bomber.

Although the F-117 stealth fighter had not been publicly announced in 1979, tests on the F-117 proved the stealth concept was feasible and would greatly improve survival probabilities against Soviet air defenses. Two manufacturers provided stealth bomber proposals—Lockheed and Northrop. Lockheed's proposal built upon its experience with the F-117. Northrop went back to 1946 when their "flying wing" XB-35 flew. The XB-35 aircraft was discontinued after suffering stability problems leading to an accident. By the late '70s, the aviation industry knew how to eliminate stability problems through modern electronics. The flying wing design provided the opportunity to build a long-range, large-payload stealthy bomber. That bomber today is known as the B-2.

Gaining the required military and political support for acquiring a stealth bomber proved to be an insurmountable problem while Carter was president. When McNamara had been SecDef, he established a rigidly enforced budget system controlled by political appointees. The annual Five-Year Defense Plans were organized by function and rigidly enforced. If the Air Force required a new R&D program for strategic forces, negotiating the change with the other services in the JCS arena where military judgments might prevail or moving money from an Air Force program listed under general purpose forces was not the protocol. Instead, the action shifted to negotiating with appointed civilians who might, or might not, understand the military consequences of their decisions.

Reagan campaigned for office stressing he would greatly strengthen the US military. One well-publicized weakness was SAC's lack of a modern strategic bomber. Since Carter had cancelled the B-1 only four years earlier, the Reagan administration believed the fastest and cheapest way to rebuild the bomber force was restoring B-1 production. Among the strongest supporters for the B-1 were senior retired Air Force generals with access to the Reagan administration. They were not privy to the new intelligence about Soviet R&D and were unaware of major technical obstacles that stood in the way of the B-1B becoming an effective strategic bomber.

The key Air Force leadership during the bomber selection process was loaded with experience in research and development. Secretary Mark was a PhD physicist from NASA, while the USAF chief of staff, Gen Lew Allen, had earned an MS and PhD in physics. His career afterwards consisted of important R&D management and command assignments with the NSA, OSD, and AFSC. Gen Robert Marsh became AFSC commander in 1981. All three were intelligent, highly educated, and totally familiar with R&D problems and issues. Despite their limited experiences in SAC and combat operations, we hoped they would support SAC, the using command, in our quest for a stealth bomber, not the B-1.

Secretary Mark visited SAC several times while Carter was president. He was well aware of the reasons for needing a stealthy bomber and encouraged SAC in that direction. His preference was the Northrop proposal, but he wanted the design changed to allow low-level penetrations under Soviet radar. The wear and tear on an aircraft during low-altitude flight is far greater than at high altitude. Northrop redesigned its proposal to accommodate Mark's concerns, resulting in delays and a more expensive B-2.

Verne Orr replaced Hans Mark as SECAF following Reagan's election. Orr received an MBA from Stanford and during WWII served as a Navy lieutenant in the Pacific. Following the war, he became a prominent businessman in California and was active in public service. A strong supporter and associate of President Reagan, Orr became SECAF in February 1981.

When the new secretary of defense, Casper Weinberger, visited SAC shortly after assuming the office, General Ellis seized this opportunity to acquaint him with the SAC mission, SIOP, Soviet air defense systems, and the necessity for a stealthy bomber. When I briefed Weinberger, he seemed to have an open mind, asked good questions, and expressed a strong interest in the subject.

Rockwell realized the change of administrations from Carter to Reagan put life back in its B-1 program. It updated early

B-2 stealth bomber. The KC-10 is air refueling a B-2. The unusual shape, reduced engine noise, and subdued color of the B-2 make it very difficult to detect visually. Radar and infrared detection are minimized by aircraft design and by the latest technology available in radar suppression, deflection, and absorption.

B-2 R&D. The R&D costs for the B-2 program were high, partly because of the extreme security imposed on all aspects of the program. The media quickly seized upon the B-2 as a "billion dollar bomber," and production was stopped at 21 aircraft by the Clinton administration—far short of the 100 that the USAF wanted.

briefings on the B-1A to the proposed B-1B and visited SAC with new proposals on delivery dates, performance, and so forth. Its proposal to build 100 new bombers for $20 billion with an initial operational capability in 1984 was attractive from both cost and timing viewpoints. Having flown the B-1A at Edwards AFB earlier, I would readily concede that it was a large, fast aircraft with excellent handling characteristics. I would not concede the B-1B could become a combat-ready bomber capable of penetrating the advanced air defenses of the Soviet Union. I also believed the cost and timing benchmarks claimed by Rockwell were grossly understated. It turned out later that my judgment was correct.

SAC would soon learn—but not soon enough—that Rockwell's B-1B proposal killed SAC's chances for acquiring stealth bombers in the late '80s. Unaware the die was cast, SAC kept pressing for a stealth bomber that would meet future requirements.

Chasing Rainbows

Mandatory retirement for general officers during my time in the Air Force was specified by laws and regulations. Two factors forced most three- and four-star generals to retire: age and total commissioned service. A mandatory age limit of 62 was imposed after WWII because of the rigors of wartime leadership. Total commissioned service was limited to 35 years to avoid the stagnation in promotion opportunities that existed prior to WWII. Exceptions were occasionally made for positions that were term-limited by law or practice—four years for the JCS chairman, for example.

General Ellis faced the mandatory retirement age of 62 during 1981. As my third year began as vice CINCSAC in 1980, General Ellis confided that he wanted me to be his successor at SAC. During the time remaining, he shared many of his duties and kept me informed of policy changes, USAF positions, congressional interests and concerns, and so on. There were also times during his last year on active duty when a serious illness caused him to be hospitalized, leaving me in charge.

Because SAC was the largest major air command and two-thirds of the nuclear triad during the Cold War consisted of SAC bombers and ICBMs, the new CINCSAC had always been selected from the existing list of (four-star) generals. In 1981 there were 12 USAF generals, including the JCS chairman, USAF chief of staff and vice chief of staff, deputy USCINCEUR, and chief of staff, SHAPE. The remaining seven generals commanded major air commands. Only three generals were retiring in the summer of 1981: General Ellis, General Huyser at MAC, and Gen Bryce Poe at AFLC. With no significant experience in airlift or logistics, there was no reason to believe I would replace either Huyser or Poe.

Therefore, I clung to the slim chance of replacing Ellis despite past precedence and the fact that a major air commander with a 1979 date of rank was openly seeking the job. Looking back on my prospects, I should have paid heed to the advice provided in the 92d Psalm: "An unwise man doth not well consider this, and a fool doth not understand it."

One day in April 1981, General Ellis said he had arranged for my interviews with the SECAF and deputy SecDef. After arriving at the Pentagon, we would first brief Secretary Orr on the stealth bomber. It was late in the afternoon when the SAC briefer began the stealth bomber pitch. I could see Mr. Orr was having difficulty staying awake, but he graciously thanked the briefer before asking me to join him for breakfast the next morning.

We met in the secretary's private dining room in the Pentagon for one of the more important meetings I had in my career. Mr. Orr was accompanied by his deputy, Pete Aldridge, who replaced Orr as secretary in 1986. After we exchanged pleasantries while eating, the conversation turned to the subject of a new SAC bomber.

"General Leavitt, I understand SAC wants the stealth bomber, not the B-1. Why are you opposed to the B-1?" Flashing through my mind was doubt that Mr. Orr could understand the technical and operational reasons from yesterday's briefing. Would an analogy related to his business background help him understand SAC reasoning? I knew that among his other successful business activities, Orr had owned large automobile dealerships in California.

"Mr. Secretary, I have been involved with the B-1 since 1963 when it was called AMSA and I was an analyst in the Air Staff. Now, 18 years later, your administration is considering buying 100 B-1s for SAC. Military aviation has radically changed during the past two decades. You were an automobile dealer in California. How would you feel if GM produced 20-year-old cars for your dealerships to sell?"

My comment was not intentionally rude, but was poorly stated and inappropriate. Mr. Orr smiled and was silent for a moment. Then he said something that bothered me at the time, but when the Cold War ended in our favor in 1989, I understood and accepted.

"General Leavitt, you don't understand. Ronald Reagan wants a new bomber on the ramp when he runs for reelection in 1984."

I had never dealt with political decision making and was shocked, disappointed, and a little angered by his explanation. My off-the-cuff response was ill-advised and rude. "Mr. Secretary, that is your problem, not mine."

Breakfast ended shortly thereafter, and he invited me to attend his morning staff meeting. From there, I went to the deputy SecDef's office, where he walked out with my records in his hand. He had neither questions nor comments and sent me to General Allen, Air Force chief of staff.

General Allen was alone in his office. After motioning me to a seat, General Allen asked about breakfast with the secretary. I told him exactly what happened. He thought for a moment before asking, "When you return to SAC, will you persuade General Ellis to support the B-1?" My answer effectively ended any prospect for promotion, "Sir, I won't do that." Nothing was said for a moment. Realizing my answer was uncooperative and borderline insubordinate, I broke the silence to see how much damage was done. "Will you give me a major air command?" General Allen's forthright answer cleared the air and ended the meeting. "Not as long as I am the chief of staff."

I left the chief's office immediately. The DCS for Personnel, a contemporary and longtime friend, was waiting outside. He asked about the interview with the chief. I told him. The DCS Personnel said two senior lieutenant general jobs were open for me. I could have either one—commander, Air University, or chief of staff, Pacific Command—but he needed a response in a day or two. I told him my response would be in his office the following day. On the return flight to Offutt, many conflicting thoughts ran through my mind. Did I have a future with the Air Force? Was spending at least $20 billion for an outmoded bomber worth fighting about? What would I do in civilian life? Would Anne want to move to Maxwell AFB or to Hawaii? Always before, the Air Force system called the shots. Why not let it happen again?

The next day I sent a message to DCS Personnel requesting retirement in July. It was a hasty decision and one regretted ever since.

In 1982 Charlie Gabriel became the USAF chief of staff and told me that I would have replaced him as CINC USAFE. Verne Orr was right. The first B-1B was built in time for the 1984 election. Reagan won the election and the Cold War by restocking and upgrading the American arsenal. Unit costs for the B-1B program were 40 percent above estimates, and the B-1B fleet was slow in acquiring both nuclear and conventional capabilities. Despite its limitations, the B-1B has served well in the skies over Iraq and Afghanistan; the B-2 stealth bomber was later built and met strategic requirements. Shakespeare was right—"All's well that ends well!"

Off We Go . . .

The few months since submitting my retirement request passed quickly. General Ellis retired on 31 July and left for his new job as US ambassador to the US-USSR Standing Consultative Commission. I requested to be retired the same day as General Ellis, but General Allen asked me to extend one more month to maintain continuity during the transition period for the new CINCSAC, Gen Bennie Davis. I agreed although I was uncomfortable with that arrangement because the new CINCSAC and I were contemporaries in years of service and had competed to become CINCSAC.

Anne and I were fortunate to have three wonderful persons working closely with us during our time at Offutt. Lt Col (later Col) Dick Iverson was my executive officer before becoming an FB-111 squadron commander in 1979. His replacement, Maj (later Col) George Conlan kept my many commitments and the office under control and also loved to beat this "old man" in racquetball. MSgt (later SMSgt) Delbert Coleman, enlisted aide, made our busy protocol and social schedules possible and was an invaluable friend and assistant to Anne.

The familiar strains of the Air Force song floated through the open window in our bedroom. It was 31 August 1981, a beautiful, late summer day in Nebraska. The SAC band was practicing for the parade that afternoon commemorating my retirement. While putting on my uniform this final time, my mind filled with memories of other uniforms and other experiences tracing back to 1 July 1946 when I entered West Point as a 17-year-old. These nostalgic thoughts were soon swept away by the roar of four engines signaling the takeoff of Looking Glass, SAC's EC-135 airborne command post. The takeoff runway was near our quarters. Takeoffs were loud, but jet engine noise aroused me like bagpipe music aroused Scots—to my ears, it was always the Sound of Freedom.

Friends and relatives from Omaha, Arkansas, Michigan, and Florida had arrived for the retirement ceremony and dinner party that evening. Temporary stands were filled with sightseers, SAC staff, and our guests. Squadrons on the other side of the parade ground stood at attention as the band played the national anthem and the adjutant read my retirement orders. After General Davis presented the Defense Distinguished Service Medal, the nation's highest noncombat award, he stepped back and motioned me forward. I looked up. A U-2 was approaching at low altitude, followed in a loose trail formation by an F-84F, T-33, B-52, F-4, KC-135, and SR-71 . . . each aircraft separated from the previous by a few seconds. It was a very emotional experience to see these aircraft that were the core of my life. The band played "Auld Lang Syne," and the ceremony was over. And so was a wonderful, exciting, rewarding career in the world's finest Air Force.

Anne and I left Offutt the next morning. As I drove by the flight line, the words from a hymn came to mind for coming generations of Air Force people who would be "following the flag":

> O wind of heaven, by thy might
> Save all who dare the eagle's flight,
> And keep them by thy watchful care
> From every peril in the air.

Retirement ceremony, 31 August 1981. Gen B. L. Davis, the new CINCSAC (*on Leavitt's right*), awarded General Leavitt the Defense Distinguished Service Medal.

Squadrons pass in review. General Davis asked Anne to join me after the retirement orders were read. Then he stepped back while the squadron passed in review. I returned their salutes. The band played the US Air Force song as the last squadron passed. The spectators left, and I was now officially retired.

Notes

1. Hopkins and Goldberg, *Development of Strategic Air Command, 1946–86*, 217–19.

2. Department of State, "Treaty between the United States of America and the Union of Soviet Socialist Republics."

3. Expressed by Gen Carl Spaatz, commanding general of the USAAF.

4. Gen John Shaud graduated from West Point in 1956 and served in bombers and fighters until 1968 when he joined the 12th TRS in the Vietnam War. He earned a PhD at Ohio State University, served on the faculty at ACSC, graduated from NWC, and commanded two SAC bomb wings and two SAC air divisions. He was DCS Personnel from 1985 to 1986; commander, ATC, 1986–88, and chief of staff, SHAPE, 1988–91, before retiring as a general in 1991. Awards include the Distinguished Service Medal with oak leaf cluster, Legion of Merit with oak leaf cluster, Distinguished Flying Cross, Meritorious Service Medal with oak leaf cluster, Air Medal with five oak leaf clusters, and Commendation Medal with oak leaf cluster. US Military Academy, *Register of Graduates.*

Epilogue

Business Life

The Pentagon's "Current News" headline article on 22 June 1981 was titled "Air Force in a Dogfight over Its New Bomber." It signaled that Gen Bennie Davis would replace Gen Richard Ellis as Commander in Chief, Strategic Air Command (SAC), and that I would retire before the end of the year. Following this announcement, several defense contractors contacted me. Although their offers were excellent, I was unwilling to risk conflict of interest charges by working for a USAF supplier. A friend arranged an interview with a high-tech firm in Dallas. When I arrived in a business suit, the hiring executive was sitting at his desk in an open-collar sport shirt. After a very brief introduction he said, "General, I don't believe you would be comfortable here. We are very informal, but thanks for coming." The finality of his remarks did not allow an explanation that half my adult life had been spent in a flight suit and our summer uniform in the office was an open-collar short-sleeved shirt!

On the same trip, I visited Wichita, where a banker acquaintance had arranged an interview with the chairman of an aircraft company. I welcomed the offer to be a corporate senior vice president and the general manager of a modern aircraft plant with over 8,000 employees building business jets as well as turboprop and conventional twin-engine aircraft.

I went to work there the Monday following retirement. It was a great job, and I learned many things about manufacturing. By the summer of 1982, the national recession hit aircraft sales very hard. By Christmas 1983, the large plant I managed was making only a few jets and had shrunk to about 2,000 employees. I resigned upon returning to Wichita after the Christmas break. Manufacturing aircraft was a tough but rewarding business, and I enjoyed the experience.

In 1983 I managed a quality control company in California while the owner took an extended trip around the world. Eighteen months with this company taught lessons about controlling quality that were useful later in my own businesses. In

623

1985 I bought a national franchise for selling custom software and multiuser computers to businesses. I sold the computer business in 1989 and bought an established large machine shop in northern California that made parts for high-powered electrical equipment used in communications, radars, and X-ray, MRI, and CAT scan machines. The corporation expanded through acquisitions and was quite profitable. My son, Lloyd, our chief financial officer, managed the corporation after I retired.

In retrospect, being a retired officer gave me the opportunity to apply management lessons learned in the Air Force to private business. I was not afraid to take business risks. Not all turned out well, but they made life interesting and provided a comfortable life for my wife and family.

Volunteer Work

During my fourth year in California, I was elected president of the large West Point alumni association in Los Angeles. The responsibilities were mostly social—planning Founders' Day events, finding guest speakers, and arranging boarding and transportation for visiting athletic teams and the cadet choir, as well as interviewing candidates to be cadets and keeping the association finances in order. With Anne's able direction, we also arranged a five-day mini-reunion for the Class of '50 on a cruise ship from San Pedro to Mexico and back. I also served on the vestry of Episcopal churches in Palos Verdes Estates and Palm Desert when we lived in California. As an aside, "volunteer" organizations presented a different management challenge than either the Air Force or the corporate world.

In 1991 West Point began a distinguished graduate (DG) program, with the first selectees to be announced in 1992. A board of 12 graduates no longer on active duty was appointed to make the annual selections. Nominations came from West Point societies and from past graduating classes. DGs selected could not be on active duty, a current elected official, or deceased. I was the only retired Air Force general on the board, and I served for five years, enjoying the give-and-take at our annual meetings. During the five years I served, we selected a total of 17 DGs, including five USAF recipients: 1993—Edward Rowny, Class of '41, and Robert McDermott, Class of January '43;

1995—Benjamin Davis, Class of '36, and Brent Scowcroft, Class of '47; and 1996—Frank Borman, Class of '50.

Arms Control and
Crisis Management 1984–91

Shortly after we moved to California, Cornell University asked me to participate in arms control, nuclear proliferation, and crisis management studies as a Visiting Scholar. RADM Paul Tomb, USN, retired, deputy director of command, control, and communications in the Joint Chiefs of Staff (JCS), had recommended my name to Kurt Gottfried, professor of physics and nuclear studies at Cornell. Among the many notables in these early studies were Hans Bethe, Nobel Laureate and director of theoretical physics in the Manhattan Project; Dr. Ashton Carter, now head of defense procurement in the Obama administration; Dr. Richard Garwin, who twice served on the President's Science Advisory Board; Condoleezza Rice, future secretary of state; Robert McNamara, former secretary of defense; and Henry Kendall, past chairman of the Union of Concerned Scientists and Nobel Prize winner in physics. General Wallace Nutting, USA, retired, joined the study group during the last year of the Cold War.

This was one of the most interesting phases of my post-military life. It was an opportunity to discuss nuclear weapon issues on both a national and international basis with people who were genuinely concerned about the proliferation and control of nuclear weapons but who often lacked factual knowledge. With an extensive background in areas such as nuclear weapons and weapon safeguards, I was their "hair shirt" and spent my time writing, explaining command and control issues and nuclear safety policies, questioning some assumptions and misconceptions, and defending our nuclear triad.

The long-term goal of many participants was to achieve nuclear disarmament. I believe complete nuclear disarmament of the United States was then and remains a mistaken objective for several reasons. Fifty-five years after the bombing of Hiroshima and Nagasaki ended WWII, the antinuke believers still dismiss or distort the military and political advantages gained from those two atomic bombs. In fact, far fewer Japanese casualties resulted from those two atomic bombs than from our firebombing attacks on major Japanese cities. For example, B-29s had earlier killed nearly 100,000 Japanese in one firebombing raid on Tokyo. By forcing Japan to stop fighting, the nuclear bombs allowed the United States to cancel the planned October 1945 invasion of Honshu and avoid an estimated 600,000 American casualties, as well as over 1,000,000 Japanese casualties (JCS estimates).

Nuclear disarmament advocates tend to discount the peacekeeping role that our nuclear-equipped forces have provided since WWII. The threatened, possible, or potential use of nuclear weapons places an upper limit on how far opposing nations are willing to pursue their political or military objectives. When Eisenhower threatened to use nuclear weapons to break the Korean War stalemate, that war ended. The Cuban missile crisis ended after our strategic nuclear forces went to DEFCON 2 and Kennedy threatened military action. For 45 years, North Atlantic Treaty Organization (NATO) forces equipped with nuclear weapons deterred the larger Warsaw Pact forces that threatened Western Europe. Without nuclear weapons, the free world could have changed in unimaginable ways.

Nuclear disarmament advocates know that other nations already have nuclear arsenals, including the United States, Russia, the United Kingdom (UK), France, China, Pakistan, India, and Israel. Assuming that the United States and Russia would somehow agree to strategic nuclear disarmament, do they expect that the UK, France, China, Pakistan, India, and Israel would also give up their nuclear weapons? And who would control the thousands of tactical nuclear weapons produced during the Cold War for NATO and the Warsaw Pact?

There seems to be no reliable way to enforce nuclear disarmament, short of war, if a nation decides to build a nuclear arsenal. Iraq's refusal to comply with United Nations ultimatums to disclose its nuclear weapons program resulted in Operation Iraqi Freedom, with the United States suffering more than 4,300 killed and 31,000 wounded. Today, North Korea and Iran continue pursuing their nuclear weapons programs despite economic bribery and diplomatic pressure.

Because we lack reliable ways to deny rogue nations the acquisition of nuclear weapons, Americans should recognize the *deterrent* value of our own nuclear weapons. One measure is to compare American military casualties in the wars before and after the advent of nuclear weapons. The Congressional Research Service provides the following statistics:

Before nuclear weapons were developed:
World War I—320,538 dead and wounded

Before nuclear weapons destroyed Hiroshima and Nagasaki:
World War II—1,076,885 dead and wounded

After nuclear weapons were developed and available:
Korean War—139,862 dead and wounded

It should be noted that Eisenhower's May 1953 threat to use nuclear weapons broke stalemated negotiations and resulted in the July 1953 armistice, thereby saving about 130 American casualties per day.

After nuclear weapons were developed but not used:
Vietnam War—269,721 dead and wounded

Pres. Lyndon Johnson's administration was always concerned about Chinese intervention and avoided any threat or discussion of using nuclear weapons. Pres. Richard Nixon ended the war when Linebacker II bombed Hanoi-Haiphong with conventional weapons and mined North Vietnamese ports.

Recent wars in the Middle East:
Persian Gulf War—849 dead and wounded
Operation Enduring Freedom—3,876 dead and wounded
Operation Iraqi Freedom—35,731 dead and wounded

The cumulative data shows that using nuclear weapons against Japan and keeping our nuclear arsenal have greatly reduced American casualties since nuclear deterrence became US policy. The most significant gain from nuclear deterrence was being able to end the Cold War without combat operations between NATO/the United States and the Warsaw Pact/USSR.

Cold War Conferences

During the eighties, I attended many meetings and conferences on nuclear weapons and related subjects. The meetings also revealed some interesting individual motivations. They were usually held in the United States, but several took place in Europe: Supreme Headquarters Allied Powers, Europe, Belgium; Headquarters United States Air Forces in Europe, West Germany; Stockholm University, Sweden; Geneva, Switzerland; Paris, France; London, UK; Kiev, Ukraine; Moscow, Russia; Tallinn, Estonia; and Pugwash, Nova Scotia, Canada. Conferences usually included a mix of scientists, college professors, and foreign diplomats. From a historical viewpoint, the later conferences coincided with the year-by-year death of the USSR in the eighties but not the end of US concerns about the proliferation of nuclear weapons.

At a conference in Stockholm University, a retired West German admiral and member of a radical left-wing German party went on a tirade against American foreign and military policies. After listening to his and similar remarks from other left-wing speakers and with no opportunity for rebuttal, I walked out. This Cold War conference exemplified the one-sided bias by Europe's far left.

In April 1985, General Secretary and defacto leader of the USSR, Mikhail Gorbachev, made a significant step toward arms control by suspending deployment of SS-20 intermediate-range ballistic missiles (IRBMs). In January 1986, he proposed that all IRBMs be eliminated from Europe, which led to the Reagan and Gorbachev meeting in Reykjavik, Iceland, in October 1986. No formal agreement was signed on the IRBM issue at the October meeting.

In February 1986, Mikhail Gorbachev introduced his glasnost and perestroika policies that startled the world. An arms control conference was held in Geneva during the same year. The American ambassador invited four participants to his home after adjourning. The Soviet participant was the son of longtime Soviet ambassador to the United States, Anatoly Dobrynin. Mr. Dobrynin, a Russian author, explained in careful detail that *glasnost* meant less censorship and more openness in government. *Perestroika* focused on reforming the Russian economy and certain political changes. After listening to Dobrynin, I could not believe these major policy changes could occur in the USSR without strong reactions from diehard communists. When it was time to leave, the ambassador could only get one taxi to take Dobrynin and me to our hotels. Dobrynin was clearly nervous about riding alone with a retired SAC general. During the ride, we talked about authoring books in the USSR and how he was paid in cars, not rubles. The conference and that evening suggested that the worst years of the Cold War might be ending.

Returning to the United States, I stopped in Reykjavik after the IRBM meeting had ended. A Soviet colonel general (equivalent to a US lieutenant general) called my hotel room and asked if I would meet with him privately in the conference room where Reagan and Gorbachev had met. I agreed. He explained that he was the only Russian with Gorbachev in the meeting with Reagan and heard all the discussions. Gorbachev was apparently concerned that Reagan did not believe that the Russians would give up the IRBMs, as they had tentatively agreed. Would I pass the word to Reagan's advisors that Gorbachev was serious? I agreed to do that. After returning to California, I passed the message to the highest Reagan official that I could reach. He said Reagan believed Gorbachev but was not ready to sign. The Intermediate-Range Nuclear Forces Treaty eliminating IRBMs was finally signed in Geneva on 24 November 1987.

In 1989 the Berlin Wall was torn down. Gorbachev then allowed the Eastern European nations in the Warsaw Pact to choose their own political system. A 1989 conference was held in the Moscow hotel used by diplomats. The food was bad, and the rooms were marginally functional. The Russian economy was near collapse, and the ruble had little value. People stood in long lines at food markets waiting to purchase the little food that was available. A barter economy was evident as people scrambled on Moscow's sidewalks to buy shoes and other scarce items.

Four conferees, including an East German professor and myself, went to a bistro after the meeting. The East German was happy because he thought all the money he had saved would now be worth millions in West Germany. The economist in our group dampened his spirits when he told him the real value of East German marks—next to nothing!

Although the conference subject was nuclear proliferation, at one point it shifted to the vicious Chinese suppression of student protestors in Tiananmen Square in the summer of 1989.

The Chinese delegate vigorously maintained that no one was killed and that the world press lied. When I challenged him by stating the killings were visible on TV, most delegates agreed. When I left the hotel that evening, he followed and asked to talk to me privately. He said I was correct, that many protestors had been killed, but the Chinese leadership would never do that again and wanted to put the tragic incident behind them.

A meeting in Estonia included a visit to the Russian bomber base near Tallinn after the USSR had collapsed. The airfield was in terrible disrepair. If it had belonged to SAC, it would have been closed. Aircraft spare parts came from Ukraine, and deliveries had stopped. Jet fuel was still coming by pipeline, but the Russians were emptying it into the Baltic because most aircraft were not flyable and the fuel storage area was full. We had lunch at the base Officers' Club. Obviously, people had emptied their refrigerators to feed us—every guest had a different mix of leftovers. The high point of the visit for me was when the Russian commander let me carefully exam the Backfire bomber. It seemed to be technically quite similar to SAC FB-111s.

After the Ukraine became independent, an important arms control issue arose. Which nation would own the ICBMs controlled by Russians but located in Ukraine silos? The United States and Russia were opposed to making Ukraine a nuclear power with ICBMs. We wanted Russia to control these ICBMs until they could be moved to Russia or destroyed. After a day-long meeting, the Russian ambassador asked me to join him in his hotel room and bring my colleague, Lt Gen Dick Burpee, USAF, retired. We were talking to the ambassador when a Russian air force major general left his seat from the other side of the room, walked over, and stood in front of me. We all stopped talking. The general, with a depressed look on his face, asked, "Did you fear us?" His question caused me to remember MiG Alley, Soviet interceptors chasing my U-2 over Siberia, the Cuban missile crisis, the Vietnam War and Soviet air defense systems, the Yom Kippur War, and all the other years I worried about the USSR's military capabilities. When I answered, "No, but we did respect you," a relieved look crossed his face, and he sat down. It was not the same as signing a treaty on the battleship *Missouri* or accepting a sword at Appomattox, but at that moment I knew the Cold War was finally over.

Appendix A

Personnel Actions Memorandum, 17 May 1957, with addendum

HEADQUARTERS
4080TH STRATEGIC RECONNAISSANCE WING (L) (SAC)
United States Air Force
Laughlin Air Force Base, Del Rio, Texas

PERSONNEL ACTIONS MEMORANDUM   17 May 1957
NUMBER 61

CR NR[a]	RANK	NAME AFSN[b]	DATE
N-201	CAPT	JOE R KING, AO2075990	22 Jan 57
N-202	CAPT	RAYMOND L HAUPT, AO1909717	22 Jan 57
N-203	CAPT	RICHARD S HEYSER, 26536A	22 Jan 57
N-204	CAPT	WARREN J BOYD, 27823A	22 Jan 57
N-206	IST LT	MICHAEL E STYER, 27126A	22 Jan 57
N-205	CAPT	BENEDICT A LACOMBE, AO191024	25 Feb 57
N-207	CAPT	LLOYD R LEAVITT JR, 20257A	25 Feb 57
N-209	IST LT	ANTHONY F BEVACQUA, AO3025780	25 Feb 57
N-210	IST LT	JACK M GRAVES, AO3005557	25 Feb 57
N-211	CAPT	JOHN A CAMPBELL, AO1907708	13 Mar 57
N-212	CAPT	EDWIN G EMERLING, AO935447	13 Mar 57
N-213	CAPT	RICHARD E MCGRAW, AO1908848	13 Mar 57
N-214	IST LT	KENNETH W ALDERMAN, AO2229105	13 Mar 57
N-215	IST LT	MARVIN W DOERING, AO2225826	11 May 57
N-216	CAPT	LINUS L LEE JR, AO982472	12 May 57

[a] crew rating number
[b] Air Force service number

631

Addendum:

King was killed in an auto accident after retiring.

Haupt retired as a brigadier general after serving in the U-2, A-12, and SR-71.

Heyser flew the U-2 that confirmed the Cuban missile crisis and died in 2008.

Boyd died of natural causes while on active duty.

Styer was killed ferrying an F-4 back from Vietnam.

LaCombe was killed in a U-2 accident at Laughlin AFB in 1967.

Leavitt transferred to the B-52H program in late 1960.

Bevacqua remained in the U-2 program and later served on an SR-71 aircrew.

Graves remained in the U-2 program.

Campbell was killed in a U-2 accident in 1962.

Emerling stayed in the U-2 program and flew in the Cuban missile crisis.

McGraw was transferred from the U-2 program.

Alderman remained in the U-2 program.

Doering remained in the U-2 program.

Lee became a U-2 maintenance officer.

Appendix B

Awards and Decorations

Lt Gen Lloyd R. Leavitt, USAF, Retired

Defense Distinguished Service Medal

Distinguished Service Medal (Air Force) with One Oak Leaf Cluster

Legion of Merit with Two Oak Leaf Clusters

Distinguished Flying Cross with Two Oak Leaf Clusters

Bronze Star Medal

Meritorious Service Medal

Air Medal with Thirteen Oak Leaf Clusters

Air Force Commendation Medal

Air Force Outstanding Unit Award with "V" and One Oak Leaf Cluster

World War II Victory Medal

National Defense Service Medal with Bronze Service Star

Korean Service Medal with Silver Service Star

Vietnam Service Medal with Two Bronze Service Stars

Air Force Longevity Service Award with Seven Oak Leaf Clusters

Small Arms Expert Marksmanship Ribbon

Aviador Militar "Honoris Causa"—Argentina

Republic of Korea Presidential Unit Citation

United Nations Service Medal

Republic of Vietnam Campaign Medal

Abbreviations

AAA	antiaircraft artillery
AAC	Army Air Corps
AAF	Army Air Forces
AAFCE	Allied Air Forces, Central Europe
ABAC	air battle analysis center
ABAD	air battle analysis division
ABCCC	airborne battlefield command and control center
ABM	antiballistic missile
AC	alternating current
ACLU	American Civil Liberties Union
ACSC	Air Command and Staff College
AD	air division
ADC	Air Defense Command
ADCC	air defense control center
ADVON	advanced echelon
AFB	Air Force base
AFCENT	Allied Forces Central Europe
AFLC	Air Force Logistics Command
AFM	Air Force manual
AFNORTH	Allied Forces Northern Europe
AFQT	Armed Forces Qualification Test
AFR	Air Force Reserve
AFS	Air Force station
AFSC	Air Force Systems Command
AGE	aerospace ground equipment
ALCM	air launched cruise missile
AMOC	Aircraft Maintenance Officer Course
AMSA	advanced manned strategic aircraft
ANG	Air National Guard
APOE	aerial port of embarkation
APU	auxiliary power unit
ARCT	airborne regimental combat team
ARRS	aerospace rescue and recovery squadron
ARVN	Army of the Republic of Vietnam
ATC	Air Training Command
ATCA	advanced tanker/cargo aircraft
ATOC	air tactical operations center

AWACS	Airborne Warning and Control System
AWOL	absent without leave
BOQ	bachelor officers' quarters
BTZ	below the zone
BX	base exchange
CAGE	Computer Analyzed Game of Escalation
CAS	close air support
CBU	cluster bomb unit
CCSG	Consolidated Contingency Steering Group
CCTS	combat crew training squadron
CEP	circular error probable
ChiCom	Chinese Communist
CIA	Central Intelligence Agency
CINCLANT	Commander in Chief, Atlantic Command
CINCPAC	Commander in Chief, Pacific Command
CINCSAC	Commander in Chief, Strategic Air Command
CJCS	chairman of the Joint Chiefs of Staff
CO	commanding officer
CONUS	continental United States
CPI	consumer price index
DCS	deputy chief of staff
DEFCON	defense readiness condition
DEROS	date of expected return from overseas service
DETECT	Defense Evaluation through Effectiveness and Cost Techniques
DF	direction finding
DI	Air Force chief of intelligence
DIA	Defense Intelligence Agency
DMZ	demilitarized zone
DO	deputy commander for operations
DoD	Department of Defense
DOR	date of rank
DPRK	Democratic People's Republic of Korea
DRVN	Democratic Republic of Vietnam
DSM	Distinguished Service Medal
DU	depleted uranium
ECM	electronic countermeasures
EGT	exhaust gas temperature
EMP	electromagnetic pulse
EO	electro-optical

EW	early warning
FAA	Federal Aviation Administration
FAC	forward air controller
FBG	fighter-bomber group
FBS	fighter-bomber squadron
FBW	fighter-bomber wing
FEAF	Far East Air Forces
FEW	fighter-escort wing
FIS	fighter interceptor squadron
FIW	fighter interceptor wing
FORCE	Force Option Ranking by Cost Effectiveness
FRG	Federal Republic of Germany
FY	fiscal year
GCA	ground-controlled approach
GCI	ground control intercept
GDP	gross domestic product
GDR	German Democratic Republic
G-force	gravitational force
GIB	"guy in back"
GPS	Global Positioning System
GW	George Washington (University)
HASP	high-altitude sampling program
HQ	headquarters
IAF	Israeli air force
ID	identification; infantry division
IDF	Israel Defense Forces
IG	inspector general
IGY	International Geophysical Year
IIAF	Imperial Iranian Air Force
INTERPOL	International Criminal Police Organization
IP	instructor pilot
IRBM	intermediate-range ballistic missile
JAG	judge advocate general
JCS	Joint Chiefs of Staff
JDAM	Joint Direct Attack Munition
JOC	joint operations center
JSCS	Joint Strategic Connectivity Staff
JSTPS	Joint Strategic Targeting and Planning Staff
JTF	joint task force
KIA	killed in action

LABS	Low Altitude Bombing System
LCF	launch control facility
LGB	laser-guided bomb
LORAN	long-range aid to navigation
LST	landing ship, tank
MA&E	Military Art and Engineering
MAAG	military assistance advisory group
MAC	Military Airlift Command
MACV	Military Assistance Command, Vietnam
MAD	mutually assured destruction
MBFR	Mutual and Balanced Force Reduction
MC	military committee
MCO	mobile control officer
MIA	missing in action
MIRV	multiple independently targetable reentry vehicle
mph	miles per hour
MRBM	medium-range ballistic missile
NASA	National Aeronautics and Space Administration
NATO	North Atlantic Treaty Organization
NCA	National Command Authority
NCO	noncommissioned officer
NIE	National Intelligence Estimate
NKAF	North Korean air force
NKPA	North Korean People's Army
NORAD	North American Aerospace Defense Command
NSC	National Security Council
NSWP	non-Soviet Warsaw Pact
NTM	national technical means
NVN	North Vietnam/North Vietnamese
NWC	National War College
OAS	Organization of American States
OER	officer effectiveness report
OJT	on-the-job training
ops	operations
ORI	operational readiness inspection
OSD	Office of the Secretary of Defense
OSI	Office of Special Investigations
PACAF	Pacific Air Forces
PCS	permanent change of station
PE	personal equipment

PGM	precision-guided munition
PHOTINT	photographic intelligence
PKI	Indonesian Communist Party
PLATO	Programmed Logic for Automatic Teaching Operations
POL	petroleum, oil, and lubricant
POW	prisoner of war
PRC	People's Republic of China
PSP	pierced-steel planking
PVO	Soviet Air Defense Force
QRC	Quick Reaction Certification
R&D	research and development
R&R	rest and recreation
RAF	Royal Air Force
RBS	radar bombing site
RCS	radar cross section
RDJTF	Rapid Deployment Joint Task Force
RESCAP	rescue combat air patrol
RHAW	radar homing and warning
RNAF	Royal Norwegian Air Force
ROC	Republic of China
ROCAF	Republic of China Air Force
ROE	rules of engagement
ROK	Republic of (South) Korea
ROTC	Reserve Officer Training Corps
RPM	revolution per minute
RTAFB	Royal Thai Air Force Base
RV	reentry vehicle
RVN	Republic of Vietnam
S&A	Studies and Analysis
SAC	Strategic Air Command
SACEUR	Supreme Allied Commander, Europe
SALT	Strategic Arms Limitation Talks
SAM	surface-to-air missile
SEAD	suppression of enemy air defenses
SEATO	Southeast Asia Treaty Organization
SECAF	secretary of the Air Force
SecDef	Secretary of Defense
SFW	strategic fighter wing
SHAPE	Supreme Headquarters Allied Powers, Europe

SIOP	Single Integrated Operational Plan
SLBM	submarine-launched ballistic missile
SLR	side-looking radar
SOD	senior officer of the day
SOF	special operations forces
SOS	Squadron Officer School; special operations squadron
SP	security police
SPF	Strategic Projection Force
SRAM	short-range air-to-surface attack missile
SRS(L)	strategic reconnaissance squadron, light
SRW(L)	strategic reconnaissance wing, light
STOL	short takeoff and landing
SVN	South Vietnam
TAC	Tactical Air Command
TAS	true air speed
TASIS	The American School in Switzerland
TCP	Technological Capabilities Panel
TD	time difference
TDY	temporary duty
TEW	tactical electronic warfare
TFR	terrain-following radar
TFS	tactical fighter squadron
TFW	tactical fighter wing
TRFW	tactical reconnaissance fighter wing
TRW	tactical reconnaissance wing
TTC	technical training center
UCMJ	*Uniform Code of Military Justice*
UN	United Nations
UNC	United Nations Command
UNODIR	unless otherwise directed
U-of-I	University of Illinois
USAAF	US Army Air Forces
USAFE	United States Air Forces in Europe
USAFSAAS	USAF School of Applied Aerospace Sciences
USAREUR	US Army, European Command
USN	US Navy
VAR	vertical angle release
VTOL	vertical takeoff and landing
WAF	Women in the Air Force

WCP   wing command post
WWMCCS   Worldwide Military Command and Control
                System

Bibliography

Air Force Association. *Membership Directory, 2006–2007*. Chesapeake, VA: Harris Connect, Inc., 2007.

———. *1977 Soviet Air Force Almanac Issue*. Chesapeake, VA: Harris Connect, Inc., 1997.

Anderegg, C. R. *Sierra Hotel: Flying Air Force Fighters in the Decade after Vietnam*. Washington, DC: Air Force History and Museum Program, USAF, 2001.

Anderton, David. *History of the U.S. Air Force*. New York: The Military Press, 1989.

Associates in Political Science, USAF Academy. *American Defense Policy*. Baltimore, MD: The Johns Hopkins Press, 1968.

Atkinson, Rick. *An Army at Dawn: The War in North Africa, 1942–1943*. New York: Henry Holt and Company, 2002.

Berthon, Simon, and Joanna Potts. *Warlords: An Extraordinary Re-creation of World War II through the Eyes and Minds of Hitler, Churchill, Roosevelt, and Stalin*. Cambridge, MA: De Capo Press, 2006.

Beschloss, Michael. *Presidential Courage: Brave Leaders and How They Changed America, 1789–1989*. New York: Simon and Schuster, 2007.

Blair, Bruce G. *Strategic Command and Control: Redefining the Nuclear Threat*. Washington, DC: The Brookings Institution, 1985.

Borowski, Harry, ed. *The Harmon Memorial Lectures in Military History, 1959–1987: A Collection of the First Thirty Harmon Lectures Given at the United States Air Force Academy*. Washington, DC: Office of Air Force History, 1988.

Bradley, Gen Omar, Army chief of staff. Testimony to US Congress, Committee on Appropriations. Hearings on the FY 1949 Military Appropriations Bill, 1948.

British Broadcasting Corporation (BBC). "1983: Korean Airliner 'Shot Down.'" *On This Day*, 1 September 1983. http://news.bbc.co.uk/onthisday/hi/dates/stories/september/1/newsid_2493000/2493469.stm.

Buccolo, Joseph P., ed. *Memories of West Point and Its Impact on the Class of 1950*. United States: Joseph P. Buccolo, circa 2001.

Buckwalter, David T. "The 1973 Arab-Israeli War." In *Case Studies in Policy Making & Implementation*, edited by David A. Williams, 119–37. 6th ed. Newport, RI: Naval War College, 2002.

Burns, James. *The Soldiers of Freedom: 1940–1945*. New York: History Book Club, 2006.

Bush, George H. W., and Brent Scowcroft. *A World Transformed*. New York: Vintage Books, 1998.

Caro, Robert. *The Years of Lyndon Johnson: Means of Ascent*. New York: Alfred A. Knopf, 1990.

Central Intelligence Agency. *Handbook of Economic Statistics*. Washington, DC: Office of Economic Research, 1988.

Cerami, Joseph R. "Presidential Decision Making and Vietnam: Lessons for Strategists." *Parameters* 26, no. 4 (Winter 1996–97): 66–80.

Cline, Ray S. *World Power Assessment: A Calculus of Strategic Drift*. Washington, DC: Center for Strategic and International Studies, Georgetown University, 1975.

Congressional Budget Office. *Budget and Economic Outlook: Fiscal Years 2001–2010*. Washington, DC: Congressional Budget Office, 2000.

Dallek, Robert. *Nixon and Kissinger: Partners in Power*. New York: Harper Collins Publisher, 2007.

———. *An Unfinished Life: John F. Kennedy, 1917–1963*. Boston: Little, Brown and Company, 2003.

Department of Defense. *Annual Report for Fiscal Year 1963*. Washington, DC: Government Printing Office, 1964.

———. "Principal Wars in Which the United States Participated: U.S. Military Personnel Serving and Casualties." Global security.org.

Department of State. "Treaty between the United States of America and the Union of Soviet Socialist Republics on the Limitation of Strategic Offensive Arms (SALT II)." Signed at Vienna, 18 June 1979. http://www.state.gov/t/isn/5195.htm.

Department of the Navy. "Naval Aviation Chronology, 1970–1980." http://www.history.navy.mil/branches/avchr10.htm.

———. Naval Historical Center. "Biographies in Naval History: Admiral Thomas Hinman Moorer, USN (Ret.)." http://www.history.navy.mil/bios/moorer_thomas_h.htm.

Eisenhower, Dwight D. *Mandate for Change: 1953–1956; The White House Years.* Garden City, NY: Doubleday, 1963.

Fernandes, Clinton. "Indonesia 1965: A Power Move with Far-Reaching Implications." In *Foreign Relations of the United States, 1964–68*, edited by Edward C. Keefer, 289–92. Vol. XXVI. Washington, DC: Government Printing Office, 2000.

14th Strategic Aerospace Division, *Cuban Missile Crisis Annex*, October 1962. Vol. 2. Call no. K-DIV-14-HI V.2. IRIS no. 00426145. Air Force Historical Research Agency, Maxwell AFB, AL.

Futrell, Robert Frank. *The United States Air Force in Korea, 1950–1953.* Washington, DC: Office of Air Force History, US Air Force, 1983.

———. *The United States Air Force in Southeast Asia: The Advisory Years to 1965.* Washington, DC: US Government Printing Office, 1965.

Hatchett, Ronald. *Arms Control: Problems and Prospects 1990.* College Station, TX: Texas A&M University Press, 1990.

Headquarters, Williams Air Force Base. *Willie Air Patch: Class 51-E.* Chandler, AZ: Headquarters, Williams AFB, 1951.

Headquarters SAC. *Developing an Atomic Capability in Strategic Fighter Wings.* Omaha, NE: Historical Division, Headquarters SAC, Offutt AFB, 1953. Document is now declassified.

Heiber, Helmut, and David Glantz. *Hitler and His Generals: Military Conferences 1942–1945.* New York: Enigma Books, 2003.

Hermes, Walter G. *Truce Tent and Fighting Front.* Washington, DC: Center of Military History, US Army, 2005.

Historical Evaluation and Research Organization. *A Study of Breakthrough Operations.* Dunn Loring, VA: Defense Nuclear Agency, 1976.

Hopkins, J. C., and Sheldon A. Goldberg. *The Development of Strategic Air Command, 1946–1986: The Fortieth Anniversary History.* Omaha, NE: Office of the Historian, Headquarters SAC, Offutt AFB, 1986.

Hua, Mike. "The Black Cat Squadron." *Air Power History* 49, no. 1 (Spring 2002): 4–19.

Kahn, Herman. *On Thermonuclear War.* Princeton, NJ: Princeton University Press, 1960.

Kissinger, Henry. *American Foreign Policy: Three Essays*. New York: W. W. Norton & Company, 1974.

———. *Diplomacy*. New York: Touchstone, 1994.

Knaack, Marcelle Size. *Encyclopedia of US Air Force Aircraft and Missile Systems*. Vol. 1, *Post-World War II Fighters 1945–1973*. Washington, DC: Office of Air Force History, 1978.

Lake, Jon, and David Donald, eds. *McDonnell F-4 Phantom: Spirit in the Skies*. Norwalk, CT: Airtime Publishing, Inc., 2002.

MacArthur, Douglas. *Reminiscences*. New York: McGraw Hill, 1964.

Mastny, Vojtech (project coordinator). PHP—Parallel History Project on NATO and the Warsaw Pact. Press Release, 23 May 2000: "Secret Plan for Nuclear War in Europe Published: 1964 Warsaw Pact Plan Aimed at Taking Lyon in 9 Days." http://www.gwu.edu/~nsarchiv/NSAEBB/NSAEBB 31/press.html.

McCarthy, James, and George Allison. *Linebacker II: A View from the Rock*. Maxwell AFB, AL: Airpower Research Institute, 1979.

McCullough, David. *Truman*. New York: Simon and Schuster, 1992.

Mehuron, Tamar A., ed. "The Air Force in Facts and Figures." Almanac issue. *Air Force Magazine* 86, no. 5 (May 2003): 58–93.

Menuel, Marshal Stewart. *Russian Military Power*. New York: Bonanza Books, 1980.

Message 10-049. SAC to JCS, 31 January 1979. Document is now declassified.

Military History Institute of Vietnam. *Victory in Vietnam: The Official History of the People's Army of Vietnam, 1954–1975*. Vol. 2, *The Coming of Age of the People's Army of Vietnam during the Resistance War against the Americans to Save the Nation (1954–75)*. Translated by Merle L. Pribbenow. Lawrence, KS: University Press of Kansas, 2002.

Momyer, William. *Air Power in Three Wars (WWII, Korea, Vietnam)*. Washington, DC: Government Printing Office, 1978.

Morris, Benny. *Righteous Victims*. New York: Alfred Knopf, 1999.

National War College. "Mission." http://www.ndu.edu/nwc/ History/mission.htm.

Nixon, Richard. *Leaders*. New York: Warner Books, Inc. 1982.

"Off the Record Meeting on Cuba, October 16, 1962, 6:30–7:55 PM." John F. Kennedy Papers. JFK Library, Boston, Massachusetts.

Palmer, LTG David. *Summons of the Trumpet: U.S.-Vietnam in Perspective.* Novato, CA: Presidio Press, 1978.

Parks, W. Hays. "Linebacker and the Law of War." *Air University Review* 34, no. 2 (January–February 1983): 2–30.

Pedlow, Dr. Gregory W., ed. (chief, Historical Office, Supreme Headquarters Allied Powers, Europe). MC 14/2 (Rev) (Final Decision)-23.5.1957. "Overall Strategic Concept for the Defense of the North Atlantic Treaty Organization Area." *NATO Strategy Documents 1949–69.* NATO Archives. http://www.nato.int/archives/strategy.htm.

Perry, Mark. *Partners in Command.* New York: The Penguin Press, 2007.

Pocock, Chris. *50 Years of the U-2: The Complete Illustrated History of the Legendary Dragon Lady.* Atglen, PA: Schiffer Publishing, Ltd., 2005.

Polmar, Norman. *Strategic Air Command: People, Aircraft and Missiles.* Annapolis, MD: The Nautical and Aviation Publishing Company of America, Inc., 1979.

Powell, Colin. *My American Journey.* New York: Random House, 1995.

President's news conference, 29 June 1950. Public Papers of the Presidents: Harry S. Truman, no. 179. Harry S. Truman Library and Museum, Independence, MO. http://www.truman library.org/publicpapers/index.php?pid=806&st=&st1=.

Rabinovich, Abraham. *The Yom Kippur War: The Epic Encounter That Transformed the Middle East.* New York: Schoken, 2004.

Rand McNally. *World Atlas.* New York: Barnes & Noble, 1998.

Ray, Michelle. *The Two Shores of Hell.* London: The Camelot Press, 1967.

Rostow, W. W. "The Case for the Vietnam War." *Parameters* XXVI, no. 4 (Winter 1996–97): 39–50.

SAC Controller. *Summary of SAC Operational Data.* Omaha, NE: Headquarters SAC, Offutt Air Force Base, 1955.

Sheehan, Neil. *A Bright Shining Lie: John Paul Vann and America in Vietnam.* Random House: New York, 1988.

Sifakis, Carl. *The Encyclopedia of American Crime.* New York: Facts on File, 1982.

Smith, Hedrick. *The Russians.* New York: Quadrangle, New York Times Book Company, 1976.

Sokolovski, V. D. *Soviet Military Strategy.* Englewood Cliffs, NJ: Prentice Hall, 1963.

"The Son Tay Raid." Son Tay Raiders Association. www.psywarrior .com/sontay.html.

Sorley, Lewis. *A Better War: The Unexamined Victories and Final Tragedy of America's Last Years in Vietnam.* New York: Harcourt Brace & Co., 1999.

Starr, Richard. *Communist Regimes in Eastern Europe.* Stanford, CA: Hoover Institution Press, 1977.

Statement of Dr. Wayne Sellman, director of accession policy, OSD, to House Committee on Veterans Affairs, *Project 100,000: Testimony and Report on the Study of Vietnam War Era Low Aptitude Military Recruits.* 101st Cong., 2nd sess., 28 February 1990.

Taranto, James, and Leonard Leo, eds. *Presidential Leadership: Rating the Best and the Worst in the White House.* New York: Free Press, 2004.

Taylor, Maxwell. *The Uncertain Trumpet.* New York: Harper & Brothers, 1960.

Thompson, Sir Robert Grainer Ker. *Peace Is Not at Hand.* New York: McKay, 1974.

Thompson, W. Scott, and Donaldson D. Frizzell, eds. *The Lessons of Vietnam.* New York: Crane, Russak, 1977.

Truman, Harry S. *Memoirs.* Vol. 2, *Years of Trial and Hope.* Garden City, NY: Doubleday, 1956.

Uniform Code of Military Justice. 10 US Code, subtitle A, pt. 2, chap. 47, subchap. 3, sec. 815, Art. 15 (d). "Commanding officer's non-judicial punishment." Cornell University Law School. Legal Information Institute. http://www4.law .cornell.edu/uscode/html/uscode10/usc_sec_10 _00000815----000-.html.

United States Air Force. "Biographies: Brigadier General Dennis B. Sullivan." Air Force Link. http://www.af.mil/information/ bios/bio.asp?bioID =7300.

———. "Biographies: General Daniel James Jr." Air Force Link. http://www.af.mil/information/bios/bio.asp?bioID=5932.

———. "Biographies: General George J. Eade." Air Force Link. http://www.af.mil/information/bios/bio.asp?bioID=5651.

———. "Biographies: General George Scratchley Brown." Air Force Link. http://www.af.mil/information/bios/bio.asp?bioID=4813.

———. "Biographies: General Richard H. Ellis." Air Force Link. http://www.af.mil/information/bios/bio.asp?bioID=5348.

———. "Biographies: Lieutenant General Charles C. Pattillo." Air Force Link. http://www.af.mil/information/bios/bio.asp?bioID= 6700.

———. "Biographies: Lieutenant General Walter D. Druen Jr." Air Force Link. http://www.af.mil/information/bios/bio.asp?bioID=5277.

———. "Biographies: Lieutenant General William E. Brown Jr." Air Force Link. http://www.af.mil/information/bios/bio.asp?bioID=4821.

United States Air Force Academy. *Transformation in Russian and Soviet Military History: Twelfth Military History Symposium.* Washington, DC: Office of Air Force History, USAF Academy, 1986.

United States Military Academy. Association of Graduates. *Register of Graduates and Former Cadets of the United States Military Academy.* West Point, NY: Association of Graduates, 2008.

———. Department of Military Art and Engineering. *The War in Western Europe.* West Point, NY: The Academy, 1949.

———. *The War with Japan.* West Point, NY: The Academy, 1947–48.

University of California, Santa Barbara. "John F. Kennedy: Transcript of Broadcast with Walter Cronkite." The American Presidency Project. http://www.presidency.ucsb.edu/ws/index.php?pid=9388.

"USAF Almanac 2000." *Air Force Magazine* 83, no. 5 (May 2000).

"USAF Almanac 2008." *Air Force Magazine* 91, no. 5 (May 2008).

USAF Historical Advisory Committee. *Encyclopedia of U.S. Air Force Aircraft and Missile Systems.* Vol. 1, *Post World War II Fighters, 1945–73.* Washington, DC: U.S. Government Printing Office, 1973.

US House. *Department of Defense Appropriations for 1960: Hearings before the Subcommittee of the Committee on Appropriations.* 86th Congress, 1st sess., pt. 2.

US Senate. Committee on Armed Services. *Military Situation in the Far East and the Facts Surrounding the Relief of Gen-*

eral of the Army Douglas MacArthur from His Assignments in that Area. MacArthur Hearings. 82nd Cong., 1st sess. Washington, DC: Government Printing Office, 1951.

White, Theodore. *Breach of Faith: The Fall of Richard Nixon.* New York: Reader's Digest Press, 1975.

Wolf, Richard, ed. *The United States Air Force: Basic Documents on Roles and Missions.* Washington, DC: Office of Air Force History, US Air Force, 1987.

Index

Following the Flag

An Air Force Officer Provides an Eyewitness View of
Major Events and Policies during the Cold War

Air University Press Team

Chief Editor
Jeanne K. Shamburger

Copy Editor
Carolyn Burns

Cover Art and Book Design
L. Susan Fair

Illustrations
Daniel Armstrong
L. Susan Fair

*Composition and
Prepress Production*
Ann Bailey

Print Preparation and Distribution
Diane Clark